Phonetic Analysis of Speech Corpora

Phonetic Analysis of Speech Corpora

Jonathan Harrington

WILEY-BLACKWELL
A John Wiley & Sons, Ltd., Publication

This edition first published 2010
© 2010 Jonathan Harrington

Blackwell Publishing was acquired by John Wiley & Sons in February 2007. Blackwell's publishing program has been merged with Wiley's global Scientific, Technical, and Medical business to form Wiley-Blackwell.

Registered Office
John Wiley & Sons Ltd, The Atrium, Southern Gate, Chichester, West Sussex, PO19 8SQ, United Kingdom

Editorial Offices
350 Main Street, Malden, MA 02148-5020, USA
9600 Garsington Road, Oxford, OX4 2DQ, UK
The Atrium, Southern Gate, Chichester, West Sussex, PO19 8SQ, UK

For details of our global editorial offices, for customer services, and for information about how to apply for permission to re-use the copyright material in this book please see our website at www.wiley.com/wiley-blackwell.

The right of Jonathan Harrington to be identified as the author of this work has been asserted in accordance with the UK Copyright, Designs, and Patents Act 1988.

All rights reserved. No part of this publication may be reproduced, stored in a retrieval system, or transmitted, in any form or by any means, electronic, mechanical, photocopying, recording, or otherwise, except as permitted by the UK Copyright, Designs, and Patents Act 1988, without the prior permission of the publisher.

Wiley also publishes its books in a variety of electronic formats. Some content that appears in print may not be available in electronic books.

Designations used by companies to distinguish their products are often claimed as trademarks. All brand names and product names used in this book are trade names, service marks, trademarks, or registered trademarks of their respective owners. The publisher is not associated with any product or vendor mentioned in this book. This publication is designed to provide accurate and authoritative information in regard to the subject matter covered. It is sold on the understanding that the publisher is not engaged in rendering professional services. If professional advice or other expert assistance is required, the services of a competent professional should be sought.

Library of Congress Cataloging-in-Publication Data is available

ISBN hbk: 978-1-4051-4169-7
ISBN pbk: 978-1-4051-9957-5

A catalog record for this book is available from the British Library.

Set in 10/12.5pt Galliard by Graphicraft Limited, Hong Kong
Printed and bound in Malaysia by Vivar Printing Sdn Bhd

1   2010

For Sharon

Contents

Relationship between Machine Readable (MRPA) and International
   Phonetic Alphabet (IPA) for Australian English   x
Relationship between Machine Readable (MRPA) and International
   Phonetic Alphabet (IPA) for German   xii
Downloadable Speech Databases Used in this Book   xiv
Preface   xvi
Notes on Downloading Software   xix

Chapter 1   Using Speech Corpora in Phonetics Research   1

1.1   The Place of Corpora in the Phonetic Analysis of Speech   1
1.2   Existing Speech Corpora for Phonetic Analysis   4
1.3   Designing Your Own Corpus   6
1.4   Summary and Structure of the Book   18

Chapter 2   Some Tools for Building and Querying Annotated
   Speech Databases   20

2.1   Overview   20
2.2   Getting Started with Existing Speech Databases   21
2.3   Interface between Praat and Emu   24
2.4   Interface to R   26
2.5   Creating a New Speech Database: From Praat to Emu to R   32
2.6   A First Look at the Template File   34
2.7   Summary   38
2.8   Questions   39

Chapter 3   Applying Routines for Speech Signal Processing   46

3.1   Introduction   46
3.2   Calculating, Displaying, and Correcting Formants   48
3.3   Reading the Formants into R   53

3.4	Summary	58
3.5	Questions	59
3.6	Answers	69

Chapter 4 Querying Annotation Structures — 72

4.1	The Emu **Query Tool**, Segment Tiers, and Event Tiers	72
4.2	Extending the Range of Queries: Annotations from the Same Tier	74
4.3	Inter-tier Links and Queries	77
4.4	Entering Structured Annotations with Emu	82
4.5	Conversion of a Structured Annotation to a Praat TextGrid	86
4.6	Graphical User Interface to the Emu Query Language	88
4.7	Re-querying Segment Lists	90
4.8	Building Annotation Structures Semi-automatically with Emu-Tcl	91
4.9	Branching Paths	97
4.10	Summary	101
4.11	Questions	103
4.12	Answers	108

Chapter 5 An Introduction to Speech Data Analysis in R: A Study of an EMA Database — 115

5.1	EMA Recordings and the **ema5** Database	116
5.2	Handling Segment Lists and Vectors in Emu-R	121
5.3	An Analysis of Voice-Onset Time	125
5.4	Intergestural Coordination and Ensemble Plots	132
5.5	Intragestural Analysis	139
5.6	Summary	159
5.7	Questions	161
5.8	Answers	164

Chapter 6 Analysis of Formants and Formant Transitions — 171

6.1	Vowel Ellipses in the F2 × F1 Plane	172
6.2	Outliers	177
6.3	Vowel Targets	179
6.4	Vowel Normalization	183
6.5	Euclidean Distances	190
6.6	Vowel Undershoot and Formant Smoothing	198
6.7	F2 Locus, Place of Articulation, and Variability	206
6.8	Questions	213
6.9	Answers	216

Chapter 7 Electropalatography — 220

7.1	Palatography and Electropalatography	220
7.2	An Overview of Electropalatography in Emu-R	222
7.3	EPG Data-Reduced Objects	234
7.4	Analysis of EPG Data	248

7.5	Summary	258
7.6	Questions	259
7.7	Answers	260

Chapter 8 Spectral Analysis — 264

8.1	Background to Spectral Analysis	264
8.2	Spectral Average, Sum, Ratio, Difference, Slope	288
8.3	Spectral Moments	297
8.4	The Discrete Cosine Transformation	304
8.5	Questions	316
8.6	Answers	320

Chapter 9 Classification — 327

9.1	Probability and Bayes' Theorem	327
9.2	Classification: Continuous Data	330
9.3	Calculating Conditional Probabilities	336
9.4	Calculating Posterior Probabilities	338
9.5	Two Parameters: The Bivariate Normal Distribution and Ellipses	342
9.6	Classification in Two Dimensions	347
9.7	Classifications in Higher Dimensional Spaces	352
9.8	Classifications in Time	359
9.9	Support Vector Machines	366
9.10	Summary	373
9.11	Questions	374
9.12	Answers	377

References	381
Index	394

Relationship between Machine Readable (MRPA) and International Phonetic Alphabet (IPA) for Australian English

MRPA	IPA	Example
Tense vowels		
i:	iː	h<u>ee</u>d
u:	ʉː	wh<u>o</u>'d
o:	ɔː	h<u>oar</u>d
a:	ɐː	h<u>ar</u>d
@:	ɜː	h<u>ear</u>d
Lax vowels		
I	ɪ	h<u>i</u>d
U	ʊ	h<u>oo</u>d
E	ɛ	h<u>ea</u>d
O	ɔ	h<u>o</u>d
V	ɐ	b<u>u</u>d
A	æ	h<u>a</u>d
Diphthongs		
I@	ɪə	h<u>ere</u>
E@	eə	th<u>ere</u>
U@	ʉə	t<u>our</u>
ei	æɪ	h<u>ay</u>
ai	ɐɪ	h<u>igh</u>
au	æʉ	h<u>ow</u>
oi	ɔɪ	b<u>oy</u>
ou	ɔʉ	h<u>oe</u>
Schwa		
@	ə	th<u>e</u>

Consonants

p	p	pie
b	b	buy
t	t	tie
d	d	die
k	k	cut
g	g	go
tS	tʃ	church
dZ	ʤ	judge
H	ʰ	(Aspiration/stop release)
m	m	my
n	n	no
N	ŋ	sing
f	f	fan
v	v	van
T	θ	think
D	ð	the
s	s	see
z	z	zoo
S	ʃ	shoe
Z	ʒ	beige
h	h	he
r	ɹ	road
w	w	we
l	l	long
j	j	yes

Relationship between Machine Readable (MRPA) and International Phonetic Alphabet (IPA) for German

The MRPA for German is in accordance with SAMPA (Wells 1997), the speech assessment methods phonetic alphabet.

MRPA	IPA	Example
Tense vowels and diphthongs		
2:	ø:	S<u>öh</u>ne
2:6	øɐ	st<u>ö</u>rt
a:	a:	Str<u>a</u>fe, L<u>ah</u>m
a:6	a:ɐ	H<u>aar</u>
e:	e:	g<u>eh</u>t
E:	ɛ:	M<u>ä</u>dchen
E:6	ɛ:ɐ	f<u>ähr</u>t
e:6	e:ɐ	w<u>er</u>den
i:	i:	L<u>ie</u>be
i:6	i:ɐ	B<u>ier</u>
o:	o:	S<u>oh</u>n
o:6	o:ɐ	v<u>or</u>
u:	u:	t<u>u</u>n
u:6	u:ɐ	<u>Uhr</u>
y:	y:	k<u>üh</u>l
y:6	y:ɐ	nat<u>ür</u>lich
aI	aɪ	m<u>ei</u>n
aU	aʊ	H<u>aus</u>
OY	ɔʏ	B<u>eu</u>te
Lax vowels and diphthongs		
U	ʊ	M<u>u</u>nd
9	œ	zw<u>ö</u>lf
a	a	n<u>a</u>ss

Machine Readable Phonetic Alphabet: German

a6	aɐ	Mark
E	ɛ	Mensch
E6	ɛɐ	Lärm
I	ɪ	finden
I6	ɪɐ	wirklich
O	ɔ	kommt
O6	ɔɐ	dort
U6	ʊɐ	durch
Y	ʏ	Glück
Y6	ʏɐ	würde
6	ɐ	Vater

Consonants

p	p	Panne
b	b	Baum
t	t	Tanne
d	d	Daumen
k	k	kahl
g	g	Gaumen
pf	pf	Pfeffer
ts	ts	Zahn
tS	tʃ	Cello
dZ	ʤ	Job
Q	ʔ	(Glottal stop)
h	ʰ	(Aspiration)
m	m	Miene
n	n	nehmen
N	ŋ	lang
f	f	friedlich
v	v	weg
s	s	lassen
z	z	lesen
S	ʃ	schauen
Z	ʒ	Genie
C	ç	riechen
x	x	Buch, lachen
h	h	hoch
r	r, ʁ	Regen
l	l	lang
j	j	jemand

Downloadable Speech Databases Used in this Book

Database name	Description	Language/dialect	n	S	Signal files	Annotations	Source
aetobi	A fragment of the AE-TOBI database: read and spontaneous speech	American English	17	Various	Audio	Word, tonal, break	Beckman et al. (2005); Pitrelli et al. (1994); Silverman et al. (1992)
ae	Read sentences	Australian English	7	1M	Audio, spectra, formants	Prosodic, word, phonetic, tonal	Millar et al. (1994); Millar et al. (1997)
andosl	Read sentences	Australian English	200	2M	Audio, formants	Same as **ae**	Millar et al. (1994); Millar et al. (1997)
ema5 (ema)	Read sentences	Standard German	20	1F	Audio, EMA	Word, phonetic, tongue-tip, tongue-body	Bombien et al. (2007)
epgassim	Isolated words	Australian English	60	1F	Audio, EPG	Word, phonetic	Stephenson (2003); Stephenson and Harrington (2002)
epgcoutts	Read speech	Australian English	2	1F	Audio, EPG	Word	Passage from Hewlett and Shockey (1992)
epgdorsal	Isolated words	German	45	1M	Audio, EPG, formants	Word, phonetic	Ambrazaitis and John (2004)
epgpolish	Read sentences	Polish	40	1M	Audio, EPG	Word, phonetic	Guzik and Harrington (2007)

first gerplosives	Five utterances from **gerplosives**	German	72	1M	Audio, spectra	Phonetic	Unpublished
	Isolated words in carrier sentence	German					
gt	Continuous speech	German	9	Various	Audio, f0	Word, break, tone	Utterances from various sources
kielread	Read sentences	German	200	1M, 1F	Audio, formants	Word, phonemic, phonetic	Simpson (1998); Simpson et al. (1997)
mora	Read	Japanese	1	1F	Audio	Phonetic	Unpublished
second stops	Two speakers from **gerplosives** Isolated words in carrier sentence	German	470	3M, 4F	Audio, formants	Phonetic	Unpublished
timetable	Timetable enquiries	German	5	1M	Audio	Phonetic	As **kielread**

Preface

In undergraduate courses that include phonetics, students typically acquire both skills in ear-training and an understanding of the acoustic, physiological, and perceptual characteristics of speech sounds. But there is usually less opportunity to test this knowledge on sizeable quantities of speech data, partly because putting together any database that is sufficient in extent to be able to address non-trivial questions in phonetics is very time-consuming. In the last 10 years, this issue has been offset somewhat by the rapid growth of national and international speech corpora, which has been driven principally by the needs of speech technology. But there is still usually a big gap between the knowledge acquired in phonetics from classes on the one hand and applying this knowledge to available speech corpora with the aim of solving different kinds of theoretical problems on the other. The difficulty stems not just from getting the right data out of the corpus but also from deciding what kinds of graphical and quantitative techniques are available and appropriate for the problem that is to be solved. So one of the main reasons for writing this book is a pedagogical one: it is to bridge this gap between recently acquired knowledge of experimental phonetics on the one hand and practice with quantitative data analysis on the other. The need to bridge this gap is sometimes most acutely felt when embarking for the first time on a larger-scale project, such as an honors or master's thesis, in which students collect and analyze their own speech data. But in writing this book, I also have a research audience in mind. In recent years, it has become apparent that quantitative techniques have played an increasingly important role in various branches of linguistics, in particular in laboratory phonology and sociophonetics, which sometimes depend on sizeable quantities of speech data labeled at various levels (see e.g., Bod et al. 2003 for a similar view).

This book is something of a departure from most other textbooks on phonetics in at least two ways. Firstly, and as the preceding paragraphs have suggested, I will assume a basic grasp of auditory and acoustic phonetics: that is, I will assume that the reader is familiar with basic terminology in the speech sciences, knows about the international phonetic alphabet, can transcribe speech at broad and narrow levels of detail, and has a working knowledge of basic acoustic principles such as the source-filter theory of speech production. All of this has been covered many times in various excellent phonetics texts, and the material in Clark et al. (2007), Johnson (2004), and Ladefoged (1962), for instance, provides a firm grounding for such issues that are dealt with in this book. The second way in which this book is somewhat different from others is that it is more of a workbook than a textbook. This is partly again for pedagogical reasons: it is all very well being told (or reading) certain supposed facts about the nature of speech but until you get your hands on real data and test them, they tend to mean very little (and may even be untrue!). So it is for this reason that I have tried to convey something of the sense of data exploration using existing speech corpora, supported where appropriate by exercises. From this point of view, this book is similar in approach to Baayen (in press) and Johnson (2008) who also take a workbook approach based on data exploration and whose analyses are, like those of this book, based on the R computing and programming environment. But this book is also quite different from Baayen (in press) and Johnson (2008), whose main concerns are with statistics whereas mine are with techniques. So our approaches are complementary, especially since they all take place in the same programming environment: thus the reader can apply the statistical analyses that are discussed by these authors to many of the data analyses, both acoustic and physiological, that are presented at various stages in this book.

I am also in agreement with Baayen and Johnson about why R is such a good environment for carrying out data exploration of speech: firstly, it is free; secondly, it provides excellent graphical facilities; thirdly, it has almost every kind of statistical test that a speech researcher is likely to need, all the more so since R is open-source and is used in many other disciplines beyond speech, such as economics, medicine, and various other branches of science. Beyond this, R is flexible in allowing the user to write and adapt scripts to whatever kind of analysis is needed, it is very well adapted to manipulating combinations of numerical and symbolic data (and is therefore ideal for a field such as phonetics which is concerned with relating signals to symbols).

Another reason for situating the present book in the R programming environment is that those who have worked on, and contributed to, the Emu speech database project have developed a library of R routines that are customized for various kinds of speech analysis. This development has been ongoing for about 20 years now,[1] since the time in the late 1980s when Gordon Watson suggested to me during my post-doctoral time at the Centre for Speech Technology Research, Edinburgh University that the S programming environment, a forerunner of R, might be just what we were looking for in querying and analyzing speech data and, indeed, one or two of the functions that he wrote then, such as the routine for plotting ellipses, are still used today.

I would like to thank a number of people who have made writing this book possible. Firstly, there are all of those who have contributed to the development of the Emu speech database system in the last 20 years. Foremost Steve Cassidy who was responsible for the query language and the object-oriented implementation that underlies much of the Emu code in the R library; Andrew McVeigh who first implemented a hierarchical system that was also used by Janet Fletcher in a timing analysis of a speech corpus (Fletcher & McVeigh 1991); Catherine Watson who wrote many of the routines for spectral analysis in the 1990s; Michel Scheffers and Lasse Bombien who were together responsible for the adaptation of the **xassp** speech signal processing system[2] to Emu; and Tina John who has in recent years contributed extensively to the various graphical user interfaces, to the development of the Emu database tool and to Emu-to-Praat conversion routines. Secondly, a number of people have provided feedback on using Emu and the Emu-R system, or on earlier drafts of this book, as well as supplied data for some of the corpora – these include most of the above and also Stefan Baumann, Mary Beckman, Bruce Birch, Felicity Cox, Karen Croot, Christoph Draxler, Yuuki Era, Martine Grice, Christian Gruttauer, Phil Hoole, Marion Jaeger, Klaus Jänsch, Pat Keating, Felicitas Kleber, Claudia Kuzla, Friedrich Leisch, Janine Lilienthal, Katalin Mády, Stefania Marin, Jeanette McGregor, Christine Mooshammer, Doris Mücke, Sallyanne Palethorpe, Marianne Pouplier, Tamara Rathcke, Uwe Reichel, Ulrich Reubold, Elliot Saltzman, Michel Scheffers, Florian Schiel, Lisa Stephenson, Marija Tabain, Hans Tillmann, Nils Ülzmann, and Briony Williams. I am also especially grateful to the numerous students both at the IPS, Munich and at the IPdS, Kiel for many useful comments in teaching Emu-R over the last seven years. I would also like to thank Danielle Descoteaux and Julia Kirk of Wiley-Blackwell for their encouragement and assistance in seeing the production of this book completed, Leah Morin for her extensive help in matters associated with copy-editing, and the very many helpful comments from four anonymous reviewers on an earlier version of this book, Sallyanne Palethorpe for her detailed comments in the final stages of writing, and Tina John both for contributing material for the online appendices and for producing many of the figures in the earlier chapters.

Notes

[1] For example in reverse chronological order: Bombien et al. (2006), Harrington et al. (2003), Cassidy (2002), Cassidy and Harrington (2001), Cassidy (1999), Cassidy and Bird (2000), Cassidy et al. (2000), Cassidy and Harrington (1996), Harrington et al. (1993), McVeigh and Harrington (1992).
[2] www.ipds.uni-kiel.de/forschung/xassp.de.html

Notes on Downloading Software

Both R and Emu run on Linux, Mac OS X, and Windows platforms. In order to run the various commands in this book, the reader needs to download and install software as follows.

I. Emu
1. Download the latest release of the Emu speech database system from the download section at http://emu.sourceforge.net.
2. Install the Emu speech database system by executing the downloaded file and following the on-screen instructions.

II. R
3. Download the R programming language from www.cran.r-project.org.
4. Install the R programming language by executing the downloaded file and following the on-screen instructions.

III. Emu-R
5. Start up R.
6. Enter **install.packages("emu")** after the **>** prompt to install the package. (You will only need to do this once.)
7. Enter **library(emu)** to load the installed package for the session.
8. Enter **emulink()** to link the package to the Emu installation and follow the instructions.

IV. Getting started with Emu
9. Start the Emu speech database tool.
   - Windows: choose **Emu Speech Database System** → **Emu** from the Start menu.
   - Linux: choose **Emu Speech Database System** from the Applications menu or type Emu in the terminal window.
   - Mac OS X: start Emu in the Applications folder.

V. Additional software
10 Praat
- Download Praat from www.praat.org.
- To install Praat, follow the instruction at the download page.

11 WaveSurfer, which is included in the Emu setup and installed in these locations:
- Windows: **EmuXX/bin**
- Linux: **/usr/local/bin**; **/home/'username'/Emu/bin**
- Mac OS X: **Applications/Emu.app/Contents/bin**

VI. Problems
12 See FAQ at http://emu.sourceforge.net.

1
Using Speech Corpora in Phonetics Research

1.1 The Place of Corpora in the Phonetic Analysis of Speech

One of the main concerns in phonetic analysis is to find out how speech sounds are transmitted between a speaker and a listener in human speech communication. A speech corpus is a collection of one or more digitized utterances usually containing acoustic data and often marked for annotations. The task in this book is to discuss some of the ways that a corpus can be analyzed to test hypotheses about how speech sounds are communicated. But why is a speech corpus needed for this at all? Why not instead listen to speech, transcribe it, and use the transcription as the main basis for an investigation into the nature of spoken language communication? There is no doubt, as Ladefoged (1995) has explained in his discussion of instrumentation in fieldwork, that being able to hear and re-produce the sounds of a language is a crucial first step in almost any kind of phonetic analysis. Indeed many hypotheses about the way that sounds are used in speech communication stem in the first instance from just this kind of careful listening to speech. However, an auditory transcription is at best an essential initial *hypothesis* – never an objective measure.

The lack of objectivity is readily apparent in comparing the transcriptions of the same speech material across a number of trained transcribers: even when the task is to carry out a fairly broad transcription and with the aid of a speech waveform and spectrogram, there will still be inconsistencies from one transcriber to the next; and all these issues will be considerably aggravated if phonetic detail is to be included in narrower transcriptions or if, as in much fieldwork, auditory phonetic analyses are made of a language with which transcribers are not very familiar. A speech signal on the other hand is a record that does not change: it is, then, the data against which theories can be tested. Another difficulty with building a theory of speech communication on an auditory symbolic transcription of speech is that there are so many ways in which a speech signal is at odds with a segmentation into symbols: there are often no clear boundaries in a speech signal corresponding to the divisions between a string of symbols, and least of all where a layperson might expect to find them, between words.

But, apart from these issues, a transcription of speech can never get to the heart of how the vocal organs, acoustic signal, and hearing apparatus are used to transmit simultaneously many different kinds of information between a speaker and hearer. Consider that the production of /t/ in an utterance tells the listener so much more than "here is a /t/ sound." If the spectrum of the /t/ also has a concentration of energy at a low frequency, then this could be a cue that the following vowel is rounded. At the same time, the alveolar release might provide the listener with information about whether /t/ begins or ends a syllable, a word, or a more major prosodic phrase and whether the syllable is stressed or not. The /t/ might also convey sociophonetic information about the speaker's dialect and quite possibly age group and socioeconomic status (Docherty 2007; Docherty & Foulkes 2005). The combination of /t/ and the following vowel could tell the listener whether the word is prosodically accented and also even say something about the speaker's emotional state.

Understanding how these separate strands of information are interwoven in the details of speech production and the acoustic signal can be accomplished neither by just transcribing speech, nor by analyses of recordings of *individual* utterances. The problem with analyses of individual utterances is that they risk being idiosyncratic: this is not only because of all the different ways that speech can vary according to context, but also because the anatomical and speaking-style differences between speakers all leave their mark on the acoustic signal: therefore, an analysis of a handful of speech sounds in one or two utterances may give a distorted presentation of the general principles according to which speech communication takes place.

The issues raised above and the need for speech corpora in phonetic analysis in general can be considered from the point of view of other more recent theoretical developments: that the relationship between phonemes and speech is *stochastic*. This is an important argument that has been put forward by Janet Pierrehumbert in a number of papers in recent years (e.g., 2002, 2003a, 2003b, 2006). On the one hand there are almost certainly different levels of abstraction or, in terms of the episodic/exemplar models of speech perception and production developed by Pierrehumbert and others (Bybee 2001; Goldinger 1998, 2000; Johnson 1997), *generalizations* that allow native speakers of a language to recognize that *tip* and *pit* are composed of the same three sounds but in the opposite order. Now it is also undeniable that different languages, and certainly different varieties of the same language, often make broadly similar sets of phonemic contrasts: thus in many languages, differences of meaning are established as a result of contrasts between voiced and voiceless stops, or between oral stops and nasal stops at the same place of articulation, or between rounded and unrounded vowels of the same height, and so on. But what has never been demonstrated is that two languages that make similar sets of contrasts do so phonetically in exactly the same way. These differences might be subtle, but they are nevertheless present, which means that such differences must have been learned by the speakers of the language or community.

But how do such differences arise? One way in which they are unlikely to be brought about is because languages or their varieties choose their sound systems from a finite set of universal features. At least so far, no one has been able to demonstrate that the number of possible permutations that could be derived even from the most comprehensive of articulatory or auditory feature systems could account for the myriad of ways that the sounds of dialects and languages do in fact differ. It seems instead that, although the sounds of languages undeniably conform to consistent patterns (as demonstrated in the ground-breaking study of vowel dispersion by Liljencrants & Lindblom 1972), there is also an arbitrary, stochastic component to the way in which the association between abstractions like phonemes and features evolves and is learned by children (Beckman et al. 2007; Edwards & Beckman 2008; Munson et al. 2005).

Recently, this stochastic association between speech on the one hand and phonemes on the other has been demonstrated computationally using so-called agents equipped with simplified vocal tracts and hearing systems who imitate each other over a large number of computational cycles (Wedel 2006, 2007). The general conclusion from these studies is that while stable phonemic systems emerge from these initially random imitations, there are a potentially infinite number of different ways in which phonemic stability can be achieved (and then shifted in sound change – see also Boersma & Hamann 2008). A very important idea to emerge from these studies is that the phonemic stability of a language does not require *a priori* a selection to be made from a pre-defined universal feature system, but might emerge instead as a result of speakers and listeners copying each other imperfectly (Oudeyer 2002, 2004).

If we accept the argument that the association between phonemes and the speech signal is not derived deterministically by making a selection from a universal feature system, but is instead arrived at stochastically by learning generalizations across produced and perceived speech data, then it necessarily follows that analyzing corpora of speech must be one of the important ways in which we can understand how different levels of abstraction such as phonemes and other prosodic units are communicated in speech.

Irrespective of these theoretical issues, speech corpora have become increasingly important since the 1980s as the primary material on which to train and test human–machine communication systems. Some of the same corpora that have been used for technological applications have also formed part of basic speech research (see 1.2 for a summary of these). One of the major benefits of these corpora is that they foster a much needed interdisciplinary approach to speech analysis, as researchers from different disciplinary backgrounds apply and exchange a wide range of techniques for analyzing the data.

Corpora that are suitable for phonetic analysis may become available with the increasing need for speech technology systems to be trained on various kinds of fine phonetic detail (Carlson & Hawkins 2007). It is also likely that corpora will be increasingly useful for the study of sound change as more archived speech data becomes available with the passage of time, allowing sound change to be analyzed either longitudinally in individuals (Harrington 2006; Labov & Auger 1998) or within a community using so-called real-time studies (for example, by comparing the speech characteristics of subjects from a particular age group recorded today with those of a comparable age group and community recorded several years ago – see Sankoff 2005; Trudgill 1988). Nevertheless, most types of phonetic analysis still require collecting small corpora that are dedicated to resolving a particular research question and associated hypotheses; some of the issues in designing such corpora are discussed in 1.3.

Finally, before covering some of these design criteria, it should be pointed out that speech corpora are by no means necessary for every kind of phonetic investigation, and indeed many of the most important scientific breakthroughs in phonetics in the last 50 years have taken place without analyses of large speech corpora. For example, speech corpora are usually not needed for various kinds of articulatory-to-acoustic modeling nor for many kinds of studies in speech perception in which the aim is to work out, often using speech synthesis techniques, the sets of cues that are functional – that is, relevant for phonemic contrasts.

1.2 Existing Speech Corpora for Phonetic Analysis

The need to provide an increasing amount of training and testing material has been one of the main driving forces in creating speech and language corpora in recent years. Various sites for their distribution have been established and some of the more major ones include: the Linguistic Data Consortium (Reed et al. 2008),[1] which is a distribution site for speech and language resources and is located at the University of Pennsylvania; ELRA,[2] the European Language Resources Association, established in 1995, which validates, manages, and distributes speech corpora and whose operational body is ELDA[3] (Evaluations and Language resources Distribution Agency). There are also a number of other repositories for speech and language corpora, including the Bavarian Archive for Speech Signals[4] at the University of Munich, various corpora at the Center for Spoken Language Understanding at the University of Oregon,[5] the TalkBank consortium at Carnegie Mellon University,[6] and the DOBES archive of endangered languages at the Max Planck Institute in Nijmegen.[7]

Most of the corpora from these organizations serve primarily the needs for speech and language technology, but there are a few large-scale corpora that have also been used to address issues in phonetic analysis, including the Switchboard and TIMIT corpora of American English. The Switchboard corpus (Godfrey et al. 1992) includes over 600 telephone conversations from 750 adult American English speakers of a wide range of ages and varieties from both genders and was recently analyzed by Bell et al. (2003) in a study investigating the relationship between predictability and the phonetic reduction of function words. The TIMIT database (Garofolo et al. 1993; Lamel et al. 1986) has been one of the most studied corpora for assessing the performance of speech-recognition systems since the 1980s. It includes 630 talkers and 2,342 different read speech sentences, comprising over 5 hours of speech, and has been included in various phonetic studies on topics such as variation between speakers (Byrd 1992), the acoustic characteristics of stops (Byrd 1993), the relationship between gender and dialect (Byrd 1994), word and segment duration (Keating et al. 1994a), vowel and consonant reduction (Manuel et al. 1992), and vowel normalization (Weenink 2001). One of the most extensive corpora of a European language other than English is the Dutch CGN corpus[8] (Oostdijk 2000; Pols 2001). This is the largest corpus of contemporary Dutch spoken by adults in Flanders and the Netherlands and includes around 800 hours of speech. In the last few years, it has been used to study the sociophonetic variation in diphthongs (Jacobi et al. 2007). For German, the Kiel Corpus of Speech[9] includes several hours of speech annotated at various levels (Simpson 1998; Simpson et al. 1997) and has been instrumental in studying different kinds of connected speech processes (Kohler 2001; Simpson 2001; Wesener 2001).

One of the most successful corpora for studying the relationship between discourse structure, prosody, and intonation has been the HCRC Map Task Corpus[10] (Anderson et al. 1991), containing 18 hours of annotated spontaneous speech recorded from 128 two-person conversations according to a task-specific experimental design (see below for further details). The Australian National Database of Spoken Language[11] (Millar et al. 1994, 1997) also contains a similar range of map-task data for Australian English. These corpora have been used to examine the relationship between speech clarity and the predictability of information (Bard et al. 2000), and also to investigate the way that boundaries between dialogue acts interact with intonation and suprasegmental cues (Stirling et al. 2001). More recently, two corpora have been developed primarily for phonetic and basic speech research: one is the Buckeye Corpus,[12] consisting of 40 hours of spontaneous American English speech annotated at word and phonetic levels (Pitt et al. 2005), which has recently been used to model /t, d/ deletion (Raymond et al. 2006). Another is the Nationwide Speech Project (Clopper & Pisoni 2006), which is especially useful for studying differences in American varieties. It contains 60 speakers from six regional varieties of American English and parts of it are available from the Linguistic Data Consortium.

Databases of speech physiology are much less common than those of speech acoustics, largely because they have not evolved in the context of training and testing speech-technology systems (which is the main source of funding for speech-corpus work). One exception is the ACCOR speech database (Marchal & Hardcastle 1993; Marchal et al. 1991), developed in the 1990s to investigate coarticulatory phenomena in a number of European languages and which includes laryngographic, airflow, and electropalatographic data (the database is available from ELRA). Another is the University of Wisconsin X-ray Microbeam Speech Production Database (Westbury 1994) which includes acoustic and movement data from 26 female and 22 male speakers of a Midwest dialect of American English aged between 18 and 37 years. Thirdly, the MOCHA-TIMIT[13] database (Wrench & Hardcastle 2000) is made up of synchronized movement data from the supralaryngeal articulators, electropalatographic data, and a laryngographic signal of part of the TIMIT database produced by subjects of different English varieties. These databases have been incorporated into phonetic studies in various ways: for example, the Wisconsin database was used by Simpson (2002) to investigate the differences between male and female speech, and the MOCHA-TIMIT database formed part of a study by Kello and Plaut (2003) to explore feedforward learning association between articulation and acoustics in a cognitive speech-production model.

Finally, there are many opportunities to obtain quantities of speech data from archived broadcasts (e.g., in Germany from the Institut für Deutsche Sprache in Mannheim; in the UK from the BBC). These are often acoustically of high quality. However, it is unlikely they will have been annotated, unless they have been incorporated into an existing corpus design, as was the case in the development of the Machine Readable Corpus of Spoken English (MARSEC) created by Roach et al. (1993) based on recordings from the BBC.

1.3 Designing Your Own Corpus

Unfortunately, most kinds of phonetic analysis still require building a speech corpus that is designed to address a specific research question. In fact, existing large-scale corpora of the kind sketched above are very rarely used in basic phonetic research, partly because, no matter how extensive they are, a researcher inevitably finds that one or more aspects of the speech corpus (e.g., speakers, types of materials, speaking styles) are insufficiently covered for the research question to be completed. Another problem is that an existing corpus may not have been annotated in the way that is needed. A further difficulty is that the same set of speakers might be required for a follow-up speech-perception experiment after an acoustic corpus has been analyzed, and inevitably access to the subjects of the original recordings is out of the question, especially if the corpus was created a long time ago.

Assuming that you have to put together your own speech corpus, then various issues in design need to be considered, to make sure not only that the corpus is adequate for answering the specific research questions that are required of it, but also that it is possibly re-usable by other researchers at a later date. It is important to give careful thought to designing the speech corpus, because collecting and especially annotating almost any corpus is usually very time-consuming. Some non-exhaustive issues, based to a certain extent on Schiel and Draxler (2004), are outlined below. The brief review does not cover recording acoustic and articulatory data from endangered languages which brings an additional set of difficulties as far as access to subjects and designing materials are concerned (see in particular Ladefoged 1995, 2003).

1.3.1 Speakers

Choosing the speakers is obviously one of the most important issues in building a speech corpus. Some primary factors to take into account include the distribution of speakers by gender, age, first language, and variety (dialect); it is also important to document any known speech or hearing pathologies. For sociophonetic investigations, or studies specifically concerned with speaker characteristics, a further refinement according to many other factors such as educational background, profession, or socioeconomic group (to the extent that this is not covered by variety) is also likely to be important (see also Beck 2005 for a detailed discussion of the parameters of a speaker's vocal profile based to a large extent on Laver 1980, 1991). All of the above-mentioned primary factors are known to exert quite a considerable influence on the speech signal and therefore have to be controlled for in any experiment comparing two or more speaking groups. Thus it would be inadvisable in comparing, say, speakers of two different varieties to have a predominance of male speakers in one group, and female speakers in another, or one group with mostly young and the other with mostly older speakers. Whatever speakers are chosen, it is, as Schiel and Draxler (2004) comment, of great importance that as many details of the speakers are documented as possible (see also Millar 1991), should the need arise to check subsequently whether the speech data might have been influenced by a particular speaker-specific attribute.

The next most important criterion is the number of speakers. Following Gibbon et al. (1997), speech corpora of between one and five speakers are typical in the context of speech synthesis development, while more than 50 speakers are needed for adequately training and testing systems for the automatic recognition of speech. For most experiments in experimental phonetics of the kind reported in this book, a speaker sample size within the range of 10 to 20 is usual. In almost all cases, experiments involving invasive techniques such as electromagnetic articulometry and electropalatography (discussed in Chapters 5 and 7) rarely have more than five speakers because of the time taken to record and analyze the speech data and the difficulty in finding subjects.

1.3.2 Materials

An equally important consideration in designing any corpus is the choice of materials. Four of the main parameters discussed in Schiel and Draxler (2004) according to which materials are chosen are *vocabulary, phonological distribution, domain,* and *task*.

Vocabulary in a speech-technology application such as automatic speech recognition derives from the intended use of the corpus: so a system for recognizing digits must obviously include the digits as part of the training material. In many phonetics experiments, a choice has to be made between real words of the language and non-words. In either case, it will be necessary to control for a number of phonological criteria, some of which are outlined below (see also Rastle et al. 2002 and the associated website[14] for a procedure for selecting non-words according to numerous phonological and lexical criteria). Since both lexical frequency and neighborhood density have been shown to influence speech production (Luce & Pisoni 1998; Wright 2003), then it could be important to control for these factors as well, possibly by retrieving these statistics from a corpus such as Celex (Baayen et al. 1995). Lexical frequency, as its name suggests, is the estimated frequency with which a word occurs in a language: at the very least, confounds between words of very high frequency, such as between function words which tend to be heavily reduced even in read speech, and less frequently occurring content words should be avoided. Words of high neighborhood density can be defined as those for which many other words exist by substituting a single phoneme (e.g., *man* and *van* are neighbors according to this criterion). Neighborhood density is less commonly controlled for in phonetics experiments although, as recent studies have shown (Munson & Solomon 2004; Wright 2003), it too can influence the phonetic characteristics of speech sounds.

The words that an experimenter wishes to investigate in a speech-production experiment should not be presented to the subject in a list (which induces a so-called list prosody in which the subject chunks the lists into phrases, often with a falling melody and phrase-final lengthening on the last word, but a level or rising melody on all the others); these are often displayed on a screen individually or incorporated into a so-called carrier phrase. Both of these conditions will go some way towards neutralizing the effects of sentence-level prosody, i.e., towards ensuring that the intonation, phrasing, rhythm, and accentual pattern are the same from one target word to the next. Sometimes filler words need to be included in the list, in order to draw the subject's attention away from the design of the experiment. This is important because, if any parts of the stimuli become predictable, then a subject might well reduce them phonetically, given the relationship between redundancy and predictability (Fowler & Housum 1987; Hunnicutt 1985; Lieberman 1963).

For some speech-technology applications, the materials are specified in terms of their *phonological distribution*. For almost all studies in experimental phonetics, controlling for the phonological composition of the target words, in terms of factors such as their lexical-stress pattern, number of syllables, syllable composition, and segmental context, is essential because these all exert an influence on the utterance. In investigations of prosody, materials are sometimes constructed in order to elicit certain kinds of phrasing, accentual patterns, or even intonational melodies. In Silverman and Pierrehumbert (1990), two subjects produced a variety of phrases like *Ma Le Mann, Ma Lemm,* and *Mamalie Lemonick* with a prosodically accented initial syllable and identical intonation melody: they used these materials in order to investigate whether the timing of the pitch-accent was dependent on factors such as the number of syllables in the phrase and the presence or absence of word boundaries. In various experiments by Keating and colleagues (e.g., Keating et al. 2003), French, Korean, and Taiwanese subjects produced sentences that had been constructed to control for different degrees of boundary strength. Thus their French materials included sentences in which /na/ occurred at the beginning of phrases at different positions in the prosodic hierarchy, such as initially in the accentual phrase (*Tonton, Tata, Nadia et Paul arriveront demain*) and syllable-initially (*Tonton et Anabelle . . .*). In Harrington et al. (2000), materials were designed to elicit the contrast between accented and deaccented words. For example, the name *Beaber* was accented in the introductory statement *This is Hector **Beaber***, but deaccented in the question *Do you want **Anna** Beaber or **Clara** Beaber* (in which the nuclear accents falls on the preceding first name). Creating corpora such as these can be immensely difficult, however, because there will always be some subjects who do not produce words as the experimenter wishes (for example by not fully deaccenting the target words in the last example) or, if they do, they might introduce unwanted variations in other prosodic variables. The general point is that subjects usually need to have some training in the production of materials in order to produce them with the degree of consistency required by the experimenter. However, this leads to the additional concern that the productions might not really be representative of prosody produced in spontaneous speech by the wider population.

These are some of the reasons why the production of prosody is sometimes studied using map-task corpora (Anderson et al. 1991) of the kind referred to earlier, in which a particular prosodic pattern is not prescribed, but instead emerges more naturally out of a dialogue or situational context. The map task is an example of a corpus that falls into the category defined by Schiel and Draxler (2004) of being *restricted by domain*. In the map task, two dialogue partners are given slightly different versions of the same map and one has to explain to the other how to navigate a route between two or more points along the map. An interesting variation on this is due to Peters (2006) in which the dialogue partners discuss the contents of two slightly different video recordings of a popular soap opera that both subjects happen to be interested in: the interest factor has the potential additional advantage that the speakers will be distracted by the content of the task, and thereby produce speech in a more natural way. In either case, a fair degree of prosodic variation and spontaneous speech are guaranteed. At the same time, the speakers' choice of prosodic patterns and lexical items tends to be reasonably constrained, allowing comparisons between different speakers on this task to be made in a meaningful way.

In some types of corpora, a speaker will be instructed to solve a particular *task*. The instructions might be fairly general, as in the map task or the video scenario described above, or they might be more specific, such as describing a picture or answering a set of questions. An example of a task-specific recording is in Schafer et al. (2000) who used a cooperative game task in which subjects disambiguated in their productions ambiguous sentences such as *move the square with the triangle* (meaning either: move a house-like shape consisting of a square with a triangle on top of it; or: move a square piece with a separate triangular piece). Such a task allows experimenters to restrict the dialogue to a small number of words, it distracts speakers from the task at hand (since speakers have to concentrate on how to move pieces rather than on what they are saying) while at the same time eliciting precisely the different kinds of prosodic parsings required by the experimenter in the same sequence of words.

1.3.3 Some further issues in experimental design

Experimental design in the context of phonetics is to do with making choices about the speakers, materials, number of repetitions, and other issues that form part of the experiment in such a way that the validity of a hypothesis can be quantified and tested statistically. The summary below touches only very briefly on some of the matters to be considered at the stage of laying out the experimental design, and the reader is referred to Robson (1994), Shearer (1995), and Trochim (2007) for many further useful details. What is presented here is also mostly about some of the design criteria that are relevant for the kind of experiment leading to a statistical test such as analysis of variance (ANOVA). It is quite common for ANOVAs to be applied to experimental speech data, but this is obviously far from the only kind of statistical test that phoneticians need to apply, so some of the issues discussed will not necessarily be relevant for some types of phonetic investigation.

In a certain kind of experiment that is common in experimental psychology and experimental phonetics, a researcher will often want to establish whether a **dependent** variable is affected by one or more **independent** variables. The dependent variable is what is measured – for the kind of speech research discussed in this book, the dependent variable might be any one of duration, a formant frequency at a particular time point, the vertical or horizontal position of the tongue at a displacement maximum, and so on. These are all examples of **continuous** dependent variables because, like age or temperature, they can take on an infinite number of possible values within a certain range. Sometimes the dependent variable might be **categorical**, as in eliciting responses from subjects in speech-perception experiments in which the response is a specific category (e.g., a listener labels a stimulus as either /ba/ or /pa/). Categorical variables are common in sociophonetic research in which counts are made of data (e.g., a count of the number of times that a speaker produces /t/ with or without glottalization).

The independent variable, or factor, is what you believe has an influence on the dependent variable. One type of independent variable that is common in experimental phonetics comes about when a comparison is made between two or more groups of speakers, such as between male and female speakers. This type of independent variable is sometimes (for obvious reasons) called a **between-speaker factor**, which in this example might be given a name like **Gender**. Some further useful terminology is to do with the **number of levels of the factor**. For this example, **Gender** has two levels, **male** and **female**. The same speakers could of course also be coded for other between-speaker factors. For example, the same speakers might be coded for a factor **Variety** with three levels: **Standard English**, **Estuary English**, and **Cockney**. **Gender** and **Variety** in this example are **nominal** because the levels are not rank ordered in any way. If the ordering matters, then the factor is **ordinal** (for example **Age** could be an ordinal factor if you wanted to assess the effects on increasing age of the speakers).

Each speaker that is analyzed can be assigned just one level of each between-speaker factor: so each speaker will be coded as either **male** or **female**, and as **Standard English**, **Estuary English**, or **Cockney**. This example would also sometimes be called a 2 × 3 design, because there are two factors with two (**Gender**) and three (**Variety**) levels. An example of a 2 × 3 × 2 design would have three factors with the corresponding number of levels, e.g., the subjects are coded not only for **Gender** and **Variety** as before, but also for **Age** with two levels, **young** and **old**. Some statistical tests require that the design should be approximately **balanced**: specifically, a given between-subjects factor should have equal numbers of subjects distributed across its levels. For the previous example with two factors, **Gender** and **Variety**, a balanced design would be one that had 12 speakers, 6 males and 6 females, and 2 male and 2 female speakers per variety. Another consideration is that the more between-subjects factors you include, then evidently the greater the number of speakers from which recordings have to be made. Experiments in phonetics are often restricted to no more than two or three between-speaker factors, not just because of considerations of the size of the subject pool, but also because the statistical analysis in terms of interactions becomes increasingly unwieldy for a larger number of factors.

Now suppose you wish to assess whether these subjects show differences of vowel duration in words with a final /t/ like *white* compared with words with a final /d/ like *wide*. In this case, the design might include a factor **Voice** and it has two levels: **[-voice]** (words like *white*) and **[+voice]** (words like *wide*). One of the things that make this type of factor very different from the between-speaker factors considered earlier is that subjects produce (i.e., are measured on) all of the factor's levels – that is, the subjects will produce words that are both **[-voice] and [+voice]**. **Voice** in this example would sometimes be called a within-subject or **within-speaker factor** and because subjects are measured on all of the levels of **Voice**, it is also said to be **repeated**. This is also the reason why, if you wanted to use an ANOVA to work out whether **[+voice]** and **[-voice]** words differed in vowel duration, and also whether such a difference manifested itself in the various speaker groups, you would have to use a **repeated-measures ANOVA**. Of course, if one group of subjects produced the **[-voice]** words and another group the **[+voice]** words, then **Voice** would not be a repeated factor and so a conventional ANOVA could be applied. However, in experimental phonetics this would not be a sensible approach, not just because you would need many more speakers, but also because the difference between **[-voice]** and **[+voice]** words in the dependent variable (vowel duration) would then be confounded with speaker differences. So this is why repeated or within-speaker factors are very common in experimental phonetics. Of course, in the same way that there can be more than one between-speaker factor, there can also be two or more within-speaker factors. For example, if the **[-voice]** and **[+voice]** words were each produced at a slow and a fast rate, then **Rate** would also be a within-speaker factor with two levels (**slow** and **fast**). **Rate**, like **Voice**, is a within-speaker factor because the same subjects have been measured once at a slow, and once at a fast rate.

The need to use a repeated-measures ANOVA comes about, then, because the subject is measured on all the levels of a factor and (somewhat confusingly) it has nothing whatsoever to do with **repeating the same level of a factor in speech production**, which in experimental phonetics is rather common. For example, the subjects might be asked to repeat (in some randomized design) *white* at a slow rate five times. This repetition is done to counteract the inherent variation in speech production. One of the very few uncontroversial facts of speech production is that no subject can produce the same utterance twice, even under identical recording conditions, in exactly the same way. So since a single production of a target word could just happen to be a statistical aberration, researchers in experimental phonetics usually have subjects produce exactly the same materials many times over: this is especially so in physiological studies, in which this type of inherent token-to-token variation is usually so much greater in articulatory than in acoustic data. However, it is important to remember that repetitions of the same level of a factor (the multiple values from each subject's slow production of *white*) cannot be entered into many standard statistical tests such as a repeated-measures ANOVA and so they typically need to be averaged (see Max & Onghena 1999 for some helpful details on this). So even if, as in the earlier example, a subject repeats *white* and *wide* each several times at both slow and fast rates, only four values per subject can be entered into the repeated-measures ANOVA (i.e., the four mean values for each subject of: *white* at a slow rate, *white* at a fast rate, *wide* at a slow rate, *wide* at a fast rate). Consequently, the number of repetitions of identical materials should be kept sufficiently low because otherwise a lot of time will be spent recording and annotating a corpus without really increasing the likelihood of a significant result (on the assumption that the values that are entered into a repeated-measures ANOVA averaged across 10 repetitions of the same materials may not differ a great deal from the averages calculated from 100 repetitions produced by the same subject). The number of repetitions and indeed total number of items in the materials should in any case be kept within reasonable limits because otherwise subjects are likely to become bored and, especially in the case of physiological experiments, fatigued, and these types of paralinguistic effects may well in turn influence their speech production.

The need to average across repetitions of the same materials for certain kinds of statistical test described in Max and Onghena (1999) justifiably seems bizarre to many experimental phoneticians, especially in speech physiology research in which the variation, even in repeating the same materials, may be so large that an average or median becomes fairly meaningless. Fortunately, there have recently been considerable advances in the statistics of **mixed-effects modeling** (see the special edition by Forster & Masson 2008 on emerging data analysis and various papers within that; see also Baayen 2008), which provides an alternative to the classical use of a repeated-measures ANOVA. One of the many advantages of this technique is that there is no need to average across repetitions (Quené & van den Bergh 2008). Another is that it provides a solution to the so-called language-as-fixed-effect problem (Clark 1973). The full details of this matter need not detain us here: the general concern raised in Clark's (1973) influential paper is that, in order to be sure that the statistical results generalize not only beyond the subjects of your experiment but also beyond the language materials (i.e., are not just specific to *white*, *wide*, and the other items of the word list), two separate (repeated-measures) ANOVAs need to be carried out, one so-called by-subjects and the other by-items (see Johnson 2008 for a detailed exposition using speech data in R). The output of these two tests can then be combined using a formula to compute the joint F-ratio (and therefore the significance) from both of them. By contrast, there is no need in mixed-effects modeling to carry out and to combine two separate statistical tests in this way: instead, the subjects and the words can be entered as so-called random factors into the same calculation.

Since much of the cutting-edge mixed-effects modeling research in statistics has been carried out in R in the last 10 years, there are corresponding R functions for carrying out mixed-effects modeling that can be directly applied to speech data, without the need to go through the often very tiresome complications of exporting the data, sometimes involving rearranging rows and columns for analysis using the more traditional commercial statistical packages.

1.3.4 Speaking style

A wide body of research since 1960 has shown that speaking style influences speech production characteristics: in particular, the extent of coarticulatory overlap, vowel centralization, consonant lenition and deletion are all likely to increase in progressing from citation-form speech, in which words are produced in isolation or in a carrier phrase, to read speech and to fully spontaneous speech (Moon & Lindblom 1994). In some experiments, speakers are asked to produce speech at different rates so that the effect of increasing or decreasing tempo on consonants and vowels can be studied. However, in the same way that it can be problematic to get subjects to produce controlled prosodic materials consistently (see 1.3.2), the task of making subjects vary speaking rate is not without its difficulties. Some speakers may not vary their rate a great deal in changing from "slow" to "fast" and one person's slow speech may be similar to another subject's fast rate. Subjects may also vary other prosodic attributes in switching from a slow to a fast rate. In reading a target word within a carrier phrase, subjects may well vary the rate of the carrier phrase but not the focused target word that is the primary concern of the investigation: this might happen if the subject (not unjustifiably) believes the target word to be communicatively the most important part of the phrase, as a result of which it is produced slowly and carefully at all rates of speech.

The effect of emotion on prosody is a very much under-researched area that also has important technological applications in speech-synthesis development. However, eliciting different kinds of emotion, such as a happy or sad speaking style, is problematic. It is especially difficult, if not impossible, to elicit different emotional responses to the same read material, and, as Campbell (2002) notes, subjects often become self-conscious and suppress their emotions in an experimental task. An alternative then might be to construct passages that describe scenes associated with different emotional content, but then even if the subject achieves a reasonable degree of variation in emotion, any influence of emotion on the speech signal is likely to be confounded with the potentially far greater variation induced by factors such as the change in focus and prosodic accent, the effects of phrase-final lengthening, and the use of different vocabulary. (There is also the independent difficulty of quantifying the extent of happiness and sadness with which the materials were produced.) Another possibility is to have a trained actor produce the same materials in different emotional speaking styles (e.g., Pereira 2000), but whether this type of forced variation by an actor really carries over to emotional variation in everyday communication can only be assumed and is not easily verified (however see, e.g., Campbell 2002, 2004; and Douglas-Cowie et al. 2003 for some recent progress in approaches to creating corpora for "emotion" and expressive speech).

1.3.5 Recording setup[15]

Many experiments in phonetics are carried out in a sound-treated recording studio in which the effects of background noise can be largely eliminated and in which the speaker is seated at a controlled distance from a high-quality microphone. Since, with the possible exception of some fricatives, most of the phonetic content of the speech signal is contained below 8 kHz, and taking into account the Nyquist theorem (see also Chapter 8) that only frequencies below half the sampling frequency can be faithfully reproduced digitally, the sampling frequency is typically at least 16 kHz in recording speech data. The signal should be recorded in an uncompressed or PCM (pulse code modulation) format and the amplitude of the signal is typically quantized in 16 bits: this means that the amplitude of each sampled data value occurs at one of a number of 2^{16} discrete steps, which is usually considered adequate for representing speech digitally. With the introduction of the audio CD standard, a sampling frequency of 44.1 kHz and its divider 22.05 kHz are also common. An important consideration in any recording of speech is to set the input level correctly: if it is too high, a distortion known as clipping can result, while if it is too low, then the amplitude resolution will also be too low. For some types of investigations of communicative interaction between two or more speakers, it is possible to make use of a stereo microphone as a result of which data from the separate channels are interleaved or multiplexed (in which the samples from, e.g., the left and right channels are contained in alternating sequence). However, Schiel and Draxler (2004) recommend instead using separate microphones since interleaved signals may be more difficult to process in some signal processing systems – for example, at the time of writing, the speech signal processing routines in Emu cannot be applied to stereo signals.

There are a number of file formats for storing digitized speech data including a raw format which has no header and contains only the digitized signal; NIST SPHERE defined by the National Institute for Standards and Technology, USA consisting of a readable header in plain text (7 bit US ASCII) followed by the signal data in binary form; and most commonly the WAVE file format which is a subset of Microsoft's RIFF specification for the storage of multimedia files.

If you make recordings beyond the recording studio, and in particular if this is done without technical assistance, then, apart from the sampling frequency and bit-rate, factors such as background noise and the distance of the speaker from the microphone need to be very carefully monitored. Background noise may be especially challenging: if you are recording in what seems to be a quiet room, it is nevertheless important to check that there is no other hum or interference from other electrical equipment such as an air-conditioning unit. Although present-day personal and notebook computers are equipped with built-in hardware for playing and recording high-quality audio signals, Draxler (2008) recommends using an external device such as a USB headset for recording speech data. The recording should only be made onto a laptop in battery mode, because the AC power source can sometimes introduce noise into the signal.[16]

One of the difficulties with recording in the field is that you usually need separate pieces of software for recording the speech data and for displaying any prompts and recording materials to the speaker. Recently, Draxler and Jänsch (2004) have provided a solution to this problem by developing a freely available, platform-independent software system for handling multi-channel audio recordings known as SpeechRecorder.[17] It can record from any number of audio channels and has two screens that are seen separately by the subject and by the experimenter. The first of these includes instructions about when to speak as well as the script to be recorded. It is also possible to present auditory or visual stimuli instead of text. The screen for the experimenter provides information about the recording level, details of the utterance to be recorded, and which utterance number is being recorded. One of the major advantages of this system is not only that it can be run from almost any PC, but also that the recording sessions can be done with this software over the internet. In fact, SpeechRecorder has recently been used just for this purpose (Draxler & Jänsch 2007) in the collection of data from teenagers in a very large number of schools from all around Germany. It would have been very costly to have to travel to the schools, so being able to record and monitor the data over the internet was an appropriate solution in this case. This type of internet solution would be even more useful if speech data were needed across a much wider geographical area.

The above is a description of procedures for recording acoustic speech signals (see also Draxler 2008 for further details), but it can to a certain extent be applied to the collection of physiological speech data. There is articulatory equipment for recording aerodynamic, laryngeal, and supralaryngeal activity and some information from lip movement could even be obtained with video recordings synchronized with the acoustic signal. However, video information is rarely precise enough for most forms of phonetic analyses. Collecting articulatory data is inherently complicated because most of the vocal organs are hidden and so the techniques are often invasive (see various chapters in Hardcastle & Hewlett 1999 and Harrington & Tabain 2004 for a discussion of some of these articulatory techniques). A physiological technique such as electromagnetic articulometry described in Chapter 5 also requires careful calibration; and physiological instrumentation tends to be expensive, restricted to laboratory use, and generally not easily useable without technical assistance. The variation within and between subjects in physiological data can be considerable, often requiring an analysis and statistical evaluation subject by subject. The synchronization of the articulatory data with the acoustic signal is not always a trivial matter and analyzing articulatory data can be very time-consuming, especially if data are recorded from several articulators. For all these reasons, there are far fewer experiments in phonetics using articulatory techniques than there are using acoustic techniques. At the same time, physiological techniques can provide insights into speech-production control and timing which cannot be accurately inferred from acoustic techniques alone.

1.3.6 Annotation

The annotation of a speech corpus refers to the creation of symbolic information that is related to the signals of the corpus in some way. It is always necessary for annotations to be time-aligned with the speech signals: for example, there might be an orthographic transcript of the recording and then the words might be further tagged for syntactic category, or sentences for dialogue acts, with these annotations being assigned any markers to relate them to the speech signal in time. In the phonetic analysis of speech, the corpus usually has to be **segmented and labeled**, which means that symbols are linked to the physical time scale of one or more signals. As described more fully in Chapter 4, a symbol may be either a segment that has a certain duration or else an event that is defined by a single point in time. The segmentation and labeling are often done manually by an expert transcriber with the aid of a spectrogram. Once part of the database has been manually annotated, then it can sometimes be used as training material for the automatic annotation of the remainder. The Institute of Phonetics and Speech Processing of the University of Munich makes extensive use of the Munich automatic segmentation system (MAUS) developed by Schiel (1999, 2004) for this purpose. MAUS typically requires a segmentation of the utterance in words, based on which statistically weighted hypotheses of sub-word segments can be calculated and then verified against the speech signal. Exactly this procedure was used to provide an initial phonetic segmentation of the acoustic signal for the corpus of movement data discussed in Chapter 5.

Manual segmentation tends to be more accurate than automatic segmentation and it has the advantage that segmentation boundaries can be perceptually validated by expert transcribers (Gibbon et al. 1997): certainly, it is always necessary to check the annotations and segment boundaries established by an automatic procedure before any phonetic analysis can take place. However, an automatic procedure has the advantage over manual procedures not only of complete acoustic consistency but especially that annotation is accomplished much more quickly.

One of the reasons why manual annotation is complicated is because of the continuous nature of speech: it is very difficult to make use of external acoustic evidence to place a segment boundary between the consonants and vowel in a word like *wheel* because the movement between them is not discrete but continuous. Another major source of difficulty in annotating continuous or spontaneous speech is that there will be frequent mismatches between the phonetic content of the signal and the citation-form pronunciation. Thus *run past* might be produced with assimilation and deletion as [ɹʌmpɑːs], *actually* as [aʃli] and so on (Laver 1994). One of the difficulties for a transcriber is in deciding upon the extent to which reduction has taken place and whether segments overlap completely or partially. Another is in aligning the reduced forms with citation-form dictionary entries, which is sometimes done in order to measure subsequently the extent to which segmental reduction has taken place in different contexts (see Harrington et al. 1993 and Appendix B of the website related to this book for an example of a matching algorithm to link reduced and citation forms, and Johnson 2004b for a technique which, like

Harrington et al. 1993, is based on dynamic programming for aligning the two types of transcription).

The inherent difficulty in segmentation can be offset to a certain extent by following some basic procedures in carrying out this task. One fairly obvious one is that it is best not to segment and label any more of the corpus than is necessary for addressing the hypotheses that are to be solved in analyzing the data phonetically, given the amount of time that manual segmentation and labeling take. A related point (which is discussed in further detail in Chapter 4) is that the database needs to be annotated in such a way that the speech data that is required for the analysis can be queried or extracted without too much difficulty. One way to think about manual annotation in phonetic analysis is that it acts as a form of scaffolding (which may not form part of the final analysis) allowing a user to access the data of interest. But, just like scaffolding, the annotation needs to be firmly grounded, which means that segment boundaries should be placed at relatively unambiguous acoustic landmarks if at all possible. For example, if you are interested in the rate of transition between semi-vowels and vowels in words like *wheel*, then it is probably not a good idea to have transcribers try to find the boundary at the juncture between the consonants and vowel for the reasons stated earlier that it is very difficult to do so, based on any objective criteria (leading to the additional problem that the consistency between separate transcribers might not be very high). Instead, the words might be placed in a carrier phrase so that the word onset and offset can be manually marked: the interval between the word boundaries could then be analyzed algorithmically based on objective acoustic factors such as the maximum rate of formant change.

For all the reasons discussed so far, there should never really be any need for a complete, exhaustive segmentation and labeling of entire utterances into phonetic segments: it is too time-consuming, unreliable, and is probably in any case not necessary for most types of phonetic analyses. If this type of exhaustive segmentation really is needed, as perhaps in measuring the variation in the duration of vowels and consonants in certain kinds of studies of speech rhythm (e.g., Grabe & Low 2002), then you might consider using an automatic method of the kind mentioned earlier. Even if the boundaries have not all been accurately placed using the automatic procedure, it is still generally quicker to edit them subsequently rather than to place boundaries using manual labeling from scratch. As far as manual labeling is concerned, it is once again important to adhere to guidelines, especially if the task is carried out by multiple transcribers. There are few existing manuals that provide any detailed information about how to segment and label to a level of detail greater than a broad, phonemic segmentation (but see Keating et al. 1994b for some helpful criteria in providing narrow levels of segmentation and labeling in English spontaneous speech; and also Barry & Fourcin 1992 for further details on different levels of labeling between the acoustic waveform and a broad phonemic transcription). For prosodic annotation, extensive guidelines have been developed for American and other varieties of English as well as for many other languages using the tones and break indices labeling system: see for instance Beckman et al. (2005) and other references in Jun (2005).

Labeling physiological data brings a whole new set of issues beyond those that are encountered in acoustic analysis because of the very different nature of the signal. As discussed in Chapter 5, data from electromagnetic articulometry can often be annotated automatically for peaks and troughs in the movement and velocity signals, although these landmarks are certainly not always reliably present, especially in more spontaneous styles of speaking. Electropalatographic data could be annotated at EPG landmarks such as points of maximum tongue–palate contact, but this is especially time-consuming given that the transcriber has to monitor several contacts of several palatograms at once. A better solution might be to carry out a coarse acoustic phonetic segmentation manually or automatically that includes the region where the point of interest in the EPG signal is likely to be, and then to find landmarks like the maximum or minimum points of contact automatically (as described in Chapter 7), using the acoustic boundaries as reference points.

Once the data has been annotated, then it is important to carry out some form of validation, at least of a small, but representative, part of the database. As Schiel and Draxler (2004) have noted, there is no standard way of doing this, but they recommend using an automatic procedure for calculating the extent to which segment boundaries overlap (they also point out that the boundary times and annotations should be validated separately although the two are not independent, given that, if a segment is missing in one transcriber's data, then the times of the segment boundaries will be distorted). For phoneme-size boundaries, they report that phoneme boundaries from separate transcribers are aligned within 20 ms of each other in 95 percent of read speech and 85 percent of spontaneous speech. Reliability for prosodic annotations is somewhat lower (see e.g., Jun et al. 2000; Pitrelli et al. 1994; Syrdal & McGory 2000; Yoon et al. 2004 for studies of the consistency of labeling according to the tones and break indices system). Examples of assessing phoneme labeling consistency and transcriber accuracy are given in Pitt et al. (2005), Shriberg and Lof (1991), and Wesenick and Kipp (1996).

1.3.7 Some conventions for naming files

There are various points to consider as far as file naming in the development of a speech corpus is concerned. Each separate utterance of a speech corpus usually has its own base-name with different extensions being used for the different kinds of signal and annotation information (this is discussed in further detail in Chapter 2). A content-based coding is often used in which attributes such as the language, the varieties, the speaker, and the speaking style are coded in the base-name (so **EngRPabcF.wav** might be used for English, RP, speaker **abc** who used a fast speaking style for example). The purpose of content-based file naming is that it provides one of the mechanisms for extracting the corresponding information from the corpus. On the other hand, there is a limit to the amount of information that can be coded in this way, and the alternative is to store it as part of the annotations at different annotation tiers (see Chapter 4) rather than in the base-name itself. A related problem with content-based file names discussed in Schiel and Draxler (2004) is that there may be platform- or medium-dependent length restrictions on file names (such as in ISO 9960 CDs).

The extension **.wav** is typically used for the audio data (speech pressure waveform) but other than this there are no conventions across systems for what the extensions denote, although some extensions are likely to be specific to different systems (e.g., **.TextGrid** is for annotation data in Praat; **.hlb** for storing hierarchical label files in Emu).

Schiel and Draxler (2004) recommend storing the signal and annotation data separately, principally because the annotations are much more likely to be changed than the signal data. For the same reason, it is sometimes advantageous to store separately the original acoustic or articulatory sampled speech data files obtained during the recording from other signal files (containing information such as formants or spectral information) that are subsequently derived from these.

1.4 Summary and Structure of the Book

The discussion in this chapter has covered a few of the main issues that need to be considered in designing a speech corpus. The rest of this book is about how speech corpora can be used in experimental phonetics. The material in Chapters 2 to 4 provides the link between the general criteria reviewed in this chapter and the techniques for phonetic analysis of Chapters 5 to 9.

As far as Chapters 2 to 4 are concerned, the assumption is that you may have some digitized speech data that might have been labeled and the principal objective is to get it into a form for subsequent analysis. The main topics that are covered here include some routines in digital signal processing for producing derived signals such as fundamental frequency and formant frequency data (Chapter 3) and structuring annotations in such a way that they can be queried, allowing the annotations and signal data to be read into R (Chapter 4). These tasks in Chapters 3 and 4 are carried out using the Emu system: the main aim of Chapter 2 is to show how Emu is connected both with R and with Praat (Boersma & Weenink 2005) and WaveSurfer (Sjölander 2002). Emu is used in Chapters 2 to 4 because it includes both an extensive range of signal processing facilities and a query language that allows quite complex searches to be made of multi-tiered annotated data. There are certainly other systems that can query complex annotation types of which the NITE-XML[18] system (Carletta et al. 2005) is a very good example (it too makes use of a template file for defining a database's attributes in a way similar to Emu). Other tools that are especially useful for annotating either multimedia data or dialogues are ELAN[19] (EUDICO Linguistic Annotator), developed at the Max Planck Institute for Psycholinguistics in Nijmegen, and Transcriber,[20] based on the annotation graph toolkit (Bird & Liberman 2001; see also Barras et al. 2001).[21] However, although querying complex annotation structures and representing long dialogues and multimedia data can no doubt be more easily accomplished in some of these systems than they can in Emu, none of these at the time of writing includes routines for signal processing, the possibility of handling EMA and EPG data, or the transparent interface to R that is needed for accomplishing the various tasks in the later part of this book.

Chapters 5 to 9 are concerned with analyzing phonetic data in the R programming environment: two of these (Chapters 5 and 7) are on physiological techniques; the rest make use of acoustic data. The analysis in Chapter 5 of movement data is simultaneously intended as an introduction to the R programming language. The reason for using R is partly that it is free and platform-independent, but also because of the ease with which signal data can be analyzed in relation to symbolic data, which is often just what is needed in analyzing speech phonetically. Another is that, as a recent article by Vance (2009) in *The New York Times* made clear,[22] R is now one of the main data-mining tools used in very many different fields. The same article quotes a scientist from Google who comments that "R is really important to the point that it's hard to overvalue it." As Vance (2009) correctly notes, one of the reasons why R has become so popular is because statisticians, engineers, and scientists without computer-programming skills find it relatively easy to use. Because of this, and because so many scientists from different disciplinary backgrounds contribute their own libraries to the R website, the number of functions and techniques in R for data analysis and mining continues to grow. As a result, most of the quantitative, graphical, and statistical functions that are needed for speech analysis are likely to be found in one or more of the libraries available on the R website. In addition, and as already mentioned in the preface and earlier part of this chapter, there are now books specifically concerned with the statistical analysis of speech and language data in R (Baayen, in press; Johnson 2008) and much of the cutting-edge development in statistics is now being done in the R programming environment.

Notes

[1] www.ldc.upenn.edu/
[2] www.elra.info/
[3] www.elda.org/
[4] www.phonetik.uni-muenchen.de/Bas/BasHomeeng.html
[5] www.cslu.ogi.edu/corpora/corpCurrent.html
[6] http://talkbank.org/
[7] www.mpi.nl/DOBES
[8] http://lands.let.kun.nl/cgn/ehome.htm
[9] www.ipds.uni-kiel.de/forschung/kielcorpus.en.html
[10] www.hcrc.ed.ac.uk/maptask/
[11] http://andosl.anu.edu.au/andosl/
[12] http://vic.psy.ohio-state.edu/
[13] www.cstr.ed.ac.uk/research/projects/artic/mocha.html
[14] www.maccs.mq.edu.au/~nwdb
[15] Websites that provide helpful recording guidelines are those at Talkbank and at the Phonetics Laboratory, University of Pennsylvania: www.talkbank.org/da/record.html, www.talkbank.org/da/audiodig.html, and www.ling.upenn.edu/phonetics/archive/FieldRecAdvice.htm.
[16] Florian Schiel, personal communication.
[17] See www.phonetik.uni-muenchen.de/Bas/software/speechrecorder/ to download SpeechRecorder.
[18] http://sourceforge.net/projects/nite/
[19] www.lat-mpi.eu/tools/elan/
[20] http://trans.sourceforge.net/en/presentation.php
[21] Plans are currently in progress to build an interface between ELAN and Emu annotations. There was an interface between Transcriber and Emu in earlier versions of both systems (Barras et al. 2001; Cassidy & Harrington 2001). Since, at the time of writing, Transcriber is being redeveloped, the possibility of interfacing the two will need to be reconsidered.
[22] My thanks to Andrea Sims and Mary Beckman for pointing this out to me. The same article in *The New York Times* also makes a reference to Emu.

2
Some Tools for Building and Querying Annotated Speech Databases[1]

2.1 Overview

As discussed in the previous chapter, the main aim of this book is to present some techniques for analyzing labeled speech data in order to solve problems that typically arise in experimental phonetics and laboratory phonology. This will require a labeled database, the facility to read speech data into R, and a rudimentary knowledge of the R programming language. These are the main subjects of this and the next three chapters.

The relationship between these three stages is summarized in Figure 2.1. The first stage involves creating a **speech database** which is defined in this book as consisting of one or more **utterances** that are each associated with **signal files** and **annotation files**. The signal files can include digitized acoustic data and sometimes

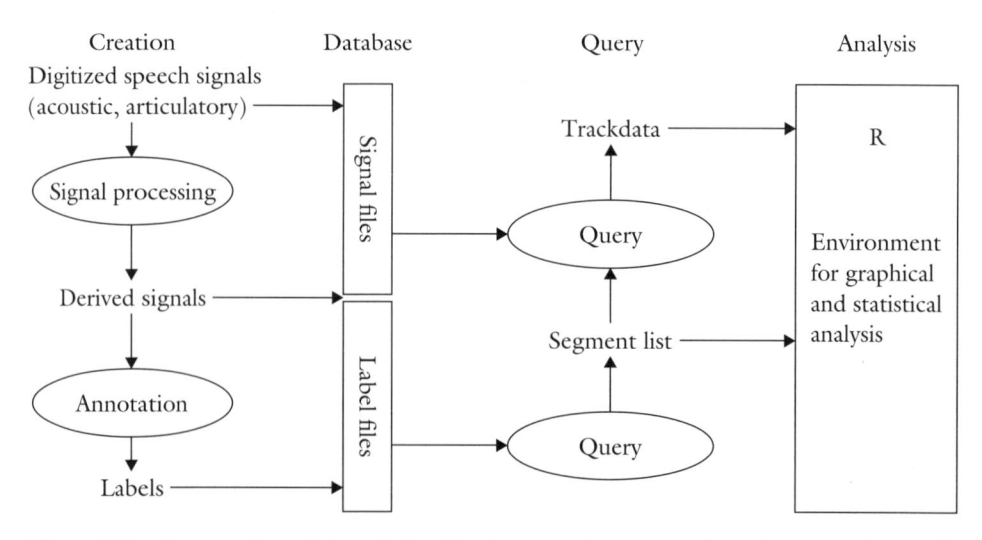

Figure 2.1 An overview of the relationship between the stages of creating, querying, and analyzing speech corpora.

articulatory data of various different activities of the vocal organs as they change in time. Signal files often include **derived signal files** that are obtained when additional processing is applied to the originally recorded data – for example to obtain formant and fundamental frequency values from a digitized acoustic waveform. Annotation files are obtained by automatic or manual labeling, as described in the preceding chapter.

Once the signal and annotation files have been created, the next step (middle section of Figure 2.1) involves **querying** the database in order to obtain the information that is required for carrying out the analysis. This book will make use of the Emu query language (Emu-QL) for this purpose, which can be used to extract speech data from structured annotations. The output of the Emu-QL includes two kinds of objects: a **segment list** that consists of annotations and their associated time-stamps and **trackdata** that is made up of sections of signal files that are associated in time with the segment list. For example, a segment list might include all the /i:/ vowels from their acoustic onset to their acoustic offset and trackdata the formant frequency data between the same time points for each such segment.

A segment list and trackdata are the structures that are read into R for analyzing speech data. Thus R is not used for recording speech data, for annotating it, or for most major forms of signal processing. But since R does have a particularly flexible and simple way of handling numerical quantities in relation to annotations, then R can be used for the kinds of graphical and statistical manipulations of speech data that are often needed in studies of experimental phonetics.

2.2 Getting Started with Existing Speech Databases

When you start up Emu for the first time, you should see a display like the one in Figure 2.2. The left and right panels of this display show the databases that are available to the system and their respective utterances. In order to proceed to the next step, you will need an internet connection. Then, open the **Database Installer** window in Figure 2.3 by clicking on **Arrange Tools** and then **Database Installer** within that menu. The display contains a number of databases that can be installed, unzipped, and configured in Emu. Before downloading any of these, you must specify a directory (**New Database Storage**) into which the database will be downloaded. When you click on the database to be used in this chapter, **first.zip**, the separate stages **download**, **unzip**, **adapt**, **configure** should light up one after the other and finish with the message: **Successful** (Figure 2.3). Once this is done, go back to the Emu **Database Tool** (Figure 2.2) and click anywhere inside the **Databases** pane: the database **first** should now be available as shown in Figure 2.4. Click on **first**, then choose **Load Database** in order to see the names of the utterances that belong to this database, exactly as in Figure 2.4.

Now double-click on **gam001** in Figure 2.4 in order to open the utterance and produce a display like the one shown in Figure 2.5.

The display consists of two signals, a waveform and a wide-band spectrogram in the 0–5,000 Hz range. For this mini-database, the aim was to produce a number of target words in a carrier sentence *ich muss* _____ *sagen* (lit. *I must* _____ *say*); the one shown in Figure 2.5 is of *guten* (*good*, dative plural) in such a carrier phrase

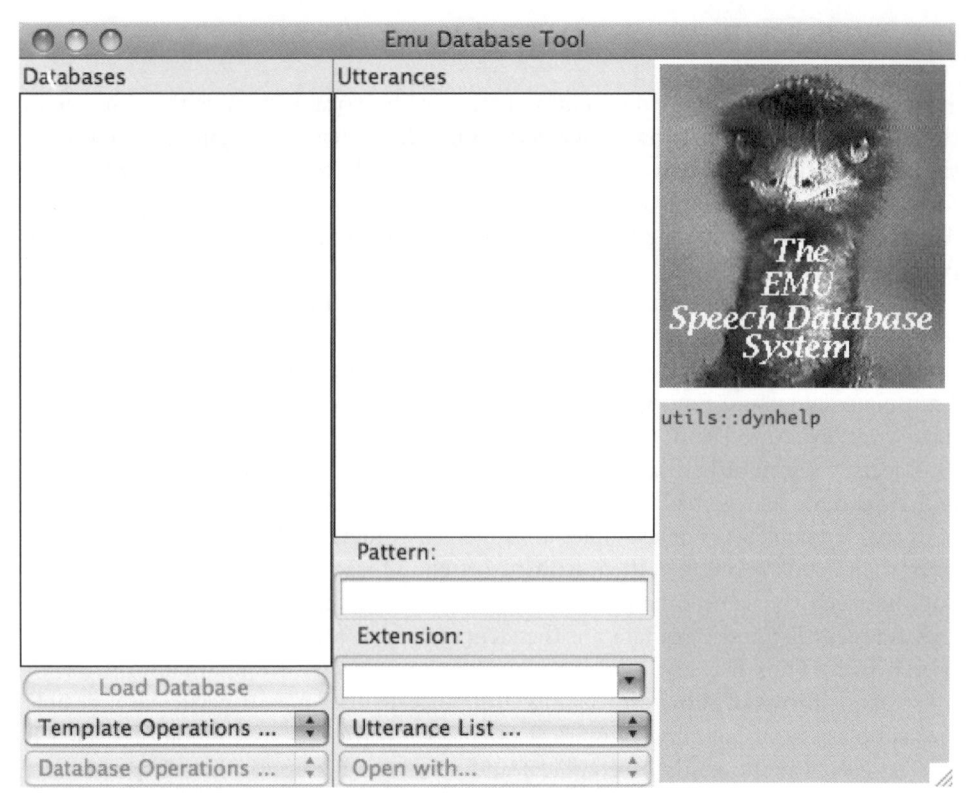

Figure 2.2 The Emu **Database Tool** as it appears when you first start up Emu. The left pane is for showing the available databases, the right pane for the utterances that each database is composed of.

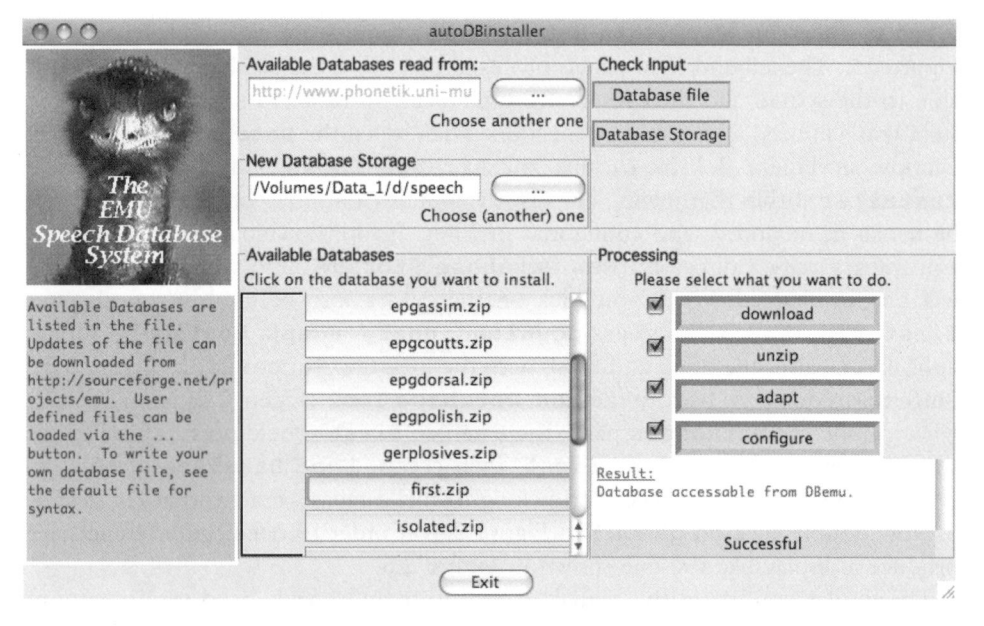

Figure 2.3 The Emu **Database Installer** is accessible from **Arrange Tools**. To install any of the available databases, first specify a path to which you want to save the data from **New Database Storage** and then click on any of the zip files. You must have an internet connection for this to work.

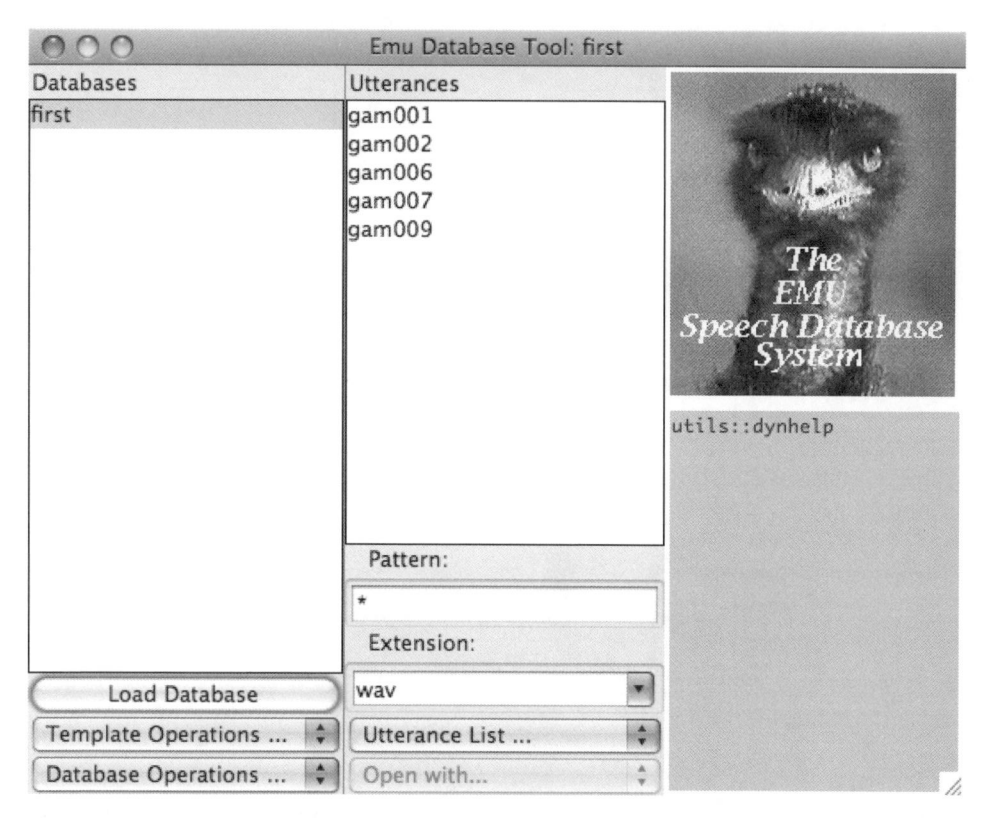

Figure 2.4 The result of following the procedure described in Figure 2.3 is access to the database **first** that is made up of five utterances shown on the right. The utterance-names are displayed by selecting **first** in **Databases** on the left followed by **Load Database**. Double-clicking any of the names in the **Utterances** pane on the right causes the utterance to be opened (Figure 2.5).

produced by a male speaker of the Standard North German variety. The display also shows annotations arranged in four separate labeling tiers. These include *guten* in the **Word** tier marking the start and end times of this word and three annotations in the **Phonetic** tier that mark the extent of velar closure (**g**), the release/frication stage of the velar stop (**H**), and the acoustic onset and offset of the vowel (**u:**). The annotations at the **Phoneme** tier are essentially the same except that the sequence of the stop closure and release are collapsed into a single segment. Finally, the label **T** at the **Target** tier marks the acoustic vowel target which is usually close to the vowel's temporal midpoint in monophthongs and which can be thought of as the time at which the vowel is least influenced by the neighboring context (see Harrington & Cassidy 1999, pp. 59–60 for a further discussion on targets).

In Emu, there are two different kinds of labeling tiers: **segment tiers** and **event tiers**. In segment tiers, every annotation has a duration and is defined by a start and end time. **Word**, **Phoneme**, **Phonetic** are segment tiers in this database. By contrast, the annotations of an event tier, of which **Target** is an example in Figure 2.5, mark only single events in time: so the **T** in this utterance marks a position in time, but has no duration.

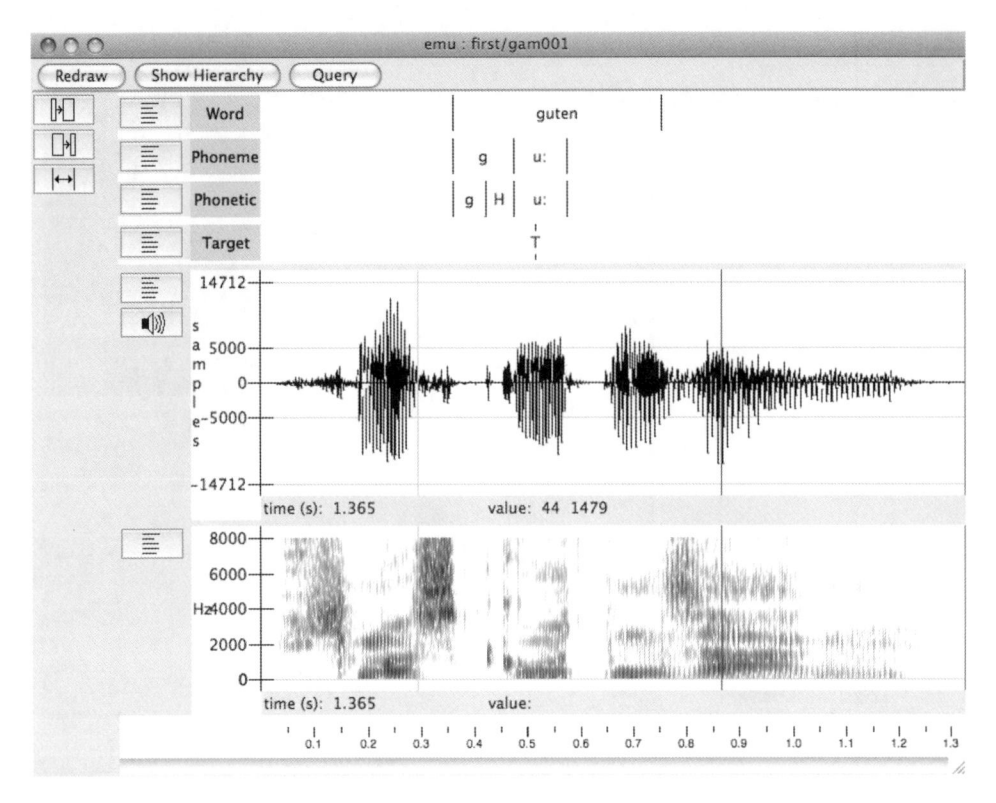

Figure 2.5 The display that appears when opening utterance **gam001** showing four labeling tiers, a waveform, and a spectrogram. The two vertical lines show a *selection*. To make a selection, position the mouse in the waveform, hold down the left button and sweep *without letting go of the left button* to the desired position later in time, then release the button. To zoom in to the selection (Figure 2.6), click the ↔ symbol in the top left of the display.

In Figure 2.6, the same information is displayed but after zooming in to the segment marks of Figure 2.5 and after adjusting the parameters, brightness, contrast, and frequency range in order to produce a sharper spectrogram. In addition, the spectrogram has been resized relative to the waveform.

2.3 Interface between Praat and Emu

The task now is to annotate part of an utterance from this small database. The annotation could be done in Emu but it will instead be done with Praat both for the purposes of demonstrating the relationship between the different software systems, and because this is the software system for speech labeling and analysis that many readers are most likely to be familiar with.

Begin by starting up Praat, then bring the Emu **Database Tool** to the foreground and select with a single mouse-click the utterance **gam002** as shown in Figure 2.7. Then select **Open with...** followed by **Praat** from the pull-out menu as shown in Figure 2.7 (NB: Praat must be running first for this to work).

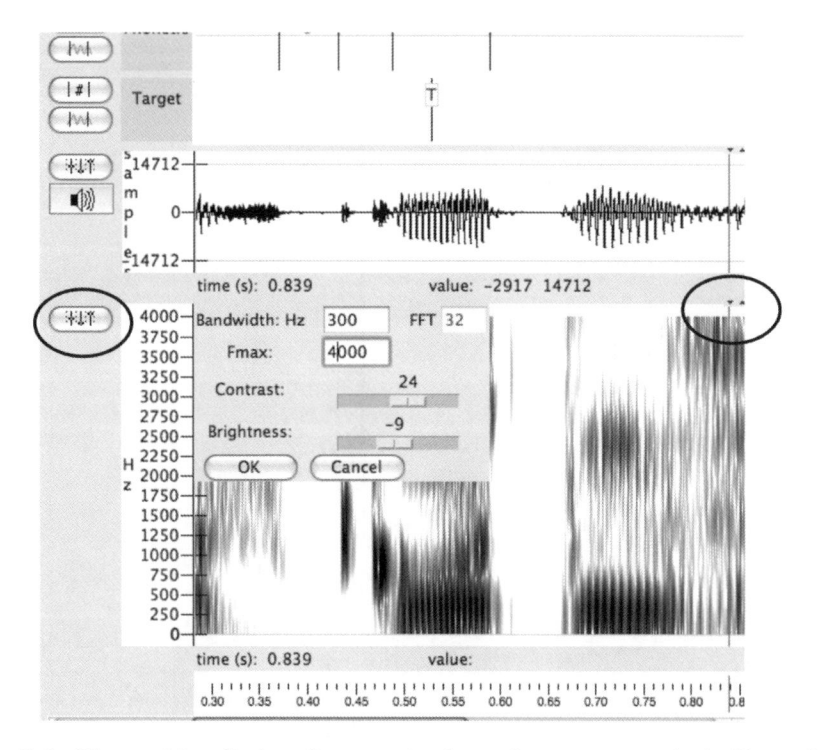

Figure 2.6 The resulting display after zooming in to the segment marks in Figure 2.5. The following further adjustments were also made. Firstly, click the button inside the ellipse on the left to get the pull-out menu shown over the spectrogram and then adjust the contrast and brightness sliders and reset the maximum spectral range to 4,000 Hz. You can also produce a narrow-band spectrogram showing harmonics by resetting the bandwidth to e.g., 45 Hz. The waveform and spectrogram windows can be made bigger/smaller using the triangles shown inside the ellipse on the right.

The result of this should be the same utterance showing the labeling tiers in Praat (Figure 2.8).

The task now is to segment and label this utterance at the **Word** tier so that you end up with a display similar to the one in Figure 2.8. The word to be labeled in this case is *Duden* (in the same carrier phrase as before). One way to do this is to move the mouse into the waveform or spectrogram window at the beginning of the closure of *Duden*; then click the circle at the top of the **Word** tier; finally, move the mouse to the end of this word on the waveform/spectrogram and click the circle at the top of the **Word** tier again. This should have created two vertical blue lines, one at the onset and one at the offset of this word. Now type in *Duden* beween these lines. The result after zooming in should be as in Figure 2.8. The final step involves saving the annotations which should be done with **Write Emulabels** from the **File** menu at the top of the display shown in Figure 2.8.

If you now go back to the Emu **Database Tool** (Figure 2.7) and double-click on the same utterance, it will be opened in Emu: the annotation that has just been entered at the **Word** tier in Praat should also be visible in Emu as in Figure 2.9.

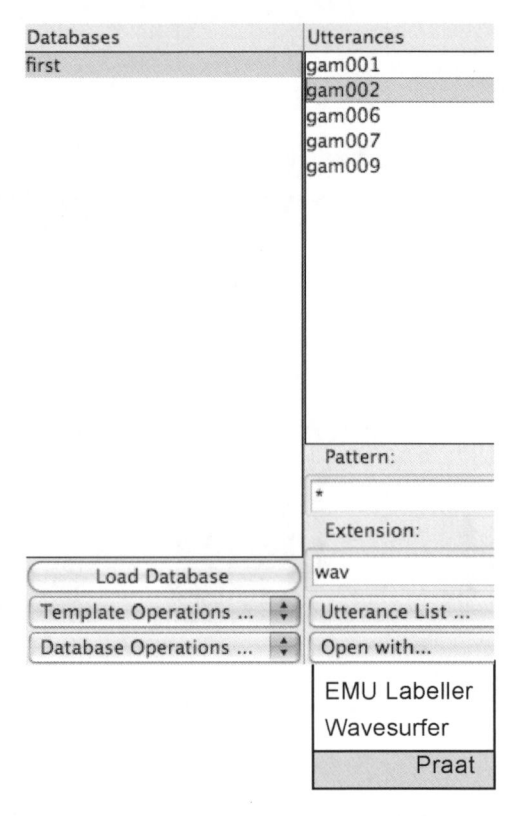

Figure 2.7 The steps for opening the utterance **gam002** in Praat from Emu. Click **gam002** in the **Utterances** pane once to select it, then Praat from the **Open with...** pull-down menu. Praat must already be running for this to work.

2.4 Interface to R

We now consider the right side of Figure 2.1 and specifically reading the annotations into R in the form of a segment list. First it will be necessary to cover a few background details about R (a more thorough treatment of R is given in Chapter 5). The reader is also encouraged to work through "An Introduction to R" from the webpage that is available after entering **help.start()** after the prompt. A very useful overview of R functions can be downloaded as a four-page reference card from the Rpad home page – see Short (2005).

2.4.1 A few preliminary remarks about R

When R is started, you begin a **session**. Initially, there will be a console consisting of a prompt after which commands can be entered:

```
> 23
[1] 23
```

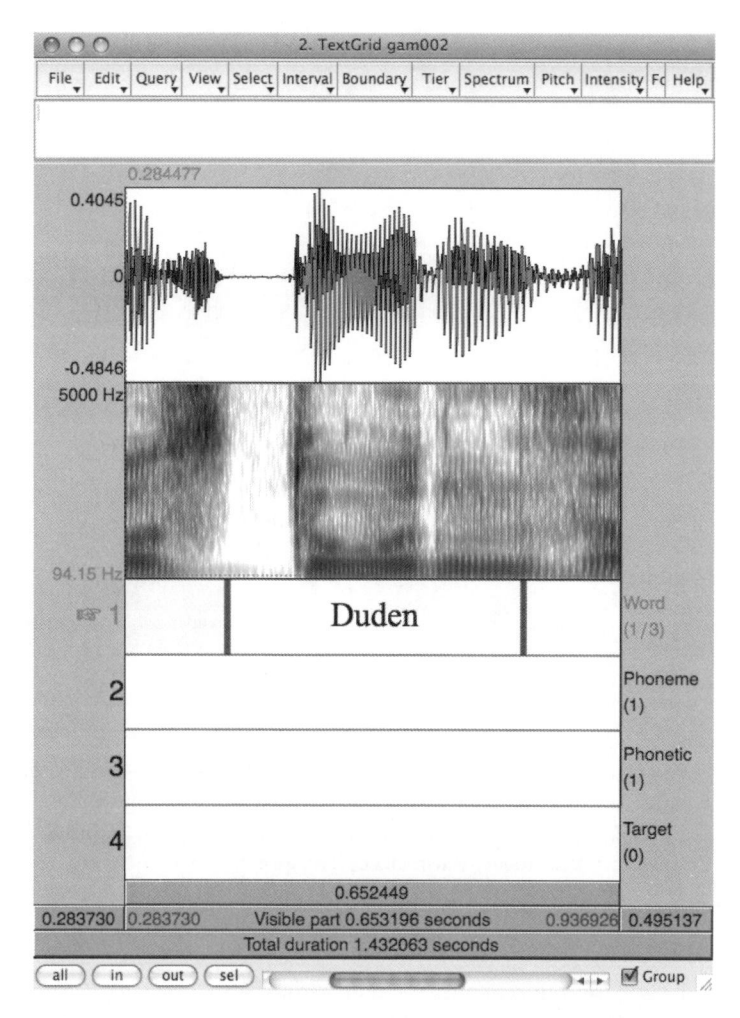

Figure 2.8 The utterance **gam002** opened in Praat and segmented and labeled at the **Word** tier.

The above shows **what is typed** in and what is returned, which will be represented in this book by these fonts respectively. The [1] denotes the first element of what is returned and it can be ignored (and will no longer be included in the examples in this book).

Anything following # is ignored by R: thus text following # is one way of including comments. Here are some examples of a few arithmetic operations that can be typed after the prompt with a following comment that explains each of them (from now on, the > prompt sign will not be included):

```
10 + 2        # Addition
2 * 3 + 12    # Multiplication and addition
54/3          # Division
pi            # π
```

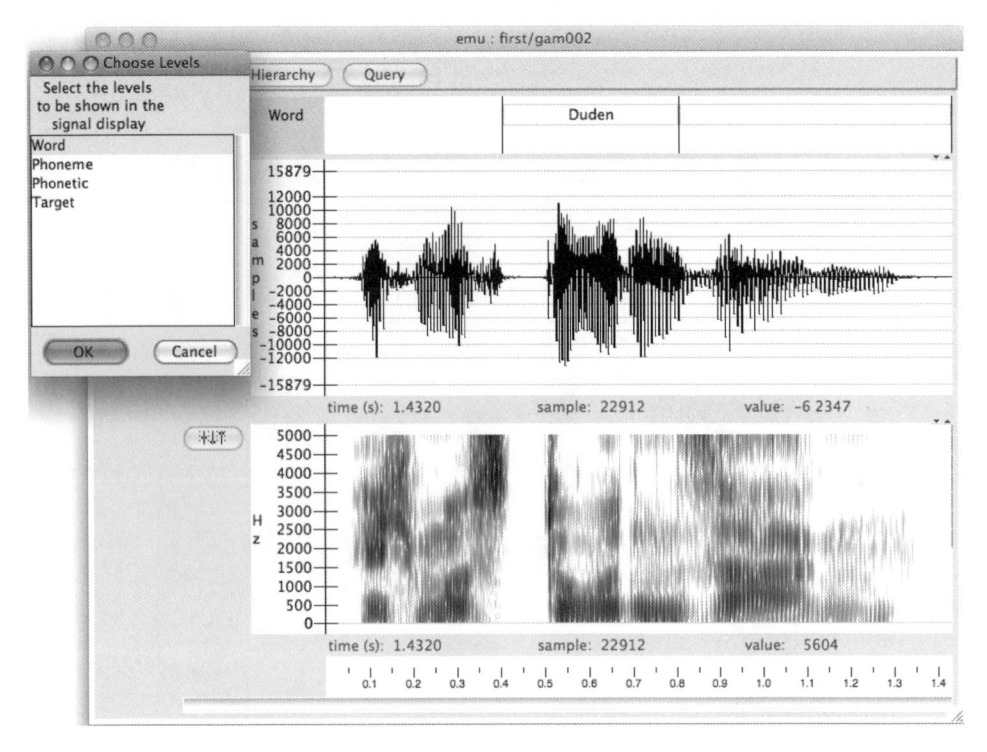

Figure 2.9 The corresponding display in Emu (obtained by double-clicking **gam002** – see Figure 2.7) after labeling the data with Praat in the manner of Figure 2.8. The other labeling tiers have been removed from the display with **Display** → **SignalViewLevels** and then by de-selecting **Phoneme**, **Phonetic**, **Target**.

```
2 * pi * 4     # Circumference of a circle, radius 4
4^2            # 4²
pi * 4^2       # Area of a circle, radius 4
```

During a session, a user can create a variety of different **objects** each with their own name using either the **<-** or the **=** operators:

newdata = 20

stores the value or element 20 in the object **newdata** so that the result of entering **newdata** on its own is:

newdata
20

newdata <- 20 can be entered instead of **newdata = 20** with the same effect. In R, the contents of an object are overwritten with another assign statement. Thus:

```
newdata = 50
```

causes **newdata** to contain the element 50 (and not 20).

Objects can be numerically manipulated using the operators given above:

```
moredata = 80
moredata/newdata
4
```

As well as being case-sensitive, R distinguishes between **numeric** and **character** objects, with the latter being created with " " quotes. Thus a character object **moredata** containing the single element **phonetics** is created as follows:

```
moredata = "phonetics"
moredata
"phonetics"
```

It is very important from the outset to be clear about the difference between a name with and without quotes. Without quotes, **x** refers to an object and its contents will be listed (if it exists); with quote marks **"x"** just means the character *x*. For example:

```
x = 20      Create a numeric object x containing 20
y = x       Copy the numeric object x to the numeric object y
y           y therefore also contains 20
20
y = "x"     Make an object y consisting of the character "x"
y           y contains the character "x"
"x"
```

Throughout this book use will be made of the extensive graphical capabilities in R. Whenever a function for plotting something is used, then a graphics window is usually automatically created. For example:

```
plot(1:10)
```

brings up a graphics window and plots integer values from 1 to 10. There are various ways of getting a new graphics window: for example, **win.graph()** on Windows, **quartz()** on a Macintosh, and **X11()** on Linux/Unix.

A **function** carries out one or more operations on objects and it can take zero or more **arguments** that are delimited by parentheses. The functions **ls()** or **objects()** when entered with no arguments can be used to show what objects are stored in the current workspace. The function **class()** with a single argument says something about the type of object:

```
newdata = 20
class(newdata)
"numeric"
```

```
newdata = "phonetics"
class(newdata)
"character"
```

Successive arguments to a function have to be separated by a comma. The function **rm()**, which can take an indefinite number of arguments, removes as many objects as there are arguments, for example:

rm(moredata)   Removes the object **moredata**
rm(moredata, newdata) Removes the objects **moredata** and **newdata**

Notice that entering the name of the function on its own without following parentheses or arguments prints out the function's code:

```
sort.list
function (x, partial = NULL, na.last = TRUE, decreasing =
FALSE,
   method = c("shell", "quick", "radix"))
{
   method = match.arg(method)
   if (!is.atomic(x))
```

... and so on.

To get out of trouble in R (e.g., you enter something and nothing seems to be happening), use control-C or press the ESC key and you will be returned to the prompt.

In order to quit an R session, enter **q()**. This will be followed by a question: **Save Workspace Image?** Answering **yes** means that all the objects in the workspace are stored in a file **.Rdata** that can be used in subsequent sessions (and all the commands used to create them are stored in a file **.Rhistory**) – otherwise all created objects will be removed. So if you answered **yes** to the previous question, then when you start up R again, the objects will still be there (enter **ls()** to check this). The directory to which these R data and history of commands are saved is given by **getwd()** with no arguments.

One of the best ways of storing your objects in R is to make a file containing the objects using the **save()** function. The resulting file can then also be copied and accessed in R on other platforms (so this is a good way of exchanging R data with another user). For example, suppose you want to save your objects to the file name **myobjects** in the directory **c:/path**. The following command will do this:

save(list=ls(), file="c:/path/myobjects")

Assuming you have entered the last command, quit R with the **q()** function and answer **no** to the prompt **Save Workspace Image?**, then start up R again. You can access the objects that you have just saved with:

attach("c:/path/myobjects")

In order to inspect which objects are stored in **myobjects**, find out where this file is positioned in the so-called R search path:

```
search()
[1] ".GlobalEnv"         "file:/Volumes/Data_1/d/myobjects"
[3] "tools:RGUI"         "package:stats"
[5] "package:graphics"   "package:grDevices"
```

Since in the above example **myobjects** is the second in the path, you can list the objects that it contains with **ls(pos=2)**.

The previous command shows that many objects and functions in R are pre-stored in a set of **packages**. These packages are available in three different ways. Firstly, entering **search()** shows the packages that are available in your current session. Secondly, there will be packages available on your computer but not necessarily accessible in your current session. To find out which these are enter:

```
library()
```

or

```
.packages(all.available = TRUE)
```

You can make a package from this second category available in your current session by passing the name of the package as an argument to **library()**: thus **library(emu)** and **library(MASS)** make these packages accessible to your current session (assuming that they are included when you enter the above commands). Thirdly, a very large number of packages is included at R archive network (**http://cran.r-project.org/**) and, assuming an internet connection is present, these can be installed directly with the **install.packages()** function. Thus, assuming that, for instance, the package **AlgDesign** is not yet stored on your computer then:[2]

```
install.packages("AlgDesign")
library(AlgDesign)
```

stores the package on your computer and makes it available as part of your current session.

R comes with an extensive set of help pages that can be illustrated in various ways. Try **help(pnorm)** or **?pnorm**, **example(density)**, **apropos("spline")**, **help.search("norm")**. As already mentioned, the function **help.start()** on its own provides an HTML version of R's online documentation.

2.4.2 Reading Emu segment lists into R

Start up R and then enter **library(emu)** after the R prompt. The function for making a segment list is **emu.query()** and it takes three arguments that are:

- the name of the database from which the segments are to be extracted;
- the utterances in the database over which the search is to be made;
- the pattern to be searched in terms of a labeling tier and segments.

The two labeled segments *guten* from **gam001** and *Duden* from **gam002** can be extracted with this function as follows:

```
emu.query("first", "*", "Word = guten | Duden")
Read 2 records
segment list from database: first
query was: Word = guten | Duden
  labels   start    end     utts
1 guten   371.64  776.06  gam001
2 Duden   412.05  807.65  gam002
```

The meaning of the command is: search through all utterances of the database **first** for the annotations *guten* or *Duden* at the **Word** tier. The next command does the same, but additionally saves the output to an object, **w**:

```
w = emu.query("first", "*", "Word = guten | Duden")
```

If you enter **w** on its own, then the same information about the segments shown above is displayed after the prompt.

As discussed more fully in Chapter 5, a number of functions can be applied to segment lists, and one of the simplest is **dur()** for finding the duration of each segment, thus:

```
dur(w)
404.42 395.60
```

shows that the duration of *guten* and *Duden* are 404 ms and 396 ms respectively.

2.5 Creating a New Speech Database: From Praat to Emu to R

You may already have labeled data in Praat that you would like to convert into Emu in order to read it into R. This section explains how to do this and will also provide some information about the way that Emu controls the attributes of each database in the form of a "blueprint" known as a **template file**. It will be assumed for the purposes of this section that you have some familiarity with how to segment and label speech data using Praat.

Begin by finding the directory to which you downloaded the database **first.zip** and the file **msajc023.wav**. If you downloaded **first.zip** to the directory **x**, then you will find this file in **x/first/msajc023.wav**. It should be pointed out that this audio file has nothing to do with the database **first** that was labeled in the preceding section: it has simply been put into that directory as a

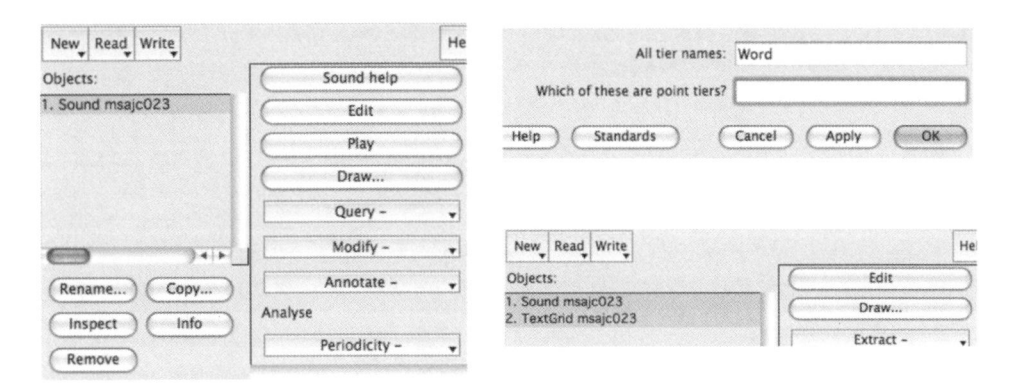

Figure 2.10 Opening files in Praat. Open the utterance `msajc023.wav` with **Read → Read from File** in the left pane, then select **to TextGrid** from the **Annotate** pull-down menu to bring up the pane shown top right and enter **Word** as a segment tier. After clicking the **OK** button in the top right pane, the TextGrid object will appear in the Praat objects window as shown bottom right. Select both the sound file and this TextGrid object together to derive the initially unlabeled waveform and spectrogram in Figure 2.11.

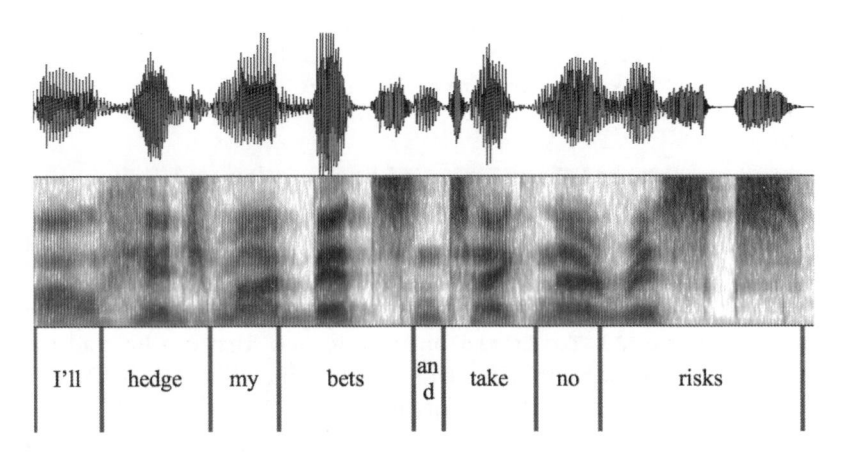

Figure 2.11 The audio file `msajc023.wav` segmented and labeled into words. Save the TextGrid to the same directory where `msajc023.wav` is located with **File → Write TextGrid to text file**.

convenient way to access an audio file for analyzing in further detail the relationship between Praat and Emu.

Start up Praat and load the file `msajc023.wav` and create a TextGrid file with a segment tier called **Word** in the manner of Figure 2.10.

Now segment and label this file into its words as shown in Figure 2.11 and save the TextGrid to the same directory in which the audio file is located.

The task will be to convert this TextGrid file into a format that can be read by Emu (and therefore also by R). To do this, start up Emu and choose **Convert Labels** from the **Arrange Tools** pull-down menu. Then select **Praat 2 Emu** from the

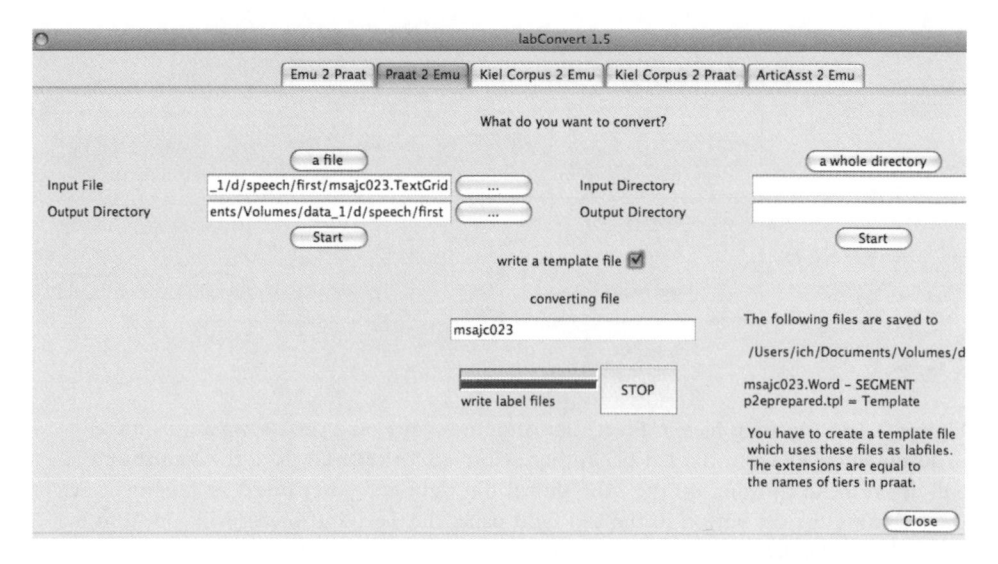

Figure 2.12 The **labConvert** window for inter-converting between Emu and Praat label files. Click on **Praat 2 Emu** to bring up this window, and enter the full path and file name for **msajc023.TextGrid** under **Input File** as shown. Then choose a directory into which the output of the conversion is to be written. Make sure you check the box **write a template file** as shown in order to create an Emu template during the conversion. Begin the conversion with **Start**.

labConvert (**graphical label convertor**) window and convert the TextGrid in the manner shown in Figure 2.12.

If you saved the TextGrid file to the same directory **first** that contains the audio file **msajc023.wav**, then the directory will now contain the files shown in Figure 2.13. The file **msajc023.Word** is a plain text file that contains the same information as **msajc023.TextGrid** but in a format[3] that can be read by Emu. The extension is always the same as the name of the annotation tier: so the extension is **.Word** in this case because the annotation tier in Praat was called **Word** (see Figure 2.10). If there had been several annotation tiers in Praat, then the conversion in Figure 2.12 would have produced as many files as there are annotation tiers, each with separate extensions and with the same **base-name** (**msajc023**). The file **p2epreparedtpl.tpl** (Praat-to-Emu prepared template) is the (plain text) Emu template file that is the output of the conversion and which defines the attributes of the database.

An important change now needs to be made to the template file before the database is accessible to Emu and this, together with some other attributes of the template, is discussed in the next section.

2.6 A First Look at the Template File

If you carried out the conversion of the Praat TextGrid in the same directory where the audio file **msajc023.wav** is located, i.e., in the **first** directory that was

Building and Querying Annotated Databases 35

Figure 2.13 The files in the **first** directory after converting the Praat TextGrid. At this point, you should rename the template file **p2epreparedtpl.tpl** as something else e.g., **jec.tpl**.

downloaded as part of the initial analysis in this chapter, then a template file called **p2epreparedtpl** should be available when you open the Emu **Database Tool**. However, it is a good idea to rename the template file as something else so that there is no conflict with any other data, should you carry out another conversion from Praat TextGrids at some later stage. When you rename **p2epreparedtpl.tpl** in the directory listing in Figure 2.13 as something else, be sure to keep the extension **.tpl**. I have renamed the template file[4] **jec.tpl** so that opening the Emu **Database Tool** shows the database with the corresponding name, as in Figure 2.14.

At this stage, Emu will not be able to find any utterances for the **jec** database because it does not know where the audio file is located. This, as well as other information, needs to be entered in the template file for this database, which is accessible with **Edit Template** from the **Template Operations...** menu (Figure 2.14). This command activates the **Graphical Template Editor** which allows various attributes of the database to be incorporated via the following sub-menus:

Levels:	The annotation tiers (in this case **Word**).
Labels:	Annotation tiers that are parallel to the main annotation tiers (discussed in further detail in Chapter 4).
Labfiles:	Information about the type of annotation tier (segment or event) and its extension.
Legal Labels:	Optionally defined features for annotations of a given tier.
Tracks:	The signal files for the database, their extension and location.
Variables:	Further information including the extension over which to search when identifying utterances.
View:	The signals and annotation tiers that are viewed upon opening an utterance.

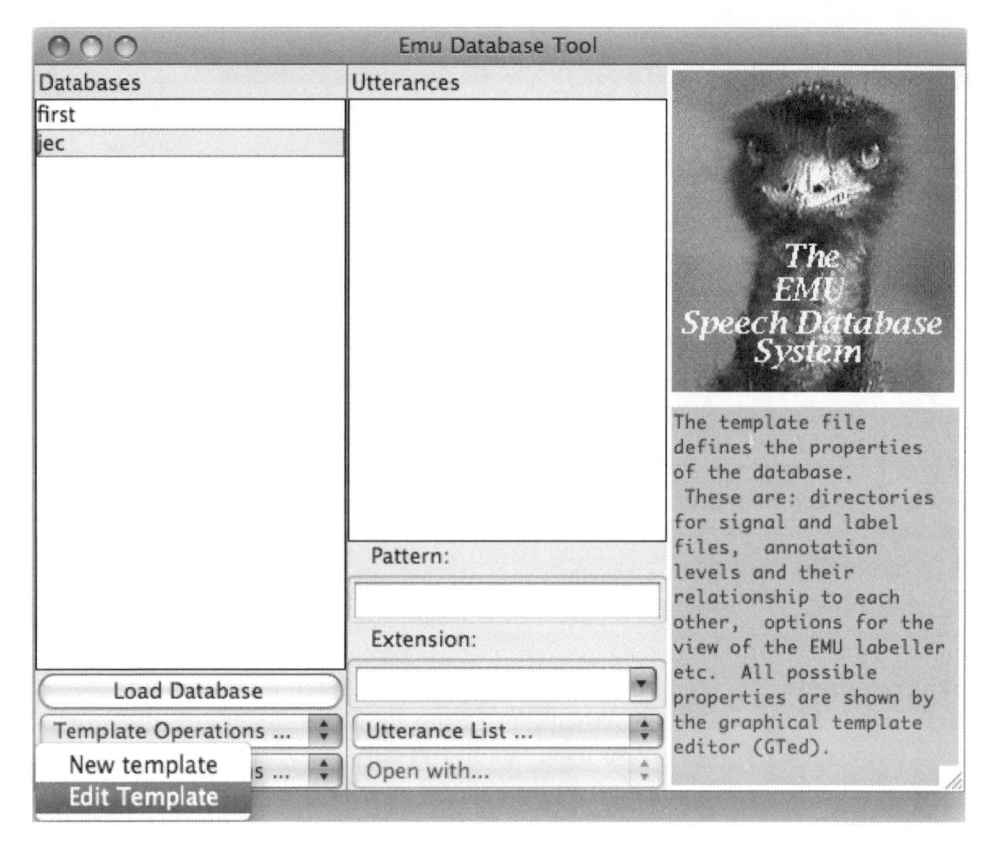

Figure 2.14 The Emu **Database Tool** showing the new database whose template should be edited with **Edit Template**.

The two sub-menus that are important for the present are **Tracks** and **Variables**. These need to be changed in the manner shown in Figure 2.15.

Changing the **Tracks** pane (Figure 2.15) has the effect of saying firstly what the extension of the audio files is (**wav** for this database) and secondly where the audio files are located. Setting the primary extension to **wav** in the **Variables** pane is the means by which the base-names are listed under **Utterances** in the Emu **Database Tool**. (More specifically, since for this example the primary extension is set to **wav** and since files of extension **wav** are found in **x/first** according to the **Tracks** pane, then any files with that extension and in that directory show up as base-names, i.e., utterance-names in the Emu **Database Tool**.)

The effect of changing the template in this way is to make the utterance available to Emu as shown in Figure 2.16: when this utterance is opened, then the audio signal as well as the labels that were marked in Praat will be displayed.

Finally, the database and utterance should now also be accessible from R following the procedure in 2.4.2. The following commands in R can be used to obtain the word durations:[5]

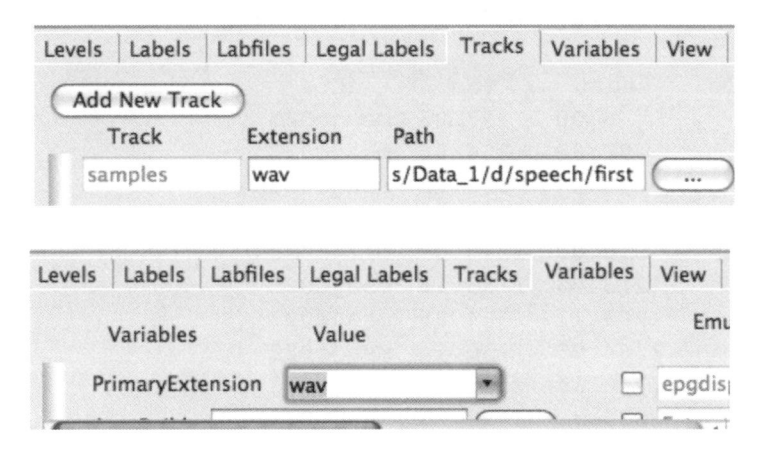

Figure 2.15 The **Tracks** (top) and **Variables** (bottom) panes of the template file for the database **jec**. Specify the extension as **wav** and the path as **x/first**, where **x** is the directory in which **msajc023.wav** is stored. For the **Variables** pane, specify the primary extension as **wav**: the utterances of the database will then be defined to be all **wav** files that are found under **Path** in the **Tracks** pane.

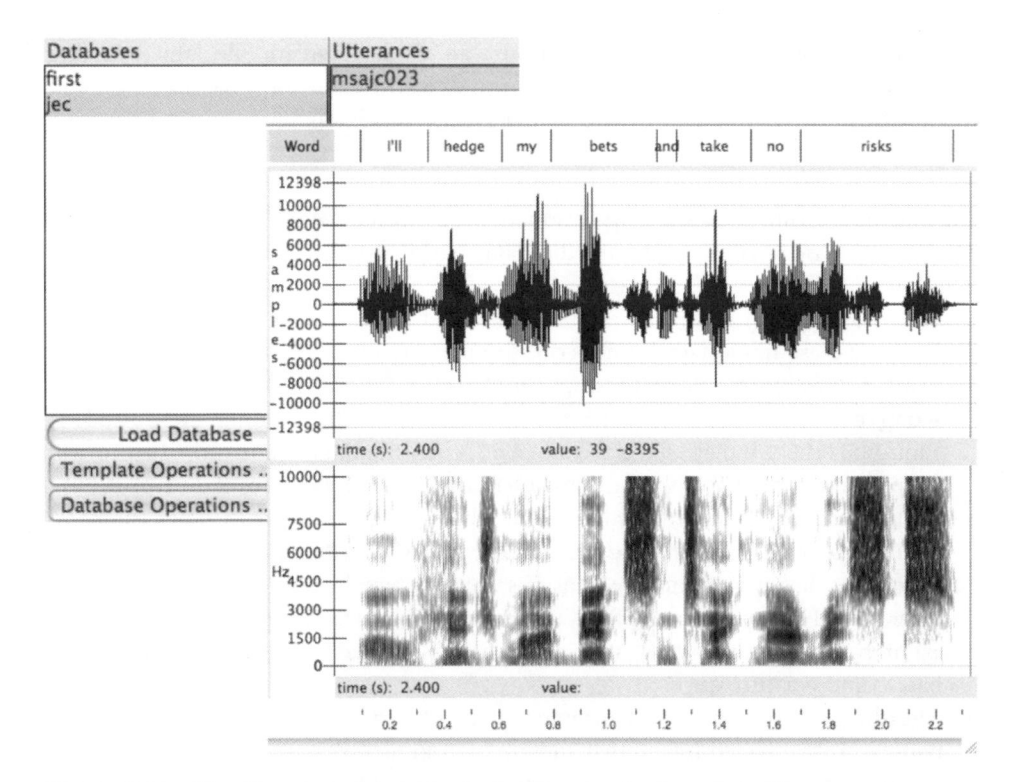

Figure 2.16 The Emu **Database Tool** showing the database **jec**. The utterances are accessible after editing the template file as shown in Figure 2.15 and then selecting **Load Database**. Double-clicking on the utterance-name opens the utterance in Emu as shown on the right.

```
words = emu.query("jec", "*", "Word!=x")
words
    labels    start      end      utts
1    *          0.00    97.85   msajc023
2    I'll      97.85   350.94   msajc023
3    hedge    350.94   628.72   msajc023
4    my       628.72   818.02   msajc023
5    bets     818.02  1213.09   msajc023
6    and     1213.09  1285.11   msajc023
7    take    1285.11  1564.95   msajc023
8    no      1564.95  1750.14   msajc023
9    risks   1750.14  2330.39   msajc023
10   *       2330.39  2428.25   msajc023

dur(words)
97.85 253.09 277.78 189.30 395.07 72.02 279.84 185.19 580.25 97.86
```

2.7 Summary

This introductory chapter has covered some details of file structure in a database, the organization of annotations, an Emu template file, the interface between Praat, Emu, and R, and some of the different Emu tools for accessing and annotating data. A summary of the salient points within these main headings is as follows.

File structure Emu makes a sharp distinction between a database, the utterances of which a database is composed, and the data that is associated with each utterance, as follows:

- Each database has a name and a corresponding template file which has the same name followed by the extension **.tpl**. Thus, if there is a database called **simple**, then there will also be a template file with the name **simple.tpl**. If Emu finds the template file **simple.tpl**, then the database name **simple** will appear under databases in the Emu **Database Tool** (Figures 2.2, 2.4, 2.14).
- Each utterance has a name or base-name that precedes any prefix. Thus the base-name of **a.wav, a.fms, a.epg, a.hlb, a.lab, a.TextGrid** is in each case **a** and the files with various extensions are different forms of data for the same utterance. The base-names of the utterances appear in the right of the display of Figures 2.2, 2.4, and 2.14 after a database is loaded, and there is always one base-name per utterance.
- The different variants of an utterance (i.e., the different extensions of a base-name) can be divided into signal and annotation files. A signal file is any digitized representation of the speech. The types of signal file typically include an audio file (often with extension **.wav**), and signal files derived from the audio file. An annotation file includes one or more annotations with time-markers linked to the signal files.

Organization of annotations

- There is a basic distinction between segment tiers (each annotation has a certain duration) and event or point tiers (each annotation marks a single point in time but is without duration).
- Annotations are organized into separate tiers.
- In Emu, there is one annotation file (see above) per segment or point tier. Thus if an utterance is labeled in such a way that words, phonemes, and tones are each associated with their separate times, then in Emu there will be three annotation files, each with their own extension for that utterance. In Praat all of this information is organized into a single TextGrid.

Template file An Emu template file defines the attributes of the database. A template file includes various kinds of information such as the annotation tiers and how they are related to each other, the types of signal file in the database, where all the different signal and annotation files of a database are physically located, and the way that an utterance is to be displayed when it is opened in Emu.

Praat–Emu interface The Praat–Emu interface concerns only annotations, not signals. The time-based annotations discussed in this chapter are inter-convertible so that the same utterance and its annotation(s) can be viewed and edited usually with no loss of information in Praat and Emu.

Emu–R interface R is a programming language and environment and the Emu-R library is a collection of functions for analyzing speech data that is accessible within R using the command **library(emu)**. Emu annotations are read into R using the Emu query language (Emu-QL) in the form of segment lists. Praat TextGrids can also be read into R as segment lists via the Praat–Emu interface defined above.

Emu tools discussed in this chapter Various Emu tools associated with different tasks have been made use of in this chapter. These and a number of other tools are accessible from the Emu **Database Tool**, which is also the central tool in Emu for listing the databases and for opening utterances. The other tools that were discussed include:

- the **Database Installer** for installing via an internet link existing annotated databases for use in this book (accessible from **Arrange Tools**);
- the **graphical template editor** for inspecting and editing the template file of a database (accessible from **Template Operations**);
- the **graphical label convertor** for inter-converting between Praat TextGrids and Emu annotations (accessible from **Arrange Tools**).

2.8 Questions

A. This question is designed to extend familiarity with annotating speech data in Emu and with Emu template files. It also provides an introduction to the Emu

configuration editor which is responsible for making template files on your system available to Emu. The exercise involves annotating one of the utterances of the **first** database with the two different annotation tiers, **Word** and **Phoneme**, as shown in Figure 2.17. Since the annotation tiers are different, and since the existing annotations of the **first** database should not be overwritten, a new template file will be needed for this task.

A.1 Begin by creating a directory on your system for storing the new annotations which will be referred to as "your path" in the question below.

A.2 Start up the Emu **Database Tool** and choose **New template** from the **Template Operations...** menu.

A.3 Enter the new annotation tiers in the manner shown in Figure 2.17. Use the **Add New Level** button to provide the fields for entering the **Phoneme** tier. Enter the path of the directory you created in A.1 for the so-called **hlb** or hierarchical label files. (This is an annotation file that encodes information about the relationship between tiers and is discussed more fully in Chapter 4.)

A.4 Select the **Labfiles** pane and enter the information about the annotation tiers (Figure 2.18). To do this, check the **labfile** box, specify both **Word** and **Phoneme** as segment tiers, enter your chosen path for storing annotations from A.1, and specify an extension for each tier. Note that the choice of extension names is arbitrary: in Figure 2.18, these have been entered as **w** and **phon**, which means that files of the form **basename.w** and **basename.phon** will be created containing the annotations from the **Word** and **Phoneme** tiers respectively.

A.5 Select the **Tracks** pane (Figure 2.19) and enter the path where the sampled speech data (audio files) are stored. In my case, I downloaded the database **first.zip** to **/Volumes/Data/d/speech** so the audio files, **gam001.wav** to **gam009.wav**, are in **/Volumes/Data/d/speech/first/signals**, which is also the path entered in the **Tracks** pane in Figure 2.19. The location of these files in your case depends on the directory to which you downloaded **first.zip**. If you

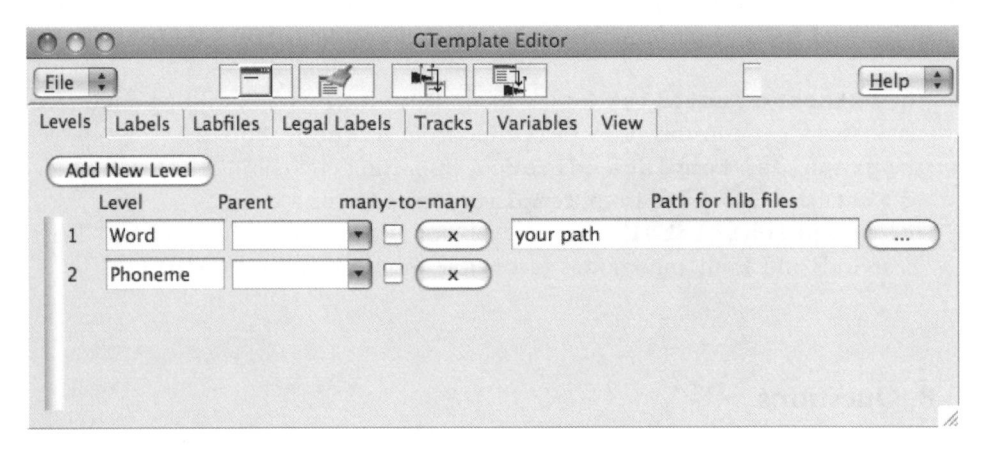

Figure 2.17 The information to be entered in the **Levels** pane.

Building and Querying Annotated Databases 41

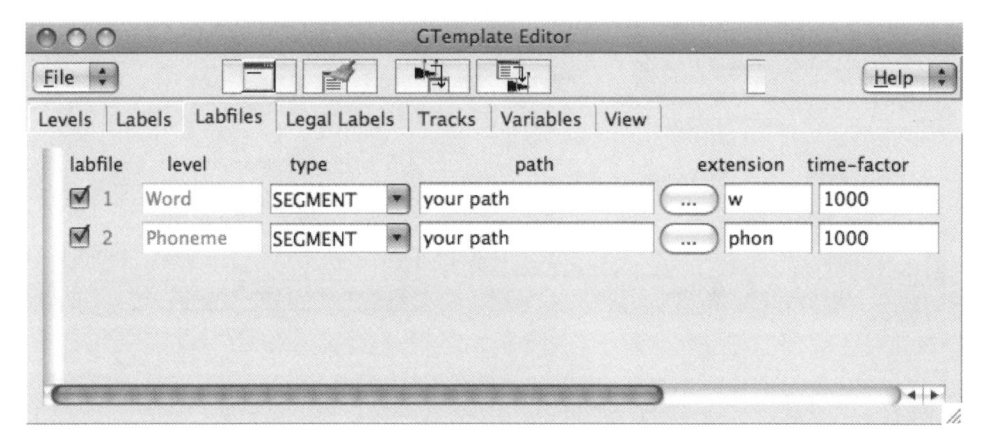

Figure 2.18 The information to be entered in the **Labfiles** pane.

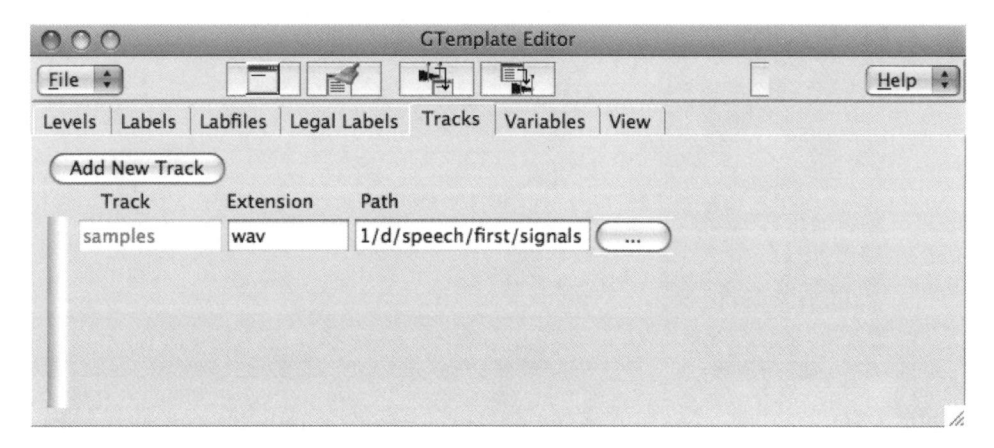

Figure 2.19 The information to be entered in the **Tracks** pane.

downloaded it to the directory **x**, then enter **x/first/signals** under **Path** in Figure 2.19. The extension also needs to be specified as **wav** because this is the extension of the speech audio files.

A.6 Select the **Variables** pane (Figure 2.20) and choose **wav** as the primary extension. This will have the effect that any files with **.wav** in the path specified in Figure 2.20 will show up as utterances when you open this database.

A.7 Save the template file (see the top left corner of Figures 2.17 to 2.20) with a name of your choice, e.g., **myfirst.tpl** and be sure to include the extension **.tpl** if this is not supplied automatically. For the purposes of the rest of this question, I will refer to the path of the directory to which you have stored the template as **pathtemplate**.

A.8 The location of the template now needs to be entered into Emu. To do this, make sure Emu is running and then open the configuration editor from inside the file

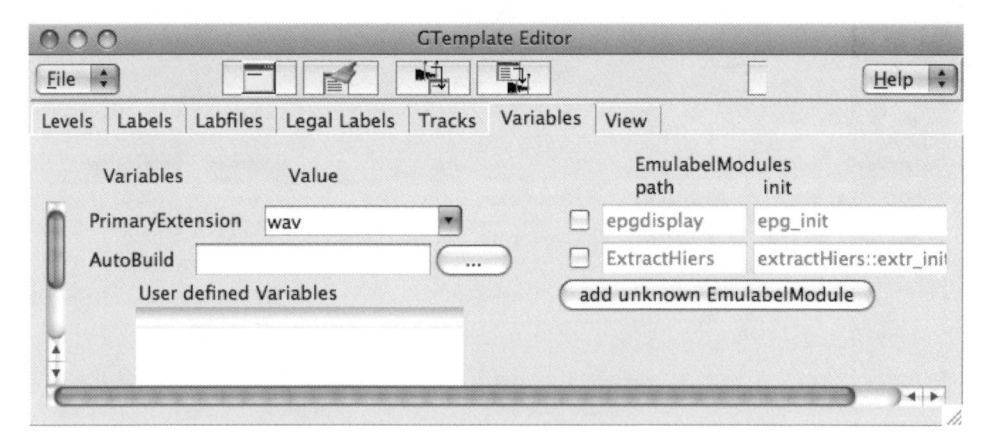

Figure 2.20 The information to be entered in the **Variables** pane.

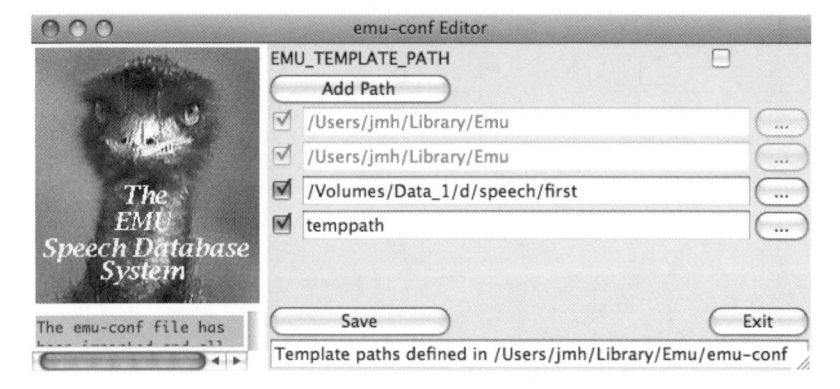

Figure 2.21 The Emu **configuration editor** showing the paths for the template files.

menu of the Emu **Database Tool**, which will bring up the display in Figure 2.21. This display should already include at least one path which is the location of the template file for the database **first.zip** that was downloaded at the beginning of this chapter. Select **Add Path** then enter the path in A.7 where you stored **myfirst.tpl** (which I have indicated as **temppath** in Figure 2.21).

A.9 If you have entered the above information correctly, then when you next click in the **databases** pane of the Emu **Database Tool**, your database/template file should appear as in Figure 2.22. If it does not, then this can be for various reasons: the path for the template file was not entered correctly (A.8); the paths for the signal files have not been entered correctly (A.3–5); **.tpl** was not included as an extension in the template file; the primary extension (A.6) has not been specified.

Assuming, however, that all is well, double-click on **gam007** to bring up the display (initially without labels) in Figure 2.23 whose spectrogram image was also manually sharpened as described earlier in Figure 2.6.

A.10 There is a way of segmenting and labeling in Emu which is quite similar to Praat and this will be the form that is explained here. Position the mouse either in

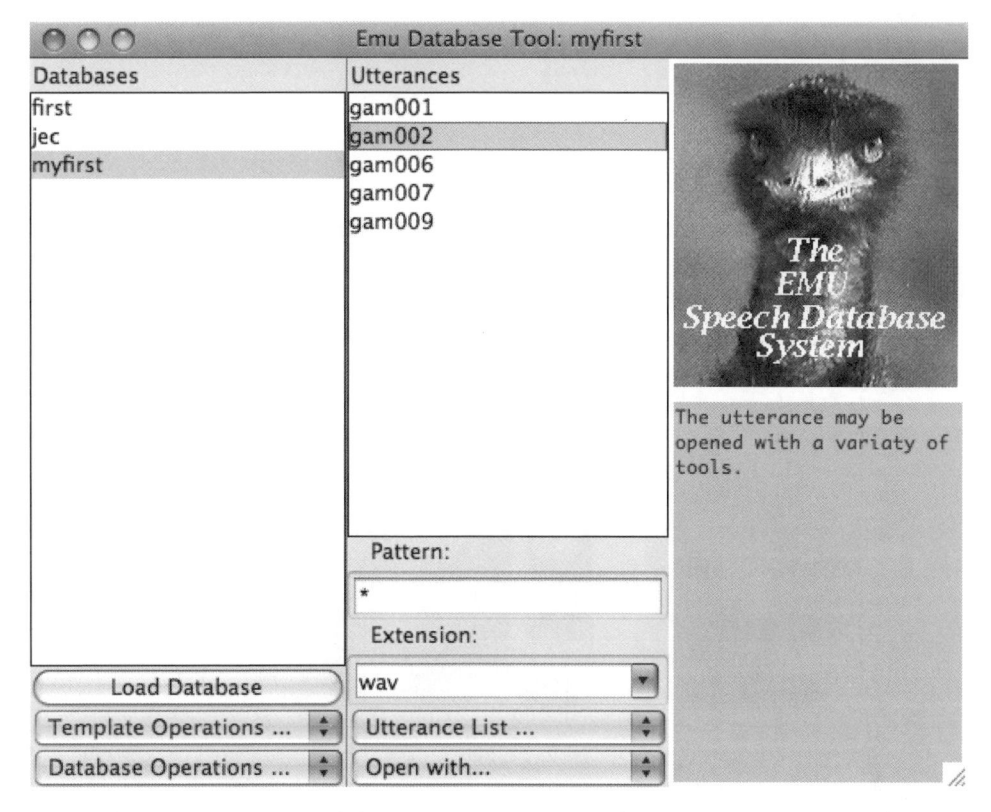

Figure 2.22 The Emu **Database Tool** showing the **myfirst** database and associated utterances.

the waveform or in the spectrogram window at the beginning of the first word *ich* and click with the left mouse button. This will bring up two vertical blue bars in the **Word** and **Phoneme** tiers. Move the mouse to the blue vertical bar at the **Word** tier and click on it. This will cause the blue bar at the **Word** tier to turn black and the one at the **Phoneme** tier to disappear. Now move the mouse back inside the waveform or spectrogram window to the offset of *ich* and click once to bring up two blue vertical bars again. Move the mouse to the blue bar you have just created at the **Word** tier and click on it. The result should be two black vertical bars at the onset and offset of *ich* and there should also be a gray rectangle between them into which you can type text: click on this gray rectangle, enter *ich* followed by carriage return. Proceed in the same way until you have completed the segmentation and labeling, as shown in Figure 2.23. Then save your annotations with **File → Save**.

A.11 Verify that, having saved the data, there are annotation files in the directory that you specified in A.1. If you chose the extensions shown in Figure 2.18, then there should be three annotation files in that directory: **gam007.w**, **gam007.phon**, and **gam007.hlb** containing the annotations at the **Word** tier, annotations at the **Phoneme** tier, and a code relating the two respectively.

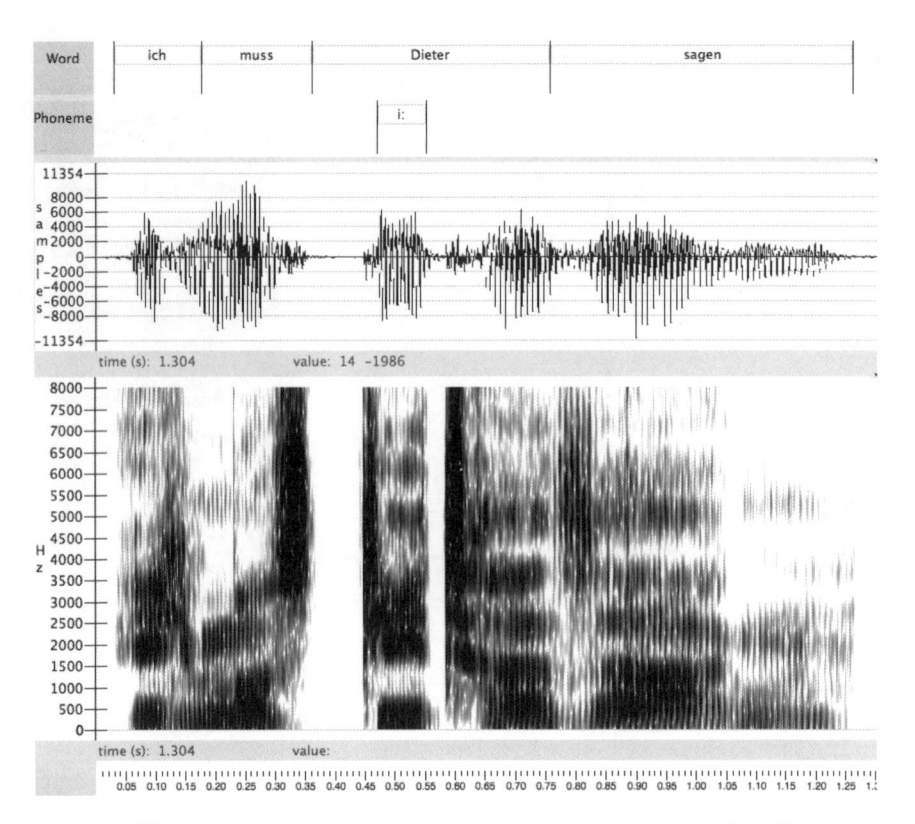

Figure 2.23 The utterance **gam007** showing a segmentation into words and a single **i:** segment at the **Phoneme** tier.

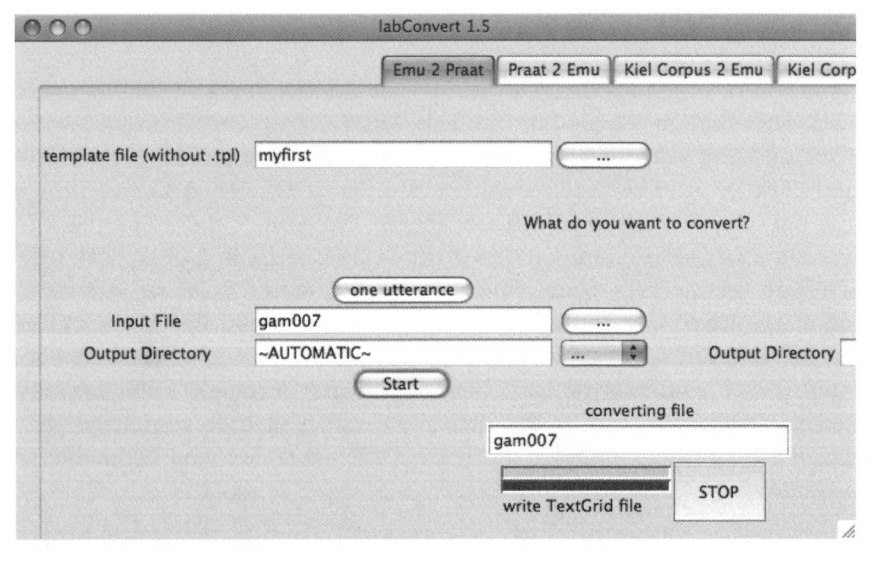

Figure 2.24 The **labConvert** window to convert the Emu annotations into a Praat TextGrid. Select **myfirst** from the **...** pull-down menu at the top, then **gam007** from the **...** menu in the middle, and then choose **Automatic** to save the TextGrid to the same directory in which the Emu annotations are stored. Finally select **Start**.

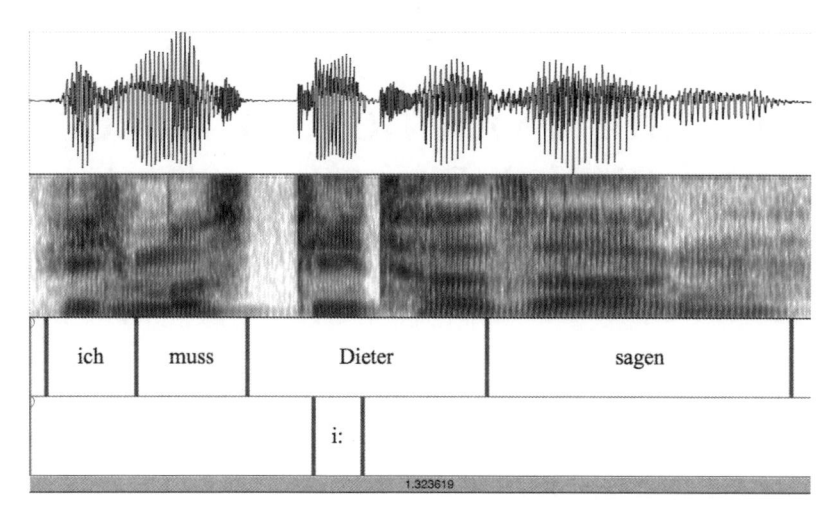

Figure 2.25 The same utterance and annotations as in Figure 2.23, here as a Praat TextGrid.

A.12 The task now is to convert these annotations into a Praat TextGrid. To do this, start up the Emu **Database Tool** then select **Arrange Tools** → **Convert Labels** followed by **Emu 2 Praat** in the **labConvert** window (Figure 2.24).

A.13 Verify that **gam007.TextGrid** has been created in the directory given in A.1 and then open the TextGrid and the audio file in Praat as in Figure 2.25.

Notes

[1] Much of the material in this chapter is based on Bombien et al. (2006), Cassidy and Harrington (2001), and Harrington et al. (2003).
[2] On some systems: **install.packages("AlgDesign", "path", "http://cran.r-project.org")** where **path** is the name of the directory for storing the package.
[3] In fact, for historical reasons, it is in the format used by ESPS/Waves.
[4] After the first author, John Clark of Clark et al. (2007) who produced this utterance as part of the Australian National Speech Database in 1990.
[5] Remember to enter **library(emu)** first.

3
Applying Routines for Speech Signal Processing

3.1 Introduction

The task in this chapter will be to provide a brief introduction to the signal processing capabilities in Emu with a particular emphasis on the formant analysis of vowels. As is well known, the main reason why listeners hear phonetic differences between two vowels is because they have different positions in a two-dimensional space of *vowel height* and *vowel backness*. These phonetic dimensions are loosely correlated respectively with the extent of mouth opening and the location of the maximum point of narrowing or *constriction location* in the vocal tract. Acoustically, these differences are (negatively) correlated with the first two resonances or formants of the vocal tract: thus, increases in phonetic height are associated with a decreasing first formant frequency (F1) and increasing phonetic backness with a decreasing F2. All of these relationships can be summarized in the two-dimensional phonetic *backness × height* space shown in Figure 3.1.

The aim in this chapter is to produce plots for vowels in the F1 × F2 plane of this kind and thereby verify that, when plotting the acoustic vowel space in this way, the

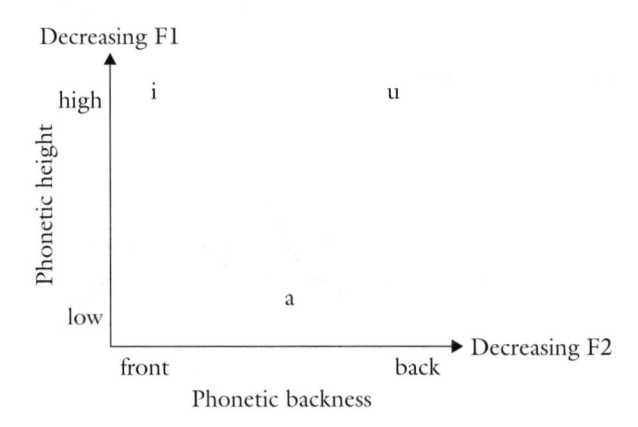

Figure 3.1 A schematic view of the phonetic vowel quadrilateral and its relationship to the first two formant frequencies.

vowel quadrilateral space emerges. In the acoustic analysis to be presented in this chapter, there will be several points, rather than just a single point per vowel as in Figure 3.1 and so each vowel category will be characterized by a two-dimensional *distribution*. Another aim will be to determine whether the scatter in this vowel space causes any overlap between the categories. In one of the final parts of this chapter (3.5) a male and female speaker will be compared on the same data in order to begin to assess some of the ways in which vowel formants are influenced by gender differences (an issue that is explored in more detail in Chapter 6); and the procedures for applying signal processing to calculating formants that will be needed in the body of the chapter will be extended to other parameters including fundamental frequency, intensity, and zero-crossing-rate.

Before embarking on the formant analysis, some comments need to be made about the point in time at which the formant values are to be extracted. Vowels have, of course, a certain duration, but judgments of vowel quality from acoustic data are often made from values at a single time point that is at, or near, the vowel's acoustic midpoint. This is done largely because, as various studies have shown, the contextual influence from neighboring sounds tends to be least at the vowel midpoint. The vowel midpoint is also temporally close to what is sometimes known as the *acoustic vowel target* which is the time at which the vocal tract is most "given over" to vowel production: thus F1 reaches a target in the form of an inverted parabola near the midpoint in non-high vowels, both because the vocal tract is often maximally open at this point, and because the increase in vocal tract opening is associated with a rise in F1 (Figure 3.2). In high vowels, F2 also reaches a maximum (in [i]) or

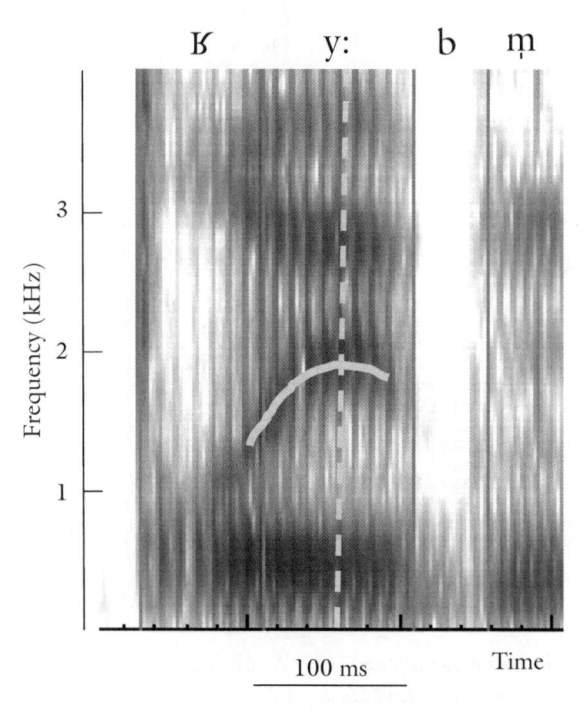

Figure 3.2 Spectrogram and superimposed second formant frequency of a production by a male speaker of the German word *drüben* with phonetic segments and boundaries shown. From Harrington (2010).

minimum (in [u]) near the temporal midpoint which is brought about by the narrowing at the palatal zone for [i] and at labial-velar regions of articulation for [u]. Figure 3.2 shows an example of how F2 reaches a maximum in the front rounded vowel [y:] in the region of the vowel's temporal midpoint.[1]

3.2 Calculating, Displaying, and Correcting Formants

Start up Emu and download the database **second.zip** exactly as shown in Figure 2.3 of the preceding chapter and then load the database as shown in Figure 2.4. This database is a larger version of the one downloaded in Chapter 2 and contains utterances from a female speaker (**agr**) and a male speaker (**gam**). The materials are the same as for the **first** database and include trochaic words of the form /CVC(ə)n/ such as *baten*, *Duden*, *geben*, and so on. It is the formants of the vowels that are the subject of the analysis here. The main initial task will be to analyze those of the male speaker whose utterances can be accessed by entering **gam*** as a pattern in the Emu **Database Tool**, as shown in Figure 3.3.

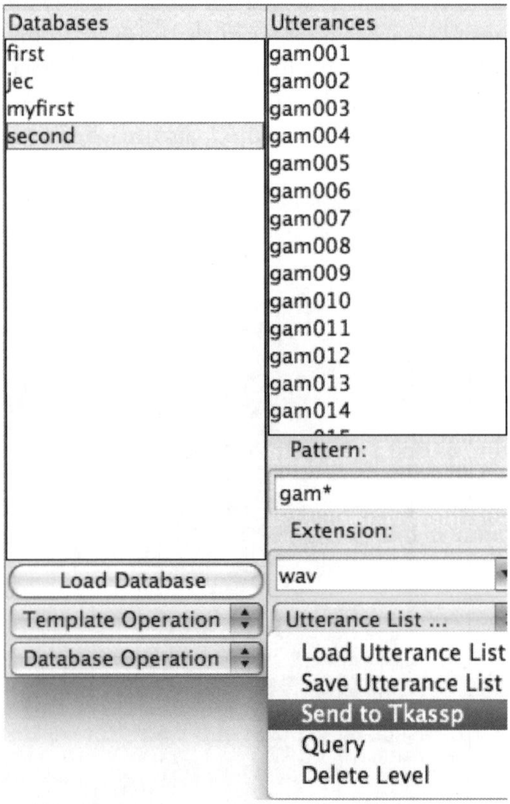

Figure 3.3 The Emu **Database Tool** after downloading the database **second.zip**. Enter **gam*** and confirm with the **ENTER** key to select all utterances beginning with **gam** (the male speaker) then select **Send to Tkassp** from the **Utterance List...** menu to bring up the **tkassp** window in Figure 3.4.

Opening any of these utterances produces a waveform, spectrogram, and annotation tiers at various levels, exactly as described in the previous chapter. The task is now to calculate the formant frequencies for the speaker **gam** and this is done by entering the corresponding pattern in the Emu **Database Tool** to select those utterances for this speaker and then passing them to the **tkassp** routines in the manner shown in Figure 3.3. The resulting **tkassp** window (a Tcl/Tk interface to acoustic speech signal processing) shown in Figure 3.4 includes a number of signal processing routines written by Michel Scheffers of the Institute of Phonetics and Speech Processing, University of Kiel. Selecting **samples** as the input track causes the utterances to be loaded. The formants for these utterances can then be calculated following the procedure described in Figure 3.4.

The result of applying signal processing in **tkassp** is as many derived files as input files to which the routines were applied. So, in this case, there will be one derived file containing the formant frequencies for utterance **gam001**, another for **gam002**, and so on. Moreover, these derived files are by default stored in the same directory that contains the input sampled speech data files and they have an extension that can be set by the user, but which is also supplied by default. As Figure 3.4 shows, formants are calculated with the default extension **.fms** and so the output of calculating the formants for these utterances will be files **gam001.fms**, **gam002.fms** . . . corresponding to, and in the same directory as, the audio files **gam001.wav**, **gam002.wav** . . .

Figure 3.4 also shows that there are other parameters that can be set in calculating formants. Two of the most important are the **window shift** and the **window size** or window length. The first of these is straightforward: it specifies how many sets of formant frequency values or **speech frames** are calculated per unit of time. The default in **tkassp** is for formant frequencies to be calculated every 5 ms. The second is the duration of sampled speech data that the algorithm sees in calculating a single set of formant values. In this case, the default is 25 ms which means that the algorithm sees 25 ms of the speech signal in calculating F1–F4. The window is then shifted by 5 ms, and a quadruplet of formants is calculated based on the next 25 ms of signals that the algorithm sees. This process is repeated every 5 ms until the end of the utterance.

The times at which the windows actually occur are a function of both the window shift and the window length. More specifically, the start time of the first window is $(t_S - t_L) / 2$, where t_S and t_L are the window shift and size respectively. Thus, for a window shift of 5 ms and a window size of 25 ms, the left edge of the first window is $(5 - 25) / 2 = -10$ ms and its right edge is 15 ms (an advancement of 25 ms from its left edge).[2] The next window has these times plus 5 ms, i.e., it extends from -5 ms to 20 ms, and so on. The derived values are then positioned at the center of each window. So, since the first window extends in this example from -10 ms to 15 ms, then the time at which the first quadruplet of formants occurs is $(-10 + 15) / 2 = 2.5$ ms. The next quadruplet of formants is 5 ms on from this at 7.5 ms (which is also $(-5 + 20) / 2$), etc.

Although formant tracking in Emu usually works very well from the default settings, one of the parameters that you do sometimes need to change is the **nominal F1** frequency. This is set to 500 Hz because this is the estimated first formant frequency from a lossless straight-sided tube 17.5 cm in length that serves well as a

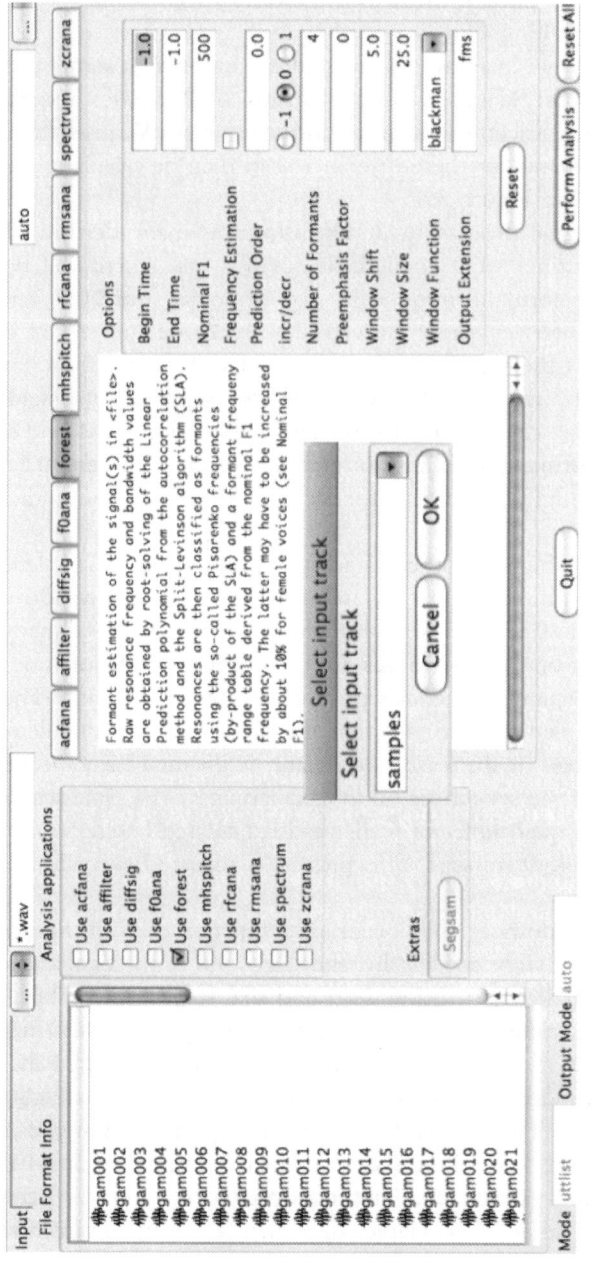

Figure 3.4 Upon selecting **Send to Tkassp** (Figure 3.3) a window (shown in the middle of this figure) appears asking whether **samples** should be selected as the input track. Selecting **OK** causes the sampled speech data (audio files) of the utterances to appear in the pane on the left. Check the **forest** box as shown to calculate formants and choose the **forest** tab (at the top of the display) to see the default parameters. Leaving the default output as **auto** (top right) causes the formants to be stored in the same directory as the audio files from which the formants have been calculated. The calculation of formants is done with the default settings (shown on the right) which include a window size of 25 ms and a window shift of 5 ms. The formant files are created with an extension **.fms**. When you are ready to calculate the formants, select **Perform Analysis**.

model for a schwa vowel for an adult male speaker. The length of 17.5 cm is based on the presumed total vocal tract length and so, since female speakers have shorter vocal tracts, their corresponding model for schwa has F1 at a somewhat higher value. Therefore, when calculating formants from female speakers, the formant-tracking algorithm generally gives much better results if nominal F1 is set to 600 Hz or possibly even higher.

There are still other parameters that for most purposes you do not need to change.[3] Two of these, the **prediction order** and the **pre-emphasis factor**, are to do with the algorithm for calculating the formants, linear predictive coding (LPC).[4] The first is set in relation both to the number of formant frequencies to be calculated and to the sampling frequency; the second is to do with factoring in "lumped" vocal tract losses in a so-called all-pole model. Another parameter that can be set is the **window function**. In general, and as described in further detail in Chapter 8 on spectra, there are good reasons for attenuating (reducing in amplitude) the signal progressively towards the edges of the window in applying many kinds of signal processing (such as the one needed for formant calculation), and most of the windows available such as the Blackman, Hanning, Hamming, and cosine in **tkassp** have this effect. The alternative is not to change the amplitude of the sampled speech data prior to calculating formants, which can be done by specifying the window to be rectangular.

In order to display the formants, it is necessary to edit the template file (Figures 2.14 and 2.15) so that Emu knows where to find them for this database. The relevant panes that need to be edited are shown in Figure 3.5. The same path is entered for the formants as for the audio files if the default setting (**auto**) was used for saving the formants (Figure 3.4). The track (name) should be set to **fm** because this tells Emu that these are formant data which are handled slightly differently from other

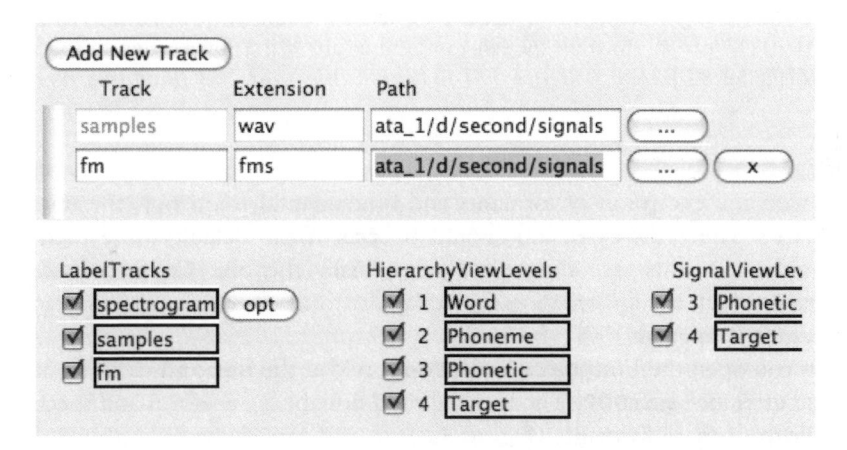

Figure 3.5 The additions to the **Tracks** (above) and **View** (below) panes that are needed for displaying the formants. Select **Add New Track** then enter **fm** under **Track**, **fms** for the extension, and copy the path from the audio file (the path next to **wav**). In the **View** pane, check the **fm** box which will have the effect of overlaying formants on the spectrograms. Finally, save the template file.

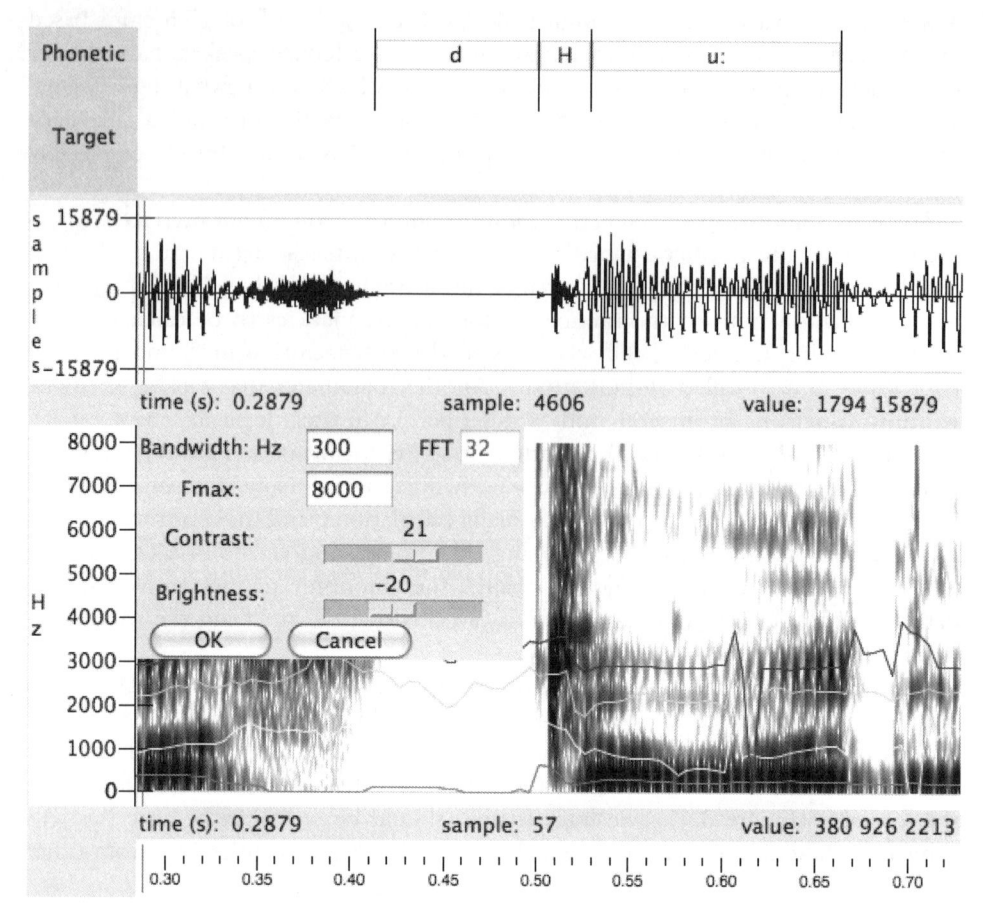

Figure 3.6 The utterance **gam002** with overlaid formants and spectrogram parameters readjusted as shown in the figure. There is an evident tracking error in F2, F3, and F4 at time 0.61 s. The pen buttons on the left can be used for manual correction of the formants (Figure 3.7).

tracks (with the exception of formants and fundamental frequency, the track name is arbitrary). The track extension should be **fms** if the defaults were used in calculating the formants (see Figure 3.3) and finally the box **fm** is checked in the **View** pane, which is an instruction to overlay the formants on the spectrogram when an utterance is opened.

When you open the Emu **Database Tool**, reload the **second** database and then open the utterance **gam002**. The result should now be a waveform and spectrogram display with overlaid formants (Figure 3.6).

As Figure 3.6 shows, there is evidently a formant-tracking error close to 0.61 s, which can be manually corrected in Emu following the procedure shown in Figure 3.7. When the manual correction is saved as shown in Figure 3.7, then the formant file of the corresponding utterance is automatically updated (the original formant file is saved to the same base-name with extension **fms.bak**).

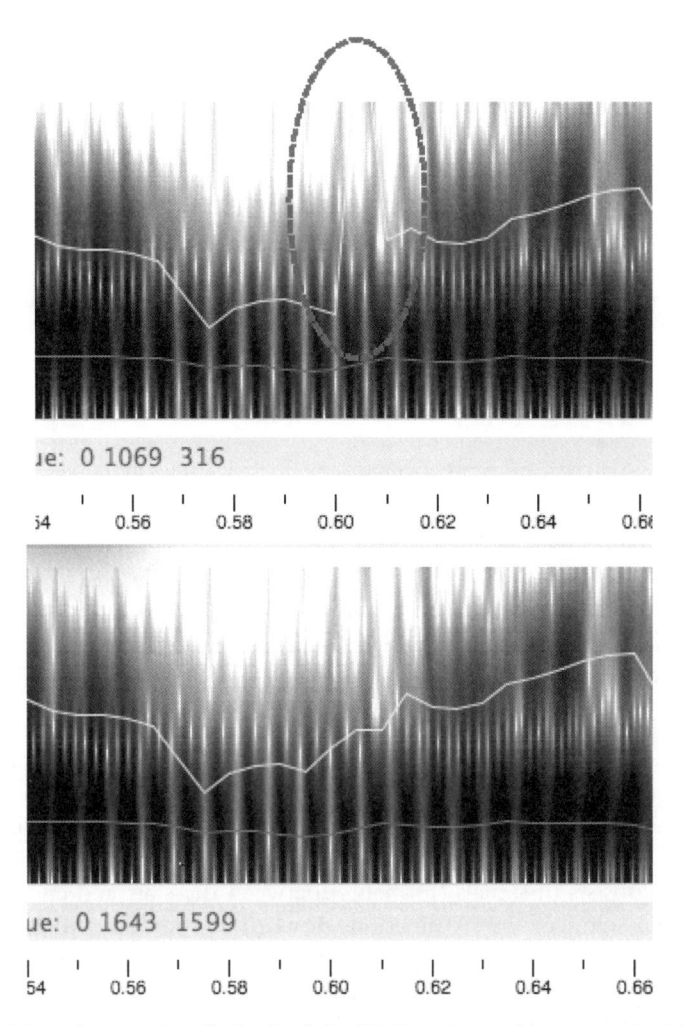

Figure 3.7 Manual correction (below) of the F2-formant-tracking error (inside the ellipse). The spectrogram is from the same utterance as in Figure 3.6 but with the frequency range set to 0–1,500 Hz. Selecting the pen color corresponding to that of F2 has the effect of showing the F2 values on the track as points. In order to change the F2 values manually, hold down the left mouse button without letting go and sweep across the spectrogram, either from left to right or from right to left slowly in order to reposition the point(s). When you are done, release the mouse and select the same pen color again. You will then be prompted to save the data. Choosing **yes** causes the formant file to be overwritten. Choosing **no** will still have the effect of redrawing the track according to your manual correction, but when you close the window, you will be asked again to save the data. If you choose **no** again, then the formant changes will not be saved.

3.3 Reading the Formants into R

The task now is to read the calculated formants and annotations into R in order to produce the F1 × F2 displays for the separate vowel categories. The procedure

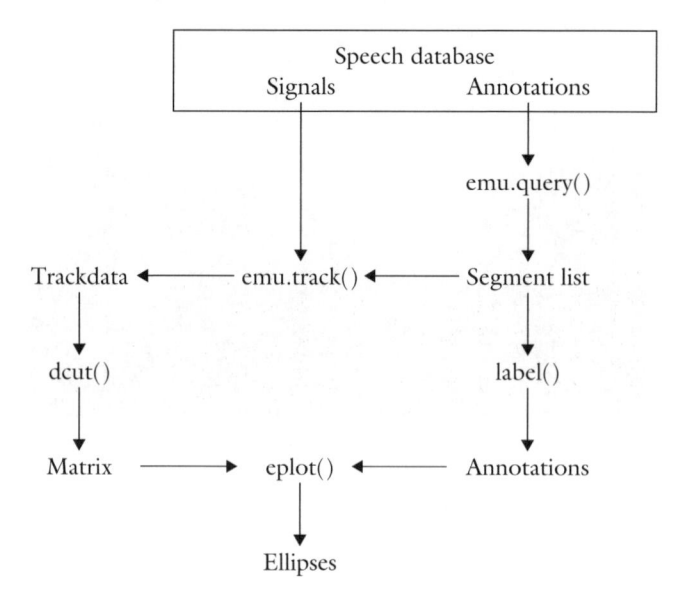

Figure 3.8 A flow diagram showing the relationship between signals, annotations, and the output, ellipses. Entries followed by () are functions in the Emu-R library. Remember to enter **library(emu)** at the R prompt to make use of any of these functions.

for doing so is sketched in Figure 3.8, the top half of which also represents a more general procedure for getting signals and annotations from Emu into R.

As Figure 3.8 shows, signals (in this case formant data) are read into R in the form of what is called **trackdata** but always from an existing segment list: as a result, the trackdata consists of signals (formants) between the start and end times of each segment in the segment list. A function, **dcut()** is then used to extract formant values at the segment's midpoint and these data are combined with annotations to produce the required ellipse plots. The procedure for creating a segment list involves using the **emu.query()** function which has already been touched upon in the preceding chapter. In the following, a segment list (**vowels.s**) is made of five of speaker **gam**'s monophthong categories, and then the formant data (**vowels.fm**) are extracted from the database relative to these monophthongs' start and end times (remember to enter **library(emu)** after starting R):

```
vowels.s = emu.query("second", "gam*", "Phonetic=i: | e: |
a: | o: | u:")
vowels.fm = emu.track(vowels.s, "fm")
```

The **summary()** function can be used to provide a bit more information on both of these objects:

```
summary(vowels.s)
segment list from database: second
query was: Phonetic=i: | e: | a: | o: | u:
with 45 segments
```

Segment distribution:

```
a:  e:  i:  o:  u:
9   9   9   9   9
```

summary(vowels.fm)
Emu track data from 45 segments

Data is 4 dimensional from track fm
Mean data length is 29.82222 samples

From this information, it can be seen that the segment list consists of nine of each of the monophthongs while the trackdata object is said to be four-dimensional (because there are four formants), extracted from the track **fm**, and with just under 30 data frames on average per segment. This last piece of information requires some further qualification. As already shown, there are 45 segments in the segment list and their average duration is:

mean(dur(vowels.s))
149.2712

i.e., just under 150 ms. Recall that the window shift in calculating formants was 5 ms. For this reason, a segment can be expected to have on average 149 / 5 – i.e., a fraction under 30 – sets of formant quadruplets (speech frames) spaced at intervals of 5 ms between the segment's start and end times.

It is important at this stage to be clear how the segment list and trackdata relate back to the database from which they were derived. Consider for example the fourth segment in the segment list. The information about its label, start time, end time, and utterance from which it was taken is given by:

vowels.s[4,]
```
segment list from database: second
query was: Phonetic=i: | e: | a: | o: | u:
 labels    start    end     utts
 4  i:    508.578  612.95  gam006
```

A plot[5] of the extracted formant data between these times (Figure 3.9, left panel) is given by:

plot(vowels.fm[4,])

or equivalently with **plot(vowels.fm[4,], type="l")** to produce a line plot. These are the same formant values that appear in Emu between 508 ms and 613 ms in the utterance **gam006**, as the panel in the right of Figure 3.9 shows.

Another important point about the relationship between a segment list and trackdata is that the speech frames are always extracted between or *within* the boundary times of segments in a segment list. Therefore the first speech frame in the fourth segment above must be fractionally after the start time of this segment at 508 ms

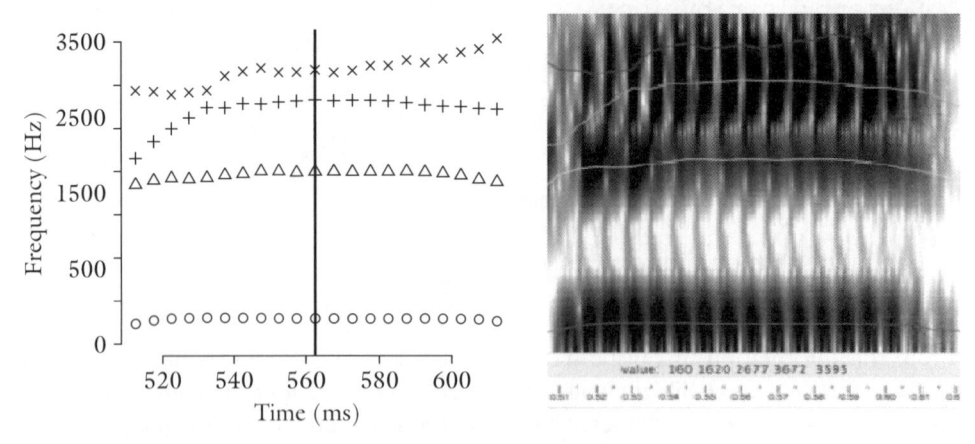

Figure 3.9 A display of the first four formants in R (left) and the corresponding formant display in Emu (right) for an [i:] vowel from the **gam006** utterance. The vertical line in the display on the left marks the temporal midpoint of the vowel at 562.5 ms and can be marked with **abline(v=562.5)**, once the formant data have been plotted.

and the last speech frame must be fractionally before its end time at 613 ms. This is confirmed by using the **start()** and **end()** functions to find the times of the first and last data frames for this segment:

```
start(vowels.fm[4,])
512.5
end(vowels.fm[4,])
612.5
```

Thus the times of the first (leftmost) quadruplet of formants in Figure 3.9 is 512.5 ms and of the last quadruplet 612.5 ms. These times are also found in **tracktimes(vowels.fm[4,])**, which returns the times of *all* the data frames of the fourth segment:

```
tracktimes(vowels.fm[4,])
512.5 517.5 522.5 527.5 532.5 537.5 542.5 547.5 552.5 557.5 562.5
567.5 572.5 577.5 582.5 587.5 592.5 597.5 602.5 607.5 612.5
```

The above once again shows that the times are at intervals of 5 ms. Further confirmation that the start and end times of the trackdata are just inside those of the segment list from which it is derived is given by subtracting the two:

```
start(vowels.fm) - start(vowels.s)
end(vowels.s) - end(vowels.fm)
```

The reader will see upon entering the above instructions in R that all of these subtracted times from all 45 segments are positive (thus showing that the start and end times of the trackdata are within those of the segment list from which it was derived).

As discussed at the beginning of this chapter, the task is to plot the ellipses at the temporal midpoint of the vowels and, to do this, the **dcut()** function is needed to extract these values from the trackdata (Figure 3.8). This is done as follows:

```
mid = dcut(vowels.fm, 0.5, prop=T)
```

The object **mid** is a matrix of 45 rows and 4 columns containing F1–F4 values at the segments' temporal midpoints. Here are F1–F4 at the temporal midpoint in the first eight segments (i.e., the formants at the midpoints of the segments in **vowels.s[1:8,]**):

```
mid[1:8,]
        T1    T2    T3    T4
542.5  260   889  2088  2904
597.5  234   539  2098  2945
532.5  287   732  2123  2931
562.5  291  1994  2827  3173
512.5  282  1961  2690  2973
532.5  291   765  2065  2838
562.5  595  1153  2246  3262
592.5  326   705  2441  2842
```

It looks as if there are five columns of formant data, but in fact the one on the far left is not a column in the sense that R understands it but a **dimension name** containing the times at which these formant values occur. In order to be clear about this, the fourth row (highlighted above) shows four formant values, F1 = 291 Hz, F2 = 1,994 Hz, F3 = 2,827 Hz, and F4 = 3,173 Hz that occur at time 562.5 ms. These are exactly the same values that occur just after 560 ms identified earlier in the utterance **gam006** and marked at the vertical line in the left panel of Figure 3.9.

A plot of all these formant data at the vowel midpoint could now be given by **plot(mid[,1:2])** or equivalently **plot(mid[,1], mid[,2])**, where the integers after the comma index the first and second column respectively. However, in order to differentiate the points by vowel category, a vector of their labels is needed and, as the flow diagram in Figure 3.8 shows, the vector can be obtained from the segment list using the **label()** function. Here the segment labels are stored as a vector **vowels.lab**:

```
vowels.lab = label(vowels.s)
```

The command **plot(mid[,1:2], pch=vowels.lab)** now differentiates the points by category label. However, these data are not the right way round as far as the more familiar vowel quadrilateral is concerned. In order to rotate the plot such that the vowels are arranged in relation to the vowel quadrilateral (i.e., as in Figure 3.1), a plot of − F2 vs − F1 on the *x*- and *y*-axes needs to be made. This could be done as follows:

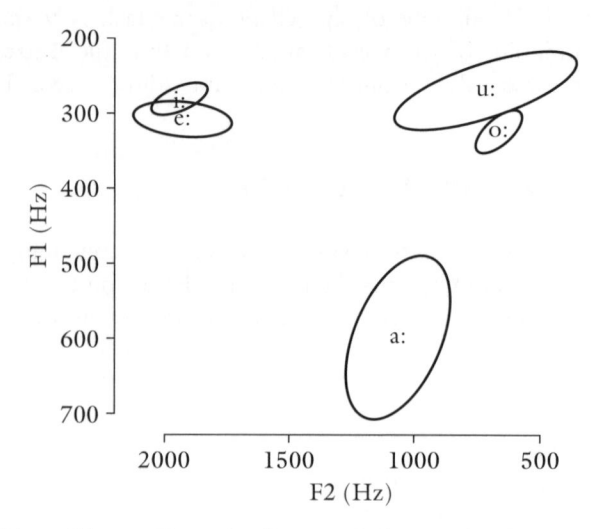

Figure 3.10 95% confidence ellipses for five vowels from isolated words produced by a male speaker of Standard German.

```
plot(-mid[,2:1], pch=vowels.lab)
```

The same can be achieved more simply with the **eplot()** function for ellipse drawing in the Emu-R library by including the argument **form=T**. The additional argument **centroid=T** of **eplot()** plots a symbol per category at the center (whose coordinates are the mean of formants) of the ellipse (Figure 3.10):

```
eplot(mid[,1:2], vowels.lab, centroid=T, form=T)
```

The ellipses include at least 95 percent of the data points by default and so are sometimes called 95 percent confidence ellipses – these issues are discussed more fully in relation to probability theory in the last chapter of this book. You can also plot the points with **dopoints=T** and take away the ellipses with **doellipse=F**, thus:

```
eplot(mid[,1:2], vowels.lab, dopoints=T, doellipse=F, form=T)
```

gives the same display (albeit color-coded by default) as **plot(-mid[,2:1], pch=vowels.lab)** given earlier.

3.4 Summary

The main points that were covered in this chapter and that are extended in the exercises below are as follows.

Signal processing

- Signal processing in Emu is applied with the **tkassp** toolkit. If signal processing is applied to the file **x.wav**, then the output is **x.ext** where **ext** is an extension

that can be set by the user and which by default depends on the type of signal processing that is applied. The files derived from **tkassp** are by default stored in the same directory as those to which the signal processing was applied.
- Signal processing is applied by calculating a single speech frame at a single point in time for a given window size. The window size is the duration of the speech signal seen at any one time by the signal processing routine in calculating the speech frame. A speech frame is often a single value (such as an intensity value or a fundamental frequency value) or a set of values (such as the first four formants). The window shift defines how often this calculation is made. If the window shift is set to 5 ms, then one speech frame is derived every 5 ms.
- One of the parameters in calculating formants that often needs to be changed from its default is **Nominal F1**, which is set to 500 Hz on the assumption that the speaker has a vocal tract length of 17.5 cm. For female speakers, this should be set to around 600 Hz.

Displaying signal processing in Emu

- In order to display the output of **tkassp** in Emu, the template file needs to be edited to tell Emu where the derived signal files are located (and whether they should be displayed when Emu utterances from the database are opened).
- In Emu, formants, fundamental frequency, and some other signals can be manually corrected.

Interface to R

- Speech signal data that is the output of **tkassp** is read into R as a **trackdata** object. A trackdata object can only ever be created relative to a segment list. For this reason, a trackdata object contains signal data within the start and end times of each segment in the segment list.
- Various functions can be applied to trackdata objects including **plot()** for plotting trackdata from individual segments and **dcut()** for extracting signal data at a specific time point.
- Ellipses can be plotted for two parameters at a single point of time with the **eplot()** function. An option is available within **eplot()** for plotting data from the first two formants in such a way that the vowel categories are arranged in relation to the height and backness dimensions of the vowel quadrilateral.

3.5 Questions

A. The task in this question is to obtain ellipse plots as in the left panel of Figure 3.11 for the female speaker **agr** from the **second** database analyzed in this chapter. The male speaker **gam** and the female speaker **agr** are speakers of the same North German variety.

A.1 Follow the procedure exactly as outlined in Figures 3.3 and 3.4 (except substitute **agr** for **gam** in Figure 3.3) and calculate formants for the female speaker **agr** with a default nominal F1 of 600 Hz.

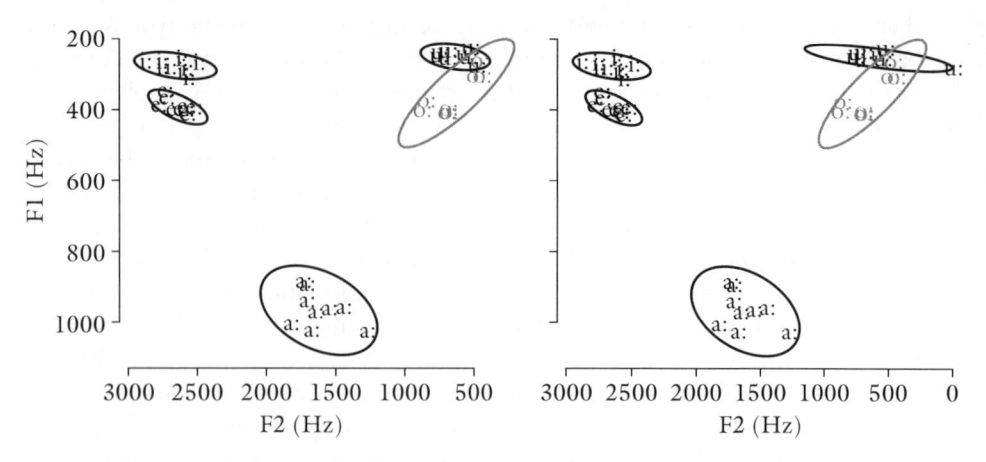

Figure 3.11 Vowels for the female speaker **agr** in the F2 × F1 plane (values extracted at the temporal midpoint of the vowel), after (left) and before (right) correction of an outlier (at F2 = 0 Hz) for [u:].

A.2 Start up R and, after entering `library(emu)`, enter commands analogous to those given for the male speaker to produce the ellipses for the female speaker **agr** as shown in the right panel of Figure 3.11. Create the following objects as you proceed with this task:

`vowelsF.s`	Segment list of speaker **agr**'s vowels
`vowelsF.l`	Vector of labels
`vowelsF.fm`	Trackdata object of formants
`vowelsF.fm5`	Matrix of formants at the temporal midpoint of the vowel

(See the answers at the end of the exercises if you have difficulty with this.)

A.3 You will notice from your display in R and from the right-hand panel of Figure 3.11 that there is evidently a formant-tracking error for one of the [u:] tokens that has F2 at 0 Hz. The task is to use R to find this token and then Emu to correct it in the manner described earlier. Assuming you have created the objects in A.2, then the outlier can be found in R using an object known as a logical vector (covered in detail in Chapter 5) that is **True** for any **u:** vowel that has F2 less than 100 Hz:

```
temp = vowelsF.fm5[,2] < 100 & vowelsF.l == "u:"
```

The following verifies that there is only one such vowel:

```
sum(temp)
[1]
```

This instruction identifies the outlier:

```
vowelsF.s[temp,]
segment list from database: second
query was: Phonetic=i: | e: | a: | o: | u:
labels   start      end        utts
33  u:   560.483    744.803    agr052
```

The above shows that the formant-tracking error occurred in **agr052** between times 560 ms and 745 ms (so since the data plotted in the ellipses were extracted at the temporal midpoint, then the value of F2 = 0 Hz must have occurred close to (560 + 745) / 2 = 652 ms). Find these data in the corresponding utterance in Emu (shown below) and correct F2 manually to an appropriate value.

A.4 Having corrected F2 for this utterance in Emu, produce the ellipses again for the female speaker. Your display should now look like the one in the left panel of Figure 3.11.

A.5 According to Fant (1966), the differences between males and females in the ratio of the mouth-to-pharynx cavity length cause greater formant differences in some vowels than in others. In particular, back-rounded vowels are predicted to show much less male–female variation than most other vowels. To what extent is this consistent with a comparison of the male (**gam**) and female (**agr**) formant data?

A.6 The function **trackinfo()** with the name of the database gives information about the signals that are available in a database that can be read into R. For example: **trackinfo("second")** returns **"samples"** and **"fm"**. Where is this information stored in the template file?

A.7 You could make another trackdata object of formants for just the first three segments in the segment list you created in A.1 as follows:

```
newdata = emu.track(vowelsF.s[1:3,], "fm")
```

Given the information in A.6, how would you make a trackdata object, **audiowav**, of the audio waveform of the first three segments? How would you use this trackdata object to plot the waveform of the third segment?

A.8 As was shown in Chapter 2, a segment list of the word *guten* from the **Word** tier in the utterance **gam001** can be read into R as follows:

```
guten = emu.query("first", "gam001", "Word=guten")
```

How can you use the information in A.6 to show that this:

```
emu.track(guten, "fm")
```

must fail?

B. The following question extends the use of signal processing to two parameters, intensity (dB-RMS) and zero-crossing-rate (ZCR). The first of these gives an indication of the overall energy in the signal and is therefore very low at stop closures, high at the release of stops, and higher for most vowels than for fricatives. The second, which is less familiar in phonetics research, is a calculation of how often the audio waveform crosses the *x*-axis per unit of time. In general, there is a relationship between ZCR and the frequency range at which most of the energy is concentrated in the signal. For example, since [s] has most of its energy concentrated in a high-frequency range, ZCR is usually high (the audio waveform for [s] crosses

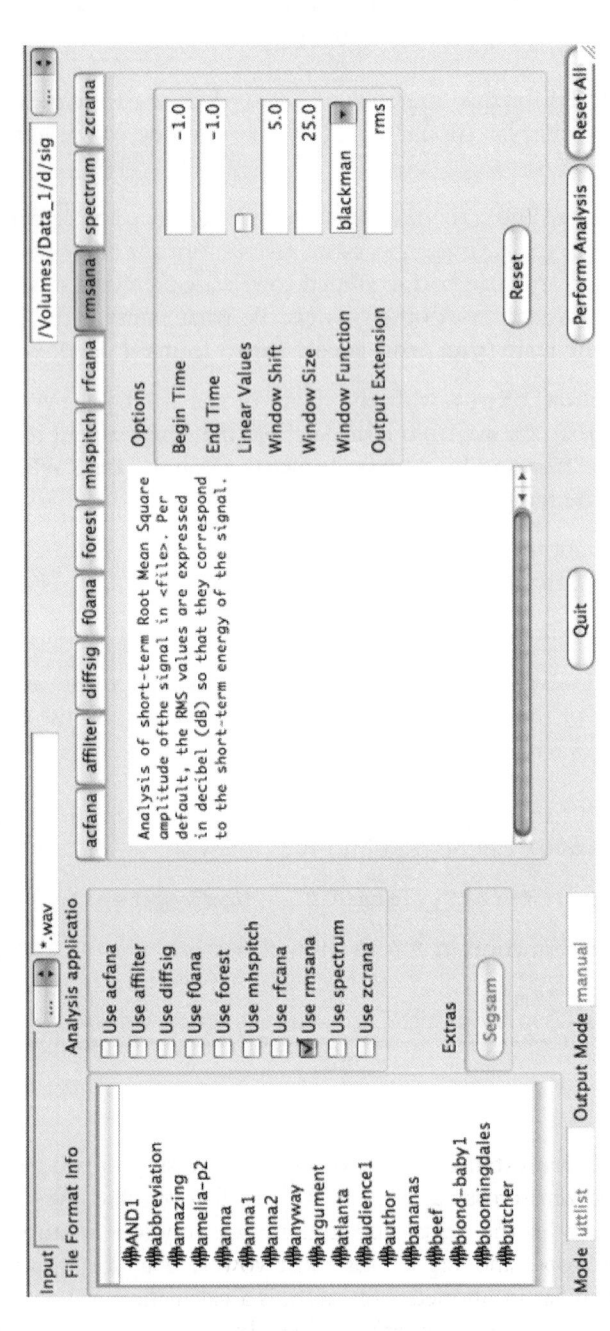

Figure 3.12 The **tkassp** window for calculating intensity data for the **aetobi** database. Select the **...** button in the top right corner then choose **manual** and from that the directory into which you want to store the intensity data. Make a note of the directory (path) because it will need to be included in the template file to tell Emu where these intensity data are located on your system.

the x-axis frequently). But since on the other hand most sonorants have their energy concentrated below 3,000 Hz, the audio waveform crosses the x-axis much less frequently and ZCR is comparably lower. Therefore, ZCR can give some indication about the division of an audio speech signal into fricative- and sonorant-like sounds.

B.1 Download the **aetobi** database. Calculate using **rmsana** (Figure 3.12) the intensity signals for all the utterances in this database using the defaults. Rather than using the default setting for storing the RMS data, choose a new directory (and create one if need be) for storing the intensity signals. Then follow the description shown in Figure 3.12.

B.2 When the intensity data is calculated (select **Perform Analysis** in Figure 3.12), then the corresponding files should be written to whichever directory you entered into the **tkassp** window. Verify that this is so.

B.3 The task now is to modify the template file to get Emu to see these intensity data following exactly the procedure established earlier in this chapter (Figure 3.5). More specifically, you will need to enter the information shown in Figure 3.13 in the **Track** and **View** panes of the **aetobi** template file.

B.4 Verify that when you open any utterance of the **aetobi** database in Emu, the intensity signal is visible together with the spectrogram as in Figure 3.14. Why is the waveform not displayed? (Hint: look at the **View** pane of the template file in Figure 3.13.)

B.5 Change the display to show only the **Word** tier and intensity contour as shown in Figure 3.15. This is done with: **Display → SignalView Levels → Word** and **Display → Tracks... → rms**

B.6 The calculation of intensity has so far made use of the defaults with a window size and shift of 25 ms and 5 ms respectively. Change the defaults by setting the window shift to 2 ms and the window size to 10 ms (Figure 3.16). The output extension should be changed to something other than the default, e.g., to **rms2** as in Figure 3.16, so that you do not overwrite the intensity data you calculated in B.2. Save the data to the same directory in which you stored the intensity files in the calculation in B.2 and then recalculate the intensity data.

B.7 Edit the template file so that these new intensity data with the shorter time window and shift are accessible to Emu and so that when you open any utterance in Emu you display only the two intensity contours as in Figure 3.17. (The required template modifications are in the answers.)

B.8 Explain why the intensity contour analyzed with the shorter time window in Figure 3.17 seems to be influenced to a greater extent by short-term fluctuations in the speech signal.

C. Using **zcrana** in **tkassp**, calculate the zero-crossing-rate (ZCR) for the **aetobi** database. Edit the template file in order to display the ZCR data for the utterance **bananas** as shown in Figure 3.18. What classes of speech sound in this utterance have the highest ZCR values (e.g., above 1.5 kHz) and why?

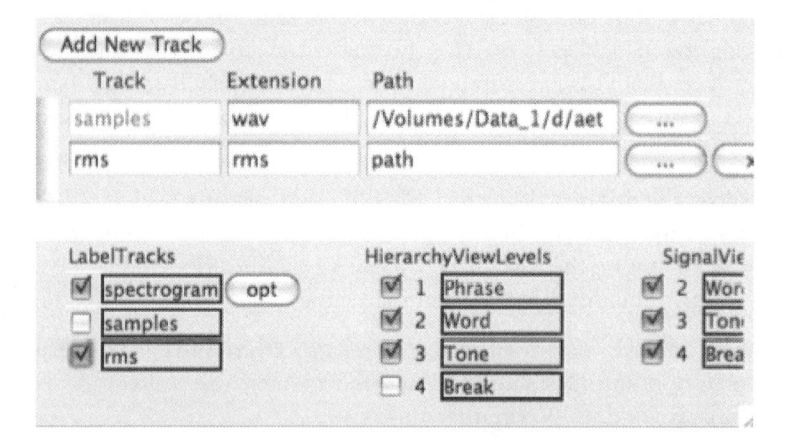

Figure 3.13 The required modifications to the **aetobi** template file in order to display intensity data in Emu in the **Tracks** (top) and **View** (bottom) panes. The path entered in the **Tracks** pane is the one to which you wrote the intensity data in Figure 3.12.

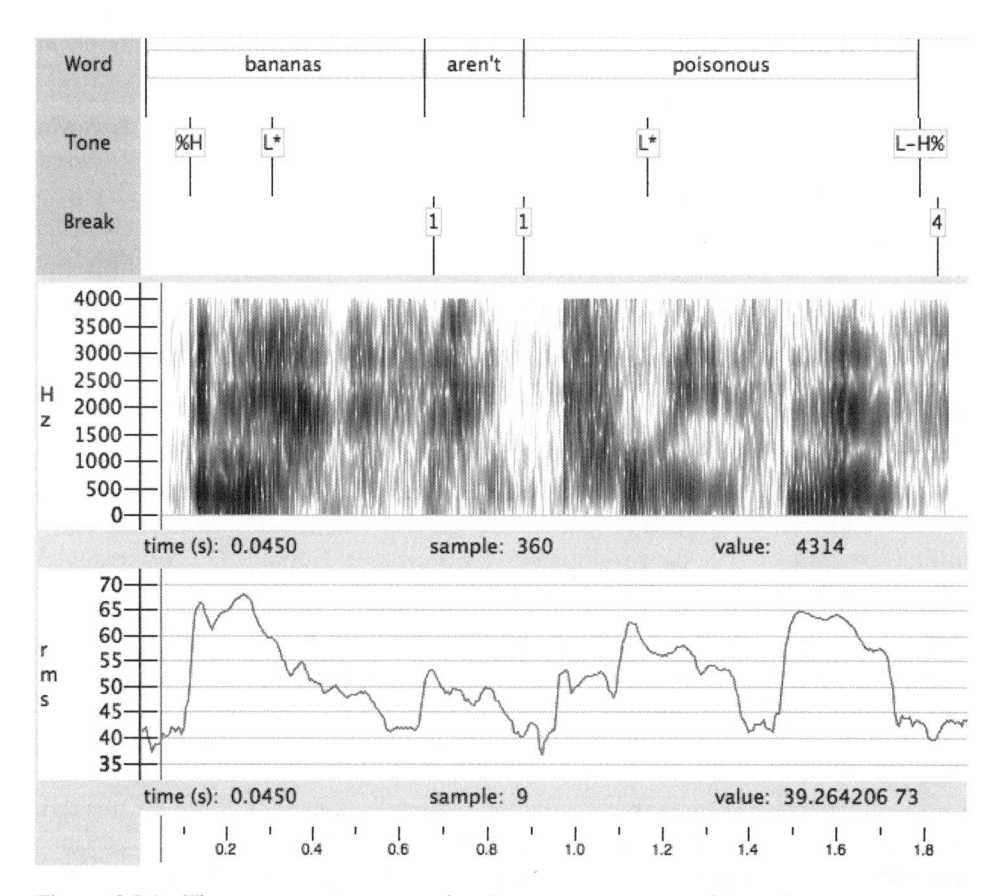

Figure 3.14 The utterance **bananas** showing a spectrogram and intensity contour.

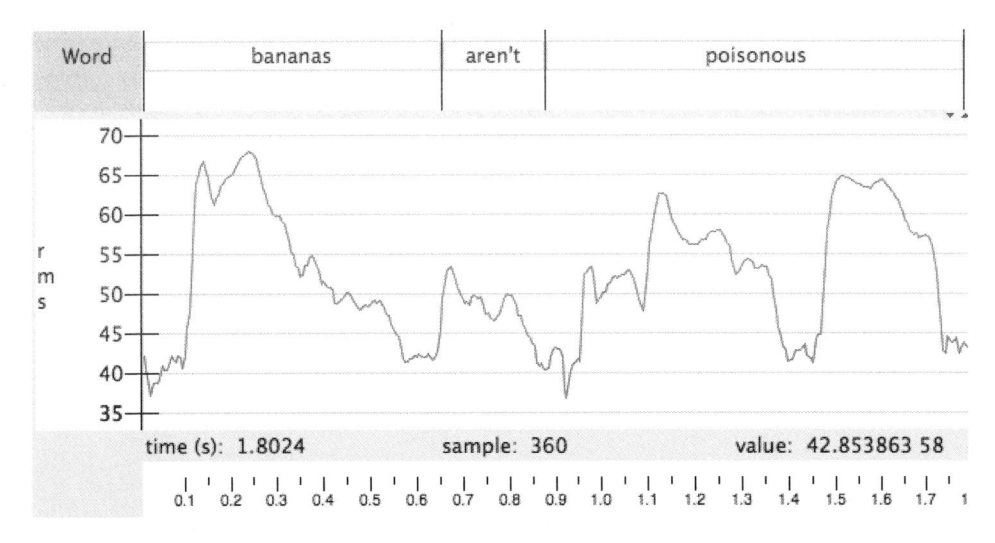

Figure 3.15 The same utterance as in Figure 3.14 showing only the **Word** tier and intensity contour.

Figure 3.16 The defaults of the **rmsana** pane set to a window shift and size of 2 ms and 10 ms respectively and with an output extension **rms2**. These data will be saved to the same directory as the one selected in Figure 3.13.

D. Calculate the fundamental frequency (use the **f0ana** pane in **tkassp**) and formant frequencies for the **aetobi** database in order to produce a display like the one shown in Figure 3.19 for the **argument** utterance (male speaker) beginning at 3.2 seconds (NB: in modifying the **Tracks** pane of the template file, you must enter **F0** (capital **F**) under **Track**s for fundamental frequency data and, as already discussed, **fm** for formant data, so that Emu knows to treat these displays somewhat differently from other signals).

E. In order to obtain trackdata for a database, the procedure has so far been to use **tkassp** to calculate signals for the entire, or part of the, database and then to

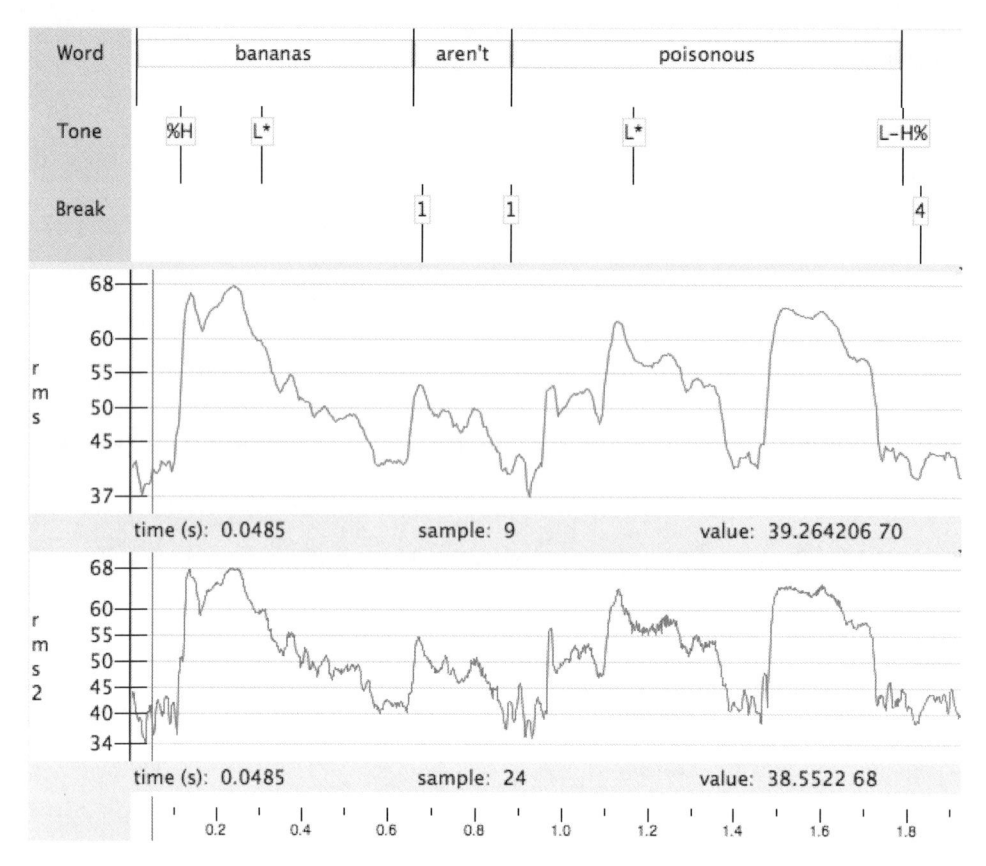

Figure 3.17 The utterance **bananas** showing intensity contours calculated with a window size and shift of 25 ms and 5 ms (above) and 10 ms and 2 ms (below) respectively.

edit the template file so that Emu knows where to locate the new signal files. However, it is also possible to obtain trackdata for a segment list without having to derive new signals for the entire database and make changes to the template file. This can be especially useful if the database is very large but you only need trackdata for a handful of segments; and it also saves a step in not having to change the template file. This procedure is illustrated below in obtaining fundamental frequency data for speaker **gam**'s [i:] vowels from the **second** database. Begin by making a segment list in R of these vowels:

```
seg.i = emu.query("second", "gam*", "Phonetic = i:")
```

Now write out the segment list as a plain text file **seg.txt** to a directory of your choice using the **write.emusegs()** function. NB: use only forward slashes in R and put the name of the directory in " " inverted commas (e.g., on Windows `"c:/documents/mydata/seg.txt"`).

```
write.emusegs(seg.i, "your chosen directory/seg.txt")
```

The plain text segment list created by the above command should look like this:

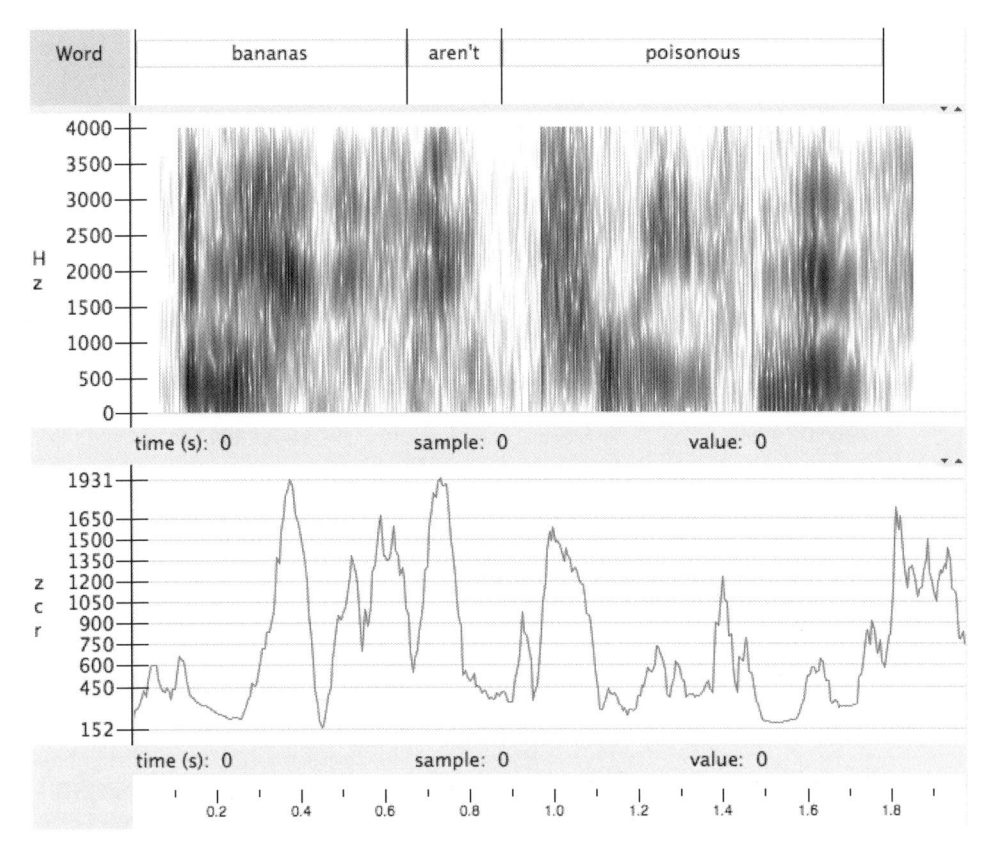

Figure 3.18 A spectrogram and synchronized zero-crossing-rate for the **bananas** utterance showing word segmentations.

```
database:second
query:Phonetic = i:
type:segment
#
i:   508.578   612.95    gam006
i:   472.543   551.3     gam007
i:   473.542   548.1     gam016
i:   495.738   644.682   gam022
i:   471.887   599.255   gam026
i:   477.685   589.961   gam035
i:   516.33    618.266   gam038
i:   459.79    544.46    gam055
i:   485.844   599.902   gam072
```

Start up Emu and then access **tkassp** from **Signal Processing** → **Speech Signal Analysis**. Then follow the instructions shown in Figure 3.20 to calculate f0 data. The result of running **tkassp** in the manner shown in Figure 3.20 is

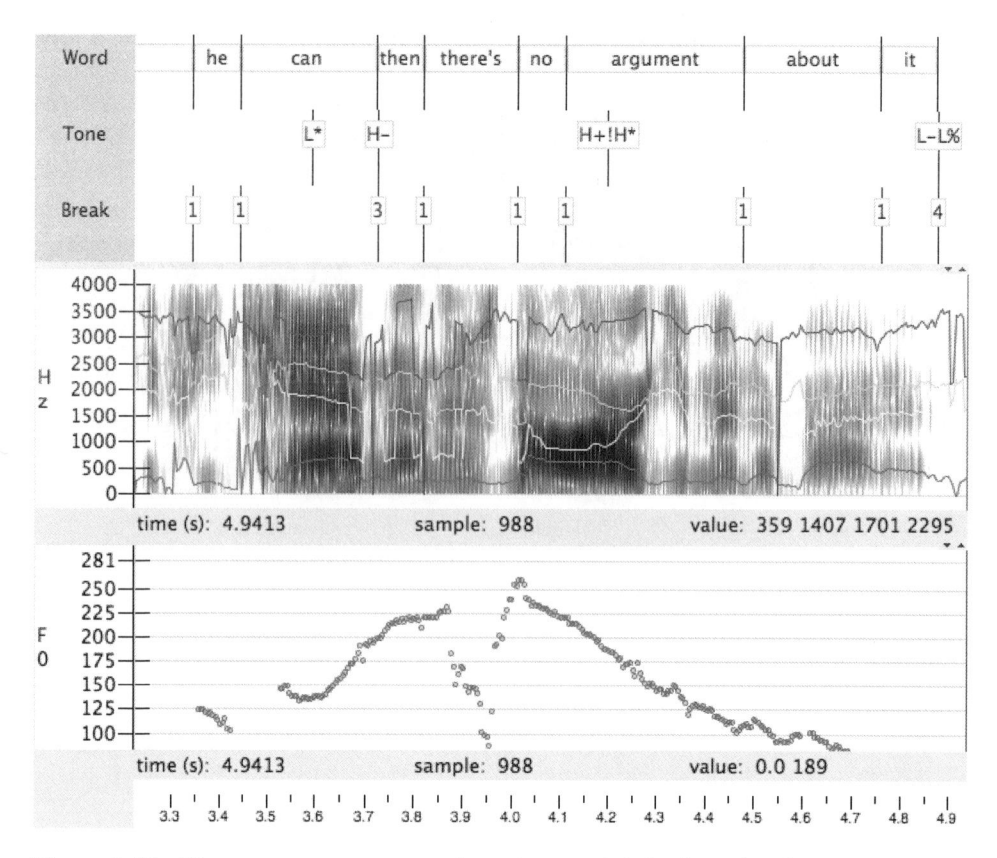

Figure 3.19 The **argument** utterance from the **aetobi** database showing a spectrogram with overlaid formants and a synchronized f0 contour.

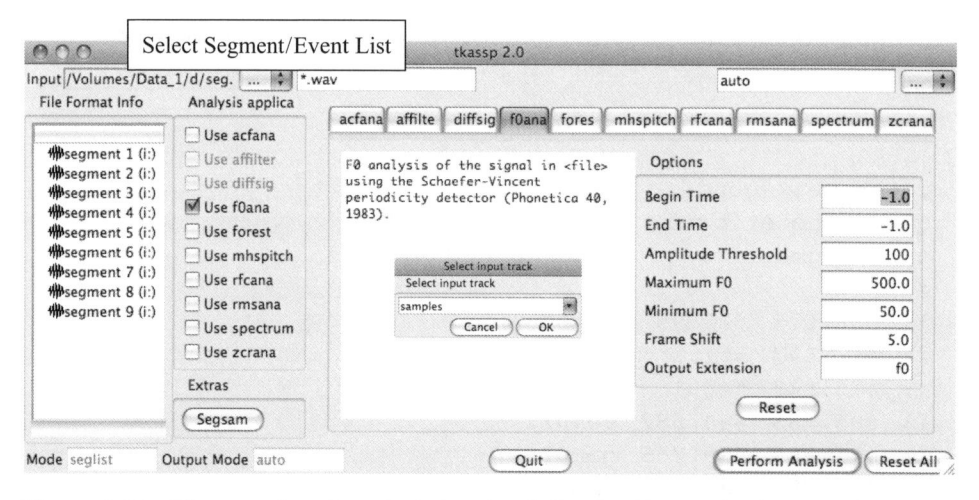

Figure 3.20 The procedure for calculating signal files, in this case fundamental frequency data from a segment list. This **tkassp** window is accessed from **Signal Processing → Speech Signal Analysis** after starting Emu. Import the segment list using the **Input ...** button in the top left and choose **Select Segment/Event**, then select **path/seg.txt** where **path** is the directory where **seg.txt** is stored, then **OK** to **samples**. This should bring up the list of segments shown in the left part of the figure. Choose **Use f0ana**, inspect the **f0ana** pane if you wish, and finally click on **Perform Analysis**. If the input was the plain text file **seg.txt**, then the output will be **seg-f0.txt**, containing the fundamental frequency data in the same directory (by default) as **seg.txt**.

to create another text file in the same directory as the segment list to which you applied **tkassp** and with the name **seg.f0-txt**. This can be read into R with **read.trackdata()** and stored as the trackdata object **seg.f0**:

```
seg.f0 = read.trackdata("your chosen directory/
seg-f0.txt")
```

Verify with the **summary()** function that these are trackdata from nine segments and plot the f0 data from the third segment. Which utterance are these data from?

3.6 Answers

A.2

```
# Segment list
vowelsF.s = emu.query("second", "agr*", "Phonetic=i: | e: |
a: | o: | u:")

# Vector of labels
vowelsF.l = label(vowelsF.s)

# Trackdata of formants
vowelsF.fm = emu.track(vowelsF.s, "fm")

# Formants at the temporal midpoint of the vowel
vowelsF.fm5 = dcut(vowelsF.fm, 0.5, prop=T)

# Ellipse plots in the formant plane
eplot(vowelsF.fm5[,1:2], vowelsF.l, form=T, dopoints=T,
xlab="F2 (Hz)", ylab="F1 (Hz)")
```

A.4 You will need to read the formant data into R again since a change has been made to the formants in Emu (but not the segment list if you are still in the same R session), i.e., repeat last three commands from A.2.

A.5 A comparison of Figures 3.10 (male speaker **gam**) and 3.11 (female speaker **agr**) shows that there is indeed comparatively little difference between the male and female speaker in the positions of the high back vowels [o:, u:] whereas F2 for [i:, e:] and F1 for [a:] have considerably higher values for the female speaker. Incidentally, the mean category values for the female on F2, for instance, can be obtained from:

```
tapply(vowelsF.fm5[,2], vowelsF.l, mean)
```

A.6 You get the same information with **trackinfo()** as is given under **Track** in the **Tracks** pane of the corresponding template file.

A.7

```
audiowav = emu.track(vowelsF.s[1:3,], "samples")
plot(audiowav[3,], type="l")
```

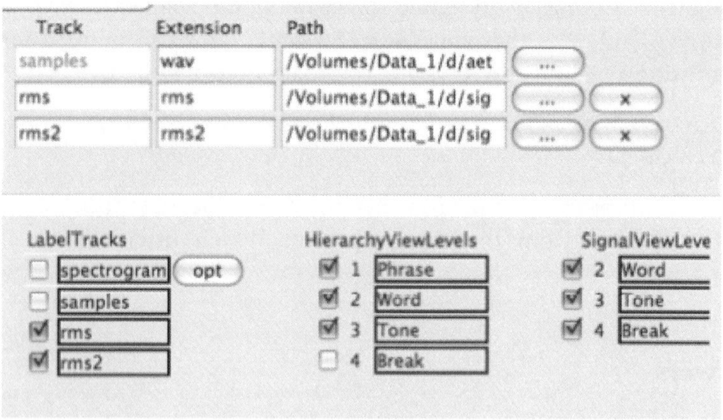

Figure 3.21 The **Track** (above) and **View** (below) panes of the **aetobi** database edited to include the new intensity parameter.

A.8

```
trackinfo("first")
```

shows that the track name **fm** is not listed, i.e., there is no formant data available for this database, as looking at the **Tracks** pane of this database's template file will confirm.

B.4 The waveform is not displayed because the **samples** box is not checked in the **View** pane of the template file.

B.7 The **Tracks** and **Variables** panes of the template file need to be edited as shown in Figure 3.21.

B.8 The longer the window, the greater the probability that variation over a small time interval is smoothed out.

C. ZCR is above 1.5 kHz at points in the signal where there is acoustic frication caused by a turbulent airstream. Notice that this does *not* mean that ZCR is high in *phonological* fricatives and low in phonological vowels in this utterance. This is because this utterance was produced with a high degree of frication verging on laughter (for pragmatic effect, i.e., to convey surprise/astonishment at the interlocutor's naivety) resulting in, for instance, fricative energy around 2 kHz and a comparatively high ZCR in the second vowel of *bananas*. ZCR is also high in the release of [t] of *aren't* and in the release/aspiration of the [p] and in the final [s] of *poisonous*. Notice how ZCR is lower in the medial /z/ than the final /s/ of *poisonous*. This does not necessarily come about because of phonetic voicing differences between these segments (in fact, the signal is more or less aperiodic for /z/ as shown by an absence of vertical striations on the spectrogram) but probably instead because this production of /z/ does not have as much energy in the same high-frequency range as does the final /s/ (see Chapter 8 for a further example of this).

E.

`summary(seg.f0)`

should confirm that there are nine segments. The fundamental frequency for the third segment is plotted with:

`plot(seg.f0[3,])`

The information about the utterance is given in the corresponding segment list:

```
seg.i[3,]
segment list from database: second
query was: Phonetic = i:
labels   start    end     utts
3  i:    473.542  548.1   gam016
```

i.e., the f0 data plotted in R are from utterance **gam016**.

Notes

[1] However, the acoustic vowel target need not necessarily occur at the midpoint, as the example from Australian English in the exercises to Chapter 6 shows.

[2] All of the signal's values preceding its start time are presumed to be zero: thus the first window is "buffered" with zeros between its left edge at $t = -10$ ms and the actual start time of the signal at $t = 0$ ms (see Chapter 8 for some details of zero padding).

[3] Some further points on the relationship between accuracy of formant estimation, prediction order, and nominal F1 frequency (Michel Scheffers, personal communication) are as follows. Following Markel and Gray (1976), the prediction order for accurate estimation of formants should be approximately equal to the sampling frequency in kHz based on an adult male vocal tract 17.5 cm in length (taking the speed of sound to be 35,000 cm/s). In **tkassp**, the default prediction order is the smallest even number greater than p in:

(1) $p = fs / (2F1_{nom})$

where fs is the sampling frequency and $F1_{nom}$ the nominal F1 frequency in kHz. Thus, for a sampling frequency of 20 kHz and nominal F1 of 0.5 kHz, $p = 20$ and so the prediction order is 22, this being the smallest even number greater than p. (The extra two coefficients are intended for modeling the additional resonance often found in nasalized vowels and/or for compensating for the fact that the vocal tract is not a lossless tube.) (1) shows that increasing the nominal F1 frequency causes the prediction order to be decreased, as a result of which the lossless model of the vocal tract is represented by fewer cylinders and therefore fewer formants in the same frequency range (which is appropriate for shorter vocal tracts). Should two formants still be individually unresolved after adjusting $F1_{nom}$, then the prediction order could be increased in the **forest** pane, either by entering the prediction order itself, or by selecting **1** from **incr/decr**: this second action would cause the default prediction order for a sampling frequency of 20 kHz to be increased by 2 from 22 to 24.

[4] LPC is not covered in this book – see Harrington and Cassidy (1999), Chapter 8 for a fairly non-technical treatment.

[5] For the sake of simplicity, I have reduced the command for plotting the formants to the minimum. The various options for refining the plot are discussed in Chapter 5. The plot command actually used here was `plot(vowels.fm[4,], bty="n", ylab="Frequency (Hz)", xlab="Time (ms)", col=F, pch=1:4)`.

4
Querying Annotation Structures

The purpose of this chapter is to provide an overview both of the different kinds of annotation structures that are possible in Emu and of some of the main types of queries for extracting annotations from them. This will take in a discussion of how annotations from different tiers can be linked, their relationship to a Praat TextGrid, and the way in which they can be entered and semi-automated in Emu. This chapter will begin with a brief review of the simplest kinds of queries that have been used in the preceding chapters to make segment lists.

4.1 The Emu **Query Tool**, Segment Tiers, and Event Tiers

As already discussed, whenever annotations are queried in Emu the output is a segment list containing the annotations, their start and end times, and the utterances from which they were taken. One of the ways of making segment lists is with the **emu.query()** function in the R programming language. For example, this function was used in the preceding chapter to make a segment list from all utterances beginning with **gam** (i.e., for the male speaker) in the **second** database of five types of vowels annotated at the **Phonetic** tier:

```
emu.query("second", "gam*", "Phonetic = i: | e: | a: | o: | u:")
```

The other equivalent way to make a segment list is with the Emu **Query Tool**, which is accessed with **Database Operations** followed by **Query Database** from the Emu **DB** window as shown in Figure 4.1. Once you have entered the information in Figure 4.1, save the segment list to the file name **seg.txt** and in a directory of your choice. You will then be able to read this segment list into R with the **read.emusegs()** function as follows:

```
read.emusegs("path/seg.txt")
```

gam001	Modify the Utterance List
gam002	
gam003	Add/Delete utterances matching pattern: gam*
gam004	Extension to use when finding utterances: wav
gam005	
gam006	Add to list Delete from list
gam007	
gam008	Delete All Utterances
gam009	
gam010	Query this utterance list
gam011	graphical query
gam012	Phonetic = i: | e: | a: |o: | u: Search

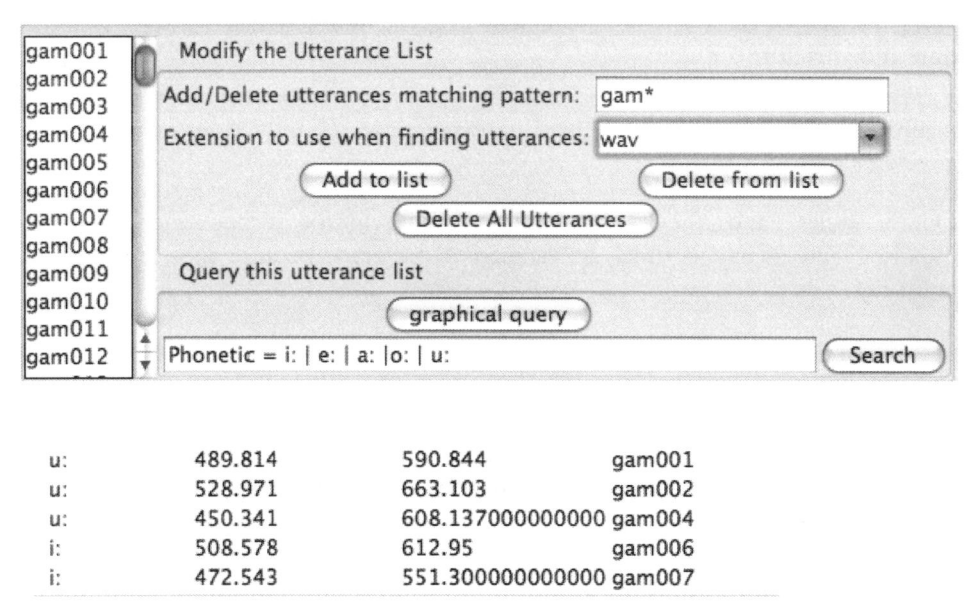

```
u:      489.814      590.844              gam001
u:      528.971      663.103              gam002
u:      450.341      608.137000000000     gam004
i:      508.578      612.95               gam006
i:      472.543      551.300000000000     gam007
```

Figure 4.1 The Emu **Query Tool** accessed from **Database Operations** followed by **Query Database** (above) and the segment list (below) that results from the query.

where **path** is the name of the directory to which you saved **seg.txt**. This will give exactly the same output as you get from the **emu.query()** function above (and therefore illustrates the equivalence of these two methods).

In Chapter 2, a distinction was made between a **segment** tier whose annotations have durations and an event or **point** tier in which an annotation is marked by a single point in time. The commands for querying annotations from either of these tiers is the same but what is returned in the first case is a **segment list** and in the second a variation on a segment list called an **event list** in which the end times are zero. An example of both from the **author** utterance of the **aetobi** database is as follows:

```
state.s = emu.query("aetobi", "author", "Word = state")
state.s
segment list from database: aetobi
query was: Word = state
  labels   start    end       utts
1  state   2389.44  2689.34   author

bitonal = emu.query("aetobi", "author", "Tone = L+H*")
bitonal
event list from database: aetobi
query was: Tone = L+H*
  labels   start    end   utts
1  L+H*    472.51   0     author
2  L+H*    1157.08  0     author
```

Since the first of these is from a segment tier, the annotation has a start and end time and therefore a duration:

```
dur(state.s)
299.9
```

On the other hand, the two annotations found in the second query have no duration (and their end times are defined to be zero) because they are from an event tier:

```
dur(bitonal)
0 0
```

4.2 Extending the Range of Queries: Annotations from the Same Tier

As shown by various examples so far, the most basic query is of the form **T = x** where **T** is an annotation tier and **x** an annotation at that tier. The following extensions can be made to this basic query command for querying annotations from the *same* tier. In all cases, as before, the output is either a segment list or an event list.

4.2.1 The | (or) operator and classes (features)

An example of this has already been given: **Phonetic = i: | e: | a: | o: | u:** makes a segment list of all these vowels. A very useful way of simplifying this type of instruction is to define annotations in terms of *classes* (or features). In Emu, classes can be set up in the **Legal Labels** pane of the template file. For example, a number of annotations have been grouped for the **second** database at the **Phonetic** tier into the classes shown in Figure 4.2. Consequently, a query for finding all rounded vowels can be more conveniently written as follows:

```
emu.query("second", "gam*", "Phonetic=round")
```

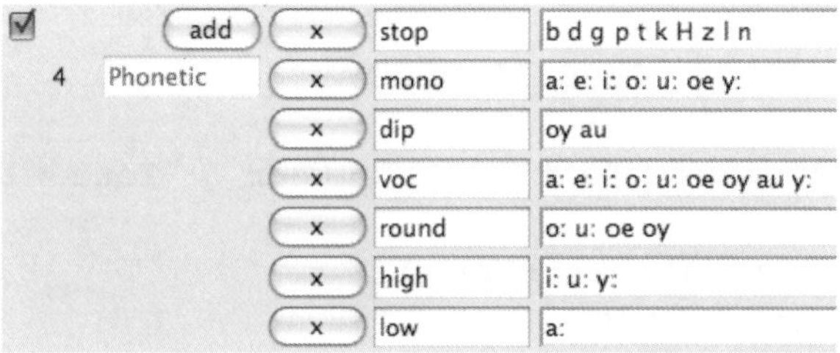

☑	add	x	stop	b d g p t k H z l n
4	Phonetic	x	mono	a: e: i: o: u: oe y:
		x	dip	oy au
		x	voc	a: e: i: o: u: oe oy au y:
		x	round	o: u: oe oy
		x	high	i: u: y:
		x	low	a:

Figure 4.2 The **Legal Labels** pane of the **Graphical Template Editor** showing how the annotations at the **Phonetic** tier are grouped into different classes (features).

4.2.2 The != operator

T != a means all annotations except **a**. So one way to get at all annotations in tier **T** in the database is to put the right-hand side equal to an annotation that does not occur at that tier. For example, since **abc** is not an annotation that occurs at the **Phonetic** tier in the **second** database, then **Phonetic != abc** returns all annotations from that tier. In the following example, this instruction is carried out for speaker **gam** in R and then the **label()** and **table()** functions are used to tabulate all the corresponding annotations:

```
seg.all = emu.query("second", "gam*", "Phonetic != abc")
table(label(seg.all))
 H   a:  au  b   d   e:  g   i:  o:  oe  oy  u:
 72  9   9   24  24  9   24  9   9   9   9   9
```

4.2.3 The & operator

Apart from its use for queries between linearly linked tiers discussed in 4.3, this operator is mostly useful for defining annotations at the intersection of features. For example, the following feature combinations can be extracted from the **second** database as follows:

rounded high vowels
Phonetic = round & Phonetic = high

unrounded high vowels
Phonetic != round & Phonetic = high

mid vowels
Phonetic != high & Phonetic != low

mid rounded vowels
Phonetic != high & Phonetic != low & Phonetic = round

Such definitions are then equivalent to those found in some distinctive feature notations in phonology and linguistic phonetics. Thus the last instruction defines vowels that are [−high, −low, +round] and they can be read into R using **emu.query()** in the same manner as before:

```
midround = emu.query("second", "*", "Phonetic != high &
Phonetic != low & Phonetic = round")
table(label(midround))
o:  oe  oy
18  18  18
```

4.2.4 The -> operator

Any two queries at the same tier can be joined together with the **->** operator which finds either a sequence of annotations, or an annotation in the context of another annotation. There are three cases to consider:

1. Make a segment list of **a b** (the segment list has a start time of **a** and end time of **b**)

    [T = a -> T = b]

2. Make a segment list of **a** if **a** precedes **b**

    [#T = a -> T = b]

3. Make a segment list of **b** if **b** follows **a**

    [T = a -> #T = b]

For example:

(i) A segment list of any word followed by *of* in the **aetobi** database:

```
emu.query("aetobi", "*", "[Word != x -> Word = of]")
    labels     start      end      utts
1   kind->of   2867.88   3106.87   amazing
2   lot->of    5315.62   5600.12   amazing
3   author->of 296.65    894.27    author
```

(ii) A segment list of all words preceding *of*:

```
emu.query("aetobi", "*", "[#Word != x -> Word = of]")
segment list from database: aetobi
query was: [#Word != x -> Word = of]
    labels   start      end      utts
1   kind     2867.88   3016.44   amazing
2   lot      5315.62   5505.39   amazing
3   author   296.65    737.80    author
```

(iii) As above, but here the segment list is of the second word *of*:

```
emu.query("aetobi", "*", "[Word != x -> #Word = of]")
segment list from database: aetobi
query was: [Word != x -> #Word = of]
    labels   start      end      utts
1   of       3016.44   3106.87   amazing
2   of       5505.39   5600.12   amazing
3   of       737.80    894.27    author
```

4.3 Inter-tier Links and Queries

An **inter-tier query** is, as its name suggests, any query that spans two or more annotation tiers. For the **aetobi** database, an example of an inter-tier query is: "find pitch-accented words." This is an inter-tier query because all annotations at the **Word** tier have to be found, but only if they are **linked** to annotations at the **Tone** tier. For this to be possible, some of the annotations between tiers must already have been linked (since otherwise Emu cannot know which words are associated with a pitch-accent). So the first issue to be considered is the different kinds of links that can be made between annotations of different tiers.

An initial distinction needs to be made between two tiers that are **linearly** and **non-linearly** linked. The first of these is straightforward: when two tiers are linearly linked, then one tier **describes** or **enriches** another. For example, a tier **Category** might be included as a separate tier from **Word** for marking words' grammatical category membership (thus each word might be marked as one of adjective, noun, verb, etc.); or information about whether or not a syllable is stressed might be included on a separate **Stress** tier. In both cases, the tiers are linearly linked because, for every annotation at **Word** or **Syllable** tiers, there are exactly corresponding annotations at the **Category** or **Stress** tiers. Moreover, the linearly linked annotations have the same times. In the downloadable database **gt**, which contains utterances labeled more or less according to the conventions of the German Tones and Break Indices system GToBI (Grice et al. 2005), the tiers **Word** and **Break** are linearly linked. The **Break** tier contains annotations for so-called break-indices which define the phonetic juncture at word boundaries. Each word is associated with a break on a scale from 0 to 5, with lower numbers corresponding to less juncture. So if there is a full pause between two words, then the word before the pause on the **Break** tier is marked with a high value, e.g., 4 or 5. On the other hand, the first word in *did you* when produced as the assimilated form [dɪdʒə] would be 0 to denote the substantial overlap at the word boundary. Whereas **Break** and **Word** are linearly linked, all of the other tiers in the **gt** database stand in a non-linear relationship to each other. In Figure 4.3, the relationship between **Tone** and **Word** (and therefore also between **Tone** and **Break**) must be non-linear, because there is evidently not one pitch-accent per word (not one annotation at the **Tone** tier for every annotation at the **Word** tier).

Figure 4.3 also shows the organization of the utterance into a prosodic hierarchy. In an annotation of this kind, an utterance (tier **Utt**) is made up of one or more intonation phrases (tier **I**). An intonation phrase is made up of at least one intermediate phrase (tier **i**) and an intermediate phrase is made up of one or more words. (Intonation and intermediate phrases are collectively referred to as *prosodic phrases*.) The criteria for marking these groupings depend to a certain extent on phonetic juncture. Thus, there is a greater juncture between word pairs that are in different phrases (*morgen/fährt, Thorsten/ja*, and *Studio/bei* in Figure 4.3) than those within a prosodic phrase. Moreover, the break between adjacent words in different intonation phrases (*Studio/bei*) is greater than that between adjacent words in different intermediate phrases.

The non-linear association extends beyond those tiers that are in a parent–child relationship.[1] Thus since **I** is a parent of **i** and since the relationship between **i** and

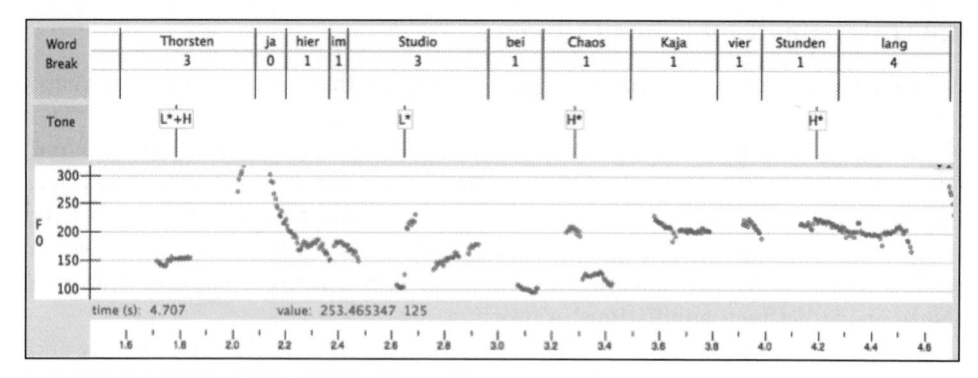

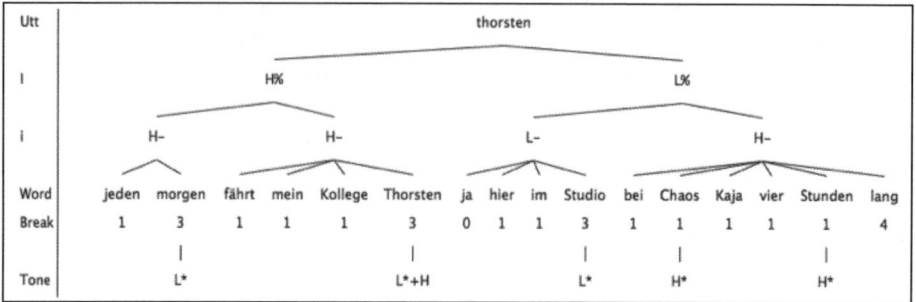

Figure 4.3 A fragment of the utterance **thorsten** from the downloadable **gt** database showing signal (top) and hierarchy (bottom) views. The signal view has been set to display only the f0 contour (**Display → Tracks → F0**) and in the range 100–300 Hz by the use of the slider buttons to the left of the f0 pane. The hierarchy window is accessible from the signal window using either the **Show Hierarchy** button or **Display → Detach hierarchy** to display both windows simultaneously.

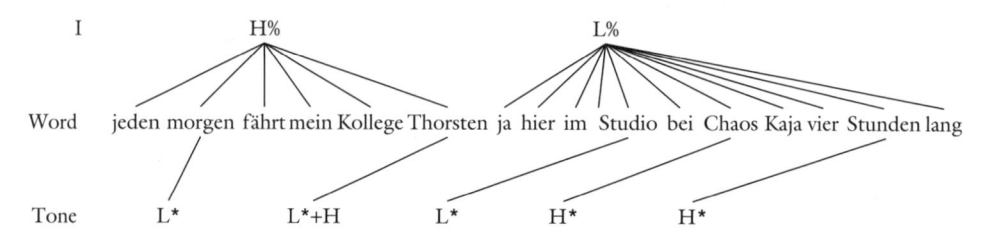

Figure 4.4 The association between **I**, **Word**, and **Tone** tiers for the same utterance as in Figure 4.3. This display was produced with **Display → Hierarchy Levels** and then by de-selecting the other tiers.

Word is non-linear, then the grandparent–child relationship between **I** and **Word** is also necessarily non-linear. This becomes completely clear in skipping the **i** tier and displaying the links between **I** and **Word** that fall out from these relationships, as in Figure 4.4.

There are two further parameters that need to be mentioned, which both only apply to non-linear relationships between tiers. The first is whether a non-linear

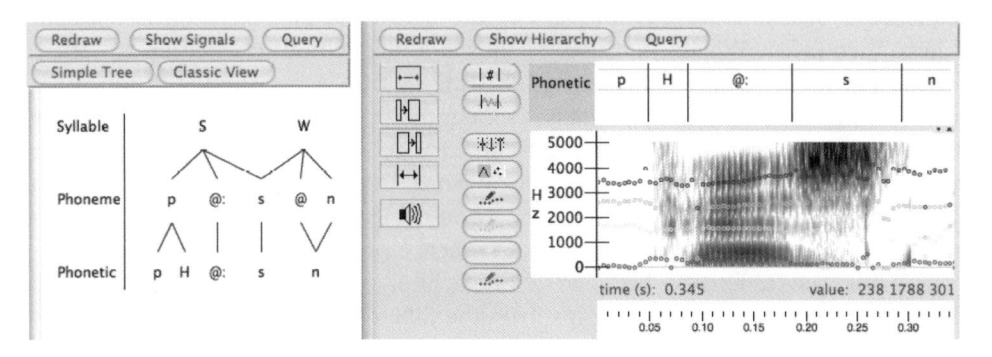

Figure 4.5 An example of an annotation of the word *person* showing many-to-many relationships between both **Phonetic** and **Phoneme**, and between **Phoneme** and **Syllable** tiers. In addition, the tiers are in a hierarchical relationship in which **Syllable** immediately dominates **Phoneme**, which immediately dominates **Phonetic**.

association is **one-to-many** or **many-to-many**. All of the relationships between tiers in Figure 4.3 are one-to-many because an annotation at a parent tier maps onto one or more annotations at a child tier, but not the other way round: thus an intermediate phrase can be made up of one or more words, but a word cannot map onto more than one intermediate phrase. In a many-to-many relationship, by contrast, an annotation at the parent tier can map onto one or more annotations at the child tier, and vice versa. Two examples of this type of many-to-many association are shown in Figure 4.5. Firstly, the final syllable was produced with a final syllabic nasal (that is with no discernible weak vowel in the final syllable) but, in order to express the idea that this word could (in a more careful speech production) be produced with a weak vowel as [ən], the word is annotated as such at the **Phoneme** tier and both segments are linked to the single **n** annotation at the child tier. Since two annotations from a parent tier can map onto a child tier and vice versa, the inter-tier relationship is many-to-many. Secondly, to express the idea inherent in some prosodic models that the medial /s/ in (non-rhotic varieties of) *person* is ambisyllabic (e.g., Gussenhoven 1986; Kahn 1976), the single **s** annotation is linked to both **S** and **W** (*strong* and *weak*) annotations at the **Syllable** tier. Evidently, **Syllable** and **Phoneme** also stand in a many-to-many relationship to each other because a syllable can be made up of more than one phoneme, but a phoneme can also map onto two syllables.

The final parameter that needs to be mentioned is whether the non-linear association between two tiers is **hierarchical** or **autosegmental** (see also Bird & Liberman 2001 and Taylor 2001 for a similar distinction in query languages). Two tiers are defined in Emu to be in a hierarchical relationship when the annotations of a parent tier are **composed of** those from the child tier (or seen from the bottom upwards, when the annotations of the child tier can be **parsed** into those of the parent tier). For example, syllables stand in a hierarchical relationship to phonemes in Figure 4.5 because syllables are made up of a sequence of phonemes (phonemes are parsed into syllables). In the autosegmental-metrical model of intonation (Beckman & Pierrehumbert 1986; Ladd 1996; Pierrehumbert 1980), words are made up of a sequence of syllables and, for this reason, the tiers stand in a hierarchical relationship to each other. Where → means "stands in a hierarchical relationship to" then, for the GToBI annotation in Figure 4.3, **Utt** → **I** → **i** → **Word**. On the other hand, the meaning of autosegmental is "belongs to" or "is associated with." In Figure 4.3, **Word** and **Tone** stand in an autosegmental relationship to each other. Their relationship is not hierarchical because a word is evidently not made up of a sequence of pitch-accents (the units at the **Tone** tier) in the same way that it is always composed of a sequence of syllables or a sequence of phonemes.

In Emu, the difference between a hierarchical or autosegmental relationship depends on whether the time stamps from the different tiers can be predicted from each other. In an autosegmental relationship they cannot. For example, given a pitch-accent, it is not possible to say anything about the start and end times of the word with which it is associated nor vice versa (beyond the vague statement that a pitch-accent is likely to be annotated at a point on the f0 contour somewhere near the word's rhythmically strongest vowel). On the other hand, given that a word is composed of a sequence of syllables, then the start and end times of a word are necessarily predictable from those of the first and last syllable. Similarly, given the hierarchical relationship **Utt** → **I** → **i** → **Word** in Figure 4.3, then the duration of the first **H%** at tier **I** in this figure extends from the onset of the first word to the offset of the last word that it dominates, i.e., between the start time of *jeden* and the end time of *Thorsten*; similarly, the duration of the first **H-** at level **i** extends from the beginning to the end of *jeden morgen* that it dominates, and so on.

Specifying a relationship as hierarchical *and* many-to-many allows hierarchies to overlap with each other in time at their edges. For example, since the **Syllable** and **Phoneme** tiers are hierarchically related to each other in Figure 4.5, then the duration of the first syllable (**S**) of *person* extends across the segments that it dominates, i.e., from the onset of **p** to the offset of **s**; but since the second syllable (**W**) also extends across the segments it dominates, then its duration is from the onset of the same **s** to the end of the word: that is, the two syllables overlap in time across the durational extent of the medial **s**. For analogous reasons, since **@** (schwa) and **n** at the **Phoneme** tier both map onto the same **n** annotation at the **Phonetic** tier, and since **Phoneme** and **Phonetic** stand in a hierarchical relationship to each other, then these annotations are both defined to have the same start times and they both have the same end times: thus, since both **@** and **n** inherit their times from the same annotation at the **Phonetic** tier, they are defined to be temporally overlapping.

When two tiers, **T** and **U**, are non-linearly (therefore either autosegmentally or hierarchically) linked, then their annotations can be queried with **[T = a ^ U = b]** where **a** and **b** are annotations at those tiers: such a query finds all **a** annotations at tier **T** that are linked to **b** annotations at tier **U**. Some examples with respect to the **thorsten** utterance of the **gt** database (Figure 4.3) are given below. As discussed earlier, these search instructions can be entered either in the Emu **Query Tool** in the manner shown in Figure 4.1, or by using the **emu.query()** function in R. For example, the search instruction

```
[Tone=L* ^ Word=morgen | Studio]
```

(i) All **L*** tones at the **Tone** tier linked to either *morgen* or *Studio* at the **Word** tier.

```
emu.query("gt","thorsten","[Tone=L* ^ Word=morgen |
Studio]")
labels   start     end   utts
1   L*   325.625    0    thorsten
2   L*   2649.770   0    thorsten
```

(ii) As (i), but return the corresponding words.

```
[Tone = L* ^ #Word = morgen | Studio]
   labels     start     end      utts
1  morgen    250.366   608.032   thorsten
2  Studio    2438.090  2962.670  thorsten
```

The **!=** operator discussed in 4.2 can be used to find *all* annotations. For example, the following search instruction finds all pitch-accented words, i.e., any annotation at the **Word** tier that is linked to any annotation at the **Tone** tier:

```
[Word != x ^ Tone != x]
1  morgen     250.366   608.032   thorsten
2  Thorsten   1573.730  2086.380  thorsten
3  Studio     2438.090  2962.670  thorsten
4  Chaos      3165.340  3493.200  thorsten
5  Stunden    3982.010  4274.110  thorsten
```

Queries can be made across intervening tiers as long as all the tiers are linked. Thus, since tiers **i** and **Tone** are linked via **Word**, a query such as "find any intermediate phrase containing an **L***" (any annotation at tier **i** that is linked to **L*** at the **Tone** tier) is defined for this database:

```
[i != x ^ Tone = L*]
   labels   start     end       utts
1  H-       47.689    608.032   thorsten
2  L-       2086.380  2962.670  thorsten
```

Two intermediate phrases are returned, which are the two that are associated with **L*** via the **Word** tier (see Figure 4.3). Notice that, although the query is made with respect to an event which has no duration (**L***), since the intermediate phrases inherit their durations from the **Word** tier, they have a duration equal to the words that they dominate.

It is possible to nest non-linear queries inside other non-linear queries. For example, the following query finds the words that occur in an **H-** intermediate phrase and in an **L%** intonational phrase (any annotation at the **Word** tier linked both to **H-** at the **i** tier and to **L%** at the **I** tier):

```
[ [ Word != x ^ i = H- ] ^ I = L% ]
1  bei      2962.67  3165.34  thorsten
2  Chaos    3165.34  3493.20  thorsten
3  Kaja     3493.20  3815.10  thorsten
4  vier     3815.10  3982.01  thorsten
5  Stunden  3982.01  4274.11  thorsten
6  lang     4274.11  4691.39  thorsten
```

The following does the same but under the additional condition that the words should be pitch-accented (linked to an annotation at the **Tone** tier):

```
[[[Word !=x ^ Tone !=x] ^ i = H-] ^ I = L%]
```

or equivalently:

```
[[[ Tone !=x ^ # Word!=x] ^ i = H-] ^ I = L%]
1  Chaos    3165.34  3493.20  thorsten
2  Stunden  3982.01  4274.11  thorsten
```

4.4 Entering Structured Annotations with Emu

A helpful first step in entering annotations such as the one shown in Figure 4.3 is to summarize the inter-tier relationships for a database in a **path** as in Figure 4.6. In this Figure, **(S)** and **(E)** denote segment and event tiers which, for convenience,

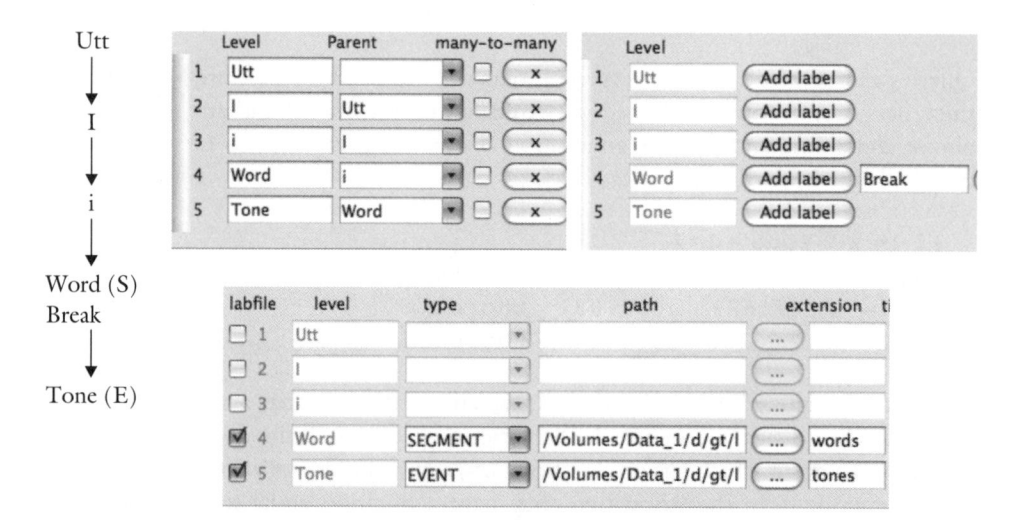

Figure 4.6 The path for the **gt** database (far left) showing the inter-tier relationships. **(S)** and **(E)** denote segment and event tiers respectively, all other tiers are timeless. A downward arrow denotes a non-linear, one-to-many relationship. The figure also shows the information in the **Levels** (top left), **Labels** (top right), and **Labfiles** (below) panes of the template file for encoding this path.

can be collectively referred to as **time tiers**. All other tiers (**Utt**, **I**, **i**, **Break**) are (initially) **timeless**, i.e., they inherit their times from another tier. An arrow between two tiers means that they stand in a non-linear relationship to each other, either one-to-many (a single downward arrow) or many-to-many (a double arrow). Any adjacent two tiers not connected by an arrow stand in a linear relationship to each other (**Word**, **Break**). When a single or double arrow extends between any two time tiers (**Word**, **Tone**) then the relationship is autosegmental; otherwise, if either one (**i**, **Word**) or both (**Utt**, **I** and **I**, **i**) of the tiers is timeless, then the relationship is hierarchical. A timeless tier inherits its times from the child tier that it dominates. Thus, times percolate up the tree: **i** inherits its times from **Word**, **I** from **i**, and **Utt** from **I**. In linear relationships, a timeless tier inherits its times from the tier with which it is linearly associated (**Break** inherits its times from **Word**).

The tiers that stand in a non-linear relationship to each other are entered into Emu in the **Levels** pane of the template file (Figure 4.6) in which the child–parent relationship is specified as one-to-many or many-to-many. A tier that is linearly linked to another tier is declared in the **Labels** pane. The distinction between hierarchical and autosegmental depends on whether a tier is marked as timeless in the **Labfiles** pane. Unless a tier is defined as a segment or event tier (Figure 4.6), it is timeless. Thus **Utt** → **I** → **i** → **Word** defines a hierarchical relationship in this template file for two reasons: firstly, because of the child–parent relationships that are declared in the **Levels** pane, and secondly because **Word** is the only one of these tiers declared to be linked to times in the **Labfiles** pane. As described earlier, **Utt**, **I**, and **i** inherit their times from **Word** both because they dominate it, and because **Word** is associated with times. Moreover, because these tiers do not have their own independent times, they do not appear in the utterance's signal view window: thus when you open any utterance in the **gt** database, you will only see **Word/Break** and **Tone** in the signal view window and you have to switch to the hierarchy view window to see the other tiers (Figure 4.3).

There is one utterance in the **gt** database, **dort**, for which the non-linear links have not been set and these can be incorporated following the details below. Begin by opening the hierarchy window of this utterance in the manner described in Figure 4.3. Once you have the hierarchy window in the top panel of Figure 4.7, select **Simple Tree** so that the annotations do not overlap. The utterance *dann treffen wir uns dort am Haupteingang* (lit. *then meet we us there at the main-entrance*, i.e., *then we'll meet each other there, at the main entrance*) was produced as one intonational phrase and two intermediate phrases and with accented words *dann*, *dort*, and *Haupteingang*. The corresponding pitch-accents have already been entered at the **Tone** tier: the task, then, is to link the annotations to end up with the display shown in the lower pane of Figure 4.7. Move the mouse over the leftmost **H***, which causes the annotation to turn blue. Then hold down the left button and, without letting go, drag the mouse to the word to which this pitch-accent belongs, *treffen*. Once *treffen* is highlighted (it will also change colour to blue), then release the mouse button. This should set the link. It is quite a good idea to practice deleting the link, in case you make a mistake. To do this, select **Delete**, and move the mouse over the line you have just drawn and it will then turn red. Clicking the mouse once deletes the link. You can in fact delete not just lines but annotations in this way. When you finish deleting, select **Edit** before continuing, otherwise you will delete material

```
              Utt

               I

               i

      Word   dann  treffen  wir  uns  dort  am  haupteingang
      Break    *      *      *    *    *    *         *

      Tone           H*           L*        H*
      ─────────────────────────────────────────────────────

              Utt              dort
                                │
               I                H%
                               ╱ ╲
               i             H−    L−
                            ╱│╲    ╱╲
      Word   dann  treffen  wir  uns  dort  am  haupteingang
      Break    1      0      1    1    3    1         5

      Tone           H*           L*        H*
```

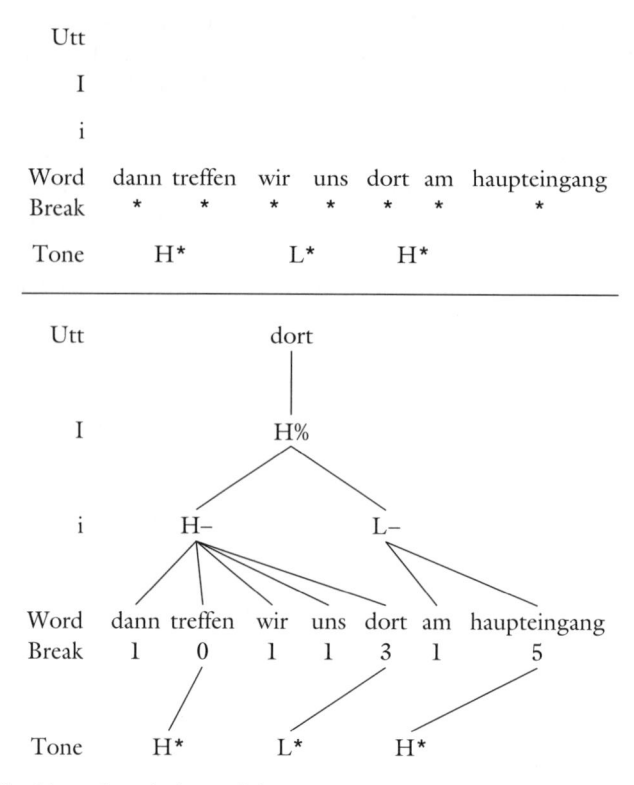

Figure 4.7 The hierarchy window of the utterance **dort** in the **gt** database before (above) and after (below) annotation.

such as links and annotations (unfortunately, there is currently no undo button – so if you accidentally delete material, close the annotation window without saving).

In order to set the links between the **i** and **Word** tiers, move the mouse anywhere to the same height in the window as the **i** tier and click twice (twice because two intermediate phrases have to be entered). This will cause two asterisks to appear. Proceed in the same way as described earlier for setting the non-linear links between the asterisks and the words as shown in Figure 4.7: thus, move the mouse to the first word *dann* until it changes to blue, then hold the mouse button down and sweep to the first asterisk until it also changes to blue. Set all of the links between these tiers in the same way. You should end up with two asterisks at the **i** tier, the first of which is linked to the first five words, the second to the last two. To enter text, click on the asterisk to get a cursor and enter the annotations. Set the labels and links at the **Utt** and **I** tier in the same manner as described above. Finally, enter the annotations of the **Break** tier (these could also be entered in the signal window because any tier that is linearly linked to a time tier – in this case to **Word** – also appears in the signal window)[2] and then save the file.

The result of saving annotations is that one file per time tier and one so-called **hierarchical label file** will be created or updated. Since, for this database, there are two time tiers, **Tone** and **Word**, then the annotations at the **Tone** tier and the annotations at the **Word** tier are stored in their own separate (plain text) files. The location of these

Querying Annotation Structures 85

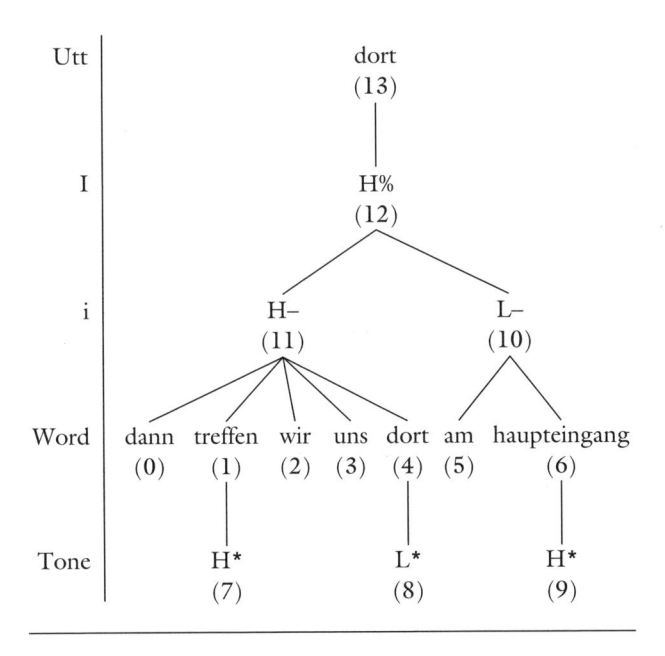

```
                                    dort
                                    (13)
                                     |
                                    H%
                                    (12)
                                    / \
                                   /   \
                                  H-    L-
                                 (11)  (10)
```

Utt — dort (13)
I — H% (12)
i — H− (11), L− (10)
Word — dann (0), treffen (1), wir (2), uns (3), dort (4), am (5), haupteingang (6)
Tone — H* (7), L* (8), H* (9)

Figure 4.8 The annotations for **dort** showing the annotation numbers (gray) coded in the corresponding **hlb** file. The annotation numbers can be displayed with **Display → Toggle Segment numbers** (from the main Emu menu). For simplicity, the **Break** tier has been removed from the display (**Display → Hierarchy Levels**).

files is given in the **Labfiles** pane of the template file (lower pane, Figure 4.6). The other annotations from timeless tiers are stored in the hierarchical label file which always has the extension **hlb** and which is stored in the path given in the **Levels** pane of the template file. As you will see if you open any (plain text) **hlb** file, the information is a code that is equivalent to the kinds of structures shown in Figure 4.8. (The actual numbers might differ depending on the order in which the annotations were created.) For example, some of the lines from **dort.hlb** might look like this:

```
0
1 7
2
3
4 8
5
6 9
7
8
9
10 5 6 9
11 0 1 2 3 4 7 8
```

The number on the left denotes a parent of any of those on the right. So **1 7** in the second line means that annotation **1** is a parent (or grandparent or great-great-grandparent, etc.) of annotation **7** while annotation **11** on the last line stands in an analogous relationship to the adjacent annotations **0, 1, 2, 3, 4, 7, 8**. The relationship between these numeric and actual annotations can be deduced from the other information in the same **hlb** file or alternatively by opening a hierarchy window and showing both types of annotations as in Figure 4.8. This figure shows that **11** corresponds to the first **H-** at tier **i** while the other numbers to the right include the annotations at the **Word** tier of which it is a parent, as well as those of the **Tone** tier of which it is a grandparent.

4.5 Conversion of a Structured Annotation to a Praat TextGrid

Although tiers whose times are predictable are structurally and implicitly coded in Emu, it is nevertheless possible to convert most Emu annotations into a Praat TextGrid in which times are explicitly represented for every annotation and for every tier. For example, the equivalent TextGrid representation for the utterance that has just been annotated is shown in Figure 4.9: in this TextGrid, the annotations of the tiers that

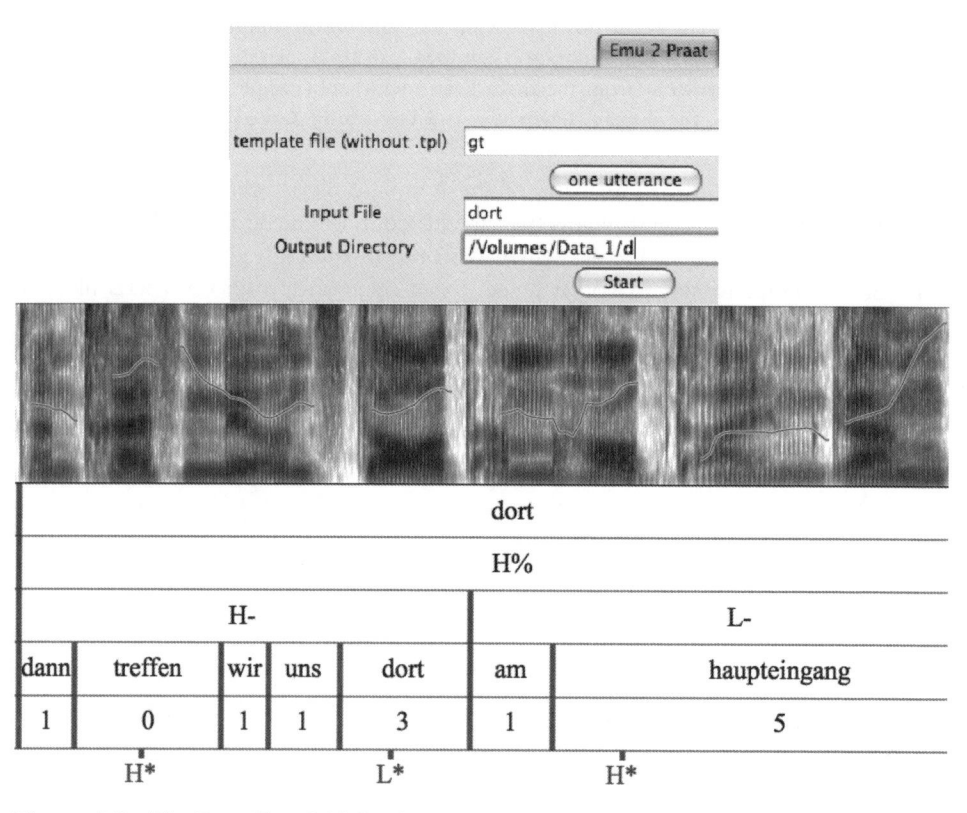

				dort			
				H%			
		H-				L-	
dann	treffen	wir	uns	dort	am	haupteingang	
1	0	1	1	3	1	5	
H*				L*		H*	

Figure 4.9 The Praat TextGrid for the utterance **dort** corresponding to the structured annotation in Emu. This TextGrid was created with the **labConvert** window shown above the Praat display (accessible from **Arrange Tools** → **Convert Labels** → **Emu2Praat**) by entering the template file (**gt**) and input file (**dort**) and specifying an output directory.

were declared to stand in a hierarchical relationship to each other in Emu have identical times at boundaries, as Figure 4.9 shows. But not every Emu annotation structure can have a corresponding representation as a Praat TextGrid. In particular, it is possible to have annotations in Emu that are completely timeless even after annotations have percolated up through the tree, in the manner described earlier. An example of this occurs in the downloadable **kielread** corpus in Figure 4.10, in which the **Kanonic** tier (used for citation-form, dictionary pronunciations) stands in a hierarchical relationship to the segment tier **Phonetic** from which it therefore inherits its times. However, since some annotations at the **Kanonic** tier are not linked to the **Phonetic** tier, then the times cannot be passed up the tree to them and so they remain timeless.

The purpose of these unlinked annotations is to express segment deletion. Thus the citation-form, isolated word production of *und* (*and*) has a final /t/, but in the read speech form that actually occurred in this utterance, the /t/ appears to have been deleted, as both the spectrogram Figure 4.10 and listening to the utterance suggest. This mismatch between the citation-form representation and what was actually spoken is given expression by representing this final /t/ at the **Kanonic** tier as being unassociated with any time. The advantage of this representation is that the user can subsequently compare analogous contexts that differ according to whether or not segment deletion has taken place. For example, although based on a similar spectrographic/auditory impression, the final /t/ in *past six* may appear to have been deleted (thereby rendering the first word apparently homophonous with *pass*), a more rigorous follow-up analysis may well show that there were, after all, fine phonetic

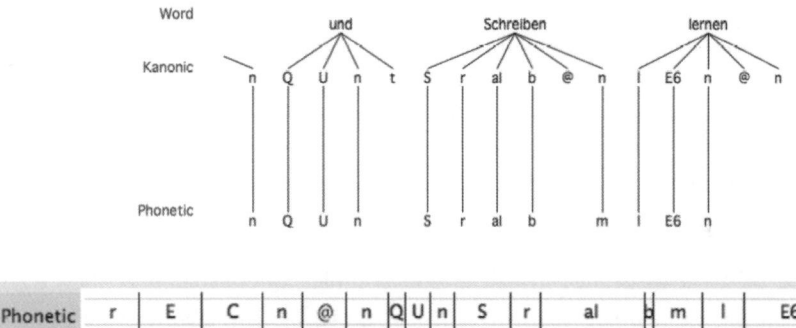

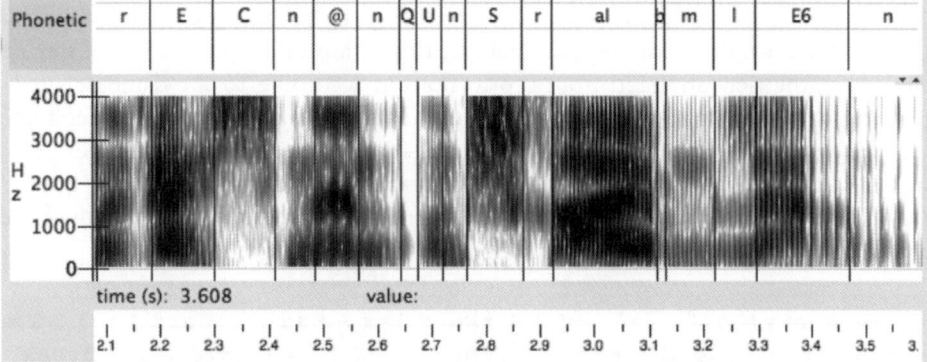

Figure 4.10 A fragment of the utterance **K67MR095** from the **kielread** corpus showing apparent segment deletion in the words *und*, *schreiben*, and *lernen*.

cues that distinguished the long [s] across the word boundary in *past six* from its occurrence in *pass six*. But in order to carry out such an analysis, it would be necessary to find in the corpus examples of [s] that do and do not precede a deleted /t/ and this will only be possible if the deletion is explicitly encoded at this more abstract level of representation, as has been done for the /t/ of *und*, the /ə/ of *schreiben* (*to write*) and the final /ən/ of *lernen* (*to learn*) in this utterance in the **kielread** corpus. Now, since annotations in Praat must be explicitly associated with times, then these kinds of timeless segments that are used to express the possibility of segment deletion will not appear in the Praat TextGrid, when the conversion is carried out in the manner shown earlier in Figure 4.9 (and a warning message is given to this effect).

4.6 Graphical User Interface to the Emu Query Language

The types of queries that have been discussed so far can be combined for more complex queries of structured annotations. A full review of the query syntax is beyond the scope of this chapter but is summarized in Cassidy and Harrington (2001) and set out in further detail in Appendix A on the website associated with this book. An example is given here of a complex query that makes use of the additional functionality for searching by position and number: "find all **L*+H** pitch-accented words that are in intermediate-phrase-final position and in **H%** intonational phrases of at least five words and such that the target words precede another word with a break index of **0** in an **L-** intermediate phrase." Such a query should find the word *Thorsten* in the **gt** database (Figure 4.3) because *Thorsten*:

- is the last word in an intermediate phrase;
- is associated with an **L*+H** pitch-accent;
- occurs in an **H%** intonational phrase of at least five words;
- precedes another word (*ja*) whose break index is **0** and which occurs in an **L-** intermediate phrase.

The graphical user interface to the Emu query language, which was written by Tina John, can be of great assistance in calculating complex queries such as these. This GUI (Figure 4.11) is opened by clicking on the **graphical query** button in the **Query Tool** window: for the **gt** database, this action brings up a form of spreadsheet with the tiers arranged from top to bottom according to the database's template file. It is a comparatively straightforward matter to enter the search criteria into this window in the manner shown in Figure 4.11. The search instruction is automatically copied into the **Query Tool** window after clicking the **Query** button. You could also copy the calculated search instruction and then enter it as the third argument of the **emu.query()** function in R thus:

```
emu.query("gt", "*", "[ [ [ #Word !=x & End ( i,Word ) = 1 ^ I =
H% & Num ( I,Word ) >= 5 ] ^ Tone = L*+H ] -> [ Word !=x & Break
= 0 ^ i = L- ] ]")
     labels      start    end     utts
1   Thorsten   1573.73  2086.38  thorsten
```

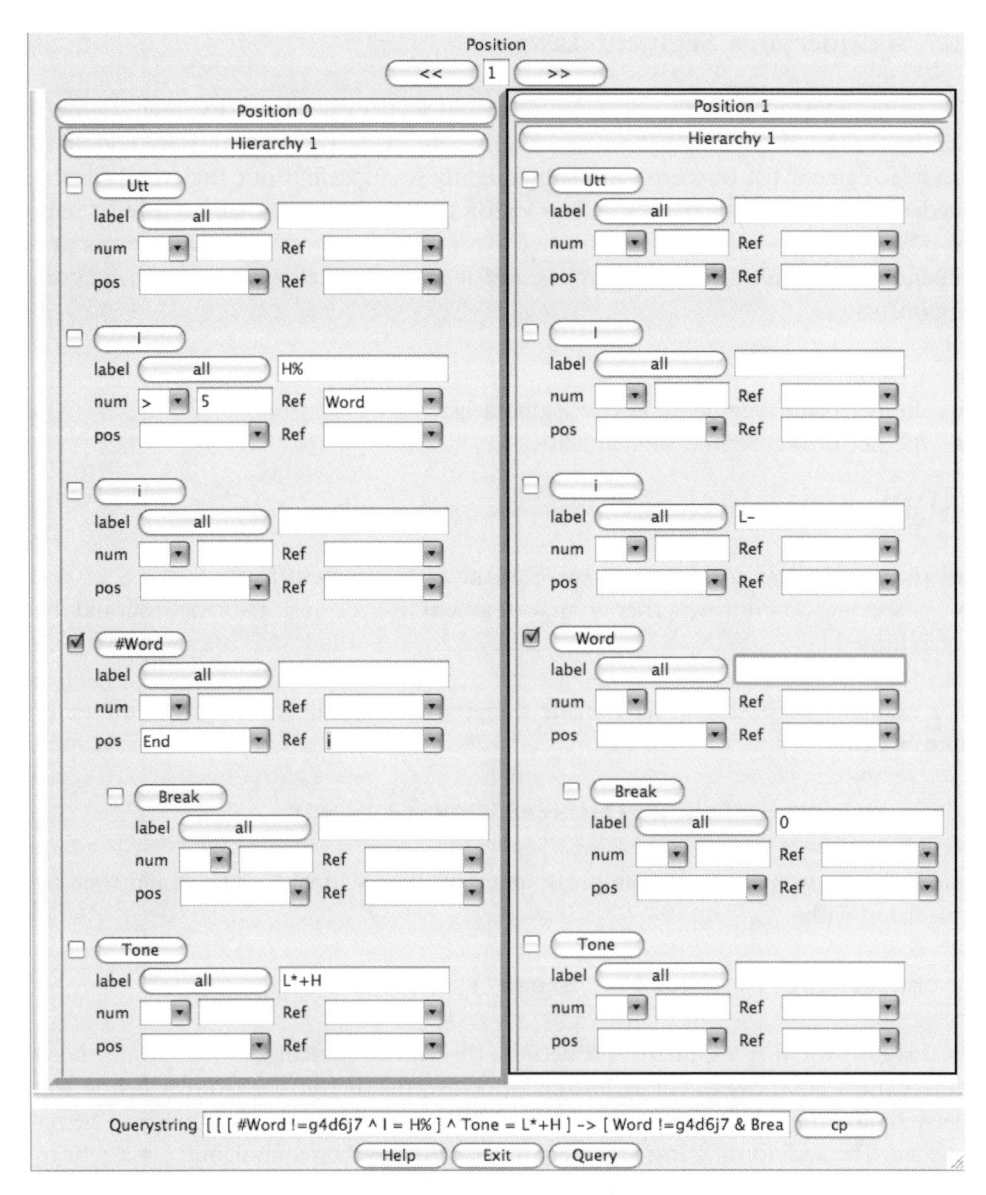

Figure 4.11 The graphical user interface to the Emu query language. Assuming you have loaded the utterances of the **gt** database, click on **graphical query** in the **Query Tool** window (Figure 4.1) to open the spreadsheet shown above (initially you will only see the pane on the left). A query of all **H%** (intonational phrases) labels that dominate more than five words is entered at tier **I**, with the label **H%** and with **num > 5 Word**. A tick mark is placed next to **Word** to make a segment list of annotations at this tier; also click on **Word** itself to get the # sign which means that a segment list should be made of words only in this position (rather than across this and the next word). Enter **End i** at the **Word** tier to search for intermediate-phrase-final words. At the **Tone** tier, enter **L*+H** to search for these annotations. Then click the **>>** arrow at the top of the spreadsheet beneath **Position** to enter the search criteria in an analogous manner for the following segment, i.e., **L-** at tier **i** and 0 at the **Break** tier. Finally select the **Query** button when you are ready and the system will calculate the search instruction (shown next to **Querystring**).

4.7 Re-querying Segment Lists

The **emu.requery()** function in the Emu-R library allows existing segment lists to be queried for position or non-linearly. This is useful if, say, you have made a segment list of words and subsequently want to find out the type of intermediate phrase in which they occurred, or the annotations that followed them, or the pitch-accents with which they were associated. The **emu.requery()** function can be used for this purpose and it takes the following three mandatory arguments:

- a segment list;
- the tier of the segments in the segment list;
- the tier of the desired segment list;

and the following two optional arguments:

- the position (as an integer) relative to the input segment list;
- a specification for whether a new segment list or just its labels should be returned.

For example, suppose you have made a segment list of all words in the utterance **thorsten**:

```
w = emu.query("gt", "thorsten", "Word != x")
```

and you now want to know the break index of these segments. This could then be calculated with:

```
emu.requery(w, "Word", "Break")
```

In this case, the first argument is **w** because this is the segment list that has just been made; the second argument is **"Word"** because this is the tier from which **w** was derived; and the third argument is **"Break"** because this is the tier that is to be re-queried. The additional fourth argument **justlabels=T** or equivalently **j = T** returns only the corresponding annotations rather than the entire segment list:

```
emu.requery(w, "Word", "Break", j=T)
"1" "3" "1" "1" "1" "3" "0" "1" "1" "3" "1" "1" "1" "1" "1" "4"
```

Thus the second annotation **"3"** in the vector of annotations highlighted above is the break index of the second segment. Exactly the same syntax can be used to re-query segment lists for annotations of non-linearly linked tiers. So **emu.requery(w, "Word", "i")** and **emu.requery(w, "Word", "I")** make segment lists of the intermediate and intonational phrases that dominate the words in the segment list **w**. Similarly, you could find which words are associated with a pitch-accent (i.e., the prosodically accented words) as follows:

```
emu.requery(w, "Word", "Tone", j=T)
"no-segment" "L*" "no-segment" ...
```

The first two words in **w** are unaccented and accented respectively because, as the above annotations show, **no-segment** is returned for the first (i.e., it is not associated with any annotation at the **Tone** level) whereas the second is associated with an **L***.

If you want to find the preceding or following segments relative to a segment then use the **seq** argument. Thus:

```
emu.requery(w, "Word", "Word", seq=-1)
```

finds the annotations at the same tier that precede the segment list (analogously, **seq=2** would be for finding annotations positioned two slots to the right, and so on). The first three segments that are returned from the above command look like this:

```
Read 16 records
segment list from database: gt
query was: requery
    labels       start     end      utts
1   no-segment   0.000     0.000    thorsten
2   jeden        47.689    250.366  thorsten
3   morgen       250.366   608.032  thorsten
```

The reason why the first segment has a **no-segment** entry is because there can be no segment that precedes the first word of the utterance.

If you want to re-query for both a different tier and a different position, then two queries are needed. Firstly, a segment list is made of the preceding word and, secondly, these preceding words are queried for pitch-accents:

```
prec.word = emu.requery(w, "Word", "Word", seq=-1)
prec.tone = emu.requery(prec.word, "Word", "Tone", j=T)
```

4.8 Building Annotation Structures Semi-automatically with Emu-Tcl

Putting together annotation structures such as the one discussed so far can be useful for subsequently searching the database, but the data entry can be cumbersome, especially for a large and multi-tiered database. For this reason, there is the facility in Emu to automate various stages of tree-building via an interface to the Tcl/Tk programming language, and there are some existing programs in the Emu-Tcl library for doing so. Since an introduction to the Tcl/Tk language is beyond the scope of this book, some examples will be given here of using very simple programs for building annotation structures automatically. Some further examples of using existing Emu-Tcl scripts are given in Appendix B of the website associated with this book.

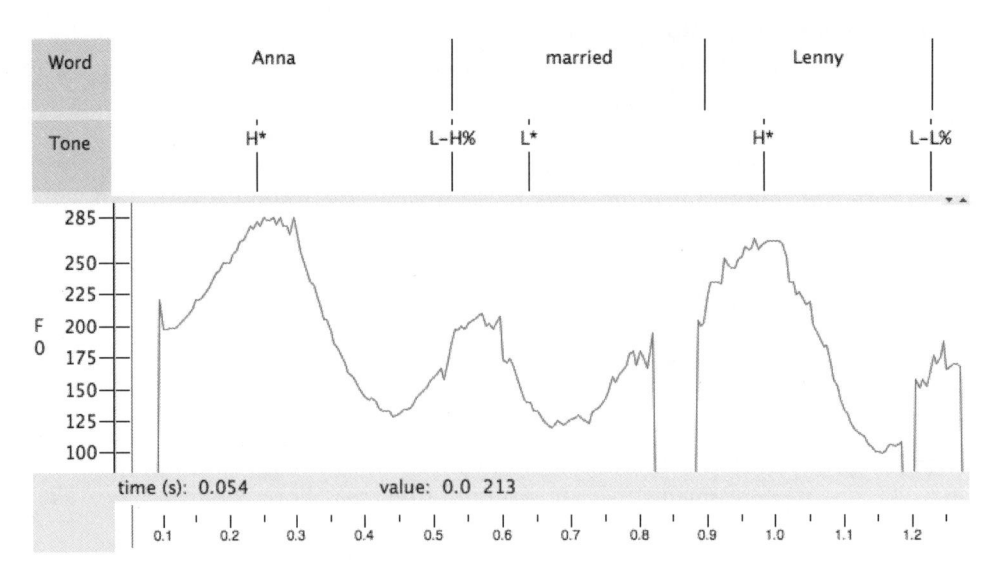

Figure 4.12 The utterance **anna1** from the **aetobi** database including the f0 contour as calculated in the exercises of Chapter 3.

For the present example, the task will be to link annotations between the **Tone** and **Word** tiers in the **aetobi** database in order to be able to make similar kinds of queries that were applied to the **gt** database above. The annotations in **aetobi** are arranged in three time tiers, **Word**, **Tone**, and **Break** that have the same interpretation as they did for the **gt** database considered earlier. Since, in contrast to the **gt** database, none of **aetobi**'s annotations are linked, then inter-tier queries are not possible. The first task will be to use an Emu-Tcl function **LinkFromTimes** to link the **Word** and **Tone** tiers based on their times in order to allow queries such as "find all pitch-accented words."

The Emu-Tcl function **LinkFromTimes** causes annotations at two tiers **T** and **U** to be linked whenever the time(s) of the annotations at tier **U** are within those of tier **T**. Therefore, **LinkFromTimes** should link the **H***, **L***, and **H*** pitch-accents to *Anna*, *married*, and *Lenny* respectively in Figure 4.12 because the times of the pitch-accents all fall within the times of these word boundaries. It is not clear what this function will do to the annotations **L-H%** and **L-L%**: in annotating these utterances, which was done in the early 1990s as part of the American English ToBI database, the task was to align all phrase and boundary tones like these with the right word boundary (so the right boundary of *Anna* and **L-H%** should have the same time) but very fine mouse control indeed would have been needed to make the boundaries coincide precisely. So it is more than likely that these boundary times are fractionally either before or after the word boundary and, for this reason, it is difficult to predict whether they will be linked with the phrase-final or phrase-initial word.

Three steps are needed to run **LinkFromTimes** function, and these are:

- write an Emu-Tcl script that includes this function;
- load the script into the template file;
- modify the template file if need be.

For the first of these, the syntax is:

```
LinkFromTimes $utt Word Tone
```

where **$utt** is a variable defining the current utterance. This command needs to be saved in a plain text file that includes a **package statement** to provide access to **LinkFromTimes** in the Emu-Tcl library. You also have to include two functions that each begin with the line **proc**. The first of these, **AutoBuildInit**, is used to initialize any datasets and variables that are needed by the second, **AutoBuild**, that does the work of building the annotation structure for the current utterance. Your plain text file should therefore include just these three commands:

```
package require emu::autobuild
proc AutoBuildInit {template} {}
proc AutoBuild {template utt} {LinkFromTimes $utt Word Tone}
```

Save this plain text file as **aetobi.txt** somewhere on your system. Now edit the template file of the **aetobi** database in the usual way in order to make two changes: firstly, **Word** must be made a parent of **Tone** because Emu will only link annotations between two tiers non-linearly if one tier is declared to be a parent of the other; and, secondly, you will have to tell Emu where to find the plain text file, **aetobi.txt**, that you have just created (Figure 4.13).

Then save the template file, reload the database and open any utterance. There will now be a new button, **Build Hierarchy**, which is used to run your Tcl script over the annotations of the utterance that you have just opened. Switch to the hierarchy view, then select **Build Hierarchy** and finally **Redraw** to see the result, which should be linked annotations between the **Word** and **Tone** tiers (Figure 4.14).

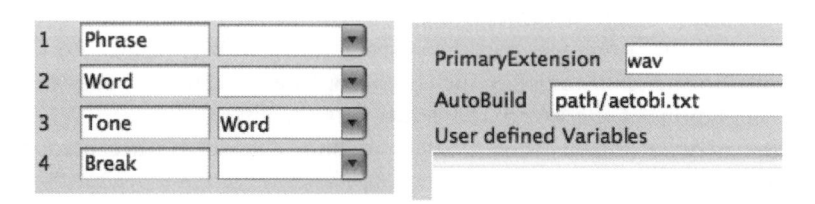

Figure 4.13 The modified **aetobi** template file. **Word** is made a parent of **Tone** (left) and **path/aetobi.txt** is the file containing the Tcl code that is entered in the **Variables** pane (right) under **AutoBuild**. Also make sure that **Word** and **Tone** are selected in **HierarchyViewLevels** of the template file's **view** pane.

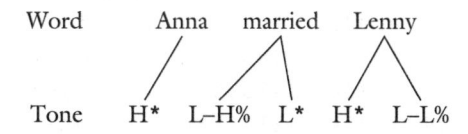

Figure 4.14 The output of the **LinkFromTimes** function showing links between annotations at the **Word** and **Tone** tiers. This display was obtained by clicking on **Build Hierarchy**.

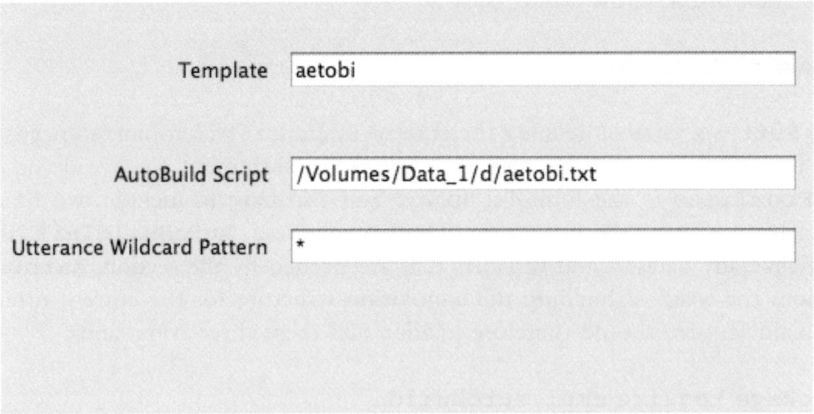

[Screenshot showing fields: Template "aetobi", AutoBuild Script "/Volumes/Data_1/d/aetobi.txt", Utterance Wildcard Pattern "*"]

Figure 4.15 The Emu **AutoBuild** tool is accessible from **Database Operations** → **AutoBuildExtern** and will automatically load any Tcl (AutoBuild) script that is specified in the template file. Follow through the instructions to apply the script to all utterances in the database.

The same figure also shows that the **L-H%** phrase-boundary tone has been linked with the second word (so the labeler evidently positioned this annotation fractionally beyond the offset of the first word *Anna*).

You could now save the utterance and then work through the entire database one utterance at a time in order to link the annotations in this way, but even for a handful of utterances this becomes tedious. Your Tcl script can instead be run over the entire database with **Database Operations** → **AutoBuildExtern**, which will bring up the Emu **AutoBuild Tool** with your Tcl script ready to be run (Figure 4.15). If you follow through the instructions in this window, the script will be applied to all the utterances and the corresponding **hlb** files saved to the directory specified in the Emu template file. If you open any utterance, you should find that the annotations at the **Word** and **Tone** tiers are linked.

Once the tiers are linked, then a query to find, e.g., all **L*** accented words is possible:

```
emu.query("aetobi", "*", "[Word != x ^ Tone = L*]")
Read 13 records
segment list from database: aetobi
query was: [Word!=x ^ Tone=L*]
      labels         start        end       utts
  1   married       529.945     897.625    anna1
  2   can          1063.330    1380.750    argument
  3   can          3441.810    3723.970    argument
  4   Atlanta      8483.270    9214.580    atlanta
  5   audience     1070.865    1473.785    audience1
  6   bananas        10.000     655.665    bananas
```

```
7    poisonous    880.825   1786.855   bananas
8    ma'am       1012.895   1276.395   beef
9    don't       2201.715   2603.025   beef
10   eat         2603.025   2867.945   beef
11   beef        2867.945   3441.255   beef
12   and         3510.095   3622.955   blond-baby1
13   pink        3785.905   4032.715   blond-baby1
```

In Cassidy et al. (2000), a more complicated Tcl program was written for converting the flat annotations of the **aetobi** database into a hierarchical form similar to that of the **gt** database considered earlier, in which intonational phrases dominate intermediate phrases which dominate words and in which words are associated with pitch-accents. In addition, and as for the **gt** database, the boundary and phrase tones are marked at the intonational and intermediate tiers and the script ensures only pitch-accents from the **Tone** tier are associated with words. The script for carrying out these operations is **tobi2hier.txt** and it is located in the top level folder of the **aetobi** database when it is downloaded.

As described above, the parent–child tier relationships need to be defined and the script has to be loaded into the template file. For the first of these, the template file has to be changed to encode the path in Figure 4.16. This path has to be entered as always in the **Levels** pane of the template file and the simplest way to do this, when there are already existing tiers, is in *text mode*, as shown in Figure 4.17. Having edited the tiers in the manner of Figure 4.17, you must also load the new Emu-Tcl program (in the **Variables** pane of the template file, as already described in the right panel of Figure 4.13). If you downloaded the **aetobi** database to the directory **path**, then the file that you need to load is **path/aetobi/tobi2hier.txt**. While you are editing the template, you should also select the new tiers **Intonational** and **Intermediate** to be displayed in the **View** pane of the template file.

Now call up the program for running this script over the entire database as in Figure 4.15, which should now load the new Emu-Tcl script **tobi2hier.txt**. After you have run this script, then the hierarchy for each utterance should be built and visible, in the manner of Figure 4.18. You will now be able to query the database

Intonational
↓
Intermediate
↓
Word (S)
↓
Tone (E)

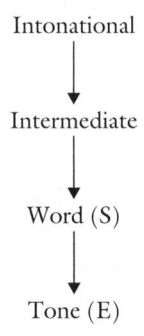

Figure 4.16 The path for representing parent–child tiers in **aetobi**.

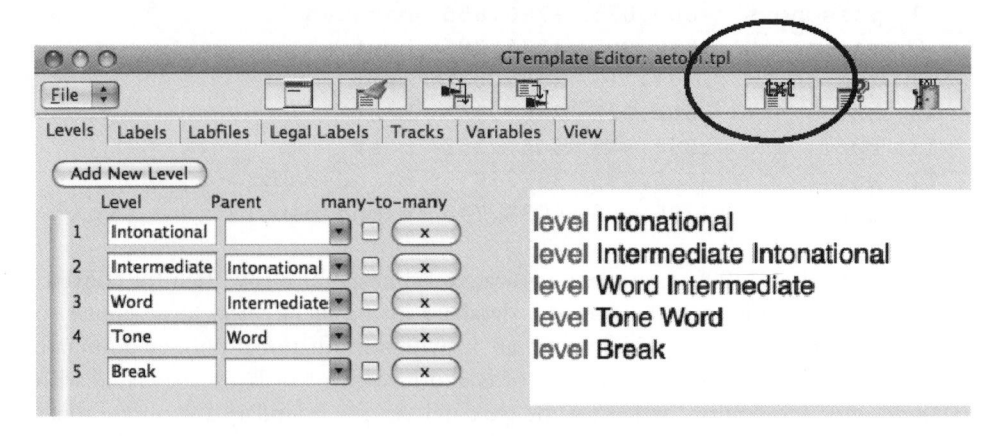

Figure 4.17 The modified **Levels** pane of the **aetobi** template file to encode the path relationships in Figure 4.16. The simplest way to do this is in text mode by clicking on **txt** (inside the ellipse), which will bring up the plain text file of the template. Then replace the existing **level** statements with those shown on the right of this figure. Once this is done, click anywhere inside the **GTemplate Editor** and answer **yes** to the prompt: **Do you want to update GTed?** to create the corresponding tiers shown here in the **Levels** pane. Finally, save the template file in the usual way. (There is no need to save the plain text file.)

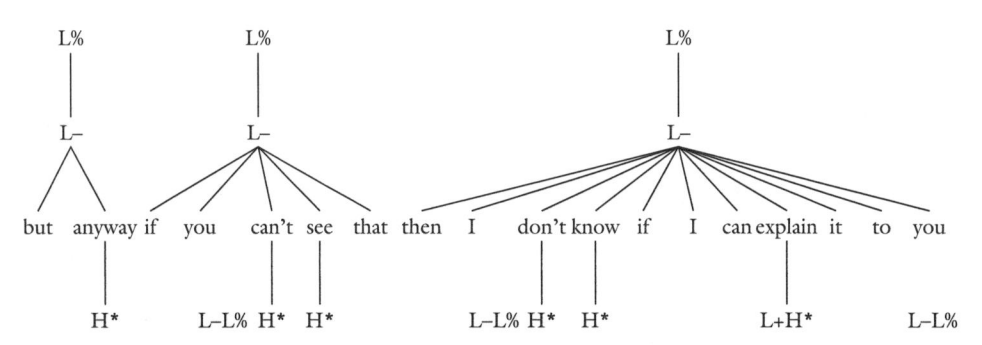

Figure 4.18 The result of running **tobi2hier.txt** on the utterance **anyway**. If the **Intonational** and **Intermediate** tiers are not visible when you open this utterance, then select them from **Display → Hierarchy Levels**.

for all the linked tiers. For example, the words associated with **H*** in **L-** intermediate and **H%** intonational phrases is given by:

```
emu.query("aetobi", "*", "[ [ [ Word != x ^ Tone = H* ] ^
Intermediate = L- ] ^ Intonational = H% ]")
  1  Anna      9.995   529.945   anna1
  2  yes      10.000  2119.570   atlanta
  3  uh     2642.280  3112.730   atlanta
  4  like   3112.730  3360.330   atlanta
  5  here's   10.000   206.830   beef
```

4.9 Branching Paths

In all the tier relationships considered in the various corpora so far, the tiers have been stacked up on top of each other in a single vertical path – which means that a tier has at most one parent and at most one child. However, there are some kinds of annotation structure that cannot be represented in this way. Consider as an example of this the relationship between various tiers below the level of the word in German. It seems reasonable to suggest that words, morphemes, and phonemes stand in a hierarchical relationship to each other because a word is composed of one or more morphemes, each of which is composed of one or more phonemes: thus *kindisch* (*childish*) unequivocally consists of a sequence of two morphemes, *kind* and *-isch*, which each maps onto its constituent phonemes. Analogously, words, syllables, and phonemes also stand in hierarchical relationship to each other. Now there is a well-known phonological process (sometimes called final devoicing) by which obstruents in German are voiceless in prosodically final position (e.g., Wiese 1996): thus, although the final consonant in *Rad* (*wheel*) may have underlying voicing by analogy to, for instance, the genitive form, *Rades*, which surfaces (is actually produced) with a voiced /d/, the final consonant of *Rad* is phonetically voiceless, i.e., produced as /ra:t/ and possibly homophonous with *Rat* (*advice*). Therefore, since *kindisch* is produced with a *voiced* medial obstruent, i.e., /kɪndɪʃ/, then the /d/ cannot be in a prosodically final position because, if it were, then *kindisch* should be produced with a medial voiceless consonant as /kɪntɪʃ/ as a consequence of final devoicing. In summary it seems, then, that there are two quite different ways of parsing the same phoneme string into words: either as morphemes *kind+isch* or as syllables *kin.disch*. But what is the structural relationship between morphemes and syllables in this case? It cannot be hierarchical in the sense of the term used in this chapter, because a morpheme is evidently not made up of one or more syllables (the first morpheme *Kind* is made up of the first syllable but only a fragment of the second) while a syllable is also evidently not made up of one or more morphemes (the second syllable consists of the second morpheme preceded by only a fragment of the first). It seems instead that, because phonemes can be parsed into words in two different ways, then there must be two different hierarchical relationships between **Phoneme** and **Word** organized into two separate paths: via **Morpheme** along one path, but via **Syllable** along another (Figure 4.19).

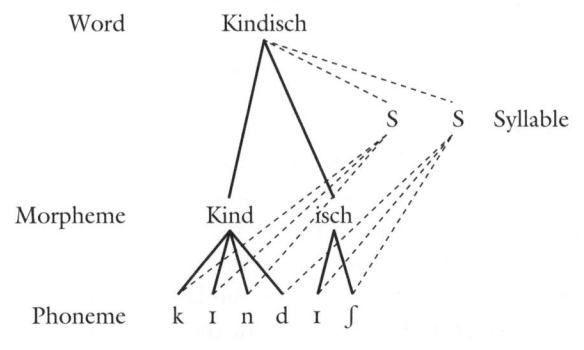

Figure 4.19 The structural relationships between **Word**, **Morpheme**, **Phoneme**, and, in a separate plane, between **Word**, **Syllable**, and **Phoneme** for German *kindisch* (*childish*).

```
        Word              Word                 Word
          │                 │                  ╱   ╲
          ▼                 ▼                 ▼     ▼
       Morpheme         Syllable    =     Morpheme  Syllable
          │                 │                 │    ╱
          ▼                 ▼                 ▼   ▼
     Phoneme (S)       Phoneme (S)         Phoneme (S)
```

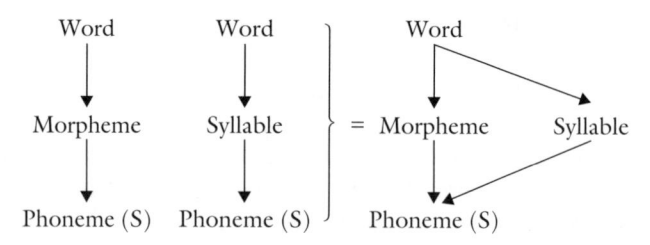

Figure 4.20 The two paths for the hierarchical structures in Figure 4.19, which can be summarized by the inter-tier relationships on the right. Since only **Phoneme** is a segment tier and all other tiers are timeless, then, where → denotes "dominates," **Word** → **Morpheme** → **Phoneme** and **Word** → **Syllable** → **Phoneme**.

This three-dimensional representation in Figure 4.19 can be translated quite straightforwardly using the notation for defining parent–child relationships between tiers discussed earlier, in which there are now two paths for this structure from **Word** to **Morpheme** to **Phoneme** and from **Word** to **Syllable** to **Phoneme** as shown in Figure 4.20. The equivalent parent–child statements that would need to be made in the **Levels** pane of an Emu template file are as follows:

```
Word
Morpheme   Word
Phoneme    Morpheme
Syllable   Word
Phoneme    Syllable
```

This type of dual path structure also occurs in the downloadable **ae** database of read sentences of Australian English in which an Abercrombian stress-foot has been fused with the type of ToBI prosodic hierarchy discussed earlier. A stress-foot according to Abercrombie (1967) is a sequence of a stressed syllable followed by any number of unstressed syllables, and it can occur across word boundaries. For example, a parsing into stress-feet for the utterance **msajc010** of the **ae** database might be:

```
It is | fu | tile to | offer | any | further re | sistance |
w  w    s    s   w    s w     s w   s   w    w    s    w
```

where **s** and **w** are strong and weak syllables respectively and the vertical bar denotes a stress-foot boundary. Evidently words and feet cannot be in a hierarchical relationship for the same reason discussed earlier with respect to morphemes and syllables: a foot is not made up of a whole number of words (e.g., *resistance*) but a word is also not composed of a whole number of feet (e.g., *further re-* is one stress-foot). In the **ae** database, the Abercrombian foot is incorporated into the ToBI prosodic hierarchy by allowing an intonational phrase to be made up of one or more feet (thus a foot is allowed to cross not only word boundaries but also intermediate boundaries, as in *futile to* in **msajc010**). The paths for the **ae** database (which also include another branching path from **Syllable** to **Tone** that has nothing to do with the incorporation of the foot discussed here) are shown in Figure 4.21 (open the **Labels**

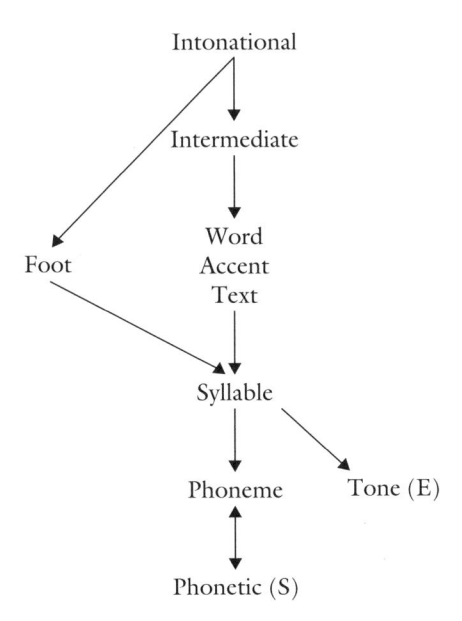

Figure 4.21 The path relationships for the **ae** database. All tiers are timeless except **Phonetic** and **Tone**.

pane of the **ae** template file to see how the child–parent relationships have been defined for these paths).

If you were to draw the structural relationships for an utterance from this database in the manner of Figure 4.19, then you would end up with a three-dimensional structure with a parsing from **Intonational** to **Foot** to **Syllable** on one plane, and from **Intonational** to **Intermediate** to **Word/Accent/Text** to **Syllable** on another. These three-dimensional diagrams cannot be displayed in Emu; on the other hand, it is possible to view the relationships between tiers on the same path, as in Figure 4.22. (Notice that, if you select two tiers like **Intermediate** and **Foot** that are *not* on the same path, then the annotations in the resulting display will, by definition, not be linked.)

Inter-tier queries can be carried out in the usual way for the kinds of structures discussed in this section, **but only as long as the tiers are on the same path**. So, in the *kindisch* example discussed earlier, queries are possible between any pairs of tiers except between **Morpheme** and **Syllable**. Similarly, all combinations of inter-tier queries are possible in the **ae** database except those between **Foot** and **Intermediate** or between **Foot** and **Word/Accent/Text**. Thus the following are meaningful and result each in a segment list:

intonational-final feet
`emu.query("ae", "msajc010", "[Foot=F & End(Intonational, Foot)=1]")`

intonational-final content words
`emu.query("ae", "msajc010", "[Word=C & End(Intonational, Word)=1]")`

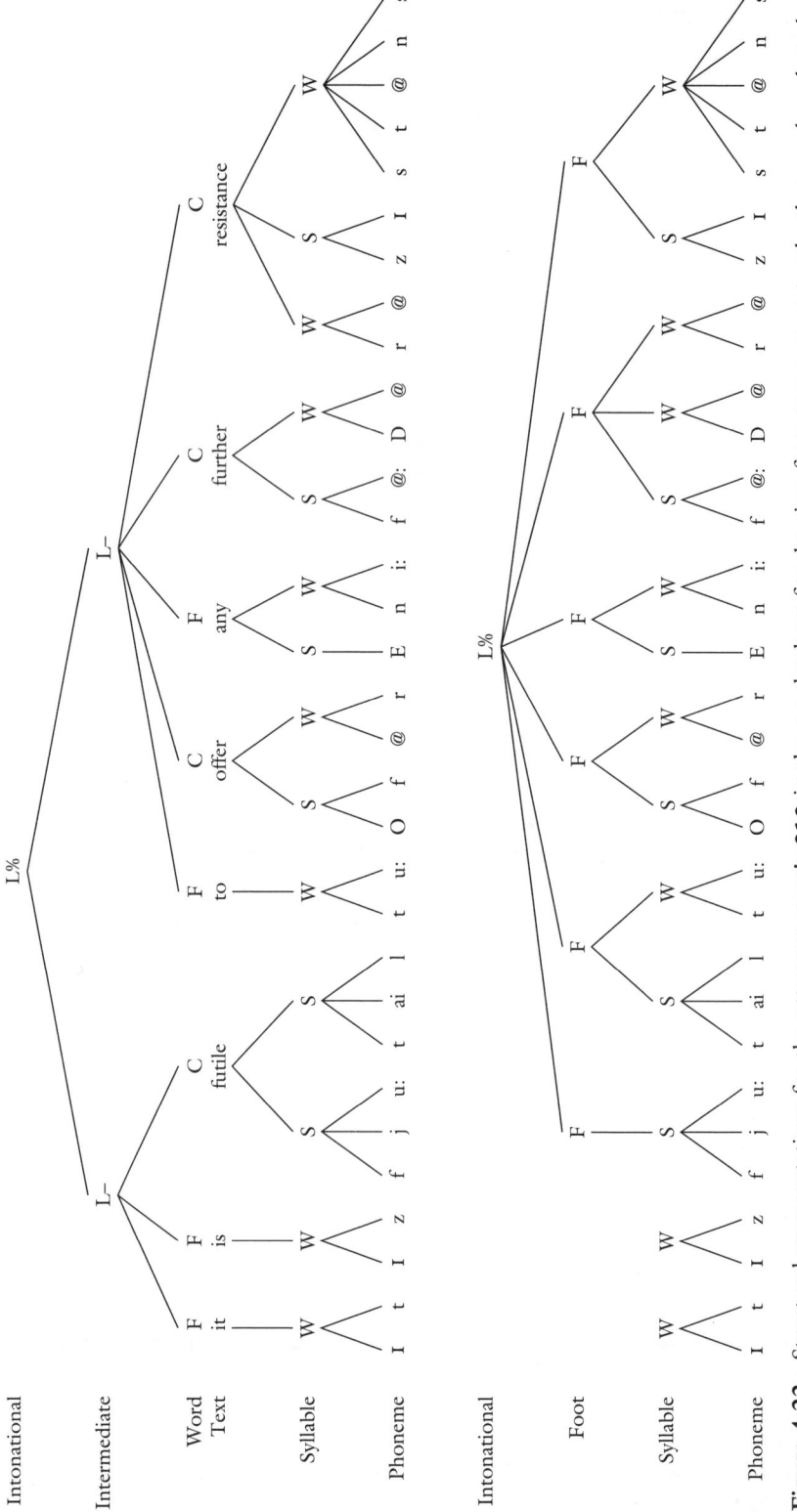

Figure 4.22 Structural representations for the utterance **msajc010** in the **ae** database for the tiers from two separate paths that can be selected from **Display → Hierarchy Levels**.

but the following produces no output because **Intermediate** and **Foot** are on separate paths:

intermediate-final feet
```
emu.query("ae", "msajc010", "[Foot=F & End(Intermediate,
Foot)=1]")

Error in emu.query("ae", "msajc010", "[Foot=F &
End(Intermediate, Foot)=1]") : Can't find the query results
in emu.query:
```

4.10 Summary

Tier types: segment, event, timeless In Emu, there is a distinction between time tiers and timeless tiers. The former includes segment tiers, in which annotations have a certain duration, and event tiers, in which annotations are marked by a single point in time. Timeless tiers inherit their times from time tiers depending on how the tiers are linked.

Linear links When two tiers are linearly linked, then their annotations stand in a one-to-one relationship to each other: that is for every annotation at one tier there is another annotation in the tier to which it is linearly linked with the same time stamp. A tier inherits the times from the tier with which it is linearly linked.

Non-linear links Two tiers are non-linearly linked if an annotation at one tier can map onto one or more annotations at another tier.

If both of the non-linearly linked tiers are also time tiers, then they stand in an autosegmental relationship to each other, otherwise the relationship is hierarchical. In an autosegmental relationship, the times of the tiers are by definition not predictable from each other. In a hierarchical relationship, the times of the parent tier are predictable and inherited from the child tier, where the parent tier is defined as the tier which is ordered immediately above a child tier.

If a single annotation in a parent tier can map onto one or more annotations at the child tier but not vice versa, the relationship between non-linearly linked tiers is additionally one-to-many; otherwise it is defined to be many-to-many. Hierarchical many-to-many links can be used to allow trees to overlap in time at their edges.

Specifying tier relationships in the template file A tier which is linearly linked to another is entered in the **Labels** pane of the template file. When two non-linearly linked tiers are entered in the **Levels** pane by specifying that one is the parent of the other, then they are non-linearly linked. The **Levels** pane is also used for specifying whether the relationship is one-to-many or many-to-many. The distinction between autosegmental and hierarchical emerges from the information included in the **Labfiles** pane: if both tiers are specified as time tiers (segment or event) the association is autosegmental, otherwise it is hierarchical.

Single and multiple paths Any set of tiers linked together in a parent–child relationship forms a path. For most purposes, the annotation structures of a database can be defined in terms of a single path in which a parent tier maps onto only one child tier and vice versa. Sometimes, and in particular if there is a need to encode intersecting hierarchies, the annotation structures of a database may be defined as two or more paths (a parent tier can be linked to more than one child tier and vice versa).

Data entry in Emu Annotations of time tiers must be entered in the signal view window. Tiers linearly linked to time tiers can be entered in either the signal view or the hierarchy window. The annotations of all other tiers as well as the links between them are entered in the hierarchy window. Use **Display** → **SignalView Levels** and **Display** → **Hierarchy Levels** to choose the tiers that you wish to see (or specify this information in the **Variables** pane of the template file). Annotations and annotation structures can also be semi-automated with the interface to Tcl. These scripts, some of which are pre-stored in the Emu-Tcl library, are loaded into the **Variables** pane of the template file. They are applied to single utterances with the **Build Hierarchy** button or to all utterances with the Emu **AutoBuild Tool**.

File output and conversion to a Praat TextGrid The result of saving the Emu annotations is one plain text annotation file per time tier. The extensions of each time tier are specified in the **Labfiles** pane of the template file. The information about annotations in timeless tiers as well as the linear and non-linear links between annotations is coded in the plain text **hlb** file (again with the utterance's base-name) whose path is specified in the template's **Levels** pane. Annotations stored in these files can be converted to an equivalent Praat TextGrid using **Arrange Tools** → **Convert Labels** → **Emu2Praat**. All annotations can be converted, even those in timeless tiers, as long as they have inherited times from a time tier. Annotations that remain timeless are not converted.

Queries Emu annotation structures can be queried with the Emu query language either directly using the Emu **Query Tool** or in R with the **emu.query()** function. The basic properties of the Emu query language are as follows:

1. **T = a** finds all **a** annotations from tier **T**. The same syntax is used to find annotations grouped by feature in the **Legal Labels** pane of the template file.
2. **T != a** finds all annotations except **a**. **T = a | b** finds **a** or **b** annotations at tier **T**.
3. Basic queries, either at the same tier or between linearly linked tiers, can be joined by **&** to denote *both* and **->** to denote *a sequence*. **T = a & U = w** finds **a** annotations at tier **T** linearly linked with **w** annotations at tier **U**. **T = a -> T = b** finds the sequence of annotations **a b** at tier **T**.
4. The **#** sign preceding a basic query causes annotations to be returned from that basic query only. Thus **T = a -> #T = b** finds **b** annotations preceded by **a** annotations at tier **T**.
5. **^** is used for queries between non-linearly linked tiers. **[T = a ^ U = w]** finds **a** annotations at tier **T** non-linearly linked (autosegmentally or hierarchically) to **w** annotations at tier **U**.

6 **Num(T, U)=n** finds annotations at tier **T** that are non-linearly linked to a sequence of *n* annotations at tier **U**. (In place of = use >, <, !=, >=, <= for *more than, less than, not equal to, greater than or equal to, less than or equal to*.)
7 **Start(T, U)=1** finds annotations at tier **U** that occur in initial position with respect to the non-linearly linked tier **T**. **End(T, U) = 1** and **Medial(T, U) = 1** do the same but for final and medial position. **Start(T, U) = 0** finds non-initial annotations at tier **U**.
8 Complex queries can be calculated with the aid of the graphical user interface.
9 An existing segment list can be re-queried in R either for position or with respect to another tier using the **emu.requery()** function.

4.11 Questions

A. This question is concerned with the **second** database.

A.1 By inspecting the **Levels**, **Labels**, and **Labfiles** panes of the template file, sketch by hand the relationship between the tiers of this database in a path analogous to that in Figure 4.6.

A.2 How are the following pairs of tiers related: autosegmentally, hierarchically, linearly, or unrelated?

Word and **Phoneme**
Word and **Phonetic**
Word and **Target**
Word and **Type**
Type and **Phoneme**
Type and **Phonetic**
Type and **Target**
Phoneme and **Phonetic**
Phoneme and **Target**
Phonetic and **Target**

A.3 Using the **emu.query()** function in R, make segment lists for utterances beginning with **agr*** (i.e., for the female speaker) in the following cases (/x/ refers to a segment at the **Phoneme** tier, [x] to a segment at the **Phonetic** tier, /x y/ to a sequence of segments at the **Phoneme** tier). If need be, make use of the graphical user interface to the Emu query language. Store the result as segment lists **s1**, **s2** ... **s12**. Question A.3.1 is given as an example.

A.3.1 [u:]
Example answer: **s1 = emu.query("second", "agr*", Phonetic=u:")**

A.3.2 The words *Duden* or *Gaben*. (Store the results in the segment list **s2**.)

A.3.3 The annotations at the **Type** tier for *Duden* or *Gaben* words

A.3.4 [u:] and [oe]

104   *Querying Annotation Structures*

A.3.5 /g u:/

A.3.6 /i:/ following /g/ or /b/

A.3.7 [H] in *Gaben*

A.3.8 [a:] in *Gaben* words of Type **L**

A.3.9 **T** at the **Target** level associated with any of /u:/, /i:/, or /y:/

A.3.10 Word-initial phonemes

A.3.11 [H] in words of at least two phonemes

A.3.12 [H] when the word-initial phoneme is /d/

A.4 Use the **emu.requery()** function to make segment lists or annotations relative to those made in A.3 in the following cases:

A.4.1 A segment list of the words corresponding to **s4**
Example answer: **emu.requery(s4, "Phonetic", "Word")**

A.4.2 A segment list of the phonemes preceding the segments in **s6**

A.4.3 The annotations at the **Type** level in **s9**

A.4.4 The annotations of the segments following **s12**

A.4.5 A segment list of the phonetic segments corresponding to **s2**

B. This question is concerned with the downloadable **ae** database.

B.1 Figure 4.21 is a summary of the paths for the **ae** database. Sketch the separate paths for the **ae** database in the manner shown on the left of Figure 4.20. Why is there an ambiguity about the times inherited by the **Syllable** tier (and hence also about all tiers above **Syllable**)?

B.2 Make segment or event lists from the **ae** database in the following cases. /x/ refers to annotations at the **Phoneme** tier, [x] to annotations at the **Phonetic** tier, orthographic annotations are at the **Text** tier. A strong (weak) syllable is coded as **S** (**W**) at the **Syllable** tier, and a prosodically accented (unaccented) word as **S** (**W**) at the **Accent** tier.

B.2.1 Annotations of *his* (from the **Text** tier)

B.2.2 /p/ or /t/ or /k/

B.2.3 All words following *his*

B.2.4 The sequence /ei k/

B.2.5 All content words (annotations at the **Text** tier associated with **C** from the **Word** tier)

B.2.6 The orthography of prosodically accented words in sequences of **W S** at the **Accent** tier

B.2.7 A sequence at the Text tier of *the* followed by any word, e.g., sequences of *the person* or *the situation* etc.

B.2.8 The phoneme /ei/ in strong syllables

B.2.9 Weak syllables containing an /ei/ phoneme

B.2.10 Word-initial /m/ or /n/

B.2.11 Weak syllables in intonational-phrase final words

B.2.12 Trisyllabic words (annotations from the **Text** tier of three syllables)

B.2.13 /w/ phonemes in monosyllabic words

B.2.14 Word-final syllables in trisyllabic content words

B.2.15 Foot-initial syllables

B.2.16 **L+H*** annotations at the **Tone** tier in foot-initial syllables in feet of more than two syllables

C. This question is concerned with the downloadable **gt** database that has been discussed in this chapter.

C.1 In some models of intonation (e.g., Grice et al. 2000), phrase tones (annotations at the intermediate tier) are hierarchical groupings of words but also have their own independent times, as in Figure 4.23. What simple modification do you need to make to the template file so that phrase tones (the annotations at Tier **i**) can be marked as an event in time as in Figure 4.23? Verify that you can annotate and save the utterance **schoen** in the manner shown in Figure 4.23 after you have edited and saved the template file.

C.2 If annotations at the intermediate tier are queried with the template file modified according to C.1, then such annotations are no longer segments but events as follows for the **schoen** utterance:

```
emu.query("gt", "schoen", "i !=x")
Read 1 records
event list from database: gt
query was: i !=x
  labels   start      end    utts
1    L-    1126.626    0     schoen
```

Why is the result now an event and not a segment list as before?

C.3 If you nevertheless also wanted to get the duration of this **L-** intermediate phrase in terms of the words it dominates as before, how could you do this in R? (Hint: use **emu.requery()**.)

D. Figure 4.24 shows the prosodic hierarchy for the Japanese word [kit:a] (*cut*, past participle) from Harrington et al. (2000) in which the relationship between word,

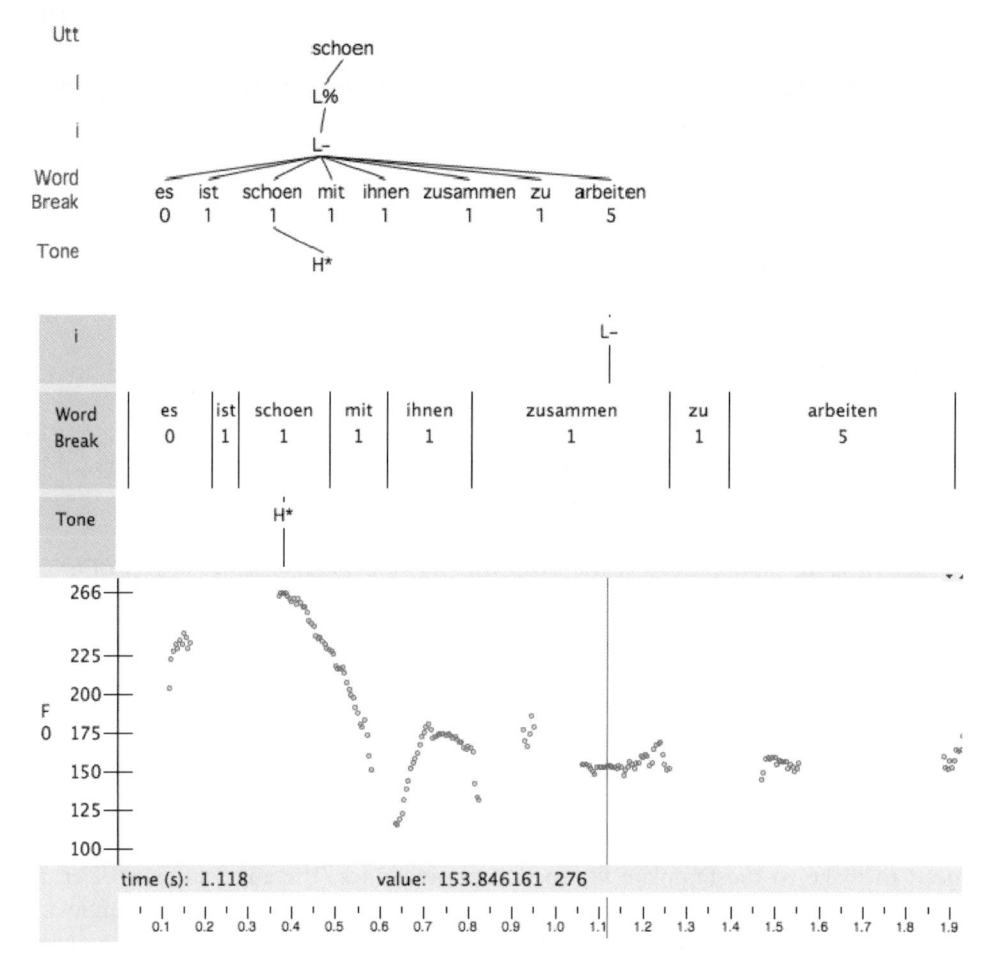

Figure 4.23 The utterance **schoen** from the **gt** database with an **L–** phrase tone marked at a point of time in the second syllable of *zusammen*.

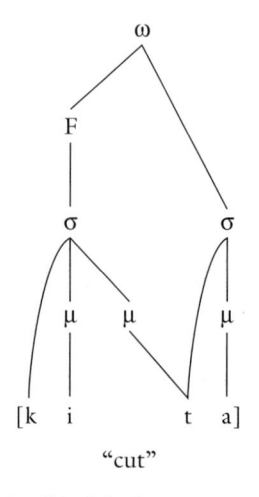

Figure 4.24 Prosodic structure for [kita] in Japanese. ω, **F**, σ, μ are respectively prosodic word, foot, syllable, and mora. From Harrington et al. (2000).

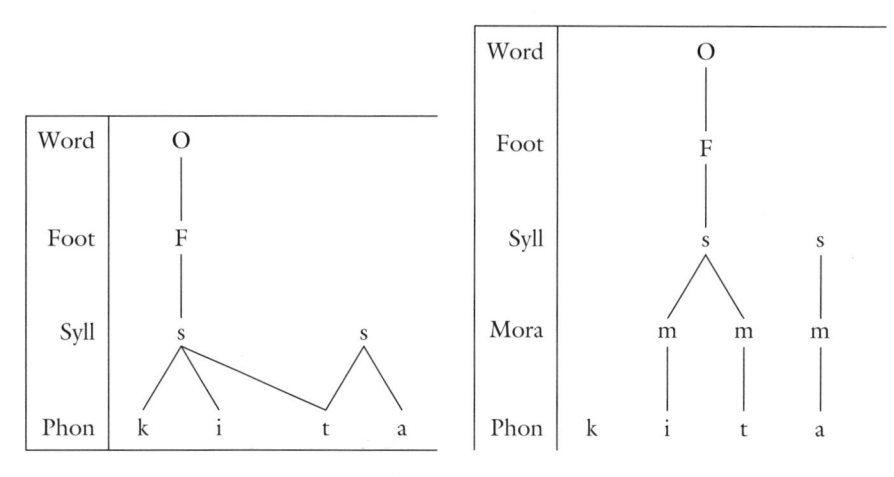

Figure 4.25 The coding in Emu of the annotations in Figure 4.24.

foot, syllable, mora, and phoneme tiers is hierarchical. (The long [t:] consonant is expressed in this structure by stating that [t] is ambisyllabic and dominated by a final mora of the first syllable.) The downloadable database **mora** contains the audio file of this word produced by a female speaker of Japanese with a segmentation into [kita] at the lowest segment tier, **Phon**.

D.1 Draw the path structure for converting this representation in Figure 4.24 into a form that can be used in a template file. Use **Word**, **Foot**, **Syll**, **Mora**, **Phon** for the five different tiers.

D.2 Modify the existing template file from the downloadable database **mora** to incorporate these additional tiers and annotate this word according to relationships given in Figure 4.24.

D.3 Verify when you have completed your annotations that you can display the relationships between annotations shown in Figure 4.25 corresponding to those in Figure 4.24.

D.4 Make five separate segment lists of the segments at the five tiers **Word**, **Foot**, **Syll**, **Mora**, **Phon**.

D.5 Verify the following by applying **emu.requery()** to the segment lists in D.4:

D.5.1 ω at the **Word** tier consists of [kita] at the **Phon** tier.

D.5.2 F at the **Foot** tier consists of [kit] at the **Phon** tier.

D.5.3 F at the **Foot** tier consists of the first two morae at the **Mora** tier.

D.5.4 The second syllable at the **Syll** tier consists only of the last mora at the **Mora** tier.

D.5.5 When you re-query the annotations at the **Phon** tier for morae, the first segment [k] is not dominated by any mora.

D.5.6 When you re-query the [t] for syllables, then this segment is dominated by both syllables.

4.12 Answers

A.1

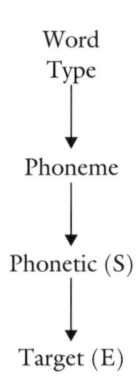

```
Word
Type
  |
  v
Phoneme
  |
  v
Phonetic (S)
  |
  v
Target (E)
```

A.2

Word and **Phoneme**	h
Word and **Phonetic**	h
Word and **Target**	a
Word and **Type**	l
Type and **Phoneme**	h
Type and **Phonetic**	h
Type and **Target**	a
Phoneme and **Phonetic**	h
Phoneme and **Target**	a
Phonetic and **Target**	a

A.3.2

```
s2 = emu.query("second", "agr*", "Word = Duden | Gaben")
```

A.3.3

```
s3 = emu.query("second", "agr*", "Type !=x & Word = Duden | Gaben ")
# OR
s3 = emu.requery(s2, "Word","Type")
```

A.3.4

```
s4 = emu.query("second", "agr*", "Phonetic=u: | oe")
```

A.3.5

```
s5 = emu.query("second", "agr*", "[Phoneme = g -> Phoneme = u:]")
```

A.3.6

```
s6 = emu.query("second", "agr*", "[Phoneme = g | b ->
#Phoneme = i:]")
```

A.3.7

```
s7 = emu.query("second", "agr*", "[Phonetic = H ^ Word =
Gaben]")
```

A.3.8

```
s8 = emu.query("second", "agr*", "[Phonetic = a: ^ Word =
Gaben & Type=L]")
```

A.3.9

```
s9 = emu.query("second", "agr*", "[Target = T ^ Phoneme =
u: | i: | y: ]")
```

A.3.10

```
s10 = emu.query("second", "agr*", "Start(Word,
Phoneme)=1")
# OR
s10 = emu.query("second", "agr*", "Phoneme !=g4d6j7 &
Start (Word, Phoneme) = 1")
```

A.3.11

```
s11 = emu.query("second", "agr*", "[Phonetic = H ^
Num(Word, Phoneme) >= 2]")
```

A.3.12

```
s12 = emu.query("second", "agr*", "[Phonetic = H ^ Phoneme
=d & Start(Word, Phoneme)=1]")
```

A.4.2

```
emu.requery(s6, "Phoneme", "Phoneme", seq=-1)
```

A.4.3

```
emu.requery(s9, "Target", "Type", j = T)
```

A.4.4

```
emu.requery(s12, "Phonetic", "Phonetic", seq=1, j=T)
```

A.4.5

```
emu.requery(s2, "Word", "Phonetic")
```

B.1 There are four separate paths as follows:

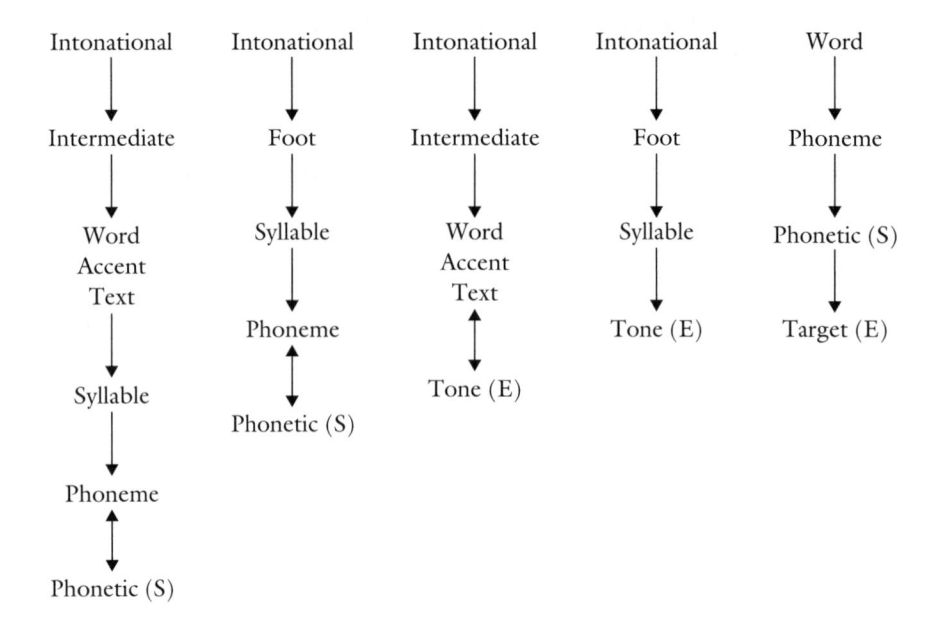

```
Intonational    Intonational    Intonational    Intonational    Word
    ↓               ↓               ↓               ↓             ↓
Intermediate     Foot          Intermediate       Foot         Phoneme
    ↓               ↓               ↓               ↓             ↓
  Word          Syllable          Word          Syllable    Phonetic (S)
  Accent           ↓              Accent           ↓             ↓
  Text          Phoneme           Text          Tone (E)     Target (E)
    ↓              ↑                ↑
 Syllable      Phonetic (S)      Tone (E)
    ↓
 Phoneme
    ↑
 Phonetic (S)
```

The ambiguity in the times inherited by the **Syllable** tier comes about because **Syllable** is, on the one hand, a (grand)parent of **Phonetic** but also, on the other hand, a parent of **Tone**. So do **Syllable** and all the tiers above it inherit segment times from **Phonetic** or event times from **Tone**? In Emu, this ambiguity is resolved by stating one of the child–parent relationships before the other in the template file. So because the child–parent relationship

Phoneme Syllable

is stated before

Tone Syllable

in the **Levels** pane of the template file, then **Syllable** inherits its times from **Phoneme** (and therefore from **Phonetic**). If the **Tone-Syllable** relationship had preceded the others, then **Syllable** would have inherited event times from **Tone**.

The resolution of this ambiguity is (indirectly) expressed in Figure 4.21 by drawing the **Syllable-Phoneme-Phonetic** tiers as the vertical path and having **Syllable-Tone** as a branching path from this main path (so whenever there is an ambiguity in time inheritance, then times are inherited along the vertical path).

B.2.1

   Text = his

B.2.2

   Phoneme = p | t | k

B.2.3

   `[Text = his -> # Text!=x]`

B.2.4

   `[Phoneme = ei -> Phoneme = k]`

B.2.5

   `Text!=x & Word = C`

B.2.6

   `[Accent = W -> # Text!=x & Accent = S]`

B.2.7

   `[Text = the -> Text!=x]`

B.2.8

   `[Phoneme = ei ^ Syllable = S]`

B.2.9

   `[Syllable = W ^ Phoneme = ei]`

B.2.10

   `Phoneme = m | n & Start(Text, Phoneme)=1`
   `# OR`
   `Phoneme = m | n & Start(Word, Phoneme)=1`

B.2.11

   `[Syllable = W ^ End(Intonational, Text)=1]`

B.2.12

   `[Text !=x & Num(Text, Syllable)=3]`
   `# OR`
   `Num(Text, Syllable)=3`

B.2.13

   `[Phoneme = w ^ Num(Text, Syllable)=1]`

B.2.14

   `[[Syllable!=x & End(Text, Syllable)=1 ^ Num(Text,`
   `Syllable)=3 ] ^ Word=C]`

B.2.15

```
[Syllable !=x & Start(Foot, Syllable)=1]
```

B.2.16

```
[[Tone = L+H* ^ Start(Foot, Syllable)=1 ] ^ Num(Foot,
Syllable) > 2]
```

C.1 Tier **i** needs to be declared an event tier in the **Labfiles** pane of the template file.

C.2 Because Tier **i** no longer inherits its times hierarchically from the **Word** tier.

C.3

```
ptone = emu.query("gt", "schoen", "i !=x")
emu.requery(ptone, "i", "Word")
```

D.1 This is a three-dimensional structure with **Foot** on a separate plane from **Word-Syll** and **Mora** on a separate plane from **Syll-Phon** as shown in the left panel of Figure 4.26. The translation into the path structure is shown on the right in which **Word** inherits its times from **Phon** via **Syll** (as a result of which the duration of ω extends over all segments [kita] that it dominates).

D.2 The parent–child relationships between the tiers need to be coded in the Emu template file as follows:

Level	Parent	
Word		
Syll	Word	
Phon	Syll	many-to-many
Foot	Word	

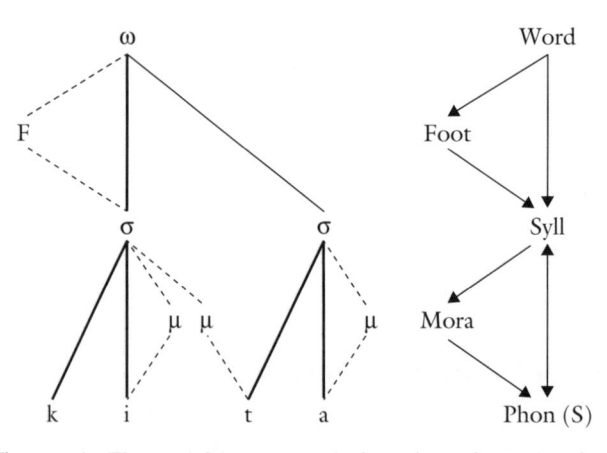

Figure 4.26 The tree in Figure 4.24 as an equivalent three-dimensional annotation structure (left) and the derivation from this of the corresponding Emu path structure (right). The path structure gives expression to the fact that the tier relationships **Word-Foot-Syll-Phon**, **Word-Syll-Phon** and **Word-Syll-Mora-Phon** are in three separate planes.

```
Syll    Foot
Mora    Syll
Phon    Mora
```

The **Syll-Phon** parent–child relationship needs to be many-to-many because /t/ at tier **Phon** is ambisyllabic. All other tier relationships are one-to-many. The **Word-Syll** relationship needs to be positioned before **Word-Foot** in the template file so that **Word** inherits its times along the **Word-Syll-Phon** path (see the note in the answer to question B.1 for further details). The tiers will be arranged in appropriate order if you select the tiers from the main path (i.e., **Word**, **Syll**, **Phon**) in the **View** pane of the template file. Alternatively, verify in text mode (see Figure 4.17 on how to do this) that the following has been included:

```
set HierarchyViewLevels Word Foot Syll Mora Phon
```

D.3 When you annotate the utterance in the different planes, then choose from **Display** → **Hierarchy Levels** to display the tiers in the separate planes as in Figure 4.26. If all fails, then the completed annotation is accessible from the template file **moraanswer.tpl**.

D.4 (You will need to choose **"moraanswer"** as the first argument to **emu.query()** if you did not complete D.1–3 above.)

```
pword = emu.query("mora", "*", "Word!=x")
foot = emu.query("mora", "*", "Foot!=x")
syll = emu.query("mora", "*", "Syll!=x")
m = emu.query("mora", "*", "Mora!=x")
phon = emu.query("mora", "*", "Phon!=x")
```

D.5.1

```
emu.requery(pword, "Word", "Phon")
k->i->t->a 634.952 1165.162 kitta
```

D.5.2

```
emu.requery(foot, "Foot", "Phon")
k->i->t 634.952 1019.549 kitta
```

D.5.3

```
emu.requery(foot, "Foot", "Mora")
m->m 763.892 1019.549 kitta
```

D.5.4

```
emu.requery(syll[2,], "Syll", "Mora")
m 1019.549 1165.162 kitta
# OR
emu.requery(m[3,], "Mora", "Syll")
s 831.696 1165.162 kitta
```

D.5.5

```
emu.requery(phon, "Phon", "Mora", j=T)
"no-segment"    "m"          "m"     "m"
```

D.5.6

```
emu.requery(phon[3,], "Phon", "Syll", j=T)
"s->s"
```

Notes

[1] A tier **T** is a parent of tier **U** if it is immediately above it in the annotation structure: so **Utt** is a parent of **I** which is a parent of **i** which is a parent of **Word** which is a parent of **Tone**.

[2] If for any reason you are not able to reproduce the final display shown in Figure 4.7, then copy **dort.tonesanswer dort.wordsanswer** and **dort.hlbanswer** in **path/gt/labels**, where path is the name of the directory to which you downloaded the **gt** database, and rename the files to **dort.tones**, **dort.words**, and **dort.hlb** respectively, overwriting any existing files if need be.

5
An Introduction to Speech Data Analysis in R: A Study of an EMA Database

In the third chapter, a relationship was established in R using some of the principal functions of the Emu-R library between segment lists, trackdata objects, and their values extracted at the temporal midpoint in the formant analysis of vowels. The task in this chapter is to deepen the understanding of the relationship between these objects, but in this case using a small database of some movement data obtained with the electromagnetic midsagittal articulograph manufactured by Carstens Medizinelektronik. These data were collected by Lasse Bombien and Phil Hoole of the IPS, Munich (Hoole et al., in press) and their aim was to explore the differences in synchronization of the /k/ with the following /l/ or /n/ in German /kl/ (in e.g., *Claudia*) and /kn/ (e.g., *Kneipe*) word-onset clusters. More specifically, one of the hypotheses that Bombien and Hoole wanted to test was whether the interval between the tongue-dorsum closure for the /k/ and the tongue-tip closure for the following alveolar was greater in /kn/ than in /kl/. A fragment of 20 utterances, 10 containing /kn/ and 10 containing /kl/ clusters, of their much larger database was made available by them for illustrating some techniques in speech analysis using R in this chapter.

After a brief overview of the articulatory technique and some details of how the data were collected (5.1), the annotations of movement signals from the tongue tip and tongue dorsum will be discussed in relation to segment lists and trackdata objects that can be derived from them (5.2). The focus of section 5.3 is an acoustic analysis of voice-onset time in these clusters which will be used to introduce some simple forms of analysis in R using segment duration. In section 5.4, some techniques for making ensemble plots are introduced to shed some light on intergestural co-ordination, i.e., on the coordination between the tongue-body and following tongue-tip raising. In section 5.5, the main aim is to explore some *intra*gestural parameters and in particular the differences between /kn/ and /kl/ in the characteristics of the tongue-dorsum raising gesture in forming the /k/ closure. This section will also include a brief overview of how these temporal and articulatory landmarks are related to some of the main parameters that are presumed to determine the shape of movement trajectories in time in the model of articulatory phonology (Browman & Goldstein 1990a, 1990b, 1990c) and task-dynamic modeling (Saltzman & Munhall 1989).

5.1 EMA Recordings and the `ema5` Database

In electromagnetic articulometry (EMA), sensors are attached with a dental cement or dental adhesive to the midline of the articulators, and most commonly to the jaw, lips, and various points on the tongue (Figure 5.1).

As discussed in further detail in Hoole and Nguyen (1999), when an alternating magnetic field is generated by a transmitter coil, it induces a signal in the receiver coil contained in the sensor that is approximately inversely proportional to the cube of the distance between the transmitter and the receiver, and it is this which allows the position of the sensor to be specified. In the so-called 5D system that has been developed at the IPS Munich (Hoole et al. 2003; Hoole & Zierdt 2006; Zierdt 2007) and which was used for the collection of the present data, the position of the sensor is obtained in a three-dimensional Cartesian space that can be related to the sensor's position in the sagittal, coronal, and transverse planes (Figure 5.3). Typically, the data are rotated relative to the occlusal plane, which is the line extending from the upper incisors to the second molars at the back and which is parallel to the transverse plane (Figure 5.3). (The rotation is done so that the positions of the articulators can be compared across different speakers relative to the same reference points.) The occlusal plane can be determined by having the subject bite onto a bite-plate with sensors attached to it. In recording the data, the subject sits inside a so-called EMA cube (Figure 5.2) so there is no need for a helmet as in earlier EMA systems. In the system that was used here, corrections for head movements were carried out in a set of processing steps sample by sample.

Up–down differences in the vertical dimension of the sagittal plane correspond most closely to stricture differences in consonants and to phonetic height differences in vowels. So, once the rotation has been done, then there should be noticeable differences in the position of the jaw sensor in moving from a bilabial closure to the open vowel in [pa]. Front–back differences in the horizontal dimension of the sagittal plane are related to movement of the articulators in the direction from the lips to the uvula. In this plane, the tongue-mid and tongue-back sensors should register a clear difference in producing a transition from a phonetically front to a back articulation in the production of [ju]. Finally, the lateral differences (horizontal dimension of the coronal plane) should register movements between right and left, as in moving the jaw or the tongue from side to side.[1]

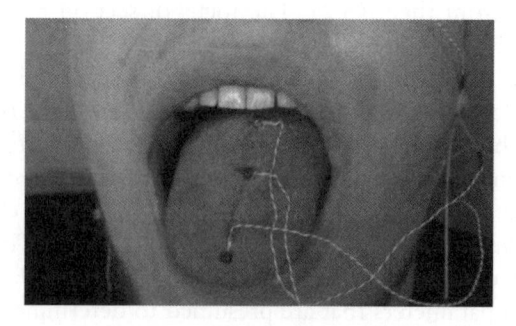

Figure 5.1 The tongue-tip (**TT**), tongue-mid (**TM**), and tongue-back (**TB**) sensors glued with dental cement to the surface of the tongue.

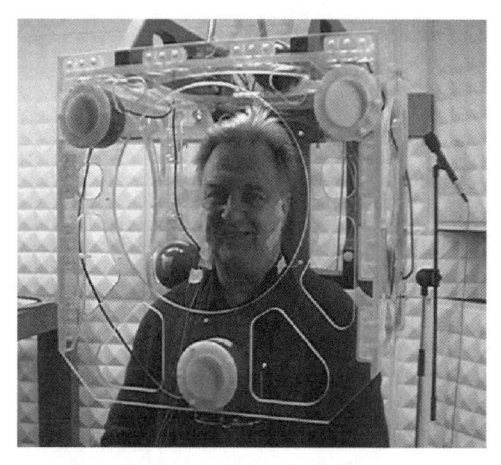

Figure 5.2 The Carstens Medizinelektronik EMA "cube" used for recording speech movement data.

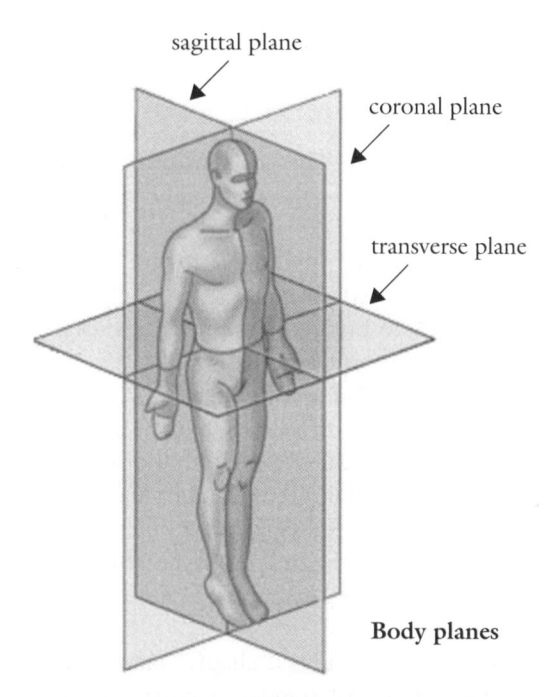

Figure 5.3 The sagittal, coronal, and transverse body planes. From http://commons.wikimedia.org/wiki/File:Human_anatomy_planes.svg.

For the data in the downloadable EMA database, movement data were recorded from sensors fixed to three points on the tongue (Figure 5.1), as well as to the lower lip, upper lip, and jaw (Figure 5.4). The sensors were all fixed in the mid-sagittal plane. The tongue-tip (TT) sensor was attached approximately 1 cm behind the tip of the tongue; the tongue-back or tongue-body (TB) sensor was positioned as far back as the subject could tolerate; the tongue-mid (TM) sensor was equidistant between

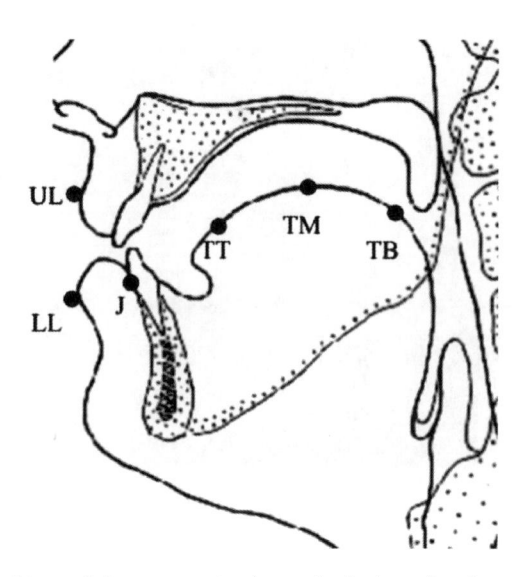

Figure 5.4 The position of the sensors in the sagittal plane for the upper lip (**UL**), lower lip (**LL**), jaw (**J**), tongue tip (**TT**), tongue mid (**TM**), and tongue back (**TB**). The reference sensors are not shown.

the two with the tongue protruded. The jaw sensor was positioned in front of the lower incisors on the tissue just below the teeth. The upper-lip (UL) and lower-lip (LL) sensors were positioned on the skin just above and below the lips respectively (so as not to damage the lips' skin). In addition, there were four reference sensors which were used to correct for head movements: one each on the left and right mastoid process, one high up on the bridge of the nose, and one in front of the upper incisors on the tissue just above the teeth.

The articulatory data were sampled at a frequency of 200 Hz in a raw file format. All signals were band-pass filtered with an FIR filter (Kaiser-window design, 60 dB at 40–50 Hz for the tongue tip, at 20–30 Hz for all other articulators, at 5–15 Hz for the reference sensors). Horizontal, vertical, and tangential velocities were calculated and smoothed with a further Kaiser-window filter (60 dB at 20–30Hz). All these steps were done in Matlab and the output was stored in self-documented Matlab files. The data was then converted using a script written by Lasse Bombien into an Emu-compatible SSFF format.[2]

The database that will be analyzed in this chapter, **ema5**, consists of 20 utterances produced by a single female speaker of Standard German. The 20 utterances are made up of five repetitions of four sentences that contain a target word in a prosodically phrase-medial, accented position containing either a /kl/ or a /kn/ cluster in onset position. The four words for which, then, there are five repetitions each (thus 10 /kl/ and 10 /kn/ clusters in total) are *Klausur* (*examination*), *Claudia* (a person's name), *Kneipe* (*bar*), and *Kneipier* (*bar attendant*). *Claudia* and *Kneipe* have primary lexical stress on the first syllable, the other two on the final syllable. When any utterance of this database is opened, the changing positions of the moving jaw, lips, and three points of the tongue are shown in relation to each other in the sagittal and transverse planes (Figure 5.5). In addition, the template file has been set up so

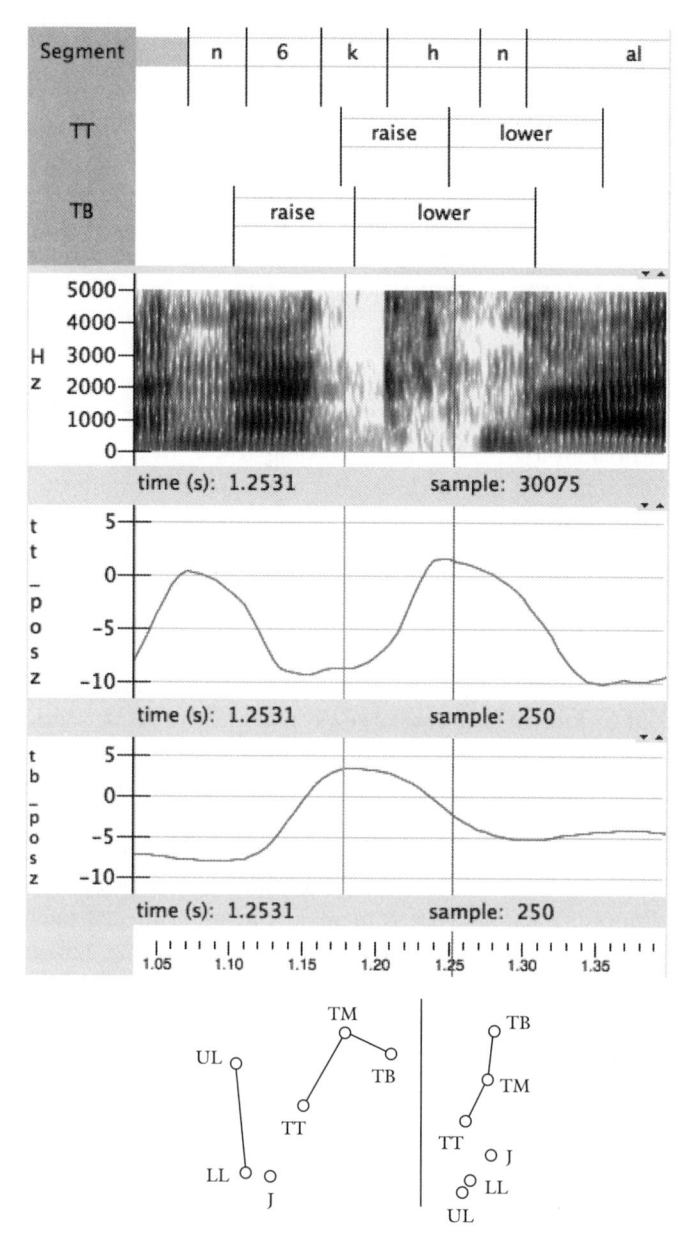

Figure 5.5 A section from the first utterance of the downloadable **ema5** database showing acoustic phonetic (**Segment**), tongue-tip (**TT**), and tongue-body (**TB**) labeling tiers, a spectrogram, vertical tongue-tip movement, and vertical tongue-body movement. Also shown are mid-sagittal (bottom left) and transverse (bottom right) views of the positions of the upper lip (**UL**), lower lip (**LL**), jaw (**J**), tongue tip (**TT**), tongue mid (**TM**), and tongue body (**TB**) at the time of the left vertical cursor (offset time of tongue-body raising, i.e., at the time of the highest point of the tongue body for /k/).

that the two movement signals, the vertical movement of the tongue tip and tongue body, are displayed. These are the two signals that will be analyzed in this chapter.

As is evident in opening any utterance of **ema5**, the database has been annotated at three tiers: **Segment**, **TT**, and **TB**. The **Segment** tier contains acoustic phonetic annotations that were derived semi-automatically with the MAUS automatic segmentation system (Schiel 2004) using a combination of orthographic text and hidden Markov models trained on phonetic-sized units. The segmentations have been manually changed to sub-segment the /k/ of the target words into an acoustic closure and following release/frication stage.

In producing a /kl/ or /kn/ cluster, the tongue body attains a maximum height in forming the velar closure for the /k/. The time at which this maximum occurs is the right boundary of **raise** at the **TB** tier (or, equivalently, at the left boundary of the following **lower** annotation). The left boundary of **raise** marks the greatest point of tongue-dorsum lowering in the preceding vowel. In producing the following /l/ or /n/, the tongue tip reaches a maximum height in forming the alveolar constriction. The time of this maximum point of tongue-tip raising is the right boundary of **raise** at the **TT** tier (left boundary of **lower**). The left boundary of **raise** marks the greatest point of tongue-tip lowering in the preceding vowel (Figure 5.5).

The annotations for this database are organized into a double path annotation structure in which **Segment** is a parent of both the **TT** and the **TB** tiers, and in which **TT** is a parent of **TB** (Figure 5.6). The annotations **raise** and **lower** at the **TT** tier are linked to **raise** and **lower** respectively at the **TB** tier and both of these annotations are linked to the word-initial /k/ of the target words at the **Segment** tier. The purpose of structuring the annotations in this way is to facilitate queries from the database. Thus, it is possible with this type of annotation structure to make a segment list of word-initial acoustic /k/ closures and then to obtain a segment list of the associated sequence of **raise lower** annotations at either the **TT** or the **TB** tier. In addition, if a segment list is made of **raise** at the **TT** tier, then this can be re-queried not only to obtain a segment list of the following **lower** annotations but also, since **TT** and **TB** are linked, of the **raise** annotation at the **TB** tier. Some examples of segment lists that will be used in this chapter are given in the next section.

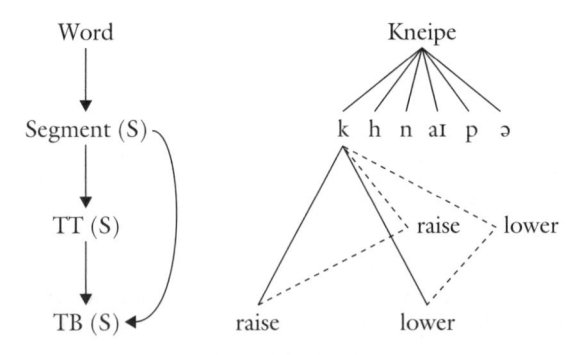

Figure 5.6 The annotation structure for the **ema5** database in which word-initial /k/ at the **Segment** tier is linked to a sequence of **raise lower** annotations at both the **TT** and **TB** tiers, and in which **raise** at the **TT** tier is linked to **raise** at the **TB** tier, and **lower** at the **TT** tier to **lower** at the **TB** tier.

5.2 Handling Segment Lists and Vectors in Emu-R

In almost all cases, whether analyzing formants in Chapter 3 or movement data in this chapter, or indeed electropalatographic and spectral data in the later parts of this book, the association between signals and annotations that is needed for addressing hypotheses almost always follows the structure which was first presented in Figure 3.8 of Chapter 3, and which is further elaborated in Figure 5.7. The first step involves making one or more segment lists using the **emu.query()** or **emu.requery()** functions. Then **emu.track()** is used to retrieve trackdata, i.e., signal data from the database with respect to the start and end times of any segment list that has been made. The purpose of **start()**, **end()**, and **dur()** is to obtain basic durational properties from either the segment list or the trackdata object. The functions **label()** and **utt()** are used to retrieve from segment lists the annotations and utterance identifiers of the segments respectively. Finally, **dcut()** is used to slice out values from a trackdata object either over an interval, or at a specific point in time (as was done in analyzing vowel formants at the temporal midpoint in Chapter 3). These functions are at the core of all subsequent operations for analyzing and plotting data in R.

In this section, the task will be to obtain most of the necessary segment lists that will be needed for the comparison of /kn/ and /kl/ clusters and then to discuss some of the ways that segment lists and vectors can be manipulated in R: these types of manipulations will be needed for the acoustic VOT analysis in the next section and are fundamental to most preliminary analyses of speech data in Emu-R.

Using the techniques discussed in Chapter 4, the following segment lists can be obtained from the **ema5** database:

```
# Segment list of word-initial /k/
k.s = emu.query("ema5", "*", "Segment=k & Start(Word,
Segment)=1")
```

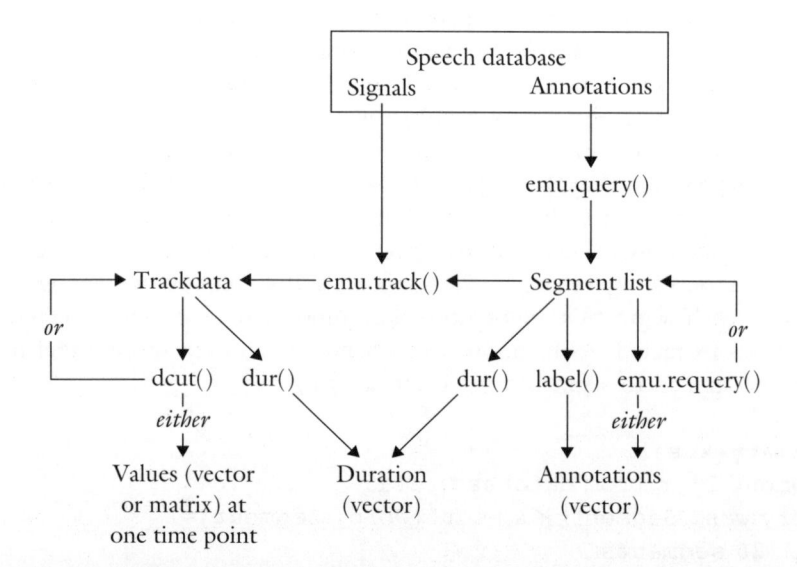

Figure 5.7 Relationship between various key functions in Emu-R and their output.

```
# Segment list of the following h (containing acoustic VOT information)
h.s = emu.requery(k.s, "Segment", "Segment", seq=1)

# Segment list of the sequence of raise lower at the TT tier
tip.s = emu.requery(k.s, "Segment", "TT")

# Segment list of the sequence raise lower at the TB tier
body.s = emu.requery(k.s, "Segment", "TB")
```

In addition, two character vectors of annotations will be obtained using the **label()** function, the first containing either **n** or **l** (in order to identify the cluster as /kn/ or /kl/) and the second of the word annotations. Finally, a numeric vector is obtained with the **dur()** function of the duration of the **h** segments, i.e., of voice-onset time.

```
# Vector consisting of n or l (the segments are two positions to the right of
  word-initial /k/)
son.lab = emu.requery(k.s, "Segment", "Segment", seq=2, j=T)

# Word annotations
word.lab = emu.requery(k.s, "Segment", "Word", j=T)

# Acoustic VOT
h.dur = dur(h.s)
```

It is useful at this point to note that segment lists on the one hand and vectors on the other are of different types and need to be handled slightly differently. As far as R is concerned, a segment list is a type of object known as a **data frame**. As far as the analysis of speech data in this book is concerned, the more important point is that segment lists **share many properties with matrices**: that is, many operations that can be applied to matrices can also be applied to segment lists. For example, **nrow()** and **ncol()** can be used to find out how many rows and columns there are in a matrix. Thus, the matrix **bridge** in the Emu-R library has 13 rows and 3 columns and this information can be established with **nrow(bridge)**, **ncol(bridge)**, and **dim(bridge)**: the last of these returns the number of both rows and columns (and is therefore **13 3** in this case). The same functions can be applied to segment lists. Thus **dim(h.s)** returns **20 4** because, as will be evident by entering **h.s** on its own, there are 20 segments and 4 columns containing information about each segment's annotation, start time, end time, and utterance from which it was extracted. As mentioned in Chapter 3, an even more useful function that can be applied to segment lists is **summary()**:

```
summary(k.s)
segment list from database: ema5
query was: Segment=k & Start(Word, Segment)=1
with 20 segments
```

```
Segment distribution:

k
20
```

which, apart from listing the number segments and their annotations (all **k** in this case), also gives information about the database from which they were derived and the query that was used to derive them.

In contrast to segment lists and matrices, vectors have no dimensions, i.e., no rows or columns, and this is why **dim(word.lab)**, **nrow(son.lab)**, and **ncol(word.lab)** all return **NULL**. Moreover, these three vectors can be divided into two types: **character vectors** like **word.lab** and **son.lab** whose elements all contain characters in " " quotes or **numeric vectors** to which various arithmetic, statistical, and mathematical operations can be applied and whose elements are not in quotes. You can use various functions beginning with **is.** as well as the **class()** function to test the type/class of an object thus:

```
# Is k.s a segment list?
is.seglist(k.s)
TRUE

# What type of object is h.s?
class(h.s)
# Both a segment list and a data frame
"emusegs" "data.frame"

# Is son.lab a vector?
is.vector(son.lab)
TRUE

# Is h.dur of mode character?
is.character(h.dur)
FALSE

# Is h.dur of mode numeric?
is.numeric(h.dur)
TRUE

# Is word.lab both of mode character and a vector (i.e., a character vector)?
is.character(word.lab) & is.vector(word.lab)
TRUE
```

A very important idea in all of the analyses of speech data with Emu-R in this book is that objects used for solving the same problem usually need to be **parallel to each other**. This means that, if you extract n segments from a database, then the nth row of a segment list, of a matrix, and, as will be shown later, of a trackdata object, and the *n*th element of a vector **all provide information about the same segment**. Data for the *n*th segment can be extracted or indexed using integers inside a square bracket notation, thus:

```
# The fifteenth segment in the segment list
h.s[15,]
```

```
# The corresponding duration of this segment (h.dur is a vector)
h.dur[15]
```

```
# The corresponding word label (word.lab is a vector)
word.lab[15]
```

The reason for the comma in the case of a matrix or segment list is because **the entries before and after the comma index rows and columns respectively** (so since a vector has no rows or columns, there is no comma). More specifically, **h.s[15,]** means all columns of row 15 which is why **h.s[15,]** returns four elements (because **h.s** has four columns). If you just wanted to pick out row 15 of column 2, then this would be **h.s[15,2]** (and only one element is returned). Analogously, entering nothing *before* the comma indexes all rows and so **h.s[,2]** returns 20 elements, i.e., all elements of column 2 (i.e., the segments' start, or left boundary, times). Since **1:10** in R returns the integers 1 through 10, then the command to obtain the first 10 rows of **h.s** is given by **h.s[1:10,]** while the same notation is used for the first 10 elements of a vector, but again without the comma, thus **word.lab[1:10]**, **h.dur[1:10]**, etc. If you want to pull out non-sequential segment numbers, then first make a vector of these numbers with **c()**, the concatenate function, thus:

```
# Make a numeric vector of three elements
n = c(2, 5, 12)
```

```
# Rows 2, 5, 12 of h.s
h.s[n,]
```

```
# Or in a single line
h.s[c(2,5,12),]
```

```
# The corresponding word labels
word.lab[n]
```

A negative number inside the square bracket notation denotes **all except**. So **h.s[-2,]** means all rows of **h.s** except the second row, **h.s[-(1:10),]** all rows except the first 10, **word.lab[-c(2, 5, 12)]** all elements of **word.lab** except the second, fifth, and twelfth and so on.

When analyses of speech fail in R (i.e., an error message is returned), it is often because the various objects that are used for solving a particular problem may have become out of step with each other so that the condition of being parallel is no longer met. There is no test for whether objects are parallel to each other as far as I know but, when an analysis fails, it is a good idea to check that all the segment lists have the same number of rows and that there is the same number of elements in the vectors that have been derived from them. This can be done with the logical operator == which amounts to asking a question about equality, thus:

```
# Is the number of rows in k.s the same as the number of rows in h.s?
nrow(k.s) == nrow(h.s)
TRUE

# Is the number of rows in k.s the same as the number of elements in
word.lab?
nrow(k.s) == length(word.lab)
TRUE

# Do word.lab and h.dur have the same number of elements?
length(word.lab) == length(h.dur)
TRUE
```

5.3 An Analysis of Voice-Onset Time

There are very many in-built functions in R for applying descriptive statistics whose function names usually speak for themselves, e.g., **mean()**, **median()**, **max()**, **min()**, **range()** and they can be applied to numeric vectors. It is therefore a straightforward matter to apply any of these functions to durations extracted from a segment list. Thus **mean(h.dur)** gives the mean VOT duration calculated across all segments, **max(dur(k.s))** gives the maximum /k/-closure duration, **range(dur(k.s))** the range (minimum and maximum value) of closure durations, etc. However, a way has to be found of calculating these kinds of quantities separately for the /kn/ and /kl/ categories. It might also be interesting to do the same for the four different word types. You can remind yourself which these are by applying the **table()** function to the character vector containing them:

```
table(word.lab)
 Claudia  Klausur   Kneipe  Kneipier
       5        5        5         5
```

The same function can be used for cross-tabulations when more than one argument is included, for example:

```
table(son.lab,word.lab)
son.lab  Claudia  Klausur   Kneipe  Kneipier
      1        5        5        0         0
      n        0        0        5         5
```

One way to get the mean VOT separately for /kn/ or /kl/, or separately for the four different kinds of words, is with a for-loop. A better way is with another type of object in R called **logical vectors**. A logical vector consists entirely of True (**T**) and False (**F**) elements that are returned in response to applying a **comparison operator**. One of these, **==**, has already been encountered above in asking whether the number of rows in two segment lists were the same. The other comparison operators are as follows:

!=	Is not equal to
<	Is less than
>	Is greater than
<=	Is less than or equal to
>=	Is greater than or equal to

As already described, making use of a comparison operator implies asking a question. So typing **h.dur > 45** is to ask: which segment has a duration greater than 45 ms? The output is a logical vector, with one True or False per segment thus:

```
h.dur > 45
TRUE FALSE FALSE TRUE FALSE TRUE TRUE FALSE TRUE TRUE FALSE
TRUE TRUE TRUE TRUE FALSE TRUE TRUE TRUE TRUE
```

The first two elements that are returned are **True** and **False** because the first two segments do and do not have durations greater than 45 ms respectively, as shown by the following:

```
h.dur[1:2]
63.973 43.907
```

Since the objects for comparing /kn/ with /kl/ are all parallel to each other in the sense discussed earlier, then the position number of the **T** and **F** elements can be used to find the corresponding segments or other labels for which VOT is, or is not, greater than 45 ms. For example, since there is, among others, a **T** element in the first, fourth, sixth, and seventh positions, then these words must have segments with VOTs greater than 45 ms:

```
word.lab[c(1, 4, 6, 7)]
"Kneipe" "Kneipier" "Kneipe" "Kneipier"
```

and it is equally easy to find in which utterances these words occur by indexing the corresponding segment lists (and inspecting the fourth column):

```
k.s[c(1, 4, 6, 7),]
segment list from database: ema5
query was: Segment=k & Start(Word, Segment)=1
```

```
  labels    start        end              utts
1   k     1161.944    1206.447    dfgspp_mo1_prosody_0020
4   k     1145.785    1188.875    dfgspp_mo1_prosody_0063
6   k     1320.000    1354.054    dfgspp_mo1_prosody_0140
7   k     1306.292    1337.196    dfgspp_mo1_prosody_0160
```

The corresponding rows or elements can be more easily retrieved by putting the logical vector within square brackets. Thus:

```
# Logical vector when h.dur is greater than 45 ms
temp = h.dur > 45

# The corresponding durations
h.dur[temp]

# The corresponding word-labels
word.lab[temp]
"Kneipe" "Kneipier" "Kneipe" "Kneipier" "Claudia" Kneipier"
"Kneipe" "Kneipier" "Claudia" "Kneipe" "Claudia" "Klausur"
"Kneipe" "Kneipier"
```

An important point to remember is **that when you combine a logical vector with a matrix or segment list, then it has to be followed by a comma**, if you want to pull out the corresponding rows. Thus **h.s[temp,]** identifies the rows in **h.s** for which VOT is greater than 45 ms. A logical vector could be used in a similar way to extract columns. For example, **h.s[,c(F, T, F, T)]** extracts columns 2 and 4 (the start time and utterance identifier). Also, changing **temp** to **!temp** gets at the rows or elements for which the duration is *not* greater than (less than or equal to) 45 ms, i.e., those rows/elements for which the logical vector is **False**, e.g., **h.dur[!temp]**, **word.lab[!temp]**, **k.s[!temp,]**. Finally, three useful functions when applied to logical vectors are **sum()**, **any()**, and **all()**, which find out respectively how many, whether any, or whether all elements of a logical vector are **True**. For example:

```
lvec = c(T, F, F)
sum(lvec)
1

any(lvec)
TRUE

all(lvec)
FALSE
```

The same can be applied to **False** elements by preceding the logical vector with an exclamation mark. Thus **any(!lvec)** returns **True** because there is at least one

F element in **lvec**. With regard to the earlier example, these functions could be used to work out how many segments have VOT greater than 45 ms (**sum(h.dur > 45)**), whether any segments have a duration greater than 45 ms (**any(h.dur > 45)**), and whether all segments have a duration greater than 45 ms (**all(h.dur > 45)**).

There is now easily sufficient computational machinery in place to find out something about the distributional VOT differences between /kn/ and /kl/. The first step might be to make a logical vector to identify which elements correspond to /kn/: this could then be applied to **h.dur** to get the corresponding VOT values. Since there are only two label categories, then the **F** elements of the logical vector could be used to find the VOT values for /kl/, thus:

```
# Logical vector which is True for the n elements in son.lab
temp = son.lab == "n"

# Mean VOT (ms) for /kn/
mean(h.dur[temp])
74.971

# Mean VOT (ms) for /kl/
mean(h.dur[!temp])
44.9015
```

The above analysis shows that the mean VOT is about 30 ms greater in /kn/ than in /kl/. What if you wanted to work out the mean duration of the preceding velar closure? This can be done by applying the logical vector to the durations of the segment list **k.s**. In this case, you have to remember to include the comma because **k.s** is a segment list requiring rows to be identified:

```
# Mean duration (ms) of /k/ closure in /kn/
mean(dur(k.s[temp,]))
38.0994

# Mean duration (ms) of /k/ closure in /kl/
mean(dur(k.s[!temp,]))
53.7411
```

In fact this result is not without interest because it shows that the closure duration of /kn/ is somewhat less than that of /kl/. Thus the difference between /kn/ and /kl/, at least as far as voicing onset is concerned, seems to be one of *timing*.

What if you now wanted to compare the ratio of closure duration to VOT? Consider first the two main ways in which arithmetic operations can be applied to vectors:

```
# Make a vector of three elements
x = c(10, 0, 5)

# Subtract four from each element
x - 4
```

```
# Make another vector of three elements
y = c(8, 2, 11)

# Subtract the two vectors element by element
x - y
```

In this first case, the effect of **x - 4** is to subtract **4** from every element of **x**. In the second case, the subtraction between **x** and **y** is done element by element. These are the two main ways of doing arithmetic in R and in the second case it is important to check that the vectors are of the same length (**length(x) == length(y)**) because, if they are not, a warning message is given and the values of the shorter vector are recycled in a way that is usually not at all helpful for the problem that is to be solved. Logical vectors can be applied in the same two ways. In the earlier example of **h.dur > 45**, each element of **h.dur** was compared with 45. But two vectors can also be compared element by element if they are of the same length. In **x > y** (assuming you have entered **x** and **y** as above), the first element of **x** is compared with the first element of **y** to see if it is greater, then the same is done for the second element, then for the third. The output is therefore **T F F** because **x** is greater than **y** only in its first element.

The ratio of the closure duration to VOT can now be worked out by dividing one vector by the other, thus:

```
h.dur/dur(k.s)
1.4374986  0.9140436  0.6911628...
```

The first value returned is 1.4 because the VOT of the first segment, given by **h.dur[1]** (63.9 ms) is about 1.4 times the size of its preceding closure duration given by **dur(k.s[1,])** (44.5 ms): more generally, what is returned by the above command is **h.dur[n]/dur(k.s[n,])** where **n** is the *n*th segment. You could also work out the proportion of VOT taken up by the total closure duration plus VOT duration. This is:

```
h.dur/(h.dur + dur(k.s))
0.5897434  0.4775459  0.4086909...
```

So, for the second segment, VOT takes up about 48 percent of the duration between the onset of the closure and the onset of periodicity.

In order to compare /kn/ with /kl/ on any of these measures, a logical vector needs to be applied as before. Thus to compare /kn/ with /kl/ on this proportional measure, apply the logical vector either to each object or to the result of the proportional calculation. Here are the two possibilities:

```
# Logical vector to identify /kn/
temp = son.lab== "n"

# Mean proportional VOT duration for /kn/
mean(h.dur[temp]/(h.dur[temp] + dur(k.s[temp,])))
0.6639655
```

```
# Equivalently
mean((h.dur/(h.dur + dur(k.s)))[temp])
0.6639655
```

The second of these is perhaps easier to follow if the proportional calculation on each segment is initially stored in its own vector:

```
prop = h.dur/(h.dur + dur(k.s))

# Proportional VOT for /kn/
mean(prop[temp])
0.6639655

# Proportional VOT for /kl/
mean(prop[!temp])
0.4525008
```

So the proportion of VOT taken up by the interval between the closure onset and onset of periodicity is some 20 percent less for /kl/ compared with /kn/.

What if you wanted to compare the four separate words with each other on any of these measures? Recall that the annotations for these words are stored in **word.lab**:

```
table(word.lab)
Claudia  Klausur  Kneipe  Kneipier
   5        5        5       5
```

One possibility would be to proceed as above and to make a logical vector that was **True** for each of the categories. However, a much simpler way is to use **tapply (x, lab, fun)**, which applies a function (the third argument) to the elements of a vector (the first argument) separately per category (the second argument). Thus the mean VOT separately for /kn/ and /kl/ is also given by:

```
tapply(h.dur, son.lab, mean)
    l         n
44.9015   74.9710
```

The third argument is any function that can be sensibly applied to the numeric vector (first argument). So you could calculate the standard deviation separately for the closure durations of /kn/ and /kl/ as follows:

```
tapply(dur(k.s), son.lab, sd)
    l         n
5.721609  8.557875
```

Thus the mean VOT duration (ms) for each separate word category is:

```
tapply(h.dur, word.lab, mean)
 Claudia  Klausur   Kneipe  Kneipier
 49.5272  40.2758  66.9952  82.9468
```

So the generalization that the mean VOT of /kn/ is greater than that of /kl/ seems to hold across the separate word categories. Similarly, **tapply()** can be used to work out separately per category the mean proportion of the interval between the onset of the closure and the periodic onset of the sonorant taken up by aspiration/frication:

```
prop = h.dur/(h.dur + dur(k.s))
tapply(prop, word.lab, mean)
  Claudia    Klausur     Kneipe   Kneipier
0.4807916  0.4242100  0.6610947  0.6668363
```

The results showing differences between the categories on means need to be followed up with analyses of the distribution of the tokens about each category. One of the most useful displays for this purpose, of which extensive use will be made in the rest of this book, is a boxplot which can be used per category to produce a display of the median, the interquartile range, and the range. The median is the 50 percent quantile, and the pth quantile ($0 \leq p \leq 100$) is in the index position **1+p*(n-1)/100** after the data has been sorted in rank order. For example, here are 11 values randomly sampled between −50 and 50:

```
g = sample(-50:50, 11)
-46  41  23   4  -33  46  -30  18  -19  -38  -32
```

They can be rank-order sorted with the **sort()** function:

```
g.s = sort(g)
g.s
-46  -38  -33  -32  -30  -19   4  18  23  41  46
```

The median is the sixth element from the left in this rank-order sorted data, because 6 is what is returned by **1+50*(11-1)/100**: thus the median of these random numbers is **g.s[6]**, which is −19. The same is returned by **median(g)** or **quantile(g, .5)**. The interquartile range is the difference between the 75 percent and 25 percent quantiles, i.e., **quantile(g, .75) - quantile(g, .25)** or equivalently **IQR(g)**. In the corresponding boxplot, the median appears as the thick horizontal line and the upper (75 percent) and lower (25 percent) quartiles as the upper and lower limits of the rectangle. A boxplot for the present VOT data can be produced with (Figure 5.8):

```
boxplot(h.dur ~ son.lab, ylab = "VOT (ms)")
```

The operation ~ means "given that" and often forms part of a formula that is used in very many statistical tests in R. The boxplot shows fairly conclusively that VOT is greater in /kn/ than in /kl/ clusters.

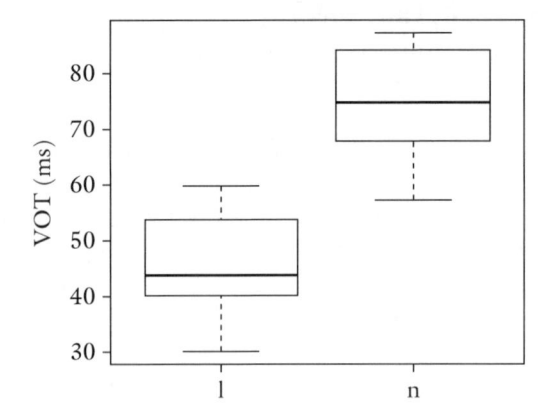

Figure 5.8 Boxplots showing the median (thick horizontal line), interquartile range (extent of the rectangle), and range (the extent of the whiskers) for VOT in /kl/ (left) and /kn/ (right).

5.4 Intergestural Coordination and Ensemble Plots

The task in this section is to produce synchronized plots of tongue-dorsum and tongue-tip movement in order to ascertain whether these are differently coordinated for /kn/ and /kl/. The discussion will begin with some general remarks about trackdata objects (5.4.1), then overlaid plots from these two movement signals will be derived (5.4.2); finally, so-called ensemble plots will be discussed in which the same movement data from several segments are overlaid and averaged separately for the two categories. All the movement data are in millimetres and the values are relative to the origin [0, 0, 0] which is a point on the occlusal plane just in front of the teeth.

5.4.1 Extracting trackdata objects

As shown in the flow diagram in Figure 5.7, signal or trackdata is extracted from a database relative to the start and end times of a segment list using the **emu.track()** function. The first argument to **emu.track()** is the segment list itself and the second argument is any track that has been declared to be available in the template file. You can check which tracks are available, either by inspecting the **Tracks** pane of the template file, or with **trackinfo()** in R using the name of the database as an argument:

```
trackinfo("ema5")
```

```
"samples" "tm_posy" "tm_posz" "ll_posz" "tb_posz" "jw_posy"
"jw_posz" "tt_posz" "ul_posz"
```

The movement data is accessed from any track name containing **posz** for vertical movement (i.e., height changes) or **posy** for anterior–posterior movement (i.e., for front–back changes to mark e.g., the extent of tongue-front/backing between the palatal and uvular regions). The initial **ll**, **tb**, **tm**, **jw**, **tt**, and **ul** are codes for lower lip, tongue body, tongue mid, jaw, tongue tip, and upper lip respectively. Here the concern will be almost exclusively with the analysis of **tt_posz** and **tb_posz** (vertical tongue-tip and tongue-body movement in the coronal plane). Thus, assuming you have created the segment list **tip.s** as set out in 5.2, trackdata of the vertical tongue-tip movement over the durational extent of the **raise lower** annotations at the **TT** tier is obtained as follows:

```
tip.tt = emu.track(tip.s, "tt_posz")
```

tip.tt is a trackdata object as can be verified with **is.trackdata(tip.tt)** or **class(tip.tt)**.

Trackdata objects are **lists** but, because of an implementation using object-oriented programming in Emu-R, they **behave like matrices** and therefore just like segment lists as far as both indexing and the application of logical vectors are concerned. Therefore, the same operations for identifying one or more segment numbers can also be used to identify their corresponding signal data in the trackdata objects. For example, since **tip.s[10,]** denotes the tenth segment, then **tip.tt[10,]** contains the tongue-tip movement data for the tenth segment. Similarly, **tip.s[c(10, 15, 18),]** are segment numbers 10, 15, 18 in the segment list and **tip.tt[c(10, 15, 18),]** access the tongue-tip movement data for the same segments. Logical vectors can be used in the same way. So, in the previous section, the /kn/ segments in the segment list could be identified with a logical vector:

```
# Logical vector: True for /kn/, False for /kl/
temp = son.lab == "n"

# /k/ closures in /kn/
k.s[temp,]

# A segment list of raise lower associated with /kn/
tip.s[temp,]
```

The corresponding tongue-tip movement data for the above segments is analogously given by **tip.tt[temp,]**.

As already foreshadowed in Chapter 3, **emu.track()** retrieves signal data within the start and end time of the segment list. For this reason, the duration measured from a trackdata object is always fractionally less than the durations obtained from the corresponding segment list. In both cases, the duration can be obtained with **dur()** (Figure 5.7). Here this function is used to confirm that the trackdata durations are less than the segment durations for all 20 segments. More specifically, the following command asks: are there any segments for which the trackdata duration is greater than or equal to the duration from a segment list?

```
any(dur(tip.tt) >= dur(tip.s))
FALSE
```

5.4.2 Movement plots from single segments

Each segment in a trackdata object is made up of a certain number of frames of data or **speech frames**[3] that occur at equal intervals of time depending on the rate at which they were sampled or the **frame rate**. For example, if formants are calculated at intervals of 5 ms and if a segment is 64 ms in duration, then that segment should have at least 12 speech frames of formant frequencies between its start time and end time at intervals of 5 ms. The function **frames()** and **tracktimes()** applied to a trackdata object retrieve the speech frames and the times at which they occur, as already shown in Chapter 3. The generic **plot()** function when applied to any single segment of trackdata plots the frames as a function of time. For example, the speech frames of the fifth segment, corresponding to **tip.s[5,]**, are given by:

```
frames(tip.tt[5,])
       T1
1405   -12.673020
1410   -12.631612
1415   -12.499837
1420   -12.224785...
```

and the times at which these occur by:

```
tracktimes(tip.tt[5,])
1405  1410  1415  1420  1425  1430...
```

These data could be inspected in Emu by looking at the corresponding segment in the segment list:

```
tip.s[5,]
5 raise->lower 1404.208 1623.48 dfgspp_mo1_prosody_0132
```

i.e., the speech frames occur between times 1,404 ms and 1,623 ms in the utterance **dfgspp_mo1_prosody_0132**.

The data returned by **frames()** looks as if it has two columns, but there is only one, as **ncol(frames(tip.tt[5,]))** shows: the numbers on the left are **row names** and they are the track times returned by **tracktimes(tip.tt[5,])**. When **tracktimes()** is applied to **tip.tt** in this way, it can be seen that the frames occur at 5 ms intervals and so the frame rate is $1{,}000 / 5 = 200$ Hz.

The commands **start(tip.tt[5,])** and **end(tip.tt[5,])** return the times of the first and last speech frame of the fifth segment. A plot of the speech frames as a function of the times at which they occur is given by **plot(tip.tt[5,])**. You can additionally set a number of plotting parameters (see **help(par)** for which ones). In this example, both lines and points are plotted (**type="b"**) and labels are supplied for the axes:

```
plot(tip.tt[5,], type="b", ylab ="Tongue tip vertical
position (mm)", xlab="Time (ms)")
```

In order to investigate tongue-body and tongue-tip synchronization, the movement data from both tracks need to be plotted in a single display. One way to do this is to retrieve the tongue-body data for the same segment list and then to use the **cbind()** (column-bind) function to make a new trackdata object consisting of the tongue-tip and tongue-body movement data. This is done in the following two instructions, firstly by obtaining the tongue-body data from the same segment list from which the tongue-tip data has already been obtained, and then, in the second instruction, column-binding the two trackdata objects.[4] The third instruction plots these data:

```
tip.tb = emu.track(tip.s, "tb_posz")
both = cbind(tip.tt, tip.tb)
plot(both[5,], type="l")
```

If you are familiar with R, then you will recognize **cbind()** as the function for concatenating vectors by column, thus:

```
a = c(0, 4, 5)
b = c(10, 20, 2)
w = cbind(a, b)
w
  a  b
  0 10
  4 20
  5  2
```

As already mentioned, trackdata objects are not matrices but lists. Nevertheless, many of the functions for matrices can be applied to them. Thus the functions intended for matrices, **dim(w)**, **nrow(w)**, **ncol(w)**, also work on trackdata objects. For example, **dim(both)** returns **20 2** and has the meaning not that there are 20 rows and 2 columns (as it would if applied to a matrix) but, firstly, that there are 20 segments' worth of data (also given by **nrow(both)**) and, secondly, that there are two tracks (also given by **ncol(both)**). Moreover, a new trackdata object consisting of just the second track (tongue-body data) could now be made with **new = both[,2]**; or a new trackdata object of the first 10 segments and first track only with **both[1:10,1]**, etc.

In the previous example, the movement data from both tongue tracks extended over the interval **raise lower** annotated at the tongue-*tip* (**TT**) tier. If you wanted to superimpose the tongue-body movement extracted over a corresponding interval from the tongue-*body* (**TB**) tier, then the data needs to be extracted from this segment list made earlier at the **TB** tier:

```
body.s = emu.requery(k.s, "Segment", "TB")
body.tb = emu.track(body.s, "tb_posz")
```

It is not possible to apply **cbind()** to join together **tip.tt[5,]** and **body.tb[5,]** in the manner used before because **cbind()** presupposes that the segments in the trackdata objects are of the same duration, and this will only be so if they have been extracted from the same segment list. The plots must therefore be made separately for the tongue-tip and tongue-body data and superimposed using **par(new=T)**, after setting the ranges for the *x*- and *y*-axes to be the same:

```
# Find the y-range for the vertical axis in mm
ylim = range(frames(tip.tt[5,]), frames(body.tb[5,]))

# Find the x-range for times in ms
xlim = range(tracktimes(tip.tt[5,]),
tracktimes(body.tb[5,]))
plot(tip.tt[5,], xlim=xlim, ylim=ylim, xlab="", ylab="",
type="l")
par(new=T)
plot(body.tb[5,], xlim=xlim, ylim=ylim, xlab="Time (ms)",
ylab="Vertical tongue position", type="l", lty=2)
```

The first of these commands for finding the *y*-range concatenates the speech frames from the tongue tip and tongue body into a single vector and then finds the range. The second command does the same but after concatenating the times at which the frames occur. The **plot()** function is then called twice with the same *x*- and *y*-ranges. In the first plot command, **xlab** and **ylab** are set to "" which means print nothing on the axis labels. The command **par(new=T)** means that the next plot will be drawn on top of the first one. Finally, the argument **lty=2** is used to create the dotted line in the second plot. The result is the plot of synchronized tongue-tip and tongue-body data, extending from the onset of tongue-body raising for the /k/ closure to the offset of tongue-tip lowering for the /l/, as shown in Figure 5.9.

5.4.3 Ensemble plots

A visual comparison between /kn/ and /kl/ on the relative timing of tongue-body and tongue-tip movement can best be made by looking not at single segments but

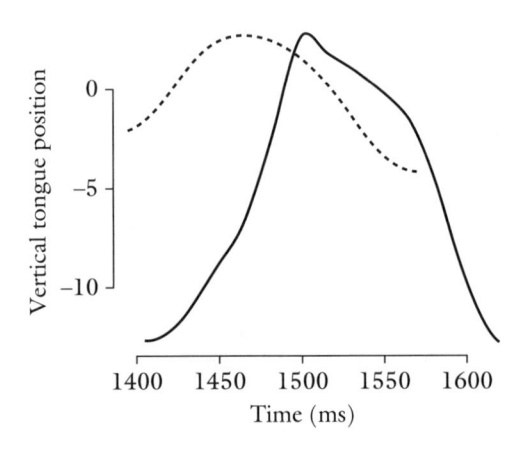

Figure 5.9 Positions of the tongue body (dashed) and tongue tip (solid) between the onset of tongue-dorsum raising and the offset of tongue-tip lowering in a /kl/ token.

at multiple segments from each category in what are sometimes called *ensemble plots*. The function for creating these is **dplot()** in the Emu-R library. This function has **trackdata as an obligatory argument**; two other important optional arguments are a **parallel set of annotations** and the **temporal alignment** point. Assuming you have created the trackdata objects in the preceding section, then **dplot(tip.tt)** plots the tongue-tip data from multiple segments superimposed on each other and time-aligned by default at their onset ($t = 0$ ms). The command **dplot(tip.tt, son.lab)**, which includes a parallel vector of labels, further differentiates the plotted tracks according to segment type. The argument **offset** can be used for the alignment point. This is by default 0 and without modifying other default values it can be set to a proportional value which varies between 0 and 1, denoting that the trackdata are to be synchronized at their onsets and offsets respectively. Thus **dplot(tip.tt, son.lab, offset=0.5)** synchronizes the tracks at their temporal midpoint, which is then defined to have a time of 0 ms. You can also synchronize each segment according to a millisecond time by including the argument **prop = F** (proportional time is **False**). Therefore, **dplot(tip.tt, son.lab, prop=F, offset=end(tip.tt)-20)** synchronizes the tongue-tip movement data at a time point 20 ms before the segment offset. The way in which the synchronization point is evaluated per segment is as follows. For the first segment, the times of the frames are **tracktimes(tip.tt[1,])** which are reset to:

```
tracktimes(tip.tt[1,]) - ( end(tip.tt[1,]) - 20)

-150 -145 -140 -135 -130 -125 -120 -115 -110 -105 -100 -95 -90
-85 -80 -75 -70 -65 -60 -55 -50 -45 -40 -35 -30 -25 -20 -15 -10
-5 0 5 10 15 20
```

As a result, the synchronization point at $t = 0$ ms is four frames earlier than the offset (which is also apparent if you enter, e.g., **dplot(tip.tt[1,], offset=end(tip.tt[1,])-20, prop=F, type="b")**).

In order to compare /kl/ and /kn/ on the relative timing of tongue-body and tongue-tip movement, an ensemble plot could be made of the tongue-tip data but synchronized at the time at which the tongue-*body* displacement for the /k/ is a maximum. Recall that, in labeling the movement trajectories, the tongue-body trajectory was segmented into a sequence of **raise** and **lower** annotations such that the time of maximum tongue-body raising was at the boundary between them. It is not possible to use the segment list **body.s** to obtain these times of maximum tongue-dorsum raising for /k/, because this segment list extends over *both* **raise** and **lower** without marking the boundary between. Instead, therefore, a new segment list needs to be made just of the **raise** annotations at the **TB** tier and then the offset times extracted from these with **end()**. Since there is only one **raise** annotation per segment, the segment list could be made with:

```
tbraise.s = emu.query("ema5", "*", "TB=raise")
```

But a safer way is to query the **raise** annotation at the **TB** tier subject to it also being in word-initial position. This is because all the other segment lists (and

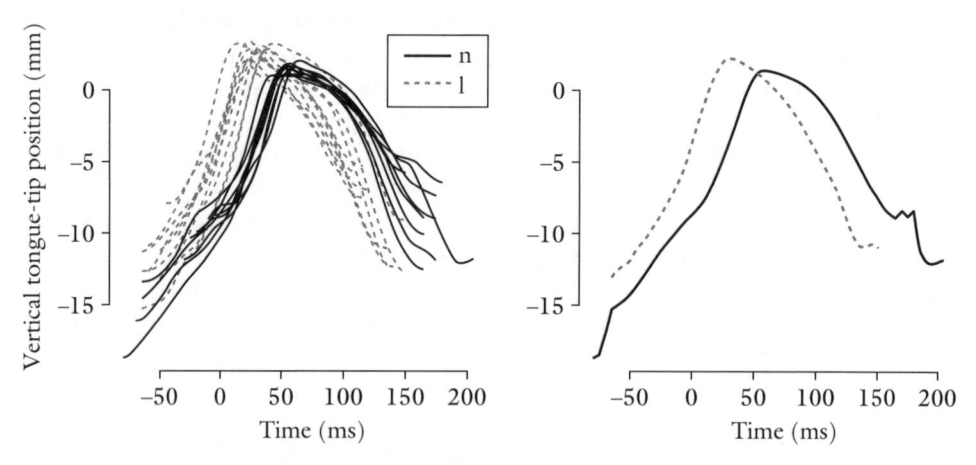

Figure 5.10 Vertical position of the tongue tip in /kn/ and /kl/ clusters synchronized at the point of maximum tongue-body raising in /k/ ($t = 0$ ms) and extending between the tongue-tip raising and lowering movements for /n/ (solid) or /l/ (dashed). The plot on the right is an average of the one on the left.

trackdata objects derived from these) have been obtained in this way and so there is then absolutely no doubt that the desired segment list of **raise** annotations is parallel to all of these:

```
tbraise.s = emu.query("ema5", "*", "[TB=raise ^ Start(Word,
Segment)=1]")
```

An ensemble plot[5] of the tongue-tip movement synchronized at the point of maximum tongue-dorsum raising (Figure 5.10, left panel) can be produced with:

```
dplot(tip.tt, son.lab, prop=F, offset=end(tbraise.s))
```

The same function can be used to produce ensemble-averaged plots in which all of the speech frames at equal time points are averaged separately per annotation category. It should be remembered that the data in an ensemble-averaged plot are less representative of the mean for points progressively further away in time from the synchronization point (because fewer data points tend to be averaged at points further away in time from $t = 0$ ms). The ensemble-averaged plot is produced in exactly the same way as the left panel of Figure 5.10, but by adding the argument **average=T** (Figure 5.10, right panel).

In order to produce ensemble plots of both tongue-tip and tongue-body data together in the manner of Figure 5.9, the same method can be used of overlaying one (ensemble) plot on the other as shown in Figure 5.11. For the x-axis range, specify the desired duration as a vector consisting of two elements, a negative and a positive value on either side of the synchronization point. The y-range is determined, as before, across both sets of data. Figure 5.11 was produced as follows:

```
# Set the x- and y-ranges
xlim = c(-100, 100); ylim = range(frames(tip.tt),
frames(body.tb))
```

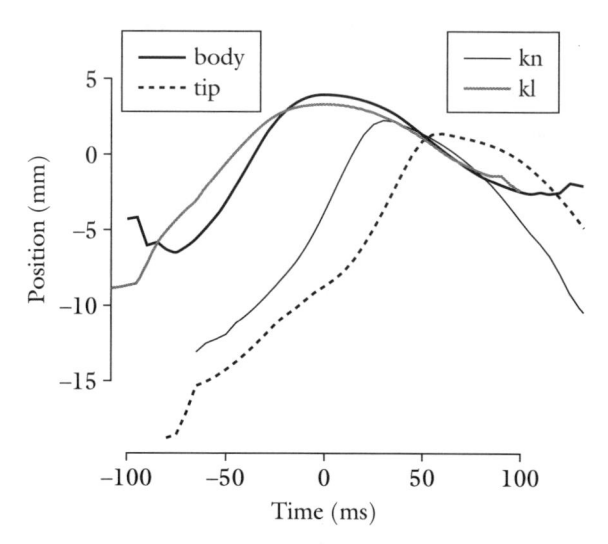

Figure 5.11 Tongue-body (solid) and tongue-tip (dashed) trajectories averaged separately for /kn/ (black) and /kl/ (gray) after synchronization at $t = 0$ ms, the time of maximum tongue-body raising for /k/.

```
# Tongue-tip data coded for /n/ or /l/ with no surrounding box, black and
slate-gray colors,
# double line thickness, dashed, and no legend
dplot(tip.tt, son.lab, prop=F, offset=end(tbraise.s),
average=T, xlim=xlim, ylim=ylim, ylab="Position (mm)",
xlab="Time (ms)", bty="n", col=c(1, "slategray"), lwd=2,
lty=2, legend=F)

# Put appropriate legends at the top left and top right of the display
legend("topleft", c("body", "tip"), lty=c(1,2), lwd=2)
legend("topright", paste("k", unique(son.lab), sep=""),
col=c(1,"slategray"), lty=1, lwd=2)
par(new=T)

# The tongue-body data
dplot(body.tb, son.lab, prop=F, offset=end(tbraise.s),
average=T, xlim=xlim, ylim=ylim, legend=F, col=c(1,
"slategray"), lwd=2, bty="n")
```

5.5 Intragestural Analysis

The task for the rest of this chapter will be to compare /kn/ with /kl/ on the movement and velocity of tongue-dorsum raising in /k/. To do so requires a bit more discussion both of the numerical and logical manipulation of trackdata objects and of the way in which functions can be applied to them. This is covered in 5.5.1. Then in 5.5.2 some of these operations from 5.5.1 are applied to movement data in order to derive their velocity as a function of time.[6] Finally, in 5.5.3, the various movement and velocity parameters are interpreted in terms of the output of a critically damped system that forms part of the model of articulatory phonology (Browman & Goldstein 1990a, 1990b, 1990c) in order to try to specify more precisely the ways in which these clusters may or may not differ in tongue-body raising. It is emphasized here that, although the analyses are conducted from the perspective of movement data, the types of procedures are just as relevant for many of the subsequent investigations of formants, electropalatography, and spectra in the remaining chapters of the book.

5.5.1 Manipulation of trackdata objects

Arithmetic Earlier in this chapter two methods for carrying out simple arithmetic were presented. The first involved applying an arithmetic operation to a single element of a vector and in the second the operation was applied to two vectors of the same length. Here are the two methods again.

```
# Make a vector of four values
x = c(-5, 8.5, 12, 3)

# Subtract four from each value
x - 4
-9.0 4.5 8.0 -1.0

# Make another vector of the same length
y = c(9, -1, 12.3, 5)

# Multiply the vectors element by element
x * y
-45.0 -8.5 147.6 15.0
```

Trackdata objects can be handled more or less in an analogous way. Consider the operation **tip.tt - 20**. In this case, 20 is subtracted from every speech frame. Therefore, if you save the results:

```
new = tip.tt - 20
```

and then compare **new** and **tip.tt**, you will find that they are the same except that in **new** the *y*-axis scale has been shifted down by 20 (because 20 has been subtracted from every speech frame). This is evident if you compare **new** and **tip.tt** on any segment, e.g.,

```
par(mfrow=c(1,2))
plot(new[10,])
plot(tip.tt[10,])
```

If you enter **tip.tt[10,]** on its own you will see that it consists of three components (which is why it is a list): **index**, **ftime**, and **data**. The last of these contains the speech frames: therefore those of the tenth segment are accessible with either **tip.tt[10,]$data** or (more conveniently) with **frames(tip.tt[10,])**. Thus, because of the way that trackdata objects have been structured in R, the arithmetic just carried out **affects only the speech frames** (only the values in **$data**). Consider as another example the trackdata object **vowlax.fdat** containing the first four formant frequencies of a number of vowels produced by two speakers. The fact that this object contains four tracks in contrast to **tip.tt** which contains just one is evident if you use **ncol(vowlax.fdat)** to ask how many columns there are, or **dim(vowlax.fdat)** to find out the number of segments and columns. If you wanted to add 100 Hz to all four formants, then this is **vowlax.fdat + 100**. The following two commands can be used to make a new trackdata object, **newform**, in which 150 Hz is added only to F1:

```
newf1 = vowlax.fdat[,1]+150
newform = cbind(newf1, vowlax.fdat[,2:4])
```

Can arithmetic operations be applied to two trackdata objects in a similar way? The answer is yes, **but only if the two trackdata objects are from the same segment list**. So **tip.tt + tip.tt**, which is the same as **tip.tt * 2**, causes the speech frames to be added to themselves. Analogously, **d = vowlax.fdat[,2]/vowlax.fdat[,1]** creates another trackdata object, **d**, whose frames contain F2 divided by F1 only. As before, it is only the speech frames that are subject to these operations. Suppose then you wanted to subtract the jaw height from the tongue-tip height in order to estimate the extent of tongue-tip movement independently of the jaw. The trackdata object **tip.tt** for tongue movement was derived from the segment list **tip.s**. Therefore, the vertical movement of the jaw must first be derived from the same segment list:

```
jaw = emu.track(tip.s, "jw_posz")
```

The difference between the two is then:

```
tipminusjaw = tip.tt - jaw
```

The derived trackdata object can now be plotted in all the ways described earlier, thus:

```
par(mfrow=c(1,3))
# Tongue-tip movement (for the fifteenth segment)
plot(tip.tt[15,])

# Jaw movement for the same segment
plot(jaw[15,])

# Tongue-tip movement with jaw height subtracted out for the same segment
plot(tipminusjaw[15,])
```

The fact that it is the speech frames to which this operation is applied is evident from asking the following question: are all speech frames of the fifteenth segment in **tipminusjaw** equal to the difference between the tongue-tip and jaw speech frames?

```
all(frames(tipminusjaw[15,]) == frames(tip.tt[15,]) -
frames(jaw[15,]))
TRUE
```

The types of arithmetic functions that show this parallelism between vectors on the one hand and trackdata on the other are given in **help(Ops)** (under **Arith**). So you will see from **help(Ops)** that the functions listed under **Arith** include ^ for raising. This means that there must be parallelism between vectors and trackdata objects for this operation as well:

```
x = c(-5, 8.5, 12, 3)
# Square the elements in x
x^2

# Square all speech frames of the tongue-tip trackdata object
tipsquared = tip.tt^2
```

Comparison operators There is also to a certain extent a similar parallelism between vectors and trackdata objects in using comparison operators. Recall from the analysis of acoustic VOT in 5.3 that logical vectors return **True** or **False**. Thus:

```
x = c(-5, 8.5, 12, 3)
x < 9
TRUE TRUE FALSE TRUE
```

When logical vectors are applied to trackdata objects, then they operate on speech frames. For example, **vowlax.fdat[10,1] > 600** returns a logical vector for any F1 speech frames in the tenth segment greater than 600 Hz: exactly the same result is produced by entering **frames(vowlax.fdat[10,1]) > 600**. Similarly, the command **sum(tip.tt[4,] >= 0)** returns the number of frames in the fourth segment that are greater than zero. To find out *how many* frames are greater than zero in the entire trackdata object, use the **sum()** function without any subscripting, i.e., **sum(tip.tt > 0)**; the same quantity expressed as a proportion of the total number of frames is **sum(tip.tt > 0)/length(tip.tt > 0)** or **sum(tip.tt > 0)/length(frames(tip.tt))**.

The analogy to vectors also holds when two trackdata objects are compared with each other. For example for vectors:

```
# Vectors
x = c(-5, 8.5, 12, 3)
y = c(10, 0, 13, 2)
x > y
FALSE TRUE FALSE TRUE
```

For trackdata objects, the following instruction:

```
temp = tip.tt > tip.tb
```

compares every frame of tongue-tip data with every frame of tongue-body data that occurs at the same time and returns **True** if the first is greater than the second. Therefore, **sum(temp)/length(temp)** can be subsequently used to find the proportion of frames (as a fraction of the total) for which the tongue-tip position is greater (higher) than the position of the back of the tongue.

All logical vectors show this kind of parallelism between vectors and trackdata objects and they are listed under **Compare** in **help(Ops)**. However, there is one important sense in which this parallelism does not work. In the previous example with vectors, **x[x > 9]** returns those elements in **x** for which **x** is greater than nine. Although (as shown above) **tip.tt > 0** is meaningful, **tip.tt[tip.tt > 0]** is not. This is because **tip.tt** indexes *segments* whereas **tip.tt > 0** indexes *speech frames*. So if you wanted to extract the speech frames for which the tongue tip has a value greater than zero, this would be **frames(tip.tt)[tip.tt > 0]**. You can get the times at which these occur with **tracktimes(tip.tt)[tip.tt > 0]**. To get the utterances in which they occur is a little more involved, because the utterance identifiers are not contained in the trackdata object. For this reason, the utterance labels of the corresponding segment list have to be expanded to the same length as the number of speech frames. This can be done with **expand_labels()** in the Emu-R library whose arguments are the index list of the trackdata object and the utterances from the according segment list:

```
uexpand = expand_labels(tip.tt$index, utt(tip.s))
```

A table listing per utterance the number of speech frames for which the position of the tongue tip is greater than 0 mm could then be obtained with **table (uexpand[tip.tt > 0])**.

Math and summary functions There are many math functions in R that can be applied to vectors including those that are listed under **Math** and **Math2** in **help(Ops)**. The same ones can be applied directly to trackdata objects and once again they operate on speech frames. So **round(x, 1)** rounds the elements in a numeric vector **x** to one decimal place and **round(tip.tt, 1)** does the same to all speech frames in the trackdata object **tip.tt**. Since **log10(x)** returns the common logarithm of a vector **x**, then **plot(log10(vowlax.fdat[10,1:2]))** plots the common logarithm of F1 and F2 as a function of time for the tenth segment of the corresponding trackdata object. There are also a couple of so-called summary functions including **max()**, **min()**, and **range()** for finding the maximum, minimum, and range that can be applied in the same way to a vector or trackdata object. Therefore **max(tip.tt[10,])** returns the speech frame with the highest tongue-tip position for the tenth segment and **range(tip.tt[son.lab == "n",])** returns the range of tongue-tip positions across all /kn/ segments (assuming you created **son.lab** earlier).

Finally, if a function is not listed under **help(Ops)**, then it does *not* show a parallelism with vectors and must therefore be applied to speech frames directly. So, while **mean(x)** and **sd(x)** return the mean and standard deviation respectively of the numeric elements in a vector **x**, since neither **mean()** nor **sd()** are functions listed under **help(Ops)**, then this syntax does not carry over to trackdata objects. Thus **mean(frames(tip.tt[1,]))** and not **mean(tip.tt[1,])** returns the mean of the frames of the first segment; and **sd(frames(tip.tt[1:10,]))** and not **sd(tip.tt[1:10,])** returns the standard deviation across all the frames of the first 10 segments, and so on.

Applying a function segment by segment to trackdata objects With the exception of **mean()**, **max()**, and **min()** all the functions in the preceding sections for carrying out arithmetic and math operations have two things in common when they are applied to trackdata objects:

1. The resulting trackdata object has the same number of frames as the trackdata object to which the function was applied.
2. The result is unaffected by the fact that trackdata contains values from multiple segments.

Thus, according to the first point above, the number of speech frames in e.g., **tip.tt - 20** or **tip.tt^2** is the same as in **tip.tt**; or the number of frames in **log(vowlax.fdat[,2]/vowlax.fdat[,1])** is the same as in **vowlax.fdat**. According to the second point, the result is the same whether the operation is applied to all segments in one go or to one segment at a time: **the segment divisions are therefore transparent** as far as the operation is concerned. So the result of applying the cosine function to three segments:

```
res = cos(tip.tt[1:3,])
```

is exactly the same as if you were to apply the cosine function separately to each segment:

```
res1 = cos(tip.tt[1,])
res2 = cos(tip.tt[2,])
res3 = cos(tip.tt[3,])
resall = rbind(res1, res2, res3)
```

The equivalence between the two is verified with:

```
all(res == resall)
TRUE
```

Now clearly there are a number of operations in which the division of data into segments does matter. For example, if you want to find the mean tongue-tip position separately for each segment, then evidently **mean(frames(tip.tt))** will not work because this will find the mean across *all* 20 segments, i.e., the mean value calculated across all speech frames in the trackdata object **tip.tt**. It would instead be necessary to obtain the mean separately for each segment:

```
m1 = mean(frames(tip.tt[1,]))
m2 = mean(frames(tip.tt[2,]))
...
m20 = mean(frames(tip.tt[20,]))
```

Even for 20 segments, entering these commands separately becomes tiresome, but in programming this problem can be more manageably solved using **iteration** in which the same function, **mean()** in this case, is applied repeatedly to each segment. As the words of the penultimate sentence suggest ("obtain the mean separately *for each* segment") one way to do this is with a for-loop applied to the speech frames per segment, thus:

```
vec = NULL
for(j in 1:nrow(tip.tt)){
m = mean(frames(tip.tt[j,]))
vec = c(vec, m)
}
vec
-3.818434 -4.357997 -4.845907...
```

A much easier way, however, is to use **trapply()** in the Emu-R library, which applies a function (in fact using just such a for-loop) separately to the trackdata for each segment. The single-line command will accomplish this and produce the same result:

```
trapply(tip.tt, mean, simplify=T)
-3.818434 -4.357997 -4.845907...
```

So to be clear: the first value returned above is the mean of the speech frames of the first segment, i.e., it is **mean(frames(tip.tt[1,]))** or the value shown by the horizontal line in:

```
plot(tip.tt[1,], type="b")
abline(h= mean(frames(tip.tt[1,])))
```

The second value, −4.357997, has the same relationship to the tongue-tip movement for the second segment and so on.

The first argument to **trapply()** is, then, a trackdata object and the second argument is a function like **mean()**. What kinds of functions can occur as the second argument? The answer is any function, **as long as it can be sensibly applied to a segment's speech frames**. So the reason why **mean()** is valid is because it produces a sensible result when applied to the speech frames for the first segment:

```
mean(frames(tip.tt[1,]))
-3.818434
```

Similarly **range()** can be used in the **trapply()** function because it too gives meaningful results when applied to a segment's speech frames, returning the minimum and maximum:

```
range(frames(tip.tt[1,]))
-10.124228  1.601175
```

Moreover, you could write your own function and pass it as the second argument to **trapply()** as long as your function gives a meaningful output when applied to any segment's speech frames. For example, supposing you wanted to find out the average values of just the first three speech frames for each segment. The mean of the first three frames in the data of, say, the tenth segment is:

```
fr = frames(tip.tt[10,])
mean(fr[1:3])
-14.22139
```

Here is a function to obtain the same result:

```
mfun <- function(frdat, k=3)
{
  # frdat are speech frames, k the number of frames to be averaged
  (default is 3)
    mean(frdat[1:k])
}

mfun(frames(tip.tt[10,]))
-14.22139
```

Can **mfun()** be applied to a segment's speech frames? Evidently it can, as the preceding command has just shown. Consequently, the function can be used as the second argument to **trapply()** to calculate the mean of the first three elements for each segment separately:

```
res = trapply(tip.tt, mfun, simplify=T)
res[10]
-14.22139
```

The purpose of the third argument, **simplify=T**, is to simplify the result as a vector or a matrix (otherwise, for reasons explained below, the output is a list). This third argument can, and should, be used if you are sure **that the function will return the same number of numeric elements per segment**. It was therefore appropriate to use **simplify=T** in all of the above examples, because in each case the number of values returned is the same for each segment: both **mean()** and **mfun()** always return one numeric value per segment and **range()** always returns two values per segment. Whenever one value is returned per segment, then **simplify=T** causes the output to be converted to a vector, otherwise, as when using **range()**, the output is a matrix.

Using **simplify=T** would not be appropriate if the function returns neither a vector nor a matrix. Consider for example **ar()** for calculating autocorrelation coefficients. This function produces meaningful output when applied to speech frames for any segment:

```
auto = ar(frames(tip.tt[9,]))
auto
Call:
ar(x = frames(tip.tt[9, ]))

Coefficients:
   1
0.9306

Order selected 1  sigma^2 estimated as  3.583
```

Therefore, **ar()** could be applied iteratively to each segment using **trapply()**. But as both the above output and **class(auto)** show, the output is neither a vector nor a matrix. Consequently, **simplify=T** should not be included as the third argument. When **simplify=T** is not included (equivalent to **simplify=F**), the output for each segment is collected as a list and the data corresponding to any segment number is accessible using the double-bracket notation, thus:

```
a = trapply(tip.tt, ar)
summary(a[[9]])
             Length Class  Mode
order          1    -none- numeric
ar             1    -none- numeric
var.pred       1    -none- numeric
x.mean         1    -none- numeric
aic           17    -none- numeric
n.used         1    -none- numeric
order.max      1    -none- numeric
partialacf    16    -none- numeric
resid         40    -none- numeric
method         1    -none- character
series         1    -none- character
frequency      1    -none- numeric
call           2    -none- call
asy.var.coef   1    -none- numeric
```

5.5.2 Differencing and velocity

Another perhaps more common case in which **simplify=T** is not appropriate is if the function does not return the same number of elements per segment. This is going to happen in, for example, differencing speech frames because the number of frames per segment is not the same for each segment (because segments are not of the same duration). Differencing is often a useful operation in many kinds of speech research and when speech *movement* data is differenced, the result is a signal containing an estimate for any point in time of the articulator's velocity. In differencing a signal, element at time $n - 1$ in a digital signal is subtracted from element at time n. The relationship can be written as an equation relating the differenced signal y[n] to the signal x[n] to which differencing is applied:

(1) $y[n] = x[n] - x[n-1]$

(1) can be carried out in R straightforwardly using the **diff()** function:

```
x = c(10, 0, -2, 4, 12, 5)
y = diff(x)
y
-10 -2 6 8 -7
```

(1) is an example of first-order (backward) differencing and the output always has one value less than the number of elements in the signal to which differencing is applied. The estimation of velocity from movement data is, however, often more reliably obtained from **three-point central differencing**. The equation for this is:

(2) $y[n] = \frac{1}{2}(x[n] - x[n-2])$

(2) could be translated into R as **0.5 * diff(x, 2)**. The same result can be obtained by convolving the input signal with the coefficients of a finite impulse response (FIR) filter. The coefficients are the weights on the signal delays: thus **c(0.5, 0, -0.5)** in this case because 0.5 is the coefficient of x[n], 0 is the coefficient on x[n – 1] (i.e., there is no x[n – 1]), and – 0.5 is the coefficient on x[n – 2]. So in R the three-point central differencing equation in (2) can be implemented using the **filter()** function as:

```
y = filter(x, c(0.5, 0, -0.5))
y
NA -6.0 2.0 7.0 0.5 NA
```

In three-point central differencing, two values are lost, one at the beginning and the other at the end:[7] this is why the output has an initial and final **NA** (not applicable). The other values are synchronized with those of the original signal: thus the second value **y[2]** is an estimate of the velocity at time point 2, **y[3]** at time point 3, and so on. This is another advantage of three-point central differencing: in contrast to first-order differencing, no further synchronization of the differenced and the original signal is necessary.

Consider now the effect of differencing on a cosine wave which can be produced with **cr()** in the Emu-R library. In Figure 5.12, a single-cycle sinusoid (a phase-shifted cosine wave) consisting of 48 points was produced and plotted as follows:

```
coswav = cr(N=48, p=pi/2, values=T, plotf=F)
times = 0:47
plot(times, coswav, type="b", xlab="Time (number of
points)", ylab="Displacement")
```

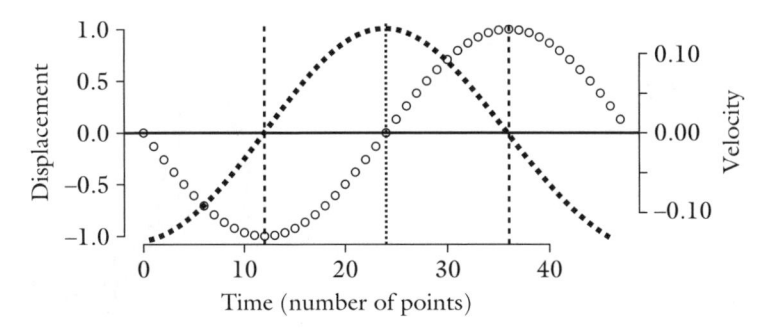

Figure 5.12 A sinusoid (open circles) and the rate of change of the sinusoid (diamonds) obtained by central differencing. The dashed vertical lines are the times at which the rate of change is zero. The dotted vertical line is the time at which the rate of change is maximum.

For reasons that will be clear in a moment, vertical lines are marked at both the trough, or minimum, and the following peak, or maximum, which occur at times 12 and 36:

```
abline(v=c(12, 36), lty=2)
```

Then central differencing is applied to this sinusoid and the result is plotted on top:

```
coswav.d = filter(coswav, c(0.5, 0, -0.5))
par(new=T)
plot(times, coswav.d, axes=F, type="b", xlab="", ylab="",
pch=18)
axis(side=4); mtext("Velocity", side=4, line=2)
```

The values for which the first differenced signal is zero can be seen by plotting a horizontal line with **abline(h=0)**. Finally, **abline(v=24)** marks the time at which the differenced signal has a maximum value (Figure 5.12).

Now it is evident from Figure 5.12 that, whenever there is a peak (maximum) or trough (minimum) in the sinusoid, then the differenced signal is zero-valued. This is as it should be because the sinusoid is **stationary** at these times, i.e., the rate at which the sinusoid changes at these times is zero. In addition, the time at which the differenced signal has a peak is when the sinusoid has the greatest range of change (which is when the amplitude interval between two points of the sinusoid is greatest).

One of the remarkable discoveries in speech research since the 1980s, which is brought out so well by EMA analyses, is that the movement of the supralaryngeal articulators – the jaw, lips, different points on the tongue – as a function of time often bears quite a close resemblance to the sinusoidal movement shown on the left in Figure 5.12. For example, there is a quasi-sinusoidal shape to the movement of the tongue body over the interval of the tongue-body raising and lowering for the /k/ in the fifth segment in Figure 5.13. These data can be plotted with **plot(body.tb[5,])**, assuming that the tongue-body trackdata has been derived from the corresponding segment list:

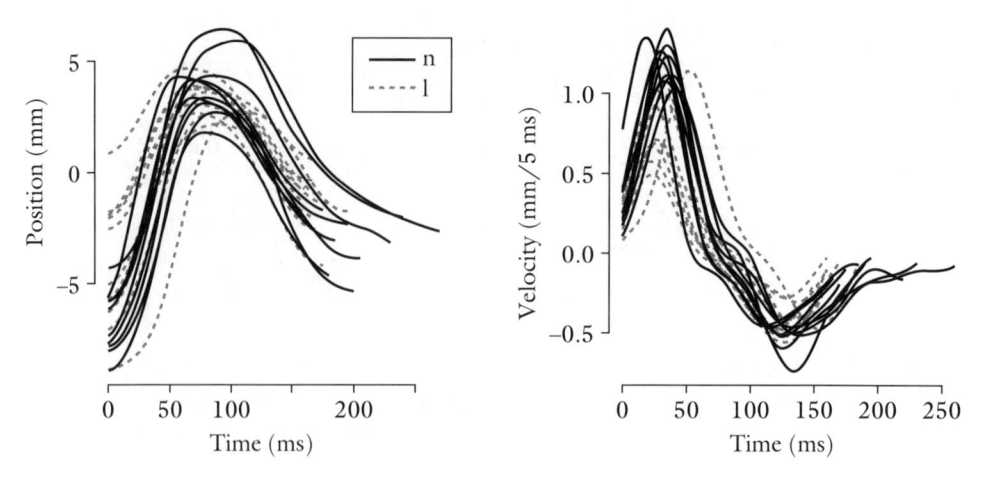

Figure 5.13 Tongue-body position (left) and velocity (right) as a function of time over an interval of tongue-body raising and lowering in the /k/ of /kn/ (solid) and of /kl/ (dashed, gray) clusters.

```
body.s = emu.query("ema5", "*", "[TB=raise -> TB = lower]")
body.tb = emu.track(body.s, "tb_posz")
plot(body.tb[5,])
```

The velocity of the tongue body can be derived using the same central differencing procedure described above. In the procedure below, the **filter()** function is put inside another function, **cendiff()**, which removes the first and last **NA**. The arguments to this function are the speech frames and the coefficients set by default to those for central differencing:

```
cendiff <- function(spframes, coeffs=c(0.5, 0, -.5))
{
times = tracktimes(spframes)
result = filter(spframes, coeffs)
temp = is.na(result)
result = cbind(result[!temp])
rownames(result) <- times[!temp]
result
}
```

The function can be applied to speech frames, as this example shows:

```
cendiff(frames(body.tb[5,]))
     [,1]
1400 0.2107015
1405 0.3403330
1410 0.4507700
1415 0.5315820
1420 0.5738020
```

The same function can therefore also be used inside **trapply()** for deriving the velocity from multiple segments. For all the reasons discussed in the preceding section, **simplify=T** must not be included because the number of differenced values is not the same from one segment to the next, given that the durations of segments vary. However, if the function outputs values as a function of time – as is necessarily the case in differencing a time signal – then the argument **returntrack=T** can be included, which will cause the output to be built as a trackdata object, if possible. The advantage of doing this is that all the functionality for manipulating trackdata objects becomes available for these differenced data. The command is:

```
body.tbd = trapply(body.tb, cendiff, returntrack=T)
```

A plot of tongue-body velocity as a function of time is then given by **plot(body.tbd[5,])**. Ensemble plots (Figure 5.13) for the movement and velocity data separately per category, synchronized at the beginning of the raising movement for all segments, can be produced with:

```
par(mfrow=c(1,2))
dplot(body.tb, son.lab)
dplot(body.tbd, son.lab)
```

The scale of the velocity data is mm/T where T is the duration between speech frames. Since in this case T is 5 ms, the scale is mm/5 ms.[8]

As the right panel of Figure 5.13 shows, there are maxima and minima in the velocity data corresponding to the times at which the rate of change of tongue-body raising and lowering is greatest. The same figure also shows that the velocity is around zero close to 75 ms: this is the time around which the tongue-body raising for the /k/ closure is at a maximum in many segments.

The left panel of Figure 5.13 suggests that the peak velocity of the raising movement might be greater for /kn/ than for /kl/. In order to bring out such differences between the clusters more clearly, it would be helpful to align the trajectories at the time of the peak velocity itself. This in turn means that these times have to be found, which will require writing a function to do so. For the data in question, the speech frames of any segment number n are given by **frames(body.tb[n,])** and the times at which they occur by **tracktimes(body.tb[n,])**. The required function needs to find the time at which the speech frames for any segment attain a maximum. This can be done by using the **which.max()** function to find the speech frame number at which the maximum occurs and then applying it to the times of the speech frames. For example, for the fifth segment:

```
num = which.max(frames(body.tbd[5,]))
times = tracktimes(body.tbd[5,])
times[num]
1420
```

These lines can now be packed into a function that can be applied to speech frames. The function has been written so that it defaults to finding the time of the maximum if **maxtime** is **True**; if not, it finds the time of the minimum:

```
peakfun <- function(fr, maxtime=T)
{
if(maxtime) num = which.max(fr)
else num = which.min(fr)
tracktimes(fr)[num]
}
```

Now verify that you get the same result as before:

```
peakfun(frames(body.tbd[5,]))
1420
```

The time of the peak-velocity *minimum* is, incidentally:

```
peakfun(frames(body.tbd[5,]), F)
1525
```

Since this function can evidently be applied to speech frames, then it can also be used inside **trapply()** to get the peak-velocity maximum for each segment. In this case, **simplify=T** can be set because there should only be one peak-velocity time per segment:

```
pkraisetimes = trapply(body.tbd, peakfun, simplify=T)
```

If you wanted to get the times of the peak-velocity minima for each segment corresponding to the peak velocity of tongue-body lowering, then just append the argument **F** after the function name in **trapply()**, thus:

```
pklowertimes = trapply(body.tbd, peakfun, F, simplify=T)
```

The movement or velocity trackdata objects can now be displayed in an ensemble plot synchronized at the peak-velocity maximum (Figure 5.14):

```
par(mfrow=c(1,2))
dplot(body.tbd, son.lab, offset=pkraisetimes, prop=F)
dplot(body.tbd, son.lab, offset=pkraisetimes, prop=F,
average=T)
```

These data are quite interesting because they show that the peak velocity of the tongue-body movement is not the same in /kn/ and /kl/ clusters and noticeably greater in /kn/, a finding that could never be established from a spectrogram or an acoustic analysis alone.

5.5.3 Critically damped movement, magnitude, and peak velocity

The purpose in this final section is to explore in some further detail the origin of the evidently faster movement in closing the /k/ in /kn/ than in /kl/. To do so,

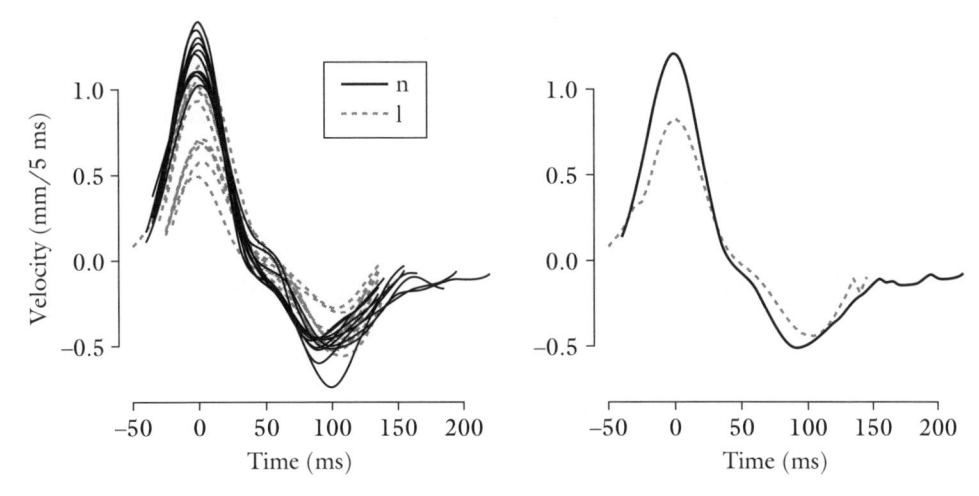

Figure 5.14 The same data as in the right panel of Figure 5.13, but additionally synchronized at the time of the peak-velocity maximum in the tongue-back raising gesture of individual segments (left) and averaged after synchronization by category (right).

a bit more needs to be said about the way in which movements are modeled in articulatory phonology (e.g., Browman & Goldstein 1990a, 1990b, 1990c, 1992a; Saltzman & Munhall 1989). In the preceding section, it was noted that the movement of an articulator such as the tongue tip or jaw often follows a quasi-sinusoidal pattern as a function of time. In articulatory phonology, this type of pattern is presumed to come about because articulatory dynamics are controlled by the same kind of dynamics that control the movement of a mass in a mass–spring system (e.g., Byrd et al. 2000).

In such a system, imagine that there is a mass attached to the end of a spring. You pull down on the mass and let it go and then measure its position as a function of time as it approaches rest position. The way that the mass approaches the rest, or equilibrium, position depends on a number of parameters, some of which are factored out by making the simplification firstly that the mass is of unit size and secondly that the mass–spring system is what is called *critically damped*. In a critically damped system, the spring does not overshoot its rest position or oscillate before coming to rest but approaches it exponentially and in the shortest amount of time possible. This system's equation of motion is defined as follows (Byrd et al. 2000; Saltzman & Munhall 1989):

(3) $\ddot{x} + 2\omega\dot{x} + \omega^2(x - x_{targ}) = 0$

where x, $\ddot{x}$, and $\dot{x}$ are the position, velocity, and acceleration of the mass, ω is the spring's natural frequency (and equal to the square root of the spring's stiffness), and x_{targ} is the position of the spring at rest position. The system defined by (3) is dynamically autonomous in that there are no explicit time-dependent, but only state-dependent, forces. For this critically damped mass–spring system, the position of the mass as a function of time can be computed using the solution equation in (4), in which time is explicitly represented and in which the starting velocity is assumed to be zero:[9]

(4) $\quad x(t) = (A + Bt)e^{-\omega t}$

where $A = x(0) - x_{targ}$ and $B = v(0) + A\omega$. In this equation, ω and x_{targ} have the definition as before, and $x(t)$ and $v(t)$ are the position and velocity of the mass at time t ($t \geq 0$). Equation (4) can be converted into an equivalent function in R as follows, in which $x(0)$, x_{targ}, $v(0)$, ω, and t are represented in the function by **xo**, **xtarg**, **vo**, **w**, and **n** respectively:

```
critdamp <- function(xo=1, xtarg=0, vo=0, w=0.05, n=0:99)
{
A = xo - xtarg
B = vo + w * A
(A + B * n) * exp(-w * n)
}
```

The defaults are set in such a way that the starting position of the mass is 1, the initial velocity is zero, and such that the mass approaches, but does not attain, the rest (target) position of zero over an interval between 0 and 99 time points. The position of the mass (articulator) as a function of time[10] for the defaults is shown in the left panel of Figure 5.15. The figure was produced with:

```
position = critdamp()
plot(0:99, position)
```

The velocity, shown in the right panel of Figure 5.15, can be calculated from the movement as before with central differencing:

```
plot(0:99, filter(position, c(0.5, 0, -0.5)))
```

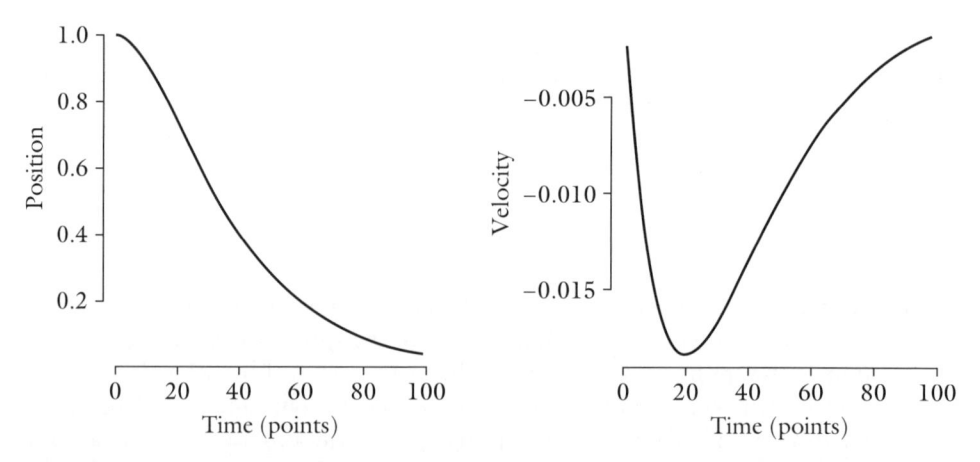

Figure 5.15 The position (left) and velocity (right) of a mass in a critically damped mass–spring system with parameters in equation (4) $x(0) = 1$, $\omega = 0.05$, $v(0) = 0$, $x_{targ} = 0$.

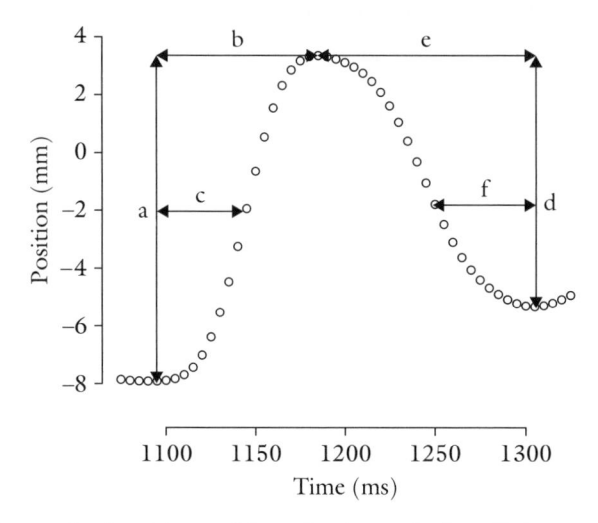

Figure 5.16 Tongue-body raising and lowering in producing /k/ – a: magnitude of the raising gesture; b: duration of the raising gesture; c: time to peak velocity in the raising gesture; d: magnitude of the lowering gesture; e: duration of the lowering gesture; f: time to peak velocity in the lowering gesture.

In some implementations of the model of articulatory phonology (e.g., Byrd et al. 2000), there is presumed to be a two-parameter specification of just this kind for each so-called **gesture**. In the present data, raising and lowering the tongue body in producing the /k/ closure (Figure 5.16) are the result of tongue-dorsum constriction-formation and constriction-release gestures that are separately determined by their own two-parameter specifications that are input to an equation such as (3). There then has to be a further parameter defining how these two gestures are timed or **phased** relative to each other. This phasing is not the concern of the analysis presented here – but see e.g., Beckman et al. (1992), Fowler and Saltzman (1993), Harrington et al. (1995), and more recently Nam (2007) for further details.

Although varying the parameters x_0 and ω can result in a potentially infinite number of gestural shapes, they all conform to the following four generalizations (Beckman et al. 1992; Byrd et al. 2000):

i The **magnitude of a gesture** is affected by x_0: the greater x_0, the greater the magnitude. In Figure 5.15, the magnitude is 1 because this is the absolute difference between the highest and lowest positions. In tongue-body raising for producing the /k/ closure, the magnitude is the extent of movement from the tongue-body minimum in the preceding vowel to the maximum in closing the /k/ (a in Figure 5.16).

ii The **peak velocity of a gesture** is influenced by both x_0 and ω.

iii The **time at which the peak velocity occurs** relative to the onset of the gesture (c or f in Figure 5.16) is influenced only by ω, the articulatory stiffness.

iv The **gesture duration** (b or e in Figure 5.16) is the time taken between the tongue-body minimum and following maximum in closing the /k/: this is not explicitly specified in the model but arises intrinsically as a consequence of specifying x_o and ω.

Both (ii) and (iii) can be derived from algebraic manipulation of (1) and demonstrated graphically. As far as the algebra is concerned, it can be shown that the time at which the peak velocity occurs, t_{pkvel}, is the reciprocal of the natural frequency:

(5) $t_{pkvel} = 1 / \omega$

Therefore, the higher the value of ω (i.e., the stiffer the spring/articulator), the smaller $1/\omega$ and the earlier the time of the peak velocity. Also, since (5) makes no reference to x_o, then changing x_o can have no influence on t_{pkvel}. Secondly, the peak velocity (ii), *pkvel*, is given by:

(6) $pkvel = -x_o \omega / e$

Consequently, an increase either in x_o or in ω (or both) causes the absolute value of *pkvel* to increase because in either case the right-hand side of (6) increases (in absolute terms).

An illustration of the consequences of (5) and (6) is shown in Figure 5.17. In column 1, **critdamp()** was used to increase x_o in equal steps with the stiffness parameter held constant: in this case, there is a progressive increase in both the magnitude (between 0.75 and 1.5) and the peak velocity, but the time of the peak

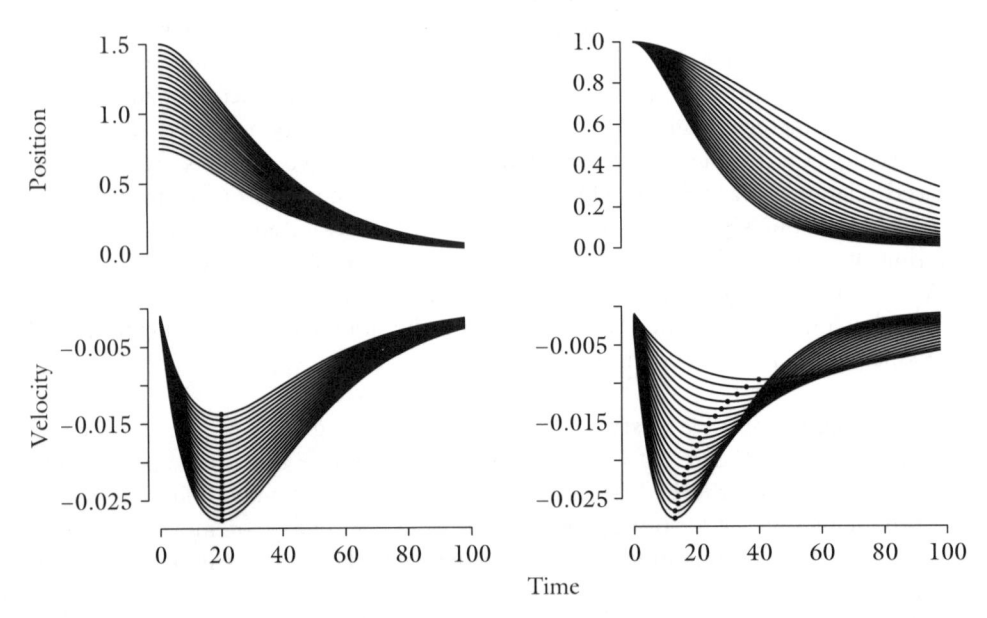

Figure 5.17 Position (row 1) and velocity (row 2) as a function of time in varying the parameters x_o and ω of equation (3). In column 1, x_o was varied in 20 equal steps between 0.75 and 1.5 with constant $\omega = 0.05$. In column 2, ω was varied in 20 equal steps between 0.025 and 0.075 while keeping x_o constant at 1. The peak velocity is marked by a point on each velocity trajectory.

velocity is unchanged at $1/\omega$. In column 2, x_o was held constant and ω was varied in equal steps. In this case, the magnitude is the same, the peak velocity increases, and the time of the peak velocity relative to movement onset decreases.

The issue to be considered now is which parameter changes can best account for the observed faster tongue-body raising movement shown in Figure 5.14 for /kn/ compared with /kl/. This is at first sight not self-evident since, as shown in Figure 5.17, the greater peak velocity could have been brought about by a change either to x_o or to ω or to both. However, based on the above considerations the following two predictions can be made:

1. If the faster tongue-body movement in /kn/ is due to a change in stiffness and not in the target, then the time at which the peak velocity occurs should be earlier in /kn/ than in /kl/.
2. If the faster tongue-body movement in /kn/ is due to a change in the target and not in the stiffness, then the ratio of the magnitude of the movement to the peak velocity should be about the same for /kn/ and /kl/. The evidence for this can be seen in column 1 of Figure 5.17, which shows a progressive increase in the peak velocity, *as the magnitude increases.* It is also evident from algebraic considerations. Since by (6) $pkvel = -x_o\omega/e$, then the ratio of the magnitude to the peak velocity is $-x_o/(x_o\omega/e) = -e/\omega$. Consequently, if ω is the same in /kn/ and /kl/, then this ratio for both /kn/ and /kl/ is the same constant which also means that the tokens of /kn/ and /kl/ should fall on a line with approximately the same slope of $-e/\omega$ when they are plotted in the plane of the magnitude as a function of the peak velocity.

In order to adjudicate between these hypotheses – whether the faster tongue movement is brought about by a change to the target or to stiffness or quite possibly both – then the parameters for the raising gesture shown in Figure 5.16 need to be extracted from the trackdata object. Recall that a segment list over the interval defined by tongue-body raising was made earlier:

```
tbraise.s = emu.query("ema5", "*", "TB=raise")
```

A trackdata object of tongue-body raising over this raising interval is given by:

```
tbraise.tb = emu.track(tbraise.s, "tb_posz")
```

The function **dur()** could now be used to retrieve the duration of the raising gesture (b in Figure 5.16) from this trackdata object:

```
# Raising gesture duration
raise.dur = dur(tbraise.tb)
```

For the raising gesture magnitude (a in Figure 5.16), the positions at the onset and offset of the raising gesture need to be retrieved from the trackdata object and subtracted from each other. The retrieval of values at a single time point in a trackdata object can be done with **dcut()** in the Emu-R library. For example, the start time of the raising gesture for the first segment is given by **start(tbraise.tb[1,])**, which is 1,105 ms so the position at that time is **dcut(tbraise.tb[1,], 1105)**. The corresponding positions for all segments can be extracted by passing the entire vector of start times to **dcut()** as the second argument, thus:

```
pos.onset = dcut(tbraise.tb, start(tbraise.tb))
```

The positions at the offset of the raising gesture can be analogously retrieved with:

```
pos.offset = dcut(tbraise.tb, end(tbraise.tb))
```

The magnitude is the absolute difference between the two:

```
magnitude = abs(pos.onset - pos.offset)
```

The function **dcut()** could also be used to extract the times of the peak velocity. The first three lines repeat the commands from 5.5.2 for creating the peak velocity trackdata object. The last line extracts the times of maximum peak velocity:

```
body.s = emu.query("ema5", "*", "[TB=raise -> TB = lower]")
body.tb = emu.track(body.s, "tb_posz")
body.tbd = trapply(body.tb, cendiff, returntrack=T)
pkvel = dcut(body.tbd, pkraisetimes)
```

Finally, the fourth parameter that is needed is the duration between the movement onset and the time of the peak velocity. Using the objects created so far, this is:

```
timetopkvel = pkraisetimes - start(body.tbd)
```

If the faster tongue-body movement in /kn/ is due to a change in articulatory stiffness, then the time to the peak velocity should be earlier than for /kl/. Assuming you have created the objects **k.s** and **son.lab** (section 5.2), then the boxplot in Figure 5.18 can be created with:

```
boxplot(timetopkvel ~ son.lab)
```

The boxplot shows no evidence that the time to the peak velocity is earlier in /kn/, although it is difficult to conclude very much from these results, given the small number of tokens and somewhat skewed distribution for /kn/ (in which the median and upper quartile have nearly the same value).

The same figure shows /kn/ and /kl/ in the plane of the magnitude as a function of the peak velocity. The figure was plotted with:

```
plot(pkvel, magnitude, pch=son.lab)
```

The resulting display suggests that the tokens of /kn/ and /kl/ may well fall on the same line. Thus, although there are insufficient data to be conclusive, the pattern

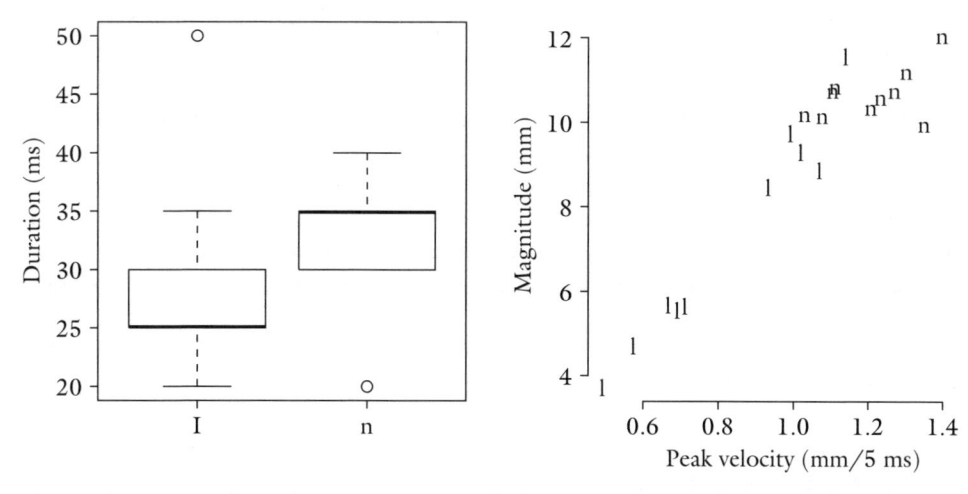

Figure 5.18 Data from the raising gesture of /kl/ and /kn/. Left: boxplot of the duration between the movement onset and the time to peak velocity. Right: the magnitude of the raising gesture as a function of its peak velocity.

of results in the right panel of Figure 5.17 is consistent with the view that the ratio of the displacement to the peak velocity is quite similar for both /kn/ and /kl/.

These data support the view, then, that the faster tongue movement is the result of changes not to articulatory stiffness but instead to the target: informally, this brief analysis suggests that the raising gesture for the velar stop in /kn/ is bigger and faster than in /kl/.

5.6 Summary

The main purpose of this chapter has been to make use of movement data in order to illustrate some of the principal ways that speech can be analyzed in Emu-R. The salient points of this chapter are as follows.

Segment lists and trackdata objects A segment list is derived from an annotated database with **emu.query()** and it includes for each segment information about its annotation, its start time, its end time, and the utterance from which it was extracted. The functions **label()** and **utt()** operate on a segment list to retrieve respectively the annotation and utterance name in which the segment occurs.

The function **trackinfo()** gives information about which signals are available for a database, i.e., which trackdata objects can be made. The **summary()** function provides an overview of the contents either of a segment list or of a trackdata object.

A trackdata object contains speech frames and is always derived from a segment list. For each segment, the times of the first and last speech frame are also within the boundary times of the segment list. Successive speech frames are stored in rows and can be retrieved with the function **frames()** and their times with **tracktimes()**. The functions **start()**, **end()**, and **dur()** can be applied to segment lists or trackdata objects to obtain the segments' start times, end times, and durations. There may be several columns of speech frames if several signal files are read into the same trackdata object (as in the case of formants for example).

Indexing and logical vectors   Emu-R has been set up so that vectors, matrices, segment lists, and trackdata objects can be indexed in broadly the same way. The annotation or duration of the *n*th segment is indexed with **x[n]**, where x is a vector containing the segments' annotations or durations. Data for the *n*th segment from matrices, segment lists, and trackdata objects are indexed with **x[n,]**.

Logical vectors are the output of comparison operators and can be used to index segments in an analogous way: if **temp** is logical, **x[temp]** retrieves information about the annotations and durations of segments from vectors; and **x[temp,]** retrieves segment information from segment lists and trackdata objects.

Plotting speech data from trackdata objects   The function **plot()** (in reality **plot.trackdata()** when applied to a trackdata object) can be used to produce a plot of the speech frames as a function of time for any individual segment. The function **dplot()** is used for ensemble plots of speech frames as a function of time for several segments.

Numerical, mathematical, and logical operations on trackdata objects   Trackdata objects can be handled arithmetically, logically, and mathematically in very similar way to vectors for the functions listed under **Arith**, **Compare**, **Ops**, **Math**, **Math2**, and **Summary** in **help(Ops)**. In all cases, these operations are applied to speech frames.

Applying functions to trackdata objects   **trapply()** can be used to apply a function to a trackdata object. **tapply()** is for applying a function to a vector separately for each category; and **apply()** can be used for applying a function separately to the rows and columns of a matrix.

Extracting data from trackdata objects at particular points in time   Speech frames are extracted from a trackdata object with **dcut()** either at a single point in time or over an interval.

Analysis of movement data   In many cases, the movement of the supralaryngeal articulators in speech production exhibits characteristics of a damped sinusoid with a minimum and maximum displacement at articulatory landmarks. In the task-dynamic model, the movement between these extreme points of articulatory movement is the result of producing an articulatory gesture according to the same sets of parameters that control a critically damped mass–spring system. The time interval between these points of minimum and maximum displacement corresponds to the gesture's duration. The absolute difference in position between the minimum and maximum displacement is the gesture's magnitude. Since the movement ideally follows a sinusoidal trajectory, there is one point at which the velocity is a maximum, known as the peak velocity. The peak velocity can be found by finding the time at which the movement's rate of change has a peak. The times of the maximum or minimum displacement are the same as the times at which the velocity is zero.

In the equation of a critically damped mass–spring system that defines the gesture's trajectory, time is not explicitly represented but is instead a consequence of specifying two parameters: the stiffness (or the spring/the articulator) and the target (change from equilibrium position). Changing the stiffness increases peak velocity but does not affect the magnitude. When the target is changed, then the peak velocity and magnitude change proportionally.

/kn/ vs /kl/ clusters The interval between the tongue-dorsum and tongue-tip closures is greater for /kn/ than for /kl/. In addition, /kn/ was shown to have a greater acoustic voice-onset time as well as a bigger (and proportionately faster) tongue-dorsum closing gesture compared with /kl/.

5.7 Questions

A. This question is about exploring whether the data show a relationship between the extent of jaw lowering and the first formant frequency in the first [a] component of [aɪ] of *Kneipe* and *Kneipier*, or of [aʊ] of *Claudia* and *Klausur*. In general, a more open vocal tract can be expected to be associated with both F1 raising and a lower jaw position (Lindblom & Sundberg 1971).

A.1 Calculate the first two formants of this database (**ema5**) and store these in a directory of your choice. Modify the template file in the manner described in Chapter 2 so that they are visible to the database **ema5**. Since this is a female speaker, use a nominal F1 of 600 Hz.

A.2 Assuming the existence of the segment list **k.s** of word-initial /k/ segments as defined at the beginning of this chapter and repeated below:

```
k.s = emu.query("ema5", "*", "Segment=k & Start(Word,
Segment)=1")
```

how could you use **emu.requery()** to make a segment list, **vow**, containing the diphthongs in the same words, given that these are positioned three segments to the right in relation to these word-initial /k/ segments? Once you have made **vow**, make a trackdata object **vow.fm**, for this segment list containing the formants. (You will first need to calculate the formants in the manner described in Chapter 3. Use a nominal F1 of 600 Hz.)

A.3 Make a vector of word labels, **word.1**, either from **k.s** or from the segment list **vow** you created in A.2. A table of the words should look like this:

```
table(word.1)
word.1
Claudia Klausur Kneipe Kneipier
   5       5      5       5
```

A.4 Make a trackdata object, **vow.jaw**, containing vertical jaw-movement data (in track **jw_posz**) for the segment list you made in A.2.

A.5 The jaw height should show a trough in these diphthongs somewhere in the first component as the jaw lowers and the mouth opens. Use **trapply()** and **peakfun()** given below (repeated from section 5.5.2) to find the time at which the jaw height is at its lowest point in these diphthongs.

```
peakfun <- function(fr, maxtime=T)
{
if(maxtime) num = which.max(fr)
else num = which.min(fr)
tracktimes(fr)[num]
}
```

A.6 Verify that the times you have found in A.5 are appropriate by making an ensemble plot of **vow.jaw** color-coded for the diphthong type and synchronized at time of maximum jaw lowering found in A.5.

A.7 Using **dcut()** or otherwise, extract (i) the first formant frequency and (ii) the jaw height at these times. Store the first of these as **f1** and the second as **jaw**.

A.8 Plot F1 as a function of the jaw-height minimum showing the word labels at the corresponding points. This can be done either with:

```
plot(f1, jaw, type="n", xlab="F1 (Hz)", ylab="Jaw position
(mm)")
text(f1, jaw, word.1)
```

or with:

```
eplot(cbind(f1, jaw), word.1, dopoints=T, doellipse=F,
xlab="F1 (Hz)", ylab="Jaw position (mm)")
```

where **word.1** is the vector of word labels you make in A.3. To what extent would you say that there is a relationship between F1 and jaw height?

B. This question is about lip aperture and tongue movement in the closure of [p] of *Kneipe* and *Kneipier*.

B.1 Make a segment list, **p.s**, of the acoustic [p] closure (**p** at the **Segment** tier) of *Kneipe* or *Kneipier*.

B.2 Make a vector of word labels **pword.1**, parallel to the segment list in B.1.

B.3 Make two trackdata objects from **p.s**: (i) **p.ll**, of the vertical position of the lower lip (track **ll_posz**) and (ii) **p.ul**, of the vertical position of the upper lip (track **ul_posz**).

B.4 One way to approximate the lip aperture using EMA data is by subtracting the vertical lower-lip position from the vertical upper-lip position. Create a new trackdata object **p.ap** consisting of this difference between upper- and lower-lip position.

B.5 Use **peakfun()** from A.5 to create a vector, **p.mintime**, of the time at which the lip aperture in **p.ap** is a minimum.

B.6 Make an ensemble plot of the position of the lip-aperture as a function of time from **p.ap** color-coded for *Kneipe* vs *Kneipier* and synchronized at the time of minimum lip aperture.

B.7 How could you work out the mean proportional time in the acoustic closure at which the lip-aperture minimum occurs separately for *Kneipe* and *Kneipier*? For example, if the acoustic [p] closure extends from 10 to 20 ms and the time of the minimum lip aperture is 12 ms, then the proportional time is $(12 - 10) / (20 - 10) = 0.2$. The task is to find two mean proportional times, one for *Kneipe* and the other for *Kneipier*.

B.8 How would you expect the vertical and horizontal position of the tongue-mid (Figure 5.4) sensor to differ between the words in the closure of [p], given that the segment following the closure is [ɐ] in *Kneipe* and [j] or [ɪ] in *Kneipier*? Check your predictions by producing two ensemble plots over the interval of the acoustic [p] closure and color-coded for these words (i) of the vertical tongue-mid position and (ii) of the horizontal tongue-mid position synchronized at the time of the lip-aperture minimum obtained in B.7. (NB: the horizontal movement of the tongue-mid sensor is in **tm_posy**; and lower values obtained from the horizontal movement of sensors denote more forward, anterior positions towards the lips.)

C. The following question is concerned with the production differences between the diphthongs [aʊ] and [aɪ] in the first syllables respectively of *Klausur/Claudia* and *Kneipe/Kneipier*.

C.1 Make a boxplot of F2 (second formant frequency) at the time of the jaw-height minimum (see A.5) separately for each diphthong (i.e., there should be one boxplot for [aʊ] and one for [aɪ]).

C.2 Why might either tongue backing or a decreased lip aperture contribute to the tendency for F2 to be lower in [aʊ] at the time point in C.1? Make ellipse plots separately for the two diphthong categories with the horizontal position of the tongue-mid sensor on the *x*-axis and the lip aperture (as defined in B.4) on the *y*-axis, and with both of these parameters extracted at the time of the jaw-height minimum identified in C.1. To what extent might these data explain the lower F2 in [aʊ]?

D. This question is about the relationship between jaw height and duration in the first syllable of the words *Kneipe* and *Kneipier*.

D.1 *Kneipe* has primary lexical stress on the first syllable, but *Kneipier* has it on the last. It is possible that these lexical-stress differences are associated with a greater duration in the first syllable of *Kneipe* than that of *Kneipier*. Make a segment list of these words between the time of maximum tongue-tip raising in /n/ and the time of minimum lip aperture in /p/. (The way to do this is to make use of the segment list of the **lower** annotations for these words at the **TT** tier, and then to replace its third column, i.e., the end times, with **p.mintime** obtained in B.5.) Before you make this change, use **emu.requery()** to obtain a parallel vector of word labels (so that each segment can be identified as *Kneipe* or *Kneipier*).

D.2 Calculate the mean duration of the interval defined by the segment list in D.1 separately for *Kneipe* and *Kneipier*.

D.3 If there is less time available for a phonetic segment or for a syllable to be produced, then one possibility according to Lindblom (1963) is that the target is undershot, i.e., not attained. If this production strategy is characteristic of the shorter first syllable in *Kneipier*, then how would you expect the jaw position as a function of time over this interval to differ between these two words? Check your predictions by making an ensemble plot of the position of the jaw height color-coded according to these two words.

D.4 Derive by central differencing from D.3 a trackdata object **vz** of the velocity of jaw height over this interval.

D.5 Use **emu.track()** to make a trackdata object of the *horizontal* position of the jaw (**jw_posy**) over this interval and derive the velocity of horizontal jaw movement, **vy**, from this trackdata object.

D.6 The *tangential velocity* in some analyses of EMA data is the rate of change of the Euclidean distance in the plane of vertical and horizontal movement which can be defined by:

$$(7) \quad \sqrt{v_z^2 + v_y^2}$$

in which v_z is the velocity of vertical movement (i.e., the trackdata object in D.4 for this example) and v_y the velocity of horizontal movement (the trackdata object in D.5). Derive the tangential velocity for these jaw-movement data and make an ensemble plot of the tangential velocity averaged and color-coded for the two word categories (i.e., one tangential velocity trajectory as a function of time averaged across all tokens of *Kneipe* and another superimposed tangential velocity trajectory averaged across all tokens of *Kneipier*).

5.8 Answers

A.2

```
vow = emu.requery(k.s, "Segment", "Segment", seq=3)
vow.fm = emu.track(vow, "fm")
```

A.3

```
word.l = emu.requery(vow, "Segment", "Word", j=T)
```

A.4

```
vow.jaw = emu.track(vow, "jw_posz")
```

A.5

```
jawmin = trapply(vow.jaw, peakfun, F, simplify=T)
```

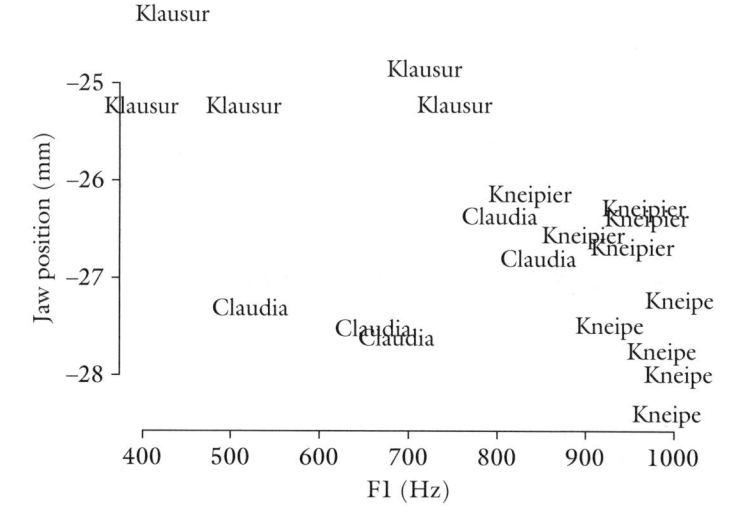

Figure 5.19 Jaw position as a function of the first formant frequency at the time of the lowest jaw position in two diphthongs showing the corresponding word label at the points.

A.6

```
dplot(vow.jaw, label(vow), offset=jawmin, prop=F)
```

A.7

```
f1 = dcut(vow.fm[,1], jawmin)
jaw = dcut(vow.jaw, jawmin)
```

A.8

Figure 5.19 shows that the variables are related: in very general terms, lower jaw positions are associated with higher F1 values. The (negative) correlation is, of course, far from perfect (in fact, −0.597 and significant, as given by **cor.test(f1, jaw)**).

B.1

```
p.s = emu.query("ema5", "*", "[Segment = p ^ Word=Kneipe | Kneipier]")
```

B.2

```
pword.l = emu.requery(p.s, "Segment", "Word", j=T)
```

B.3

```
p.ll = emu.track(p.s, "ll_posz")
p.ul = emu.track(p.s, "ul_posz")
```

B.4

```
p.ap = p.ul - p.ll
```

B.5

```
p.mintime = trapply(p.ap, peakfun, F, simplify=T)
```

B.6

```
dplot(p.ap, pword.1, offset=p.mintime, prop=F)
```

B.7

```
prop = (p.mintime-start(p.s))/dur(p.s)
tapply(prop, pword.1, mean)
 Kneipe  Kneipier
 0.3429   0.2607
```

B.8 You would expect the tongue-mid position to be higher and fronter in *Kneipier* due to the influence of the preceding and following palatal segments and this is supported by the evidence in Figure 5.20.[11]

```
p.tmvertical = emu.track(p.s, "tm_posz")
p.tmhorz = emu.track(p.s, "tm_posy")
par(mfrow=c(1,2))
dplot(p.tmvertical, pword.1, offset=p.mintime, prop=F,
ylab="Vertical position (mm)", xlab="Time (ms)", legend=F)
```

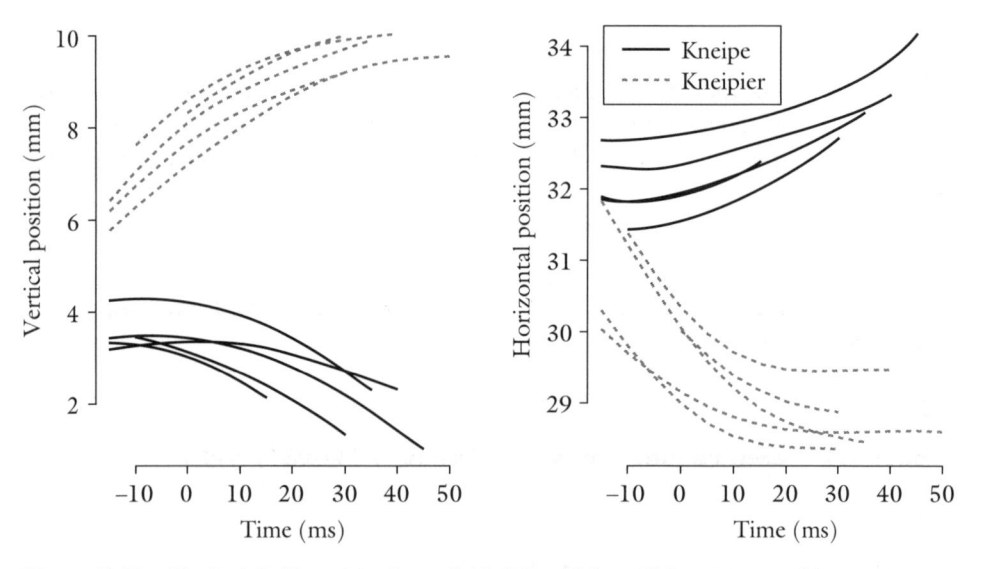

Figure 5.20 Vertical (left) and horizontal (right) position of the tongue-mid sensor over the interval of the acoustic closure of [p] synchronized at the time of the lip-aperture minimum in *Kneipe* (black) and *Kneipier* (dashed, gray).

```
dplot(p.tmhorz, pword.1, offset=p.mintime, prop=F,
ylab="Horizontal position (mm)", xlab="Time (ms)",
legend="topleft")
```

C.1

```
f2jaw = dcut(vow.fm[,2], jawmin)
boxplot(f2jaw ~ label(vow))
```

C.2

```
vow.tmhor = emu.track(vow, "tm_posy")
vow.ul = emu.track(vow, "ul_posz")
vow.ll = emu.track(vow, "ll_posz")
vow.ap = vow.ul - vow.ll
tongue = dcut(vow.tmhor, jawmin)
ap = dcut(vow.ap, jawmin)
d = cbind(tongue, ap)
eplot(d, label(vow), dopoints=T, xlab="Horizontal tongue
position (mm)", ylab="Lip aperture (mm)")
```

Overall, there is evidence from Figure 5.22 of a more retracted tongue position or decreased lip aperture at the jaw-height minimum in [aʊ], which could be due to the phonetically back and rounded second component of this diphthong. Either of these factors is likely to be associated with the observed lower F2 in Figure 5.21. In addition, Figure 5.22 shows that [aʊ] seems to cluster into two groups and these are probably tokens from the two words *Claudia* and *Klausur*. Thus, the data show either that the lip aperture in [aʊ] is less than in [aɪ] (for the cluster of points

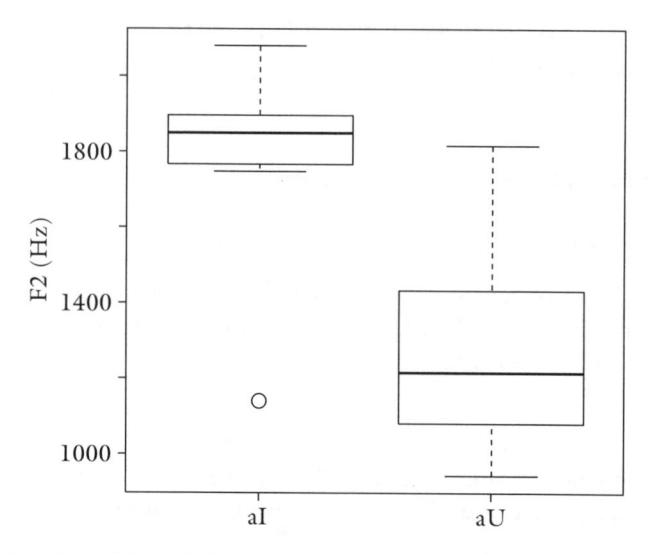

Figure 5.21 Boxplot of F2 in [aɪ] and [aʊ] at the time of the lowest position of the jaw in these diphthongs.

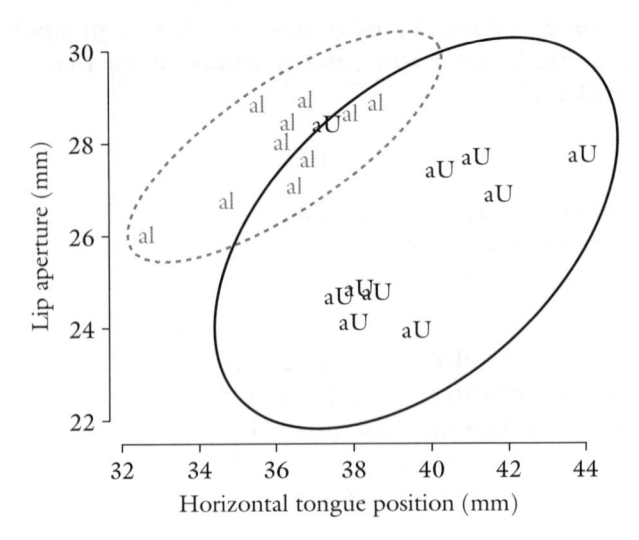

Figure 5.22 95% confidence ellipses for two diphthongs in the plane of the horizontal position of the tongue-mid sensor and lip aperture with both parameters extracted at the time of the lowest vertical jaw position in the diphthongs. Lower values on the *x*-axis correspond to positions nearer to the lips. The lip aperture is defined as the difference in position between the upper- and lower-lip sensors.

around 24 mm on the *y*-axis) or that the tongue is retracted (for the points around 27–8 mm on the *y*-axis) relative to [aɪ] (but not both).

D.1

```
syll.s = emu.query("ema5", "*", "[TT = lower ^ Word = Kneipe |
Kneipier]")
word.l = emu.requery(syll.s, "TT", "Word", j=T)
syll.s[,3] = p.mintime
```

D.2

```
tapply(dur(syll.s), word.l, mean)
  Kneipe    Kneipier
201.6592    161.0630
```

Yes: the first syllable of *Kneipier*, where syllable is defined as the interval between tongue-tip raising in /n/ and the point of minimum lip aperture in /p/, is some 40 ms less than that of *Kneipe*.

D.3

```
syll.jaw = emu.track(syll.s, "jw_posz")
dplot(syll.jaw, word.l, ylab="Position (mm)")
```

There does seem to be evidence for target undershoot of vertical jaw movement, as Figure 5.23 suggests.

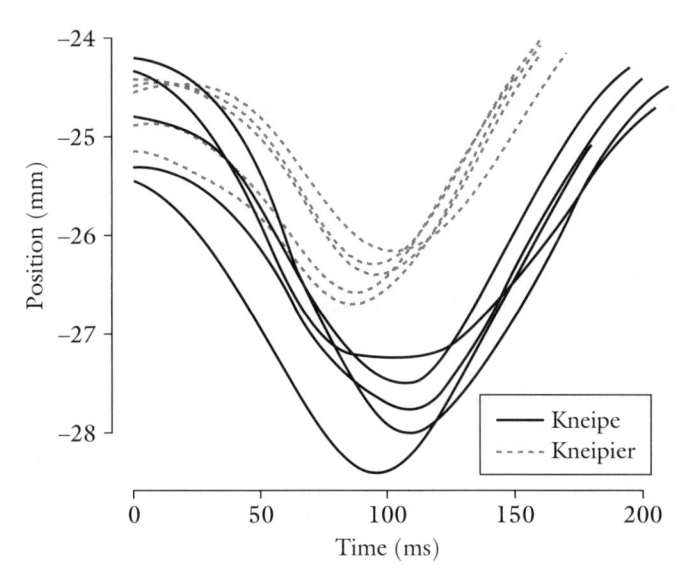

Figure 5.23 Jaw-height trajectories over the interval between the maximum point of tongue-tip raising in /n/ and the minimum jaw aperture in /p/ for *Kneipe* (solid) and *Kneipier* (gray, dashed).

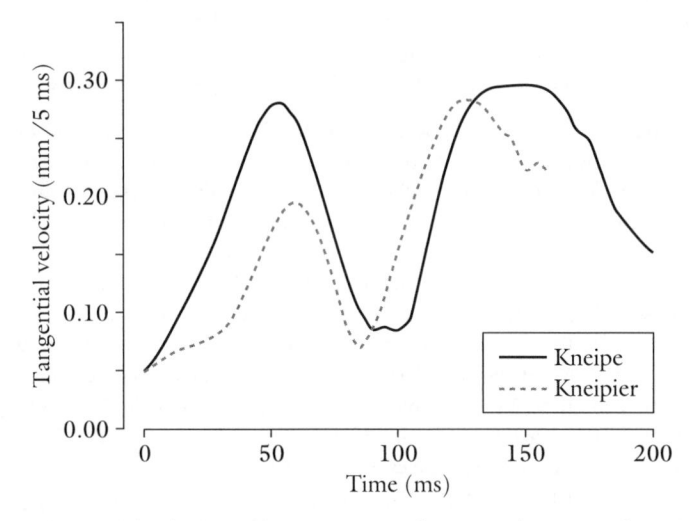

Figure 5.24 Tangential velocity of jaw movement between the time of maximum tongue-tip raising in /n/ and the lip-aperture minimum in /p/ averaged separately in *Kneipe* (solid) and *Kneipier* (dashed, gray).

D.4

```
vz = trapply(syll.jaw, cendiff, returntrack=T)
```

D.5

```
syll.jawx = emu.track(syll.s, "jw_posy")
vy = trapply(syll.jawx, cendiff, returntrack=T)
```

D.6

```
tang = sqrt(vz^2 + vy^2)
dplot(tang, word.1, average=T, ylab="Tangential velocity
(mm/5 ms)", xlab="Time (ms)")
```

Notes

[1] See www.phonetik.uni-muenchen.de/~hoole/5d_examples.html for some examples.
[2] The script is **mat2ssff.m** and is available in the top directory of the downloadable **ema5** database.
[3] The term speech frame will be used henceforth for these data to distinguish them from a type of object in R known as a data frame.
[4] Both trackdata objects must be derived from the same segment list for **cbind()** to be used in this way.
[5] For the sake of brevity, I will not always include the various options (see **help(par)**) that can be included in the plotting function and that were needed for camera-ready black-and-white images in this book. Thus Figure 5.10 was actually produced as follows:

```
par(mfrow=c(1,2)); lwd=lty=c(1,2); col=c(1, "slategray")
xlab = "Time (ms)"; ylab="Vertical tongue tip position (mm)"
dplot(tip.tt, son.lab, prop=F, offset=end(tbraise.s), bty="n",
ylab=ylab, xlab=xlab, col=col, lwd=lwd, lty=lty)
dplot(tip.tt, son.lab, prop=F, offset=end(tbraise.s), average=T,
bty="n", xlab=xlab, col=col, lwd=lwd, lty=lty, legend=F)
```

[6] The velocity signals are also available in the same directory to which the **ema5** database was downloaded, although they have not been incorporated into the template file. They could be used to find peaks and troughs in the movement signals, as described in section 5.5.2.
[7] This is because three-point central differencing is the average of the forward and backward difference. For example, suppose there is a signal **x = c(1, 3, 4)**. At time point 2, the forward difference is **x[2] - x[1]** and the backward difference is **x[3] - x[2]**. The average of these is **0.5 * (x[2] - x[1] + x[3] - x[2])** or **0.5 * (x[3]-x[1])** or 1.5. At time point 1, the three-point central difference would therefore be **0.5 * (x[2] - x[0])**. But this gives **numeric(0)** or **NA** because **x[0]** is undefined (there is no sample value preceding **x[1]**). At time point 3, the output of **0.5 * (x[4]-x[2])** is **NA** for the same reason that **x[4]** is undefined (the signal is of length 3). Consequently, **filter(x, c(0.5, 0, -0.5))** gives **NA 1.5 NA**.
[8] If you want to convert this to cm/s, then divide by 5 to get to ms, multiply by 1,000 to get to seconds, and divide by 10 to get to cm: the combined effect of these operations is that the trackdata object has to be multiplied by 20, which can be done with **body.tbd = body.tbd * 20**.
[9] My thanks to Elliot Saltzman for assistance in relating (3) to (4).
[10] The units are not important for this example but, in fact, if the sampling frequency **fs** is defined, then the natural frequency is **w * fs/(2 * pi)** Hz (see e.g., Harrington & Cassidy 1999, p. 160). Thus, if the default of 100 points in the **critdamp()** function is assumed to take up 1 s (i.e., **fs = 100** Hz), then the default **w = 0.05** has a frequency in Hz of **0.05 * 100/(2 * pi)**, i.e., just under 0.8 Hz.
[11] The following additional plotting parameters were used: **col=c(1, "slategray")**, **lwd=c(1,2)**, **lty=c(1,2)**, **bty="n"**.

6

Analysis of Formants and Formant Transitions

The aim of this chapter is to extend some of the techniques presented in Chapter 3 for the analysis of formant frequencies as well as some methods for analyzing the way in which formants change in time. The discussion is centered predominantly on vowels and the type of acoustic information that is available for distinguishing between them. Sections 6.1 to 6.3 are for the most part concerned with representing vowels in terms of their first two formant frequencies extracted at the vowel targets. A technique known as **kmeans clustering** for assessing the influence of context is briefly reviewed as well as some methods for locating vowel targets automatically from vowel-formant data. Outliers that can arise as a result of formant-tracking errors are discussed, as well as methods for removing them.

As is well known, the formants of the same phonetic vowel vary not only because of context, but also due to speaker differences, and in 6.4 some techniques of vowel normalization are applied to some vowel data in order to determine how far they reduce the different formant characteristics of male and female vowels.

The final sections of this chapter deal with vowel reduction, undershoot, and coarticulatory influences. In 6.5, some metrics for measuring the Euclidean distance are introduced and applied to determining the expansion of the vowel space relative to its center: this method is especially relevant for modeling the relationship between vowel positions and vowel hyperarticulation (see e.g., Moon & Lindblom 1994; Wright 2003). But Euclidean distance measurements can also be used to assess how close one vowel space is to another and this is found to have an application in quantifying sound change that is relevant for sociolinguistic investigations.

Whereas all the techniques in 6.1–6.5 are static, in the sense that they rely on applying analyses to formants extracted at a single point in time, in section 6.6 the focus is on the shape of the entire formant movement **as a function of time**. In this section, the coefficients of the parabola fitted to a formant are used both for quantifying vowel undershoot and also for smoothing formant frequencies. Finally, the concern in section 6.7 is with the second formant frequency transition as a cue to the place of the articulation of consonants and the way that so-called **locus equations** can be used to measure the coarticulatory influence of a vowel on a preceding or following consonant.

6.1 Vowel Ellipses in the F2 × F1 Plane

There is extensive evidence going back to the nineteenth and early part of the twentieth century that vowel-quality distinctions depend on the first two, or first three, resonances of the vocal tract (see Ladefoged 1967 and Traunmüller & Lacerda 1987 for reviews). Since the first formant frequency is negatively correlated with phonetic vowel height, and since F2 is correlated with vowel backness, then a shape resembling the vowel quadrilateral emerges by plotting vowels in the (decreasing) F1 × F2 plane. Essner (1947) and Joos (1948) were amongst the first to demonstrate this relationship and, since then, many different kinds of experimental studies have shown that this space is important for making judgments of vowel quality (see e.g., Harrington & Cassidy 1999, pp. 60–78).

The first task will be to examine some formant data from a male speaker of Standard German using some objects from the **vowlax** dataset stored in the Emu-R library:[1]

vowlax	Segment list of four German lax vowels
vowlax.fdat	Trackdata object of F1–F4
vowlax.l	Vector of parallel vowel labels
vowlax.left	Vector of labels of the segments preceding the vowels
vowlax.right	Vector of labels of the segments following the vowels
vowlax.spkr	Vector of speaker labels
vowlax.word	Vector of word labels for the vowel

The dataset includes the vowels **I, E, O, a** from two speakers of Standard German, one male (speaker 67) and one female (speaker 68) who each produced the same 100 read sentences from the Kiel Corpus of Read Speech (the data are in the downloadable **kielread** database). In the following, a logical vector is used to extract the data from the above for the male speaker:

`temp = vowlax.spkr == "67"`	Logical vector – True for speaker 67
`m.fdat = vowlax.fdat[temp,]`	Formant data
`m.s = vowlax[temp,]`	Segment list
`m.l = vowlax.l[temp]`	Vowel labels
`m.left = vowlax.left[temp]`	Left context
`m.right = vowlax.right[temp]`	Right context
`m.word = vowlax.word[temp]`	Word labels

In plotting vowels in the F1 × F2 plane, a decision has to be made about the time point from which the data are to be extracted. Usually, the extraction point should be at or near the **vowel target**, which can be considered to be the point in the vowel at which the formants are least influenced by context and/or where the formants change minimally in time (Chapter 3, Figure 3.2). Some issues to do with the vowel target are discussed in 6.3. For the present, the target is taken to be at the temporal midpoint of the vowel, on the assumption that this is usually the time point nearest to which the target occurs (Figure 6.1):

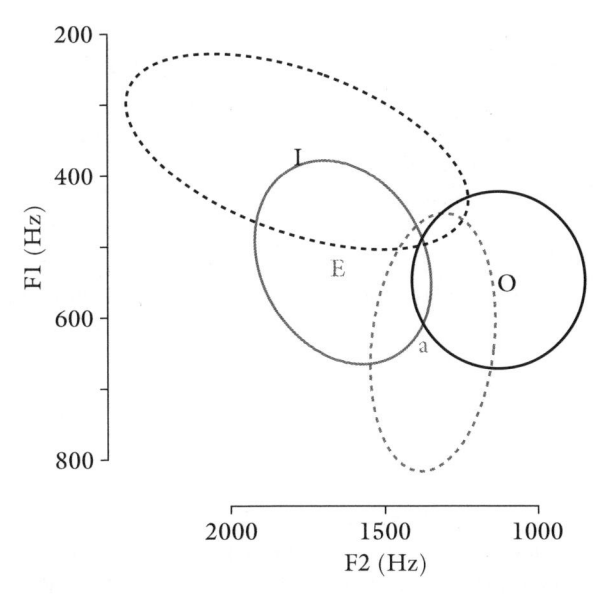

Figure 6.1 95% ellipse contours for F1 × F2 data extracted from the temporal midpoint of four German lax vowels produced by one speaker.

```
m.fdat.5 = dcut(m.fdat, .5, prop=T)
eplot(m.fdat.5[,1:2], m.l, centroid=T, form=T, xlab="F2
(Hz)", ylab="F1 (Hz)")
```

Note that in using **eplot()**, the number of rows of data must be the same as the number of elements in the parallel label vector. This can be checked as follows:

```
nrow(m.fdat.5[,1:2]) == length(m.l)
[1] TRUE
```

The **centroid=T** argument displays the means of the distributions using the corresponding character label; and, as discussed in Chapter 3, the **form=T** argument rotates the space so that the *x*-axis has decreasing F2 and the *y*-axis decreasing F1 as a result of which the vowels are positioned analogously to the phonetic backness and height axes of the vowel quadrilateral. As discussed in more detail in connection with probabilistic classification in Chapter 9, an ellipse is a contour of equal probability. In the default implementation of the **eplot()** function, each ellipse includes at least 95 percent of the data points corresponding to just under 2.45 ellipse standard deviations.

Those researchers who tend not to look very much at data from continuous speech may find the extent of overlap between vowels shown in Figure 6.1 quite alarming because in laboratory speech of isolated word data, the ellipses of one speaker are usually quite well separated. The overlap arises, in part, because vowel targets in continuous speech are affected by different contexts and prosodic factors. It might be helpful then to look at [I] in further detail according to the left context (Figure 6.2):

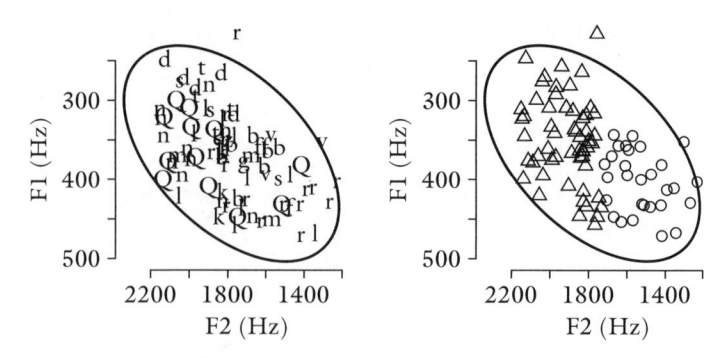

Figure 6.2 Left: the [I] ellipse from Figure 6.1 with the left-context labels superimposed on the data points. Right: the same data partitioned into two clusters using kmeans clustering.

```
temp = m.l== »I» ; par(mfrow=c(1,2))
eplot(m.fdat.5[temp,1:2], m.l[temp],m.left[temp],
dopoints=T, form=T, xlab="F2 (Hz)", ylab="F1 (Hz)")
```

There is not an immediately obvious pattern to the data in Figure 6.2 and nor can one be reasonably expected, given that it does not take account of some other variables, especially of the right context. Nevertheless, when the preceding context is alveolar, it does seem that [I] is mostly positioned in the top left of the display with low F1 and high F2. There are also a number of Q labels with a high F2: these denote vowels that are preceded by a glottal stop, i.e., syllable or word-initial [ʔI] (vowels in a domain-initial position in German are usually glottalized).

The technique of **kmeans clustering** can be applied to the data to give an indication of whether the variability is affected by different types of context. This technique partitions the data into k different clusters in such a way that the distance from the data points to the centroids (means) of the derived clusters of which they are members is minimized. An example of how this algorithm works is shown for 10 data points (those in `bridge[1:10,1:2]`) which are divided into two clusters. Initially, a guess is made of two means shown by X_1 and Y_1 in the left panel of Figure 6.3. Then the straight-line (Euclidean) distance is calculated from each point to each of these two means (i.e., two distance calculations per point) and each point is classified depending on which of these two distances is shortest. The results of this initial classification are shown in the central panel of the same figure: thus the four values at the bottom of the central panel are labeled x because their distance is less to X_1 than to Y_1. Then the centroid (mean value on both dimensions) is calculated separately for the points labeled x and those labeled y: these are shown as X_2 and Y_2 in the middle panel. The same step as before is repeated in which two distances are calculated from each point to X_2 and Y_2 and then the points are reclassified depending on which of the two distances is the shortest. The results of this reclassification (right panel, Figure 6.3) show that two additional points are labeled x because these are nearer to X_2 than to Y_2. The means of these new classes are X_3 and Y_3 and, since there is no further shift in the

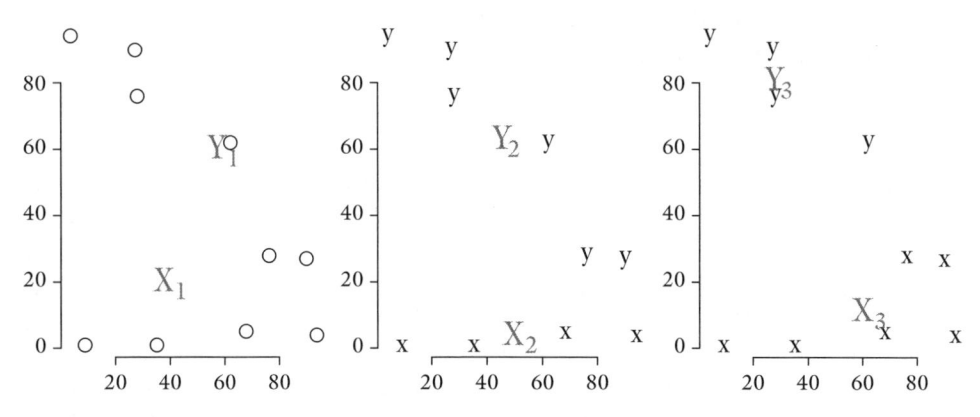

Analysis of Formants and Formant Transitions 175

Figure 6.3 An illustration of the steps in kmeans clustering for 10 points in two dimensions. X_1 and Y_1 in the left panel are the initial guesses of the means of the two classes. *x* and *y* in the middle panel are the same points classified based on whichever Euclidean distance to X_1 and Y_1 is least. In the middle panel, X_2 and Y_2 are the means (centroids) of the points classified as *x* and *y*. In the right panel, *x* and *y* are derived by reclassifying the points based on the shortest Euclidean distance to X_2 and Y_2. The means of these two classes in the right panel are X_3 and Y_3.

derived means by making the same calculations again, these are the final means and final classifications of the points. They are also the ones that are given by **kmeans(bridge[1:10,1:2], 2)**.

When kmeans clustering is applied to the [I] data shown in the left panel of Figure 6.2, the result is a split of the data into two classes, as the right panel of the same figure shows. This figure was produced with the following commands:

```
temp = m.l=="I"
k = kmeans(m.fdat.5[temp,1:2], 2)
eplot(m.fdat.5[temp,1:2], m.l[temp], k$cluster, dopoints=T,
form=T, xlab="F2 (Hz)", ylab="F1 (Hz)")
```

As is apparent from the right panel of Figure 6.2, the algorithm has split the data according to whether F2 is less, or greater, than roughly 1,800 Hz. We can see whether this also partitions the data along the lines of the left context as follows:

```
temp = m.l == "I"
# Left context preceding [I]
m.left.I = m.left[temp]

# Left context preceding [I] in cluster 1 (the circles in Figure 6.2, right panel)
temp = k$cluster==1
table(m.left.I[temp])
 Q  b  d  k  l  m  n  r  s  t  z
10  3  6  3 10  1 10  6  2  4  1
```

```
# Left context preceding [ɪ] in cluster 2
table(m.left.I[!temp])
Q b f g l m n r s v
2 4 3 1 3 2 1 9 1 3
```

So, as these results and the right panel of Figure 6.2 show, cluster 1 (the circles in Figure 6.2) includes all of [d, t], 10 / 11 of [n] and 10 / 12 [ʔ] ("Q"). Cluster 2 tends to include more contexts like [ʁ] ("r") and labials (there are more [b, f, m, v] in cluster 2 that, for reasons to do with their low F2 locus, are likely to have a lowering effect on F2).

Thus the left context obviously has an effect on F2 at the formant midpoint of [ɪ]. Just how much of an effect can be seen by plotting the entire F2 trajectory between the vowel onset and vowel midpoint for two left contexts that fall predominantly in cluster 1 and cluster 2 respectively. Here is such a plot comparing the left contexts [ʔ] with the labiodentals [f, v] (Figure 6.4):

```
# Logical vector that is True when the left context of [ɪ] is one of [ʔ, f, v]
temp = m.l == "I" & m.left %in% c("Q", "f", "v")

# The next two lines relabel "f" and "v" to a single category "LAB"
lab = m.left[temp]
lab[lab %in% c("f", "v")] = "LAB"
dplot(m.fdat[temp,2], lab, ylab="F2 (Hz)", xlab="Duration
(ms)")
```

Apart from two [ʔɪ] trajectories, there is a separation in F2 throughout the vowel depending on whether the left context is [ʔ] or a labiodental fricative. But before these very clear F2 differences are attributed just to left context, the word label (and hence the right context) should also be checked. For example, for [ʔ]:

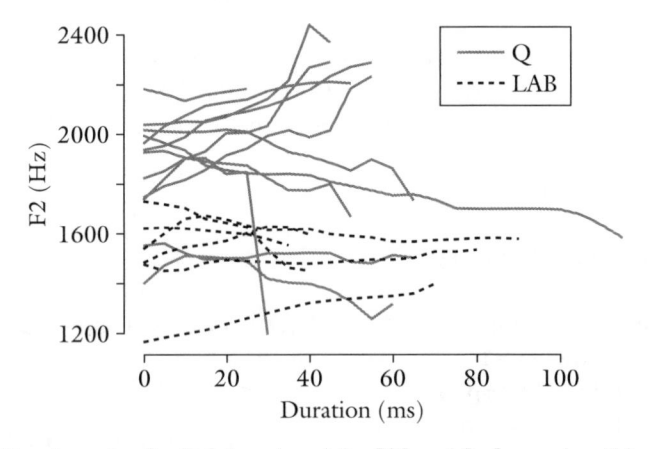

Figure 6.4 F2 trajectories for [ʔɪ] (gray) and for [fɪ] and [vɪ] together (black, dashed) synchronized at the temporal onset.

Analysis of Formants and Formant Transitions

```
table(vowlax.word[m.left=="Q" & m.l=="I"])
 ich  Ich   In  Inge  Iss  isst  ist
  4    4    2    4     2    2     6
```

So the words that begin with [ʔɪ] almost all have a right context which is likely to contribute to the high F2, i.e., [ç] in [ɪç] (*I*) or [s] in [ɪs], [ɪst] (*eat, is*): that is, the high F2 in [ʔɪ] is unlikely to be due just to left context alone.

6.2 Outliers

When a formant tracker is run over speech data in the manner described in Chapter 3, there will inevitably be errors due to formant tracking, especially for large speech corpora. Errors are especially common at the boundaries between voiceless and voiced segments and whenever two formants, such as F1 and F2 for back vowels, are close together in frequency. If such errors occur, then it is likely that they will show up as outliers in ellipse plots of the kind examined so far. If the outliers are far from the ellipse's center, then they can have quite a dramatic effect on the ellipse orientation.

Figure 6.5 shows two outliers from the [ɪ] vowels of the male speaker for the data extracted at the onset of the vowel:

```
# Speaker 67's [I] vowels
temp = vowlax.spkr=="67" & vowlax.l=="I"

# Segment list thereof
m.seg = vowlax[temp,]

# F1 and F2 at the segment onset
m.Ion = dcut(vowlax.fdat[temp,1:2], 0, prop=T)
```

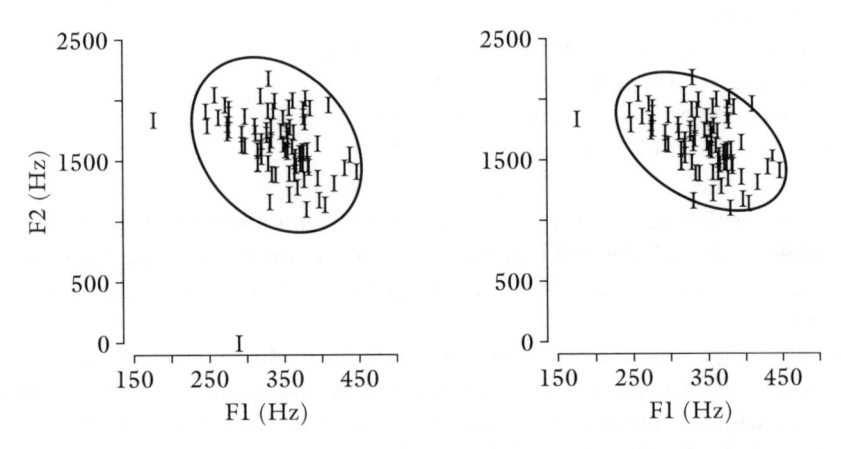

Figure 6.5 95% confidence intervals ellipses for [ɪ] vowels of speaker **67** at segment onset in the F1 × F2 plane before (left) and after (right) removing the outlier at F2 = 0 Hz.

```
# Set x- and y-ranges to compare two plots to the same scale
xlim = c(150,500); ylim =c(0,2500); par(mfrow=c(1,2))

# Ellipse plot with outliers
eplot(m.Ion, label(m.seg), dopoints=T, xlim=xlim,
ylim=ylim, xlab="F2 (Hz)", ylab="F1 (Hz)")
```

As the left panel of Figure 6.5 shows, there are two outliers: one of these is where F2 = 0 Hz at the bottom of the plot and is almost certainly due to a formant-tracking error. The other outlier has a very low F1 but it is not possible to conclude without looking at the spectrogram whether this is a formant error or the result of a context effect. The first of these outliers can, and should, be removed by identifying all values that have F2 less than a certain value, say 50 Hz. This can be done with a logical vector that is also passed to **eplot()** to produce the plot on the right without the outlier. The command in the first line is used to identify F2 values less than 50 Hz:

```
temp = m.Ion[,2] < 50
eplot(m.Ion[!temp,], label(m.seg[!temp,]),dopoints=T,
xlim=xlim, ylim=ylim, xlab="F2 (Hz)")
```

Because the outlier was a long way from the center of the distribution, its removal has shrunk the ellipse size and also changed its orientation slightly.

It is a nuisance to have to constantly remove outliers with logical vectors, so a better solution than the one in Figure 6.5 is to locate its utterance identifier and redraw the formant track by hand in the database from which these data were extracted (following the procedure in 3.1). The utterance in which the outlier occurs as well as its time stamp can be found by combining the logical vector with the segment list:

```
temp = m.Ion[,2] < 50
m.seg[temp,]
segment list from database: kielread
query was: Kanonic=a | E | I | O
    labels   start     end       utts
194   I     911.563  964.625   K67MR096
```

That is, the outlier occurs somewhere between 911 ms and 964 ms in the utterance **K67MR096** of the **kielread** database. The corresponding spectrogram shows that the outlier is very clearly a formant-tracking error that can be manually corrected as in Figure 6.6.

Manually correcting outliers when they are obviously due to formant-tracking errors as in Figure 6.6 is necessary. But this method should definitely be used sparingly: the more manual intervention is used, the greater the risk that the researcher might unwittingly bias the experimental data.

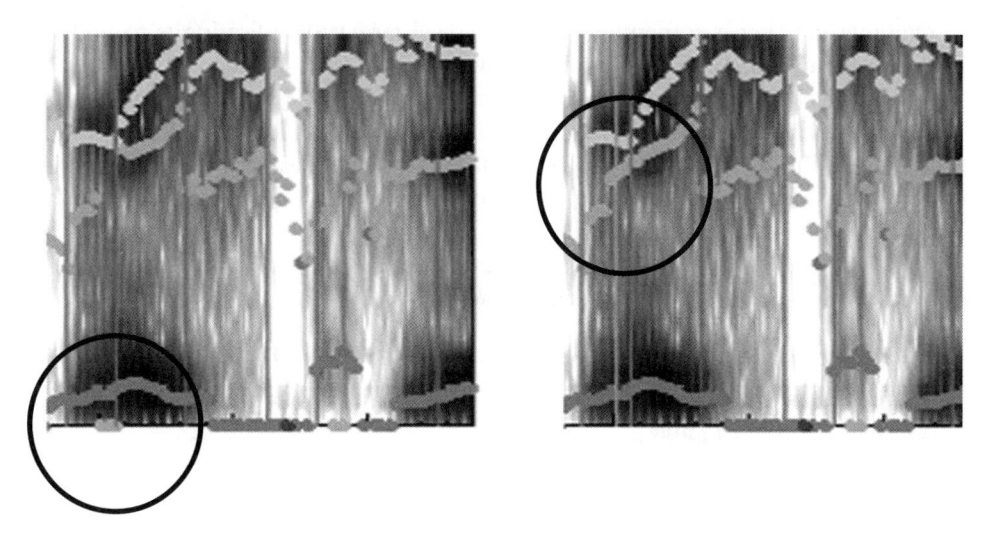

Figure 6.6 Spectrogram (0–3,000 Hz) from the utterance K67MR096 showing an [ɪ] vowel with superimposed F1–F3 tracks; the miscalculated F2 values are redrawn on the right. The redrawn values can be saved – which has the effect of overwriting the signal file data containing the formant track for that utterance permanently. See Chapter 3 for further details.

6.3 Vowel Targets

As discussed earlier, the vowel target can be considered to be the section of the vowel that is least influenced by consonantal context and most similar to a citation-form production of the same vowel. It is also sometimes defined as the most **steady-state** part of the vowel: that is, the section of the vowel during which the formants (and hence the phonetic quality) change minimally (see e.g., Broad & Wakita 1977; Schouten & Pols 1979). It is, however, not always the case that the vowel target is at the temporal midpoint. For example, in most accents of Australian English, in particular the broad variety, the targets of the long high vowels in *heed* and *who'd* occur late in the vowel and are preceded by a long onglide (Cox & Palethorpe 2007). Apart from factors such as these, the vowel target could shift proportionally because of coarticulation. For example, Harrington et al. (1995) present articulatory data showing that, in prosodically unaccented vowels (that is those produced without sentence stress), the final consonant is timed to occur earlier in the vowel than in prosodically accented vowels (with sentence stress). If the difference between the production of accented and unaccented vowels has an influence on the final transition in the vowel, then the effect would be that the vowel target occurs proportionally somewhat later in the same word when it is unaccented. For reasons such as these, the vowel target cannot always be assumed to be at the temporal midpoint. At the same time, some studies have found that different strategies for locating the vowel target have not made a great deal of difference to classifying vowels from formant data (see e.g., van Son & Pols 1990 who compared three different methods for vowel target identification in Dutch).

One method that is sometimes used for vowel target identification is to find **the time point at which the F1 is at a maximum**. This is based on the idea that vowels reach their targets when the oral tract is maximally open, which often coincides with an F1 maximum, at least in non-high vowels (Lindblom & Sundberg 1971). The time of the F1 maximum can be obtained using the same function for finding the first maximum or minimum in the speech frames of a single segment presented in 5.5.2. Here is the function again:

```
peakfun <- function(fr, maxtime=T)
{
if(maxtime) num = which.max(fr)
else num = which.min(fr)
tracktimes(fr)[num]
}
```

Following the procedure discussed in 5.5.2, the time at which F1 reaches a maximum in the fifth segment of the trackdata object **m.fdat** is:

```
peakfun(frames(m.fdat[5,1]))
2117.5
```

Since the function can evidently be applied to speech frames, then it can be used inside the **trapply()** function to find the time of the F1 maximum in all segments. However, it might be an idea to constrain the times within which the F1 maximum is to be found, perhaps by excluding the first and last 25 percent of each vowel from consideration, given that these intervals are substantially influenced by the left and right contexts. This can be done, as discussed in 5.5.3 of the preceding chapter, using **dcut()**:

```
# Create a new trackdata object between the vowels' 25 percent and 75 percent
time points
m.fdat.int = dcut(m.fdat, .25, .75, prop=T)
```

```
# Get the times at which the F1 maximum first occurs in this interval
m.maxf1.t = trapply(m.fdat.int[,1], peakfun, simplify=T)
```

The calculated target times could be checked by plotting the trackdata synchronized at these calculated target times (Figure 6.7, left panel):

```
# Logical vector to identify all [a] vowels
temp = m.l == "a"
```

```
# F1 and F2 of [a] synchronized at the F1-maximum time
dplot(m.fdat[temp,1:2], offset=m.maxf1.t[temp], prop=F,
ylab="F1 and F2 (Hz)", xlab="Duration (ms)")
```

The alignment can also be inspected segment by segment using a for-loop.

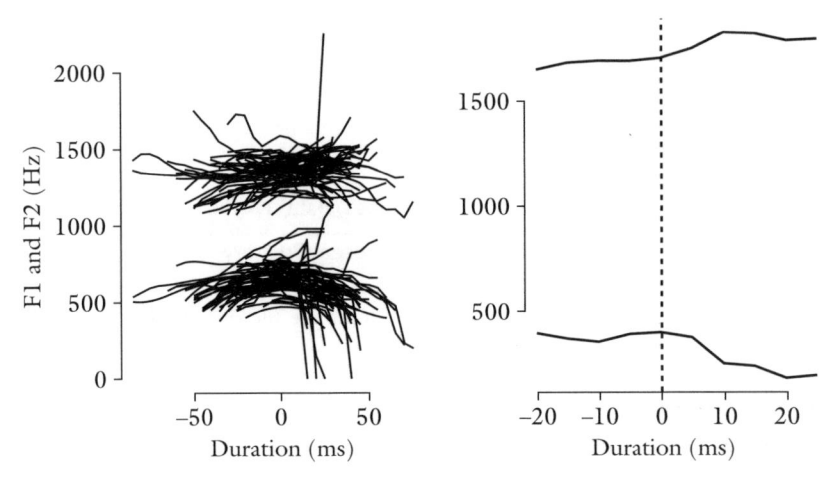

Figure 6.7 Left: F1 and F2 of [a] for a male speaker of standard German synchronized at time $t = 0$, the time of the F1 maximum. Right: F1 and F2 from segment onset to offset for an [a]. The vertical line marks the time within the middle 50% of the vowel at which F1 reaches a maximum.

```
# For the first five [a] segments separately . . .
for(j in 1:5){

# plot F1 and F2 as a function of time with the vowel label as the main title
dplot(m.fdat[temp,1:2][j,], main=m.l[temp][j], offset=
m.maxf1.t[temp][j], prop=F, ylab="F1 and F2 (Hz)")

# Draw a vertical line at the F1 maximum
abline(v = 0, col=2)

# Left button to advance
locator(1)
}
```

The result of the last iteration is shown in the right panel of Figure 6.7.

It will almost certainly be necessary to change some of these target times manually but this should be done in Praat or Emu, not in R. To do this, the vector of times needs to be exported so that the times are stored separately in different annotation files. The **makelab()** function can be used for this. The following writes out annotation files so that they can be loaded into Emu. You have to supply the name of the directory where you want all these annotation files to be stored as the third argument to **makelab()**.

```
path = "directory for storing annotation files"
makelab(m.maxf1.t, utt(m.s), path, labels="T")
```

This will create a number of files, one per utterance, in the specified directory. For example, a file **K67MR001.xlab** will be created that looks like this:

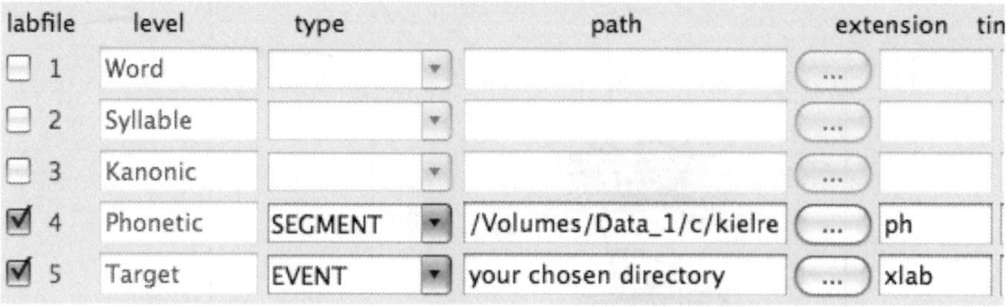

labfile	level	type	path	extension	tin
☐ 1	Word			...	
☐ 2	Syllable			...	
☐ 3	Kanonic			...	
☑ 4	Phonetic	SEGMENT	/Volumes/Data_1/c/kielre	...	ph
☑ 5	Target	EVENT	your chosen directory	...	xlab

Figure 6.8 The revised **labfiles** pane in the template file of the **kielread** database to include a new **Target** tier.

```
signal K67MR001
nfields 1
#
0.8975   125   T
1.1225   125   T
1.4775   125   T
1.6825   125   T
2.1175   125   T
```

The template file for the database **kielread** must now be edited in the manner described in 2.6 of Chapter 2 so that the database can find these new label files. In Figure 6.8, this is done by specifying a new level called **Target** that is (auto-segmentally) associated with the **Phonetic** tier:

As a result of modifying the template, the target times are visible and can be manipulated in either Emu or Praat.

The function **peakfun()**, which has so far been used to find the time at which the F1 maximum occurs, can also be used to find the time of the F1 minimum:

```
m.minf2.t = trapply(m.fdat.int[,2], peakfun, F, simplify=T)
```

What if you want to find the vowel target in a vowel-specific way – based on the F1 maximum for the open and half-open vowels [a, ɛ], on the F2 maximum for the mid-high vowel [ɪ], and on F2 minimum for the back-rounded vowel [ɔ]? In order to collect up the results so that the vector of target times is parallel to all the other objects, a logical vector could be created per vowel category and used to fill up the vector successively by vowel category. The commands for doing this and storing the result in the vector **times** are shown below:

```
# A vector of zeros the same length as the label vector (and trackdata object)
times = rep(0, length(m.l))

# Target times based on F2 max for [ɪ]
temp = m.l=="I"
times[temp] = trapply(m.fdat.int[temp,2], peakfun,
simplify=T)
```

```
# Target time based on F1 max for [a, ɛ]
temp = m.l %in% c("E", "a")
times[temp] = trapply(m.fdat.int[temp,1], peakfun,
simplify=T)

# Target time based on F2 min for [ɔ]
temp = m.l == "O"
times[temp] = trapply(m.fdat.int[temp,2], peakfun, F,
simplify=T)
```

6.4 Vowel Normalization

Much acoustic variation comes about because speakers have different sized and shaped vocal organs. This type of variation was demonstrated spectrographically in Peterson and Barney's (1952) classic study of vowels produced by men, women, and children and the extensive speaker-dependent overlap between formants was further investigated in Peterson (1961), Ladefoged (1967) and Pols et al. (1973) (see also Adank et al. 2004 for a more recent investigation).

The differences in the distribution of the vowels for the male speaker and female speaker can be examined once again with ellipse plots. These are shown together with the data points in Figure 6.9 and they were created with the following commands:

```
# Set the ranges for the x- and y-axes to plot two panels in one row and two
columns
xlim = c(800,2800) ; ylim = c(250, 1050) ; par(mfrow=c(1,2))

# Logical vector for identifying the male speaker; !temp is the female speaker
temp = vowlax.spkr=="67"
```

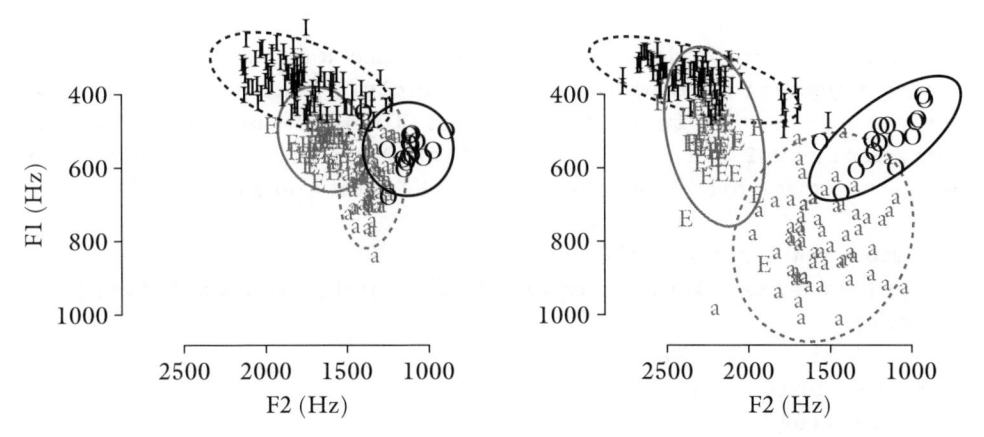

Figure 6.9 German lax monophthongs produced by a male (left) and a female (right) speaker in the F2 × F1 plane. Data extracted at the temporal midpoint of the vowel.

```
eplot(vowlax.fdat.5[temp,1:2], vowlax.l[temp], dopoints=T,
form=T, xlim=xlim, ylim=ylim, xlab="F2 (Hz)", ylab="F1 (Hz)")
eplot(vowlax.fdat.5[!temp,1:2], vowlax.l[!temp], dopoints=T,
form=T, xlim=xlim, ylim=ylim, xlab="F2 (Hz)", ylab="")
```

The differences are quite substantial, especially considering that these are speakers of the same Standard North German variety producing the same read sentences! The figure shows, in general, how the formants of the female speaker are higher in frequency than those of the male, which is to be expected because female vocal tracts are on average shorter. But, as argued in Fant (1966), because the ratio of the mouth cavity to the pharyngeal cavity lengths is different in male and female speakers, the changes to the vowels due to gender are *non-uniform*: this means that the male–female differences are greater in some vowels than others. Figure 6.9 shows that, whereas the differences between the speakers in [ɪ] are not that substantial, those between [a] on F1 and F2 are quite considerable. Also the F2 differences are much more marked than those in F1, as a comparison of the relative positions of [ɪ, ɛ] between the two speakers shows. Finally, the differences need not be the result entirely of anatomical and physiological differences between the speakers. Some differences may be as a result of speaking style: indeed, for the female speaker, there is a greater separation between [ɪ, ɛ] on the one hand and [ɔ, a] on the other than for the male speaker, and this may be because there is greater vowel hyperarticulation for this speaker – this issue will be taken up in more detail in the analysis of Euclidean distances in 6.5.

An overview of the main male–female vowel differences can be obtained by plotting a polygon that connects the means (centroids) of each vowel category for the separate speakers on the same axes. The first step is to get the speaker means. As discussed in 5.3, **tapply()** applies a function to a vector per category. So the F1 category means for speaker 67 are:

```
temp = vowlax.spkr=="67"
tapply(vowlax.fdat.5[temp,1], vowlax.l[temp], mean)
      a         E         I         O
635.9524  523.5610  367.1647  548.1875
```

However, in order to calculate these category means for a *matrix* of F1 and F2 vowels, **tapply()** could be used inside the **apply()** function. The basic syntax for applying a function, **fun()**, to the columns of a matrix is **apply(matrix, 2, fun, arg1, arg2 ... argn)** where **arg1, arg2 ... argn** are the arguments of the function that is to be applied. So the F1 and F2 category means for speaker 67 are:

```
temp = vowlax.spkr=="67"
apply(vowlax.fdat.5[temp,1:2], 2, tapply, vowlax.l[temp],
mean)
        T1          T2
E   523.5610   1641.073
I   367.1647   1781.329
O   548.1875   1127.000
a   635.9524   1347.254
```

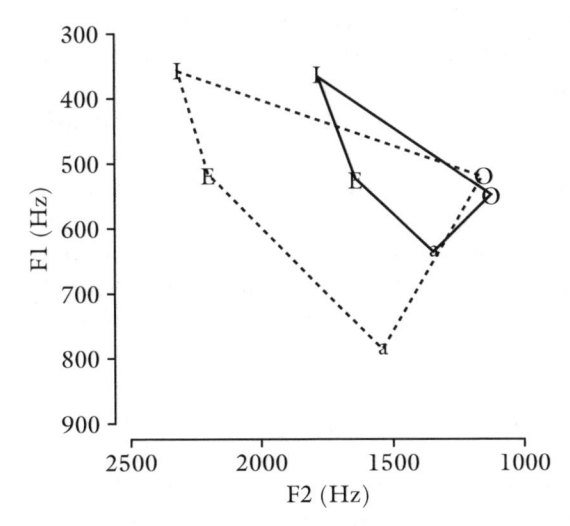

Figure 6.10 Mean F2 × F1 values for the male (solid) and female (dashed) data from Figure 6.9.

The desired polygon (Figure 6.10) could be plotted first by calling **eplot()** with **doellipse=F** (don't plot the ellipses) and then joining up these means using the **polygon()** function. The *x*- and *y*-ranges need to be set in the call to **eplot()**, in order to superimpose the corresponding polygon from the female speaker on the same axes:

```
xlim = c(1000, 2500); ylim = c(300, 900)
eplot(vowlax.fdat.5[temp,1:2], vowlax.l[temp], form=T,
xlim=xlim, ylim=ylim, doellipse=F, col=F, xlab="F2 (Hz)",
ylab="F1 (Hz)" )
m = apply(vowlax.fdat.5[temp,1:2], 2, tapply,
vowlax.l[temp], mean)

# Negate the mean values because this is a plot in the − F2 × − F1 plane
polygon(-m[,2], -m[,1])
```

Then, since the logical vector, **temp**, is **True** for the male speaker and **False** for the female speaker, the above instructions can be repeated with **!temp** for the corresponding plot for the female speaker. The line **par(new=T)** is for superimposing the second plot on the same axes and **lty=2** in the call to **polygon()** produces dashed lines:

```
par(new=T)
eplot(vowlax.fdat.5[!temp,1:2], vowlax.l[!temp], form=T,
xlim=xlim, ylim=ylim, doellipse=F, col=F, xlab="", ylab="")
m = apply(vowlax.fdat.5[!temp,1:2], 2, tapply,
vowlax.l[!temp], mean)
polygon(-m[,2], -m[,1], lty=2)
```

Strategies for vowel normalization are designed to reduce the extent of these divergences due to the speaker and they fall into two categories: **speaker-dependent** and **speaker-independent**. In the first of these, normalization can only be carried out using statistical data from the speaker **beyond the vowel that is to be normalized** (for this reason, speaker-dependent strategies are also called **extrinsic**, because information for normalization is extrinsic to the vowel that is to be normalized). In a speaker-independent strategy by contrast, all the information needed for normalizing a vowel is **within the vowel itself,** i.e., intrinsic to the vowel.

The idea that normalization might be extrinsic can be traced back to Joos (1948) who suggested that listeners judge the phonetic quality of a vowel in relation to a speaker's point vowels [i, a, u]. Some evidence in favor of extrinsic normalization is provided in Ladefoged and Broadbent (1957) who found that the listeners' perceptions of the vowel in the same test word shifted when the formant frequencies in a preceding carrier phrase were manipulated. On the other hand, there were also various perception experiments in the 1970s and 1980s showing that listeners' identifications of a speaker's vowels were not substantially improved if they were initially exposed to the same speaker's point vowels (Assmann et al. 1982; Verbrugge et al. 1976).

Whatever the arguments from studies of speech perception for or against extrinsic normalization (Johnson 2005), there is evidence to show that, when extrinsic normalization is applied to acoustic vowel data, the differences due to speakers can often be quite substantially reduced (see e.g., Disner 1980 for an evaluation of some extrinsic vowel-normalization procedures). A very basic and effective extrinsic normalization technique is to **transform the data to z-scores** by subtracting the speaker's mean and dividing by the speaker's standard deviation for each parameter separately. The technique was first used by Lobanov (1971) for vowels and so is sometimes called **Lobanov normalization**. The transformation has the effect of centering each speaker's vowel space at coordinates of zero (the mean); the axes are then the **number of standard deviations away from the speaker's mean**. So for a vector of values:

```
vec = c(-4, -9, -4, 7, 5, -7, 0, 3, 2, -3)
```

their Lobanov-normalized equivalents are:

```
(vec - mean(vec)) / sd(vec)
-0.5715006  -1.5240015  -0.5715006   1.5240015   1.1430011
-1.1430011   0.1905002   0.7620008   0.5715006  -0.3810004
```

A function that will carry out Lobanov normalization when applied to a vector is as follows:

```
lob <- function(x)
{

# transform x to z-scores (Lobanov normalization); x is a vector
(x - mean(x))/sd(x)
}
```

Thus **lob(vec)** gives the same results as above. But, since there is more than one parameter (F1, F2), the function needs to be applied to a matrix. As discussed earlier, **apply(matrix, 2, fun)** has the effect of applying a function, **fun()**, separately to the columns of a matrix. The required modifications can be accomplished as follows:

```
lobnorm <- function(x)
{

# transform x to z-scores (Lobanov normalization); x is a matrix
lob <- function(x)
{
(x - mean(x))/sd(x)
}
apply(x, 2, lob)
}
```

In **lobnorm()**, the function **lob()** is applied to each column of **x**. Thus, the Lobanov-normalized F1 and F2 for the male speaker are now:

```
temp = vowlax.spkr == "67"
norm67 = lobnorm(vowlax.fdat.5[temp,])
```

and those for the female speakers can be obtained with the inverse of the logical vector, i.e., **lobnorm(vowlax.fdat.5[!temp,])**. However, as discussed in 5.2, it is always a good idea to keep objects that belong together (segment list, trackdata, label files, matrices derived from trackdata, normalized data derived from such data, etc.) parallel to each other, as a result of which they can all be manipulated in relation to segments. Here is one way to do this:

```
# Set up a matrix of zeros with the same dimensions as the matrix to be
Lobanov-normalized
vow.norm.lob = matrix(0, nrow(vowlax.fdat.5),
ncol(vowlax.fdat.5))
temp = vowlax.spkr == "67"
vow.norm.lob[temp,] = lobnorm(vowlax.fdat.5[temp,])
vow.norm.lob[!temp,] = lobnorm(vowlax.fdat.5[!temp,])
```

The same effect can be achieved with a for-loop and, indeed, this is the preferred approach if there are several speakers whose data is to be normalized (but it works just the same when there are only two):

```
vow.norm.lob = matrix(0, nrow(vowlax.fdat.5),
ncol(vowlax.fdat.5))
for(j in unique(vowlax.spkr)){
temp = vowlax.spkr==j
vow.norm.lob[temp,] = lobnorm(vowlax.fdat.5[temp,])
}
```

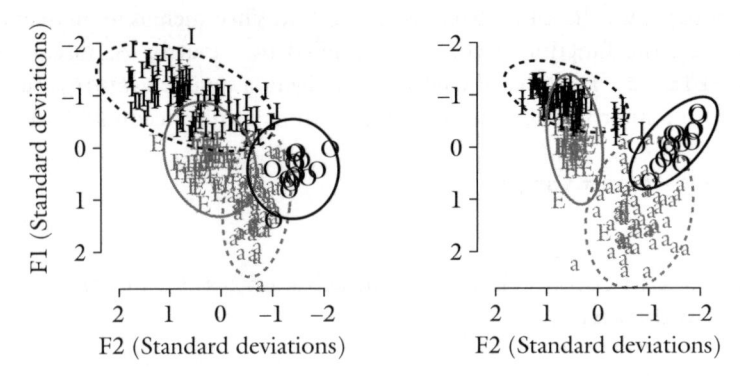

Figure 6.11 Lobanov-normalized F1 and F2 of the data in Figure 6.9. The axes are numbers of standard deviations from the mean.

Since **vow.norm.lob** is parallel to the vector of labels **vowlax.l**, then **eplot()** can be used in the same way as for the non-normalized data to plot ellipses (Figure 6.11).

```
xlim = ylim = c(-2.5, 2.5); par(mfrow=c(1,2))
temp = vowlax.spkr=="67"
eplot(vow.norm.lob[temp,1:2], vowlax.l[temp], dopoints=T,
form=T, xlim=xlim, ylim=ylim, xlab="F2 (normalized)",
ylab="F1 (normalized)")
eplot(vow.norm.lob[!temp,1:2], vowlax.l[!temp],
dopoints=T, form=T, xlim=xlim, ylim=ylim, xlab="F2
(normalized)", ylab="")
```

The point [0,0] in Figure 6.11 is the mean or **centroid** across all the data points per speaker and the axes are the numbers of standard deviations away from [0,0]. Compared with the raw data in Figure 6.9, it is clear enough that there is a much closer alignment between the vowel categories of the male and female speakers in these normalized data. For larger studies, the mean and standard deviation should be based on those of not just a handful of lax vowels, but a much wider selection of vowel categories.

Another extrinsic normalization technique is due to Nearey (see e.g., Assmann et al. 1982; Nearey 1989). The version demonstrated here is the one in which normalization is accomplished by subtracting a **speaker-dependent constant** from the logarithm of the formants. This speaker-dependent constant is obtained by working out (a) the mean of the logarithm of F1 (across all tokens for a given speaker) and (b) the mean of the logarithm of F2 (across the same tokens), and then averaging (a) and (b). An expression for the speaker-dependent constant in R is therefore **mean(apply(log(mat), 2, mean))**, where **mat** is a two-columned matrix of F1 and F2 values. So, for the male speaker, the speaker-dependent constant is:

```
temp = vowlax.spkr == "67"
mean(apply(log(vowlax.fdat.5[temp,1:2]), 2, mean))
6.755133
```

This value must now be subtracted from the logarithm of the raw formant values separately for each speaker. This can be done with a single-line function:

```
nearey <- function(x)
{
# Function for extrinsic normalization according to Nearey
# x is a two-columned matrix
log(x) - mean(apply(log(x), 2, mean))
}
```

Thus **nearey(vowlax.fdat.5[temp,1:2])** gives the Nearey-normalized formant (F1 and F2) data for the male speaker. The same methodology as for Lobanov-normalization above can be used to obtain Nearey-normalized data that is parallel to all the other objects – thereby allowing ellipse and polygon plots to be drawn in the F2 × F1 plane in the manner described earlier.

Lobanov and Nearey normalization are, then, two examples of speaker-dependent strategies that require data beyond the vowel that is to be normalized. In speaker-*independent* strategies all the information for normalization is supposed to be in the vowel itself. Earlier speaker-independent strategies made use of formant ratios (Peterson 1961; Potter & Steinberg 1950; see also Miller 1989) and they often copy some aspects of the auditory transformations to acoustic data that are known to take place in the ear (Bladon et al. 1984). These types of speaker-independent auditory transformations are based on the idea that two equivalent vowels, even if they are produced by different speakers, result in a similar pattern of motion along the basilar membrane, even if the actual position of the pattern varies (Potter & Steinberg 1950; see also Chiba & Kajiyama 1941). Since there is a direct correspondence between basilar membrane motion and a sound's frequency on a scale known as the **Bark scale**, a transformation to an auditory scale like the Bark scale (or ERB scale: see e.g., Glasberg & Moore 1990) is usually the starting point for speaker-independent normalization. Independently of these normalization issues, many researchers transform formant values from hertz to Bark before applying any further analysis, on the grounds that an analogous translation is presumed to be carried out in the ear.

There is a function **bark(x)** in the Emu-R library to carry out such a transformation, where **x** is a vector, matrix, or trackdata object of hertz values. (The same function with the **inv=T** argument converts Bark back into hertz.) The formulae for these transformations are given in Traunmüller (1990) and they are based on analyses by Zwicker (1961).

A graph of the relationship between the two scales (up to 10 kHz) with horizontal lines at intervals of 1 Bark superimposed on the Hz axis can be drawn as follows (Figure 6.12):

```
plot(0:10000, bark(0:10000), type="l", xlab="Frequency
(Hz)", ylab="Frequency (Bark)")
abline(v=bark(1:22, inv=T), lty=2)
```

Figure 6.12 shows that the interval corresponding to 1 Bark becomes progressively wider for values higher up the hertz scale (the Bark scale, like the Mel scale – Fant

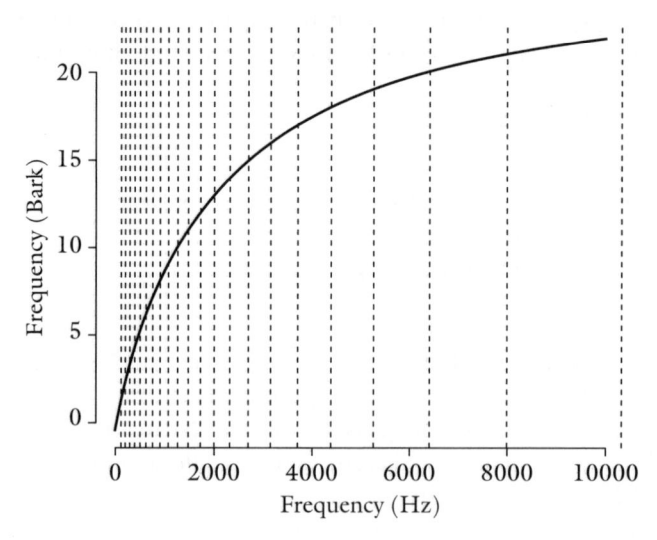

Figure 6.12 Relationship between the hertz and Bark scales. The vertical lines mark interval widths of 1 Bark.

1968 – is roughly linear up to 1 kHz and then quasi-logarithmic thereafter). Ellipse plots analogous to those in Figure 6.11 can be created by converting the matrix into Bark values (thus the first argument to **eplot()** for the male speaker is **bark(vowlax.fdat.5[temp,1:2])**) or else by leaving the values in Hz and adding the argument **scaling="bark"** in the **eplot()** function. A detailed exploration of Bark-scaled vowel formant data is given in Syrdal and Gopal (1986).

6.5 Euclidean Distances

6.5.1 Vowel-space expansion

Various studies in the last 50 years have been concerned with phonetic vowel reduction, that is with the changes in vowel quality brought about by segmental, prosodic, and situational contexts. In Lindblom's (1990) hyper- and hypoarticulation theory, speech production varies along a continuum from clear to less clear speech. According to this theory, speakers make as much effort to speak clearly as is required by the listener for understanding what is being said. Thus, the first time that a person's name is mentioned, the production is likely to be clear because this is largely unpredictable information for the listener; but subsequent productions of the same name in an ongoing dialogue are likely to be less clear, because the listener can more easily predict its occurrence from context (Fowler & Housum 1987).

A vowel that is spoken less clearly tends to be reduced, which means that there is a deviation from its position in an acoustic space relative to either a clear, or a citation-form production. The deviation is often manifested as **centralization**, in which the vowel is produced nearer to the center of the speaker's vowel space than in clear speech. Equivalently, in clear speech there is an **expansion of the vowel space**. There is articulatory evidence for this type of vowel-space expansion when vowels occur in

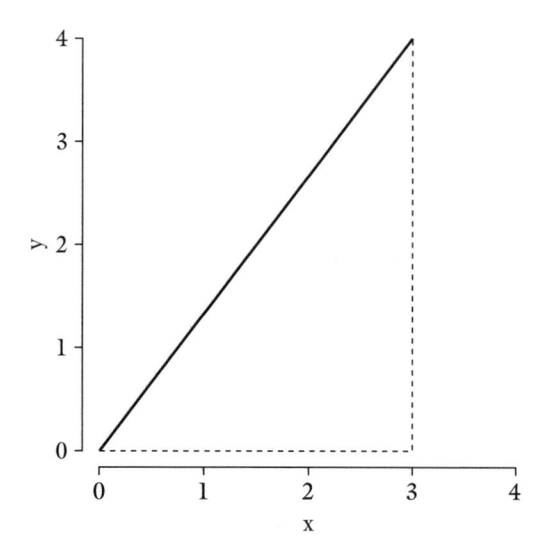

Figure 6.13 A 3–4–5 triangle. The length of the solid line is the Euclidean distance between the points (0, 0) and (3, 4). The dotted lines show the horizontal and vertical distances that are used for the Euclidean distance calculation.

prosodically accented words, often because these tend to be points of information focus, that is points of the utterance that are especially important for understanding what is being said (de Jong 1995; Harrington et al. 2000).

One of the ways of quantifying vowel-space expansion is to measure the Euclidean or straight-line distance between a vowel and the center of the vowel space. Wright (2003) used just such a measure to compare so-called *easy* and *hard* words on their distances to the center of the vowel space. Easy words are those that have high lexical frequency (i.e., occur often) and low neighborhood density (there are few words that are phonemically similar). Since such words tend to be easier for the listener to understand, then, applying Lindblom's (1990) model, the vowels should be more centralized compared with hard words which are both infrequent and high in neighborhood density.

In a two-dimensional space, the Euclidean distance is calculated by summing the square of the horizontal and vertical distances between the points and taking the square root. For example, the expressions in R for horizontal and vertical distances between the two points (0, 0) and (3, 4) in Figure 6.13 are **(0 - 3)^2** and **(0 - 4)^2** respectively. Thus the Euclidean distance between them is:

```
sqrt( (0 - 3)^2 + (0 - 4)^2 )
5
```

Because of the nice way that vectors work in R, the same result is given by:

```
a = c(0, 0)
b = c(3, 4)
sqrt( sum( (a - b)^2 ))
5
```

So a function to calculate the Euclidean distance between any two points **a** and **b** is:

```
euclid <- function(a, b)
{

# Function to calculate Euclidean distance between a and b;
# a and b are vectors of the same length
sqrt(sum((a - b)^2))
}
```

In fact, this function works not just in a two-dimensional space, but in an *n*-dimensional space. So, if there are two vowels, **a** and **b**, in a three-dimensional F1, F2, F3 space with coordinates for vowel **a** F1 = 500 Hz, F2 = 1,500 Hz, F3 = 2,500 Hz and for vowel **b** F1 = 220 Hz, F2 = 2,400 Hz, F3 = 3,000 Hz, then the straight-line Euclidean distance between **a** and **b** is just over 1,066 Hz as follows:

```
a = c(500, 1500, 2500)
b = c(220, 2400, 3000)
euclid(a, b)
1066.958
```

Exactly the same principle (and hence the same function) works in 4, 5, . . . *n* dimensional spaces even though any space higher than three dimensions cannot be seen or drawn. The only obligation on the function is that the vectors should be of the same length. The function can be made to break giving an error message, if the user should try to do otherwise:

```
euclid <- function(a, b)
{

# Function to calculate Euclidean distance between a and b;
# a and b are vectors of the same length
if(length(a) != length(b))
stop("a and b must be of the same length")
sqrt(sum((a - b)^2))
}

a = c(3, 4)
b = c(10, 1, 2)
euclid(a, b)
Error in euclid(a, b) : a and b must be of the same length
```

For the present task of assessing vowel-space expansion, the distance of all the vowel tokens to the center of the space will have to be measured. For illustrative purposes, a comparison will be made between the male and female speakers on the lax-vowel data considered so far, although, in practice, this technique is more likely to be used to compare vowels in easy and hard words or in accented and unaccented words as described earlier. The question we are asking is: is there any evidence that the lax vowels of the female speaker are more expanded, that is more distant from the center of the vowel space than those of the male speaker in Figures 6.9 and 6.10? A glance at Figure 6.10 in particular must surely suggest that the answer to this question is "yes" and, indeed, the greater area of the polygon for the female speaker partly comes about because of the female's higher F1 and F2 values.

In order to quantify these differences, a single point that is at the center of the speaker's vowel space, known as the **centroid**, has to be defined. This could be taken across a much larger sample of the speaker's vowels than is available in these datasets: for the present, it will be taken to be the mean across all of the speaker's lax vowels. For the male and female speaker these are:

```
temp = vowlax.spkr == "67"
m.av = apply(vowlax.fdat.5[temp,1:2], 2, mean)
m.av
      T1         T2
495.1756   1568.8098

f.av = apply(vowlax.fdat.5[!temp,1:2], 2, mean)
f.av
      T1         T2
533.8439   1965.8293
```

But there are good grounds for objecting to these means: in particular, the distribution of vowel tokens across the categories is not equal, as the following shows for the male speaker (the distribution is the same for the female speaker):

```
table(vowlax.l[temp])
 a   E   I   O
63  41  85  16
```

In view of the relatively few back vowels, the centroids are likely to be biased towards the front of the vowel space. As an alternative, the centroids could be defined as the mean of the vowel means, which is the point that is at the center of the polygons in Figure 6.10. Recall that for the female speaker the mean position of all the vowels was given by:

```
temp = vowlax.spkr == "67"
f = apply(vowlax.fdat.5[!temp,1:2], 2, tapply,
vowlax.l[!temp], mean)
f
        T1          T2
a   786.1429   1540.159
E   515.9268   2202.268
I   358.0941   2318.812
O   520.0000   1160.813
```

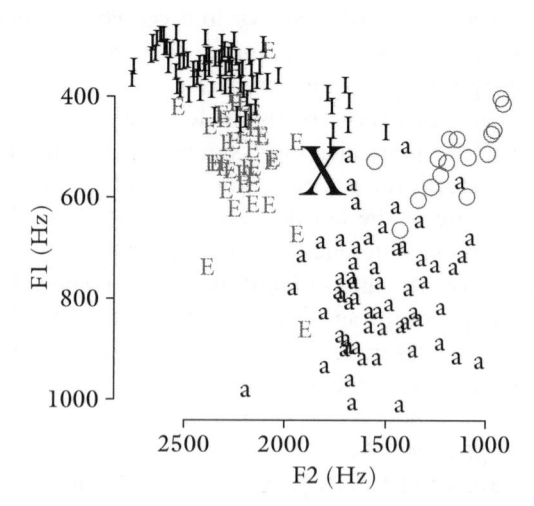

Figure 6.14 Lax monophthongs in German for the female speaker in the F2 × F1 plane for data extracted at the vowels' temporal midpoint. X is the centroid defined as the mean position of the same speaker's mean across all tokens of the four vowel categories.

So the mean of these means is:

```
f.av = apply(f, 2, mean)
f.av
    T1        T2
545.041   1805.51
```

The centroid is shown in Figure 6.14 and was produced as follows:

```
temp = vowlax.spkr=="68"
eplot(vowlax.fdat.5[temp,1:2], vowlax.l[temp], dopoints=T,
form=T, xlab="F2 (Hz)", ylab="F1 (Hz)", doellipse=F)
text(-f.av[2], -f.av[1], "X", cex=3)
```

The Euclidean distances of each data point to **X** in Figure 6.14 can be obtained by applying **euclid()** to the rows of the matrix using **apply()** with a second argument of **1** (meaning apply to rows):

```
temp = vowlax.spkr=="68"
e.f = apply(vowlax.fdat.5[temp,1:2], 1, euclid, f.av)
```

The same technique as in 6.4 could be used to keep all the various objects that have something to do with lax vowels parallel to each other, as follows:

```
# Vector of zeros to store the results
edistances = rep(0, nrow(vowlax.fdat.5))
```

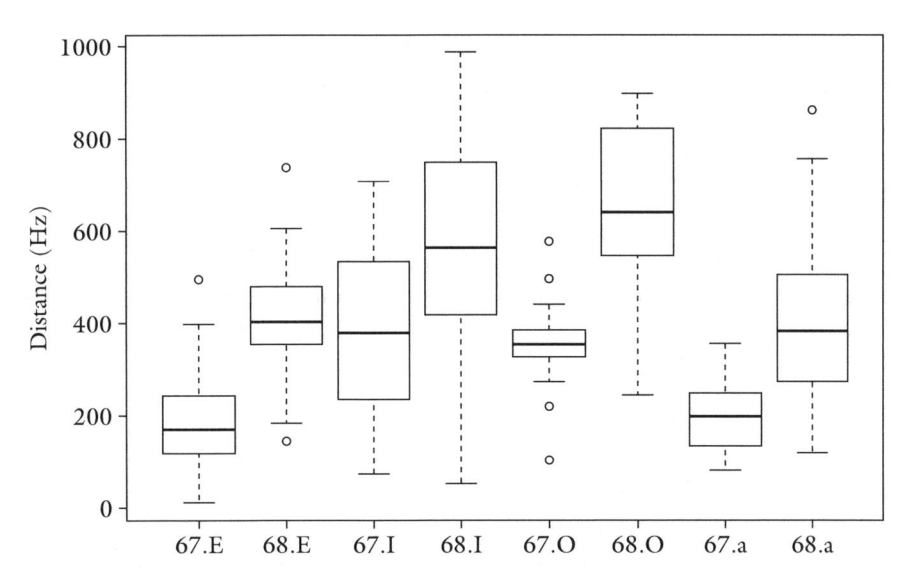

Analysis of Formants and Formant Transitions 195

Figure 6.15 Boxplots of Euclidean distances (Hz) to the centroid for speaker 67 (male) and speaker 68 (female) for four lax vowel categories in German.

```
# Logical vector to identify speaker 67
temp = vowlax.spkr == "67"

# The next two commands give the male speaker's centroid analogous to f.av
m = apply(vowlax.fdat.5[temp,1:2], 2, tapply,
vowlax.l[temp], mean)
m.av = apply(m, 2, mean)

# Distances to the centroid for the male speaker
edistances[temp] = apply(vowlax.fdat.5[temp,1:2], 1,
euclid, m.av)

# Distances to the centroid for the female speaker
edistances[!temp] = apply(vowlax.fdat.5[!temp,1:2], 1,
euclid, f.av)
```

Since all the objects are parallel to each other, it only takes one line to produce a boxplot of the results comparing the Euclidean distances for the male and female speakers separately by vowel category (Figure 6.15):

```
boxplot(edistances ~ factor(vowlax.spkr) *
factor(vowlax.l), ylab= "Distance (Hz)")
```

Figure 6.15 confirms what was suspected: the Euclidean distances are greater on every vowel category for the female speaker.

6.5.2 Relative distance between vowel categories

In the study of dialect and sound change, there is often a need to compare the relative position of two vowel categories in a formant space. The sound change can sometimes be linked to age and social class, as the various pioneering studies by Labov (1994, 2001) have shown. It might be hypothesized that a vowel is in the process of fronting or raising: for example, the vowel in *who'd* in the standard accent of English has fronted in the last 50 years (Harrington et al. 2008; Hawkins & Midgley 2005), there has been a substantial rearrangement of the front lax vowels in New Zealand English (Maclagen & Hay 2007), and there is extensive evidence in Labov (1994, 2001) of numerous diachronic changes to North American vowels.

Vowels are often compared across two different age groups so that, if there is a vowel change in progress, the position of the vowel in the older and younger groups might be different (this type of study is known as an **apparent time study**: see e.g., Bailey et al. 1991). Of course, independently of sound change, studies comparing different dialects might seek to provide quantitative evidence for the relative differences in vowel positions: whether, for example, the vowel in Australian English *head* is higher and/or fronter than that of Standard Southern British English.

There are a number of ways of providing quantitative data of this kind. The one to be illustrated here is concerned with determining whether the position of a vowel in relation to other vowels is different in one set of data compared with another. I used just this technique (Harrington 2006) to assess whether the long, final lax vowel in words like *city*, *plenty*, and *ready* was relatively closer to the tense vowel in [i] (*heed*) than in the lax vowel in [ɪ] (*hid*) in the more recent Christmas messages broadcast by Queen Elizabeth II over a 50-year period.

For illustrative purposes, the analysis will again make use of the lax-vowel data. Figure 6.10 suggests that [ɛ] is closer to [ɪ] than it is to [a] in the female than in the male speaker. Perhaps this is a sound change in progress; perhaps the female subject does not speak exactly the same variety as the male speaker; perhaps it has something to do with differences between the speakers along the hyper- and hypo-articulation continuum; or perhaps it is an artifact of anatomical differences in the vocal tract between the male and female speaker. Whatever the reasons, it is just this sort of problem that can arise in sociophonetics in dealing with gradual and incremental sound change.

The way of addressing this issue based on Harrington (2006) is to work out two Euclidean distances: d_1, the distance of all the [ɛ] tokens to the centroid of [ɪ]; and d_2, the distance of all the same [ɛ] tokens to the centroid of [a]. The ratio of these two distances, d_1 / d_2 is indicative of how close (in terms of Euclidean distances) the [ɛ] tokens are to [ɪ] in relation to [a]. The logarithm of this ratio, which will be termed E_{RATIO}, gives the same information but in a more convenient form. More specifically, since

(1) $\quad E_{RATIO} = \log(d_1 / d_2)$
$\qquad\qquad\; = \log(d_1) - \log(d_2)$

the following three relationships hold for any single token of [ɛ]:

1. if an [ɛ] token is exactly equidistant between the [ɪ] and [a] centroids, then $\log(d_1) = \log(d_2)$, and so E_{RATIO} is zero.
2. if an [ɛ] token is closer to the centroid of [ɪ], then $\log(d_1) < \log(d_2)$ and so E_{RATIO} is negative.
3. if an [ɛ] token is closer to [a] than to [ɪ], $\log(d_1) > \log(d_2)$ and so E_{RATIO} is positive.

The hypothesis to be tested is that the female speaker's [ɛ] vowels are closer to her [ɪ] than to her [a] vowels compared with those for the male speaker. If so, then the female speaker's E_{RATIO} should be smaller than that for the male speaker. The Euclidean distance calculations will be carried out as before in the F2 × F1 vowel space using the **euclid()** function written in 6.5.1. Here are the commands for the female speaker:

```
# Next two lines calculate the centroid of female [ɪ]
temp = vowlax.spkr == "68" & vowlax.l=="I"
mean.I = apply(vowlax.fdat.5[temp,1:2], 2, mean)

# Next two lines calculate the centroid of female [a]
temp = vowlax.spkr == "68" & vowlax.l=="a"
mean.a = apply(vowlax.fdat.5[temp,1:2], 2, mean)

# Logical vector to identify all the female speaker's [ɛ] vowels
temp = vowlax.spkr == "68" & vowlax.l=="E"

# This is d₁ above, i.e., the distance of [ɛ] tokens to [ɪ] centroid
etoI = apply(vowlax.fdat.5[temp,1:2], 1, euclid, mean.I)

# This is d₂ above, i.e., the distance of [ɛ] tokens to [a] centroid
etoa = apply(vowlax.fdat.5[temp,1:2], 1, euclid, mean.a)

# E_RATIO for the female speaker
ratio.log.f = log(etoI/etoa)
```

Exactly the same instructions can be carried out for the male speaker except that **68** should be replaced with **67** throughout in the above instructions. For the final line for the male speaker, **ratio.log.m** is used to store the male speaker's E_{RATIO} values. A histogram of the E_{RATIO} distributions for these two speakers can then be created as follows (Figure 6.16):

```
par(mfrow=c(1,2)); xlim = c(-3, 2)
col = "steelblue"; xlab=expression(E[RATIO])
hist(ratio.log.f, xlim=xlim, col=col, xlab=xlab,
main="Speaker 67")
hist(ratio.log.m, xlim=xlim, col=col, xlab=xlab,
main="Speaker 68")
```

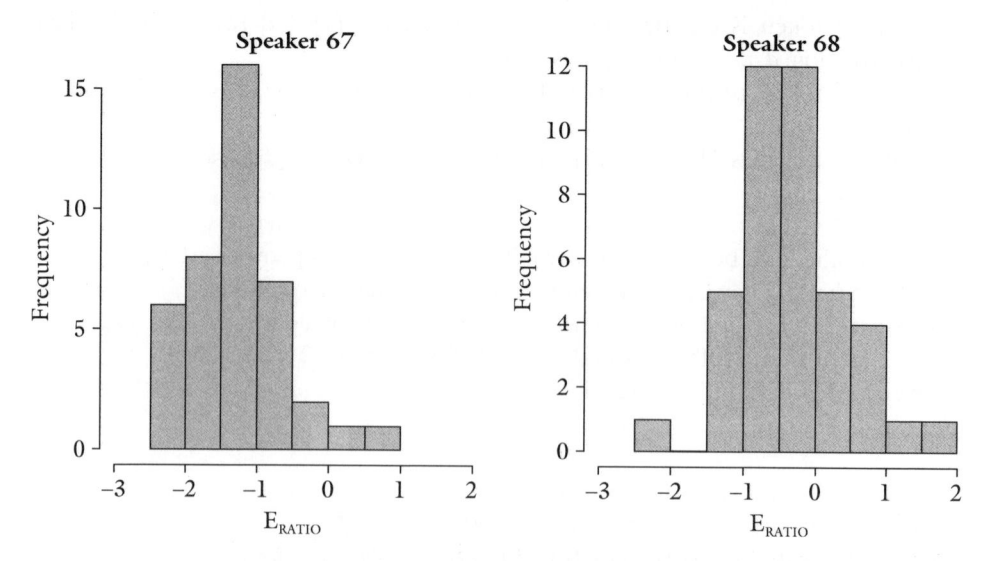

Figure 6.16 Histograms of the log. Euclidean distance ratios obtained from measuring the relative distance of [ɛ] tokens to the centroids of [ɪ] and [a] in the F1 × F2 space separately for a male (left) and a female (right) speaker.

It is clear enough that the E_{RATIO} values are smaller for the female than for the male speaker as a statistical test would confirm: (e.g., assuming the data are normally distributed, `t.test(ratio.log.f, ratio.log.m)`). So compared with the male speaker, the female speaker's [ɛ] is relatively closer to [ɪ] in a formant space than it is to [a].

6.6 Vowel Undershoot and Formant Smoothing

The calculation of the Euclidean distance to the center of the vowel space discussed in 6.5.1 is one of the possible methods for measuring vowel undershoot, a term first used by Lindblom (1963) to refer to the way in which vowels failed to reach their targets due to contextual influences such as the flanking consonants and stress. But, in such calculations, the extent of vowel undershoot (or expansion) is being measured only at a **single time point**. The technique to be discussed in this section is based on a parameterization of the **entire formant trajectory**. These parameterizations involve reducing an entire formant trajectory to a set of **coefficients** – this can be thought of as the **analysis** mode. A by-product of this reduction is that, if the formant trajectories are reconstructed from the coefficients that were obtained in the analysis mode, then a smoothed formant contour can be derived – this is the **synthesis** mode and it is discussed more fully at the end of this section.

The type of coefficients to be considered are due to van Bergem (1993) and involve fitting a parabola, that is an equation of the form $F = c_0 + c_1 t + c_2 t^2$, where F is a formant from the start to the end of a vowel that changes as a function of time t. As the equation shows, there are three coefficients c_0, c_1, and c_2 that have to be calculated for each vowel separately from the formant's trajectory. The shape of a parabola is necessarily curved in an arc, either ∪-shaped if c_2 is positive, or ∩-shaped if c_2 is negative. The principle that lies behind fitting such an equation is as follows. The shape of a formant trajectory, and in particular that of F2, over the extent of a vowel, is influenced mostly both by the vowel and by the immediately preceding and following sounds: that is by the **left and right contexts**. At the vowel target, which for most monophthongs is nearest the vowel's temporal midpoint, the shape is predominantly determined by the phonetic quality of the vowel, but it is reasonable to assume that the influence from the context increases progressively nearer the vowel onset and offset (e.g., Broad & Fertig 1970). Consider for example the case in which the vowel has no target at all. Just this hypothesis has been suggested for schwa vowels by Browman and Goldstein (1992b) in an articulatory analysis and by van Bergem (1994) using acoustic data. In such a situation, a formant trajectory might approximately follow a straight line between its values at the vowel onset and vowel offset: this would happen if the vowel target has no influence so that the trajectory's shape is entirely determined by the left and right contexts. On the other hand, if a vowel has a prominent target, as is often the case if it is emphasized or prosodically accented (Pierrehumbert & Talkin 1990), then it is likely to deviate considerably from a straight line joining its onset and offset. Since a formant trajectory often follows reasonably well a parabolic trajectory (Lindblom 1963), one way to measure the extent of deviation from the straight line and hence to estimate how much it is undershot is to fit a parabola to the formant and then measure the parabola's **curvature**. If the formant is heavily undershot and follows more or less a straight-line path between its endpoints, then the curvature will be almost zero; on the other hand, the more prominent the target, the greater the deviation from the straight line, and the greater the magnitude of the curvature, in either a positive or a negative direction.

The way that the parabola is fitted in van Bergem (1993) is essentially to rescale the time axis of a trajectory linearly between $t = -1$ and $t = 1$. This rescaled time axis can be obtained using the **seq()** function, if the length of the trajectory in data points is known. As an example, the length of the F2 trajectory for the first segment in the lax-vowel data is given by:

```
N = length(frames(vowlax.fdat[1,2]))
N
18
```

So the linearly rescaled time axis between $t = \pm 1$ is given by:

```
times = seq(-1, 1, length=N)
```

Since a precise estimate of the formant will need to be made at time $t = 0$, the number of data points that supports the trajectory could be increased using **linear interpolation** with the **approx()** function. The shape of the trajectory stays exactly the same, but the interval along the time axis becomes more fine-grained (this procedure is sometimes known as **linear time-normalization**). For example, the F2 trajectory for the first segment in the lax-vowel dataset could be given 101 rather than 17 points as in Figure 6.17, which was created as follows (an odd number of points is chosen here, because this makes sure that there will be a value at $t = 0$):

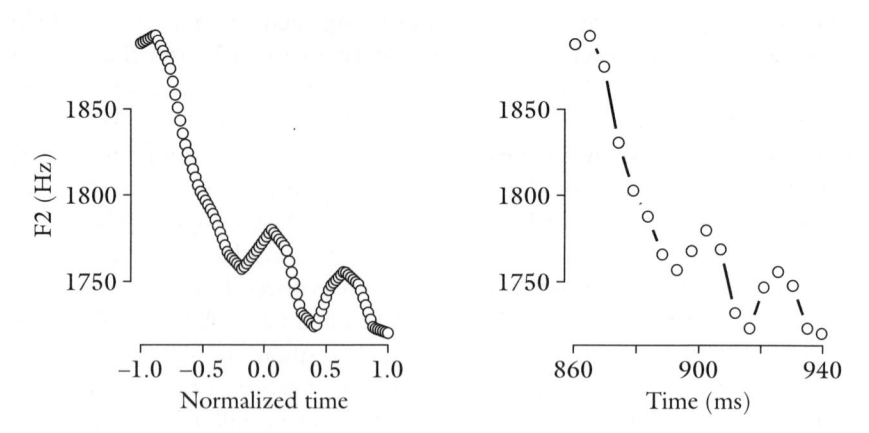

Figure 6.17 An F2 trajectory (right) and its linearly time-normalized equivalent using 101 data points between $t = \pm 1$.

```
N = 101
F2int = approx(frames(vowlax.fdat[1,2]), n=N)
times = seq(-1, 1, length=N)
par(mfrow=c(1,2));
plot(times, F2int$y, type="b", xlab="Normalized time",
ylab="F2 (Hz)")

# The original F2 for this segment
plot(vowlax.fdat[1,2], type="b", xlab="Time (ms)", ylab="")
```

There are three unknown coefficients to be found in the parabola $F = c_0 + c_1 t + c_2 t^2$ that is to be fitted to the data of the left panel in Figure 6.17, and this requires inserting three sets of data points into this equation. It can be shown (van Bergem 1993) that, when the data is extended on the time axis between $t = \pm 1$, the coefficients have the following values:

```
# c0 is the value at t = 0
c0 = F2int$y[times==0]

# c1 is half of the difference between the first and last data points
c1 <- 0.5 * (F2int$y[N] - F2int$y[1])

# c2 is half of the sum of the first and last data points minus c0
c2 <- 0.5 * (F2int$y[N] + F2int$y[1]) - c0
```

If you follow through the example in R, you will get values of 1,774, − 84, and 30 for c_0, c_1, and c_2 respectively. Since these are the coefficients, the parabola over the entire trajectory can be calculated by inserting these coefficients' values into the equation $c_0 + c_1 t + c_2 t^2$. So, for this segment, the values of the parabola are:

```
c0 + c1 * times + c2 * (times^2)
```

These values could be plotted as a function of time to obtain the fitted curve. However, there is a function in the Emu-R library, **plafit()**, that does all these steps. So, for the present data, the coefficients are:

```
plafit(frames(vowlax.fdat[1,2]))
  c0    c   c2
1774  -84   30
```

Moreover, the additional argument **fit=T** returns the formant values of the fitted parabola linearly time-normalized back to the same length as the original data to which the **plafit()** function was applied. So a superimposed plot of the raw and parabolically smoothed F2 track for this first segment is:

```
# Calculate the values of the parabola
F2par = plafit(frames(vowlax.fdat[1,2]), fit=T)
ylim = range(c(F2par, frames(vowlax.fdat[1,2])))
xlab="Time (ms)"; ylab="F2 (Hz)"

# Plot the raw values
plot(vowlax.fdat[1,2], type="b", ylim=ylim, xlab=xlab,
ylab=ylab)

# Superimpose the smoothed values
par(new=T)
plot(as.numeric(names(F2par)), F2par, type="l", ylim=ylim,
xlab=xlab, ylab=ylab, lwd=2)
```

The fitted parabola (Figure 6.18) always passes through the first and last points of the trajectory and through whichever point is closest to the temporal midpoint. The coefficient c_0 is the y-axis value at the temporal midpoint. The coefficient c_1, being the average of the first and last values, is negative for falling trajectories and positive for rising trajectories. As already mentioned, c_2 measures the trajectory's curvature: positive values on c_2 mean that the parabola has a ∪-shape, as in Figure 6.18, negative values that it is ∩-shaped. Notice that these coefficients encode the trajectory's shape **independently of time**. So the above trajectory extends over a duration of about 80 ms; however, even if the duration were 1/10th or 100 times as great, the coefficients would all be the same, if the trajectory's shape were unchanged. So it would be wrong to say that very much can be inferred about the rate of change of the formant (in Hz/s) from c_1 (or to do so, c_1 would have to be divided by the formant's duration).

The task now is to explore a worked example of measuring formant curvatures in a larger sample of speech. The analysis of the vowel spaces in the F2 × F1 plane, as well as the Euclidean distance measurements in 6.5, has suggested that the female speaker produces more distinctive vowel targets or, in terms of Lindblom's (1990) H&H theory, her vowels show greater evidence of hyperarticulation and less of a tendency to be undershot. Is this also reflected in a difference in the extent of formant curvature?

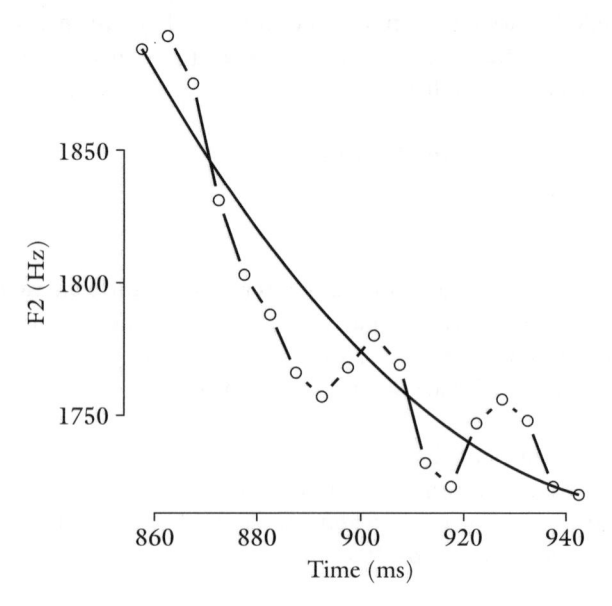

Figure 6.18 A raw F2 trajectory (points) and a fitted parabola.

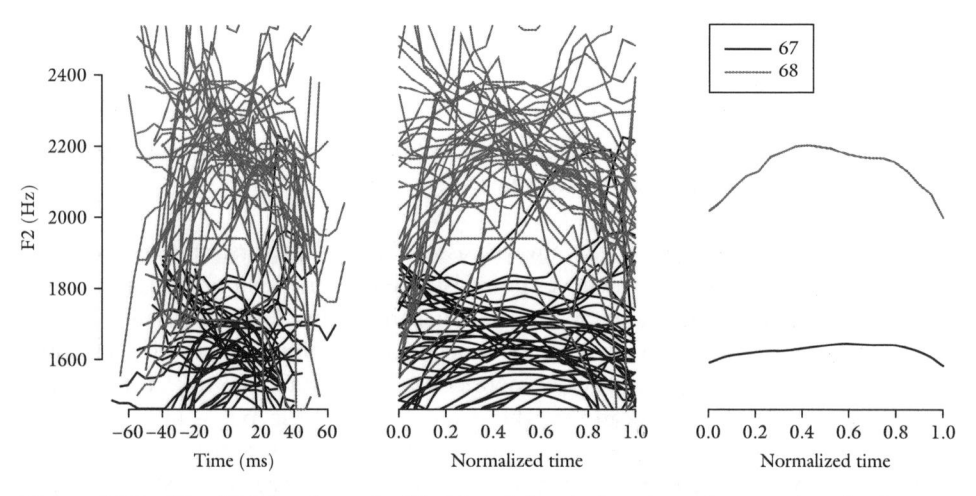

Figure 6.19 F2 of [ɛ] for the male (black) and female (gray) speakers synchronized at the temporal midpoint (left), linearly time-normalized (center), and linearly time-normalized and averaged (right).

In order to address this question, the two speakers' [ɛ] vowels will be compared. Before applying an algorithm for quantifying the data, it is always helpful to look at a few plots, if this is possible (if only because a gross inconsistency between what is seen and what is obtained numerically often indicates that there is a mistake in the calculation!). A plot of all the F2 trajectories lined up at the temporal midpoint and shown separately for the two speakers does not seem to be especially revealing (Figure 6.19, left panel), perhaps in part because the trajectories have different durations and, as was mentioned earlier, in order to compare whether one trajectory is more curved than another, they need to be time-normalized to the same length. The argument **norm=T** in the **dplot()** function does just this by linearly stretching and compressing the trajectories so that they extend in time between 0 and 1. There is some suggestion from the time-normalized data (Figure 6.19, center) that the female's F2 trajectories are more curved than for the male speaker. This emerges especially clearly when the linearly time-normalized, male and female F2 trajectories are separately averaged (Figure 6.19, right). However, the average is just that: at best a trend, and one that we will now seek to quantify by calculating the c_2 coefficients of the fitted parabola. Before doing this, here are the instructions for producing Figure 6.19:

```
temp = vowlax.l == "E"
par(mfrow=c(1,3)); ylim = c(1500, 2500)

# F2 of E separately for M and F synchronized at the midpoint
dplot(vowlax.fdat[temp,2], vowlax.spkr[temp], offset=.5,
ylab="F2 (Hz)", ylim=ylim, xlab="Time (ms)",legend=F)

# As above with linear time-normalization
dplot(vowlax.fdat[temp,2], vowlax.spkr[temp], norm=T,
xlab="Normalized time", ylim=ylim, legend=F)

# As above and averaged
dplot(vowlax.fdat[temp,2], vowlax.spkr[temp], norm=T,
average=T, ylim=ylim, xlab="Normalized time")
```

The **plafit()** function can be applied to any vector of values, just like the **euclid()** function created earlier. For example, this instruction finds the three coefficients of a parabola that have been fitted to 10 random numbers.

```
r = runif(10)
plafit(r)
```

Since **plafit()** evidently works on frames of speech data (see the instructions for creating Figure 6.18), then, for all the reasons given in 5.5.1 of the preceding chapter, it can also be used inside **trapply()**. Moreover, since the function will return the same number of elements per segment (three in this case), then, for the further reasons discussed in 5.5.1, the argument **simplify=T** can be set, which has the effect of returning a matrix with the same number of rows as there are segments:

```
# Logical vector to identify E vowels
temp = vowlax.l == "E"

# Matrix of coefficients, one row per segment
coeffs = trapply(vowlax.fdat[temp,2], plafit, simplify=T)
```

coeffs has three columns (one per coefficient) and the same number of rows as there are [ɛ] segments (this can be verified with **nrow(coeffs) == sum(temp)**).

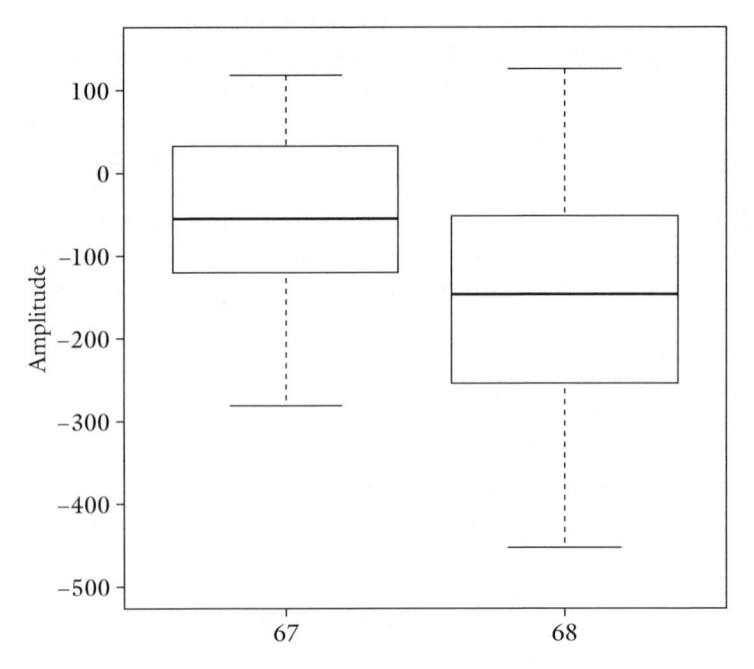

Figure 6.20 Boxplots of the c_2 coefficient of a parabola fitted to F2 of [ɛ] for the male (left) and female (right) speaker.

Figure 6.20 compares the F2 curvatures of the male and female speakers using a boxplot. There are two outliers (both for the female speaker) with values less than −500 (as **sum(coeffs[,3] < -500)** shows), and these have been excluded from the plot by setting the *y*-axis limits:

```
ylim = c(-550, 150)
boxplot(coeffs[,3] ~ factor(vowlax.spkr[temp]),
ylab="Amplitude", ylim=ylim)
```

Figure 6.20 shows greater negative values on c_2 for the female speaker, which is consistent with the view that there is indeed greater curvature in the female speaker's F2 of [ɛ] than for the male speaker.

As foreshadowed at various stages in this section, the **fit=T** argument applies the function in synthesis mode: it works out the corresponding fitted formant parabola as a function of time. In order to smooth an entire trackdata object, **trapply()** can once again be used, but this time with the argument **returntrack=T** to build a trackdata object (see 5.5.2):

```
# Calculate the fitted F2 parabolas for all the vowel data
vow.sm2 = trapply(vowlax.fdat[,2], plafit, T,
returntrack=T)
```

The smoothed and raw F2 data can be superimposed on each other for any segment as in Figure 6.21 and in the manner described below.

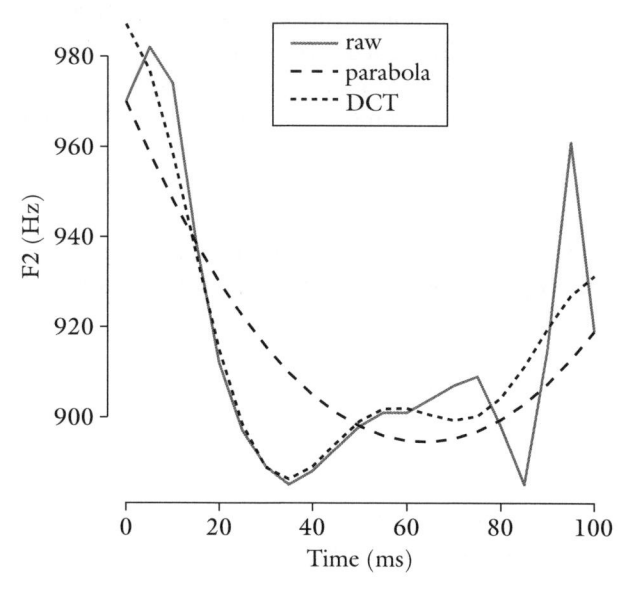

Figure 6.21 A raw F2 formant trajectory of a back vowel [ɔ] (solid, gray) produced by a male speaker of Standard German and two smoothed contours of the raw signal based on fitting a parabola following van Bergem (1993) (dashed) and the first five coefficients of the discrete cosine transformation (dotted).

Although fitting a parabola is an effective method of data reduction that is especially useful for measuring formant curvature and hence undershoot, there are two disadvantages as far as obtaining a smoothed contour are concerned:

- not every formant trajectory has a parabolic shape;
- parabolic fitting of the kind illustrated above forces a fit at the segment onset, offset, and midpoint as is evident from Figure 6.21.

One way around both of these problems is to use the **discrete cosine transformation** (see e.g., Harrington 2006; Harrington et al. 2008; Watson & Harrington 1999), which will be discussed more fully in Chapter 8. This transformation decomposes a trajectory into a set of coefficients (this is the *analysis* mode) that are the amplitudes of half-cycle cosine waves of increasing frequency. The number of coefficients derived from the discrete cosine transformation (DCT) is the same as the length of the trajectory. If, in *synthesis* mode, all of these cosine waves are summed, then the original, raw trajectory is exactly reconstructed. However, if only the first few lowest-frequency cosine waves are summed, then a smoothed trajectory is derived. Moreover, the fewer the cosine waves that are summed, the greater the degree of smoothing. Therefore, an advantage of this type of smoothing over that of fitting parabolas is that it is possible to control the degree of smoothing. Another advantage is that the DCT does not necessarily force the smoothed trajectory to pass through the values at the onset, offset, and midpoint and so is not as prone to producing a wildly inaccurate contour, if formant onsets and offsets were inaccurately tracked (which is often the case, especially if there is a preceding or following voiceless segment).

There is a function in the Emu-R library for computing the DCT coefficients, **dct()**, which, just like **plafit()** and **euclid()**, takes a vector of values as its main argument. The function can be used in an exactly analogous way to the **plafit()** function in synthesis mode for obtaining smoothed trajectories from the coefficients that are calculated in analysis mode. In the example in Figure 6.21, a smoothed F2 trajectory was calculated from the first five DCT coefficients as follows:

```
# Calculate a smoothed trajectory based on the lowest five DCT coefficients
vow.dct2 = trapply(vowlax.fdat[,2], dct, fit=T, 4,
returntrack=T)
```

Figure 6.21 containing the raw and two types of smoothed trajectories for the eighth segment in the segment list was produced with the following commands:

```
j = 8
# A label vector to identify the trajectories
lab = c("raw", "parabola", "DCT")

# Row-bind the three trajectories into one trackdata object
dat = rbind(vowlax.fdat[j,2], vow.sm2[j,], vow.dct2[j,])
dplot(dat, lab, ylab="F2 (Hz)", xlab="Time (ms)")
```

6.7 F2 Locus, Place of Articulation, and Variability

In the production of an oral stop the vocal tract is initially sealed, during which time air pressure builds up and is then released. At the point of release, the shape of the vocal tract has a marked influence on the acoustic signal and this influence extends at least to the beginning of the formant transitions, if the following segment is a vowel. Since the shape of the vocal tract is quite different for labial, alveolar, and velar places of articulation, the way in which the acoustic signal is influenced following the release differs correspondingly. If the influence extends to the onset of periodicity for the following vowel, then the formant onset frequencies of the same phonetic vowel should be different when it occurs after consonants at different places of articulation.

As a study by Potter et al. (1947) had shown, different places of articulation have their greatest influence on the onset of the second formant frequency. But it was the famous perception experiments using hand-painted spectrograms at the Haskins Laboratories that gave rise to the concept of an **F2 locus**. In these experiments, Liberman and colleagues (Delattre et al. 1955; Liberman et al. 1954; Liberman et al. 1958) showed that the origin of the second formant frequency influenced the perception of the place of articulation of the following consonant. More specifically, if the F2 onset was low and at around 700 Hz, listeners would predominantly hear /b/; if it was roughly in the 1,800 Hz region, they would hear /d/; while if the F2 onset began near 3,000 Hz, listeners would perceive /g/ before front vowels. The locus frequency was not at the acoustic vowel onset itself, but at some point prior to it during the consonantal closure. More specifically, in synthesizing a consonant–vowel (CV) transition, formants would be painted from the F2-locus somewhere in the consonant closure to the F2-vowel target and then the first part of the transition up to where the voicing for the vowel began would be erased. With these experiments, Liberman and colleagues also demonstrated that the perception of place of articulation was categorical, and this finding was interpreted in favor of the famous motor theory of speech perception (see e.g., Hawkins 1999 for a thorough review of these issues).

In the years following the Haskins Laboratories experiments, various large-scale acoustic studies were concerned with finding evidence for an F2 locus (including e.g., Fant 1973; Kewley-Port 1982; Lehiste & Peterson 1961; Öhman 1966). These studies showed that the most stable F2 locus was for alveolars (i.e., alveolars exhibit the least F2-onset variation of the three places of articulation) whereas velars, which exhibit a great deal of variability depending on the backness of the following vowel, showed no real evidence from acoustic data of a single F2 locus.

From the early 1990s, Sussman and colleagues applied the concept of a **locus equation** to suggest that F2 transitions might in some form provide invariant cues to the place of articulation (see e.g., Sussman et al. 1991; Sussman et al. 1995), a position that has also not been without its critics (e.g., Brancazio & Fowler 1998; Löfqvist 1999).

Locus equations were first investigated systematically by Krull (1987, 1989) and they provide a numerical index of the extent to which vowels exert a coarticulatory influence on a consonant's place of articulation. Thus, whereas in studies of vowel undershoot, the concern is with the way in which context influences vowel targets, here it is the other way round: that is, the aim is to find out the extent to which vowel targets exert a coarticulatory influence on the place of articulation of flanking consonants.

The basic idea behind a locus equation is illustrated with some made-up data in Figure 6.22 showing two hypothetical F2-trajectories for [bɛb] and [bob]. In the trajectories on the left, the extent of influence of the vowel on the consonant is nil. This is because, in spite of very different F2 vowel targets, the F2 frequencies of [ɛ] and of [o] both converge to exactly the same F2 locus at 700 Hz for the bilabial – that is, the F2-onset frequency is determined entirely by the consonant with no influence from the vowel. The other (equally unlikely) extreme is shown on the right. In this case, the influence of the vowel on the consonant's place of articulation is maximal so that there is absolutely no convergence to any locus and therefore no transition.

A locus equation is computed by transforming F2 frequencies (top row, Figure 6.22) as a function of time into the plane of F2 target × F2 onset (bottom row, Figure 6.22) in order to estimate the extent of coarticulatory influence of the vowel on the consonant. Firstly, when there is no vowel-on-consonant coarticulation (left), the locus equation, which is the line that connects [bɛb] and [bob], is horizontal: this is because they both converge to the same locus frequency and so F2-onset is 700 Hz in both cases. Secondly, when vowel-on-consonant coarticulation is at a maximum (right), then the locus equation is a diagonal in this plane because the locus frequency is equal to the target frequency.

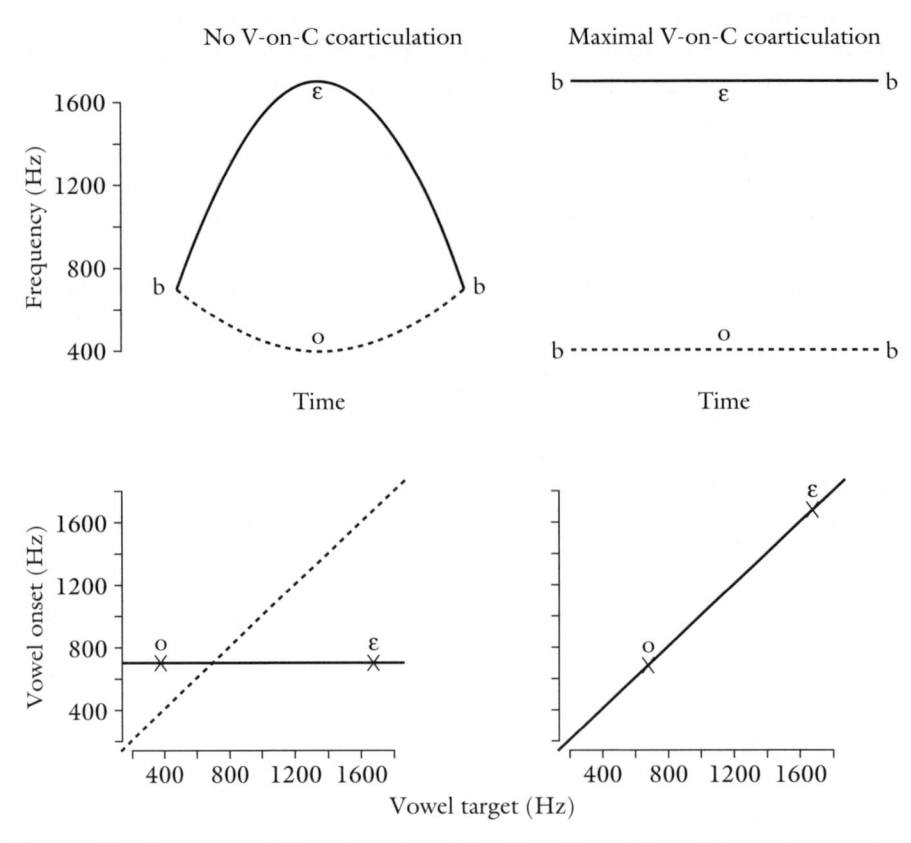

Figure 6.22 Hypothetical F2 trajectories of [bɛb] (solid) and [bob] (dashed) when there is no V-on-C coarticulation (left) and when V-on-C coarticulation is maximal (right). First row: the trajectories as a function of time. Second row: a plot of the F2 values in the plane of the vowel target × vowel onset for the data in the first row. The dotted line bottom left is the line $F2_{Target} = F2_{Onset}$ that can be used to estimate the locus frequency. From Harrington (2010).

A fundamental difference between these two extreme cases of coarticulation is in the slope of the locus equation. On the left, the slope in this plane is zero (because the locus equation is horizontal) and on the right it is one (because $F2_{Target} = F2_{Onset}$). Therefore, for real speech data, the slope of the locus equation can be used as a measure of the extent of vowel-on-consonant coarticulation: the closer the slope is to one, the more the consonant's place of articulation is influenced by the vowel (and the slope must always lie between 0 and 1 since these are the two extreme cases of zero and maximal coarticulation). Finally, it can be shown (with some algebraic manipulation: see Harrington & Cassidy 1999, pp. 128–30) that the locus frequency itself, that is the frequency towards which transitions tend to converge, can be estimated by establishing where the locus equation and the line $F2_{Target} = F2_{Onset}$ bisect. This is shown for the case of zero vowel-on-consonant coarticulation on the left in Figure 6.22: this line bisects the locus equation at the frequency at which the transitions in the top left panel of Figure 6.22 converge, i.e. at 700 Hz, which is the locus frequency. On the right, the line $F2_{Target} = F2_{Onset}$ cannot bisect the locus equation, because it is the same as the locus equation. Because these lines do not bisect, there is no locus frequency, as is of course obvious from the "transitions" in Figure 6.22 top right that never converge.

This theory can be applied to some simple isolated word data produced by the first author of Clark et al. (2007). In 1991, John Clark produced a number of isolated /dVd/ words where the V is one of the 13 possible monophthongs of Australian English. The relevant dataset which is part of the Emu-R library includes a segment list of the vowel in these words (**isol**), a vector of vowel labels (**isol.l**), and a trackdata object of the first four formant frequencies between the vowel onset and offset (**isol.fdat**).

The task is to investigate whether the coarticulatory influence of the vowel is greater on the final, than on the initial, consonant. There are various reasons for expecting this to be so. Foremost are the arguments presented in Ohala (1990) and Ohala and Kawasaki (1984) that initial CV transitions tend to be a good deal more salient than VC transitions: compatibly, there are many more sound changes in which the vowel and syllable-final consonant merge resulting in consonant loss (such as the nasalization of vowels and associated final nasal consonant deletion in French) than is the case for initial CV syllables. This would suggest that synchronically a consonant and vowel are more sharply delineated from each other in CV than in VC syllables and again there are numerous aerodynamic and acoustic experiments to support this view. Secondly, there are various investigations (Butcher 1989; Hoole et al. 1990) which show that in V_1CV_2 sequences where C is an alveolar, the perseverative influence of V_1 on V_2 is greater than the anticipatory influence of V_2 on V_1. This suggests that the alveolar consonant resists coarticulatory influences of the following V_2 (so the alveolar has a blocking effect on the coarticulatory influences of a *following* vowel) but is more transparent to the coarticulatory influences of the preceding V_2 (so the alveolar does not block the coarticulatory influences of a *preceding* vowel to the same extent). Therefore, the vowel-on-consonant coarticulatory influences can be expected to be weaker when the vowel follows the alveolar in /dV/ than when it precedes it in /Vd/.

Before proceeding to the details of quantification, it will be helpful as always to plot the data. Figure 6.23 shows the second formant frequency trajectories synchronized at the vowel onset on the left and at the vowel offset on the right. The trajectories are of F2 of the separate vowel categories and there is only one token per vowel category, as **table(isol.l)** shows.[2] The plots can be obtained by setting the **offset** argument in this function to **0** (for alignment at the segment onset) and to **1** (for alignment at the segment offset).

```
par(mfrow=c(1,2))
dplot(isol.fdat[,2], offset=0, ylab = "F2 (Hz)", xlab="Time
(ms)")
dplot(isol.fdat[,2], offset=1, xlab="Time (ms)")
```

It seems clear enough from Figure 6.23 that there is greater convergence of the F2 transitions at the alignment point on the left (segment onset) than on the right (segment offset). So far, the hypothesis seems to be supported.

The task now is to switch to the plane of F2 target × F2 onset (F2 offset) and calculate locus equations in these two planes. The vowel target is taken to be at the

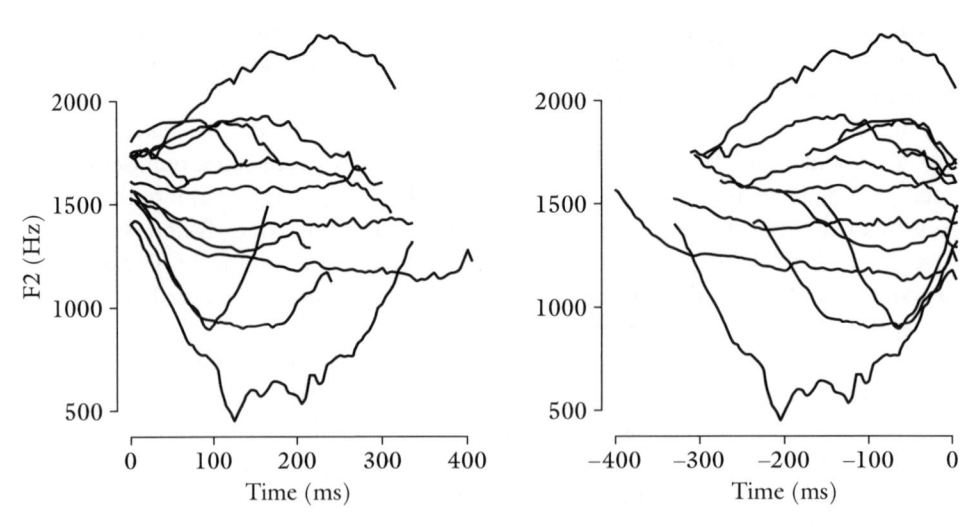

Figure 6.23 F2 trajectories in isolated /dVd/ syllables produced by a male speaker of Australian English for a number of different vowel categories synchronized at the vowel onset (left) and at the vowel offset (right).

temporal midpoint of the vowel. The following three vectors are F2 at the vowel onset, target, and offset respectively:

```
f2onset = dcut(isol.fdat[,2], 0, prop=T)
f2targ = dcut(isol.fdat[,2], .5, prop=T)
f2offset= dcut(isol.fdat[,2], 1, prop=T)
```

The next step is to plot the data and then to calculate a straight line of best fit known as a **regression line** through the scatter of points: that is, there will not be two points that lie on the same line as in the theoretical example in Figure 6.22, but several points that lie close to a **line of best fit**. The technique of linear regression, which for speech analysis in R is described in detail in Johnson (2008), is to calculate such a line, which is defined as the line to which the distances of the points are minimized. The function **lm()** is used to do this. Thus for the vowel-onset data, the second and third commands below are used to calculate and draw the straight line of best fit:

```
plot(f2targ, f2onset)
regr = lm(f2onset ~ f2targ)
abline(regr)
```

The information about the slope is stored in **$coeff**, which also gives the intercept (the value at which the regression line cuts the *y*-axis, i.e., the F2-onset axis). The slope of the line is just over 0.27:

```
regr$coeff
 (Intercept)     f2targ
1217.8046955   0.2720668
```

Analysis of Formants and Formant Transitions

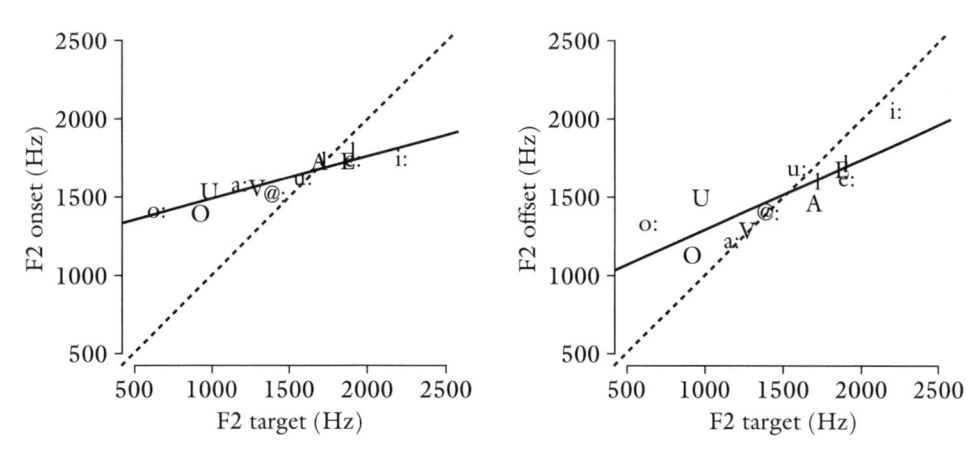

Figure 6.24 Locus equations (solid lines) for /dVd/ words produced by a male speaker of Australian English for F2 onset (left) and F2 offset (right) as a function of F2 target. The dotted line is $y = x$ and is used to estimate the locus frequency at the point of intersection with the locus equation.

Recall that the best estimate of the locus is where the line $F2_{Target} = F2_{Onset}$ cuts this regression line. Such a line can be superimposed on the plot as follows:

```
abline(0, 1, lty=2)
```

There is a function in the Emu-R library, **locus()**, that carries out all these operations. The first two arguments are for the data to be plotted on the *x*- and *y*-axes (in this case the F2 target and the F2 onset respectively) and there is a third optional argument for superimposing a parallel set of labels. In this example, the vowel labels are superimposed on the scatter and the *x*- and *y*-ranges are set to be identical (Figure 6.24):

```
xlim = c(500, 2500); ylim = xlim; par(mfrow=c(1,2))
xlab = "F2-target (Hz)"; ylab = "F2-onset (Hz)"
stats.on = locus(f2targ, f2onset, isol.1, xlim=xlim,
ylim=ylim, xlab=xlab, ylab=ylab)
stats.off = locus(f2targ, f2offset, isol.1, xlim=xlim,
ylim=ylim, xlab=xlab)
```

Figure 6.24 shows that the regression line (locus equation) is not as steep for the F2-onset compared with the F2-offset data. The following two commands show the actual values of the slopes (and intercepts), firstly in the F2-target × F2-onset plane and secondly in the F2-target × F2-offset plane:

stats.on$coeff
```
(Intercept)     target
1217.8046955    0.2720668
```

stats.off$coeff
```
(Intercept)     target
850.4935279     0.4447689
```

The **locus()** function also calculates the point at which the regression line and the lines $F2_{Target} = F2_{Onset}$ (Figure 6.24, left) and $F2_{Target} = F2_{Offset}$ (Figure 6.24, right) bisect, thus giving a best estimate of the locus frequency. These estimates are in **$locus** and the calculated values for the data in the left and right panels of Figure 6.24 respectively are 1,673 Hz and 1,532 Hz. In fact, the locus frequency can also be derived from:

(2) $\quad L = c / (1 - \alpha)$

where L is the locus frequency and c and α are the intercept and slope of the locus equation respectively (Harrington 2010). Thus the estimated locus frequency for the CV syllables is equivalently given by:

```
1217.8046955/(1 - 0.2720668)
1672.962
```

The reason why there is this 141 Hz difference in the calculation of the locus frequencies for initial as opposed to final /d/ is not immediately clear; but nevertheless, as Figure 6.23 shows, these are reasonable estimates of the point at which the F2 transitions tend, on average, to converge. Finally, statistical diagnostics on the extent to which the regression line could be fitted to the points is given by the summary function:

```
summary(stats.on)
Call:
lm(formula = onset ~ target)

Coefficients:
            Estimate Std. Error t value Pr(>|t|)
(Intercept) 1.218e+03  5.134e+01  23.721  8.51e-11 ***
target      2.721e-01  3.308e-02   8.224  5.02e-06 ***
---
Signif. codes: 0 '***' 0.001 '**' 0.01 '*' 0.05 '.' 0.1 ' ' 1

Residual standard error: 53.12 on 11 degrees of freedom
Multiple R-squared: 0.8601, Adjusted R-squared: 0.8474
F-statistic: 67.64 on 1 and 11 DF, p-value: 5.018e-06
```

The probability that the regression-line slope accounts for the data is given by the results of *t*-test in the line beginning **target**. The null hypothesis is that there is no relationship at all between the F2 onset and F2 target (which would mean that the slope of the regression line would be zero): the *t*-test computes the likelihood that this could be the case. This probability is shown to be **5.02e-06** or 0.00000502, i.e., very small. So the null hypothesis is rejected. The other important diagnostic is given under **Adjusted R-squared** which is a measure of how much of the variance is explained by the regression line. It shows that for these data, just over 86 percent of the variance is explained by the regression line and the probability that this value is different from zero is given by the results of an F-test in the next line beginning **F-statistic**.

The analysis of these (very limited) data lends some support to the view that the coarticulatory influence of the vowel on an alveolar stop is greater when the consonant is in final than when it is in initial position. However, data from continuous speech and above all from other consonant categories will not always give such clear results, so the locus equation calculations must be used with care. In particular, an initial plot of the data to check the formant transitions for any outliers due to formant-tracking errors is essential. If the slope of the line is negative or greater than one, then it means either that the data could not be reliably modeled by any kind of regression line and/or that no sensible locus frequency could be computed (i.e., the formant transitions do not converge, and the resulting locus-frequency calculation is likely to be absurd).

6.8 Questions

These questions make use of existing objects in the Emu-R library.

A. Plotting vowel ellipses and removing outliers (sections 6.1 and 6.2)

A.1 Extract the formant data at the temporal midpoint from the trackdata object **vowlax.fdat** and convert the Hz values to Bark.

A.2 F3 – F2 in Bark was suggested by Syrdal and Gopal (1986) as an alternative to F2 in Hz for representing vowel backness. Make a plot like the one in Figure 6.25 of the female speaker's (speaker 68) **E** vowels in the plane of –F1 in Bark (*y*-axis) and F3 – F2 in Bark (*x*-axis) showing the data points.

A.3 Using a logical vector, create a matrix that is the same as the one in A.1 (of Bark values at the temporal midpoint) but which excludes the very obvious outlier shown in the upper left of Figure 6.25.

A.4 Use the same logical vector as in A.3, make a vector of speaker labels from **vowlax.spkr** and a vector of vowel labels from **vowlax.l** that are each parallel to the matrix that you created in A.3.

A.5 Make two plots as shown in Figure 6.26 of the male and female speakers' data in the plane scaled to the same axes as in Figure 6.25.

B. Finding targets (section 6.3)

B.1 The trackdata object **vowlax.rms** contains dB-RMS data that is parallel to the segment list **vowlax** and the other objects associated with it. Use **peakfun()** from 6.3 to find for each segment the time within the vowel at which the dB-RMS reaches a maximum value.

B.2 Extract the F1 and F2 data from the trackdata object **vowlax.fdat** for the male speaker 67 at the target time defined by B.1 and make a plot of the vowels in the F2 × F1 plane.

B.3 The objects **dip** (segment list), **dip.fdat** (trackdata objects of F1 – F4), **dip.l** (vector of diphthong labels), and **dip.spkr** (vector of speaker labels) are available for three diphthongs in German [aɪ, aʊ, ɔʏ] for the same two speakers as for the

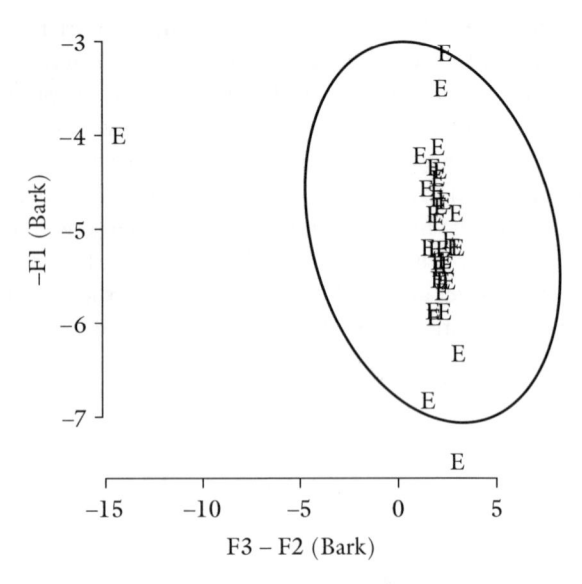

Figure 6.25 The female speaker's [ɛ] vowels in the plane of F3 − F2 Bark and − F1 Bark.

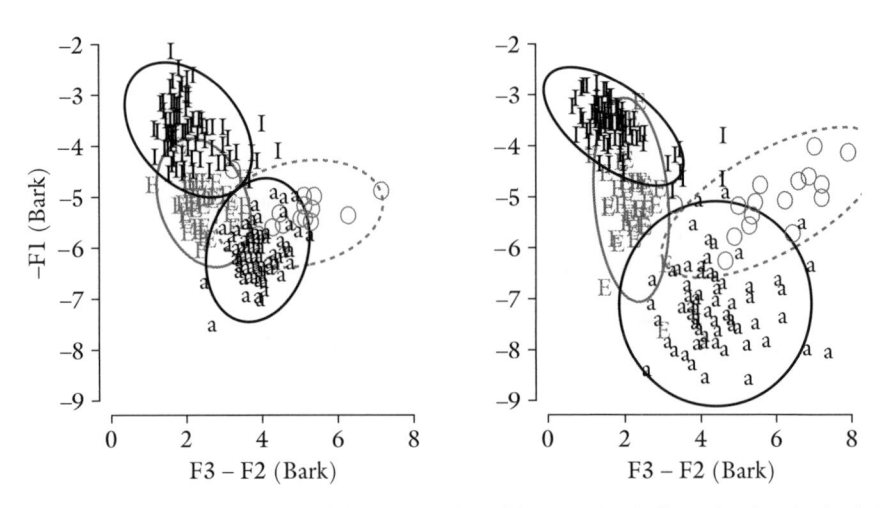

Figure 6.26 German lax monophthongs produced by a male (left) and a female (right) speaker in the plane of F3 − F2 Bark and − F1 Bark. Data extracted at the temporal midpoint of the vowel.

lax-vowel data presented in this chapter. Make a plot of F1 as a function of time for the male speaker's [aʊ] thereby verifying that F1 seems to reach a target/plateau in the first half of the diphthong.

B.4 Make a matrix of the F1 and F2 values at the time at which F1 reaches a maximum in the first half of [aʊ]. Create a vector of [aʊ] labels that is parallel to this matrix (i.e., a vector of the same length as there are rows in the matrix and consisting entirely of **aU, aU, aU...**).

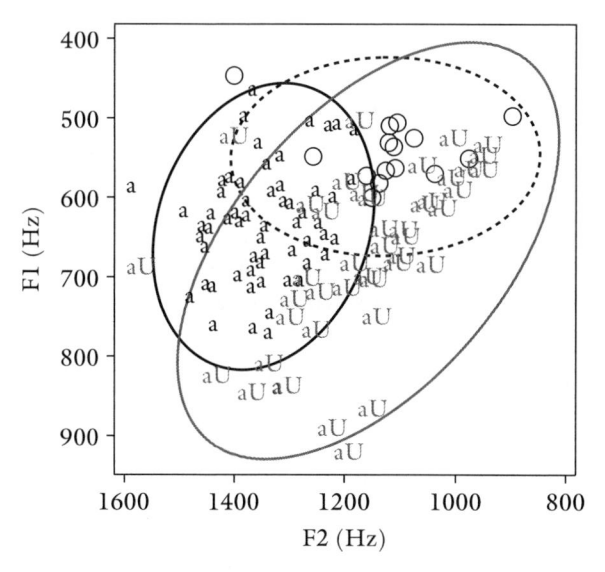

Figure 6.27 95% confidence ellipses in the plane of F2 × F1 at the temporal midpoint of [a, ɔ] and at the time at which F1 reaches a maximum in [aʊ] for a male speaker of Standard German.

B.5 The task is to check how close the quality of the diphthong at the alignment point in B.4 is to the same speaker's (67) lax [a, ɔ] (**a, O**) vowels extracted from F1 and F2 data at the temporal midpoint. Using the data from B.4 above in combination with the R objects of these lax monophthongs in A.1, make a plot of the kind shown in Figure 6.27 for this purpose. What can you conclude about the quality of the first target of this diphthong? What phonetic factor might cause it to have lower F2 values than the lax monophthong [a]?

C. Formant curvature and undershoot (section 6.6)

C.1 Which diphthong, [aɪ] or [ɔʏ], would you expect to have greater curvature in F1 and why?

C.2 Produce a linearly time-normalized plot of F1 of the female speaker's [aɪ] and [ɔʏ] diphthongs. Does this match your predictions in C1?

C.3 Fit parabolas to F1 of the diphthongs for both speakers (i.e., create a matrix of coefficients that is parallel to the R objects for the diphthong segments). Based on the evidence of the hyperarticulation differences between the speakers presented in this chapter, which speaker is expected to show less formant F1 curvature in the diphthongs?

C.4 Produce on one page four boxplots (analogous to Figure 6.15) of the curvature parameter for the label combinations **aI.67** (the male speaker's [aɪ]), **OY.67** (the male speaker's [ɔʏ]), **aI.68** (the female speaker's [aɪ]), and **OY.68** (the female speaker's [ɔʏ]).

D. F2 loci (section 6.7)

D.1

D.1.1 How would you expect the slope of the locus equation to be different in continuous speech compared with the type of isolated, citation-form production examined in 6.7 above?

D.1.2 If the female speaker 68 hyperarticulates compared with the male speaker 67, i.e., produces more distinctive consonant and vowel targets, how might their locus equation slopes differ for the same place of articulation?

D.1.3 Check your predictions by calculating and plotting locus equations in the plane of $F2_{Onset} \times F2_{Target}$ for /d/ preceding the lax vowels in the segment list **vowlax** separately for both speakers (the left context labels are given in **vowlax.left**; take F2 at the temporal midpoint for F2-target values). Set the ranges for the x- and y-axes to be between 1,000 Hz and 2,500 Hz in both cases.

D.2 How would you expect (a) the estimated F2-locus frequency and (b) the slope of the locus equation for initial [v] to compare with those of initial [d]? Check your hypotheses by making F2-locus equations based on vowels following initial [v] analogous to the ones above for initial [d] and compare the F2 loci and slopes between these places of articulation for both speakers.

D.3 Make a time-aligned plot color-coded for [v] or [d] of F2 trajectories for the male speaker following these two consonants (a plot like the one in Figure 6.23 but in which the trajectories are of F2 for the vowels following [d] or [v]). Is the plot consistent with your results from D2 (i.e, locus differences and slope differences)?

6.9 Answers

A.1

```
mid = dcut(vowlax.fdat, .5, prop=T)
mid = bark(mid)
```

A.2

```
temp = vowlax.spkr=="68" & vowlax.l=="E"
eplot(cbind(mid[temp,3]-mid[temp,2], -mid[temp,1]),
vowlax.l[temp], dopoints=T, ylab="- F1 (Bark)", xlab="F3 - F2
(Bark)")
```

A.3

```
temp = vowlax.spkr=="68" & vowlax.l=="E" & mid[,3]-mid[,2] < -12
mid = mid[!temp,]
```

A.4

```
mid.sp = vowlax.spkr[!temp]
mid.l = vowlax.l[!temp]
```

A.5

```
temp = mid.sp=="67"
par(mfrow=c(1,2)); xlim = c(0, 8); ylim = c(-9, -2)
ylab="- F1 (Bark)"; xlab="F3 - F2 (Bark)"
eplot(cbind(mid[temp,3]-mid[temp,2], -mid[temp,1]),
mid.l[temp], dopoints=T, xlim=xlim, ylim=ylim, xlab=xlab,
ylab=ylab)
eplot(cbind(mid[!temp,3]-mid[!temp,2], -mid[!temp,1]),
mid.l[!temp], dopoints=T, xlim=xlim, ylim=ylim, xlab=xlab)
```

B.1

```
mtime = trapply(vowlax.rms, peakfun, simplify=T)
```

B.2

```
form = dcut(vowlax.fdat[,1:2], mtime)
temp = vowlax.spkr == "68"
eplot(form[temp,], vowlax.l[temp], centroid=T, form=T)
```

B.3

```
temp = dip.l == "aU"
dplot(dip.fdat[temp,1], ylab="F1 (Hz)")
```

B.4

```
maxf1 = trapply(dcut(dip.fdat[,1], 0, 0.5, prop=T), peakfun,
simplify=T)
temp = dip.l == "aU"
formau = dcut(dip.fdat[temp,1:2], maxf1[temp])
labsau = dip.l[temp]
```

B.5 [ʊ] has a backing effect on [a] in the diphthong [aʊ], thus lowering F2.

```
temp = vowlax.l %in% c("a", "O") & vowlax.spkr == "67"
mono.f.5 = dcut(vowlax.fdat[temp,1:2], .5, prop=T)
both = rbind(mono.f.5, formau)
both.l = c(vowlax.l[temp], labsau)
eplot(both, both.l, form=T, dopoints=T, xlab="F2 (Hz)",
ylab="F1 (Hz)")
```

C.1 [aɪ] because the change in openness of the vocal tract between the two component vowels is greater than for [ɔʏ].

C.2

```
temp = dip.l %in% c("aI", "OY") & dip.spkr == "68"
dplot(dip.fdat[temp,1], dip.l[temp], norm=T)
```

Yes

C.3 Speaker 67

```
coeff = trapply(dip.fdat[,1], plafit, simplify=T)
```

C.4

```
temp = dip.l %in% c("aI", "OY")
boxplot(coeff[temp,3] ~ dip.l[temp] * dip.spkr[temp])
```

D.1

D.1.1 The slope in continuous speech should be higher because of the greater coarticulatory effects.

D.1.2 The slopes for speaker 68 should be lower.

D.1.3

```
temp = vowlax.left=="d" & vowlax.spkr == "67"
on.m = dcut(vowlax.fdat[temp,2], 0, prop=T)
mid.m = dcut(vowlax.fdat[temp,2], .5, prop=T)

temp = vowlax.left=="d" & vowlax.spkr == "68"
on.f = dcut(vowlax.fdat[temp,2], 0, prop=T)
mid.f = dcut(vowlax.fdat[temp,2], .5, prop=T)

par(mfrow=c(1,2)); xlim=ylim=c(1000, 2500)
l.m.d = locus(mid.m, on.m, xlim=xlim, ylim=ylim)
l.f.d = locus(mid.f, on.f, xlim=xlim, ylim=ylim)
```

D.2

D.2.1 The locus frequency for [v] should be lower because labials according to the locus theory have a lower F2 locus than alveolars.

D.2.2 The slope of the locus equation for [v] should be higher. This is because alveolars are supposed to have the most stable locus of labials, alveolars, and velars, i.e., the place of articulation for alveolars, and hence the F2 locus, shifts the least due to the effects of vowel context.

```
temp = vowlax.left=="v" & vowlax.spkr == "67"
on.m = dcut(vowlax.fdat[temp,2], 0, prop=T)
mid.m = dcut(vowlax.fdat[temp,2], .5, prop=T)

temp = vowlax.left=="v" & vowlax.spkr == "68"
on.f = dcut(vowlax.fdat[temp,2], 0, prop=T)
mid.f = dcut(vowlax.fdat[temp,2], .5, prop=T)

par(mfrow=c(1,2)); xlim=ylim=c(1000, 2500)
l.m.v = locus(mid.m, on.m, xlim=xlim, ylim=ylim)
l.f.v = locus(mid.f, on.f, xlim=xlim, ylim=ylim)
```

The F2 locus for [v] (given by `l.m.v$locus` and `l.f.v$locus`) for the male and female speakers respectively are, rounded to the nearest Hz, 749 Hz and 995

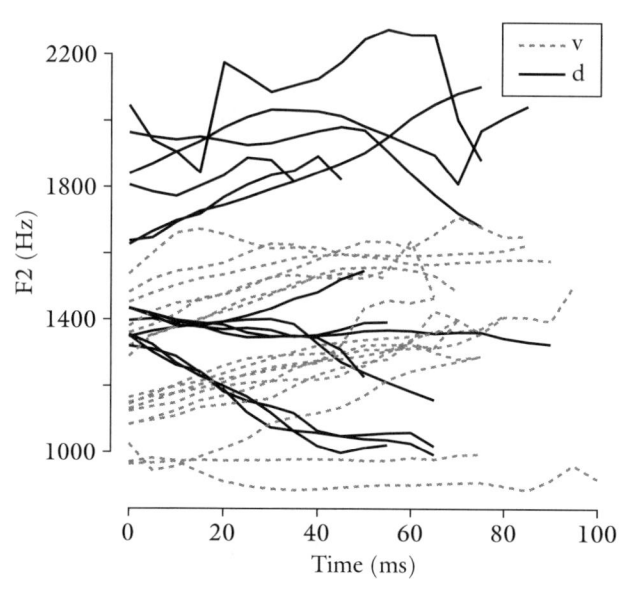

Analysis of Formants and Formant Transitions 219

Figure 6.28 F2 transitions for a male speaker of Standard German following [d] (solid) and [v] (dashed, gray).

Hz, i.e., markedly lower than for alveolars. The slopes of the locus equations for [v] (given by entering **l.m.v** and **l.f.v**) are 0.794 and 0.729 for the male and female speakers respectively and these are both higher than for the alveolar.

D.3

```
temp = vowlax.left %in% c("v", "d") & vowlax.spkr=="67"
dplot(vowlax.fdat[temp,2], vowlax.left[temp], ylab="F2 (Hz)")
```

Yes. The [v] and [d] transitions point to different loci as Figure 6.28 shows. Figure 6.28 also shows that the locus equation slope for [d] is likely to be lower because, even though the F2 range at the vowel target is quite large (over 1,000 Hz) from time point 50 ms, the F2-transitions for [d] nevertheless converge to about 1,600–700 Hz at F2 onset (*t* = 0 ms). There is much less evidence of any convergence for [v] and this is why the locus equation slope for [v] is higher than for [d].

Notes

[1] All these objects can be re-created from scratch: see Appendix C for further details.
[2] The relationship between the machine readable and phonetic alphabet for Australian vowels is given at the beginning of the book.

7
Electropalatography

7.1 Palatography and Electropalatography

Palatography is the general term given to the experimental technique for obtaining records of where the tongue makes a contact with the roof of the mouth. The earliest types of palatographic techniques were static, allowing recordings to be made of a single consonant typically produced between vowels. In static palatography, which is still very useful especially in fieldwork (Ladefoged 2003), the roof of the mouth is coated in a mixture of olive oil and powdered charcoal and the subject produces a consonant. Details of the consonant's place of articulation and stricture are obtained from a photograph taken of the roof of the mouth showing where the powder was wiped off and sometimes also of the tongue (which is coated in the powder at the point where tongue–palate contact was made). Dynamic electropalatography (Hardcastle 1972; Hardcastle et al. 1991) is an extension of this technique in which tongue–palate contacts are recorded as a function of time. In dynamic palatography, an acrylic palate is custom-made for each subject and fixed to the roof of the mouth using clasps placed over the teeth. The palate is very thin and contains a number of electrodes that are exposed to the surface of the tongue (Figure 7.1).

Each electrode is connected to a wire and all the wires from the electrodes are passed out of the corner of the subject's mouth in two bundles. The wires are fed into a processing unit whose job it is to detect whether or not there is electrical activity in any of the electrodes. The choice is binary in all cases: either there is activity or there is not. Electrical activity is registered whenever the tongue surface touches an electrode because this closes an electrical circuit that is created by means of a small electrical current passed through the subject's body via a hand-held electrode.

Three electropalatography (EPG) systems that have been commercially available include the Reading EPG3 system developed at the University of Reading and now sold by Articulate Instruments; a Japanese system produced by the Rion corporation and an American system that has been sold by Kay Elemetrics Corporation (see Gibbon & Nicolaidis 1999 for a comparison of the three systems).

The palate of the Reading EPG3 system, which is the system that is compatible with Emu-R, contains 62 electrodes, as shown in Figure 7.1, which are arranged in

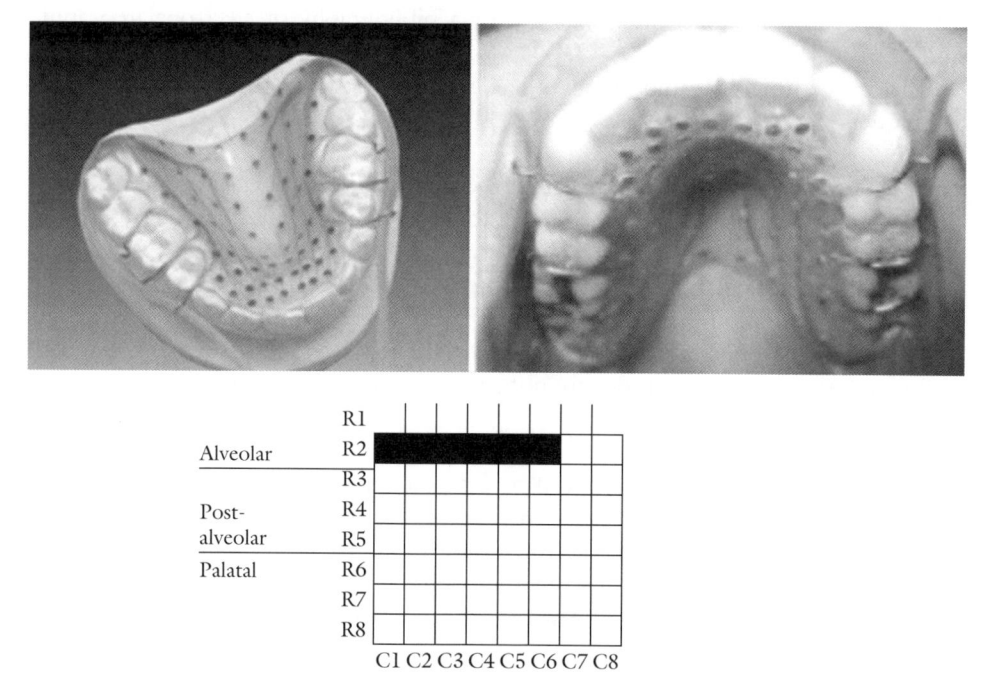

Figure 7.1 The palate of the EPG3 system in a plaster cast impression of the subject's upper teeth and roof of the mouth (left) and fixed in the mouth (right). Pictures from the Speech Science Research Centre, Queen Margaret University College, Edinburgh, www.qmuc.ac.uk/ssrc/DownSyndrome/EPG.htm. Below is a figure of the palatographic array as it appears in R showing 6 contacts in the second row. The relationship to phonetic zones and to the row (R1–R8) and column (C1–C8) numbers is also shown.

eight rows. The first row, at the front of the palate and just behind the upper front teeth, contains six electrodes, and the remaining rows each have eight electrodes. There is a greater density of electrodes in the dental-alveolar than in the dorsal region to ensure that the fine detail of lingual activity that is possible in the dental, alveolar, and post-alveolar zones can be recorded. The last row is generally positioned at the junction between the subject's hard and soft palate.

Figure 7.1 also shows the type of display produced by the EPG-system; the cells are either black (1), when the corresponding electrode is touched by the tongue surface, or white (0) when it is not. This type of display is known as a **palatogram** and the EPG3 system typically produces palatograms at a sampling frequency of 100 Hz, i.e., one palatogram every 10 ms. As Figure 7.1 shows, the palate is designed to register contacts extending from the alveolar to palatal articulations with divisions broadly into alveolar (rows 1–2), post-alveolar (rows 3–4), palatal (rows 5–7), and post-palatal (row 8).

Electropalatography is an excellent tool for studying consonant-cluster overlap and timing. It also has an important application in the diagnosis and the treatment of speech disorders. There is mostly a reasonably transparent relationship between phonetic quality and EPG output: a [t] really does show up as contacts in the alveolar zone, the different groove widths between [s] and [ʃ] are usually very clearly manifested in EPG displays, and coarticulatory and assimilatory influences can often be seen and quantified. (See Gibbon 2005 for a bibliography of electropalatographic studies since 1957.)

At the same time, it is important to be clear about some of the limitations of this technique:

- A separate palate (involving a visit to the dentist for a plaster-cast impression of the roof of the mouth) has to be made for each subject, which can be both time-consuming and expensive.
- As with any articulatory technique, subject-to-subject variation can be considerable. This variation can come about not only because subjects may invoke different articulatory strategies for producing the same phonetic segment, but also because the rows of electrodes are not always aligned with exactly the same articulatory landmarks across subjects.
- EPG can obviously give no direct information about labial consonants (apart from coarticulatory effects induced by other segments) and there is usually only limited information for places of articulation beyond a post-palatal or pre-velar articulation: that is, /k/ in English shows up clearly in *key*, but for many subjects there may be scarcely any recorded activity for the retracted /k/ in *call*.
- EPG can only give limited information about vowels. It does register contact at the sides of the palate in non-low front vowels, but provides little information about tongue position and velocity.
- Some older EPG systems have fixed sampling rates of 100 Hz and 10 kHz for the palatograms and acoustic signal respectively. A 100 Hz palatogram rate is often too slow to record details of rapid articulatory movements; a 10,000 Hz sampling frequency with the associated 5,000 Hz cut-off is often too low for carrying out articulatory-acoustic modeling of fricatives.

7.2 An Overview of Electropalatography in Emu-R

The databases listed at the beginning of this book whose names begin with **epg** include electropalatographic data and they can all be downloaded following the procedure discussed in 2.2. When an utterance is opened from any of these databases, a palatographic frame appears at the time point of the cursor (Figure 7.2). The electropalatographic data that is compatible with Emu is derived from the 62-electrode EPG system manufactured by Articulate Instruments.[1] If you already have your own EPG data from this system, then the files need to be converted into an SSFF (simple signal file format) to read them into Emu: this can be done after starting Emu from **Arrange Tools** and then **EPG2SSFF**.

Once an EPG database is available in Emu, then the EPG signal files of the database are accessible to Emu-R in all the ways that have been described in the preceding chapters. In addition, there are some functions that are specific to an EPG analysis in Emu-R, and these and the relationship between them are summarized in Figure 7.3.

As Figure 7.3 shows, there are four main components to the EPG analysis in Emu-R.

1 **Accessing the database**. The EPG data is accessed from the database in the usual way from a segment list via the **emu.track()** function.

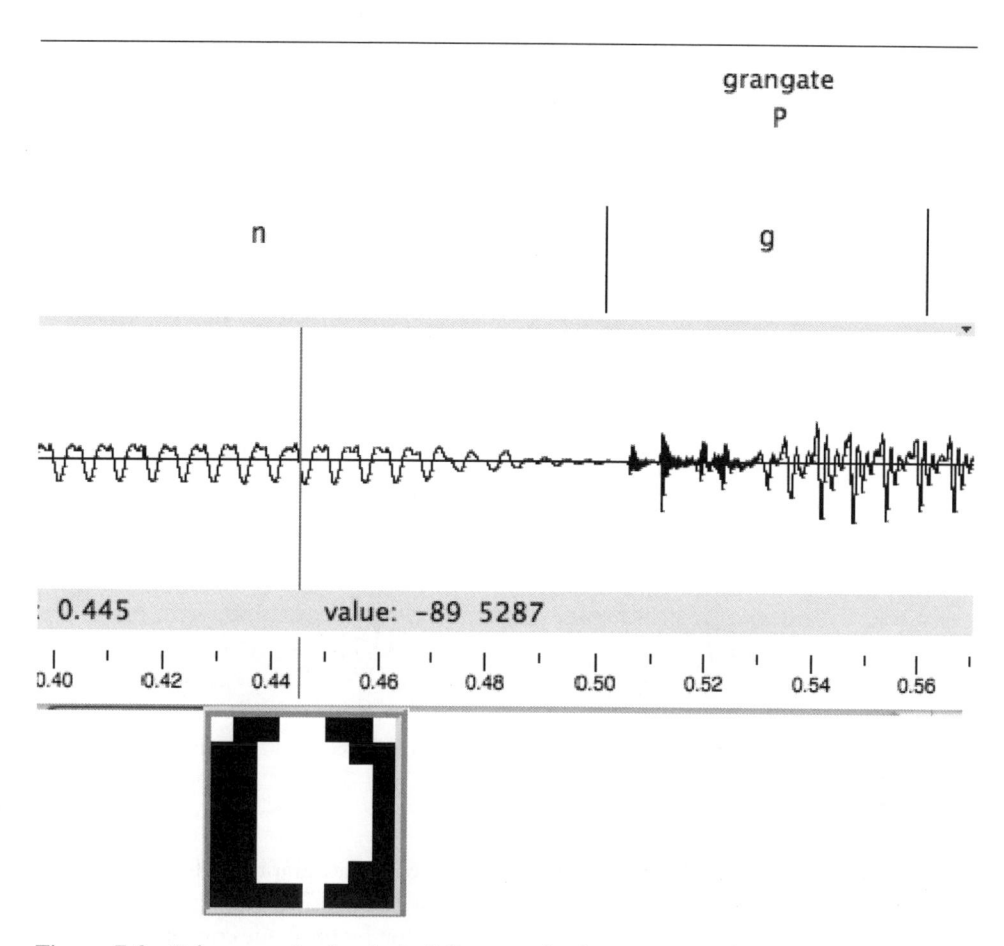

Figure 7.2 Palatogram in the /n/ of *Grangate* in the utterance of the same name from the **epgassim** database. The palatogram is at the time point shown by the vertical line in the waveform.

2. **EPG objects**. The EPG data that is read into R with **emu.track()** is an EPG-compressed trackdata object (Figure 7.3, box 2, A) which compresses the 62 zero and one values of each palatogram into a vector of just eight values. Since this is a trackdata object, then it is amenable to **dcut()** for obtaining an EPG-compressed matrix at a single time point (Figure 7.3, box 2, B). Both of these EPG-compressed objects can be uncompressed in R (using the **palate()** function) to produce a **3D palatographic array** (Figure 7.3, box 2, C): that is, an array of palatograms containing 0 s and 1 s in an 8 × 8 matrix.

Any of the objects listed under 2 are then amenable to two kinds of analysis: plotting or further parameterization, as follows:

3. **EPG plots**. Two kinds of plots are possible: either the palatograms showing their time-stamps, or a three-dimensional grayscale plot that represents the frequency of contact over two or more palatograms.

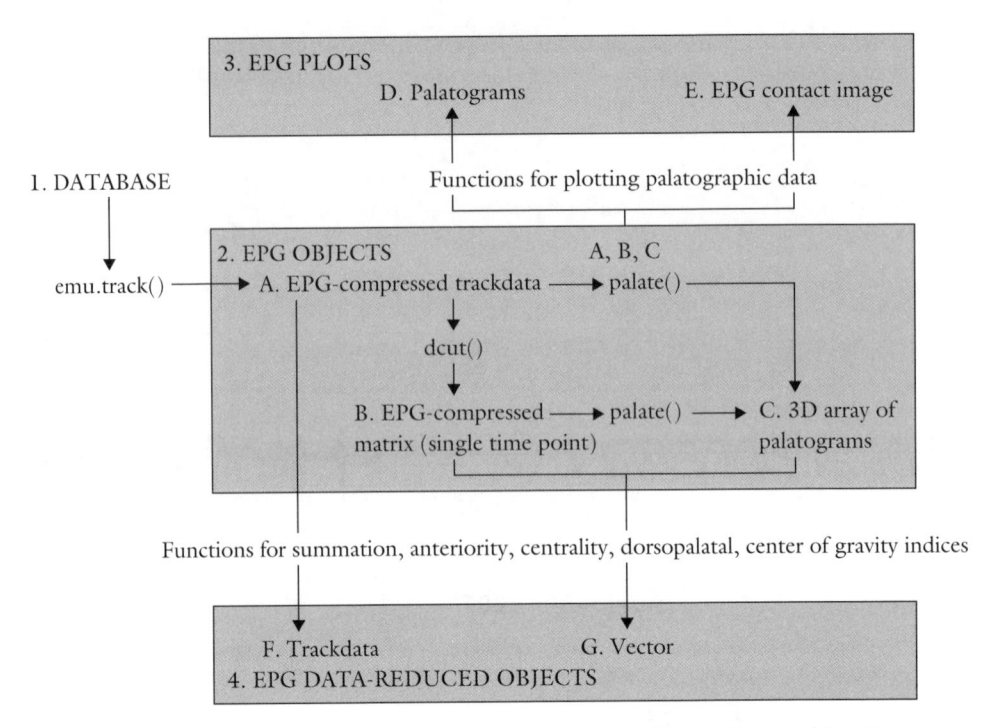

Figure 7.3 Schematic outline of the relationship between electropalatographic objects and functions in R.

4 **EPG data-reduced objects**. In this case, the 62 palatographic values from each palatogram are reduced to a single value. As will be shown later in this chapter, these data-reduced objects can be very useful for quantifying consonantal overlap and coarticulation.

It will be helpful to begin by looking in some further detail at the types of R objects in box 2 (EPG objects) of Figure 7.3, because they are central to all the other forms of EPG analysis, as the figure shows. All the EPG databases that are pre-stored and accessible within the Emu-R library and used as examples in this chapter are initially in the form of EPG-compressed trackdata objects (A. in Figure 7.3) and this is also always the way that you would first encounter EPG data in R if you were using your own database obtained from the Articulate Instruments EPG system. One of the available EPG database fragments is **epgcoutts**, recorded by Sallyanne Palethorpe, and it includes the following R objects:

coutts   Segment list of the sentence *just relax said Coutts* (one segment per word)
coutts.sam Sampled speech trackdata object of **coutts**
coutts.epg EPG-compressed trackdata object of **coutts** (frame rate 5 ms)

The segment list, **coutts**, consists of four words of a sentence produced by a female speaker of Australian English and the sentence forms part of a passage that was constructed by Hewlett and Shockey (1992) for investigating (acoustically) coarticulation in /k/ and /t/. Here is the segment list:

```
coutts
segment list from database: epgcoutts
query was: [Word!=x ^ Utterance=u1]
   labels      start      end         utts
1  just       16018.8    16348.8    spstoryfast01
2  relax      16348.8    16685.7    spstoryfast01
3  said       16685.7    16840.1    spstoryfast01
4  Coutts     16840.1    17413.7    spstoryfast01
```

The EPG-compressed trackdata object **coutts.epg** therefore also necessarily consists of four segments, as can be verified with **nrow(coutts.epg)**. Thus the speech frames of EPG data for the first word in the segment list, *just*, are given by **frames(coutts.epg[1,])**. The command **dim(frames(coutts.epg[1,]))** shows that this is a 66×8 matrix: 66 rows because there are 66 palatograms between the start and end time of *just* and 8 columns which provide the information about palatographic contacts in columns 8 to 1 respectively. As for all trackdata objects, the times at which these EPG frames of data occur are stored as row names (accessible with **tracktimes(coutts.epg)**) and for this example they show that palatographic frames occur at intervals of 5 ms (i.e., at times 16,020 ms, 16,025 ms, etc.).

Each of the EPG frames can be unpacked into a series of zeros and ones corresponding to the absence and presence of contact in the palatogram. The unpacking is done by converting these values into binary numbers after adding 1 (one). More specifically, consider e.g., the twenty-third EPG frame of the first segment:

```
frames(coutts.epg[1,])[23,]
 T1   T2   T3   T4   T5  T6 T7 T8
195  195  131  131  129   1  0  0
```

The first value, corresponding to row 8, is 195. In order to derive the corresponding palatographic contacts for this row, $195 + 1 = 196$ is converted into binary numbers. In binary form, 196 is 11000011 and so this is the contact pattern for the last (eighth) row of the palate at time 16,020 ms (i.e., there is lateral contact and no contact at the center of the palate). Since the next entry is also 195, then row 7 evidently has the same contact pattern.

This job of converting EPG frames into binary values and hence palatographic contacts is done by the **palate()** function. So the palatogram for all 66 rows of data in **coutts.epg[1,]**, i.e., of the word *just* extending in time from 16,020 ms to 16,340 ms is obtained as follows:

p = palate(coutts.epg[1,])

p is a three-dimensional array of palatograms, as shown by the following:

```
dim(p)
8  8  66
```

The first element that is returned by **dim(p)** refers to the **number of palatographic rows** and the second to the **number of palatographic columns**: these are therefore always both 8 because each palatogram contains contacts defined over an 8 × 8 grid. The third entry is **the number of palatograms**. The result here is 66 because, as has just been shown, this is the number of palatograms between the start and end times of *just*.

A three-dimensional palatographic array is indexed in R with **[r, c, n]** where **r** and **c** are the row and column number of the palatogram and **n** is the frame number (from 1 to 66 in the present example). In order to get at the entire palatogram, omit the **r** and **c** arguments. So the first palatogram at the onset of the word *just* (at time 16,020 ms corresponding to the first row of **frames(coutts.epg[1,])** is:

```
p[,,1]
      C1  C2  C3  C4  C5  C6  C7  C8
  R1   0   1   1   1   1   1   0   0
  R2   1   1   1   1   1   1   1   1
  R3   1   1   1   0   0   1   1   1
  R4   1   1   1   0   0   0   1   1
  R5   1   1   0   0   0   0   0   1
  R6   1   1   0   0   0   0   1   1
  R7   1   1   0   0   0   0   1   1
  R8   1   1   0   0   0   0   1   1
```

In this type of array, the row and column numbers are given as the respective dimension names. Since the first row of the EPG3 palate has six contacts (i.e., it is missing the two most lateral contacts), the values both in row 1 column 1 and in row 1 column 8 are always zero.

The indexing on the palatograms works as for matrices, but since this is a 3D array, *two* preceding commas have to be included to get at the palatogram number: so **p[,,1:3]** refers to the first three palatograms, **p[,,c(2, 4)]** to palatograms 2 and 4, **p[,,-1]** to all palatograms except the first one, and so on. It is worthwhile getting used to manipulating these kinds of palatographic arrays because this is often the primary data that you will have to work with, if you ever need to write your own functions for analyzing EPG data (all the functions for EPG plotting and EPG data reduction in boxes 3 and 4 of Figure 7.3 are operations on these kinds of arrays). One way to become familiar with these kinds of arrays is to make up some palatographic data. For example:

```
# Create 4 empty palatograms
fake = array(0, c(8, 8, 4))

# Give fake appropriate row and dimension names for a palatogram
rownames(fake) = paste("R", 1:8, sep="")
colnames(fake) = paste("C", 1:8, sep="")
```

```
# Fill up row 2 of the third palatogram with contacts
fake[2,,3] = 1

# Fill up row 1, columns 3-6, of the third palatogram only with contacts
fake[1,3:6,3] = 1

# Look at the third palatogram
fake[,,3]
     C1  C2  C3  C4  C5  C6  C7  C8
R1   0   0   1   1   1   1   0   0
R2   1   1   1   1   1   1   1   1
R3   0   0   0   0   0   0   0   0
R4   0   0   0   0   0   0   0   0
R5   0   0   0   0   0   0   0   0
R6   0   0   0   0   0   0   0   0
R7   0   0   0   0   0   0   0   0
R8   0   0   0   0   0   0   0   0

# Give contacts to rows 7-8, columns 1, 2, 7, 8 of palatograms 1, 2, 4
fake[7:8, c(1, 2, 7, 8), c(1, 2, 4)] = 1

# Look at rows 5 and 7, columns 6 and 8, of the palatograms 2 and 4
fake[c(5,7), c(6, 8), c(2,4)]

, , 1
     C6  C8
R5   0   0
R7   0   1

, , 2
     C6  C8
R5   0   0
R7   0   1
```

The times at which palatograms occur are stored as the names of the third dimension and they can be set as follows:

```
# Assume that these four palatograms occur at times 0, 5, 10, 15 ms
times = seq(0, by=5, length=4)

# Store these times as dimension names of fake
dimnames(fake)[[3]] = times
```

This causes the time values to appear instead of the index number. So the same instruction as the previous one now looks like this:[2]

```
, , 5
    C6 C8
R5  0  0
R7  0  1

, , 15
    C6 C8
R5  0  0
R7  0  1
```

Functions can be applied to the separate components of arrays in R using the **apply()** function. For 3D arrays, 1 and 2 in the second argument to **apply()** refer to the rows and columns (as they do for matrices) and 3 to the third dimension of the array, for example:

```
# Sum the number of contacts in the four palatograms
apply(fake, 3, sum)
0  0  12  0
```

```
# Sum the number of contacts in the columns
apply(fake, c(2,3), sum)
    0  5  10  15
C1  2  2   1   2
C2  2  2   1   2
C3  0  0   2   0
C4  0  0   2   0
C5  0  0   2   0
C6  0  0   2   0
C7  2  2   1   2
C8  2  2   1   2
```

Notice that the above command returns a matrix whose columns refer to palatograms 1–4 respectively (at times 0, 5, 10, 15 ms) and whose rows show the summed values per palatographic column. So the entries in the first line mean: the number of contacts in column 1 of the palatograms occurring at 0, 5, 10, 15 ms are 2, 2, 1, 2 respectively. If you want to sum (or to apply any meaningful function) by row or column **across all palatograms together**, then the second argument has to be 1 (for rows) or 2 (for columns) on its own. Thus:

```
apply(fake, 1, sum)
R1 R2 R3 R4 R5 R6 R7 R8
 4  8  0  0  0  0 12 12
```

The first returned entry under **R1** means that the sum of the contacts in row 1 of all four palatograms together is four (which is also given by **sum(fake[1,,])**).

As already mentioned, arrays can be combined with logical vectors in the usual way – but take great care where to place the comma! For example, suppose that these are four palatograms corresponding to the labels **k**, **k**, **t**, **k** respectively. Then the palatograms for **k** can be given by:

```
lab = c("k", "k", "t", "k")
temp = lab=="k"
fake[,,temp]
```

and rows 1–4 of the palatograms for **t** are:

```
fake[1:4,,!temp]
```

and so on. Finally, in order to apply the functions in boxes 3 and 4 of Figure 7.3 to made-up data of this kind, the data must be declared to be of class "EPG" (this tells the functions that these are EPG objects). This is done straightforwardly as:

```
class(fake) = "EPG"
```

Having established some basic attributes of EPG objects in R, the two functions for plotting palatograms can now be considered. As Figure 7.4 shows, palatograms can be plotted directly from EPG-compressed trackdata objects or from time slices extracted from these using **dcut()**, or else from the 3D palatographic arrays of the kind discussed above. We will begin by looking at EPG data from the third and fourth segments *said Coutts*. This is given by **epgplot(coutts.epg[3:4,])** (or by **epgplot(palate(coutts.epg[3:4,]))**) and the corresponding waveform, from which the palatograms are derived, by **plot(coutts.sam[3:4,], type="l")**.

Some of the main characteristics of the resulting palatograms shown in Figure 7.4 are:

- The alveolar constriction for the fricative [s] of *said* is in evidence in the first seven palatograms between 16,690 ms and 16,720 ms.
- The alveolar constriction for [d] of *said* begins to form at 16,800 ms and there is a complete alveolar closure for eight palatograms, i.e., for 40 ms.
- There is clear evidence of a doubly articulated [d̂k] in *sai̱d̲ ̲C̲outts* (i.e., a stop produced with simultaneous alveolar and velar closures) between 16,825 ms and 16,835 ms.
- [k] of *Coutts* is released at 16,920 ms.
- The aspiration of *Coutts* and the following [ʉ] vowel extend through to about 17,105 ms.
- The closure for the final alveolar [t] of *Coutts* is first completed at 17,120 ms. The release of this stop into the final [s] is at 17,205 ms.

The interval including at least the doubly articulated [d̂k] has been marked by vertical lines on the waveform in Figure 7.5. This was done with the **locator()** function that allows any number of points on a plot to be selected and the values in either *x*- or *y*-dimension to be stored (these commands must be entered after those used to plot Figure 7.5):

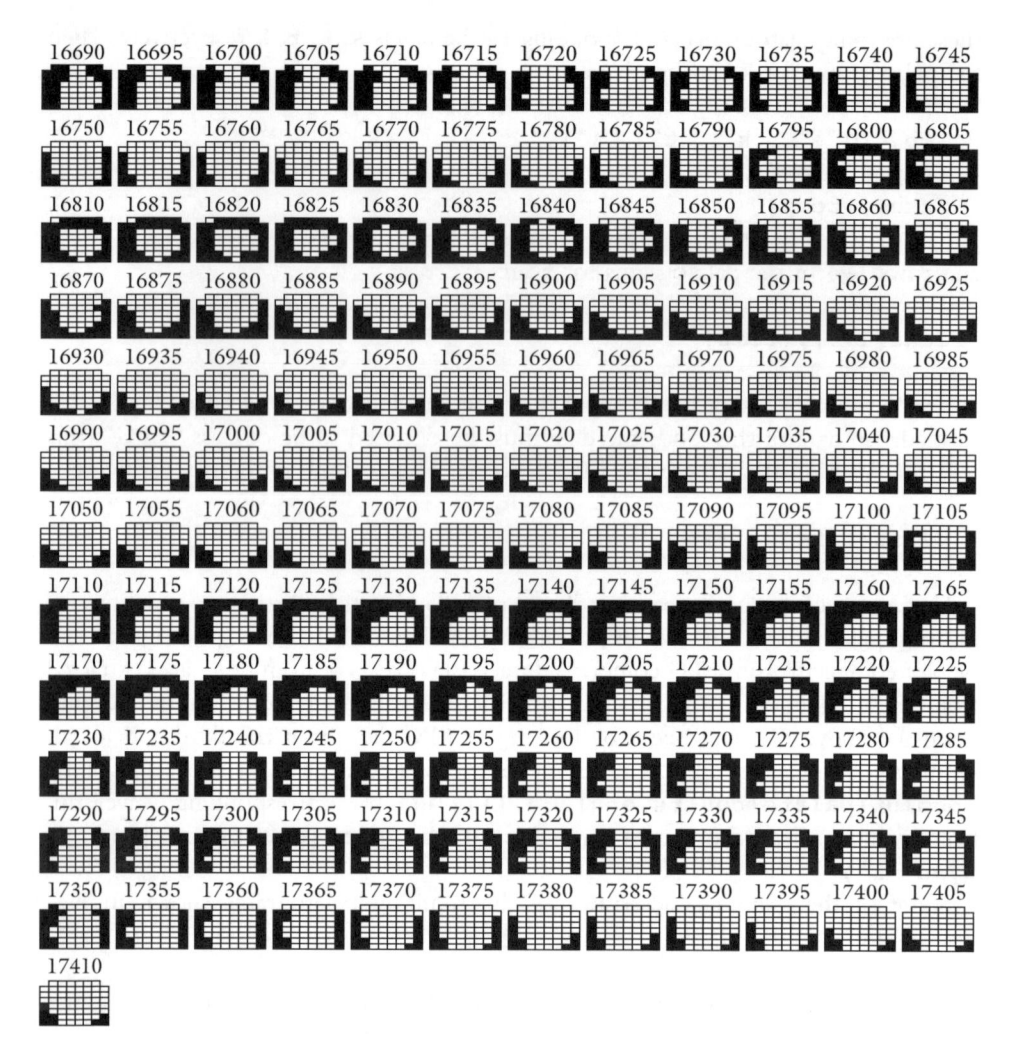

Figure 7.4 Palatograms of *said Coutts* showing the times (ms) at which they occurred.

```
# Select two time points and store the x-coordinates
times = locator(2)$x

# The vertical boundaries in Figure 7.5 are at these times
times
16828.48 16932.20
abline(v=times)
```

The **xlim** argument can be used to plot the palatograms over this time interval and optionally the **mfrow** argument to set the number of rows and columns (you will also often need to sweep out the graphics window in R to get an approximately square shape for the palatograms):

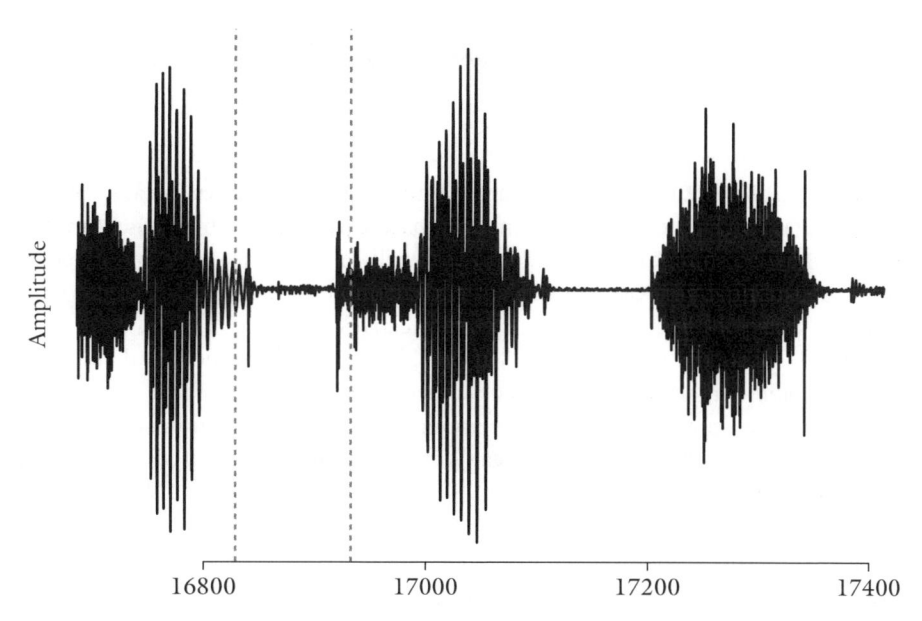

Figure 7.5 Waveform over the same time interval as the palatograms in Figure 7.4. The vertical dotted lines mark the interval that is selected in Figure 7.6.

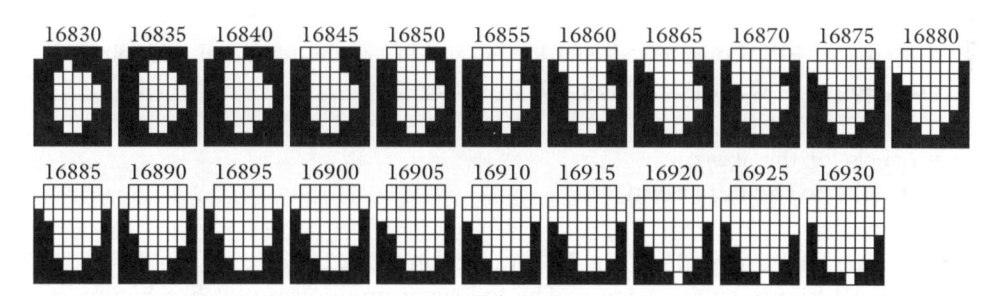

Figure 7.6 Palatograms over the interval marked by the vertical lines in Figure 7.5.

```
# A 2 × 11 display of palatograms plotted between the interval defined by times
epgplot(coutts.epg, xlim=times, mfrow=c(2,11))
```

The next example of manipulating and plotting electropalatographic data is taken from a fragment of a database of Polish fricatives that was collected in Guzik and Harrington (2007). This database was used to investigate the relative stability of fricatives in word-final and word-initial position. Four fricatives were investigated: the alveolar [s], a post-alveolar [ʃ], an alveolo-palatal [ɕ], and a velar [x]. They were produced in word pairs in all possible combinations with each other across word boundaries. So there are sequences like [s#ʃ] (in *wlos szary*), [ʃ#ɕ] (in *pytasz siostre*), [x#s] (in *dach sali*) and so on for all possible 4 × 4 cross-word boundary combinations, including the homorganic sequences [s#s], [ʃ#ʃ], [ɕ#ɕ], [x#x]. The database fragment **polhom** is of the homorganic sequences produced by one native, adult male speaker of Polish. The palatographic data was sampled at 100 Hz:

polhom	Segment list of Polish homorganic fricatives
polhom.l	A parallel vector of labels (**s**, **S**, **c**, **x**, for [s#s], [ʃ#ʃ], [ç#ç], [x#x])
polhom.epg	Parallel EPG trackdata

As **table(polhom.l)** shows, there are 10 homorganic fricatives in each category. If you have accessed the corresponding database **epgpolish** from the **Arrange tools** → **DB Installer** in Emu, then you will see that the segment boundaries in the segment list **polhom** extend approximately from the acoustic onset to the acoustic offset of each of these homorganic fricatives.

The first task will be to compare [s] with [ʃ] as far as differences and similarities in palatographic contact patterns are concerned and this will be done by extracting the palatographic frames closest to the temporal midpoint of the fricatives. The data for [s] and [ʃ] are accessed with a logical vector, and **dcut()** is used for extracting the frames at the midpoint:

```
# Logical vector to identify [s] and [ʃ]
temp = polhom.l %in% c("s", "S")

# EPG-compressed trackdata for [s] and [ʃ]
cor.epg = polhom.epg[temp,]

# Matrix of EPG-compressed data for [s] and [ʃ] at the temporal midpoint
cor.epg.5 = dcut(cor.epg, 0.5, prop=T)

# Labels for the above
cor.l = polhom.l[temp]
```

sum(temp) shows that there are 20 fricatives and **table(cor.l)** confirms that there are 10 fricatives per category. The following produces a plot like Figure 7.7 of the palatograms at the temporal midpoint, firstly for [s], then for [ʃ]. Rather than displaying the times at which they occur, the palatograms have been numbered with the **num=T** argument:

```
temp = cor.l =="s"
epgplot(cor.epg.5[temp,], num=T)
epgplot(cor.epg.5[!temp,], num=T)
```

As expected, the primary stricture for [s] is further forward than for [ʃ] as shown by the presence of contacts for [s] but not for [ʃ] in row 1. A three-dimensional, grayscale image can be a useful way of summarizing the differences between two different types of segments: the function for doing this is **epggs()**:

```
par(mfrow=c(1,2))
epggs(cor.epg.5[temp,], main="s")
epggs(cor.epg.5[!temp,], main="S")
```

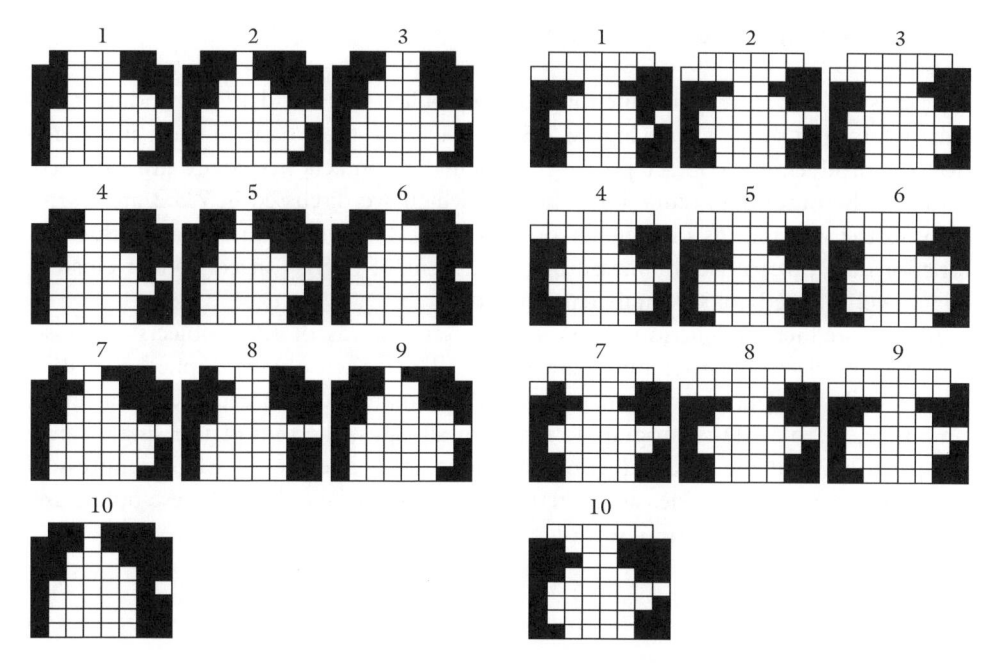

Figure 7.7 Palatograms for 10 [s] (left) and 10 [ʃ] (right) Polish fricatives extracted at the temporal midpoint from homorganic [s#s] and [ʃ#ʃ] sequences produced by an adult male speaker of Polish. (The electrode in column 8 row 5 malfunctioned and was off throughout all productions.)

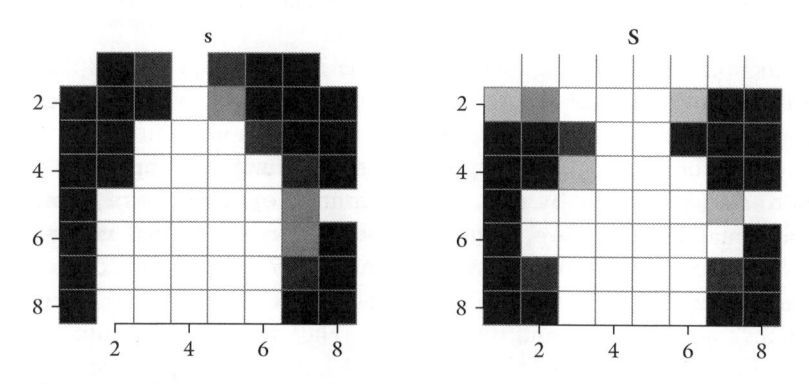

Figure 7.8 Grayscale images of the data in Figure 7.7 for [s] (left) and [ʃ] (right). The darkness of a cell is proportional to the number of times that the cell was contacted.

At the core of **epggs()** is a procedure for calculating **the proportional number of times a cell was contacted**. When a cell is black, then it means that it was contacted in all the palatograms over which the function was calculated, and when a cell is white, then there were no contacts. Thus for [s] in Figure 7.8, the entire first column is black in this three-dimensional display because, as Figure 7.7 shows, all ten palatograms for [s] have their contacts on in column 1; and columns 3 and 5 of rows 1 for [s] are dark gray, because, while most [s] palatograms had a contact for these cells (numbers 2, 5, 6, 9, 10 in Figure 7.7), others did not.

7.3 EPG Data-Reduced Objects

As discussed earlier, various functions can be applied to EPG data that reduce each palatogram to a single value (Figure 7.3, box 4). The most basic of these is a function for producing a contact profile in which the contacts per palate are summed (7.3.1). The other data-reduction functions which are discussed in 7.3.2 are essentially further operations on contact profiles. In 7.4, some of these data-reduction functions are put to use for measuring the extent of overlap in consonant clusters and vowel-induced consonantal coarticulation.

All data-reduction functions work on the same kinds of EPG objects as those for plotting electropalatographic data in 7.3. Thus, they can be applied to EPG-compressed trackdata objects, a matrix of EPG-compressed data extracted at a single time slice, or to a 3D-palatographic array. In all cases, the output is a single value per palatogram: if the data-reduction functions are applied to an EPG-compressed trackdata object, these values are structured into a trackdata object. These points are elaborated further in the next section.

7.3.1 Contact profiles

A contact profile is a form of data reduction in which palatographic data are summed by row(s) and/or by column(s). Contact profiles have a number of applications in phonetics: they can be used to distinguish between stops and fricatives at the same place of articulation (by summing the number of contacts in certain rows) or between different places of articulation (by summing contacts in different rows).

The function for calculating a contact profile is **epgsum()** and its default is to **sum all the contacts per palate**. Thus for the 3D-array **fake** created earlier, **epgsum(fake)** gives the same result as the operation applied in 7.2 for summing contacts in the four palatograms, **apply(fake, 3, sum)**.[3] But **epgsum()** can also be used to **sum selectively by row and column**. So **epgsum(fake, rows=1:4)** sums the contacts in rows 1–4, **epgsum(fake, rows=1:4, columns=c(1, 2, 7, 8))** sums contacts in rows 1–4 of columns 1, 2, 7, and 8. The additional argument **inactive=T** can be used to **sum the inactive electrodes** (the zeros of the palatograms) also by row and by column. The default is to sum the entire palatogram (in selected rows and/or columns) but it is also possible to show the summations for the separate rows or columns using a second argument of 1 (for rows) or 2 (for columns). For example, in the previous section it was shown how **apply(fake, c(2,3), sum)** gives the sum of the contacts in the columns: an equivalent way of doing this is **epgsum(fake, 2)**. See **help(epgsum)** for further examples.

In Figure 7.4, the separate palatograms at 5 ms intervals were shown for the words *said Coutts*. By making a display of the summed contacts in rows 1–3, the articulations in the front part of the palate should become very clearly visible, while a summation in the back two rows over columns 3–6 should produce a display which is associated with the degree of tongue-dorsum contact in /k/ of *Coutts*. Here are these two contact profiles:

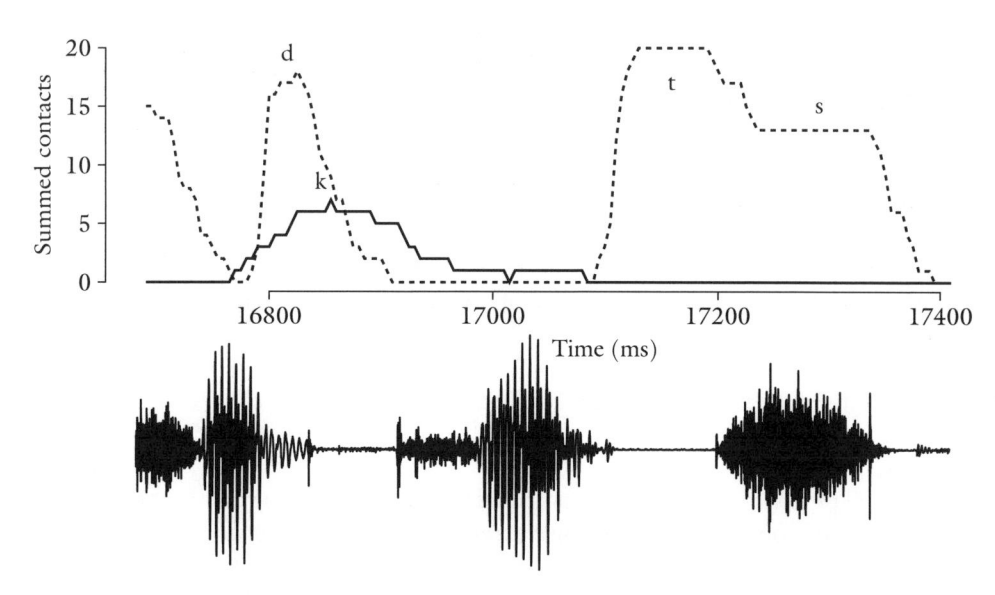

Figure 7.9 Sum of the contacts in rows 1–3 (dashed) and in rows 6–8 (solid) showing some phonetic landmarks synchronized with an acoustic waveform in *said Coutts* produced by an adult female speaker of Australian English.

```
# Sum rows 1-3 of the EPG trackdata object over said
fsum = epgsum(coutts.epg[3:4,], rows=1:3)

# Sum rows 7-8, columns 3-6 of the EPG trackdata object over said Coutts
bsum = epgsum(coutts.epg[3:4,], rows=7:8, columns=3:6)
```

A plot of the contact profiles superimposed on each other together with the waveform is shown in Figure 7.9 and can be produced as follows:

```
# Column-bind the trackdata objects
both = cbind(fsum, bsum)

# Save the defaults for setting graphical parameters
oldpar = par(no.readonly = TRUE)

par(mfrow=c(2,1)); par(mar=c(1,4,1,1))
xlim = c(start(coutts[3,]), end(coutts[4,]))
plot(both, type="l", ylab="Summed contacts", xlab="",
axes=F, xlim=xlim)
axis(side=2); axis(side=1)
mtext("Time (ms)", side=1, at=17300)

# Superimpose some symbols
text( c(16816, 16846, 17158, 17291), c(19.6, 8.7, 17.1,
15.0), c("d", "k", "t", "s"))
```

```
# Plot the synchronized acoustic waveform
plot(coutts.sam[3:4,], type="l", axes=F, xlab="Time (ms)",
ylab="", xlim=xlim)

# Restore the margin defaults
par(mar = oldpar$mar)
```

The synchronized contact profiles in Figure 7.9 provide a great deal of information about the overlap and lenition of the alveolar and velar articulations. For example:

- The tongue dorsum for [k] already begins to rise during [ɛ] of *said*.
- The maximum overlap between [d] and [k] is at the point of the final stop release in *said*.
- The [t] of *Coutts* is less lenited compared with [d] of *said*, as shown by the greater number of contacts for the former extending over a greater duration.

Contact profiles could be used to distinguish between the Polish [s, ʃ] fricatives discussed earlier according to the **central groove width** which could be defined as the smallest number of inactive electrodes in any row over the central columns 3–6. For example, in the first five palatograms of [s] in Figure 7.7, this central groove width is 3, 1, 2, 2, 1 respectively. For the first five [ʃ] palatograms in Figure 7.7, the central groove width is usually at least one inactive contact greater.

In order to obtain groove widths for the data in Figure 7.7, the first step is to count the number of *inactive* electrodes (i.e., those with a value of zero) over a particular row and column range: we will restrict this to the first four rows and to columns 3–6, since, as Figure 7.7 shows, this is the region of the palate within which the point of maximum narrowing occurs:

```
# Commands repeated from before
temp = polhom.l %in% c("s", "S")
cor.epg = polhom.epg[temp,]
cor.epg.5 = dcut(cor.epg, 0.5, prop=T)
cor.l = polhom.l[temp]

# Count the number of inactive electrodes in rows 1–4, columns 3–6
in.sum = epgsum(cor.epg.5, 1, rows=1:4, columns=3:6,
inactive=T)

# Show the first two rows of in.sum
in.sum[1:2,]
      R1  R2  R3  R4
2120   3   3   4   4
1170   1   1   3   4
```

So that it is completely clear what is being counted, the first two palatograms of the array are listed below. The count on the right is of the zeros in bold:

```
p = palate(cor.epg.5)
p [,,1:2]

, , 2120

    C1 C2 C3 C4 C5 C6 C7 C8
R1   0  1  0  0  0  1  1  0   3
R2   1  1  0  0  0  1  1  1   3
R3   1  1  0  0  0  0  1  1   4
R4   1  1  0  0  0  0  0  1   4
R5   1  0  0  0  0  0  0  0
R6   1  0  0  0  0  0  0  1
R7   1  0  0  0  0  0  0  1
R8   1  0  0  0  0  0  1  1

, , 1170

    C1 C2 C3 C4 C5 C6 C7 C8
R1   0  1  1  0  1  1  1  0   1
R2   1  1  1  0  1  1  1  1   1
R3   1  1  0  0  0  1  1  1   3
R4   1  1  0  0  0  0  1  1   4
R5   1  0  0  0  0  0  0  0
R6   1  0  0  0  0  0  0  1
R7   1  0  0  0  0  0  0  1
R8   1  0  0  0  0  0  1  1
```

A function is needed to get the *minimum* groove width – that is, the function should return 3 and 1 respectively for the above two palatograms. Since **in.sum** is a matrix, this can be done with the **apply()** function:

```
# Find the row with the fewest zeros and return the number of zeros for
that row
min.groove = apply(in.sum, 1, min)
```

```
# Minima for the first two palatograms above: this is correct (see the
palatograms above)
min.groove[1:2]
2120  1170
   3     1
```

The histogram in Figure 7.10 of the minimum groove width provides some limited evidence that it is less for [s] than for [ʃ]. The histogram was created with the following commands:

```
xlim = c(1,3); ylim = c(0, 6); par(mfrow=c(1,2))
xlab = "Min groove width"
```

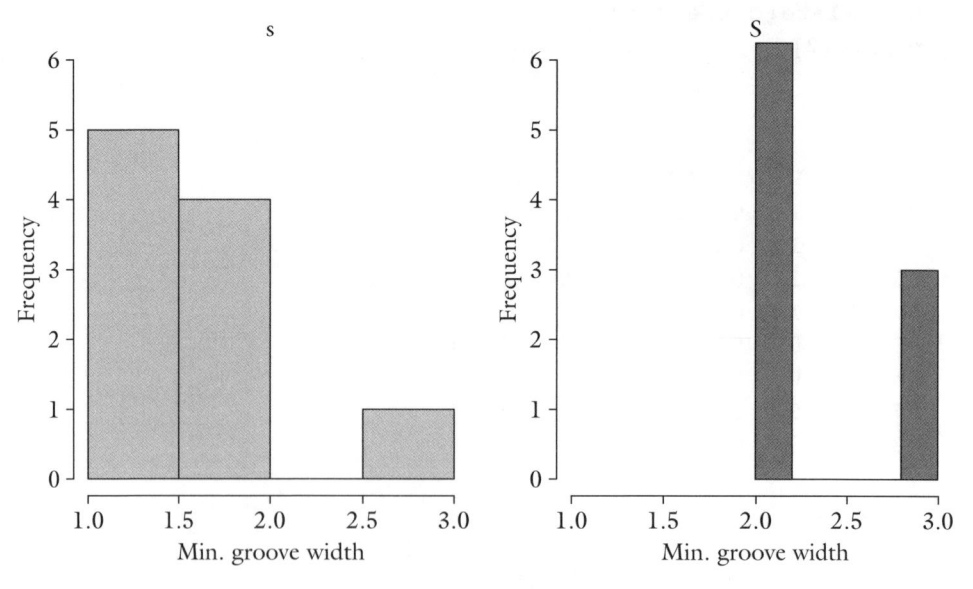

Figure 7.10 A histogram of the distribution of the minimum groove width shown separately for palatograms of Polish [s, ʃ]. The minimum groove width is obtained by finding whichever row over rows 1–5, columns 3–6 has the fewest number of inactive electrodes and then summing the inactive electrodes.

```
# Logical vector that is True for [s]
temp = cor.l=="s"
hist(min.groove[temp], col="gray", main="s", xlim=xlim,
ylim=ylim, xlab=xlab)
hist(min.groove[!temp], col="slategray", main="S",
xlim=xlim, ylim=ylim, xlab=xlab)
```

The above analysis was for one single palatogram per segment extracted at the temporal midpoint. The same kind of analysis could be carried out for *every* palatogram between the temporal onset and offset of these fricatives. This would allow us to see not only if there is a difference in minimum groove width between [s, ʃ], but also whether groove width decreases from the fricative margins towards the fricatives' temporal midpoint (this is to be expected given that the homorganic fricatives were flanked by vowels and given that the extent of stricture in fricative production tends to increase from the margins towards the temporal midpoint).

The first step is to count the number of inactive electrodes in rows 1–4 and columns 3–6 as before, but this time for all the palatograms contained in the entire EPG-compressed trackdata object. This is done in the following command by summing the number of inactive electrodes from the onset to the offset for all segments in the EPG-trackdata object **polhom.epg** and storing the count separately by row:

```
in.sum.all = epgsum(polhom.epg, 1, rows=1:4, columns=3:6,
inactive=T)
```

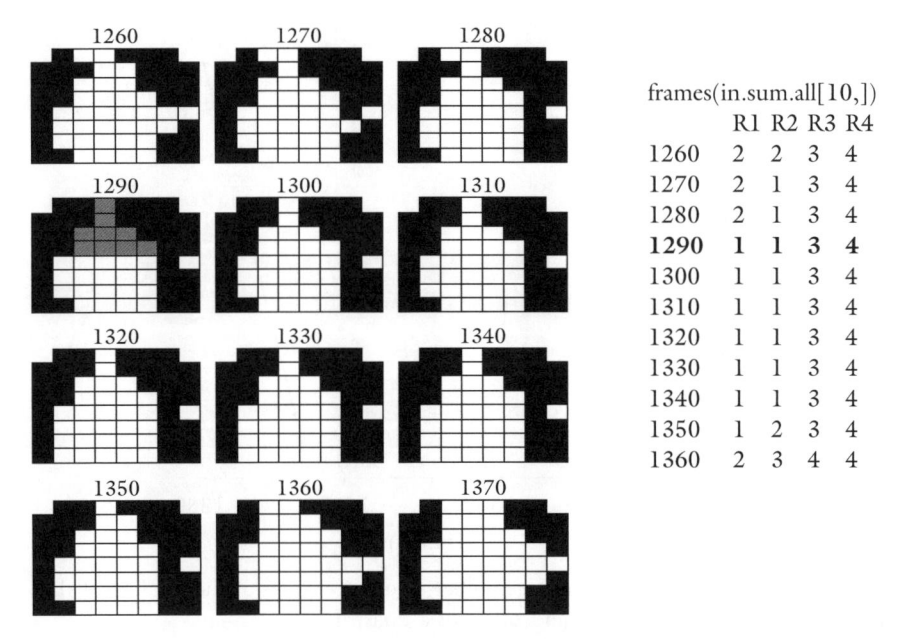

Figure 7.11 Palatograms for the first 12 frames between the acoustic onset and offset of a Polish [s]. On the right is the number of inactive electrodes for each palatogram in rows 1–7. The count of inactive electrodes for the palatogram 1290 ms is highlighted.

```
frames(in.sum.all[10,])
     R1 R2 R3 R4
1260  2  2  3  4
1270  2  1  3  4
1280  2  1  3  4
1290  1  1  3  4
1300  1  1  3  4
1310  1  1  3  4
1320  1  1  3  4
1330  1  1  3  4
1340  1  1  3  4
1350  1  2  3  4
1360  2  3  4  4
```

The object **in.sum.all** is four-dimensional (as shown by **summary(in.sum.all)**) and consists of the sum of inactive electrodes in rows 1–4 of columns 3–6 for every palatogram between the onset and offset of each fricative. So that it is clear what has just been calculated, Figure 7.11 shows the EPG data for the tenth segment (given by **epgplot(polhom.epg[10,])**), together with the corresponding minimum groove widths (given by **frames(in.sum.all[10,])**). Thus, the values of the rows at 1,290 ms in the matrix on the right of Figure 7.11 are 1, 1, 3, 4 because this is the count of inactive electrodes in rows 1–4, columns 3–6 of the palatogram shown on the left at that time. A function is now needed similar to the one before to find the minimum value per row in the EPG frames:

```
minfun <- function(contacts)
{

# Find the minimum per row
apply(contacts, 1, min)
}
```

When this function is applied to the data of the tenth segment, the minimum groove widths of the palatograms at intervals of 10 ms between the start and end time of the tenth segment are returned:

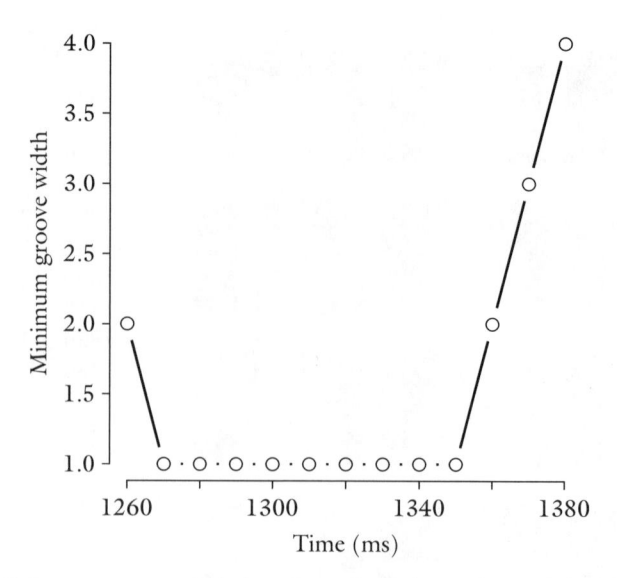

Figure 7.12 Minimum groove width (number of off electrodes in the midline of the palate) between the acoustic onset and offset of a Polish [s].

```
minfun(frames(in.sum.all[10,]))
1260 1270 1280 1290 1300 1310 1320 1330 1340 1350 1360 1370 1380
  2    1    1    1    1    1    1    1    1    1    2    3    4
```

This function must now be applied to every segment, which can be done using the **trapply()** function with **returntrack=T** to build a corresponding trackdata object (see 5.5.2):

```
groove.min = trapply(in.sum.all, minfun, returntrack=T)
```

A plot of the tenth segment of this trackdata object should give the same values as those returned by **minfun(frames(in.sum.all[10,])**, which is indeed the case (Figure 7.12).

```
plot(groove.min[10,], type="b", ylab="Minimum groove
width", xlab="Time (ms)")
```

Finally, a plot from segment onset to segment offset should show both the differences on this parameter between [s] and [ʃ] and also a progressively decreasing minimum groove width towards the temporal midpoint of the segments, as the fricative's stricture is increased. Such a plot can be produced with **dplot()** and, in this example, the 10 fricatives per category are averaged after linear time normalization (Figure 7.13):

```
temp = polhom.l %in% c("s", "S")
dplot(groove.min[temp,], polhom.l[temp], norm=T, average=T,
ylab="Minimum groove width", xlab="Normalized time",
leg="topleft")
```

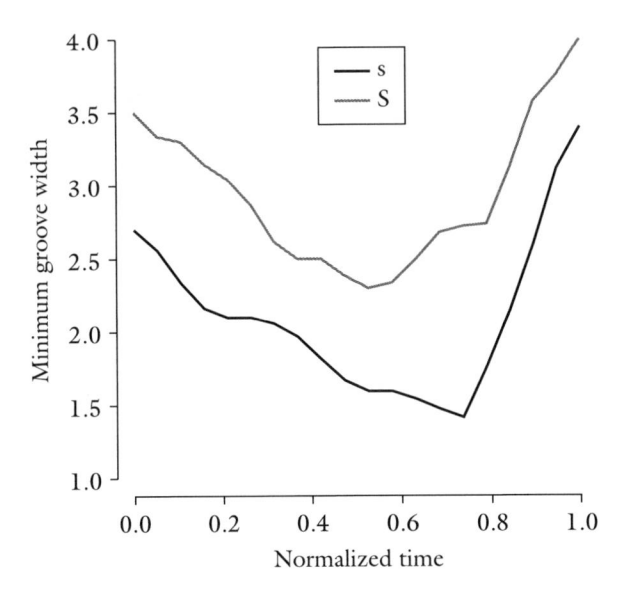

Figure 7.13 Minimum groove width between the acoustic onset and offset of Polish [s] (black) and [ʃ] (gray) averaged after linear time normalization.

Evidently, the groove width decreases on average towards the temporal midpoint for [ʃ] and somewhat after the temporal midpoint for [s]. Figure 7.13 also shows that the groove width for [s] is well below that of [ʃ] at equal proportional time points from segment onset to segment offset.

7.3.2 Contact distribution indices

As discussed in Gibbon and Nicolaidis (1999), various EPG parameters have been devised for quantifying both the distribution and the extent of tongue–palate contacts. Almost all of these are based on some form of summation of the palates (see e.g., Hardcastle et al. 1991 and Recasens et al. 1993 for details). These are the **anteriority index** (AI), the **centrality index** (CI), the **dorsopalatal index** (DI), and the **center of gravity index** (COG). The first three of these all vary between 0 and 1 and COG varies between 0.5 and 7.5. The R functions in the Emu-R library for calculating them are **epgai()**, **epgci()**, **epgdi()**, and **epgcog()** respectively.

The anteriority index quantifies how far forward the contacts are on the palate in rows 1–5. Rows 6–8 are not taken into account in this calculation. AI is especially useful for quantifying the place of articulation as far back as the post-alveolar zone (row 5), and can also be used to quantify the degree of stricture for two consonants at the same place of articulation. The data in Figure 7.14 shows AI for various made-up palatograms. (Details of how to produce these are given at the end of this chapter in the exercises.) Four general principles are involved in calculating AI (Figure 7.14):

1 The further forward the contacts in any row, the higher AI. Thus, the palatogram with the filled row of contacts in row 1 in (a) has a higher AI value

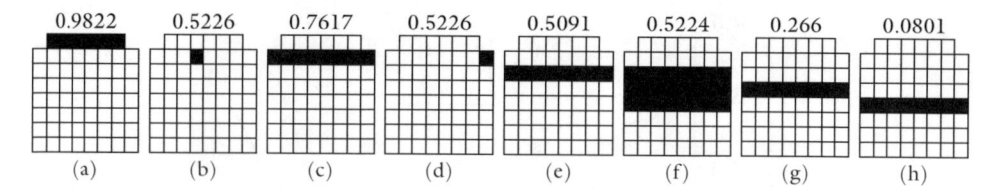

0.9822	0.5226	0.7617	0.5226	0.5091	0.5224	0.266	0.0801
(a)	(b)	(c)	(d)	(e)	(f)	(g)	(h)

Figure 7.14 Palatograms with corresponding values on the anteriority index shown above.

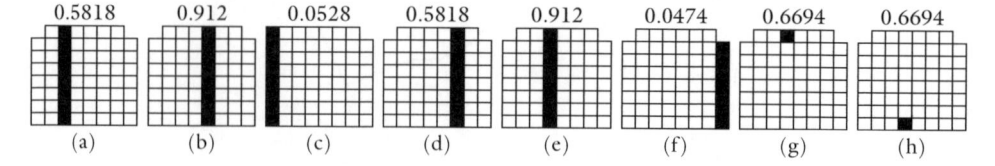

0.5818	0.912	0.0528	0.5818	0.912	0.0474	0.6694	0.6694
(a)	(b)	(c)	(d)	(e)	(f)	(g)	(h)

Figure 7.15 Palatograms with corresponding values on the centrality index shown above.

than (c) for which the contacts are filled in row 2. AI decreases from 0.9822 (filled row of contacts in row 1) to 0.0801 (filled row of contacts in row 5). Any palatogram with contacts exclusively in rows 6–8 has an AI of 0.

2 Any single contact in row i always has a higher AI than any number of contacts in row j, where $i < j$. So the AIs for palatograms (b) and (d) that each have a single contact in row 2 are greater than the AI of palatogram (e) in which all contacts are filled in a lower row number, row 3.

3 The same number of contacts in any row has the same AI irrespective of their lateral distribution (distribution by column). So the fact that the lateral distribution of the single contact is different in palatograms (b) and (d) makes no difference as far as AI is concerned, since both palatograms have a single contact in row 2.

4 The greater the number of contacts, the higher AI – but only up to the limit specified by (2) above. So palatogram (f), which has rows 3–5 completely filled, has a higher AI than palatogram (e), in which only row 3 is filled; but since palatogram (f) has no contacts forward of row 3, its AI is lower than those of (b) or (d) that have a single contact in row 2.

The **centrality index** (CI), as its name suggests, measures the extent of contact at the center of the palate and varies between 0 and 1. In general, the more the contacts are laterally distributed, the lower the value of CI. This parameter could be used to distinguish between consonants that have a narrow vs wide central groove, as in the [s, ʃ] fricatives discussed earlier. The actual calculation of CI can be explained in terms of a set of principles that are very similar to those of AI, except that they are based on columns and the relative lateralization of contacts:

1 In the case of a single filled column of contacts, CI is higher nearer the center of the palate: thus higher for filled columns 4 or 5 (palatograms (b), (e) in Figure 7.15) than for the more laterally filled columns 3 or 6 (palatograms (a), (d)).

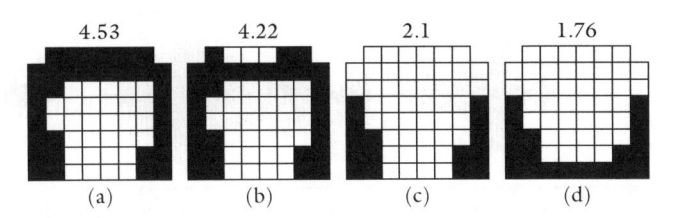

Figure 7.16 Palatograms with corresponding center of gravity values shown above.

2 Any single contact in a given column has a higher CI than a palatogram filled with any number of contacts in more lateral columns. So the CIs for palatograms (g) and (h), which have a single contact in column 4, are higher than those of palatograms (a) and (d), in which all contacts are filled in the more lateral columns 3 and 6.
3 The same number of contacts in any column has the same CI irrespective of the distribution by row: thus, palatograms (g) and (h) have the same CI.
4 The greater the number of contacts, the higher CI – but only up to the limit specified by (2) above.

The **dorsopalatal index** (DI) also varies between 0 and 1 and is a measure of the extent of contact in the last three rows, i.e., in the palatal and post-palatal region. It is a simple proportional measure: when all 24 electrodes are contacted in rows 6–8, then DI has a value of 1; if 12 are contacted, then DI is 0.5, etc.

Finally, the **center of gravity index** (COG) is a measure of the distribution of the place of articulation between the front and back of the palate: further advanced/retracted places of articulation are associated with higher/lower COG values. COG varies between 7.5 (when row 1 alone is filled) to 0.5 (when row 8 alone is filled). COG is calculated from a weighted average of the sum of contacts in the rows, where the weights on rows 1–8 are 7.5, 6.5 . . . 0.5. For example, for palatogram (c) in Figure 7.16, COG is calculated as follows:

```
# Sum of the contacts in rows 1–8 for (c) in Figure 7.16
contacts = c(0, 0, 0, 2, 2, 3, 4, 4)

# Weights on rows 1–8
weights = seq(7.5, 0.5, by = -1)

# COG for (c)
sum(contacts * weights)/sum(contacts)
2.1
```

In Figure 7.16, (a) and (b) have the same contact patterns, except that in (b) some contacts in the first row are missing. Thus, the overall distribution of contacts is further towards the front in (a) than in (b) and so COG is higher. In (c) and (d), there are no contacts in the first three rows and so the COG values are lower than those of either (a) or (b). Finally, (c) and (d) have the same pattern of contacts except

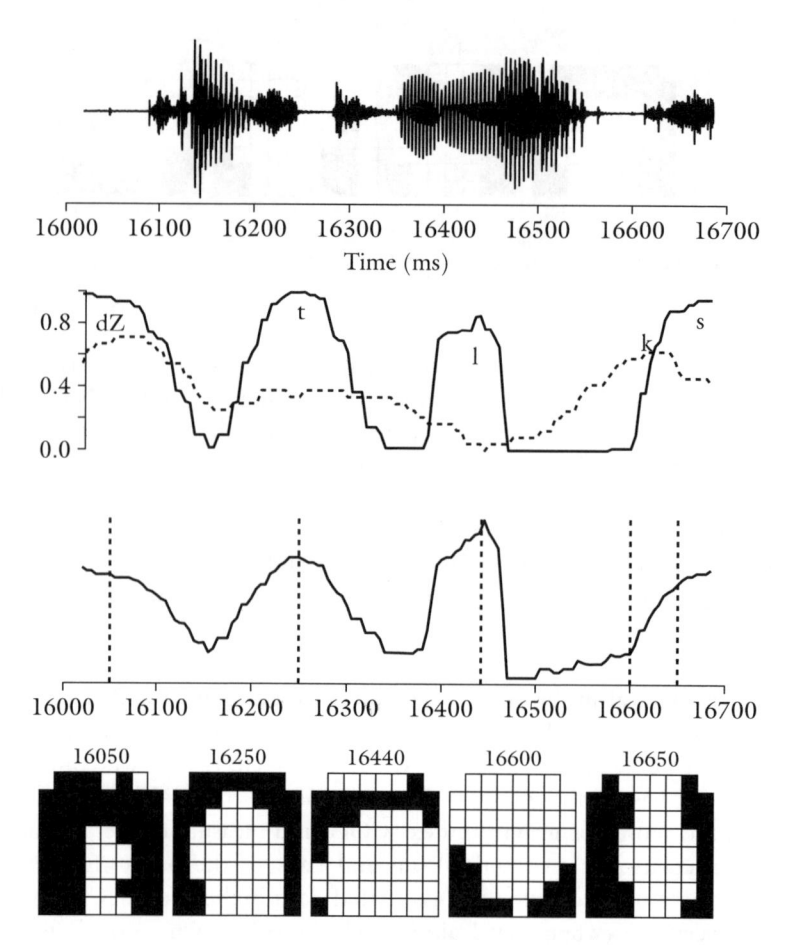

Figure 7.17 Synchronized waveform (top), anteriority index (middle panel, solid), dorsopalatal index (middle panel, dashed), center of gravity (lower panel) for *just relax*. The palatograms are those that are closest to the time points marked by the vertical dotted lines in the segments [ʤ] and [t] of *just*, and in [l], [k], [s] of *relax*.

that in (d) the last row is filled: consequently the overall distribution of contacts in (d) is furthest towards the back of all the palatograms and so it has the lowest COG of all.

An example of how AI, DI, and COG vary is shown in Figure 7.17 for the first two words *just relax* from the **epgcoutts** database considered earlier. AI, DI, and COG for the first two segments are obtained as follows:

```
ai = epgai(coutts.epg[1:2,])
di = epgdi(coutts.epg[1:2,])
cog = epgcog(coutts.epg[1:2,])

# Save the default graphical parameters
oldpar = par(no.readonly=TRUE)
```

```
# Set the display for a 3 x 1 plot and define the margins
par(mfrow=c(3,1)); par(mar=c(1, 2, 1, 1))

# Waveform
plot(coutts.sam[1:2,], type="l", axes=F, ylab="Amplitude")
axis(side=1)
mtext("Time (ms)", side=1, at=16600, line=-1)

# AI and DI
plot(cbind(ai, di), type="l", axes=F)
axis(side=2, line=-1)

# Some superimposed labels
text(c(16048, 16250, 16434, 16616, 16674), c(0.80, 0.88,
0.60, 0.69, 0.82), c("dZ", "t", "l", "k", "s"))

# COG
plot(cog, type="l", axes=F, ylab="COG")
axis(side=1)

# Mark in some time values
times = c(16050, 16250, 16442, 16600, 16650)
abline(v=times)

# Restore the plotting device defaults
par(oldpar)

# Plot palatograms at these time values
epgplot(coutts.epg[1:2,], times, mfrow=c(1,5))
```

The contact profiles in Figure 7.17 lead to the following conclusions:

- AI is somewhat lower for the lateral of *relax* than either [ʤ] (**dZ**) or [st] of *just* because, in contrast to these segments, [l] has only one contact in the first row, as the palatogram at 16,440 ms shows.
- DI has a high value during [ʤ] and this is because, as the palatogram at 16,050 ms shows, there is quite a lot of contact in the back three rows.
- COG often tends to track AI quite closely and this is also evident for the data in Figure 7.17. However, unlike AI, COG takes account of the overall distribution of the contacts from front to back; and, unlike AI, COG is not biased towards giving a higher ranking if there is a single contact in a low row number. Therefore, because the two leftmost palatograms in Figure 7.17 have contacts in the first row, they have high AI values, which are higher than those of the third palatogram from the left at 16,440 ms during [l]. But of these three, the leftmost palatogram at 16,050 ms has the lowest COG because of the large number of contacts in the back rows.

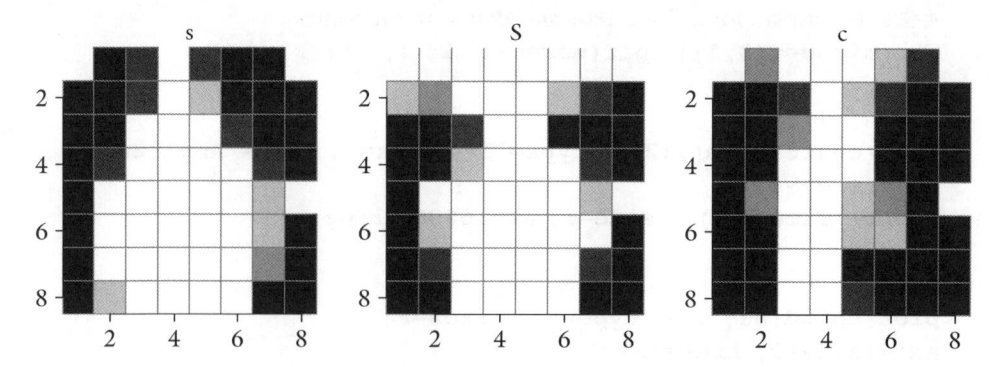

Figure 7.18 Grayscale images for 10 tokens each of the Polish fricatives [s, ʃ, ɕ].

Finally, some of these data-reduction parameters will be applied to the Polish fricatives considered earlier. For this analysis, the data from the alveolo-palatal [ɕ] is included, as well as that from [s, ʃ]. Here again is a grayscale palatographic display, this time averaged over the middle third of each fricative:

```
par(mfrow=c(1,3))
for(j in c("s", "S", "c")){
   temp = polhom.l == j
   epggs(dcut(polhom.epg[temp,], .33, .67, prop=T), main=j)
}
```

These grayscale palatographic displays in Figure 7.18 can be used to make various predictions about how these three places of articulation might be separated on some of the EPG data-reduction parameters:

- AI: highest for [s] (greatest number of contacts in rows 1 and 2) and possibly higher for [ɕ] than for [ʃ] (more contacts in rows 1–2)
- DI: highest for [ɕ] (greatest number of contacts in rows 5–8)
- CI: lowest for [ʃ] (least number of contacts medially in columns 4–5)
- COG: highest for [s], possibly with little distinction between [ʃ] and [ɕ] since the distribution of contacts from front to back is about the same for these fricatives

In the example in Figure 7.19, these parameters were calculated across the entire temporal extent of the homorganic fricatives. Since the fricatives were flanked by vowels, then the parameters might be expected to rise towards the temporal midpoint in most cases. The commands for creating Figure 7.19 are as follows.

```
# AI, DI, CI, COG
ai = epgai(polhom.epg); di = epgdi(polhom.epg)
ci = epgci(polhom.epg); cog = epgcog(polhom.epg)
```

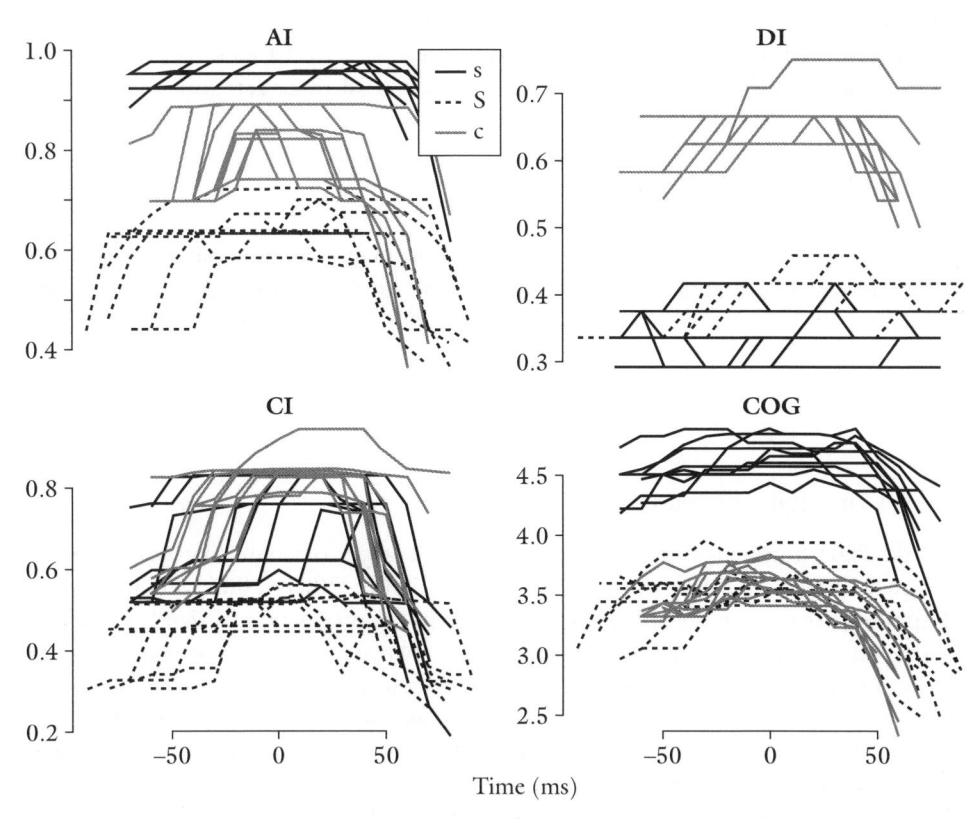

Figure 7.19 Anteriority (AI), dorsopalatal (DI), centrality (CI), and center of gravity (COG) indices for 10 tokens each of the Polish fricatives [s, ʃ, ɕ] (solid, dashed, gray) synchronized at their temporal midpoints.

```
# Logical vector to identify the three fricatives
temp = polhom.l %in% c("s", "S", "c")

par(mfrow=c(2,2)); par(mar=c(1,2,1.3,1))
dplot(ai[temp,], polhom.l[temp], offset=.5, axes=F,
main="AI", bty="n")
axis(side=2)
dplot(di[temp,], polhom.l[temp], offset=.5, axes=F,
legend=F, main="DI", bty="n")
axis(side=2)
dplot(ci[temp,], polhom.l[temp], offset=.5, legend=F,
axes=F, main="CI", bty="n")
axis(side=1, line=-1); axis(side=2)
mtext("Time (ms)", side=1, at=120, line=0)
dplot(cog[temp,], polhom.l[temp], offset=.5, legend=F,
axes=F, main="COG", bty="n")
axis(side=1, line=-1); axis(side=2)
```

Three of the parameters distinguish one fricative category from the other two: thus DI separates [ɕ] from [s, ʃ], CI separates [ʃ] from [s, ʃ, ɕ], COG separates [s] from [ɕ, ʃ] while AI produces a clear distinction between all three categories.

7.4 Analysis of EPG Data

The mechanisms are now in place to carry out many different kinds of analysis using electropalatographic data. Two common kinds of investigation to which an EPG analysis is particularly suited are presented in this section: an investigation into the extent of consonant overlap in alveolar–velar consonant clusters (7.4.1); and vowel-induced place of articulation variation in dorsal fricatives and stops (7.4.2).

7.4.1 Consonant overlap

The database fragment in this section is part of a larger database that was collected and analyzed by Lisa Stephenson (Stephenson 2003, 2004, 2005; Stephenson & Harrington 2002) in studying consonant overlap in the production of blends in English and Japanese. In her experiments, subjects saw two hypothetical town names on a screen and had to produce a blend from the two words as quickly as possible after seeing them. They might see for example *Randon* and *Pressgate* and the task was to produce a blend by combining the first syllable of the first word with the second syllable of the second word, thus *Rangate*.

Stephenson's database included a number of blends formed with combinations of /n/ and a following consonant and, in the analysis in this section, two of these types will be compared: blends formed with /nk, ng/ and blends formed with /sk, sg/ clusters. No differentiation will be made between the voicing status of the final consonant: so the comparison is between /nK/ vs /sK/ where /K/ stands for either /k/ or /g/. The question that is addressed is the following: is the extent of alveolar–velar overlap the same in /nK/ and /sK/?

As an initial hypothesis, it is reasonable to expect more overlap in /nK/ for at least two reasons. Firstly, because of the well-known tendency for /n/ to assimilate in this context (see e.g., Hardcastle 1994), whereas /s/ does not audibly retract its place of articulation in e.g., *mascot* or *must get* and is often resistant to coarticulatory influences (e.g., Recasens 2004). Secondly, whereas it is quite possible to sustain an alveolar [n] production when there is tongue-dorsum contact at the velum for [k] or for [g], this type of overlapping or double-articulation is likely to be more difficult in [sk] or [sg]: this is because, if there is substantial velar closure during the production of the alveolar, then the airflow through the oral cavity will be inhibited as a result of which it will be difficult to sustain the high aerodynamic power required for the production of the sibilant fricative [s].

The available database fragment is **epgassim** and there are the usual sets of parallel R objects associated with this:

engassim	Segment list from the acoustic onset to the acoustic offset of the entire [nk, ng, sk, sg] sequences
engassim.l	Label vector of the above – **nK** for [nk, ng] vs **sK** for [sk, sg]

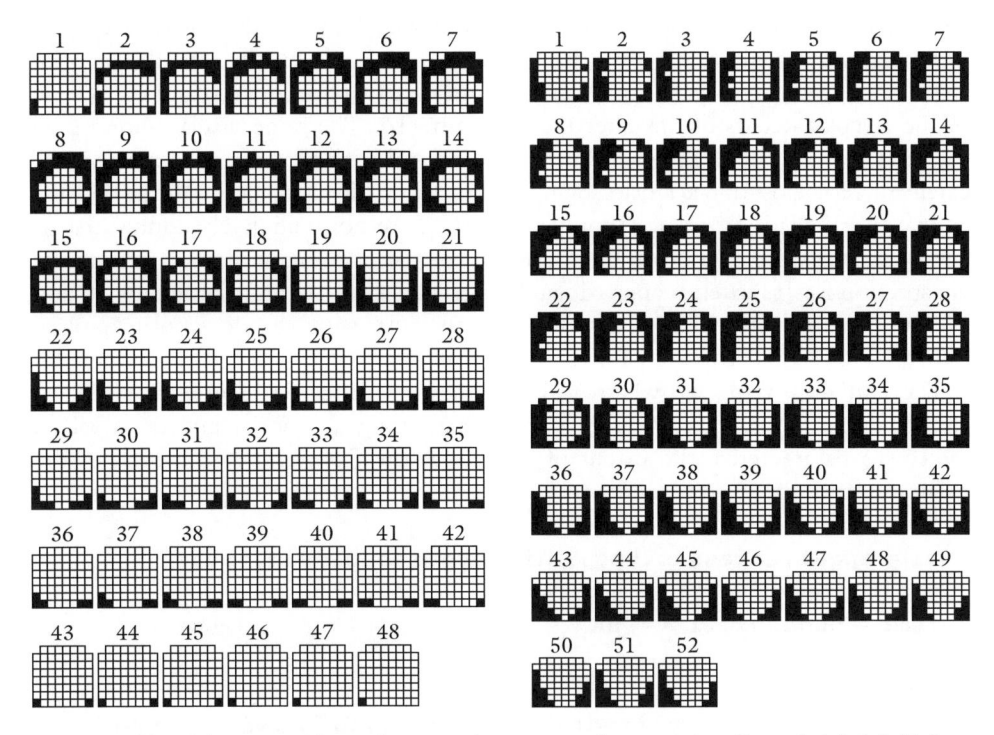

Figure 7.20 Palatograms from the acoustic onset to the acoustic offset of /nk/ (left) in the blend *duncourt* and /sk/ (right) in the blend *bescan* produced by an adult female speaker of Australian English.

    engassim.w   Label vector of the words from which the sequences were derived
    engassim.epg   Parallel EPG trackdata at a frame rate of 5 ms

In 7.3 it was shown how the anteriority and dorsopalatal indices tend to provide positive evidence for productions at alveolar and velar places of articulation respectively. The data will therefore be analyzed for these parameters but, as with any more complicated parametric analysis, it is always a good idea to look at some samples of the data first. A plot of all the **nK** data separately per segment and from the onset of the [n] to the offset of the velar can be produced as follows. (Use the left mouse button to advance through each plot; you will have to do this 17 times, since there are 17 **nK** segments. Use the same commands to get the corresponding **sK** data, but replace **temp** with its logical inverse **!temp**.) The EPG frames from the first run through the loop (for the first **nK** and **sK** segments) are shown in Figure 7.20:

```
temp = engassim.l == "nK"
for(j in 1:sum(temp)){
   # Show palate numbers rather than times
   epgplot(engassim.epg[temp,][j,], numbering=T)
   # Left mouse button to advance
   locator(1)
}
```

Palatograms from two segments are shown in Figure 7.20: on the left is /nk/ from *duncourt* and on the right, /sk/ from *bescan*. For /nk/ on the left, the alveolar stricture increases from palatogram 2. It is complete by palatogram 6 and the release of the alveolar occurs 50 ms after that by frame 16. The same display shows how the velar closure begins to form during this interval such that the maximum visible extent of velar closure takes place by frame 16. Evidently then, although the alveolar and velar articulations are not simultaneous (i.e., are not completely doubly articulated), they overlap a good deal. Consider now /sk/ in Figure 7.20. The alveolar constriction for [s] extends approximately over 115 ms between palatograms 10 and 23, but the greatest degree of narrowing for the velar stop /k/ does not take place until well after this at frame 31.

The aim now is to see whether there is any evidence for a greater extent of alveolar–velar overlap in **nK** in all of the data, using anteriority and dorsopalatal indices to parameterize the extent of contact at the front and at the back of the palate respectively:

```
ai = epgai(engassim.epg); di = epgdi(engassim.epg)
par(mfrow=c(1,2))
temp = engassim.l == "nK"

# Data for nK
dplot(ai[temp,], ylim=c(0,1), main="/nK/", lwd=2, leg=F)
par(new=T)
dplot(di[temp,], ylim=c(0,1), col="slategray", lwd=2, leg=F)

# Data for sK
dplot(ai[!temp,], ylim=c(0,1), main="/sK/", lwd=2, leg=F)
par(new=T)
dplot(di[!temp,], ylim=c(0,1), col="slategray", lwd=2, leg=F)
```

It is apparent from Figure 7.21 that the tongue-dorsum activity for [k] is timed to occur a good deal earlier relative to the preceding consonant in the clusters with [n] compared with those of [s]. In particular, the left panel of Figure 7.20 shows how the dorsopalatal index rises throughout the AI plateau for [n]; by contrast, there is a dorsopalatal trough for most of the AI plateau for [s] between roughly 40 ms and 100 ms on the right.

The differences in the extent of alveolar–velar overlap could be further highlighted by producing grayscale EPG images at about 50 ms after the acoustic onset of the consonant cluster: as Figure 7.20 shows, this is approximately the time at which the AI maxima are first attained in **nK** and **sK**.

```
par(mfrow=c(1,2))
temp = engassim.l == "nK"
epggs(dcut(engassim.epg[temp,],
start(engassim[temp,])+50), main="/nK/")
epggs(dcut(engassim.epg[!temp,],
start(engassim[!temp,])+50), main="/sK/")
```

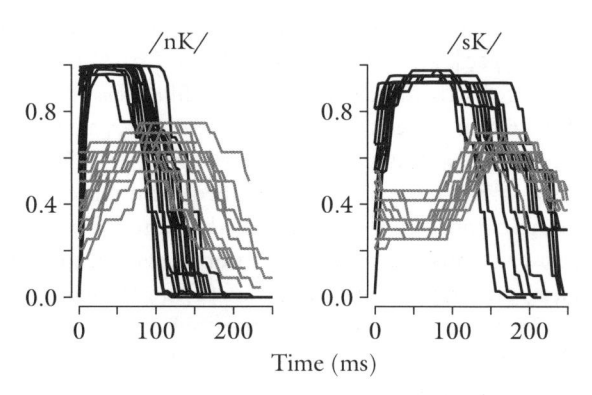

Figure 7.21 Anteriority (black) and dorsopalatal (gray) indices for 17 /nK/ (left) and 15 /sK/ (right) sequences (K = /k, g/) produced by an adult female speaker of Australian English.

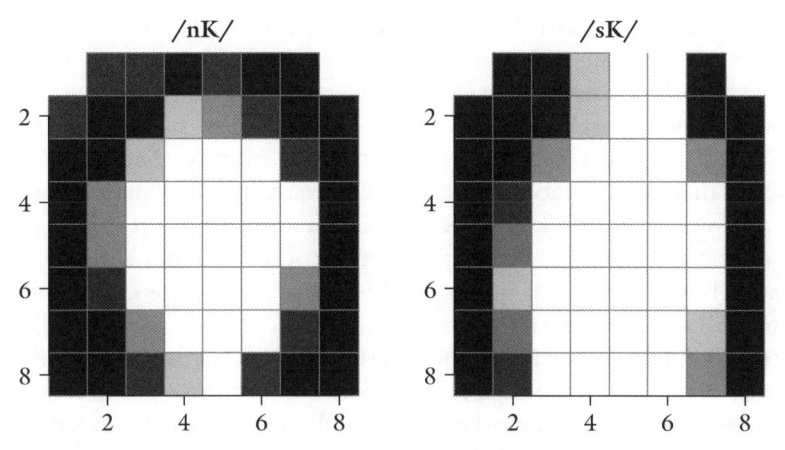

Figure 7.22 Grayscale EPG images for the /nK/ (left) and the /sK/ (right) for the data in Figure 7.21 extracted 50 ms after the acoustic onset of the cluster.

The grayscale images in Figure 7.22 show greater evidence of alveolar–velar overlap for /nK/ which, in contrast to /sK/, has more filled cells in the last two rows.

7.4.2 VC coarticulation in German dorsal fricatives

The analysis in this section is concerned with dorsal fricative assimilation in German and more specifically with whether the influence of a vowel on the following consonant is greater when the consonant is a dorsal fricative, which, for compatibility with the machine readable phonetic alphabet, will be denoted phonemically as /x/, compared with an oral stop, /k/. This analysis was carried out in a seminar at the IPDS, University of Kiel, and then further developed in a paper by Ambrazaitis and John (2004).

In German, a post-vocalic dorsal fricative varies in place of articulation depending largely on the backness of a preceding tautomorphemic vowel. After front vowels,

/x/ is produced in Standard German and many German varieties as a palatal fricative (e.g., [riːç], [lɪçt], [pɛç]; *riech/smell, Licht/light, Pech/bad luck* respectively), as a velar fricative after high back vowels (e.g., [buːx], *Buch/book*), and quite possibly as a uvular fricative after central or back non-high vowels (e.g., [maχ], *mach/make*; [lɔχ], *Loch/hole*). In his extensive analysis of German phonology, Wiese (1996) raises the interesting point that, while this type of vowel-dependent place of articulation in the *fricative* is both audible and well documented, the same cannot be said for analogous contexts with /k/. Thus, there are tautomorphemic sequences of /iːk, ɪk, ɛk/ (*flieg/fly, Blick/view, Fleck/stain*), of /uːk, ɔk/ (*Pflug/plough, Stock/stick*), and of /ak/ (*Lack/paint*). However, it is not so clear either auditorily or from any experimental analysis whether there is the same extent of allophonic variation between palatal and uvular places of articulation.

We can consider two hypotheses as far as these possible differences in coarticulatory influences on /x/ and /k/ are concerned. Firstly, if the size of coarticulatory effects is entirely determined by the phonetic quality of the preceding vowel, then there is indeed no reason to expect there to be any differences in the variation of place of articulation between the fricative and the stop: that is, the extent of vowel-on-consonant coarticulation should be the same for both. However, perhaps the coarticulatory variation is simply much less audible in the case of /k/ because the release of the stop, which together with the burst contains most of the acoustic cues to place of articulation, is so much shorter than in the fricative. The alternative hypothesis is that there is a categorical distinction between the allophones of the fricative, but not between those of /k/. Under this hypothesis, we might expect not only a sharper distinction in speech production between the front and back allophones of the fricative but also that the variation *within* the front or back allophones might be less for the fricative than for the stop.

It is certainly difficult to answer this question completely with the available fragment of the database of a single speaker, but it is nevertheless possible to develop a methodology that could be applied to many speakers in subsequent experiments. The database fragment here is **epgdorsal**, which forms part of a corpus recorded by phonetics students at the IPDS Kiel in 2003 and is also part of the study by Ambrazaitis and John (2004). The EPG data was recorded at a frame rate of 10 ms at the Zentrum für allgemeine Sprachwissenschaft in Berlin. For the recording, the subject had to create and produce a street name by forming a blend of a hypothetical town name and a suffix that were shown simultaneously on a screen. For example, the subject was shown RIEKEN and –UNTERWEG at the same time, and had to produce RIE<u>KUN</u>TERWEG as quickly as possible. In this example, the underlined part of this blend includes /iːkʊ/. Blends were formed in an analogous way to create /V_1CV_2/ sequences where V_1 included vowels varying in backness and height, C = /k, x/, and V_2 = /ʊ, ɪ/. In all cases, primary stress is necessarily on V_2. To take another example, the subject produced RE<u>CHIN</u>SKIWEG in response to RECHEN and –INSKIWEG, resulting in a blend containing /ɛxɪ/ over the underlined segments.

For the database fragment to be examined here, there are six different V_1 vowels whose qualities are close to IPA [iː, ɪ, ɛ, a, ɔ, ʊ] (**i, I, E, a, O, U** respectively in this database) and that vary phonetically in backness more or less in the order shown. So assuming that the following V_2 = /ʊ, ɪ/ has much less influence on the dorsal fricative than the preceding vowel, which was indeed shown to be the case in

Ambrazaitis and John (2004), we can expect a relatively front allophone of the fricative or stop after the front vowels [i:, ɪ, ɛ] but a back allophone after [ɔ, ʊ].

The following parallel objects are available in the dataset **dorsal** for investigating this issue. With the exception of **dorsal.bound**, which marks the time of V_1C acoustic boundary, their boundary times extend from the acoustic onset V_1 to the acoustic offset of C (the acoustic offset of the dorsal):

dorsal	Segment list of V_1C (C = /k, x/)
dorsal.epg	EPG-compressed trackdata of **dorsal**
dorsal.sam	Sampled waveform trackdata of **dorsal**
dorsal.fm	Formant trackdata of **dorsal**
dorsal.vlab	Label vector of V_1 (**i, I, E, a, O, U**)
dorsal.clab	Label vector of C (**k** or **x**)
dorsal.bound	Event times of the acoustic V_1C boundary

There were two tokens per /V_1CV_2/ category (two tokens each of /i:kɪ/, /i:kʊ/, /i:xɪ/, /i:xʊ/, etc.), giving four tokens for each separate V_1 in /V_1k/ and four tokens per /V_1x/ (although, since V_1 was not always realized in the way that was intended – e.g., /ɪ/ was sometimes produced instead of /i:/ – there is some deviation from this number, as **table(label(dorsal))** shows). In order to be clear about how the above R objects are related, Figure 7.23 shows the sampled waveform and electropalatographic data over the third segment in the database which, as **label(dorsal[3,])** shows, was **ak**:[4]

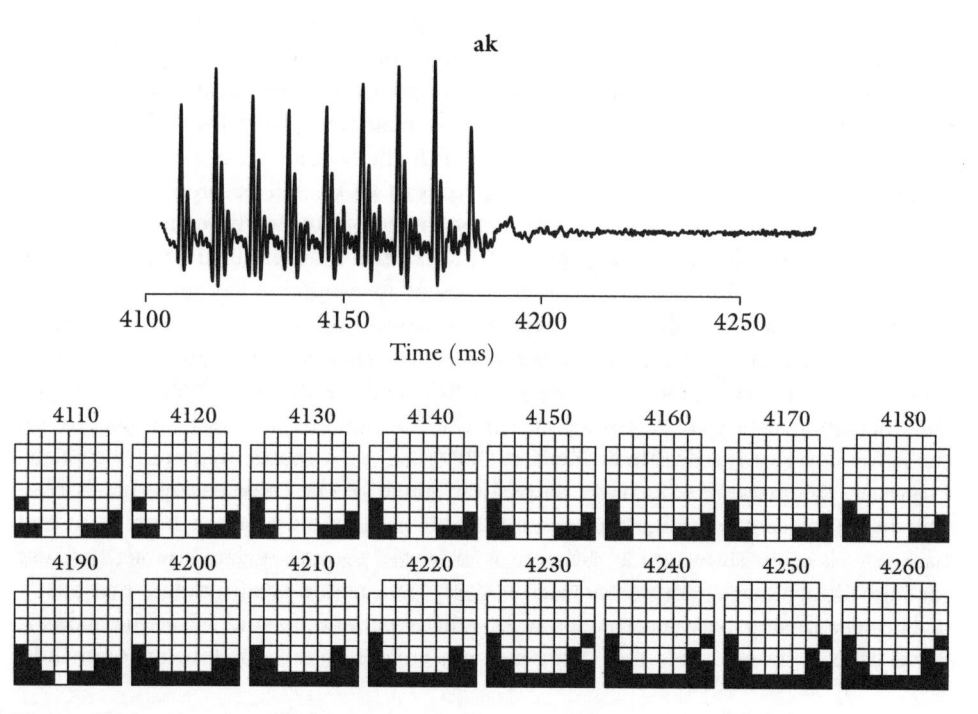

Figure 7.23 Acoustic waveform (top) of /ak/ produced by an adult male speaker of Standard German and the palatograms over the same time interval.

```
plot(dorsal.sam[3,], type="l", main="ak", xlab="Time (ms)",
ylab="", axes=F, bty="n")
axis(side=1)
epgplot(dorsal.epg[3,], mfrow=c(2,8))
```

For the investigation of the variation in place of articulation in dorsal consonants, the anteriority index is not appropriate because this only registers contact in rows 1–5. The dorsopalatal index might shed more light on place of articulation variation; however, given that it is based on summing the number of contacts in the back three rows, it is likely to register differences between the lesser stricture of the fricatives rather than the stops. But this is not what is needed. Instead, we need a parameter that is affected mostly by shifting the tongue from front to back along the palate and which does so in more or less the same way for the fricative and the stop categories.

The parameter that is most likely to be useful here is the EPG center of gravity (COG) which should show decreasing values as the primary dorsal stricture moves back along the palate. COG should also show a predictable relationship by vowel category. It should be highest for a high front vowel like [iː] that tends to have a good deal of contact laterally in the palatal region and decrease for [ɪ, ɛ] which have a weaker palatal contact. It should have the lowest values for [ʊ, ɔ] in which contacts are expected at the back of the palate.

COG should show some relationship to the vowel's second formant frequency, since F2 of [iː] is higher than F2 of [ɪ, ɛ] and since of course F2 of front vowels is greater than F2 of low, central, and back vowels. These relationships between COG, vowel category, and F2 can be examined during the interval for which sensible formant data is available, i.e., during the voiced part of the vowel. Given that the interest in this analysis is in the influence of the vowel on the following consonant, we will consider data extracted at the vowel–consonant boundary close to the vowel's last glottal pulse, i.e. close to the time at which the voiced vowel gives way to the (voiceless) fricative or stop. Two different types of COG will be presented. In one, COG is calculated as in section 7.3 over the entire palate; in the other, which will be called the **posterior center of gravity** (P-COG), the COG calculations are restricted to rows 5–8. P-COG is relevant for the present investigation because the study is concerned exclusively with sounds made in the dorsal region such as vowels followed by dorsal consonants. It should be mentioned at this point that this version of P-COG is not quite the same as the one in Gibbon and Nicolaidis (1999), who restrict the calculations not only to rows 5–8 but also to columns 3–6 (see the picture on the jacket cover of Hardcastle & Hewlett 1999), i.e., to a central region of the palate. However, this parameter is likely to exclude much of the information that is relevant in the present investigation, given that the distinction between high front and back vowels often shows up as differences in *lateral* tongue–palate contact (present for high front vowels, absent for back vowels), i.e., at the palatographic margins.

The relationship between the center of gravity parameters and F2 at the acoustic vowel offset is shown in Figure 7.24, which was created with the following commands:

```
# COG and P-COG, from the onset to the offset of VC
cog = epgcog(dorsal.epg); pcog = epgcog(dorsal.epg, rows=5:8)
```

Electropalatography 255

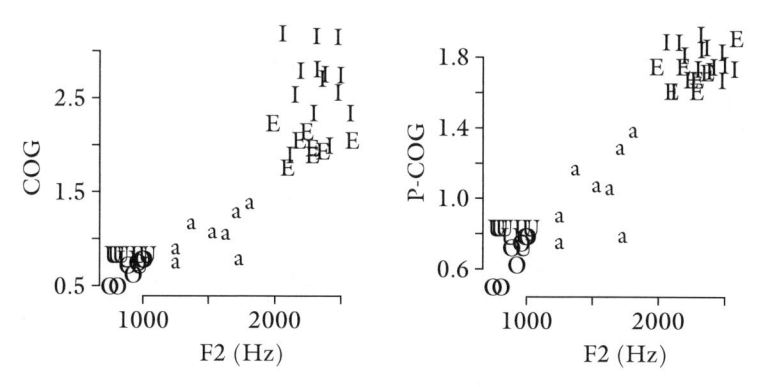

Figure 7.24 COG (left) and P-COG (right) extracted at the acoustic vowel offset and plotted as a function of F2 for data pooled across /x/ and /k/. The vowel labels are shown at the data points.

```
# COG and P-COG at the VC boundary
cog.voffset = dcut(cog, dorsal.bound)
pcog.voffset = dcut(pcog, dorsal.bound)

# F2 at the VC boundary
f2.voffset = dcut(dorsal.fm[,2], dorsal.bound)
par(mfrow=c(1,2))
plot(f2.voffset, cog.voffset, pch=dorsal.vlab, xlab="F2
(Hz)", ylab="COG")
plot(f2.voffset, pcog.voffset, pch=dorsal.vlab, xlab="F2
(Hz)", ylab="PCOG")
```

As Figure 7.24 shows, both COG and P-COG show a fairly linear relationship to the second formant frequency at the vowel offset. They also show a clear separation between vowel categories, with the low back vowels appearing at the bottom left of the display and the high and mid-high front vowel in the top right. For this particular speaker, these relationships between acoustic data, articulatory data, and vowel category emerge especially clearly. It must be emphasized that this will not always be so for all speakers! P-COG shows a slightly better correlation with the F2-data than COG (as **cor.test(f2.voffset, pcog.voffset)** and **cor.test(f2.voffset, cog.voffset)** show). However, COG shows a clearer distinction within the front vowel categories [i:, ɪ, ɛ] – and this could be important in determining whether the coarticulatory influences of the vowel on the consonant are more categorical for /x/ than for /k/ (if this were so, then we would expect less variation in /x/ following these different front vowels, if /x/ is realized as basically the same front allophone in all three cases). The subsequent analyses are all based on COG – some further calculations with P-COG are given in the exercises.

In order to get some insight into how /k, x/ vary with the preceding vowel context, a plot of COG will be made 30 ms on either side of the vowel boundary. This is shown in Figure 7.25 and was produced as follows:

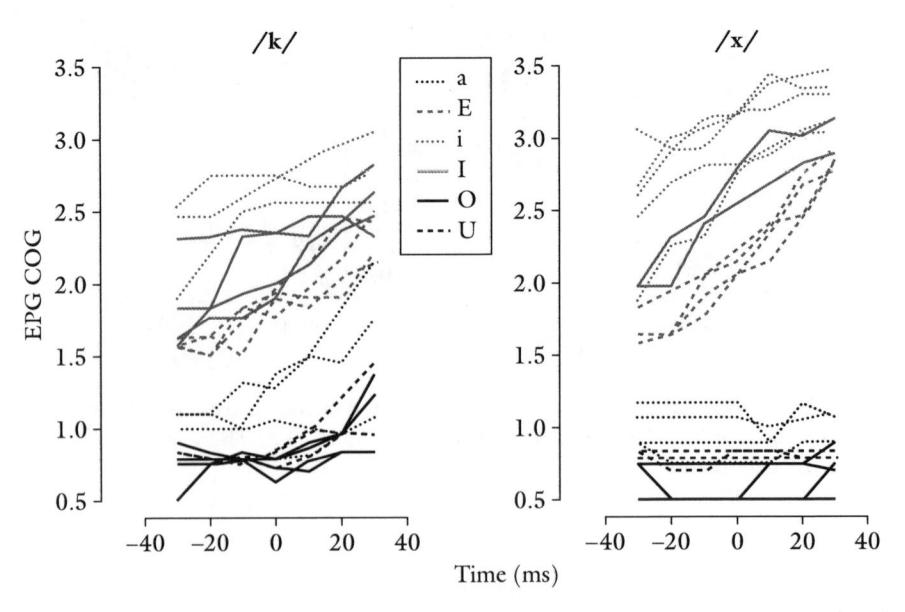

Figure 7.25 COG calculated 30 ms on either side of the acoustic V₁C boundary for /k/ (left) and /x/ (right) shown separately as a function of time by V_1 category.

```
# Cut the EPG data to ± 30 ms either side of V₁C boundary
epg30 = dcut(dorsal.epg, dorsal.bound-30, dorsal.bound+30)

# Calculate COG
cog30 = epgcog(epg30)

# Logical vector that is True when the consonant is /k/ as opposed to /x/
temp = dorsal.clab=="k"
ylim = c(0.5, 3.5); xlim=c(-50, 50)
par(mfrow=c(1,2))
dplot(cog30[temp,], dorsal.vlab[temp], offset=.5,
xlim=xlim, ylim=ylim, leg="topright", ylab="EPG COG",
main="/k/", bty="n")
mtext("Time (ms)", side=1, line=1, at=70)
dplot(cog30[!temp,], dorsal.vlab[!temp], offset=.5,
xlim=xlim, ylim=ylim, leg=F, main="/x/", bty="n")
```

As Figure 7.25 shows, there is a clearer separation (for this speaker at least) on this parameter between the front vowels [i, ɪ, ɛ] on the one hand and the non-front /a, ɔ, ʊ/ in the context of /x/ on the other hand; the separation is much less in evidence, however, in the context of /k/. A histogram of COG 30 ms after the acoustic VC boundary brings out the greater categorical separation between these allophone groups preceding /x/ quite clearly.

```
# COG values at 30 ms after the VC boundary. Either:
cog30end = dcut(cog30, 1, prop=T)
```

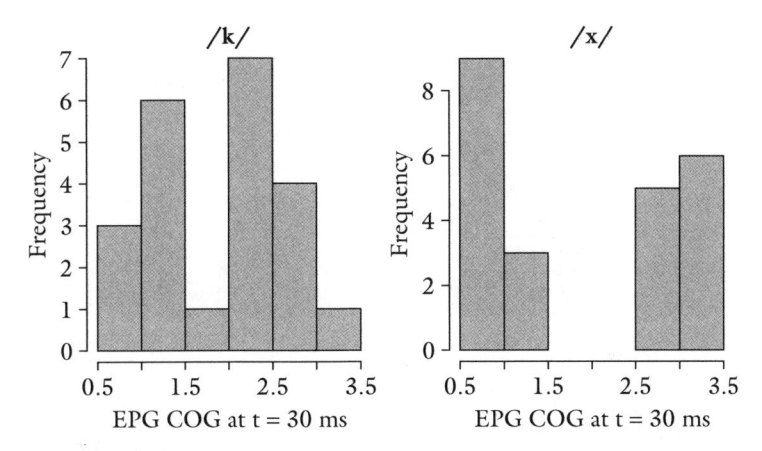

Figure 7.26 COG for /k/ (left) and /x/ (right) at the V₁C boundary.

```
# Or:
cog30end = dcut(cog30, dorsal.bound+30)

# Logical vector, T when clab is /k/, F when clab is /x/
temp = dorsal.clab=="k"
par(mfrow=c(1,2))

# Histogram of EPG COG 30 ms after the VC boundary for /k/
hist(cog30end[temp], main="/k/", xlab="EPG-COG at t = 30
ms", col="blue")

# As above but for /x/
hist(cog30end[!temp], main="/x/", xlab="EPG-COG at t = 30
ms", col="blue")
```

There is evidently a bimodal distribution on COG 30 ms after the VC boundary for both /x/ and /k/, but this is somewhat more pronounced for /x/: such a finding is consistent with the view that there may be a more marked separation into front and non-front allophones for /x/ than for /k/. In order to test this hypothesis further, the EPG COG data are plotted over the extent of the consonant (over the fricative or the stop closure) in Figure 7.27:

```
# Center of gravity from acoustic onset to offset of the consonant
cogcons = epgcog(dcut(dorsal.epg, dorsal.bound,
end(dorsal.epg)))

# Logical vector that is True when dorsal.clab is k
temp = dorsal.clab=="k"
par(mfrow=c(1,2)); ylim = c(0.5, 3.5); xlim=c(-60, 60)
col = c(1, "slategray", "slategray", 1, 1, "slategray")
```

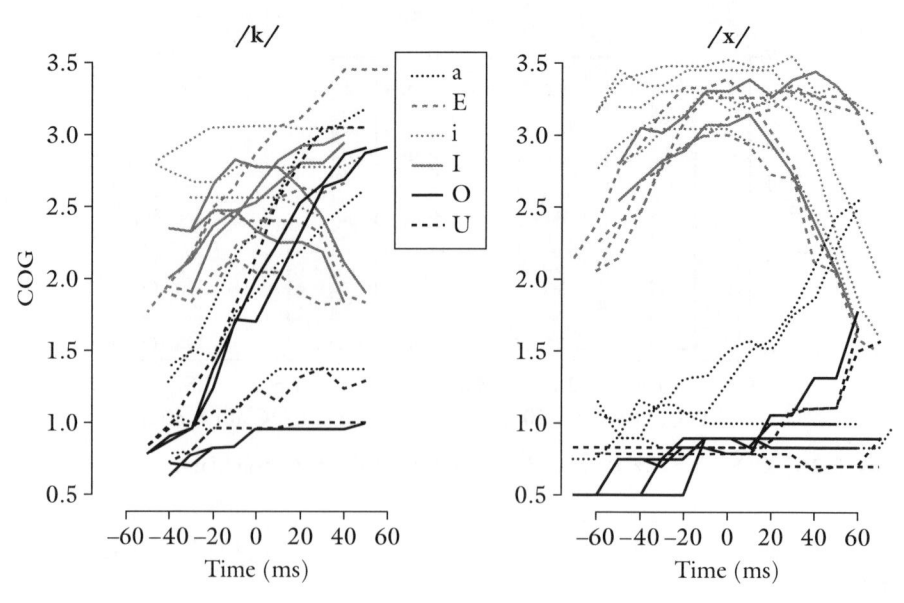

Figure 7.27 COG over the extent of the /k/ closure (left) and /x/ frication (right) shown by vowel category and synchronized at the consonants' acoustic temporal midpoints.

```
linet=c(1,1,5,5,1,1) ; lwd=c(2,2,1,1,1,1)
dplot(cogcons[temp,], dorsal.vlab[temp], offset=.5,
leg="topleft", ylab="COG", ylim=ylim, xlim=xlim,
main="/k/", col=col, lty=linet, lwd=lwd)
dplot(cogcons[!temp,], dorsal.vlab[!temp], offset=.5,
ylim=ylim, xlim=xlim, leg=F, main="/x/", col=col,
lty=linet, lwd=lwd)
```

There is once again a clearer separation of EPG COG in /x/ depending on whether the preceding vowel is front or back. Notice in particular how COG seems to climb to a target for /ɛx/ and reach a position that is not very different from that for /ix/ or /ɪx/.

For this single speaker, the data does indeed suggest a greater categorical allophonic distinction for /x/ than for /k/.

7.5 Summary

One of the central concerns in experimental phonetics is with how segments overlap and the way in which they are coordinated with each other. The acoustic speech signal provides a rich source of information allowing these types of processes in speech production to be inferred indirectly. However, it is clear that acoustics is of little use for the kind of study presented in the latter part of this chapter in analyzing how the tongue moves due to the influence of context during an acoustic stop closure. Also, it is very difficult and probably impossible to quantify reliably from speech acoustics the way in which the tongue is repositioned from an alveolar to a velar place of articulation in the kinds of /nk/ sequences that were examined earlier, largely because this kind of subtle change is very difficult to detect in the acoustics of nasal consonants. Moreover, an acoustic analysis could not reveal the differences in segmental coordination between /sk/ and /nk/ that were in evidence in analyzing these productions electropalatographically.

As discussed earlier, electropalatography is much more limited than a technique like electromagnetic articulometry (EMA) presented in Chapter 5, because it cannot provide as much information about the dynamics of tongue movement; and EPG in comparison with EMA has little to offer in analyzing vowels or consonants produced beyond the hard/soft palate junction. On the other hand, EPG tracks can often be more transparently related to phonetic landmarks than the data from EMA, although critics of EPG also argue (not unjustifiably) that the EPG parameters like AI, DI, and COG are too simplistic for inferring the complexities of speech motor control.

A central aim in this chapter has been to show how many of the procedures for handling acoustic data in R can be applied to data-reduced versions of the EPG signal. Thus the tools for plotting and quantifying EPG data are, for the most part, the same as those that were used in the analysis of movement and formant data in the preceding two chapters and for spectral data to be discussed in the next chapter. As a result, the mechanisms are in place for carrying out various kinds of articulatory-acoustic relationships, of which one example was provided earlier (Figure 7.24). In addition, the extensive resources for quantifying data that are available from the numerous R libraries can also be applied to further analyses of palatographic data.

7.6 Questions

A. Make a 3D palatographic array for creating the figure in Figure 7.14, then plot Figure 7.14 and use the made-up array to verify the values for the anteriority index.

B. Write R commands to display the first, fourth, and seventh palatograms at the acoustic temporal midpoint of [ɕ] (**c**) in the **epgpolish** database fragment with the R objects (dataset) **polhom**.

C. The R dataset **coutts2** of the database fragment **epgcoutts** contains the same utterance produced by the same speaker as **coutts** but at a slower rate. The R objects for **coutts2** are:

coutts2	Segment list of words
coutts2.l	Vector of word labels
coutts2.epg	EPG-compressed trackdata object
coutts2.sam	Trackdata of the acoustic waveform

Produce palatographic plots over a comparable extent as in Figure 7.6 from the /d/ of *said* up to the release of /k/ in *said Coutts*. Comment on the main ways the timing of /d/ and /k/ differ in the normal and slow database fragments.

D. For the **polhom** dataset of Polish homorganic fricatives (segment list, vector of labels, and trackdata **polhom**, **polhom.l**, **polhom.epg** respectively), write R expressions for the following:

D.1 For each segment onset, the sum of the contacts in rows 1–3.

D.2 For each segment, the sum of all palatographic contacts at 20 ms after the segment onset.

D.3 For each segment, the sum of the contacts in rows 1–3 and columns 1–2 and 7–8 at the segment midpoint.

D.4 For each **s** segment, the anteriority index at the segment offset.

D.5 For each **s** and **S** segment, the dorsopalatal index 20 ms after the segment midpoint.

D.6 An ensemble plot as a function of time of the sum of the contacts in rows 2 and 4 for all segments, color-coded for segment type (i.e., a different color or line type for each of **s**, **S**, **c**, **x**) and synchronized at the temporal midpoint of the segment.

D.7 An ensemble plot as a function of time of the sum of the inactive electrodes in columns 1, 2, 7, and 8 and rows 2–8 for all **S** and **c** segments for a duration of 40 ms after the segment onset and synchronized 20 ms after segment onset.

D.8 An averaged, and linearly time-normalized ensemble plot for **c** and **x** as a function of time of the posterior center of gravity P-COG (see 7.4.2).

D.9 For each segment, the median of the anteriority index between segment onset and offset.

D.10 A boxplot of the center of gravity index averaged across a 50 ms window, 25 ms on either side of the segment's temporal midpoint, for **s** and **S** segments.

E. For the **engassim** dataset, the AI and DI indices were calculated as follows:

```
ai = epgai(engassim.epg); di = epgdi(engassim.epg)
```

Calculate over these data AI_{TMAX}, the time at which AI first reaches a maximum value and DI_{TMAX}, the time at which DI first reaches a maximum value. Make a boxplot of the difference between these times, $DI_{TMAX} - AI_{TMAX}$, to show that the duration between these two maxima is greater for **sK** than for **nK**.

7.7 Answers

A.

```
palai = array(0, c(8, 8, 8))
palai[1,2:7,1] = 1
palai[2,4,2] = 1
```

```
palai[2,,3] = 1
palai[2,8,4] = 1
palai[3,,5] = 1
palai[3:5,,6] = 1
palai[4,,7] = 1
palai[5,,8] = 1
class(palai) = "EPG"
aivals = round(epgai(palai), 4)
aivals
epgplot(palai, mfrow=c(1,8), num=as.character(aivals))
```

B.

```
# EPG data at the midpoint
polhom.epg.5 = dcut(polhom.epg, 0.5, prop=T)
```

```
# EPG data at the midpoint of c
temp = polhom.l == "c"
polhom.epg.c.5 = polhom.epg.5[temp,]
```

```
# Plot of the first, fourth, and seventh c segments at the midpoint
epgplot(polhom.epg.c.5[c(1,4,7),], mfrow=c(1,3))
```

C.

```
epgplot(coutts2.epg, xlim=c(end(coutts2)[3]-120,
start(coutts2)[4]+120))
```

The main difference is that, in the slow rate, /d/ is released (at 14,910 ms) well before the maximum extent of dorsal closure is formed (at 14,935 ms), i.e., the stops are not doubly articulated.

D.1

```
epgsum(dcut(polhom.epg, 0, prop=T), r=1:3)
```

D.2

```
times = start(polhom)+20
epgsum(dcut(polhom.epg, times))
```

D.3

```
epgsum(dcut(polhom.epg, 0.5, prop=T), r=1:3, c=c(1, 2, 7,
8))
```

D.4

```
epgai(dcut(polhom.epg[polhom.l=="s",], 1, prop=T))
```

D.5

```
temp = polhom.l %in% c("s", "S")
times = (start(polhom[temp,])+end(polhom[temp,]))/2 + 20
epgdi(dcut(polhom.epg[temp,], times[temp]))
```

D.6

```
dplot(epgsum(polhom.epg, r=c(2,4)), polhom.l, offset=0.5)
```

D.7

```
# EPG trackdata from the onset for 40 ms
trackto40 = dcut(polhom.epg, start(polhom.epg),
start(polhom.epg)+40)
```

```
# Trackdata of the above but with rows and columns summed
esum = epgsum(trackto40, r=2:8, c=c(1, 2, 7, 8), inactive=T)
```

```
# Logical vector that is True for S or c
temp = polhom.l %in% c("S", "c")
```

```
# A plot of the summed contacts synchronized 20 ms after segment onset
dplot(esum[temp,], polhom.l[temp],
offset=start(polhom.epg[temp,])+20, prop=F)
```

D.8

```
temp = polhom.l %in% c("c", "x")
dplot(epgcog(polhom.epg[temp,], rows=5:8), polhom.l[temp],
norm=T, average=T)
```

D.9

```
trapply(epgai(polhom.epg), median, simplify=T)
```

D.10

```
# EPG trackdata from the temporally medial 50 ms
midtime = (start(polhom.epg) + end(polhom.epg))/2
trackmid = dcut(polhom.epg, midtime-25, midtime+25)
```

```
# COG index of the above
cogvals = epgcog(trackmid)
```

```
# The mean COG value per segment over this interval
mcog = trapply(cogvals, mean, simplify=T)
```

```
# A boxplot of the mean COG for s and S
temp = polhom.l %in% c("S", "s")
boxplot(mcog[temp] ~ polhom.l[temp], ylab="Average COG")
```

E.

```
# Function for calculating the time at which the maximum first occurs
peakfun <- function(fr, maxtime=T)
{
if(maxtime) num = which.max(fr)
else num = which.min(fr)
tracktimes(fr)[num]
}

ai = epgai(engassim.epg)
di = epgdi(engassim.epg)

# Get the times at which the AI and DI maxima first occur
aimax = trapply(ai, peakfun, simplify=T)
dimax = trapply(di, peakfun, simplify=T)
diffmax = dimax - aimax

boxplot(diffmax ~ engassim.l, ylab="Duration (ms)")
```

Notes

[1] www.articulateinstruments.com/
[2] However, the times do not appear as dimension names if you look at only a single palatogram because, in this special case, an array is turned into a matrix (which has only two dimensions as a result of which the third dimension name cannot be represented).
[3] As described earlier, **fake** must be an object of class EPG for this to work. So if **class(fake)** returns **array**, then enter **class(fake) = "EPG"**.
[4] The waveform and EPG data have to be created as separate plots in the current implementation of Emu-R.

8
Spectral Analysis

The material in this chapter provides an introduction to the analysis of speech data that has been transformed into a frequency representation using some form of a Fourier transformation. In the first section, some fundamental concepts of spectra including the relationship between time and frequency resolution are reviewed. In section 8.2 some basic techniques are discussed for reducing the quantity of data in a spectrum. Section 8.3 is concerned with what are called spectral moments that encode properties of the shape of the spectrum. The final section provides an introduction to the discrete cosine transformation (DCT) that is often applied to spectra and auditorily scaled spectra. As well as encoding properties of the shape of the spectrum, the DCT can also be used to remove much of the contribution of the source (vocal fold vibration for voiced sounds, a turbulent airstream for voiceless sounds) from the filter (the shape of the vocal tract). The DCT can then be used to derive a smoothed spectrum.

8.1 Background to Spectral Analysis

8.1.1 The sinusoid

The digital sinusoid, which is the building block for all forms of computationally based spectral analysis, can be derived from the height of a point above a line as a function of time as it moves in discrete jumps, or steps, at a constant speed around a circle. In deriving a digital sinusoid, there are four variables to consider: the **amplitude, frequency, phase**, and the **number of points per repetition or cycle**. Examples of digital sinusoids are shown in Figure 8.1 and were produced with the Emu-R **crplot()** function as follows:

```
par(mfrow=c(3,2)); par(mar=c(1, 2, 1, 1))
oldpar = par(no.readonly=TRUE)

# Plot a circle and its sinusoid with defaults
crplot()
```

Spectral Analysis 265

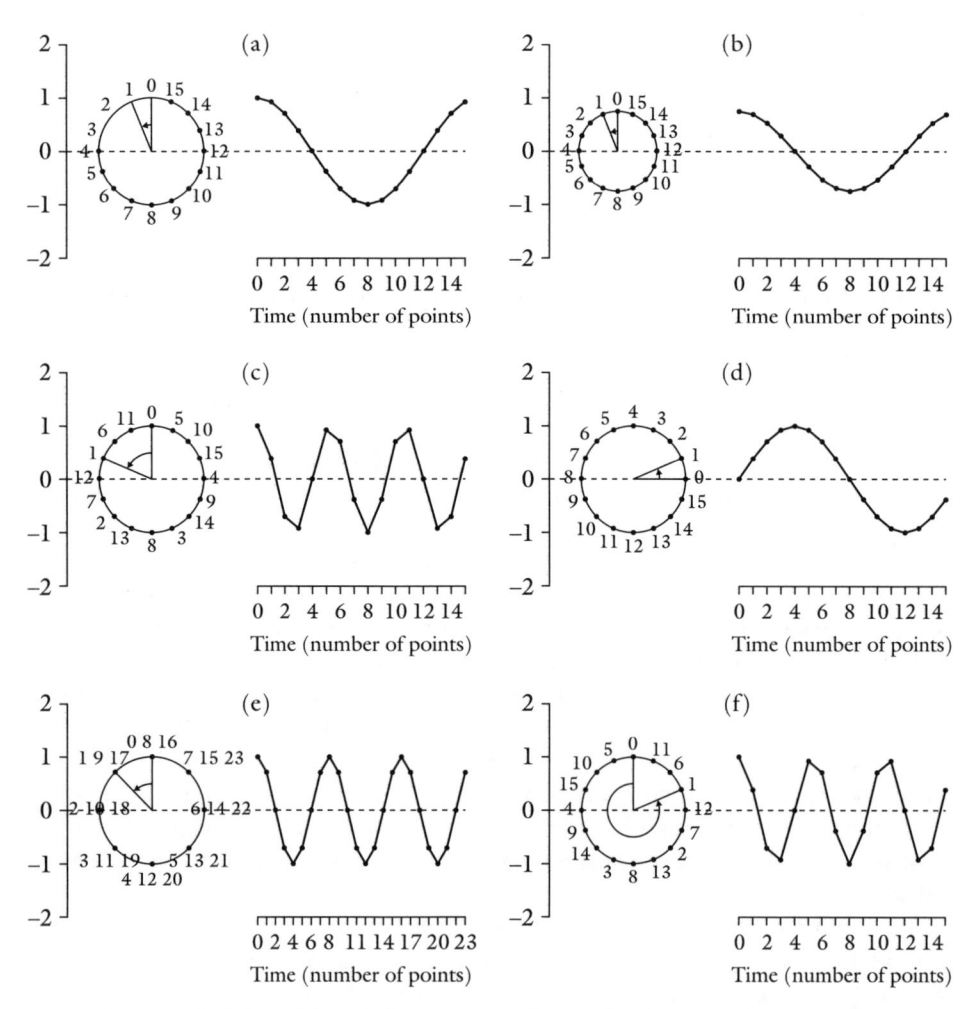

Figure 8.1 Digital sinusoids and the corresponding circles from which they were derived. The numbers correspond to the position of the point either on the circle or along the corresponding sinusoid at time point *n*. Top left: a 16-point digital cosine wave. Top right: as top left, but in which the amplitude is reduced. Middle row, left: a three-cycle 16-point cosine wave. Middle row, right: a 16-point digital sine wave. Bottom left: the same as middle row left except with 24 digital points. Bottom right: a 13-cycle, 16-point cosine wave that necessarily aliases onto a three-cycle cosine wave.

```
# Set the amplitude to 0.75
crplot(A=.75)

# Set the frequency to three cycles
crplot(k=3)

# Set the phase to − π / 2 radians
crplot(p=-pi/2)
```

```
# Set the frequency to three cycles and plot these with 24 points
crplot(k=3, N=24)

# Set the frequency to 13 cycles
crplot(k=13)
par(oldpar)
```

In the default case (Figure 8.1(a)), the point hops around the circle at a constant speed at intervals that are equally spaced on the circumference starting at the top of the circle. A plot of the height of these points about the horizontal line results in the digital sinusoid known as a **cosine wave**. The cosine wave has an amplitude that is equal to the circle's radius and it has a frequency of $k = 1$ cycle, because the point jumps around the circle once for the 16 points that are available. In Figure 8.1(b), the same cosine wave is derived but with a reduced amplitude, corresponding to a decrease in the circle's radius – but notice that all the other variables (frequency, phase, number of points) are the same. In Figure 8.1(c), the variables are the same as for Figure 8.1(a), except that the frequency has been changed to $k = 3$ cycles. Here, then, the point hops around the circle three times **given the same number of digital points** – and so necessarily the angle at the center of the circle that is made between successive hops is three times as large compared with those in Figures 8.1(a, b, d) for which $k = 1$. In Figure 8.1(d), the variable that is changed relative to Figure 8.1(a) is the **phase**, which is measured in radians. If the point begins at the top of the circle as in Figure 8.1(a–c), then the phase is defined to be zero radians. The phase can vary between $\pm \pi$ radians: at $-\pi/2$ radians, as in Figure 8.1(d), the point starts a quarter of a cycle earlier to produce what is called a **sine wave**; if the phase is $\pi/4$ radians (argument `p = pi / 4`), then the point starts at 1/8 cycle later, and so on.

The number of digital points that are available per cycle can be varied independently of the other parameters. Figure 8.1(e) is the same as Figure 8.1(c) except that the point hops around the circle three times with 24 points (8 more than in 8.1(c)). The resulting sinusoid that is produced – a three-cycle cosine wave – is the same as the one in Figure 8.1(c) except that it is supported by a greater number of digital points (and for this reason it is smoother and looks a bit more like an analog cosine wave). Since there are more points available, then the angle made at the center of the circle is necessarily smaller (compare the angles between points in Figure 8.1(c) and Figure 8.1(e)). Finally, Figure 8.1(f) illustrates the property of **aliasing** that comes about when k, the number of cycles, exceeds half the number of available data points. This is so in Figure 8.1(f) for which $k = 13$ and $N = 16$. In this case, the point has to hop 13 times around the circle **but in 16 discrete jumps**. Since the number of cycles is so large relative to the number of available data points, the angle between the hops at the center of the circle is very large. Thus, in making the first hop between time points 0 and 1, the point has to move almost all the way round the circle in order to achieve the required 13 revolutions with only 16 points. Indeed, the jump is so big that the point always ends up on the opposite side of the circle compared with the sinusoid at $k = 3$ cycles in Figure 8.1(c). For this reason, when $k = 13$ and $N = 16$, the result is not a 13-cycle sinusoid at all, but the same three-cycle sinusoid shown in Figure 8.1(c).

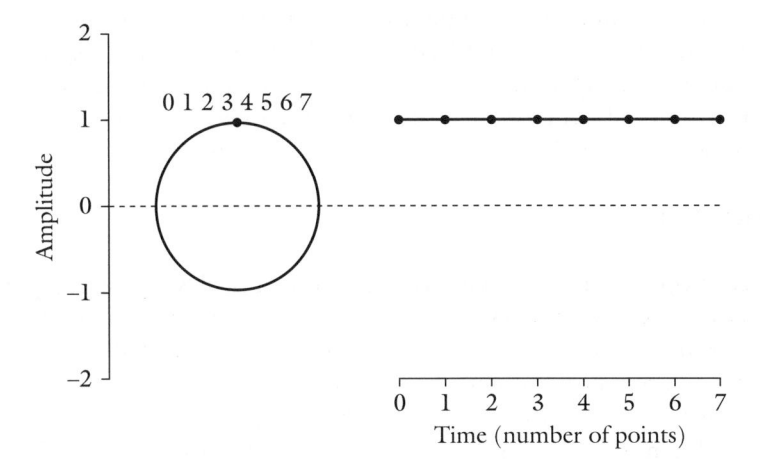

Figure 8.2 An eight-point sinusoid with frequency $k = 0$ cycles.

It is an axiom of Nyquist's theorem (1822) that it is never possible to get frequencies of more than $N/2$ cycles from N points. So, for the present example with $N = 16$, the sinusoid with the highest frequency has eight cycles (try **crplot(k=8)**), but for higher k, all the other resulting sinusoids are aliases of those at lower frequencies. Specifically, the frequencies k and $N - k$ cycles produce exactly the same sinusoids if the phase is the same: thus **crplot(k=15)** and **crplot(k=1)** both result in the same one-cycle sinusoid. The highest frequency up to which the sinusoids are unique is $k = N/2$ and this is known as the **critical Nyquist** or folding frequency. Beyond $k = N/2$, the sinusoids are aliases of those at lower frequencies.

Finally, we will sometimes come across a sinusoid with a frequency of $k = 0$. What could this look like? Since the frequency is zero, the point does not complete any cycles and so has to stay where it is: that is, for $N = 8$ points, it hops up and down eight times on the same spot. The result must therefore be a straight line, as Figure 8.2 (given by **crplot(k=0, N=8)**) shows.

8.1.2 Fourier analysis and Fourier synthesis

Fourier analysis is a technique that decomposes any signal into a set of sinusoids which, when summed, reconstructs exactly the original signal. This summation, or reconstruction, of the signal from the sinusoids into which it was decomposed is called **Fourier synthesis**.

When Fourier analysis is applied to a digital signal of length N data points, then a calculation is made of the amplitudes and phases of the sinusoids at integer frequency intervals from 0 to $N - 1$ cycles. So for a signal of a length of eight data points, the Fourier analysis calculates the amplitude and phase of the $k = 0$ sinusoid, the amplitude and phase of the $k = 1$ sinusoid, the amplitude and phase of the $k = 2$ sinusoid ... the amplitude and phase of the $k = N - 1 = 7$th sinusoid. Moreover, it does so in such a way that, if all these sinusoids are added up, then the original signal is reconstructed.

In order to get some understanding of this operation (and without going into mathematical details which would lead too far into discussions of exponentials and complex numbers), a signal consisting of eight random numbers will be decomposed into a set of sinusoids; the original signal will then be reconstructed by summing them. Here are eight random numbers between -10 and 10:

```
r = runif(8, -10, 10)
```

The principal operation for carrying out the Fourier analysis on a computer is the **discrete Fourier transform** (DFT) of which there is a faster version known as the **fast Fourier transform** (FFT). The FFT can only be used if the window length – that is the number of data points that are subjected to Fourier analysis – is exactly a power of two. In all other cases, the DFT has to be used. Since in the special case when the FFT can be used it gives exactly equivalent results to a DFT, the mathematical operation for carrying out Fourier analysis on a time signal will be referred to as the DFT, while recognizing in practice that, for the sake of speed, a window length will usually be chosen that is a power of two, thereby allowing the faster version of the DFT, the FFT, to be implemented. In R, the function for carrying out a DFT (FFT) is the function **fft()**. Thus the DFT of the above signal is:

```
r.f = fft(r)
```

r.f in the above calculation is a vector of eight complex numbers involving the square root of minus one. Each such complex number can be thought of as a convenient code that embodies the amplitude and phase values of the sinusoids from $k = 0$ to $k = 7$ cycles. To look at the sinusoids that were derived by Fourier analysis, their amplitude and phase values must be derived (the frequencies are already known: these are $k = 0, 1, \ldots 7$). The amplitude is obtained by **taking the modulus**, and the phase by **taking the argument** of the complex number representations. In R, these two operations are carried out with the functions **Mod()** and **Arg()** respectively:

```
r.a = Mod(r.f)    Amplitudes
r.p = Arg(r.f)    Phases
```

So a plot can now be produced of the sinusoids into which the eight random numbers were decomposed using the **cr()** function for plotting sinusoids (Figure 8.3):

```
par(mfrow=c(8,1)); par(mar=c(1,2,1,1))
for(j in 1:8){
  cr(r.a[j], j-1, r.p[j], 8, main=paste(j-1, "cycles"),
  axes=F)
  axis(side=2)
}
```

Following the earlier discussion, the amplitude of the sinusoid with frequency $k = 0$ cycles is a straight line, and the sinusoids at frequencies $N - k$ are aliases of those at

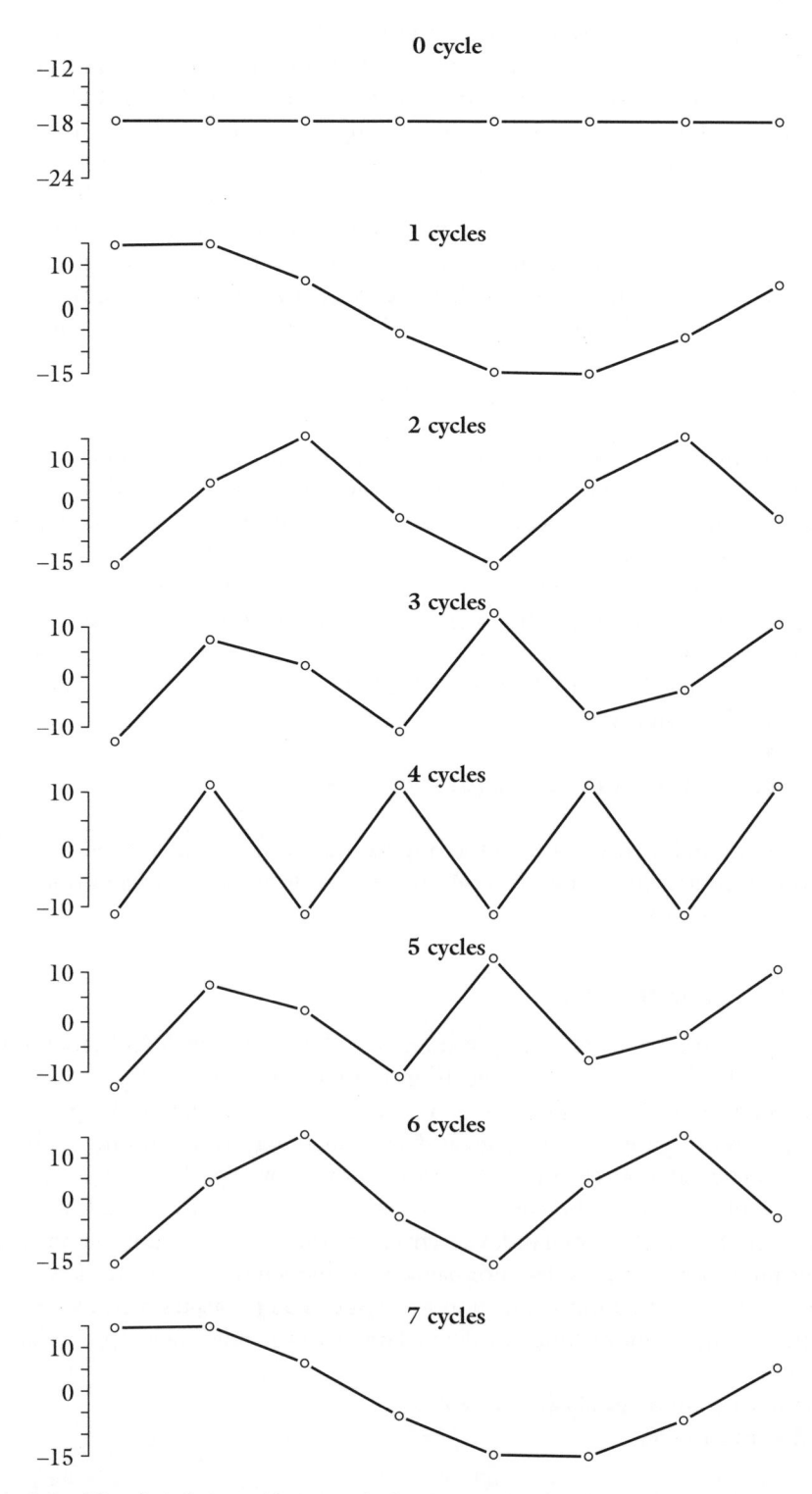

Figure 8.3 The digital sinusoids into which a sequence of eight random numbers was decomposed with a DFT.

frequencies of k (so the sinusoids for the pairs $k = 1$ and $k = 7$; $k = 2$ and $k = 6$; $k = 3$ and $k = 5$ are the same). Also, the amplitude of the $k = 0$ sinusoid[1] is equal to the sum of the values of the waveform (compare **sum(r)** and **r.a[1]**).

Carrying out Fourier synthesis involves summing the sinusoids in Figure 8.3, an operation which should exactly reconstruct the original random number signal. However, since the results of a DFT are inflated by the length of the window – that is by the length of the signal to which Fourier analysis was applied – what we get back is N times the values of the original signal. So to reconstruct the original signal, the length of window has to be normalized by dividing by N (by eight in this case). The summation of the sinusoids can also be done with the same **cr()** function as follows:

```
summed = cr(r.a, 0:7, r.p, 8, values=T)/8
```

Rounding errors apart, **summed** and the original signal **r** are the same, as can be verified by subtracting one from the other. However, the usual way of doing Fourier synthesis in digital signal processing is to carry out an **inverse Fourier transform** on the complex numbers; in R this is also done with the **fft()** function by including the argument **inverse=T**. The result is something that looks like a vector of complex numbers, but in fact the so-called imaginary part, involving the square root of minus one, is in all cases zero. To get the vector in a form without the **+0i**, take the real part using the **Re()** function. The following does this and normalizes for the length of the signal:

```
summed2 = Re(fft(r.f, inverse=T))/8
```

There is thus equivalence between the original waveform of eight random numbers, **r**, **summed2** obtained with an inverse Fourier transform, and **summed** obtained by summing the sinusoids.

8.1.3 Amplitude spectrum

An amplitude spectrum, or just spectrum, is a plot of the sinusoids' amplitudes as a function of frequency. A phase spectrum is a plot of their phase values as a function of frequency. (This chapter will only be concerned with amplitude spectra, since phase spectra do not contribute a great deal, if anything, to the distinction between most phonetic categories.) Since the information above $k = N / 2$ is, as discussed in 8.1.1, replicated in the bottom part of the spectrum, it is usually discarded. Here then (Figure 8.4) is the (amplitude) spectrum for these eight random numbers up to and including $k = N / 2$ cycles (normalized for the length of the window). In the commands below, the Emu-R function **as.spectral()** makes the objects of class "spectral" so that various functions like **plot()** can handle them appropriately.[2]

```
# Discard amplitudes above k = N / 2
r.a = r.a[1:5]
```

```
# Normalize for the length of the window and make r.a into a spectral object
r.a = as.spectral(r.a/8)
```

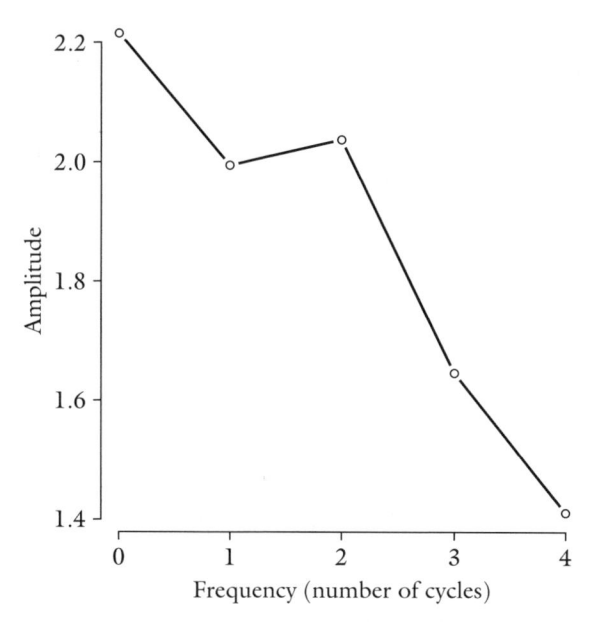

Figure 8.4 An amplitude spectrum of an eight-point signal up to the critical Nyquist frequency. These spectral values are sometimes referred to as the unreflected part of the spectrum.

```
# Amplitude spectrum
plot(r.a, xlab="Frequency (number of cycles)",
ylab="Amplitude", type="b")
```

8.1.4 Sampling frequency

So far, frequency has been represented in an integer numbers of cycles which, as discussed in 8.1.1, refers to the number of revolutions made around the circle per N points. But usually the frequency axis of the spectrum is in cycles per second or hertz and the hertz values depend on the sampling frequency. If the digital signal to which the Fourier transform was applied has a sampling frequency of f_s Hz and is of length N data points, then the frequency in Hz corresponding to k cycles is $f_s k / N$. So for a sampling frequency of 10,000 Hz and $N = 8$ points, the spectrum up to the critical Nyquist has amplitudes at frequency components in Hz of:

```
10000 * 0:4/8
0   1250   2500   3750   5000
```

From another point of view, the spectrum of an N-point digital signal sampled at f_s Hz consists of $N/2 + 1$ spectral components (has $N/2 + 1$ amplitude values) extending between 0 Hz and $f_s/2$ Hz with a frequency interval between them of f_s/N Hz.

8.1.5 dB-spectrum

It is usual in obtaining a spectrum of a speech signal to use the decibel scale for representing the amplitude values. A decibel is 10 times one bel and a bel is defined as the logarithm of the ratio of the acoustic intensity of a sound (I_S) to the acoustic intensity of a reference sound (I_R). Leaving aside the meaning of "reference sound" for the moment, the intensity of a sound is given by:

(1) $\quad I_S = 10 \log_{10}(I_S / I_R)$ dB

The acoustic or sound intensity I_S is a physical measurable quantity with units watts per square meter. Thus, to take an example, if $I_S = 10^{-8}$ watts/m² and $I_R = 10^{-4}$ watts/m², then I_S is 40 dB relative to I_R (40 decibels more intense than I_R).

More importantly for the present discussion, there is a relationship between acoustic intensity and the more familiar amplitude of air pressure which is recorded with a pressure-sensitive microphone. The relationship is $I = kA^2$, where k is a constant. Thus (1) can be rewritten as:

(2) $\quad I_S = 10 \log_{10}(kA_S^2 / kA_R^2)$ dB $= 10 \log_{10}(A_S / A_R)^2$ dB

and since $\log a^b = b \log a$ and since $\log(a / b) = \log a - \log b$, (3) is the same as (2):

(3) $\quad I_S = 20 \log_{10} A_S - 20 \log_{10} A_R$ dB

The Emu-tkassp system that is used to compute dB-spectra assumes that the amplitude of the reference sound, A_R (and hence $20 \log_{10} A_R$), is zero. So, finally, the decibel values that you will see in the spectra in this chapter and indeed in this book are $20 \log_{10} A_S$ where A_S refers to the amplitudes of sinusoids produced in Fourier analysis. Now since log (1) is always equal to zero, then this effectively means that the reference sound is a signal with an amplitude of ± 1 unit: a signal with any sequence of $+1$ or -1 like 1, 1, -1, 1, etc.

There are two main reasons for using decibels. Firstly, the decibel scale is more closely related to perceived loudness than amplitudes of air-pressure variation. Secondly, the range of amplitude of air-pressure variations within the hearing range is considerable and, because of the logarithmic conversion, the decibel scale represents this range in more manageable values (from e.g., 0 to 120 dB).

An important point to remember is that the decibel scale always expresses a **ratio of powers**: in a decibel calculation, the intensity of a signal is always defined relative to a reference sound. If the latter is taken to be the threshold of hearing, then the units are said to be dB-SPL where SPL stands for sound pressure level (and 0 dB is defined as the threshold of hearing). Independently of what we take to be the reference sound, it is useful to remember that 3 dB represents an approximate doubling of power and whenever the power is increased tenfold, then there is an increase of 10 dB (the power is the square of the amplitude of air-pressure variations).

Another helpful way of thinking of decibels is as percentages, because this is an important reminder that a decibel, like a percentage, is not an actual quantity (like

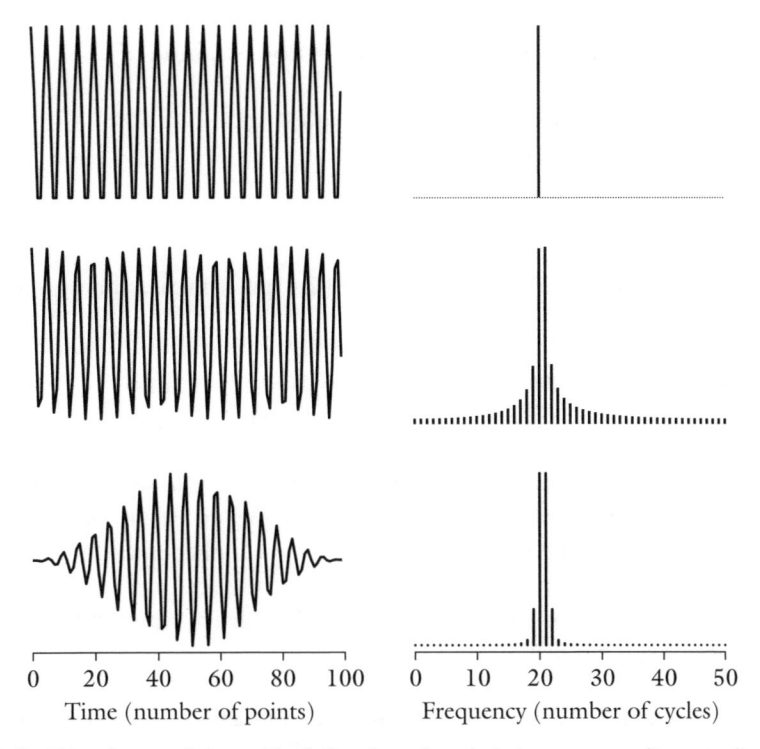

Figure 8.5 Waveforms of sinusoids (left column) and their corresponding amplitude spectra (right column). Row 1: a 20-cycle sinusoid. Row 2: a 20.5-cycle sinusoid. Row 3: as row 2 but after the application of a Hanning window.

a meter or second) but a ratio. For example, one decibel represents a power increase of 27 percent, 3 dB represents a power increase of 100 percent (a doubling of power), and 10 dB represents a power increase of 1,000 percent (a tenfold increase of power).

8.1.6 Hamming and Hann(ing) windows

If a DFT is applied to a signal that is made up exactly of an integer number of sinusoidal cycles, then the only frequencies that show up in the spectrum are the sinusoids' frequencies. For example, row 1 column 1 of Figure 8.5 shows a sinusoid of *exactly* 20 cycles, i.e., there is one cycle per five points. The result of making a spectrum of this 20-cycle waveform is a single component at the same frequency as the number of cycles (Figure 8.5, row 1, right). Its spectrum was calculated with the **spect()** function below, which simply packages up some of the commands that have been discussed in the previous section.

```
spect <- function(signal, ...)
{

# The number of points in this signal
N = length(signal)
```

```
# Apply FFT and take the modulus
signal.f = fft(signal); signal.a = Mod(signal.f)

# Discard magnitudes above the critical Nyquist and normalize
signal.a = signal.a[1:(N/2+1)]/N
as.spectral(signal.a, ...)
}
```

The 20-cycle sinusoid (Figure 8.5, row 1) and its spectrum are then given by:

```
par(mfrow=c(3,2))
a20 = cr(k=20, N=100, values=T, type="l", xlab="")
plot(spect(a20), type="h", xlab="", ylab="")
```

But the sinusoid's frequency only shows up faithfully in the spectrum in this way if the window to which the DFT is applied is made up of an **exact** number of whole sinusoidal cycles. When this is not the case, then a phenomenon called **spectral leakage** occurs, in which magnitudes show up in the spectrum, other than at the sinusoidal frequency. This is illustrated in the middle panel of Figure 8.5 for a sinusoid whose frequency is fractional at 20.5 cycles.

```
a20.5 = cr(k=20.5, N=100, values=T, type="l", xlab="")
plot(spect(a20.5), type="h", xlab="", ylab="")
```

Because a DFT can only compute amplitudes at integer values of k, the sinusoid with a frequency of 20.5 cycles falls, as it were, between the cracks: the spectrum does have a peak around $k = 20$ and $k = 21$ cycles, but there are also amplitudes at other frequencies. Obviously something is not right: a frequency of $k = 20.5$ should somehow show up in the spectrum at only that frequency and not as energy that is distributed throughout the spectrum.

What is actually happening for the $k = 20.5$ frequency is that the spectrum is being convolved with the spectrum of what is called a **rectangular window**. Why should this be so? Firstly, we need to be clear about an important characteristic of digital signals: they are finite, i.e., they have an abrupt beginning and an abrupt ending. So, although the sinusoids in the first two rows of Figure 8.5 look as if they might carry on forever, in fact they do not and, as far as the DFT is concerned, they are zero-valued outside the windows that are shown: that is, the signals in Figure 8.5 start abruptly at $n = 0$ and they end abruptly at $n = 99$. In digital signal processing, this is equivalent to saying that a sinusoid whose duration is infinite is multiplied with a rectangular window whose values are one over the extent of the signals that can be seen in Figure 8.5 (thereby leaving the values between $n = 0$ and $n = 99$ untouched, since multiplication with one gives back the same result) and multiplied by zero everywhere else. This means that any finite-duration signal that is spectrally analyzed is effectively multiplied by just such a rectangular window. But this also means that, when a DFT of a finite-duration signal is calculated, a DFT is effectively *also* being calculated of the rectangular window and it is the abrupt switch from zero to one and back to zero that causes extra magnitudes to appear in the spectrum as in the middle right panel of Figure 8.5. Now it so happens that, when the signal consists of an integer number of sinusoidal cycles so that an exact number of cycles fits into the window as in the top row of Figure 8.5, then the rectangular window has no effect on the spectrum; therefore, the sinusoidal frequencies show up faithfully in the spectrum (top right panel of Figure 8.5). However, in all other cases – and this will certainly be so for any speech signal – the spectrum is also influenced by the rectangular window.

Although such effects of a rectangular window cannot be completely eliminated, there is a way to reduce them. One way to do this is to make the transitions at the edges of the signal gradual, rather than abrupt: in this case, there will no longer be abrupt jumps between zero and one and so the spectral influence due to the rectangular window should be diminished. A common way of achieving this is to multiply the signal with some form of cosine function and two such commonly used functions in speech analysis are the Hamming window and the Hanning window (the latter is a misnomer, in fact, since the window is due to Julius von Hann). An N-point Hamming or Hanning window can be produced with the following function:

```
w <- function(a=0.5, b=0.5, N=512)
{
  n = 0: (N-1)
  a - b * cos(2 * pi * n/(N-1))
}
```

With no arguments, the above **w()** function defaults to a 512-point Hanning window that can be plotted with **plot(w())**; for a Hamming window, set **a** and **b** to 0.54 and 0.46 respectively.

The bottom left panel of Figure 8.5 shows the 20.5-cycle sinusoid of the middle left panel multiplied with a Hanning window. The spectrum of the resulting Hanning-windowed signal is shown in the bottom right of the same figure. The commands to produce these plots are as follows:

```
# Lower panel of Figure 8.5. Multiply a20.5 with a Hanning window of the same length
N = length(a20.5)
a20.5h = a20.5 * w(N=N)

# The Hanning-windowed 20.5 cycle sinusoid
plot(0:(N-1), a20.5h, type="l", xlab="Time (number of points)")

# Calculate its spectral values
a20.5h.f = spect(a20.5h)
plot(a20.5h.f, type="h", xlab="Frequency (number of cycles)", ylab="")
```

A comparison of the middle and bottom right panels of Figure 8.5 shows that, although the spectral leakage has not been eliminated, multiplication with the Hanning window has certainly caused it to be reduced.

8.1.7 Time and frequency resolution

One of the fundamental properties of any kind of spectral analysis is that time resolution and frequency resolution are inversely proportional. "Resolution" in this context defines the extent to which two events in time or two components in frequency are distinguishable. Because time and frequency resolution are inversely proportional, then if the time resolution is high (i.e., two events that occur very close together in time are distinguishable), then the frequency resolution is low (i.e., two components that are close together in frequency are indistinguishable) and vice versa.

In computing a DFT, the frequency resolution is the interval between the spectral components and, as discussed in 8.1.2, this depends on N, the length of the signal or window to which the DFT is applied. Thus, when N is large (i.e., the DFT is applied to a signal long in duration), then the frequency resolution is high, and when N is low, the frequency resolution is coarse. More specifically, when a DFT is applied to an N-point signal, then the frequency resolution is f_s / N, where f_s is the sampling frequency. So for a sampling frequency of $f_s = 16,000$ Hz and a signal of length $N = 512$ points (= 32 ms at 16,000 Hz), the frequency resolution is $f_s / N = 16,000/512 = 31.25$ Hz. Thus magnitudes will show up in the spectrum at 0 Hz, 31.25 Hz, 62.50 Hz, 93.75 Hz ... up to 8,000 Hz **and at only these frequencies** so that all other frequencies are undefined. If, on the other hand, the DFT is applied to a much shorter signal at the same sampling frequency, such as to a signal of $N = 64$ points (4 ms), then the frequency resolution is much coarser at $f_s / N = 250$ Hz and this means that there can only be spectral components at intervals of 250 Hz, i.e., at 0 Hz, 250 Hz, 500 Hz ... 8,000 Hz.

These principles can be further illustrated by computing DFTs for different values of N over the signal shown in Figure 8.6. This signal is of 512 sampled speech data points extracted from the first segment of segment list **vowlax** of German lax

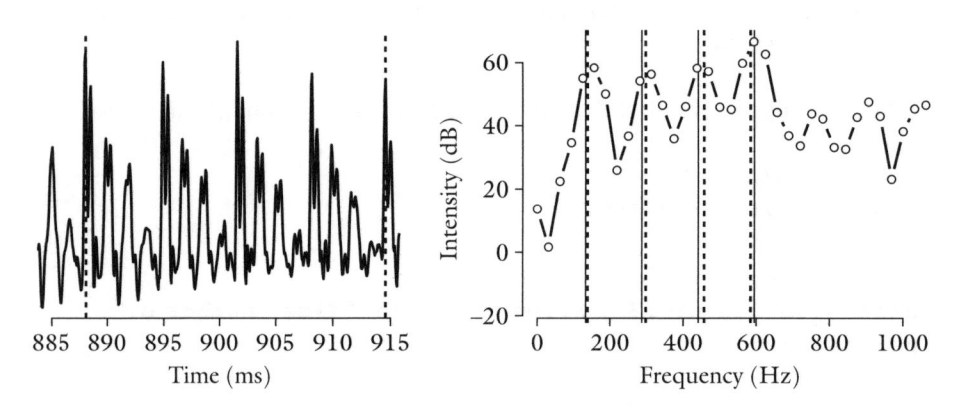

Figure 8.6 Left: a 512-point waveform of a German [ɛ] produced by a male speaker. The dashed vertical lines mark out four pitch periods. Right: a spectrum of this 512-point signal. The vertical dashed lines mark the expected frequency location of f0, the second, third, and fourth harmonics based on the closest points in the digital spectrum. The thin vertical lines show the expected f0 and harmonics at multiples of 151 Hz, which is the fundamental frequency estimated from the waveform.

monophthongs. The sampled speech data is stored in the trackdata object **v.sam** (if you have downloaded the **kielread** database, then you can (re-)create this object from **v.sam = emu.track(vowlax[1,], "samples", 0.5, 512)**). The data in Figure 8.6 was plotted as follows:

```
plot(v.sam[1,], type="l", xlab="Time (ms)",
ylab="Amplitude")

# Mark vertical lines spanning four pitch periods by clicking the mouse twice,
once at each of the time points shown in the figure
v = locator(2)$x
abline(v=v, lty=2)

# Interval (ms) between these lines
diff(v)
26.37400
```

The figure shows that four pitch periods have a duration of 26.42 ms, so the fundamental frequency over this interval is $4{,}000 / 26.42 \approx 151$ Hz. If a DFT is applied to this signal, then the fundamental frequency and its associated harmonics should show up approximately at multiples of this fundamental frequency in the resulting spectrum. In the following, the **spect()** function has been updated to include the various commands discussed earlier for calculating a dB-spectrum and for applying a Hanning window:

```
spect <- function(signal,..., hanning=T, dbspec=T)
{
# The Hanning window function
  w <- function(a=0.5, b=0.5, N=512)
  {
    n = 0: (N-1)
    a - b * cos(2 * pi * n/(N-1))
  }

# The number of points in this signal
N = length(signal)

# Apply a Hanning window
  if(hanning)
    signal = signal * w(N=N)

# Apply FFT and take the modulus
signal.f = fft(signal); signal.a = Mod(signal.f)

# Discard magnitudes above the critical Nyquist and normalize for N
signal.a = signal.a[1:(N/2+1)]/N
```

```
# Convert to dB
  if(dbspec)
    signal.a = 20 * log(signal.a, base=10)
  as.spectral(signal.a, ...)
}
```

Here is the dB-spectrum (right panel, Figure 8.6):

```
# Store the sampled speech data of the first segment in a vector for
convenience
sam512 = v.sam[1,]$data

# dB-spectrum. The sampling frequency of the signal is the second argument
sam512.db = spect(sam512, 16000)

# Plot the log-magnitude spectrum up to 1,000 Hz
plot(sam512.db, type="b", xlim=c(0, 1000), xlab="Frequency
(Hz)", ylab="Intensity (dB)")
```

Consider how the harmonics show up in the spectrum. Firstly, since f0 was estimated to be 151 Hz from the waveform in Figure 8.6, then f0 and harmonics 2–5 are to be expected at the following frequencies:

```
seq(151, by=151, length=5)
151   302   453   604   755
```

However, for a sampling frequency of 16,000 Hz and a window length of $N = 512$, the first 20 spectral magnitudes are computed only at *these* frequencies:

```
seq(0, by=16000/512, length=20)
0.00 31.25 62.50 93.75 128.00 156.25 187.50 218.75 250.00
281.25 312.50 343.75 378.00 406.25 437.50 468.75 500.00
531.25 562.50 593.75
```

Thus, there can be no peaks in the spectrum due to f0 and the harmonics at **exactly** their frequencies (because there is no frequency in the digital spectrum to support them), but instead at whichever spectral component they come closest to. These are shown in bold above and, if you count where they are in the vector, you will see that these are the sixth, eleventh, sixteenth, and twentieth spectral components. Vertical lines have been superimposed on the spectrum at these frequencies as follows:

```
abline(v=seq(0, by=16000/512, length=20)[c(6, 11, 16, 20)],
lty=2)
```

Indeed the spectrum does show peaks at these frequencies. Notice that the relationship between the expected peak location (vertical lines) and actual peaks is least accurate for the third vertical line. This is because there is quite a large deviation between

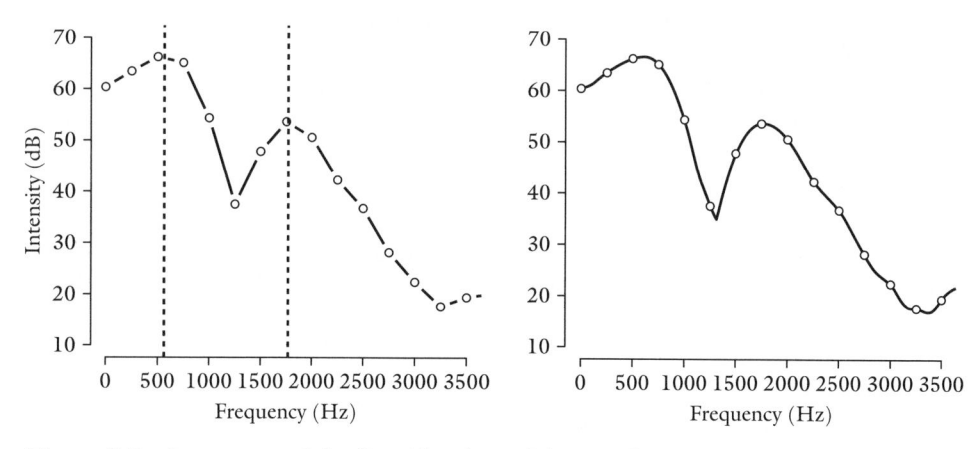

Figure 8.7 A spectrum of the first 64 points of the waveform in Figure 8.6 (left) and of the first 64 points and padded out with 192 zeros (right).

the estimated frequency of the third harmonic (453 Hz) and the (sixteenth) spectral component that is closest to it in frequency (468.75 Hz). (In fact it can be seen that the estimated third harmonic falls almost exactly halfway in frequency between two spectral components.)

The harmonics can only make their presence felt in a spectrum of voiced speech as long as the signal over which the DFT is applied includes at least two pitch periods. Consequently, harmonics can only be seen in the spectrum if the frequency resolution (interval between frequency components in the spectrum) is quite a lot less than the fundamental frequency. Consider, then, the effect of applying a DFT to just the first 64 points of the same signal. A 64-point DFT at 16,000 Hz results in a frequency resolution of 16,000 / 64 = 250 Hz, so there will be 33 spectral components between 0 Hz and 8,000 Hz at intervals of 250 Hz: that is, at a frequency interval that is greater than the fundamental frequency, and therefore too wide for the frequency and separate harmonics to have much of an effect on the spectrum. The corresponding spectrum up to 3,500 Hz in Figure 8.7 was produced as follows:

```
sam64 = sam512[1:64]
ylim = c(10, 70)
plot(spect(sam64, 16000), type = "b", xlim=c(0, 3500),
ylim=ylim, xlab="Frequency (Hz)", ylab="Intensity (dB)")
```

The influence of the fundamental frequency and harmonics is no longer visible, but instead the formant structure emerges more clearly. The first four formants, calculated with the Emu LPC-based formant tracker at roughly the same time point for which the spectrum was calculated, are:

```
dcut(vowlax.fdat[1,], 0.5, prop=T)
  T1   T2   T3   T4
 562 1768 2379 3399
```

The frequencies of the first two of these have been superimposed on the spectrum in Figure 8.7 (left) as vertical lines with **abline(v=c(562, 1768))**.

As discussed earlier, there are no magnitudes other than those that occur at f_s/N and so the spectrum in Figure 8.7 (left) is undefined except at frequencies 0 Hz, 250 Hz, 500 Hz . . . 8,000 Hz. It is possible however to interpolate between these spectral components, thereby making the spectrum smoother using a technique called **zero padding**. In this technique, a number of zero-valued data samples are appended to the speech waveform to increase its length to, for example, 256 points. (NB: these zero data values should be appended *after* the signal has been Hamming- or Hanning-windowed, otherwise the zeros will distort the resulting spectrum.) One of the main practical applications of zero padding is to fill up the number of data points of a window to a power of 2 so that the FFT algorithm can be applied to the signal data. Suppose that a user has the option of specifying the window length of a signal that is to be Fourier analyzed in milliseconds rather than points and suppose a user chooses an analysis window of 3 ms. At a sampling frequency of 16,000 Hz, a duration of 3 ms is 48 sampled data points. But if the program makes use of the FFT algorithm, there will be a problem because, as discussed earlier, the FFT requires the window length, N, to be an integer power of 2, and 48 is not a power of 2. One option then would be to append 24 zero data sample values to bring the window length up to the next power of 2, i.e., to 64.

The command lines to do the zero padding have been incorporated into the evolving **spect()** function using the argument **fftlength** that defines the length of the window to which the DFT is applied. If **fftlength** is greater than the number of points in the signal, then the signal is appended with a number of zeros equal to the difference between **fftlength** and the signal's length. (For example, if **fftlength** is 64 and the signal length is 30, then 34 zeros are appended to the signal.) The function with this modification is as follows:

```
"spect" <-
function(signal,..., hanning=T, dbspec=T, fftlength=NULL)
{
  w <- function(a=0.5, b=0.5, N=512)
  {
    n = 0: (N-1)
    a - b * cos(2 * pi * n/(N-1))
  }

# The number of points in this signal
  N = length(signal)

# Apply a Hanning window
  if(hanning)
    signal = signal * w(N=N)

# If fftlength is specified . . .
  if(!is.null(fftlength))
  {
```

```
# and if fftlength is longer than the length of the signal . . .
  if(fftlength > N)

# then pad out the signal with zeros
    signal = c(signal, rep(0, fftlength-N))
  }

# Apply FFT and take the modulus
  signal.f = fft(signal); signal.a = Mod(signal.f)

# Discard magnitudes above the critical Nyquist and normalize
  if(is.null(fftlength))
    signal.a = signal.a[1:(N/2+1)]/N
  else
    signal.a = signal.a[1:(fftlength/2+1)]/N

# Convert to dB
  if(dbspec)
    signal.a = 20 * log(signal.a, base=10)
  as.spectral(signal.a, ...)
}
```

In the following, the same 64-point signal is zero-padded to bring it up to a signal length of 256 (i.e., it is appended with 192 zeros). The spectrum of this zero-padded signal is shown as the continuous line in Figure 8.7 (right) superimposed on the 64-point spectrum:

```
ylim = c(10, 70)
plot(spect(sam64, 16000), type = "p", xlim=c(0, 3500),
xlab="Frequency (Hz)", ylim=ylim)
par(new=T)
plot(spect(sam64, 16000, fftlength=256), type = "l",
xlim=c(0, 3500), xlab="", ylim=ylim)
```

As the right panel of Figure 8.7 shows, a spectrum derived from zero padding passes through the same spectral components that were derived without it (thus, zero padding provides additional points of interpolation). An important point to remember is that zero padding does not improve the spectral resolution: zero padding does not add any new data beyond providing a few extra smooth interpolation points between spectral components that really are in the signal. Sometimes, as Hamming (1989) argues, zero padding can provide misleading information about the true spectral content of a signal.

8.1.8 Pre-emphasis

In certain kinds of acoustic analysis, the speech signal is pre-emphasized, which means that the resulting spectrum has its energy levels boosted by somewhat under

6 dB/doubling of frequency, or (just less than) 6 dB/octave. This is sometimes done to give greater emphasis to the spectral content at higher frequencies, but also sometimes to mimic the roughly 6 dB/octave lift that is produced when the acoustic speech signal is transmitted beyond the lips. Irrespective of these motivations, pre-emphasizing the signal can be useful in order to distinguish between two speech sounds that are otherwise mostly differentiated by energy at high frequencies. For example, the difference in the spectra of the release burst of a syllable-initial [t] and [d] can lie not just below 500 Hz if [d] really is produced with vocal fold vibration in the closure and release (and often in English or German it is not), but often in a high-frequency range above 4,000 Hz. In particular, the spectrum of [t] can be more intense in the upper-frequency range because the greater pressure build-up behind the closure can cause a more abrupt change in the signal from near acoustic silence (during the closure) to noise (at the release). A more abrupt change in the signal always has an effect on the higher frequencies (for example a 1,000 Hz sinusoid changes faster in time than a 1 Hz sinusoid and, of course, has a higher frequency). When I explained this [t]–[d] difference to my engineering colleagues during my time at CSTR Edinburgh in the 1980s, they suggested pre-emphasizing the bursts because this could magnify even further the spectral difference in the high-frequency range (and so lead to a better separation between these stops).

A 6 dB/octave boost in frequency can be brought about by **differencing** a speech signal where differencing has the meaning of subtracting a signal delayed by one data point from itself. You can delay a signal by k data points with the **shift()** function in the Emu-R library, which causes **x[n]** to become **x[n+1]** in the signal **x**. For example:

```
x = c(2, 4, 0, 8, 5, -4, 6)
shift(x, 1)
 6  2  4  0  8  5 -4
```

The shifting is done *circularly* by default in this function, which means that the last data point becomes the first resulting in a signal of the same length. Other than that, it is clear that the effect of delaying the signal by one point is that **x[2]** has moved to the third position, **x[3]** to the fourth position, and so on. To difference a signal, the signal is subtracted from a delayed version of itself, i.e., the differenced signal is **x - shift(x, 1)**. A spectrum of this differenced signal can be shown to have just less than a 6 dB/octave lift relative to the original signal.

This can be verified with the 64-point signal created in 8.1.7, **sam64**. To see the uncontaminated effect of the boost to higher frequencies, do not apply a Hanning window in the **spect()** function:

```
# dB-spectrum of signal
sam64.db = spect(sam64, 16000, hanning=F)

# A one-point differenced signal
dnd = sam64 - shift(sam64, 1)
```

```
# The dB-spectrum of the differenced signal
dnd.db = spect(dnd, 16000, hanning=F)

# Superimpose the two spectra
ylim = range(c(sam64.db[-1], dnd.db[-1]))
par(mfrow=c(1,2))
plot(sam64.db[-1], type="l", ylim=ylim, xlab="Frequency
(Hz)", ylab="Intensity (dB)")
par(new=T)
plot(dnd.db[-1], type="l", ylim=ylim, col="slategray",
lwd=2)

# Plot the difference between the spectra of the differenced and original signal
excluding the DC offset
plot(dnd.db[-1] - sam64.db[-1], type="l", xlab="Frequency
(Hz)", ylab="Intensity (dB)")
```

The effect of differencing is indeed to increase the energy in frequencies in the upper part of the spectrum but also to decrease them in the lower spectral range. Thus, it is as if the entire spectrum is tilted upwards about the frequency axis (Figure 8.8, left panel). The extent of the dB-change can be seen by subtracting the spectrum of the differenced signal from the spectrum of the original signal and this has been done to obtain the spectrum on the right in Figure 8.8. The meaning of an approximate 6 dB/octave change is as follows. Take any two frequencies such that one is double the other and read off the dB-levels: the difference between these dB-levels will be near 6 dB. For example, the dB-levels at 1,000, 2,000, and 4,000 Hz for the spectrum on the right are − 8.17 dB, − 2.32 dB, and 3.01 dB. So the change in dB from 1,000 to 2,000 Hz is similar to the change from 2,000 Hz to 4,000 Hz (roughly 5.5 dB). You will notice that the dB-level towards 0 Hz gets smaller and smaller and is in fact minus infinity at 0 Hz (this is why the plot on the left excludes the DC offset at 0 Hz).

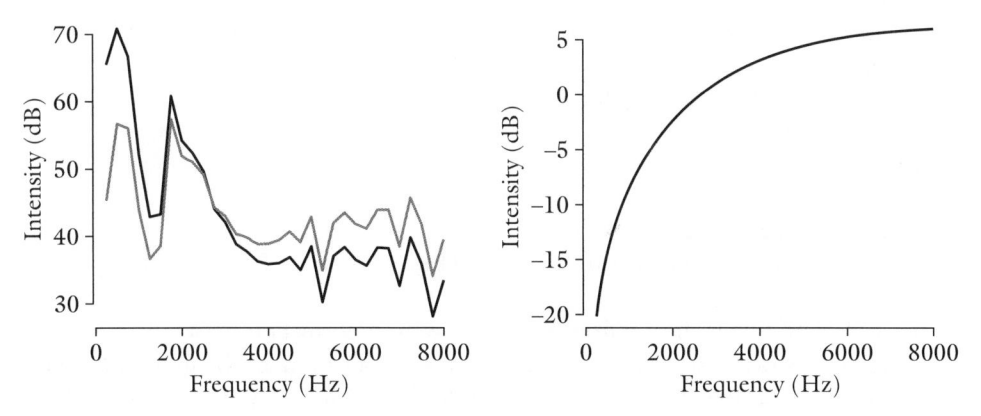

Figure 8.8 Left: a spectrum of an [i] calculated without (black) and with (gray) first differencing. Right: the difference between the two spectra shown on the left.

8.1.9 Handling spectral data in Emu-R

The usual way of getting spectral data into R is not with the functions like **spect()** of the previous section (which was created simply to show some of the different components that make up a dB-spectrum), but with the spectrum option in the Emu-tkassp toolkit (Chapter 3) for calculating spectral data allowing the DFT length, frame shift, and other parameters to be set. These routines create signal files of spectral data that can be read into Emu-R with **emu.track()**, which creates a **spectral trackdata object**.

The object **plos.dft** is such a spectral trackdata object and it contains spectral data between the acoustic closure onset and the onset of periodicity for German /b, d/ in syllable-initial position. The stops were produced by an adult male speaker of a Standard North German variety in a carrier sentence of the form *ich muss* /SVCn/ *sagen* (*I must* /SVCn/ *say*) where S is the syllable-initial /b, d/ and /SVCn/ corresponds to words like /botn/ (*boten*, past tense of *they bid*), /degn/ (*Degen, dagger*), etc. The speech data was sampled at 16 kHz so the spectra extend up to 8,000 Hz. The DFT window length was 256 points and spectra were calculated every 5 ms to derive **plos.dft**, which is part of the **plos** dataset:

plos   Segment list /b, d/ from closure onset to the periodic onset of the following vowel
plos.l   A vector of labels (**b**, **d**)
plos.w   A vector of the word labels from which the segments were taken
plos.lv   A vector of labels of the following vowels
plos.asp   Vector of times at which the burst onset occurs
plos.sam   Sampled speech data of **plos**
plos.dft   Spectral trackdata object of **plos**

You can verify that **plos.dft** is a spectral (trackdata) object by entering **is.spectral(plos.dft)**, which is to ask the question: is this a spectral object? Since the sampling frequency for this dataset was 16,000 Hz and since the window size used to derive the data was 256 points, then, following the discussion of the previous section, there should be 256 / 2 + 1 = 129 spectral components equally spaced between 0 Hz and the critical Nyquist, 8.000 Hz.

This information is given as follows:

```
ncol(plos.dft)
129
trackfreq(plos.dft)
0.0 62.5 125.0 187.5 250.0 ... 7812.5 7878.0 7937.5 8000.0
```

Compatibly with the discussion from 8.1.7, the above information shows that the spectral components occur at 0 Hz, 62.5 Hz and at intervals of 62.5 Hz up to 8,000 Hz. We were also told that the frame shift in calculating the DFT was 5 ms. So how many spectra, or spectral slices, can be expected for, e.g., the forty-seventh segment? The forty-seventh segment is a /d/ – shown below – and has a start time of 316 ms and a duration of just over 80 ms:

```
plos[47,]
labels    start      end       utts
47     d  316.948   397.214   gam070
dur(plos[47,])
80.266
```

So for this segment, around 16 spectral slices (80/5) are to be expected. Here are the times at which these slices occur:

```
tracktimes(plos.dft[47,])
317.5   322.5   327.5   332.5   337.5   ...   387.5   392.5
```

They are at 5 ms intervals and, as **length(tracktimes(plos.dft[47,]))** shows, there are indeed 16 of them. So to be completely clear: **plos.dft[47,]** contains 16 spectral slices each of 129 values and spaced on the time-axis at 5 ms intervals. A plot of the last nine of these, together with the times at which they occur, is shown in Figure 8.9 and was created as follows:

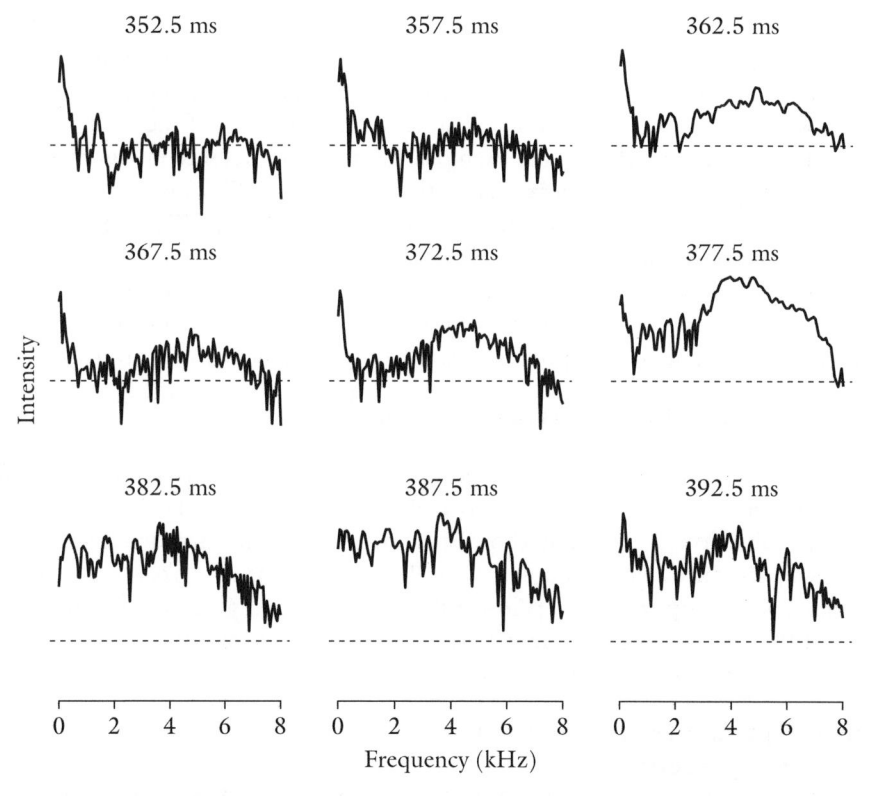

Figure 8.9 256-point spectra calculated at 5 ms intervals between the acoustic onset of a closure and the onset of periodicity of a /d/ in /daʊ/. The midpoint time of the window over which the DFT was calculated is shown above each spectrum. The release of the stop is at 378 ms (and can be related to the rise in the energy of the spectrum at 377.5 ms above 3 kHz). The horizontal dashed line is at 0 dB.

```
dat = frames(plos.dft[47,])[8:16,]
times = tracktimes(dat)
par(mfrow=c(3,3)); par(mar=c(2, 1, .4, 1))
ylim =c(-20, 50)
for(j in 1:nrow(dat)){
  plot(dat[j,], bty="n", axes=F, ylim=ylim, lwd=2)
  if(any(j == c(7:9)))
  {
    freqs = seq(0, 8000, by=2000)
    axis(side=1, at=freqs,
    labels=as.character(freqs/1000))
  }
  abline(h=0, lty=2, lwd=1)
  mtext(paste(times[j], "ms"), cex=.5)
  if(j == 8)
    mtext("Frequency (kHz)", 1, 2, cex=.5)
  if(j == 4)
    mtext("Intensity", 2, 1, cex=.75)
}
```

Since these spectral data were obtained with a DFT of 256 points and a sampling frequency of 16,000 Hz, the window length is equal to a duration of (256 × 1,000 / 16,000) = 256 / 16 = 16 ms. The temporal midpoint of the DFT window is shown above each spectral slice. For example, the sixth spectral slice in Figure 8.9 (thus the thirteenth row of **plos.dft**) has a time-stamp of 377.5 ms and so the DFT window that was used to calculate this spectrum extends from 377.5 − 8 = 369.5 ms to 377.5 + 8 = 388.5 ms.

The **dcut()** function can be used to extract trackdata between two time points, or at a single time point, either from millisecond times or proportionally (see 5.5.3). Thus spectral data at the temporal midpoint of the segment list is given by:

```
plos.dft.5 = dcut(plos.dft, .5, prop=T)
```

For spectral trackdata objects and spectral matrices, what comes after the comma within the index brackets refers not to column numbers directly, but to **frequencies**. The subscripting pulls out those spectral components that are closest to the frequencies specified. For example, the following command makes a new spectral trackdata object **spec** from **plos.dft** but containing only the frequencies 2,000–4,000 Hz. (The subsequent **trackfreq()** command verifies that these are the frequency components of the newly created object.)

```
spec = plos.dft[,2000:4000]
trackfreq(spec)
2000.0 2062.5 2125.0 2187.5 2250.0 2312.5 2375.0 2437.5
2500.0 2562.5 2625.0 2687.5 2750.0 2812.5 2875.0 2937.5
3000.0 3062.5 3125.0 3187.5 3250.0 3312.5 3375.0 3437.5
3500.0 3562.5 3625.0 3687.5 3750.0 3812.5 3875.0 3937.5
4000.0
```

Notice that **spec** now has 33 columns (given by either **ncol(spec)** or **length(trackfreq(spec))**), with each column including data from the frequencies listed above. Some further examples of handling spectral objects in Emu-R are as follows:

```
# Trackdata object 0–3,000 Hz
spec = plos.dft[,0:3000]

# As above, but of segments 1–4 only
spec = plos.dft[1:4,0:3000]
dim(spec)
4 49

# Trackdata object of the data at 1,400 Hz only
spec = plos.dft[,1400]
trackfreq(spec)
1375
ncol(spec)
1

# Trackdata object of all frequencies except 0–2,000 Hz and except
4,000–7,500 Hz
spec = plos.dft[,-c(0:2000, 4000:7500)]
trackfreq(spec)
2062.5 2125.0 2187.5 2250.0 2312.5 2375.0 2437.5 2500.0
2562.5 2625.0 2687.5 2750.0 2812.5 2875.0 2937.5 3000.0
3062.5 3125.0 3187.5 3250.0 3312.5 3375.0 3437.5 3500.0
3562.5 3625.0 3687.5 3750.0 3812.5 3875.0 3937.5 7562.5
7625.0 7687.5 7750.0 7812.5 7875.0 7937.5 8000.0

# DC offset (0 Hz), segments 1–10
spec = plos.dft[1:10,0]
```

Use minus one to get rid of the DC offset which is the spectral component at 0 Hz:

```
# All spectral components of segments 1–10, except the DC offset
spec = plos.dft[1:10,-1]
```

Exactly the same commands work on spectral matrices that are the output of **dcut()**. Thus:

```
# Spectral data at the temporal midpoint
plos.dft.5 = dcut(plos.dft, .5, prop=T)

# As above, but 1–3 kHz
spec = plos.dft.5[,1000:3000]
```

```
# A plot in the spectral range 1-3 kHz at the temporal midpoint for the
eleventh segment
plot(spec[11,], type="l")
```

Notice that, if you pull out a **single** row from a spectral matrix, the result is no longer a (spectral) **matrix** but a (spectral) **vector**: in this special case, just put the desired frequencies inside square brackets without a comma (as when indexing any vector). Thus:

```
spec = plos.dft.5[11,]
class(spec)
"numeric" "spectral"
```

```
# Plot the values between 1,000 and 3,000 Hz
plot(spec[1000:3000])
```

8.2 Spectral Average, Sum, Ratio, Difference, Slope

The aim in this section is to consider some of the ways in which spectra can be parameterized for distinguishing between different phonetic categories. A spectral parameter almost always involves some form of data reduction of the usually very large number of spectral components that are derived from the Fourier analysis of a waveform. One of the simplest forms of spectral data reduction is averaging and summing energy in frequency bands. The dataset **fric** to which these parameters will be applied is given below: these are German fricatives produced by an adult male speaker in read sentences taken from the **kielread** database. The fricatives were produced in an intervocalic environment and are phonetically (rather than just phonologically) voiceless and voiced respectively and they occur respectively in words like [bø:zə] (*böse/angry*) and [vasə] (*Wasser/water*):

fric	Segment list of intervocalic [s, z]
fric.l	Vector of (phonetic) labels
fric.w	Vector of word labels from which the fricatives were taken
fric.dft	Spectral trackdata object (256-point DFT, 16,000 Hz sampling frequency)

An ensemble plot of all the [s] and [z] fricatives at the temporal midpoint in the left panel of Figure 8.10 is given by:

```
fric.dft.5 = dcut(fric.dft, .5, prop=T)
plot(fric.dft.5, fric.l)
```

It can also be helpful to look at averaged spectral plots per category. However, since decibels are logarithms, then the addition and subtraction of logarithms really implies multiplication and division respectively; consequently, any arithmetic operation which, like averaging, involves summation, cannot (or should not) be directly applied to logarithms. For example, the average of 0 dB and 10 dB is not 5 dB.

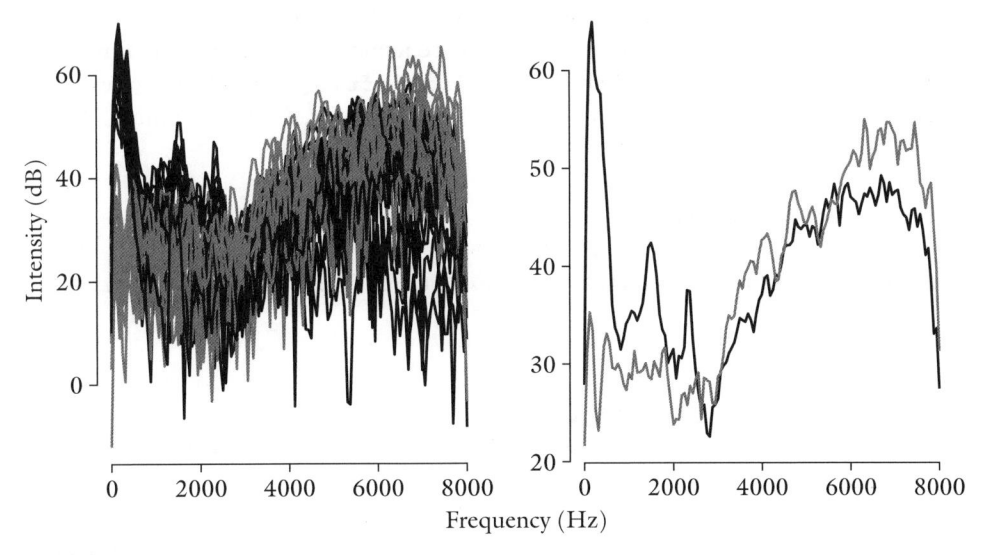

Figure 8.10 Spectra (left) and ensemble-averaged spectra (right) of [s] (gray) and [z] (black).

Instead, the values first have to be converted back into a linear scale where the averaging (or other numerical operation) takes place; the result can then be converted back into decibels. Since decibels are essentially power ratios, they could be converted to the (linear) power scale prior to averaging. This can be done by dividing by 10 and then taking the anti-logarithm (i.e., raising to a power of 10). Under this definition, the average of 0 dB and 10 dB is calculated as follows:

```
dbvals = c(0, 10)
# Convert to powers
pow = 10^(dbvals/10)

# Take the average
pow.mean = mean(pow)

# Convert back to decibels
10 * log(pow.mean, base=10)
7.403627
```

For plots of spectral data, this conversion to powers before averaging is done within the **plot()** function by including the argument **power=T**. Thus the ensemble-averaged spectra are given by:

```
plot(fric.dft.5, fric.l, fun=mean, power=T)
```

There is clearly a greater amount of energy below about 500 Hz for [z] (Figure 8.10, right), and this is to be expected because of the influence of the fundamental frequency on the spectrum in the case of voiced [z].

One way of quantifying this observed difference between [s] and [z] is to sum or to average the spectral energy in a low-frequency band using the functions **sum()** or **mean()** respectively. Thus **mean(fric.dft.5[1,0:500])** returns the mean energy value in the frequency range 0–500 Hz for the first segment. More specifically, this command returns the mean of these dB-values

```
fric.dft.5[1,0:500]
    T1      T2      T3      T4      T5      T6      T7      T8      T9
 22.4465 52.8590 63.8125 64.2507 46.0111 60.1562 57.4044 51.6558 51.6887
```

that occur respectively at these frequencies

```
trackfreq(fric.dft.5[1,0:500])
  0.0    62.5   125.0   187.5   250.0   312.5   375.0   437.5   500.0
```

In order to obtain corresponding mean values separately for the second, third, fourth ... thirty-fourth segment, a for-loop could be used around this command. Alternatively (and more simply), the **fapply(spec, fun)** function can be used for the same purpose, where **spec** is a spectral object and **fun** a function to be applied to **spec**. Thus for a single segment, **mean(fric.dft.5[1,0:500])** and **fapply(fric.dft.5[1,0:500], mean)** both return the same single mean dB-value in the 0–500 Hz range for the *first* segment. In order to calculate the mean values separately for *each* segment, the command is:

```
fapply(fric.dft.5[,0:500], mean)
```

which returns 34 mean values (arranged in a 34 × 1 matrix), one mean value per segment. The function **fapply()** also has an optional argument **power=T** that converts from decibels to power values before the function is applied: for the reasons discussed earlier, this should be done when averaging or summing energy in a spectrum. Therefore, the sum and mean energy levels in the frequency band 0–500 Hz at the midpoint of the fricatives are given by:

```
s500 = fapply(fric.dft.5[,0:500], sum, power=T)
m500 = fapply(fric.dft.5[,0:500], mean, power=T)
```

A boxplot (Figure 8.11) for the first of these, the summed energy in the 0–500 Hz band, shows that this parameter distinguishes between [s, z] very effectively:

```
boxplot(s500 ~ fric.l, ylab="dB")
```

When two categories are compared on amplitude or intensity levels, there is usually an implicit assumption that they are not artificially affected by variations in loudness caused, for example, because the speaker did not keep at a constant distance from the microphone, or because the speaker happened to produce some utterance with greater loudness than others. This is not especially likely for the present corpus, but one way of reducing this kind of artefact is to calculate the **ratio of energy levels**.

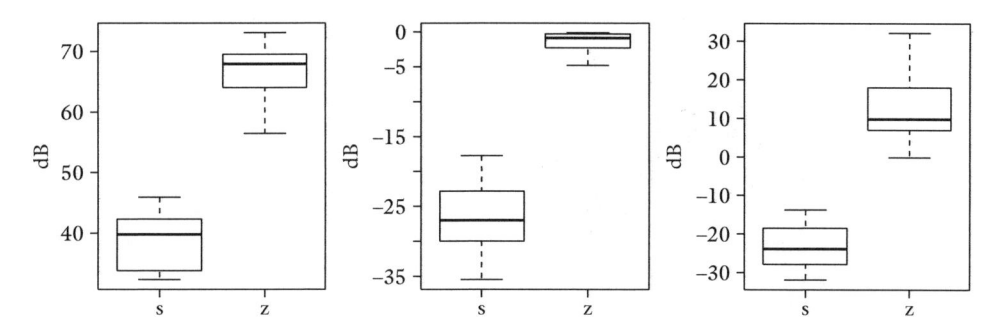

Figure 8.11 Distribution of [s] and [z] on: summed energy in the 0–500 Hz region (left), the ratio of energy in this region to that in the total spectrum (middle) and the ratio of energy in this region to the summed energy in the 6,000–7,000 Hz range (right).

More specifically, the ratio of energy in the 0–500 Hz band relative to the total energy in the spectrum should not be expected to vary too much with, say, variations in speaker distance from the microphone. The sum of the energy in the entire spectrum (0–8,000 Hz) is given by:

```
stotal = fapply(fric.dft.5, sum, power=T)
```

To get the desired energy ratio (middle panel of Figure 8.11), subtract one from the other in decibels:

```
s500r = s500 - stotal
boxplot(s500r ~ fric.l, ylab="dB")
```

The energy ratio could be calculated between two separate bands, rather than between one band and the energy in the entire spectrum, and this too would have a similar effect of reducing some of the artificially induced differences in the amplitude level discussed earlier. Since Figure 8.10 shows that [s] seems to have marginally more energy around 6,500 Hz, then the category differences might also emerge more clearly by calculating the ratio of summed energy in the 0–500 Hz band to that in the 6,000–7,000 Hz band (Figure 8.11, right panel):

```
shigh = fapply(fric.dft.5[,6000:7000], sum, power=T)
s500tohigh = s500 - shigh
boxplot(s500tohigh ~ factor(fric.l), ylab="dB")
```

Another way of normalizing for artificially induced differences in the amplitude level is to calculate **difference spectra**, obtained as its name suggests by subtracting one spectrum from another, usually in the same syllable, word, or phrase. (A difference spectrum has already been calculated in the discussion of pre-emphasis in 8.1.8.) But independently of this consideration, difference spectra have been shown to be valuable in distinguishing place of articulation in both oral (Lahiri et al. 1984) and nasal (Harrington 1994; Kurowski & Blumstein 1984) stops. A difference spectrum

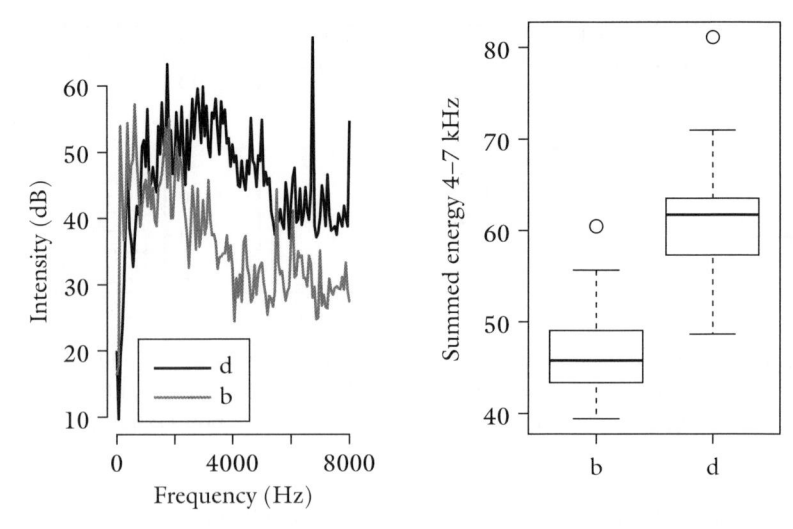

Figure 8.12 Left: ensemble-averaged difference spectra for [b] and [d] calculated from spectra taken 20 ms and 10 ms after the stop release. Right: the distributions of [b] and [d] on the change in summed energy before and after the burst in the 4,000–7,000 Hz range.

shows how the energy in the spectrum changes between two time points. For the following example, difference spectra will be calculated for the database of plosives considered earlier. More specifically, spectra are to be calculated (a) during the closure 20 ms before the release of the stop and (b) 10 ms after the release of the stop; a difference spectrum will then be obtained by subtracting (a) from (b). Because /d/ tends to have a lot more energy in the upper part of the spectrum at stop release than /b/, then such differences between these two categories should show up above about 4,000 Hz in the difference spectrum. The ensemble-averaged plot of the difference spectrum as well as the summed energy values in the difference spectrum between 4 and 7 kHz confirms this (Figure 8.12):

```
# (a) Spectra 20 ms before the stop release
before = dcut(plos.dft, plos.asp-20)

# (b) Spectra 10 ms after the stop release
after = dcut(plos.dft, plos.asp+10)

# Difference spectra: (b) – (a)
d = after - before

# Ensemble-averaged plot of the difference spectra separately for /b, d/
par(mfrow=c(1,2))
plot(d, plos.l, fun=mean, power=T, xlab="Frequency (Hz)",
ylab="Intensity (dB)", leg="bottomleft")

# Summed energy in the difference spectra 4–7 kHz
dsum = fapply(d[,4000:7000], sum, power=T)
```

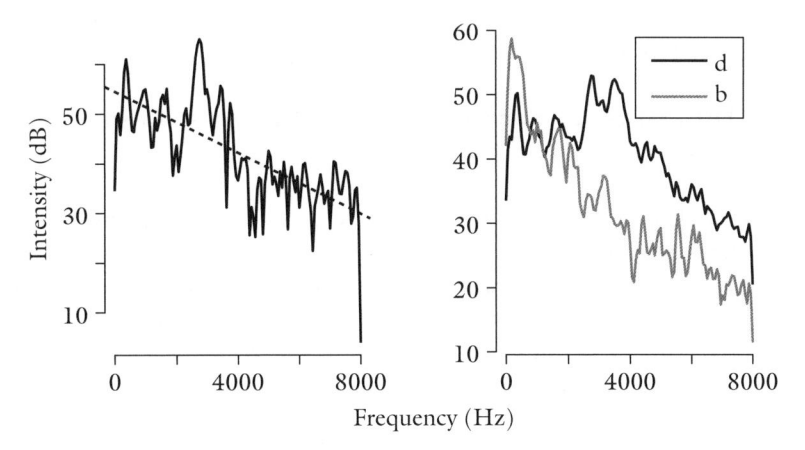

Figure 8.13 Left: a spectrum of a [d] 10 ms after the stop release showing the line of best fit (dashed) based on least squares regression. Right: ensemble-averaged spectra for [b] and [d] calculated 10 ms after the stop release.

```
# Boxplot (Figure 8.12)
boxplot(dsum ~ factor(plos.1), ylab="Summed energy 4-7 kHz")
```

The (linear) **spectral slope** is a parameter that reduces a spectrum to a pair of values, the intercept and the slope of the (straight) line of best fit through the spectral values. There is evidence that these differences in spectral slope are important for distinguishing between places of articulation in oral stops (Blumstein & Stevens 1979, 1980). The R function **lm()** can be used to compute the straight line of best fit (a linear regression based on least squares), as follows:

```
# Spectrum of the first segment 10 ms after the stop release (Figure 8.13, left)
plot(after[1,], xlab="Frequency (Hz)", ylab="Intensity (dB)")

# Calculate the coefficients of the linear regression equation
m = lm(after[1,] ~ trackfreq(after))

# Superimpose the regression equation
abline(m)
m$coeff
```

```
# The intercept and slope
  Intercept           X
54.523549132   -0.003075377
```

The slope is negative because, as Figure 8.13 (left panel) shows, the spectrum falls with increasing frequency.

A first step in parameterizing the data as spectral slopes is to look at ensemble-averaged spectra of [b, d] in order to decide roughly over which frequency range the slopes should be calculated. These are shown in the right panel of Figure 8.13, which was created as follows:

```
plot(after, plos.1, fun=mean, power=T, xlab="Frequency
(Hz)",ylab="Intensity (dB)")
```

Spectral slopes will now be calculated in the frequency range 500–4,000 Hz because, as the right panel of Figure 8.13 shows, this is where the slope differences between the categories emerge most clearly. In order to calculate slopes for the entire matrix of spectral data (rather than for a single segment, as done in the left panel of Figure 8.13), the **fapply(x, fun)** function can be used again, where **fun** is now a function that calculates the slope per spectrum. First of all, the function for calculating the slope has to be written:

```
slope <- function(x)
{

# Calculate the intercept and slope
lm(x ~ trackfreq(x))$coeff
}
```

The coefficients of the regression through the spectrum for the first segment could be obtained from:

```
slope(after[1,])
  Intercept            X
54.523549132  -0.003075377
```

The same function can be used inside **fapply()** in order to calculate the slopes separately for each segment in the 500–4,000 Hz range:

```
m <- fapply(after[,500:4000], slope)
```

The object **m** is a two-columned matrix with the intercept and slope values per segment in columns 1 and 2 respectively. So the extent to which [b, d] are distinguished by the spectral slope calculated in the 500–4,000 Hz range can be judged from the following display (Figure 8.14, left panel):

```
boxplot(m[,2] ~ plos.1, ylab="Spectral slope (dB/Hz)")
```

Compatibly with Blumstein and Stevens (1979, 1980), Figure 8.14 shows that the slope for [b] is predominantly negative whereas for [d] it is mostly positive.

It is interesting to consider the extent to which this parameter and the one calculated earlier, the sum of the energy from a difference spectrum, both contribute to the [b, d] distinction. The **eplot()** function could be used to look at the distribution of these categories on these parameters together (Figure 8.14, right panel):

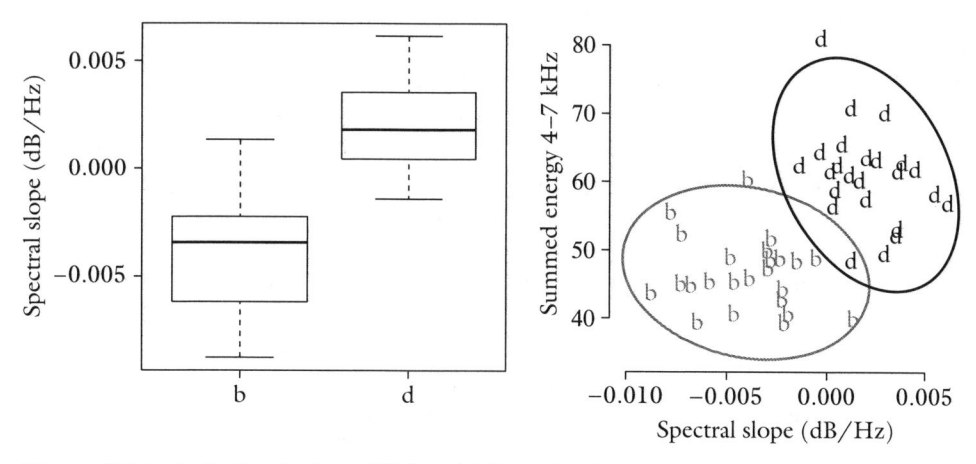

Figure 8.14 Left: distribution of [b] and [d] on the slope of the spectrum in the 500–4,000 Hz range calculated 10 ms after the stop release. Right: 95% ellipse plots on this parameter (x-axis) and the summed energy in the 4–7 kHz (y-axis) range also calculated 10 ms after stop release.

```
eplot(cbind(m[,2], dsum), plos.l, dopoints=T,
xlab="Spectral slope (dB/Hz)", ylab="Summed energy 4-7 kHz")
```

In fact, both parameters together give just about 100 percent separation between [b, d]. However, closer inspection of the right panel of Figure 8.14 shows that most of the "work" in separating them is done by the spectral slope parameter: if you draw a vertical line at around − 0.00168 (`abline(v= -0.00168)`), then you will see that only 2–3 [b] tokens fall on the wrong side (i.e., [d]) of the line. So the slope parameter separates the data more effectively than does the parameter of summed energy values.

Finally, these functions have been applied so far to spectral slices extracted from a spectral trackdata object at a *single* point in time. However, they can be just as easily applied to spectra spaced at equal time intervals in a trackdata object. Recall from the earlier discussion that the spectral trackdata object `plos.dft` has spectral data from the start time to the end time of each segment. The spectra for the first segment are given by `frames(plos.dft[1,])`, which has 24 rows and 129 columns. The rows contain spectra at the points in time given by `tracktimes(plos.dft[1,])`:

```
412.5 417.5 422.5 427.5 432.5 437.5 442.5 447.5 452.5 457.5
462.5 467.5 472.5 477.5 482.5 487.5 492.5 497.5 502.5 507.5
512.5 517.5 522.5 527.5
```

that is, they occur at 5 ms intervals. Thus at time point 412.5 ms there are 129 dB-values spanning the frequency range given between 0 and 8,000 Hz at a frequency interval of 62.5 Hz. Then, 5 ms on from this, there is another 129 dB-value over the same frequency range, and so on. Thus `plos.dft[1,]` has 24 spectral slices at 5 ms intervals: these are the spectral slices that would give rise to a spectrogram between the start and end time of the first segment in the corresponding segment list **plos[1,]**, a /d/ burst. What if we now wanted to calculate the mean dB-value for each such spectral slice? One way is to make use of the method presented so far: **fapply(frames(plos.dft[1,]), mean)** returns 24 mean values, one per spectral slice per 5 ms. However, **fapply()** can be more conveniently applied to a spectral trackdata object *directly*. Thus the same result is given, without having to use the **frames()** function, just with **fapply(plos.dft[1,], mean)**. Moreover, a major advantage of using **fapply()** in this way is that the output is also a trackdata object whose times extend over the same intervals (between 412.5 and 527.5 in this case). Since the output is a trackdata object, then a plot of the mean dB per spectral slice between the start and end time of this segment is given by **plot(fapply(plos.dft[1,], mean))**. In order to produce an ensemble plot on this parameter for all segments color-coded by segment type (and synchronized at their onsets), omit the subscripting and supply a parallel vector of annotations, thus:

```
dplot(fapply(plos.dft, mean), plos.l, type="l").
```

Consider now how this functionality could be applied to produce an ensemble plot of the spectral slope values in the 500–4,000 Hz range as a function of time between the burst's onset and offset. The first step is to apply the **slope()** function written earlier to the spectral trackdata object, thus:

```
slopetrack = fapply(plos.dft[,500:4000], slope)
```

slopetrack is now a two-dimensional trackdata object containing the intercept and slope for each spectrum at 5 ms intervals per segment between the burst onset and offset. So it is possible to inspect how the spectral slope changes between the onset and offset in, e.g., the tenth segment as follows (Figure 8.15, left panel):

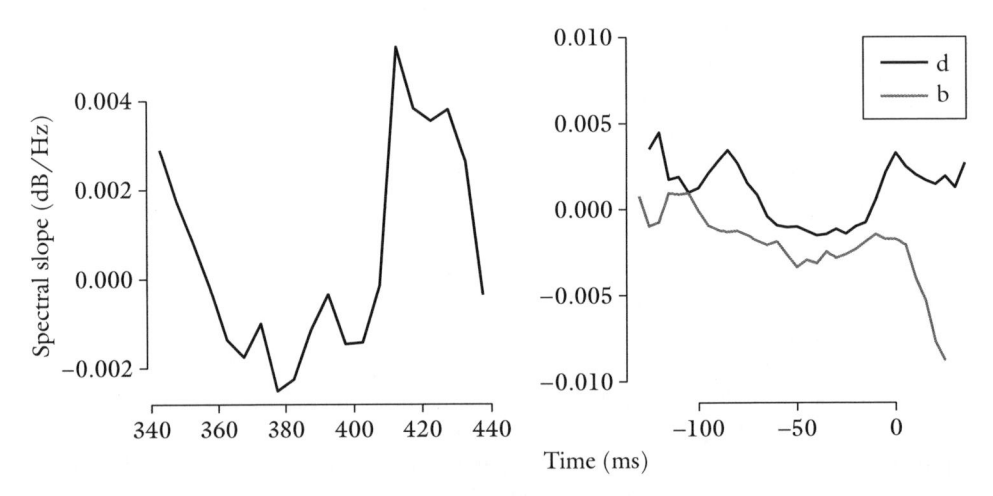

Figure 8.15 Left: the spectral slope in the 500–4,000 Hz range plotted as a function of time from closure onset to the burst offset/vowel onset for a [d] token. Right: the spectral slope over the same temporal extent averaged separately across all [b] and [d] tokens, after synchronization at the burst onset ($t = 0$ ms).

```
dplot(slopetrack[10,2], plos.l[10], xlab="Time (ms)",
    ylab="Spectral slope (dB/Hz)")
```

The right panel of Figure 8.15 shows an ensemble plot of these data averaged separately by phonetic category after synchronization at the burst onset:

```
dplot(slopetrack[,2], plos.l, plos.asp, prop=F, average = T,
    ylab="Spectral slope (dB/Hz)", xlab="Time (ms)")
```

These data show very clearly how, beyond the burst onset at $t = 0$ ms, labials have falling, but alveolars rising spectral slopes.

8.3 Spectral Moments

The types of parameters discussed in the preceding section can often effectively distinguish between spectra of different phonetic categories. Another useful way of quantifying spectral differences is to reduce the spectrum to a small number of parameters that encode basic properties of its shape. This can be done by calculating what are often called **spectral moments** (Forrest et al. 1988). The function for calculating moments is borrowed from statistics, in which the first four moments describe the **mean**, **variance**, **skew**, and **kurtosis** of a probability distribution.

Before looking at *spectral* moments, it will be helpful to consider (statistical) moments in general. The matrix **bridge** includes some hypothetical data of counts that were made on three separate days of the number of cars crossing a bridge at hourly intervals. It looks like this:

```
bridge
    Mon  Tues  Wed
0    9    1    0
1   35    1    1
2   68    5    7
3   94    4   27
...
```

The first row shows that between midday and 1 pm, 9 cars were counted on Monday, one on Tuesday, and none on Wednesday. The second row has the same meaning but is the count of cars between 1 pm and 2 pm. Figure 8.16 shows the distribution of the counts on these three separate days:

```
par(mfrow=c(1,3))
barplot(bridge[,1], ylab="Observed number of cars",
    main="Monday")
barplot(bridge[,2], xlab="Hours", main="Tuesday")
barplot(bridge[,3], main="Wednesday")
```

There are obviously overall differences in the shape of these distributions. The plot for Monday is skewed to the left; the one for Tuesday is a mirror-image of the Monday

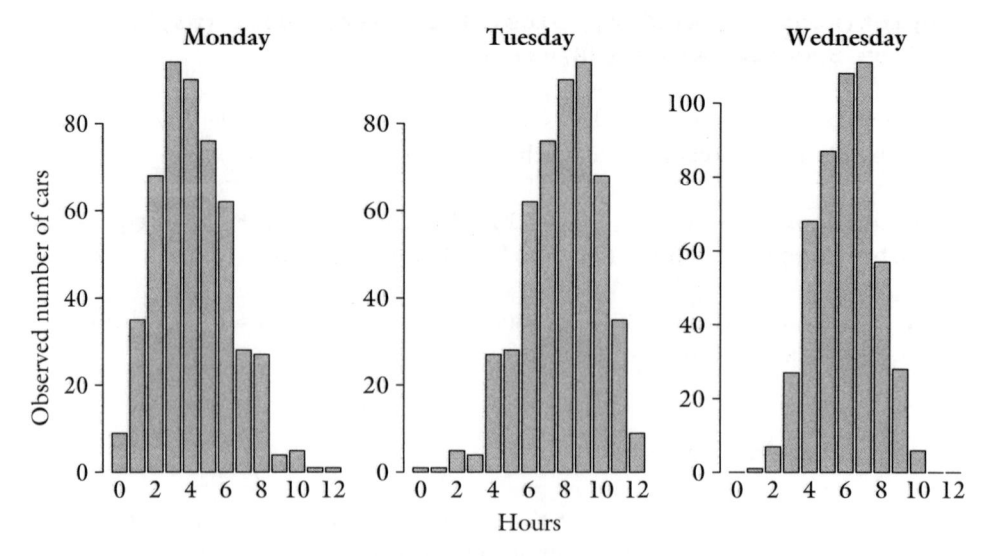

Figure 8.16 Hypothetical data of the count of the number of cars crossing a bridge in a 12-hour period.

data and is skewed to the right. The data for Wednesday is not as dispersed as for the other days: that is, it has more of its values concentrated around the mean.

Leaving aside kurtosis for the present, the following predictions can be made:

- Monday's mean (first moment) is somewhere between 4 and 5 pm, while the mean for Tuesday is a good deal higher (later), nearer 8 or 9 pm. The mean for Wednesday seems to be between these two, around 6 or 7 pm.
- The values for Wednesday are not as spread out as for Monday or Tuesday: it is likely therefore that its variance (second moment) will be lower than for those of the other two days.
- As already observed, Monday, Tuesday, and Wednesday are all likely to have different values for skew (third moment).

The core calculation of moments involves the formula:

$$(4) \quad \frac{\Sigma f(x-k)^m}{\Sigma f}$$

in which f is the observed frequency (observed number of cars in this example), x is the class (hours from 0 to 12 in our example), m is the moment ($m = 1, 2, 3, 4$), and k is a constant (see also Harrington 2010). The above formula can be translated directly into R as:

```
sum(f * (x - k)^m)/sum(f)
```

This formula can be put into a function that defaults to calculating the first moment with **m** defaulting to 1 and **k** to 0 (the constant is zero when calculating the first moment):

```
mfun <- function(x, f, k = 0, m = 1)
{
sum(f * (x - k)^m)/sum(f)
}
```

To get the mean or first moment, the class, **x**, has to be created, which in the present **bridge** data consists of the integers 0 through to 12:

```
hours = 0:12
```

So the first moment for the Monday data is

```
first = mfun(hours, bridge[,1])
```

For the other moments, the constant, **k**, is set equal to the first moment that has just been calculated, and **m**, the moment number to be calculated, is set to 2, 3, 4 respectively. Thus, for the Monday data:

```
second = mfun(hours, bridge[,1], first, 2)
third = mfun(hours, bridge[,1], first, 3)
fourth = mfun(hours, bridge[,1], first, 4)
```

Two more adjustments need to be made. The third moment has to be divided by the second moment raised to the power of 1.5:

```
third = third/second^1.5
```

and the fourth moment is divided by the square of the second moment, and then three is subtracted from the result (the subtraction of three is done to make a normal distribution have zero kurtosis):

```
fourth = fourth/second^2 - 3
```

There is a function in the Emu-R library, **moments(count, x)**, that carries out all the above calculations. In this function, **count** is the observed frequency and **x** the class. So the first four moments for the Monday data are given by **moments(bridge[,1], hours)**[3] while all four moments for Monday, Tuesday, Wednesday are given by:

```
t(apply(bridge, 2, moments, hours))
        [,1]   [,2]      [,3]         [,4]
Mon     4.172  4.422416   0.47063226   0.08290827
Tues    7.828  4.422416  -0.47063226   0.08290827
Wed     8.992  2.851936  -0.07963716  -0.39367681
```

(**t()** is the transpose function and does nothing more than turn the resulting matrix the other way round so that the days of the week appear as rows, and the first four moments are in the columns.)

As expected, the first moment (column 1) is at about 4 or 5 pm for Monday, close to 6 pm for Wednesday, and higher (later) than this for Tuesday. Also, as expected, the variance (second moment), whose unit in this example is $hours^2$, is least for Wednesday.

The skew is a dimensionless number that varies between −1 and 1. When the skew is zero, then the values are distributed evenly about the mean, as they are for a Gaussian normal distribution. When the values are skewed to the left so that there is a longer tail to the right, then it is positive (as it is for the Monday data); the skew is negative when the values are skewed to the right (as for the Tuesday data).

Finally, the kurtosis is also a dimensionless number that is zero for a normal Gaussian distribution. Kurtosis is often described as a measure of how "peaked" a distribution is. In very general terms, if the distribution is flat − that is, its shape looks rectangular − then kurtosis is negative, whereas if the distribution is peaked, then kurtosis is typically positive. However, this general assumption only applies if the distributions are not skewed (skewed distributions tend to have positive kurtosis) and kurtosis depends not just on the peak but also on whether there are high values at the extremes of the distribution (see Wuensch 2009 for some good examples of this). For all these reasons − and in particular in view of the fact that spectra are not usually symmetrical about the frequency axis − it is quite difficult to use kurtosis to make predictions about the spectral differences between phonetic categories.

When *spectral* moments are calculated, then **x** and **f** in both (4) and the corresponding R function are the frequency in Hz and the corresponding dB-values (and not the other way round!). This can be understood most easily by having another look at Figure 8.16 and pretending it is a spectrum with a horizontal axis of frequency in Hz and a vertical axis of dB. On this assumption, the calculation of the first spectral moment results in a value in Hz (analogous to a value in hours for the worked example above), and the second spectral moment a value in Hz^2, while the third and fourth spectral moments are dimensionless, as before.

Spectral moments will be investigated in the matrix of spectra at the temporal midpoint of the [s, z] fricatives extracted earlier with:

```
fric.dft.5 = dcut(fric.dft, .5, prop=T)
```

To apply the **moments(count, x)** function, **count** is a vector of dB-values and **x**, the class, contains the frequencies at which these dB-values occur. Since, for example in the third segment, the dB-values are given by **fric.dft.5[3,]** and their frequencies by **trackfreq(fric.dft.5)**, then the moments for this spectrum must be:

```
moments(fric.dft.5[3,], trackfreq(fric.dft.5))
```

However, the above command may sometimes fail. This is because some of the dB-values can be negative and yet the calculation of moments assumes that the values for the observations are positive (it would never be possible, for example, to have a negative value in counting how many cars crossed the bridge in an hourly time interval!). To overcome this problem, the dB-values are typically rescaled in calculating moments so that the minimum dB-value is set to zero (as a result of which

Spectral Analysis

all dB-values are positive and the smallest value is 0 dB). The **moments()** function does this whenever the argument **minval=T** is included. Thus:

```
moments(fric.dft.5[3,], trackfreq(fric.dft.5), minval=T)
```

Finally, since the **moments()** function can work out for itself the frequencies if it is supplied with spectral data, the second argument can be dropped. So the spectral moments for the third segment are equivalently and more simply given by:

```
moments(fric.dft.5[3,], minval=T)
```

In order to calculate spectral moments not just for the third but for all the segments, use the **fapply(x, y)** function as before. Notice in the following command how any additional arguments to **y** (in this case **minval=T** of the **moments()** function) are appended after **y**, thus:

```
m = fapply(fric.dft.5, moments, minval=T)
```

So **m[3,]** gives back the same result as **moments(fric.dft.5[3,], minval=T)**.

Since, as discussed in 8.2, **fapply()** can be used to apply a function to a track-data object, then a plot of the first spectral moment from the onset to the offset of the third segment is given by:

```
m = fapply(fric.dft, moments, minval=T)
plot(m[3,1], xlab="Time (ms)", ylab="1st spectral moment
(Hz)", type="l")
```

An ensemble plot of the first spectral moment for each segment between the acoustic onset and offset, synchronized at the temporal midpoint and coded for phonetic category (Figure 8.17), is given by:

```
dplot(m[,1], fric.l, 0.5, xlab="Time (ms)", ylab="First
spectral moment (Hz)")
```

The first spectral moment for [s] is higher than for [z] because, as Figure 8.10 showed, [s] has less energy at low frequencies and slightly more energy at high frequencies than [z].

Finally, spectral moments will also be used to assess the extent to which palatal and velar fricatives in German are separated: this was a theme presented in the preceding chapter using electropalatographic data. The dorsal fricatives in the Kiel Corpus of Read Speech were transcribed with either a front allophone [ç] (MRPA/SAMPA **C**) or with a back allophone [x] (MRPA/SAMPA **x**). Recall from the EPG analysis in Chapter 7 that there seems to be articulatory evidence for a categorical distinction between these two fricatives. The same problem will be analyzed by comparing the fricative spectra of dorsal fricatives following vowels differing in phonetic backness. The dataset in this case is acoustic data of a female speaker taken from the Kiel Corpus of Read Speech:

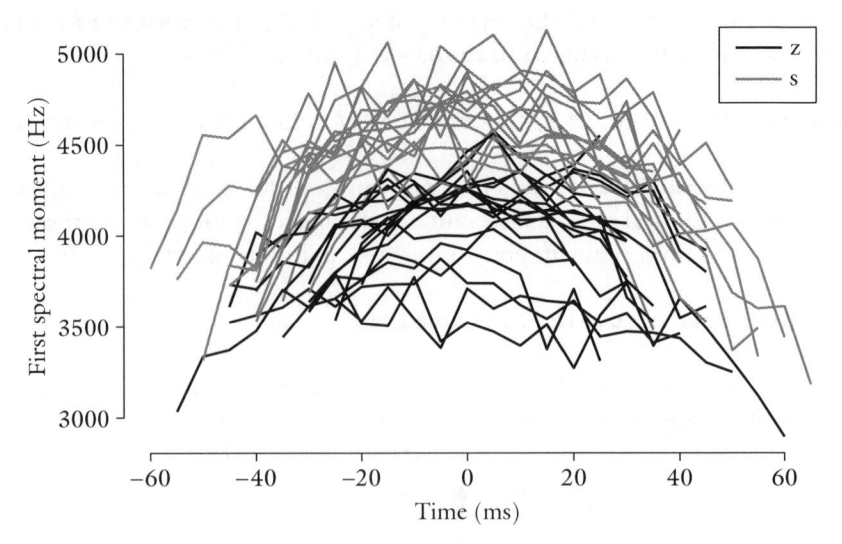

Figure 8.17 First spectral moment as a function of time for [s] (gray) and [z] (black). The tracks are synchronized at $t = 0$ ms, the segment midpoint.

dorfric   Segment list, postvocalic German dorsal fricatives
dorfric.l   A vector of their labels: **C** or **x**
dorfric.lv   A vector of the vowel labels preceding these fricatives
dorfric.w   A vector of the word labels containing these fricatives
dorfric.dft   Spectral trackdata object, 256-point DFT, 16 kHz sampling frequency

The preceding vowel types arranged from phonetically front to back are **I**, **E**, a:, O, o:, u:, corresponding to IPA [ɪ, ɛ, a:, ɔ, o:, u:] (the long [a:] and short [a] that distinguish German *Lamm* (*lamb*) and *lahm* (*lame*) have been collapsed into a single category because there was only one [a] token). As you will see from **unique(paste(dorfric.lv, dorfric.l, sep="."))**, the dorsal fricatives were transcribed in the Kiel Corpus with the palatal [ç] following [ɪ, ɛ] and with the velar [x] following the other vowels. The aim in the present analysis is to establish whether there is any acoustic justification for this. It will, as always, help to plot all the fricative spectra at the temporal midpoint separately by vowel category (Figure 8.18):

```
# Fricative spectra at the temporal midpoint
dorfric.dft.5 = dcut(dorfric.dft, .5, prop=T)

# Overlaid spectra separately by vowel category
par(mfrow=c(2,3)); par(mar=rep(2, 4))
for(j in unique(dorfric.lv)){
  temp = dorfric.lv==j
  plot(dorfric.dft.5[temp,], main=j)
}
```

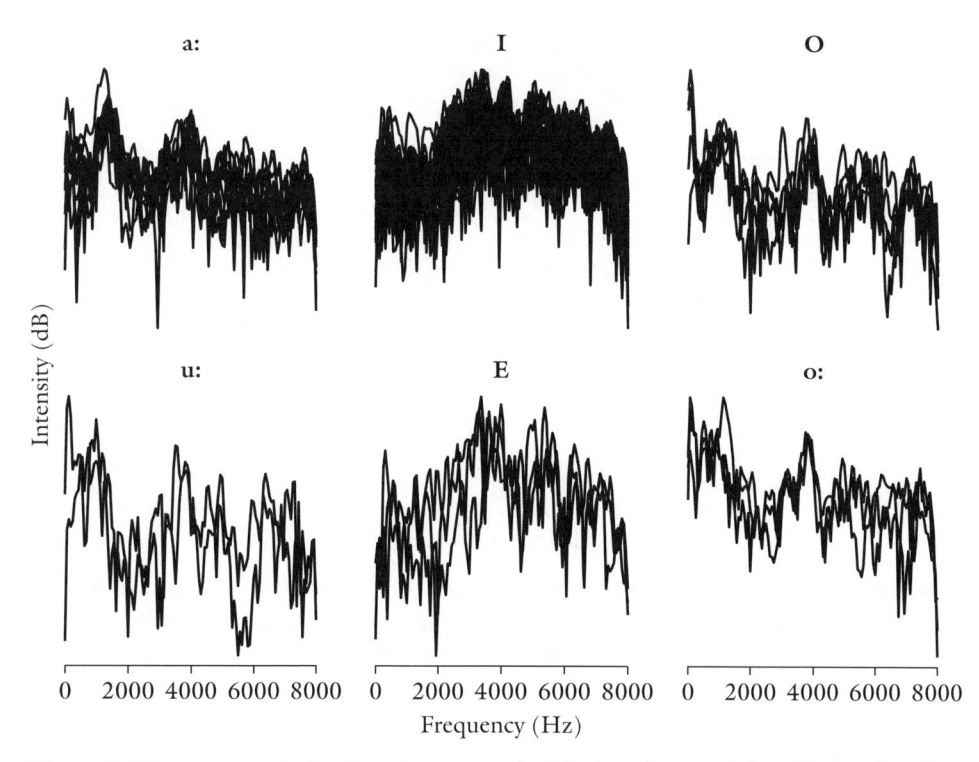

Figure 8.18 Spectra calculated at the temporal midpoint of postvocalic voiceless dorsal fricatives in German shown separately as a function of the preceding vowel context (the vowel context is shown above each spectral plot).

There do indeed seem to be differences in accordance with the transcriptions. After [ɪ, ɛ], there is a concentration of energy around 3–4 kHz whereas, after the other vowels, the spectra fall with increasing frequency and there is not the same concentration of energy at any one frequency. Based on these plots, it seems likely that the fricatives after [ɪ, ɛ] have a lower second spectral moment, because the spectral energy is not so diffuse or spread along the frequency axis as it is after the other vowel categories. It is also possible that the mean, or first spectral moment, is higher for [ɪ, ɛ] because the other fricatives have proportionally slightly more energy in the lower part (0–2,000 Hz) of the spectrum.

These predictions can be tested by calculating spectral moments for the fricatives shown in Figure 8.18. In calculating moments, researchers sometimes leave out at least the DC offset (frequency at 0 Hz), which is just the average amplitude of the spectrum multiplied by the signal length, N; and it is also a good idea to cut out the frequencies near the Nyquist frequency because these are often not very reliable. In the example, the frequencies below 500 Hz and above 7,000 Hz were removed. The second spectral moment (variance) has also been converted into the spectral standard deviation by taking its square root, in order to have more manageable values in Hz (rather than values in the region of 10^5 for Hz^2).

```
# Spectral moments 500-7,000 Hz range
m = fapply(dorfric.dft.5[,500:7000], moments, minval=T)
```

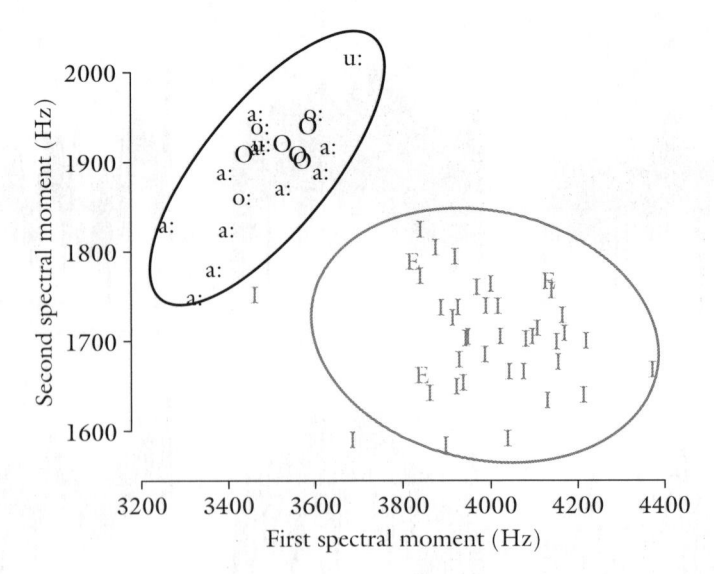

Figure 8.19 95% confidence ellipses for [ç] (gray) and [x] (black) in the plane of the first two spectral moments. The data were calculated at the fricatives' temporal midpoints. The labels of the vowels preceding the fricatives are marked at the fricatives' data points.

```
# Spectral standard deviation in Hz
m[,2] = sqrt(m[,2])
```

Figure 8.19 shows ellipse plots for these calculated spectral moments of the fricatives but showing the vowel labels at the data points:

```
eplot(m[,1:2], dorfric.l, dorfric.lv, dopoints=T,
xlab="First spectral moment (Hz)", ylab="Second spectral
moment (Hz)")
```

This figure shows that there does indeed seem to be a very good separation between the tokens labeled as **C** and **x**. Also, the relative positions according to context are roughly in accordance with the predictions made earlier from the spectra: the dorsal fricatives following the front vowels [I, ε] have a high first spectral moment; and [ɔ, o:, u:] have a higher second spectral moment than [I, ε] with the open vowel [a:] falling roughly between these vowel groups on this parameter.

8.4 The Discrete Cosine Transformation

The discrete cosine transformation (DCT) is a mathematical operation that is very much like a discrete Fourier transform: it decomposes a signal into a set of sinusoids such that, when these are summed, the same signal is reconstructed. One of the main differences between the two is that in the DCT the sinusoids are at *half*-cycles, that is, at $k = 0, 0.5, 1, 1.5 \ldots \frac{1}{2}(N-1)$ rather than, as for the DFT, at *integer* cycles ($k = 0, 1, 2, \ldots N-1$). Another is that the output of the DCT is sinusoids with no phase. But any sinusoid with no phase is a cosine wave, so we may say that a DCT decomposes a signal into a set of cosine waves at frequencies $k = 0, 0.5, 1.0, 1.5, \ldots \frac{1}{2}(N-1)$; and hence the name, discrete *cosine* transformation.

The amplitudes of these cosine waves are called **DCT coefficients** and they are usually labeled from 0 to $N-1$. So coefficient zero, k_0, is the amplitude of the $k = 0$ cosine wave; k_1, the first coefficient, is the amplitude of the $k = 0.5$ cosine wave, and so on. Now it turns out that these DCT coefficients encode global properties of the signal's shape: in particular, as will be shown below, k_0, k_1, k_2 are proportional to the signal's mean, slope, and curvature respectively. For this reason, they serve the same important function as do spectral moments that were discussed in the previous section: DCT coefficients, like spectral moments, reduce the quantity of information in a spectrum to a handful of values and, importantly, in such a way that different phonetic categories are often quite well separated (assuming these categories have differently shaped spectra).

The DCT has another useful application in phonetics: it can be used to smooth a signal. The way that this works is as follows. Suppose you are driving along a road and your task is to draw a crescent or an arc on a sheet of paper. Just as you draw the arc, the car goes over a long cattle-grid that produces a series of bumps throughout the car. You find that your drawing looks like an arc (assuming that the size of the bumps is not too big), but also has minor deviations from an arc that are caused by the regularly spaced bumps of the cattle grid. It turns out that, if you make a spectrum of what you drew, then the bits of the signal that are due to the bumps show up at high frequencies. This is to be expected: the bumps cause the pencil to change rapidly up and down above the arc that you are trying to draw. But anything that changes rapidly also shows up as a high frequency in the spectrum. Now we said that when a DCT is applied to a signal, then the signal is decomposed into cosine waves of progressively increasing frequency ($k = 0, 0.5, 1 \ldots$). Therefore, if a DCT is applied to the bumpy arc, then the bumpy part should show up at high cosine frequencies. If all the cosine waves are summed, then the same bumpy arc is reconstructed, but if only *the first few* frequencies are summed, then the influence of the bumps, which only affect the high frequencies, should be more or less removed: the net result is a smoother arc than the one that was drawn (more like the one you intended to draw), which can be called a DCT-smoothed signal. Moreover, the fewer cosine waves that are summed, the smoother the result: so a summation of the first three cosine waves at frequencies $k = 0, 0.5, 1$ is going to produce a smoother result than summing cosine waves at frequencies $k = 0, 0.5, 1, 1.5, 2$ cycles.

Now dB-spectra of speech derived using Fourier analysis techniques discussed in this chapter often have just this property of bumpiness superimposed on a trend line. In voiced speech, the trend line is due to the formants which are responsible for a number of large peaks and troughs up and down the frequency axis. However, as discussed in 8.1, there is also a superimposed jaggedness or bumpiness that is the result of the harmonics due to vocal fold vibration, which are spaced on the frequency axis at roughly pitch frequency. Thus in speech production, the filter is due to the shape of the vocal tract and produces a fairly smooth trend line in the spectrum while the source causes short-term changes (the bumpiness or sawtooth effect). Following the earlier analogy, if a DCT is applied to a spectrum of speech but only the lower-frequency cosine waves are summed, then the result will essentially be to filter out much of the bumpy part due to the source leaving predominantly the "trend line" due to the filter which is the spectrum that is due to the shape of the vocal tract.

Finally, before looking in closer detail at how the DCT can be applied in Emu-R, it should be mentioned that there is more or less an equivalence between the application of a DCT to a spectrum and **cepstral analysis**. In speech technology research, the output of a DCT applied to a spectrum is considered to be a (very close) approximation to cepstral analysis (Milner & Shao 2006), but the differences between the two are negligible for most kinds of phonetic and indeed speech signal processing analysis. Thus leaving these minor differences aside, the amplitudes of the half-cycle cosine waves into which a spectrum is decomposed by a DCT analysis are the DCT coefficients which are essentially **cepstral coefficients**. A plot of the DCT coefficients as a function of the coefficient number (a plot of k_0, k_1, k_2 ... as a function of 0, 1, 2 ...) is a **cepstrum**; and a DCT-smoothed spectrum is a cepstrally smoothed spectrum. In automatic speech recognition, speech scientists often parameterize the signal every 5 or 10 ms in terms of what they call **Mel-scaled cepstral coefficients**. These are DCT coefficients that are derived by applying a discrete cosine transformation to a Mel-scaled spectrum. This point will be explored in more detail at the end of this chapter.

8.4.1 Calculating DCT coefficients in Emu-R

In order to emphasize the very important point that the DCT is a transformation that is not specific to speech, the first example will be of a DCT applied to some of the data in **bridge** (a hypothetical count of cars crossing a bridge between midday and midnight). In the example below, the DCT is applied to the data in column 1 which is initially stored (for convenience) in a vector **x**. The function for calculating DCT coefficients is the Emu-R function **dct()**. (Formulae for the DCT are not given here, but see Harrington 2010; Harrington et al. 2008; Nossair & Zahorian 1991; Watson & Harrington 1999.)

```
x = bridge[,1]
# DCT coefficients
x.dct = dct(x)

# Round to two places for convenience
round(x.dct, 2)
    0     1      2      3     4     5     6     7    8    9    10    11    12
54.39 29.54 -26.13 -24.65 -8.77 -2.96 -0.58 -0.06 0.59 2.14 -1.75 -3.31 3.26
```

x.dct contains the DCT coefficients: remember that these are amplitudes of half-cycle cosine waves. The cosine waves into which the signal has been decomposed using the DCT can be inspected using this function:

```
cfun <- function(A, j=0)
{
```

Spectral Analysis

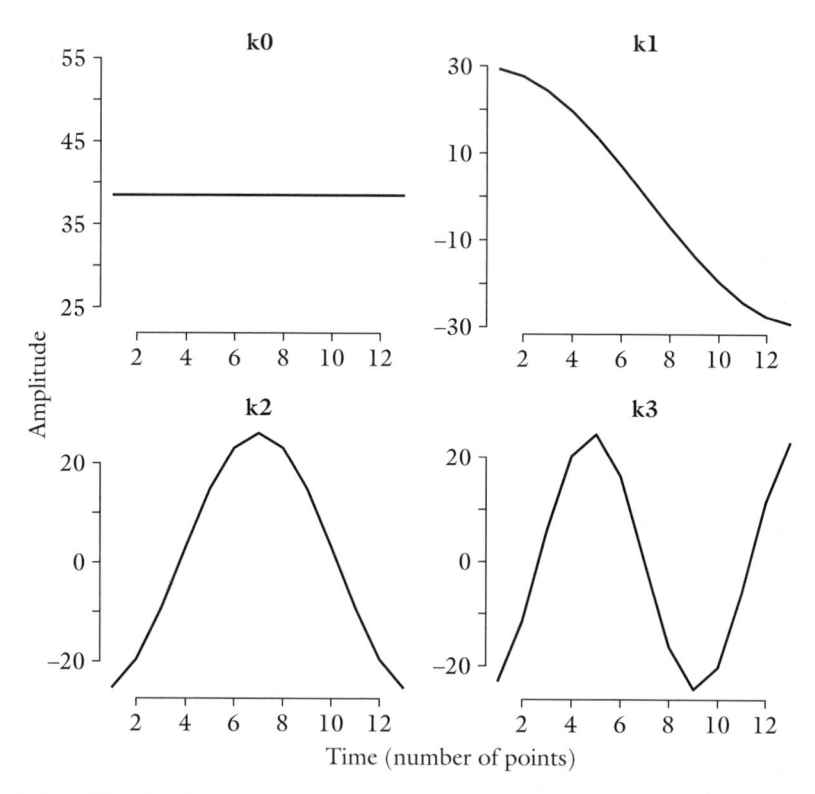

[Figure showing four plots labeled k0, k1, k2, k3 with Amplitude on y-axis and Time (number of points) on x-axis]

Figure 8.20 The first four half-cycle cosine waves that are the result of applying a DCT to the raw signal shown in Figure 8.21.

```
# A: DCT coefficients (amplitude of half-cycle cosine wave)
# j: frequency (cycles) of half-cycle cosine wave
    N = length(A)
A[1] = A[1]/sqrt(2)
    n = 0:(N-1)
k = seq(0, by=.5, length=N)

# The cosine wave corresponding to k_j
    A[j+1] * cos(2 * pi * k[j+1] * (n+0.5)/N)
}
```

Here is a plot of the first four cosine waves corresponding to k_0, k_1, k_2, k_3 (Figure 8.20):

```
par(mfrow=c(2,2)); par(mar=rep(2,4))
for(j in 0:3){
   plot(cfun(x.dct, j), type="l", xlab="", ylab="",
   main=paste("k", j, sep=""))
}
```

k_0 has a frequency of zero cycles and so, for the reasons discussed earlier (Figure 8.2), it is a straight line. Also, its amplitude is equal to the mean of the signal to which the DCT was applied. The figure also shows that cosine waves are produced at frequencies of 0.5, 1, and 1.5 cycles for the next higher coefficients respectively (the reason why k_2 and k_3 are upside-down cosine waves is because these coefficients are negative). Notice that, with the exception of k_0, the peak amplitudes of these cosine waves are equal to the corresponding DCT coefficients[4] (see **round(x.dct, 2)** given above). This is to be expected since DCT coefficients are just the (peak) amplitudes of these cosine waves.

If *all* these half-cycle cosine waves are summed, then the result is the original signal to which the DCT transformation has just been applied:

```
N = length(x.dct)
mat = rep(0, length(x.dct))
for(j in 0:(N-1)){
   mat = mat+cfun(x.dct, j)
}
```

Apart from rounding errors, **mat**, the reconstructed signal, is the same as the original signal **x**, as the following subtraction of the original from the reconstructed signal shows:

```
round(mat-x, 5)
 0  1  2  3  4  5  6  7  8  9  10  11  12
 0  0  0  0  0  0  0  0  0  0   0   0   0
```

Following the reasoning in 8.4.1 above, if only the few *lowest* frequencies are summed, e.g., the cosine waves corresponding to k_0 through to k_3 shown in Figure 8.20, then the result is a **DCT-smoothed signal**, i.e., a smoother version of the original signal. The summation could be accomplished with the for-loop given above. Alternatively, and more conveniently, the same **dct()** function can be used not just for DCT *analysis* but also for DCT *synthesis* to add up the cosine waves into which the signal was decomposed. The following adds up the first four half-cycle cosine waves shown in Figure 8.20:

```
# Sum to k_3
dctsum = dct(x, 3, T)

# The above is the same as
dctsum= rep(0, length(x.dct))
for(j in 0:3){
   dctsum = dctsum+cfun(x.dct, j)
}
```

A plot of the original signal and DCT-smoothed signal using coefficients 0–3 is shown in Figure 8.21 and is given by the following commands:

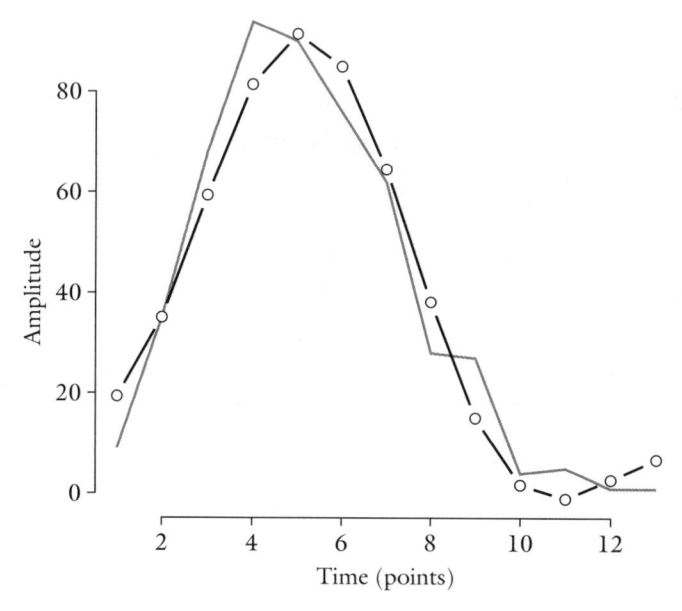

Figure 8.21 The raw signal (gray) and a superimposed DCT-smoothed signal (black showing data points) obtained by summing k_0, k_1, k_2, k_3.

```
ylim = range(c(dctsum, x))
plot(x, type="l", ylim=ylim, xlab="Time (points)", ylab="",
col="slategray", axes=F)
par(new=T)
plot(dctsum, type="b", ylim=ylim, xlab="Time (points)",
ylab="Amplitude")
```

The more coefficients that are used, the closer the DCT-smoothed signal approximates the original signal.

8.4.2 DCT coefficients of a spectrum

The leftmost panel of Figure 8.22 shows a 512-point dB-spectrum calculated at the temporal midpoint of an [ɛ] vowel sampled at 16,000 Hz (the midpoint of the first segment in **vowlax** as it happens) and plotted with **plot(e.dft, type="l")**. Following the discussion earlier in this chapter, the 512-point window is easily wide enough so that harmonics appear: there is a gradual rise and fall due to the presence of formants and superimposed on this is a jaggedness produced by the fundamental frequency and its associated harmonics. The DCT coefficients of this spectrum can be calculated following the procedure in 8.4.1. Such a calculation produces the amplitudes of the half-cycle cosine waves and a plot of them as a function of the corresponding DCT coefficient number (middle panel, Figure 8.22) is a cepstrum:

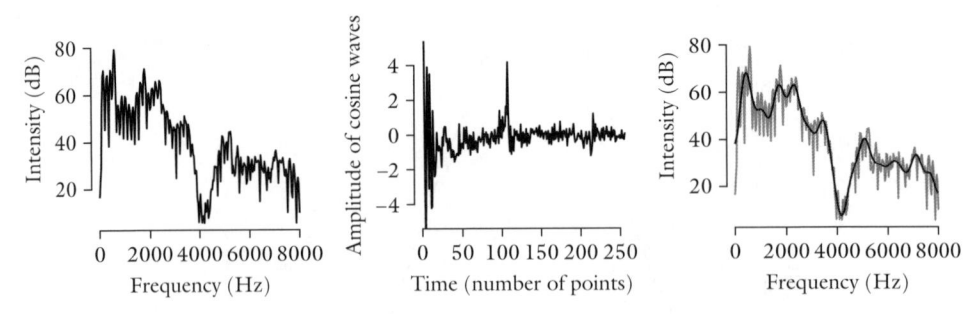

Figure 8.22 Left: a spectrum of an [ɛ] vowel. Middle: the output of a DCT-transformation of this signal (a cepstrum). Right: a DCT-smoothed signal (cepstrally smoothed spectrum) superimposed on the original spectrum in the left panel and obtained by summing the first 31 half-cycle cosine waves.

```
# DCT coefficients
e.dct = dct(e.dft)
N = length(e.dct); k = 0:(N-1)

# Cepstrum
plot(k, e.dct, ylim=c(-5, 5), type="l", xlab="Time (number
of points", ylab="Amplitude of cosine waves")
```

In the earlier example of trying to draw an arc while driving over a cattle-grid, it was argued that the deviations caused by the bumps show up at high-frequency cosine waves and that analogously so would the oscillations due to the harmonics caused by vocal fold vibration (the source) that produce the jaggedness in a spectrum. In the present example, their effect is visible as the pronounced spike in the cepstrum between 100 and 150 points. The spike occurs at the hundred and seventh DCT coefficient (k_{107}). With this information, the fundamental frequency of the signal can be estimated: 107 points corresponds to 0.0066875 s at the sampling frequency of 16,000 Hz and therefore to a fundamental frequency of 1 / 0.0066875 = 149.5 Hz. The estimated f0 can be checked against the spectrum. For example, the fourth harmonic in the spectrum in the left panel of Figure 8.22 is associated with a peak at 593.75 Hz which means that the fundamental frequency is 593.75 / 4 = 148.4 Hz, which is a value that is within about 1 Hz of the f0 estimated from the cepstrum. So this demonstrates another use of DCT (cepstral) analysis: it can be used to estimate whether or not the signal is voiced (whether there is/is not a spike) and also for estimating the signal's fundamental frequency.

A DCT or cepstrally smoothed version of the spectrum that excludes the contribution from the source signal can be obtained as long as the summation does not include the higher frequency cosine waves around k_{107} that encode the information about the fundamental frequency and harmonics. Beyond this, there can be no guidelines about how many cosine waves should be summed: the more that are summed, the more the resulting signal approximates the original spectrum. In the right panel of Figure 8.22, the first 31 coefficients have been summed and the result superimposed on the original raw spectrum as follows:

# Carry out DCT analysis then sum from k_0 to k_{30}
coeffto30 = dct(e.dft, 30, T)
```

```
# We have to tell R that this is spectral data at a sampling frequency of
16,000 Hz
coeffto30 = as.spectral(coeffto30, 16000)
ylim = range(coeffto30, e.dft)
```

```
# Raw dB-spectrum
plot(e.dft, ylim=ylim, xlab="", ylab="", axes=F,
col="slategray", type="l")
par(new=T)
```

```
# Superimposed DCT-smoothed (cepstrally smoothed) spectrum
plot(coeffto30, ylim=ylim, xlab="Frequency (Hz)",
ylab="Intensity (dB) ")
```

The smooth line through the spectrum, a cepstrally smoothed spectrum, has none of the influence due to the source. Finally, if you want to derive cepstrally smoothed spectra from either a spectral matrix or a trackdata object,[5] then this can be done using **dct()** with the argument **fit=T** inside **fapply()**. For example, a plot of cepstrally smoothed spectra using five coefficients for a spectral matrix of stop bursts is given by:

```
smooth = fapply(keng.dft.5, dct, 5, fit=T)
plot(smooth, keng.l)
```

8.4.3 DCT coefficients and trajectory shape

The lowest three DCT coefficients are, as has already been mentioned, related to the mean, slope, and curvature respectively of the signal to which the DCT transformation is applied. k_0 in the DCT algorithm that is implemented here (and discussed in Watson & Harrington 1999) is the mean of the signal multiplied by $\sqrt{2}$. k_1 is directly proportional to the linear slope of the signal. This relationship can be verified by calculating the linear slope using the **slope()** function created in 8.2 and then correlating the slope with k_1. For example, for the dorsal fricative data:

```
slope <- function(x)
{

# Calculate the intercept and slope in a spectral vector
lm(x ~ trackfreq(x))$coeff
}
```

```
# Spectra at the temporal midpoint
dorfric.dft.5 = dcut(dorfric.dft, .5, prop=T)
```
```

```
# Spectral slope (NB: the slope is stored in column 2)
sp = fapply(dorfric.dft.5, slope)

# Coefficients up to k₁ (NB: k₁ is in column 2)
k = fapply(dorfric.dft.5, dct, 1)

# How strongly is the linear slope correlated with k₁?
cor(sp[,2], k[,2])
-0.9979162
```

The above shows that there is almost complete (negative) correlation between these variables, i.e., greater positive slopes correspond to greater negative k_1 values and vice versa (this is clearly seen in **plot(sp[,2], d[,2])** where you can also see that, when the linear slope is zero, so is k_1).

k_2 is most closely related to the signal's curvature, where curvature has the definition given in 6.6 of Chapter 6, i.e., it is the coefficient c_2 in a parabola $y = c_0 + c_1 x + c_2 x^2$. Recall that the coefficient c_2 can be calculated as follows:

```
# c₂ for F1 data, lax vowels: c₂ is stored in coeffs[,3]
coeffs= trapply(vowlax.fdat[,1], plafit, simplify=T)

# The DCT coefficients: k₂ is stored in k[,3]
k = trapply(vowlax.fdat[,1], dct, 3, simplify=T)

# The correlation between c₂ and k₂ is very high
cor(coeffs[,3], k[,3])
0.939339
```

In general, there will only be such a direct correspondence between curvature in a parabola and k_2 as long as the signal has a basic parabolic shape. If it does not, then the relationship between the two is likely to be much weaker.

8.4.4 Mel- and Bark-scaled DCT (cepstral) coefficients

The Bark scale has already been discussed in the chapter on vowels: it is a scale that warps the physical frequency axis in Hz into one which corresponds more closely to the way in which frequency is processed in the ear. Another auditory scale that was more commonly used in phonetics in the 1970s and which is used in automatic speech recognition research today is the Mel scale. As discussed in Fant (1968), the Mel scale is obtained in such a way that a doubling on the Mel scale corresponds roughly to a doubling of perceived pitch. Also, 1,000 Mel = 1,000 Hz. If you want to see the relationship between Mel and Hz, then enter:

```
plot(0:10000, mel(0:10000), type="l", xlab="Frequency
(Hz)", ylab="Frequency (mels)")
```

In fact, the Bark and Mel scale warp the frequency scale in rather a similar way, especially for frequencies above about 1,000 Hz.

There are two main ways to see what a spectrum looks like when its frequency axis is converted to an auditory scale. The first just converts **trackfreq(x)** from Hz into Mel or Bark (where **x** is a spectral object). Since the auditory scales are approximately linear up to 1,000 Hz and quasi-logarithmic thereafter, the result of the first method is that there are more data points at higher frequencies in the auditorily scaled spectra: this is because the interval in Bark or Mel for the same frequency width in Hz becomes progressively smaller with increasing frequency (compare for example the difference in Bark between 7,000 Hz and 6,000 Hz given by **bark(7000) - bark(6000)** with the Bark difference between 2,000 Hz and 1,000 Hz). The second method uses a linear interpolation technique (see 6.6 and Figure 6.18) so that the data points in the spectrum are spaced at equal Mel or Bark intervals along the frequency axis. Therefore, with this second method, there is the same number of data points between 1 and 2 Bark as between 3 and 4 Bark and so on. Both methods give more or less the same spectral shape, but obviously some of the detail is lost in the high-frequency range with the second method because there are fewer data points. Here finally are the two methods for the spectrum of the [ɛ] vowel considered earlier:

```
# Method 1
plot(e.dft, freq=bark(trackfreq(e.dft)), type="l",
xlab="Frequency (Bark)")

# Method 2
plot(bark(e.dft), type="l", xlab="Frequency (Bark)")
```

A Bark-scaled DCT transformation is just a DCT transformation that is applied to a spectrum after the spectrum's frequency axis has been converted into Bark (or into Mel for a Mel-scaled DCT transformation). Only the second method, in which the data points represent equal intervals of frequency, is available for DCT analysis, and not the first.[6] This is because the DCT-analysis is predicated on the assumption that the digital points are at equal intervals (of time or of frequency).

The motivation for converting to an auditory scale is not just that this scale is obviously more closely related to the way in which frequency is perceived, but also because, as various studies in automatic speech recognition have shown, fewer Bark- or Mel-scaled DCT (cepstral) coefficients are needed to distinguish effectively between different phonetic categories than when DCT coefficients are derived from a Hz scale. In order to illustrate this point, calculate a DCT-smoothed spectrum with and without auditory scaling using only a small number of coefficients (six in this example, up to k_5), as follows:

```
# DCT (cepstrally) smoothed Hz spectrum with six coefficients
hz.dft = dct(e.dft, 5, T)
hz.dft = as.spectral(hz.dft, trackfreq(e.dft))

# DCT (cepstrally) smoothed Bark spectrum with six coefficients
bk.dft = dct(bark(e.dft), 5, T)
bk.dft = as.spectral(bk.dft, trackfreq(bark(e.dft)))
par(mfrow=c(1,2))
plot(hz.dft, xlab="Frequency (Hz)", ylab="Intensity (dB)")
plot(bk.dft, xlab="Frequency (Bark)")
```

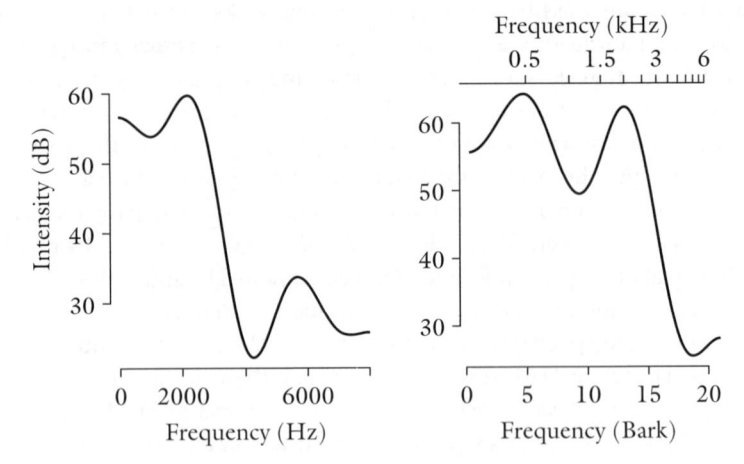

Figure 8.23 Left: a DCT-smoothed Hz spectrum of [ɛ]. Right: A DCT-smoothed, Bark-scaled spectrum of the same vowel. Both spectra were obtained by summing the first six coefficients, up to k_5. For the spectrum on the right, the frequency axis was converted to Bark with linear interpolation before applying the DCT.

```
# Superimpose a kHz axis up to 6 kHz
values = seq(0, 6000, by=500)
axis(side=3, at=bark(values),
labels=as.character(values/1000))
mtext("Frequency (kHz)", side=3, line=2)
```

The DCT-smoothed Hz spectrum (left panel, Figure 8.23) is too smooth: above all it does not allow the most important information that characterizes an [ɛ] vowel, i.e., F1 and F2, to be distinguished. The DCT-smoothed Bark spectrum seems to be as smooth and is perhaps therefore just as ineffective as the Hz spectrum for characterizing the salient acoustic properties of [ɛ]. But a closer inspection shows that this is not so. There are evidently two broad peaks in the DCT-smoothed Bark spectrum that are at 4.32 Bark and 12.63 Bark respectively. The conversion **bark(c(4.32, 12.64), inv=T)** shows that these Bark frequencies are 432 Hz and 1,892 Hz – in other words the frequency location of these peaks is strongly influenced by the first two formant frequencies.[7] So the DCT-smoothed Bark spectrum, in contrast to the DCT-smoothed Hz spectrum, seems to have given greater prominence to just those attributes of [ɛ] that are most important for identifying it phonetically.

A comparison can now be made of how the raw and auditorily transformed DCT coefficients distinguish between the same German lax vowel categories that were the subject of analysis in Chapter 6. For this purpose, there is a spectral object **vowlax.dft.5** which contains 256-point dB-spectra at the temporal midpoint of the segment list **vowlax**. The relevant objects for the present investigation include:

vowlax.dft.5	Matrix of dB-spectra
vowlax.l	Vector of vowel labels
vowlax.spkr	Vector of speaker labels
vowlax.fdat.5	F1–F4 formant frequency data at the temporal midpoint

Given that the salient acoustic information for distinguishing between vowel categories is typically between 200 and 4,000 Hz, the first few DCT coefficients will be calculated in this frequency range only:

```
# First four DCT coefficients calculated on Hz spectra
dcthz = fapply(vowlax.dft.5[,200:4000], dct, 3)

# ... on Bark-scaled spectra
dctbk = fapply(bark(vowlax.dft.5[,200:4000]), dct, 3)

# ... on Mel-scaled spectra
dctml = fapply(mel(vowlax.dft.5[,200:4000]), dct, 3)
```

Remember that at least six or seven auditorily scaled DCT coefficients are usually necessary to obtain a discrimination between vowel categories that is as effective as the one from the first two formant frequencies. Nevertheless, there is a reasonably good separation between the vowels for female speaker 68 in the plane of $k_1 \times k_2$ (the reader can experiment with other coefficients pairs and at the same time verify that the separation is not as good for the male speaker's data on these coefficients). The same vowels in the formant plane are shown for comparison in the bottom right pane of Figure 8.24.

```
temp = vowlax.spkr == "68"
par(mfrow=c(2,2))
eplot(dcthz[temp,2:3], vowlax.l[temp], centroid=T,
main="DCT-Hz")
eplot(dctbk[temp,2:3], vowlax.l[temp], centroid=T,
main="DCT-Bark")
eplot(dctml[temp,2:3], vowlax.l[temp], centroid=T,
main="DCT-mel")
eplot(dcut(vowlax.fdat[temp,1:2], .5, prop=T),
vowlax.l[temp], centroid=T, form=T, main="F1 x F2")
```

There are a couple of interesting things about the data in Figure 8.24. The first is that, in all the DCT spaces, there is a resemblance to the shape of the vowel quadrilateral, with the vowel categories distributed in relation to each other very roughly as they are in the formant plane. This is perhaps not surprising given the following three connected facts:

- A DCT transformation encodes the overall shape of the spectrum.
- The overall spectral shape for vowels is predominantly determined by F1–F3.
- F1 and F2 are proportional to phonetic height and backness respectively, and therefore to the axes of a vowel quadrilateral.

Secondly, the vowel categories are distinguished to a slightly greater extent in the auditorily transformed DCT spaces (Bark and Mel) than in the DCT-Hertz spaces. This is especially so as far as the overlap of [a] with [ɪ, ɛ] is concerned.

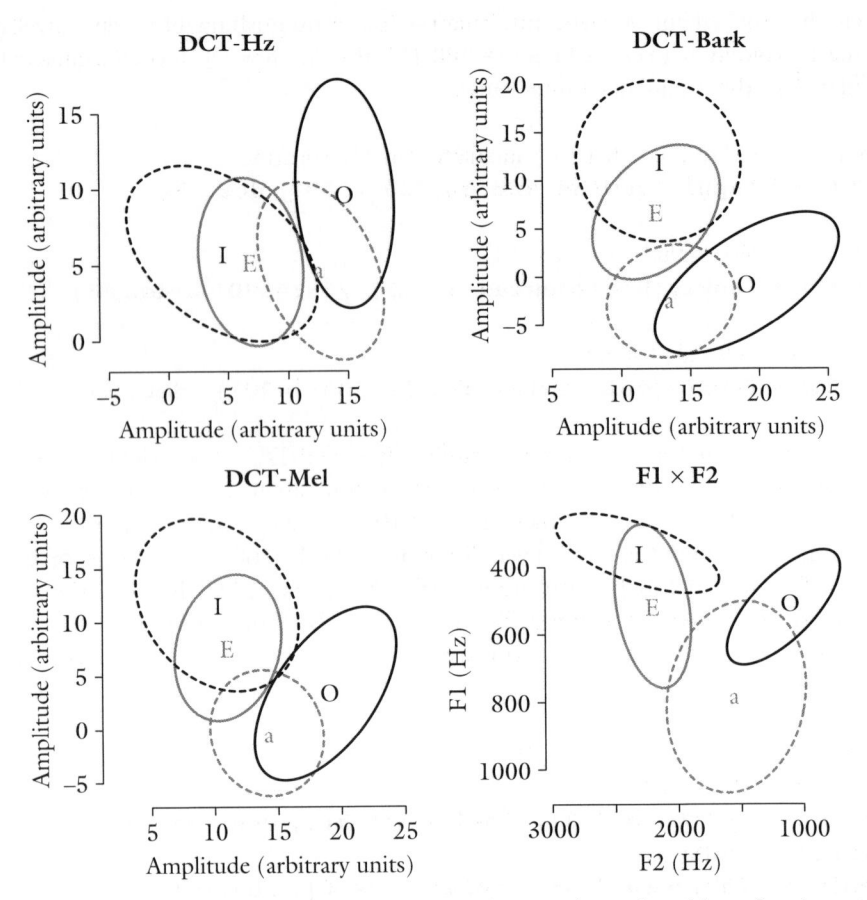

Figure 8.24 95% confidence ellipses for German lax vowels produced by a female speaker extracted at the temporal midpoint. Top left: $k_1 \times k_2$ derived from Hz-spectra. Top right: $k_1 \times k_2$ derived from Bark-spectra. Bottom left: $k_1 \times k_2$ derived from Mel-spectra.

Finally, one of the advantages of the DCT over the formant analysis is that there has been no need to use complicated formant-tracking algorithms and above all no need to make any corrections for outliers. This is one of the reasons why they are preferred in automatic speech recognition. Another is that, while it makes no sense to track formants for voiceless sounds, the same DCT coefficients, or auditorily transformed DCT coefficients, can be used for quantifying both voiced and voiceless speech.

8.5 Questions

A. This question is about digital sinusoids.

A.1 Use the **crplot()** function in the Emu-R library to plot the **alias** of the cosine wave of length 20 points and with a frequency of four cycles.

A.2 Use the `crplot()` function to plot a sine wave.

A.3 The alias also requires the phase to be opposite in sign compared with the non-aliased waveform. Use `crplot()` to plot the alias of the above sine wave.

A.4 The `cr()` function produces a plot of $A\cos((2\pi k n / N) + \phi)$ where A, k, ϕ are the cosine's amplitude, frequency (in cycles), and phase (in radians) respectively. Also, N is the length of the signal and n is a vector of integers, $0, 1, 2, \ldots N-1$. Convert the equation into an R function that takes A, k, p, N as its arguments, and verify that you get the same results as from `cr()` for any choice of amplitude, frequency, phase, and N. (Plot the cosine wave from your function against n on the x-axis.)

A.5 What is the effect of adding to a cosine wave another cosine wave that has been phase-shifted by π radians (180 degrees)? Use the `cr()` function with `values=T` (and round the result to the nearest four places) to check your assumptions.

B. According to Halle et al. (1957), the two major allophones of /k/ before front and back vowels can be distinguished by $a - b$, where a and b have the following definitions:

- a the sum of the dB-values in the 700 Hz–9,000 Hz range;
- b the sum of the dB-values in the 2,700–9,000 Hz range.

Verify (using e.g., a boxplot) whether this is so for the following data:

keng	Segment list of the aspiration of syllable-initial Australian English /k/ before front /ɪ, ɛ/ (e.g., *kin*, *kept*) and back /ɔː, ʊ/ vowels (e.g., *caught*, *could*)
keng.dft.5	Spectral matrix of the above at the temporal midpoint of the segment
keng.l	Labels of the following vowel (**front** or **back**)

C. If vowel lip-rounding has an anticipatory coarticulatory influence on a preceding consonant in a CV sequence, how would you expect the spectra of alveolar fricatives to differ preceding unrounded and rounded vowels? Plot the spectra of the German syllable-initial [z] fricatives defined below at their temporal midpoint separately in the unrounded and rounded contexts to check your predictions.

sib	Segment list, syllable-initial [z] preceding [iː, ɪ, uː, ʊ], one male and one female speaker
sib.l	A vector of labels: **f**, for [z] preceding front unrounded [iː, ɪ], **b** for [z] preceding back rounded [uː, ʊ]
sib.w	A vector of word labels
sib.dft	Spectral trackdata object (256-point DFT) from the onset to the offset of [z] with a frame shift of 5 ms

Apply a metric to the spectra that you have just plotted to see how effectively you can distinguish between [z] before unrounded and rounded vowels.

D. Here are some F2 data of Australian English and Standard German [i:] vowels, both produced in read sentences each by one male speaker.

    f2geraus   Trackdata object of F2
    f2geraus.l   Vector of labels: either **aus** or **ger** corresponding to whether the F2 trajectories in **f2geraus** were produced by the Australian or German speaker

D.1 It is sometimes said that Australian English [i:] has a "late target" (long onglide). How are the trajectories between the languages likely to differ on skew?

D.2 Produce a time-normalized, averaged plot of F2 color-coded for the language to check your predictions.

D.3 Quantify these predictions by calculating moments for these F2 trajectories (and e.g., making a boxplot of skew for the two language categories).

E. Sketch (by hand) the likely F2 trajectories of [aɪ, aʊ, a] as a function of time. How are these F2 trajectories likely to differ on skew? Check your predictions by calculating F2 moments for [aɪ, aʊ] and [a] for speaker 68. Use the following objects:

    dip.fdat   Trackdata object of formants containing the diphthongs
    dip.l   Vector of diphthong labels
    dip.spkr   Vector of speaker labels for the diphthongs
    vowlax.fdat   Trackdata object of formants containing [a]
    vowlax.l   Vector of vowel labels
    vowlax.spkr   Vector of speaker labels

Make a boxplot showing the skew for these three categories.

F. The features *diffuse* vs *compact* are sometimes used to distinguish between sounds whose energy is more distributed (diffuse) as opposed to concentrated predominantly in one region (compact) in the spectrum.

F.1 On which of the moment parameters might diffuse vs compact spectra be expected to differ?

F.2 In their analysis of stops, Blumstein and Stevens (1979) characterize (the burst of) velars as having a *compact* spectrum with mid-frequency peaks as opposed to labials and alveolars for which the spectra are *diffuse* in the frequency range 0–4,000 Hz. Check whether there is any evidence for this by plotting ensemble-averaged spectra of the bursts of [b, d, g] overlaid on the same plot (in the manner of Figure 8.10, right). All the data is contained in a spectral matrix calculated from a 256-point DFT centered 10 ms after the stop release and includes the same [b, d] spectral data as **after** derived in 8.2 as well as [g]-bursts before the non-back vowels [i:, e:, a:, aʊ].

    stops10   spectral matrix, 256-point DFT
    stops10.lab   vector of stop labels

F.3 Calculate in the 0–4,000 Hz range whichever moment you think might be appropriate for distinguishing [g] from the other two stop classes and make a boxplot of the chosen moment parameter separately for the three classes. Is there any evidence for the diffuse ([b, d]) vs compact ([g]) distinction?

G. A tense vowel is often phonetically more peripheral than a lax vowel, and acoustically this can sometimes be associated with a greater formant curvature (because there is often a greater deviation in producing a tense vowel from the center of the vowel space).

G.1 Verify whether there is any evidence for this using **dplot()** to produce time-normalized, ensemble-averaged F2 trajectories as a function of time of the German tense and lax [iː, ɪ] vowels produced by male speaker 67. The data to be plotted is from a trackdata object **dat** with a parallel vector of labels **lab** that can be created as follows:

```
temp = f2geraus.l == "ger"
# F2 trackdata of tense [i:]
dati = f2geraus[temp,]

# A parallel vector of labels
labi = rep("i:", sum(temp))

temp = vowlax.l == "I" & vowlax.spkr == "67"
# F2 trackdata of lax [I]
datI = vowlax.fdat[temp,2]

# A parallel vector of labels
labI = rep("I", sum(temp))

# Here are the data and corresponding labels to be plotted
dat = rbind(dati, datI)
lab = c(labi, labI)
```

G.2 Quantify the data by calculating k_2 and displaying the results in a boxplot separately for [iː] and [ɪ].

H. This question is concerned with the vowels [ɪ, ʊ, a] in the **timetable** database. The following objects are available from this database in the Emu-R library:

timevow	Segment list of these three vowels
timevow.dft	Spectral trackdata object of spectra between the start and end times of these vowels
timevow.l	Vector of labels

H.1 Make an ensemble-averaged spectral plot in the 0–3,000 Hz range (with one average per vowel category) of spectra extracted at the temporal midpoint of these vowels. Produce the plot with the *x*-axis proportional to the Bark scale. Look at the global shape of the spectra and try to make predictions about how the three vowel categories are likely to differ on Bark-scaled k_1 and k_2.

H.2 Calculate Bark-scaled k_1 and k_2 for these spectra and make ellipse plots of the vowels in this plane. To what extent are your predictions in H.1 supported?

H.3 Produce for the first [ɪ] at its temporal midpoint a Bark spectrum in the 0–4,000 Hz range overlaid with a smoothed spectrum calculated from the first six Bark-scaled DCT coefficients. Produce the plot with the axis proportional to the Bark scale.

8.6 Answers

A.1
```
crplot(k=16, N=20)
```

A.2
```
crplot(p=-pi/2)
```

A.3
```
crplot(k=15, p=pi/2)
```

A.4
```
cfun <- function(A, k, p, N)
{
n = 0:(N-1)
A * cos((2 * pi * k * n)/N + p)
}
```
For example:
```
res = cfun(1.5, 1.4, pi/3, 20)
n = 0:19
plot(n, res, col=2)
par(new=T)
cr(1.5, 1.4, pi/3, 20, type="l")
```

A.5 The sinusoids cancel each other out.
```
o = cr(p=c(0, pi), values=T)
round(o, 4)
0 0 0 0 0 0 0 0 0 0 0 0 0 0 0 0
```

B.
```
a = fapply(keng.dft.5[,700:9000], sum, power=T)
b = fapply(keng.dft.5[,2700:9000], sum, power=T)
```

Spectral Analysis

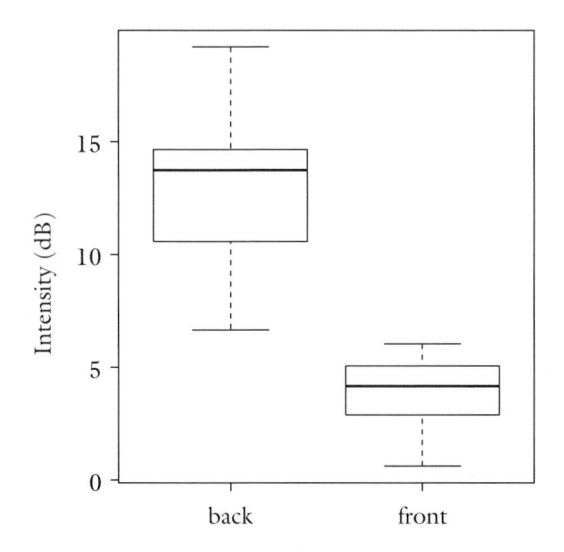

Figure 8.25 The difference in energy between two frequency bands calculated in the burst of back and front allophones of /k/.

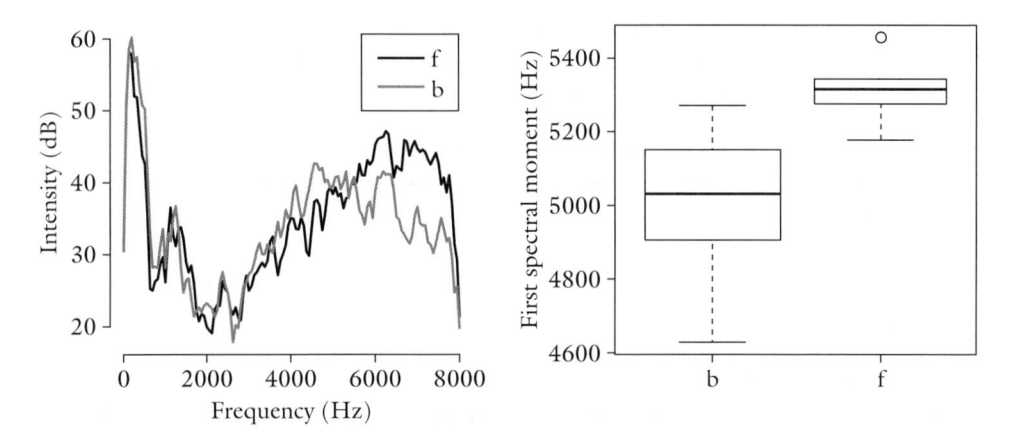

Figure 8.26 Left: averaged spectra of [z] preceding front unrounded (**f**) and back rounded (**b**) vowels. Right: boxplot of the first spectral moment of the same data calculated in the 2,000–7,700 Hz range.

```
d = a - b
boxplot(d ~ factor(keng.1), ylab="dB-difference")
```

Yes, this parameter separates the front and back allophones of /k/ quite well (Figure 8.25).

C. You would expect an overall lowering of the spectral energy: lip-rounding should produce a decrease in the spectral center of gravity or first spectral moment (Mann & Repp 1980). The parameter chosen here (Figure 8.26) is the first spectral moment in the 2,000–7,700 Hz range.

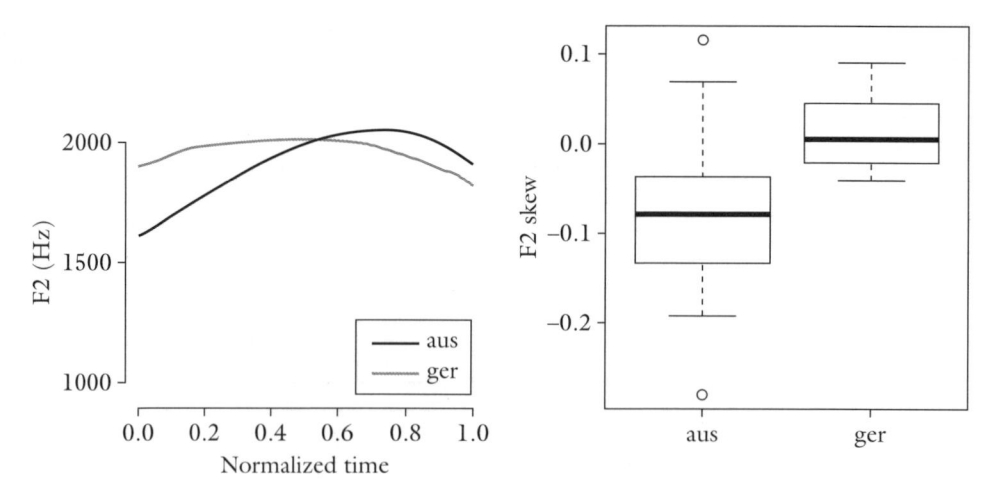

Figure 8.27 Left: averaged, time-normalized plots of F2 as a function of time for Australian English (black) and Standard German (gray) vowels. Right: boxplots of the third spectral moment calculated across the vowel trajectories from their acoustic onset to their acoustic offset.

```
sib.mid= dcut(sib.dft, .5, prop=T)
plot(sib.mid, sib.l, fun=mean, power=T, xlab="Frequency
(Hz)", ylab="Intensity (dB)")

m = fapply(sib.mid[,2000:7700], moments, minval=T)
boxplot(m[,1] ~ factor(sib.l), ylab="1st spectral moment
(Hz)")
```

D.1 The F2 trajectories for late target vowels should be skewed to the right.

D.2 The plots are shown in Figure 8.27 and were created as follows.

```
par(mfrow=c(1,2))
dplot(f2geraus, f2geraus.l, average=T, normalize=T, xlab=
"Normalized time", ylab="F2 (Hz)", leg="bottomright")
```

D.3

```
m = trapply(f2geraus, moments, simplify=T)
skew = m[,3]
boxplot(skew ~ factor(f2geraus.l), ylab="F2-skew")
```

E. [aɪ] has a late F2 peak, [aʊ] has a late F2 trough (and thus effectively an early peak), and [a] has its F2 peak near the temporal midpoint. The skew for these three categories should therefore be negative, positive, and close to zero respectively (Figure 8.28).

```
temp1 = dip.l %in% c("aI", "aU") & dip.spkr == "68"
temp2 = vowlax.l == "a" & vowlax.spkr == "68"
dat = rbind(dip.fdat[temp1,2], vowlax.fdat[temp2,2])
```

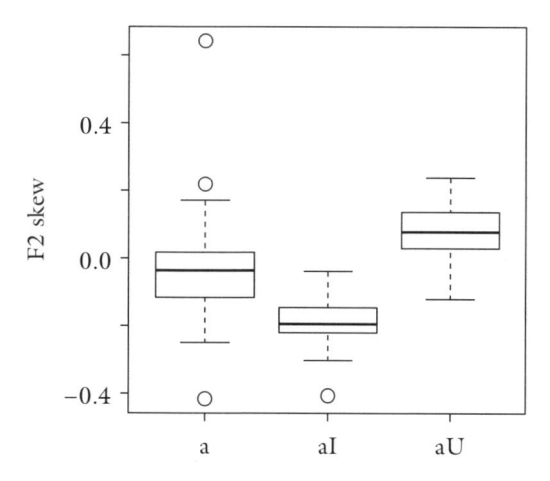

[Figure: Boxplot with y-axis "F2 skew" ranging from -0.4 to 0.4, x-axis categories "a", "aI", "aU"]

Figure 8.28 Boxplot of third moment calculated across F2 trajectories of one female speaker separately for two diphthongs and a monophthong.

```
labs = c(dip.l[temp1], vowlax.l[temp2])
coeffs = trapply(dat, moments, simplify=T)
boxplot(coeffs[,3] ~ labs, ylab="F2-skew")
```

F.1 Diffuse and compact should differ on the second moment (i.e., variance).

F.2

```
plot(stops10[,0:4000], stops10.lab, fun=mean, power=T,
xlab="Frequency (Hz)", ylab="Intensity (dB)",
leg="bottomleft")
```

The averaged spectra in Figure 8.29 do indeed seem to show a greater concentration of energy in the mid-frequency range for [g] than for the other stop categories and so the spectral variance should be less.

F.3

```
m = fapply(stops10[,0:4000], moments, minval=T)
boxplot(sqrt(m[,2]) ~ stops10.lab, ylab="Square root of
2nd moment (Hz)")
```

There is some evidence that the spectral variance is less for [g] in the right panel of Figure 8.29. However, the data for [g] is dispersed, as shown by the large interquartile range (the extent of the rectangle) in comparison with [b, d]: this probably comes about because [g] bursts occur before both front and back vowels which, of course, induce a good deal of variation in initial [g].

G.1

```
dplot(dat, lab, ylab="F2 (Hz)", norm=T, average=T,
ylim=c(1600, 2100))
```

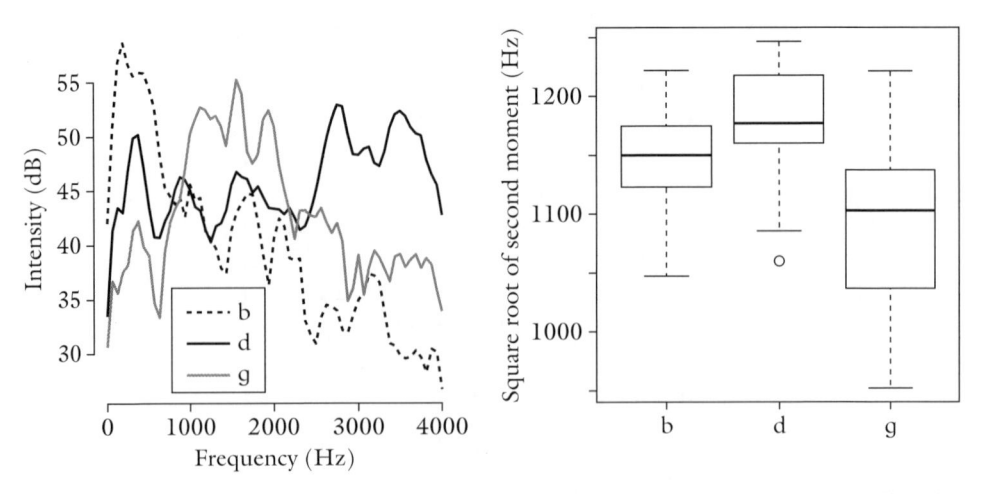

Figure 8.29 Left: averaged spectra of the bursts of [b, d, g] in isolated words produced by an adult male German speaker. The bursts were calculated with a 256-point DFT (sampling frequency 16,000 Hz) centered 10 ms after the stop release. Right: the square root of the second spectral moment for these data calculated in the 0–4,000 Hz range.

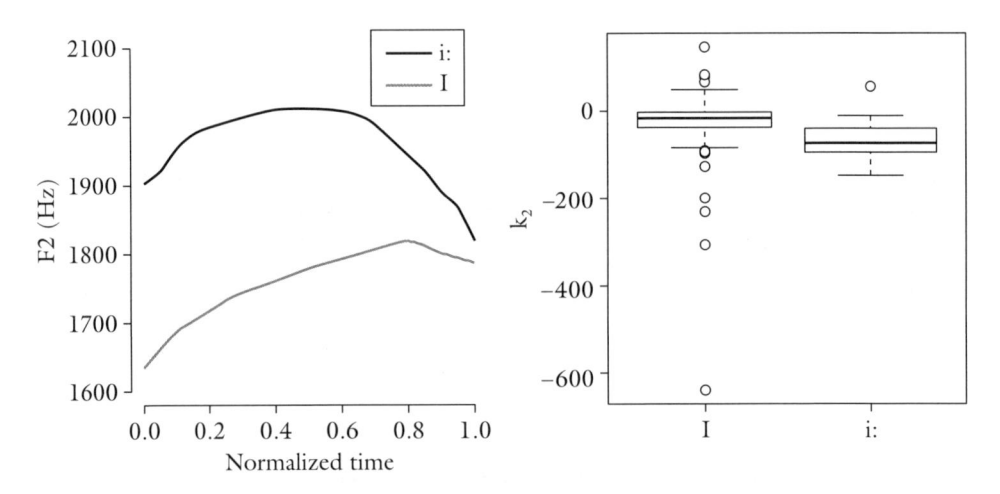

Figure 8.30 Left: linearly time-normalized and then averaged F2 trajectories for German [i:] and [ɪ]. Right: k_2 shown separately for [i:] and [ɪ] calculated by applying a discrete cosine transformation from the onset to the offset of the F2 trajectories.

There is evidence from Figure 8.30 (left) for greater curvature in [i:] as shown by the greater negative values for /i:/ on k_2.

G.2

```
m = trapply(dat, dct, 2, simplify=T)
boxplot(m[,3] ~ factor(lab), ylab="k2")
```

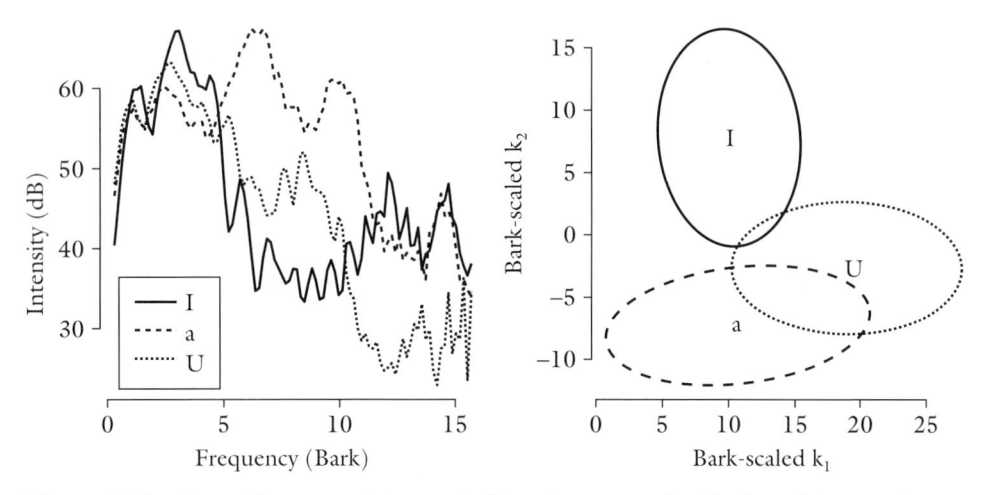

Figure 8.31 Ensemble-averaged spectra (left) at the temporal midpoint of the vowels [ɪ, a, ʊ] (solid, dashed, dotted) and a plot of the same vowels in the plane of Bark-scaled k_1 and k_2 calculated over the same frequency range.

H.1

```
mid = dcut(timevow.dft, .5, prop=T)
plot(bark(mid[,0:3000]), timevow.l, fun=mean, power=T,
xlab="Frequency (Bark)", ylab="Intensity (dB)")
```

Since the slope of the spectrum for [ʊ] in the left panel of Figure 8.31 falls more steeply than for the other vowels, it should be distinguished from them on k_1. The spectra for [ɪ, a] have a ∪-shape and ∩-shape respectively whereas that of [ʊ] shows less evidence of a parabolic shape. Therefore, k_2 should certainly distinguish [ɪ] and [a] (they might have roughly the same value on k_2 but one will be positive and the other negative) and both [ɪ] and [a] should be distinguished on k_2 from the comparatively more flat [ʊ] spectra.

H.2

```
mid.dct = fapply(bark(mid[,0:3000]), dct, 2)
eplot(mid.dct[,2:3], timevow.l, centroid=T, xlab="Bark-
scaled k1", ylab="Bark-scaled k2")
```

As Figure 8.31 shows, the predictions from H.1 are more or less supported.

H.3

```
# Logical vector for [ɪ]
temp = timevow.l == "I"

# n is an index of the first [ɪ]
n = 1:length(timevow.l)
n = n[temp][1]
```

```
# Bark spectrum for this [1] at the segment's temporal midpoint
ispec = bark(dcut(timevow.dft[n,0:4000], .5, prop=T))

# Smoothed Bark spectrum
smooth = dct(ispec, 5, fit=T)

# Equivalently
# smooth = fapply(ispec, dct, 5, fit=T)

# Row-bind the raw and smooth spectra
both = rbind(ispec, smooth)

# Make both into a spectral object with the same frequency range
fs = 2 * max(trackfreq(ispec))
both = as.spectral(both, fs)

# A plot of the raw and overlaid smoothed spectrum
plot(both, c("raw", "smooth"), xlab="Frequency (Bark)",
ylab="Intensity (dB)")
```

Notes

[1] This sinusoid at 0 Hz is equal to what is sometimes called the DC offset divided by the length of the signal (i.e., the DC offset is the mean of the signal's amplitude).

[2] Specifically, when an object of class spectral is called with **plot()**, then, as a result of an object-oriented programming implementation of spectral data in Emu-R, it is actually called with **plot.spectral()**.

[3] The **x** argument can be omitted: if it is missing, then it defaults to **0:(N-1)**, where **N** is the length of **count**. So **moments(bridge[,1])** gives the same result.

[4] For reasons to do with the implementation of the DCT algorithm (see Watson & Harrington 1999, and Harrington 2010 for formulae), k_0 is the value shown in Figure 8.20 multiplied by $\sqrt{2}$.

[5] Calculating cepstrally smoothed spectra on a spectral trackdata object is at the time of writing very slow in R. There is a signal processing routine in Emu-tkassp for calculating cepstrally smoothed spectra directly from the audio signals (LP type CSS in the spectrum pane).

[6] In fact, there is a third method. In automatic speech recognition, energy values are often summed in a filter bank at intervals of 1 Bark. This reduces a spectrum to a series of about 20 values, and it is this data-reduced form that is then subjected to a DCT (Milner & Shao 2006). The filter-bank approach is discussed in Chapter 9.

[7] Recall that this spectrum was taken at the onset of the first vowel in **vowlax**. The peaks in the Bark-smoothed cepstrum on the right of Figure 8.23 are quite close to the F1 and F2 in the first few frames of the calculated formants for this vowel given by **frames(vowlax.fdat[1,1:2])**.

9
Classification

At various stages in this book, different classes of speech sounds have been compared with each other in terms of their acoustic or articulatory proximity. In this chapter, the quantification of the similarity between speech sounds is extended by introducing some topics in classification. This will provide an additional set of tools both for establishing how effectively classes of speech sounds are separated from each other based on a number of parameters and for determining the likelihood that a given value within the parameter space belongs to one of the classes. One of the applications of this methodology in experimental phonetics is to quantify whether adding a new parameter contributes any further information to the separation between classes; another is to assess the extent to which there is a correspondence between acoustic and perceptual classification of speech data. More generally, using probability in experimental phonetics has become increasingly important in view of research advances in probabilistic linguistics (Bod et al. 2003) and developments in exemplar models of speech perception and production that are founded on a probabilistic treatment of speech signals. Probability theory has been used in recent years in forensic phonetics (Rose 2002) as a way of expressing the likelihood of the evidence given a particular hypothesis.

The introduction to this topic that is presented in this chapter will begin with a brief overview of Bayes' theorem and with the classification of single-parameter data using a Gaussian distribution. This will be extended to two parameter classifications which will provide the tools for defining an ellipse and the relationship to principal components analysis. Some consideration will also be given to a support vector machine, a non-Gaussian technique for classification. At various stages in this chapter, the problem of how to classify speech signals as a function of time will also be discussed.

9.1 Probability and Bayes' Theorem

The starting point for many techniques in probabilistic classification is Bayes' theorem, which provides a way of relating **evidence** to a **hypothesis**. In the present context, it allows questions to be answered such as: given that there is a vowel with a high second formant frequency, what is the probability that the vowel is /i/ as opposed to /e/ or /a/? In this case, "F2 is high" is the evidence and "the vowel is /i/ as opposed to /e/ or /a/" is the hypothesis.

Consider now the following problem. In a very large labeled corpus of speech, syllables are labeled categorically depending on whether they were produced with modal voice or with creak and also on whether they were phrase-final or not. After labeling the corpus, it is established that 15 percent of all syllables are phrase-final. It is also found that creak occurs in 80 percent of these phrase-final syllables and in 30 percent of non-phrase-final syllables. You are given a syllable from the corpus that was produced with creak but are not told anything about its phrase label. The task is now to find an answer to the following question: what is the probability that the syllable is phrase-final (the hypothesis) given (the evidence) that it was produced with creak?

Since the large majority of phrase-final syllables were produced with creak while most of the non-phrase-final syllables were not, it would seem that the probability that the creak token is also a phrase-final syllable is quite high. However, the probability must be computed not just by considering the proportion of phrase-final syllables that were produced with creak, but also according to both the proportion of phrase-final syllables in the corpus and the extent to which creak is found elsewhere (in non-phrase-final syllables). Bayes' theorem allows these quantities to be related and the required probability to be calculated from the following formula:

(1) $$p(H \mid E) = \frac{p(E \mid H)p(H)}{p(E)}$$

In (1), H is the hypothesis (that the syllable is phrase-final), E is the evidence (the syllable token has been produced with creak) and $p(H \mid E)$ is to be read as the probability of the hypothesis given the evidence. It can be shown that (1) can be re-expressed as (2):

(2) $$p(H \mid E) = \frac{p(E \mid H)p(H)}{p(E \mid H)p(H) + p(E \mid \neg H)p(\neg H)}$$

where, as before, H is the hypothesis that the syllable is phrase-final and $\neg H$ is the hypothesis that it is *not* phrase-final. For the present example, the quantities on the right-hand side of (2) are the following:

- $p(E \mid H)$, i.e., $p(creak \mid final)$: the probability of there being creak, given that the syllable is phrase-final, is 0.8;
- $p(H)$, i.e., $p(final)$: the probability of a syllable in the corpus being phrase-final is 0.15;
- $p(E \mid \neg H)$, i.e., $p(creak \mid not\text{-}final)$: the probability that the syllable is produced with creak, given that the syllable is phrase-medial or phrase-initial, is 0.3;
- $p(\neg H) = 1 - p(H)$, i.e., $p(not\text{-}final)$: the probability of a syllable in the corpus being phrase-initial or medial (in non-phrase-final position) is 0.85.

The answer to the question $p(H|E)$, the probability that the observed token with creak is also phrase-final, is given using (2) as follows:

```
(0.8 * 0.15) / ((0.8 * 0.15) + (0.3 * 0.85))
```

which is 0.32. Since there are two competing hypotheses (H, the syllable is phrase-final, or its negation, $\neg H$, the syllable is not phrase-final) and since the total probability must add up to one, then it follows that the probability of a syllable produced with creak being in non-phrase-final position is $1 - 0.32$ or 0.68. This quantity can also be derived by replacing H with $\neg H$ in (2), thus:

```
(0.3 * 0.85) / ((0.3 * 0.85) + (0.8 * 0.15))
0.68
```

Notice that the denominator is the same whichever of these two probabilities is calculated.

These calculations lead to the following conclusion. If you take a syllable from this corpus without knowing its phrase label, but observe that it was produced with creak, then it is more likely that this syllable was *not* phrase-final. The probability of the two hypotheses (that the syllable is phrase-final or non-phrase-final) can also be expressed as a **likelihood ratio (LR)**, which is very often used in forensic phonetics (Rose 2002). For this example:

```
LR = 0.68/0.32
LR
2.125
```

from which it follows that it is just over twice as likely for a syllable produced with creak to be non-phrase-final as it is to be phrase-final. The more general conclusion is, then, that creak is really not a very good predictor of the position of the syllable in the phrase, based on the above hypothetical corpus at least.

The above example can be used to introduce some terminology that will be used in later examples. Firstly, the quantities $p(H)$ and $p(\neg H)$ are known as the **prior probabilities**: these are the probabilities that exist independently of any evidence. Thus, the (prior) probability that a syllable taken at random from the corpus is non-phrase-final is 0.85, even without looking at the evidence (i.e., without establishing whether the syllable was produced with creak or not). The prior probabilities can have a major outcome on the posterior probabilities and therefore on classification. In all the examples in this chapter, the prior probabilities will be based on the relative sizes of the classes (as in the above examples) and indeed this is the default of the algorithms for discriminant analysis that will be used later in this chapter (these prior probabilities can be overridden, however, and supplied by the user). $p(E|H)$ and $p(E|\neg H)$ are known as **conditional probabilities**. Finally, the quantities that are to be calculated, $p(H|E)$ and $p(\neg H|E)$, which involve assigning a label given some evidence, are known as the **posterior probabilities**. Thus, for the preceding example, the posterior probability is given by:

```
conditional = 0.8
prior = 0.15
conditional.neg = 0.3
prior.neg = 1 - prior
posterior = (conditional * prior) / (( conditional * prior) +
(conditional.neg * prior.neg))
posterior
0.32
```

The idea of **training** and **testing** is also fundamental to the above example: the training data is made up of a large number of syllables whose phrase position and voice-quality labels are known while training itself consists of establishing a quantifiable relationship between the two. Testing involves taking a syllable whose phrase label is unknown and using the training data to make a probabilistic prediction about what the phrase label is. If the syllable token is taken from the same data used for training (the experimenter "pretends" that the phrase label for the syllable to be tested is unknown), then this is an example of a **closed test**. An **open test** is if the token or tokens to be tested are taken from data that was not used for training. In general, an open test gives a much more reliable indication of the success with which the association between labels and parameters has been learned in the training data. All the examples in this chapter are of **supervised learning** because the training phase is based on prior knowledge (from a database) about how the parameters are associated with the labels. An example of **unsupervised learning** is kmeans clustering, which was briefly touched upon in Chapter 6: this algorithm divides up the clusters into separate groups or classes without any prior training stage.

9.2 Classification: Continuous Data

The previous example of classification was **categorical** because the aim was to classify a syllable in terms of its position in the phrase based on whether it was produced with creak or not. The evidence, then, allows only two choices. There might be several choices (creak, modal, breathy), but this would still be an instance of a categorical classification because the evidence (the data to be tested) can only vary over a fixed number of categories. In experimental phonetics, on the other hand, the evidence is much more likely to be **continuous**: for example, what is the probability, if you observe an unknown (unlabeled) vowel with F1 = 380 Hz, that the vowel is /ɪ/ as opposed to any other vowel category? The evidence is continuous because a parameter like F1 does not jump between discrete values but can take on an infinite number of values within a certain range. So this in turn means that the basis for establishing the training data is somewhat different. In the categorical example from the preceding section, the training consisted of establishing *a priori* the probability that a phrase-final syllable was produced with creak: this was determined by counting the number of times that syllables with creak occurred in phrase-final and non-phrase-final position. In the continuous case, the analogous probability that /ɪ/ could take on a value of 380 Hz needs to be determined not by counting but by fitting a probability model to continuous data. One of the most common, robust,

Classification

and mathematically tractable probability models is based on a **Gaussian** or **normal distribution** that was first derived by Abraham de Moivre (1667–1754), but which is more commonly associated with Karl Friedrich Gauss (1777–1855) and Pierre-Simon Laplace (1749–1827). Some properties of the normal distribution and its derivation from the binomial distribution are considered briefly in the next section.

9.2.1 The binomial and normal distributions

Consider tossing an unbiased coin 20 times. What is the most likely number of times that the coin will come down heads? Intuitively for an unbiased coin this is 10 and quantitatively it is given by $\mu = np$, where μ is a theoretical quantity known as the **population mean**, n is the number of times that the coin is flipped, and p the probability of "success," i.e., of the coin coming down heads. Of course, in flipping a coin 20 times, the outcome is not always equal to the population mean of 10: sometimes there will be fewer and sometimes more, and very occasionally there may even be 20 heads from 20 coin flips, even if the coin is unbiased. This variation comes about because of the randomness that is inherent in flipping a coin: it is random simply because, if the coin is completely unbiased, there is no way to tell *a priori* whether the coin is going to come down heads or tails.

The process of flipping the coin 20 times and seeing what the outcome is can be simulated as follows in R with the **sample()** function.

```
sample(c("H", "T"), 20, replace=T)
# (You are, of course, most likely to get a different output.)
"T" "H" "H" "H" "H" "H" "H" "H" "H" "H" "T" "T" "H" "T" "H" "T"
"T" "T" "T" "T"
```

The above lines have been incorporated into the following function **coin()** with parameters **n**, the number of times the coin is tossed, and **k**, the number of trials, that is, the number of times this experiment is repeated. In each case, the number of heads is summed.

```
coin <- function(n=20, k=50)
{
# n: the number of times a coin is flipped
# k: the number of times the coin-flipping experiment is repeated
   result = NULL
   for(j in 1:k){
      singleexpt = sample(c("H", "T"), n, replace=T)
      result = c(result, sum(singleexpt=="H"))
   }
   result
}
```

Thus, in the following, a coin is flipped 20 times, the number of heads is summed, and then this procedure (of flipping a coin 20 times and counting the number of heads) is repeated eight times.

```
trials8 = coin(k=8)
trials8
# The number of heads from each of the 20 coin flips
14  5  11  8  8  11  7  8
```

Notice that (for this case) no trial actually resulted in the most likely number of Heads, $\mu = np = 10$. However, the **sample mean**, m, gets closer to the theoretical population mean, μ, as n increases. Consider now 800 trials:

```
trials800 = coin(k=800)
```

mean(trials800) is likely to be closer to 10 than **mean(trials8)**. More generally, the greater the number of trials, the more m, the sample mean, is likely to be closer to μ so that, if it were ever possible to conduct the experiment over an infinite number of trials, m would equal μ (and this is one of the senses in which μ is a theoretical quantity).

In this coin-flipping experiment there is, then, variation about the theoretical population mean, μ, in the number of heads that are obtained per 20 coin flips and, in Figure 9.1, this variation is displayed in the form of histograms for 50, 500, and 5,000 trials. The histograms were produced as follows:

```
par(mfrow=c(1,3)); col="slategray"; xlim=c(2, 18)
k50 = coin(k=50); k500 = coin(k=500); k5000 = coin(k=5000)
hist(k50,col=col,xlim=xlim, xlab="",ylab ="Frequency
count",main="k50")
hist(k500, col=col, xlim=xlim, , xlab = "", ylab = "",
main="k500")
hist(k5000, col=col, xlim=xlim, , xlab = "", ylab = "",
main="k5000")
```

In all three cases, the most frequently observed count of the number of heads is near $\mu = 10$. But, in addition, the number of heads per 20 trials falls away from 10 at about the same rate, certainly for the histograms with 500 and 5,000 trials in the

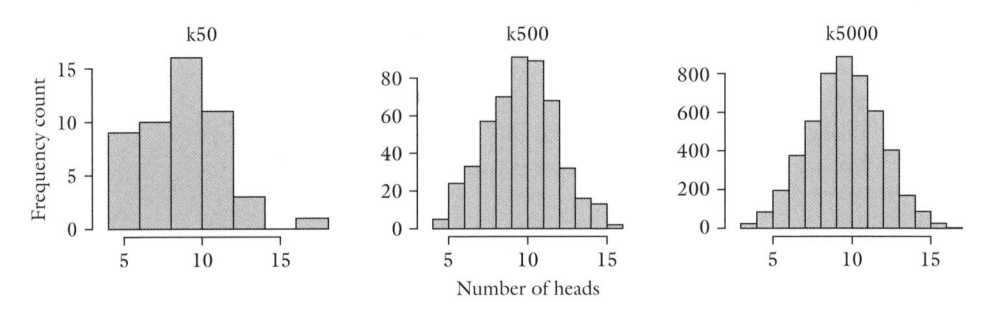

Figure 9.1 Histograms of the number of heads obtained when a coin is flipped 20 times. The results are shown when this coin-flipping experiment is repeated 50 (left), 500 (middle), and 5,000 (right) times.

middle and right panels of Figure 9.1. The rate at which the values fall away from the mean is governed by σ, the population standard deviation. In the case of flipping a coin and counting the number of heads, σ is given by $\sqrt{npq}$ where n and p have the same interpretation as before and $q = 0.5 = 1 - p$ is the probability of "failure," i.e., of getting tails. So the population standard deviation for this example is given by **sqrt(20 * 0.5 * 0.5)**, which evaluates to 2.236068. The relationship between the sample standard deviation, s, and the population standard deviation, σ, is analogous to that between m and μ: the greater the number of trials, the closer s tends to σ. (For the data in Figure 9.1, the sample standard deviations can be evaluated with the **sd()** function: thus **sd(k5000)** should be the closest to **sqrt(20 * 0.5 * 0.5)** of the three.)

When a coin is flipped 20 times and the number of heads is counted as above, then evidently there can only be any one of 21 outcomes ranging in discrete jumps from 0 to 20 heads. The probability of any one of these outcomes can be calculated from the **binomial expansion** given by the **dbinom(x, size, prob)** function in R. So the probability of getting three heads if a coin is flipped four times is **dbinom(3, 4, 0.5)** and the probability of eight heads in 20 coin flips is **dbinom(8, 20, 0.5)**. Notice that an instruction such as **dbinom(7.5, 20, 0.5)** is meaningless because this is to ask the probability of there being seven and a half heads in 20 flips (and appropriately there is a warning message that **x** is a non-integer). The binomial probabilities are, then, those of **discrete** outcomes. The **continuous** case of the binomial distribution is the Gaussian or normal distribution which is defined for all values between plus and minus infinity and is given in R by the **dnorm(x, mean, sd)** function. In this case, the three arguments are respectively the number of successful (heads) coin flips, μ, and σ. Thus the probability of there being eight heads in 20 coin flips can be *estimated* from the normal distribution with:

```
dnorm(8, 20*0.5, sqrt(20*0.5*0.5))
0.1195934
```

Since the normal distribution is continuous, then it is also defined for fractional values: thus **dnorm(7.5, 20*0.5, sqrt(20*0.5*0.5))** can be computed and it gives a result that falls somewhere between the probabilities of getting seven and eight heads in 20 coin flips. There is a slight discrepancy between the theoretical values obtained from the binomial and normal distributions (**dbinom(8, 20, 0.5)** evaluates to 0.1201344), but the values from the binomial distribution get closer to those from the normal distribution as n, the number of coin flips, tends to infinity.

The greater the number of *trials* in this coin-flipping experiment, k, the closer the sample approximates the theoretical probability values obtained from the binomial/normal distributions. This is illustrated in the present example by superimposing the binomial/normal probabilities for obtaining between 0 and 20 heads when the experiment of flipping a coin 20 times was repeated $k = 0$, 500, and 5,000 times. The plots in Figure 9.2 were produced as follows:

```
par(mfrow=c(1,3)); col="slategray"; xlim=c(2, 18); main=""
hist(k50, freq=F, main="50 trials", xlab="", col=col)
curve(dnorm(x, 20*.5, sqrt(20*.5*.5)), 0, 20, add=T, lwd=2)
```

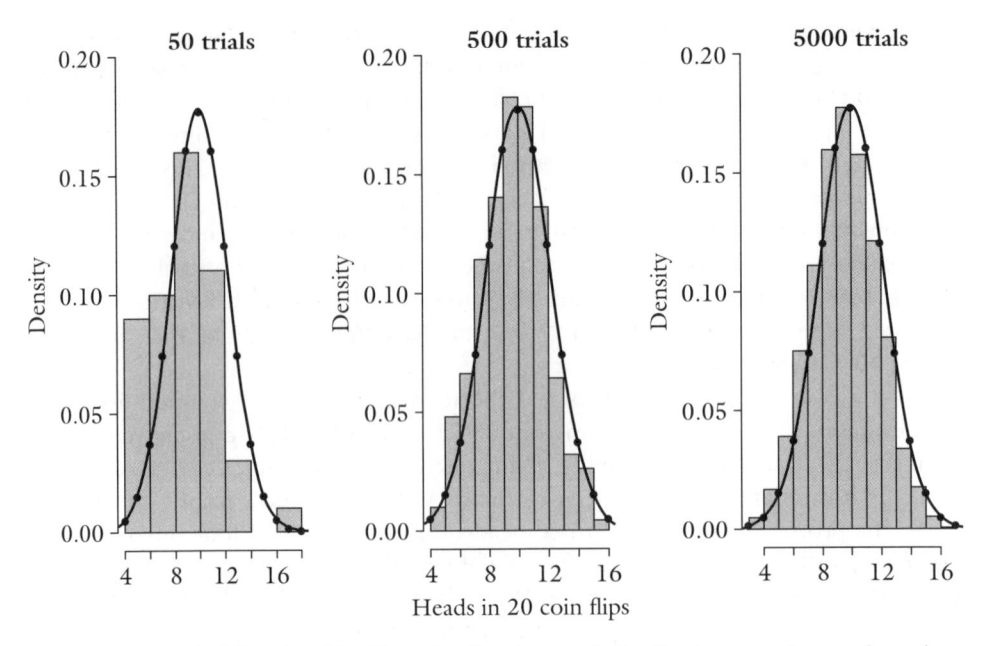

Figure 9.2 Probability densities from the fitted normal distribution superimposed on the histograms from Figure 9.1 and with the corresponding binomial probability densities shown as points.

```
# These are the probabilities of getting 0, 1 ... 20 heads from the binomial
distribution
binprobs = dbinom(0:20, 20, .5)
points(0:20, binprobs)
hist(k500, freq=F, main="500 trials", xlab="Number of Heads
in 20 coin flips", col=col)
curve(dnorm(x, 20*.5, sqrt(20*.5*.5)), 0, 20, add=T, lwd=2)
points(0:20, binprobs)
hist(k5000, freq=F, main="5000 trials", xlab="", col=col)
curve(dnorm(x, 20*.5, sqrt(20*.5*.5)), 0, 20, add=T, lwd=2)
points(0:20, binprobs)
```

The vertical axis in Figure 9.2 (and indeed the output of the **dnorm()** function) is **probability density**, and it is derived in such a way that the sum of the histogram bars is equal to one, which means that the area of each bar becomes a *proportion*. Thus, the area of the second bar from the left of the *k500* plot in Figure 9.2 is given by the probability density multiplied by the bar width, which is **0.05 * 1** or 0.05. This is also the proportion of values falling within this range: **0.05 * 500** is 25 (heads), as the corresponding bar of the histogram in the middle panel of Figure 9.1 confirms. More importantly, the correspondence between the distribution of the number of heads in the sample and the theoretical binomial/normal probabilities is evidently much closer for the histogram on the right with the greatest number of trials.

Some of the other important properties of the normal distribution are:

- the population mean is at the center of the distribution and has the highest probability;
- the tails of the distribution continue at the left and right edge to plus or minus infinity;
- the total area under the normal distribution is equal to 1;
- the probability that a value is either less or greater than the mean is 0.5.

The R function **pnorm(q, mean, sd)** calculates **cumulative probabilities**, i.e., the area under the normal curve from minus infinity to a given quantile, q. Informally, this function returns the probability that a sample drawn from the normal distribution is less than that sample. Thus, **pnorm(20, 25, 5)** returns the probability of drawing a sample of 20 or less from a normal distribution with mean 25 and standard deviation 5. To calculate the probabilities within a range of values requires, therefore, subtraction:

```
pnorm(40, 25, 5) - pnorm(20, 25, 5)
0.8399948
```

gives the probability of drawing a sample between 20 and 40 from the same normal distribution.

Here is how **qnorm()** could be used to find the range of samples whose probability of occurrence is greater than 0.025 and less than 0.975:

```
qnorm(c(0.025, 0.975), 25, 5)
15.20018  34.79982
```

In other words, 95 percent of the samples (i.e., 0.975 − 0.025 = 0.95) in a normal distribution with mean 25 and standard deviation 5 extend between 15.20018 and 34.79982.

Without the second and third arguments, the various functions for computing values from the normal distribution return so-called z-scores or the values from the **standard normal distribution** with $\mu = 0$ and $\sigma = 1$. This default setting of **qnorm()** can be used to work out the range of values that fall within a certain number of standard deviations from the mean. Thus, without the second and third arguments, **qnorm(c(0.025, 0.975))** returns the number of standard deviations for samples falling within 95 percent of the mean of *any* normal distribution, i.e., the well-known value of ± 1.96 from the mean (rounded to two decimal places). Thus the previously calculated range can also be obtained as follows:

```
# Lower range, - 1.959964 standard deviations from the mean (of 25)
25 - 1.959964 * 5
15.20018
# Upper range
25 + 1.959964 * 5
34.79982
```

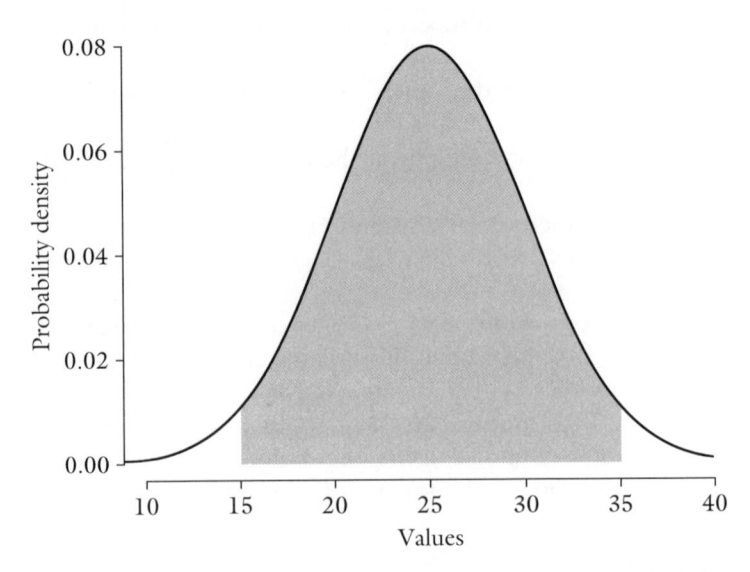

Figure 9.3 A normal distribution with parameters μ = 25, σ = 5. The shaded part has an area of 0.95 and the corresponding values at the lower and upper limits on the *x*-axis span the range within which a value falls with a probability of 0.95.

An example of the use of **dnorm()** and **qnorm()** over the same data is given in Figure 9.3, which was produced with the following commands:

```
xlim = c(10, 40); ylim = c(0, 0.08)
curve(dnorm(x, 25, 5), 5, 45, xlim=xlim, ylim=ylim, ylab="",
xlab="")
region95 = qnorm(c(0.025, 0.975), 25, 5)
values = seq(region95[1], region95[2], length=2000)
values.den = dnorm(values, 25, 5)
par(new=T)
plot(values, values.den, type="h", col="slategray",
xlim=xlim, ylim=ylim, ylab="Probability density",
xlab="Values")
```

9.3 Calculating Conditional Probabilities

Following this brief summary of the theoretical normal distribution, we can now return to the matter of how to work out the conditional probability $p(F1 = 380 \mid I)$, which is the probability that a value of F1 = 380 Hz could have come from a distribution of /ɪ/ vowels. The procedure is to sample a reasonably large size of F1 for /ɪ/ vowels and then to assume that these follow a normal distribution. Thus, the assumption here is that the sample of F1 of /ɪ/ deviates from the normal distribution simply because not enough samples have been obtained (and, analogously with summing the number of heads in the coin-flipping experiment, the normal distribution would

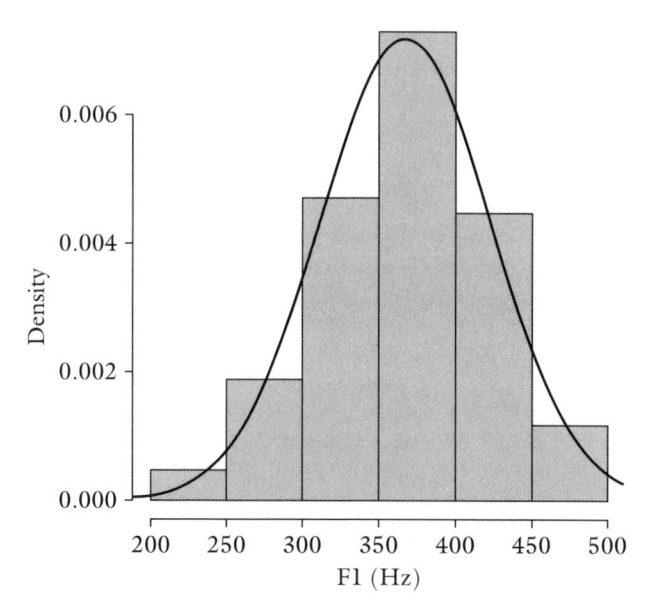

Figure 9.4 Histogram of F1 values of /ɪ/ with a fitted normal distribution.

be the theoretical distribution from an infinite number of F1 samples for /ɪ/). It should be pointed out right away that this assumption of normality could well be wrong. However, the normal distribution is fairly robust and so it may nevertheless be an appropriate probability model, even if the sample does deviate from normality; and, secondly, as outlined in some detail in Johnson (2008) and summarized again below, there are some diagnostic tests that can be applied to test the assumptions of normality.

As the discussion in 9.2.1 showed, only two parameters are needed to characterize any normal distribution uniquely, and these are μ and σ, the population mean and population standard deviation respectively. In contrast to the coin-flipping experiment, these population parameters are unknown in the F1 sample of vowels. However, it can be shown that the best estimates of these are given by m and s, the mean and standard deviation of the sample which can be calculated with the **mean()** and **sd()** functions.[1] In Figure 9.4, these are used to fit a normal distribution to F1 of /ɪ/ for data extracted from the temporal midpoint of the male speaker's vowels in the **vowlax** dataset in the Emu-R library.

```
temp = vowlax.spkr == "67" & vowlax.l == "I"
f1 = vowlax.fdat.5[temp,1]
m = mean(f1); s = sd(f1)
hist(f1, freq=F, xlab="F1 (Hz)", main="", col="slategray")
curve(dnorm(x, m, s), 150, 550, add=T, lwd=2)
```

The data in Figure 9.4 at least look as if they follow a normal distribution and, if need be, a test for normality can be carried out with the Shapiro test:

```
shapiro.test(f1)
Shapiro-Wilk normality test
data: f1
W = 0.9834, p-value = 0.3441
```

If the test shows that the probability value is greater than some significance threshold, say 0.05, then there is no evidence to suggest that these data are not normally distributed. Another way, described more fully in Johnson (2008), of testing for normality is with a quantile–quantile plot:

```
qqnorm(f1); qqline(f1)
```

If the values fall more or less on the straight line, then there is no evidence that the distribution does not follow a normal distribution.

Once a normal distribution has been fitted to the data, the conditional probability can be calculated using the **dnorm()** function given earlier (see Figure 9.3). Thus $p(F1 = 380 \mid I)$, the probability that a value of 380 Hz could have come from this distribution of /ɪ/ vowels, is given by:

```
conditional = dnorm(380, mean(f1), sd(f1))
conditional
0.006993015
```

which is the same probability given by the height of the normal curve in Figure 9.4 at F1 = 380 Hz.

9.4 Calculating Posterior Probabilities

Suppose you are given a vowel whose F1 you measure to be 500 Hz but you are not told what the vowel label is except that it is one of /ɪ, ɛ, a/. The task is to find the most likely label, given the evidence that F1 = 500 Hz. In order to do this, the three posterior probabilities, one for each of the three vowel categories, has to be calculated and the unknown is then labeled as whichever one of these posterior probabilities is the greatest. As discussed in 9.1, the posterior probability requires calculating the prior and conditional probabilities for each vowel category. Recall also from 9.1 that the prior probabilities can be based on the proportions of each class in the training sample. The proportions in this example can be derived by tabulating the vowels as follows:

```
temp = vowlax.spkr == "67" & vowlax.l != "O"
f1 = vowlax.fdat.5[temp,1]
f1.l = vowlax.l[temp]
table(f1.l)
  E   I   a
 41  85  63
```

Classification

Each of these can be thought of as vowel tokens in a bag: if a token is pulled out of the bag at random, then the prior probability that the token's label is /a/ is 63 divided by the total number of tokens (i.e., divided by 41 + 85 + 63 = 189). Thus the prior probabilities for these three vowel categories are given by:

```
prior = prop.table(table(f1.l))
prior
      E           I           a
0.2169312   0.4497354   0.3333333
```

So there is a greater prior probability of retrieving /ɪ/ simply because of its greater proportion compared with the other two vowels. The conditional probabilities have to be calculated separately for each vowel class, given the evidence that F1 = 500 Hz. As discussed in the preceding section, these can be obtained with the **dnorm()** function. In the instructions below, a for-loop is used to obtain each of the three conditional probabilities, one for each category:

```
cond = NULL
for(j in names(prior)){
   temp = f1.l==j
   mu = mean(f1[temp]); sig = sd(f1[temp])
   y = dnorm(500, mu, sig)
   cond = c(cond, y)
   }
names(cond) = names(prior)
cond
        E              I              a
0.0063654039   0.0004115088   0.0009872096
```

The posterior probability that an unknown vowel could be, e.g., /a/ given the evidence that its F1 has been measured to be 500 Hz can now be calculated with the formula given in (2) in 9.1. By substituting the values into (2), this posterior probability, denoted by $p(a\,|\,F1 = 500)$, and with the meaning "the probability that the vowel could be /a/, given the evidence that F1 is 500 Hz," is given by:

$$(3)\quad p(a\,|\,F1 = 500) = \frac{p(F1 = 500\,|\,a)p(a)}{p(F1 = 500\,|\,E)p(E) + p(F1 = 500\,|\,a)p(a) + p(F1 = 500\,|\,\textsc{i})p(\textsc{i})}$$

The denominator in (3) looks fearsome but closer inspection shows that it is nothing more than the sum of the conditional probabilities multiplied by the prior probabilities for each of the three vowel classes. The denominator is therefore **sum(cond * prior)**. The numerator in (3) is the conditional probability for /a/ multiplied by the prior probability for /a/. In fact, the posterior probabilities for *all* categories, $p(\varepsilon\,|\,F1 = 500)$, $p(\textsc{i}\,|\,F1 = 500)$, and $p(a\,|\,F1 = 500)$ can be calculated in R in one step as follows:

```
post = (cond * prior)/sum(cond * prior)
post
        E          I          a
0.72868529  0.09766258  0.17365213
```

As explained in 9.1, these sum to 1 (as **sum(post)** confirms). Thus, the unknown vowel with F1 = 500 Hz is categorized as /ɛ/ because, as the above calculation shows, this is the vowel class with the highest posterior probability, given the evidence that F1 = 500 Hz.

All the above calculations of posterior probabilities can be accomplished with **qda()** and the associated **predict()** functions in the MASS library for carrying out a quadratic discriminant analysis (you may need to enter **library(MASS)** to access these functions). Quadratic discriminant analysis models the probability of each class as a normal distribution and then categorizes unknown tokens based on the greatest posterior probabilities (Srivastava et al. 2007): in other words, much the same as the procedure carried out above.

The first step in using this function involves training (see 9.1 for the distinction between training and testing) in which normal distributions are fitted to each of the three vowel classes separately and in which they are also adjusted for the prior probabilities. The second step is the testing stage in which posterior probabilities are calculated (in this case, given that an unknown token has F1 = 500 Hz).

The **qda()** function expects a *matrix* as its first argument, but **f1** is a vector. So, in order to make these two things compatible, the **cbind()** function is used to turn the vectors into one-dimensional matrices at both the training and the testing stages. The training stage, in which the prior probabilities and class means are calculated, is carried out as follows:

```
f1.qda = qda(cbind(f1), f1.l)
```

The prior probabilities obtained in the training stage are:

```
f1.qda$prior
       E          I          a
0.2169312  0.4497354  0.3333333
```

which are the same as those calculated earlier. The calculation of the posterior probabilities, given the evidence that F1 = 500 Hz, forms part of the *testing* stage. The **predict()** function is used for this purpose, in which the first argument is the model calculated in the training stage and the second argument is the value to be classified:

```
pred500 = predict(f1.qda, cbind(500))
```

The posterior probabilities are given by:

```
pred500$post
       E          I          a
0.7286853  0.09766258  0.1736521
```

which are also the same as those obtained earlier. The most probable category, **E**, is given by:

```
pred500$class
E
Levels:  E  I  a
```

This type of single-parameter classification (single parameter because there is just one parameter, F1) results in $n - 1$ **decision points** for n categories (thus two points given that there are three vowel categories in this example): at some F1 value, the classification changes from /a/ to /ɛ/ and at another from /ɛ/ to /ɪ/. In fact, these decision points are completely predictable from the points at which the product of the prior and conditional probabilities for the classes overlap (the denominator can be disregarded in this case, because, as (2) and (3) show, it is the same for all three vowel categories). For example, a plot of the product of the prior and the conditional probabilities over a range from 250 Hz to 800 Hz for /ɛ/ is given by:

```
temp = vowlax.spkr == "67" & vowlax.l != "O"
f1 = vowlax.fdat.5[temp,1]
f1.l = vowlax.l[temp]
f1.qda = qda(cbind(f1), f1.l)

temp = f1.l=="E"; mu = mean(f1[temp]); sig = sd(f1[temp])
curve(dnorm(x, mu, sig)* f1.qda$prior[1], 250, 800)
```

Essentially, the above two lines are used inside a for-loop in order to superimpose the three distributions of the prior multiplied by the conditional probabilities, one per vowel category, on each other (Figure 9.5):

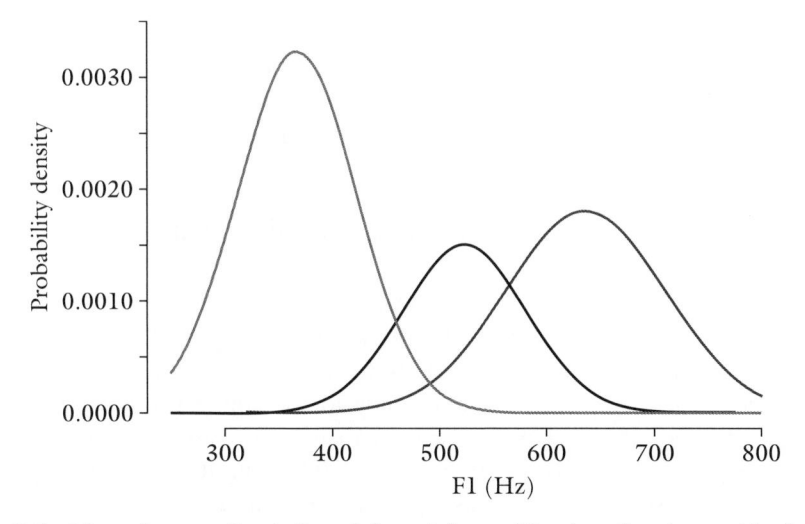

Figure 9.5 Normal curves fitted, from left to right, to F1 values for /ɪ, ɛ, a/ in the male speaker's vowels from the **vowlax** dataset.

```
xlim = c(250,800); ylim = c(0, 0.0035); k = 1;
cols = c("grey","black","lightblue")
for(j in c("a", "E", "I")){
  temp = f1.l==j
  mu = mean(f1[temp]); sig = sd(f1[temp])
  curve(dnorm(x, mu, sig)* f1.qda$prior[j],xlim=xlim,
  ylim=ylim, col=cols[k], xlab=" ", ylab="", lwd=2, axes=F)
  par(new=T)
  k = k+1
}
axis(side=1); axis(side=2); title(xlab="F1 (Hz)",
ylab="Probability density")
par(new=F)
```

From Figure 9.5, it can be seen that the F1 value at which the probability distributions for /ɪ/ and /ɛ/ bisect each other is at around 460 Hz, while for /ɛ/ and /a/ it is about 100 Hz higher. Thus any F1 value less than (approximately) 460 Hz should be classified as /ɪ/; any value between 460 and 567 Hz as /ɛ/; and any value greater than 567 Hz as /a/. A classification of values at 5 Hz intervals between 445 Hz and 575 Hz confirms this:

```
# Generate a sequence of values at 5-Hz intervals between 445 and 575 Hz
vec = seq(445, 575, by = 5)
```

```
# Classify these using the same model established earlier
vec.pred = predict(f1.qda, cbind(vec))
```

```
# This is done to show how each of these values was classified by the model
names(vec) = vec.pred$class
vec
  I   I   I   E   E   E   E   E   E   E   E   E   E   E   E
445 450 455 460 465 470 475 480 485 490 495 500 505 510 515
  E   E   E   E   E   E   E   E   E   E   a   a
520 525 530 535 540 545 550 555 560 565 570 575
```

9.5 Two Parameters: The Bivariate Normal Distribution and Ellipses

So far, classification has been based on a single parameter, F1. However, the mechanisms for extending this type of classification to two (or more) dimensions are already in place. Essentially, exactly the same formula for obtaining posterior probabilities is used, but in this case the conditional probabilities are based on probability densities derived from the bivariate (two parameters) or multivariate (multiple parameters) normal distribution. In this section, a few details will be given of the relationship between the bivariate normal and ellipse plots that have been used at various stages in this book; in the next section, examples are given of classifications from two or more parameters.

In the one-parameter classification of the previous section, it was shown how the population mean and standard deviation could be estimated from the mean and standard deviation of the sample for each category, assuming a sufficiently large sample size and that there was no evidence to show that the data did not follow a normal distribution. For the two-parameter case, there are five population parameters to be estimated from the sample: these are the two population means (one for each parameter), the two population standard deviations, and the population correlation coefficient between the parameters. A graphical interpretation of fitting a bivariate normal distribution for some F1 × F2 data for [æ] is shown in Figure 9.6. On the left is the sample of data points and on the right is a three-dimensional histogram showing the count in separate F1 × F2 bins arranged over a two-dimensional grid. A bivariate normal distribution that has been fitted to these data is shown in Figure 9.7. The probability density of any point in the F1 × F2 plane is given by the height of

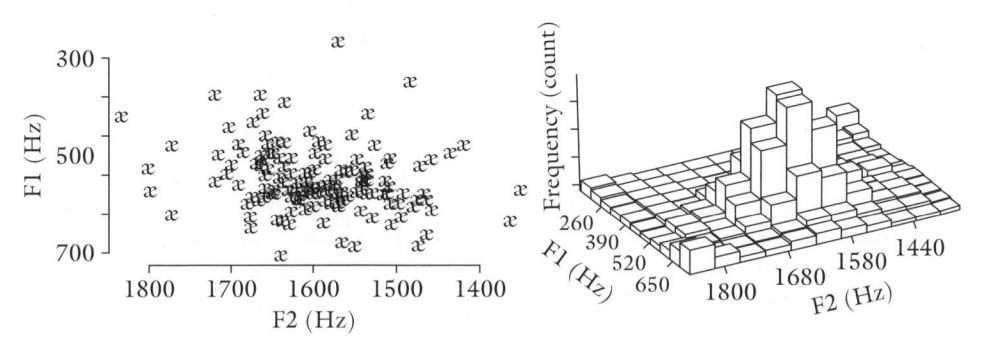

Figure 9.6 A scatter plot of the distribution of [æ] on F2 × F1 (left) and the corresponding three-dimensional histogram (right).

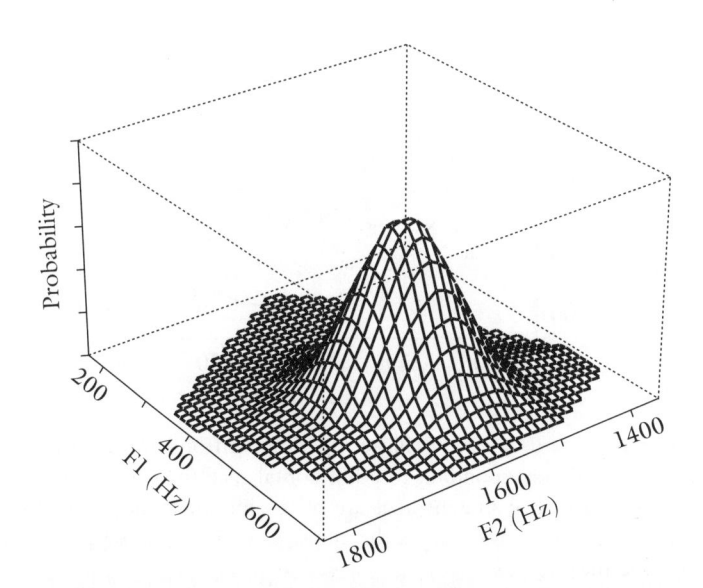

Figure 9.7 The bivariate normal distribution derived from the scatter in Figure 9.6.

the bivariate normal distribution above the two-dimensional plane: this is analogous to the height of the bell-shaped normal distribution for the one-dimensional case. The highest probability (the apex of the bell) is at the point defined by the mean of F1 and by the mean of F2: this point is sometimes known as the **centroid**.

The relationship between a bivariate normal and the two-dimensional scatter can also be interpreted in terms of an **ellipse**. An ellipse is any horizontal slice cut from the bivariate normal distribution, in which the cut is made at right angles to the probability axis. The lower down on the probability axis that the cut is made – that is, the closer the cut is made to the base of the F1 × F2 plane, the greater the area of the ellipse and the more points of the scatter that are included within the ellipse's outer boundary or circumference. If the cut is made at the very top of the bivariate normal distribution, the ellipse is so small that it includes only the centroid and a few points around it. If on the other hand the cut is made very close to the F1 × F2 base on which the probability values are built, then the ellipse may include almost the entire scatter.

The size of the ellipse is usually measured in **ellipse standard deviations from the mean**. There is a direct analogy here to the single parameter case. Recall from Figure 9.3 that the number of standard deviations can be used to calculate the probability that a token falls within a particular range of the mean. So too with ellipse standard deviations. When an ellipse is drawn with a certain number of standard deviations, then there is an associated probability that a token will fall within its circumference. The ellipse in Figure 9.8 is of F2 × F1 data of [æ] plotted at two standard deviations from the mean, and this corresponds to a cumulative probability of 0.865: this is also the probability of any vowel falling inside the ellipse (and so the probability of it falling beyond the ellipse is 1 − 0.865 = 0.135). Moreover, if

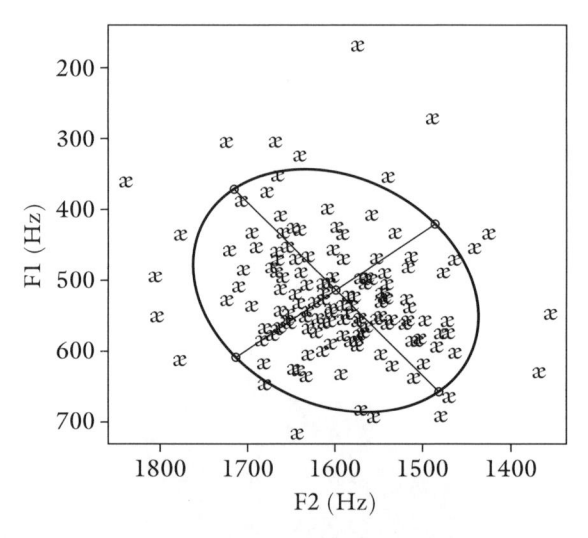

Figure 9.8 A two-standard-deviation ellipse superimposed on the F2 × F1 scatter of [æ] vowels in Figure 9.6 and corresponding to a horizontal slice through the bivariate normal distribution in Figure 9.7. The straight lines are the major and minor axes of the ellipse. The point at which these lines intersect is the ellipse's centroid, whose coordinates are the mean of F2 and the mean of F1.

[æ] is normally, or nearly normally, distributed on F1 × F2 then, for a sufficiently large sample size, approximately 0.865 of the sample should fall inside the ellipse. In this case, the sample size was 140, so roughly 140 · 0.865 ≈ 121 should be within the ellipse, and 19 tokens should be beyond the ellipse's circumference (in fact, there are 20 [æ] tokens outside the ellipse's circumference in Figure 9.8).[2]

Whereas, in the one-dimensional case, the association between standard deviations and cumulative probability was given by **qnorm()**, for the bivariate case this relationship is determined by the square root of the quantiles from the χ^2 **distribution** with two degrees of freedom. In R, this is given by **qchisq(p, df)** where the two arguments are the cumulative probability and the degrees of freedom respectively. Thus, just under 2.45 ellipse standard deviations correspond to a cumulative probability of 0.95, as the following shows:[3]

```
sqrt(qchisq(0.95, 2))
2.447747
```

The function **pchisq()** provides the same information but in the other direction. Thus the cumulative probability associated with 2.447747 ellipse standard deviations from the mean is given by:

```
pchisq(2.447747^2, 2)
0.95
```

An ellipse is a flattened circle and it has two diameters, a **major axis** and a **minor axis** (Figure 9.8). The point at which the major and minor axes intersect is the distribution's centroid. One definition of the major axis is that it is the longest radius that can be drawn between the centroid and the ellipse circumference. The minor axis is the shortest radius and it is always at right angles to the major axis. Another definition that will be important in the analysis of data reduction technique in section 9.7 is that the major ellipse axis is the **first principal component** of the data.

The first principal component is a straight line that passes through the centroid of the scatter that **explains most of the variance** of the data. A graphical way to think about what this means is to draw any line through the scatter such that it passes through the scatter's centroid. We are then going to rotate our chosen line and all the data points about the centroid in such a way that it ends up parallel to the x-axis (parallel to the F2 axis for these data). If the variance of F2 is measured before and after rotation, then the variance will not be the same: the variance might be smaller or larger after the data has been rotated in this way. The first principal component, which is also the major axis of the ellipse, can now be defined as the line passing through the centroid that produces the greatest amount of variance on the x-axis variable (on F2 for these data) after this type of rotation has taken place.

If the major axis of the ellipse is exactly parallel to the x-axis (as in the right panel of Figure 9.9), then there is an exact equivalence between the ellipse standard deviation and the standard deviations of the separate parameters. Figure 9.10 shows the rotated two-standard-deviation ellipse from the right panel of Figure 9.9 aligned with a two-standard-deviation normal curve of the same F2 data after rotation. The mean of F2 is 1,599 Hz and the standard deviation of F2 is 92 Hz. The major axis of the

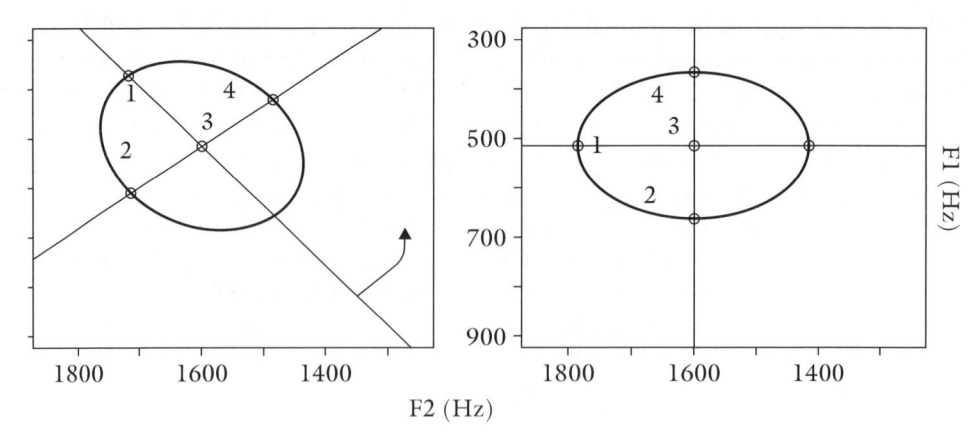

Figure 9.9 The ellipse on the right is a rotation of the ellipse on the left around its centroid such that the ellipse's major axis is made parallel with the F2 axis after rotation. The numbers 1–4 show the positions of four points before (left) and after (right) rotation.

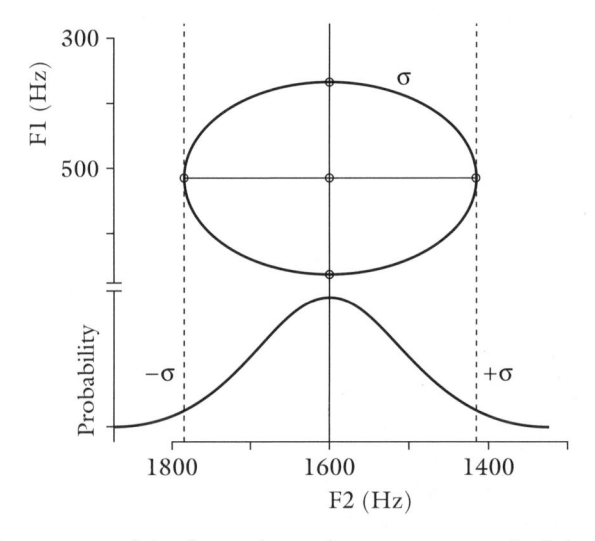

Figure 9.10 The top part of the figure shows the same two-standard-deviation ellipse as in the right panel of Figure 9.9. The lower part of the figure shows a normal curve for the rotated F2 data superimposed on the same scale. The dotted vertical lines mark $\sigma = \pm 2$ standard deviations from the mean of the normal curve which are in exact alignment with the intersection of the ellipse's major axis and circumference at two ellipse standard deviations.

ellipse extends, therefore, along the F2 parameter at ± 2 standard deviations from the mean, i.e., between $1{,}599 + (2 \cdot 92) = 1{,}783$ Hz and $1{,}599 - (2 \cdot 92) = 1{,}415$ Hz. Similarly, the minor axis extends two standard deviations in either direction from the mean of the rotated F1 data. However, this relationship only applies as long as the major axis is parallel to the x-axis. At other inclinations of the ellipse, the lengths of the major and minor axes depend on a complex interaction between the correlation coefficient, r, and the standard deviation of the two parameters.

In this special case, in which the major axis of the ellipse is parallel to the *x*-axis, the two parameters are completely uncorrelated or have **zero correlation**. As discussed in the next section on classification, the less two parameters are correlated with each other, the more information they can potentially contribute to the separation between phonetic classes. If on the other hand two parameters are highly correlated, then it means that one parameter can to a very large extent be predicted from the other: they therefore tend to provide less useful information than uncorrelated ones for distinguishing between phonetic classes.

9.6 Classification in Two Dimensions

The task in this section will be to carry out a probabilistic classification at the temporal midpoint of five German fricatives [f, s, ʃ, ç, x] from a two-parameter model of the first two spectral moments (which were shown to be reasonably effective in distinguishing between fricatives in the preceding chapter). The spectral data extends from 0 Hz to 8,000 Hz and was calculated at 5 ms intervals with a frequency resolution of 31.25 Hz. The following objects are available in the Emu-R library:

fr.dft   Spectral trackdata object containing spectral data between the segment onset and offset at 5 ms intervals
fr.l   A vector of phonetic labels
fr.sp   A vector of speaker labels

The analysis will be undertaken using the first two spectral moments calculated at the fricatives' temporal midpoints over the range 200–7,800 Hz. The data are displayed as ellipses in Figure 9.11 on these parameters for each of the five fricative

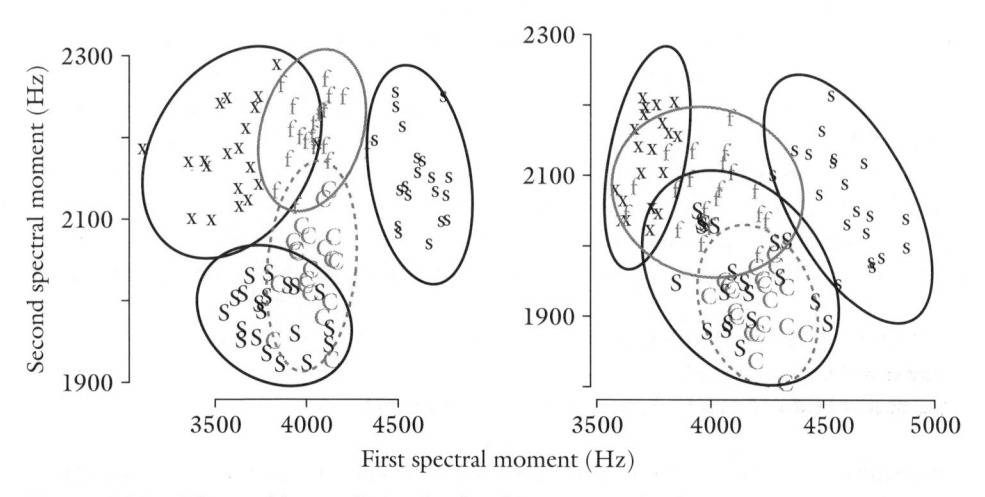

Figure 9.11 95% confidence ellipses for five fricatives on the first two spectral moments extracted at the temporal midpoint for a male (left) and female (right) speaker of Standard German.

categories and separately for the two speakers. The commands to create these plots in Figure 9.11 are as follows:

```
# Extract the spectral data at the temporal midpoint
fr.dft5 = dcut(fr.dft, .5, prop=T)

# Calculate their spectral moments
fr.m = fapply(fr.dft5[,200:7800], moments, minval=T)

# Take the square root of the second spectral moment so that the values are
# within sensible ranges
fr.m[,2] = sqrt(fr.m[,2])

# Give the matrix some column names
colnames(fr.m) = paste("m", 1:4, sep="")
par(mfrow=c(1,2))
xlab = "1st spectral moment (Hz)"; ylab="2nd spectral moment
(Hz)"

# Logical vector to identify the male speaker
temp = fr.sp == "67"
eplot(fr.m[temp,1:2], fr.l[temp], dopoints=T, ylab=ylab,
xlab=xlab)
eplot(fr.m[!temp,1:2], fr.l[!temp], dopoints=T, xlab=xlab)
```

As discussed in section 9.5, the ellipses are horizontal slices each taken from a bivariate normal distribution and the ellipse standard deviations have been set to the default such that each includes at least 95 percent of the data points. Also, as discussed earlier, the extent to which the parameters are likely to provide independently useful information is influenced by how correlated they are. For the male speaker, **cor.test(fr.m[temp,1], fr.m[temp,2])** shows that the correlation is both low ($r = 0.13$) and not significant; for the female speaker, it is significant although still quite low ($r = -0.29$). Thus the second spectral moment may well provide information beyond the first that might be useful for fricative classification and, as Figure 9.11 shows, it separates [x, s, f] from the other two fricatives reasonably well in both speakers, whereas the first moment provides a fairly good separation within [x, s, f].

The observations can now be quantified probabilistically using the **qda()** function in exactly the same way for training and testing as in the one-dimensional case:

```
# Train on the first two spectral moments, speaker 67
temp = fr.sp == "67"
x.qda = qda(fr.m[temp,1:2], fr.l[temp])
```

Classification is accomplished by calculating whichever of the five posterior probabilities is the highest, using the formula in (2) in an analogous way to one-dimensional classification discussed in section 9.4. Consider then a point [m_1, m_2] in this two-dimensional moment-space with coordinates [4,500, 2,000]. Its position in relation to the ellipses in the left panel of Figure 9.11 suggests that it is likely to be classified as /s/ and this is indeed the case:

```
unknown = c(4500, 2000)
result = predict(x.qda, unknown)

# Posterior probabilities
round(result$post, 5)
     C      S    f     s    x
0.0013 0.0468    0 0.9519    0

# Classification label
result$class
s
Levels: C S f s x
```

In the one-dimensional case, it was shown how the classes were separated by a single point that marked the decision boundary between classes (Figure 9.5). For two-dimensional classification, the division between classes is not a point but one of a family of quadratics (and hyperquadratics for higher dimensions) that can take on forms such as planes, ellipses, and parabolas of various kinds (see Duda et al. 2001, Chapter 2 for further details).[4] This becomes apparent in classifying a large number of points over an entire two-dimensional surface, which can be done with the **classplot()** function in the Emu-R library: its arguments are the model on which the data was trained (maximally two-dimensional) and the range over which the points are to be classified. The result of such a classification for a dense region of points in a plane with similar ranges as those of the ellipses in Figure 9.11 is shown in the left panel of Figure 9.12, while the right panel shows somewhat wider ranges. The first of these was created as follows:

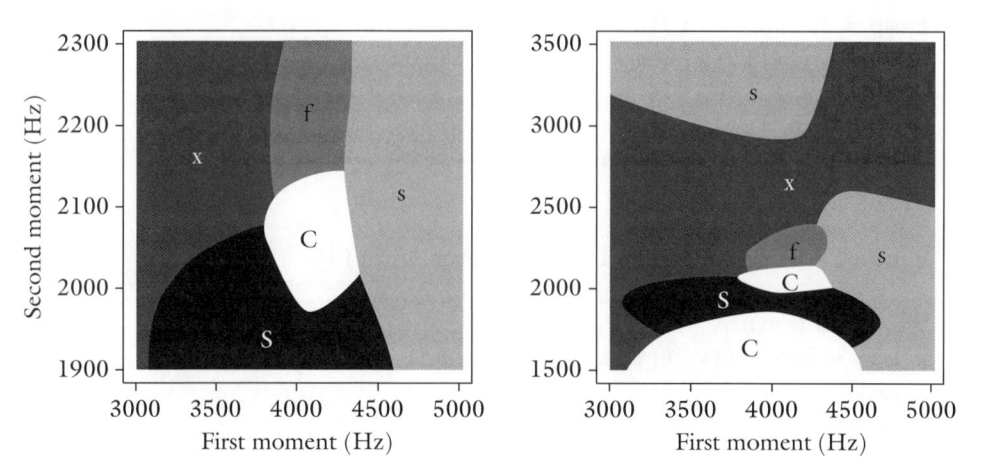

Figure 9.12 Classification plots on the first two spectral moments after training on the data in the left panel of Figure 9.11. The left and right panels of this figure differ only in the *y*-axis range over which the data points were calculated.

```
classplot(x.qda, xlim=c(3000, 5000), ylim=c(1900, 2300),
xlab="First moment (Hz)", ylab="Second moment (Hz)")
text(4065, 2060, "C", col="white"); text(3820, 1937, "S");
text(4650, 2115, "s"); text(4060, 2215, "f"); text(3380,
2160, "x")
```

It is evident from the left panel of Figure 9.12 that points around the edge of the region are classified (clockwise from top left) as [x, f, s, ʃ] with the region for the palatal fricative [ç] (the white space) squeezed in the middle. The right panel of Figure 9.12, which was produced in exactly the same way except with `ylim = c(1500, 3500)`, shows that these classifications do not necessarily give contiguous regions, especially for regions far away from the class centroids: as the right panel of Figure 9.12 shows, [ç] is split into two by [ʃ] while the territories for [s] are also non-contiguous and divided by [x]. The reason for this is to a large extent predictable from the orientation of the ellipses. Thus since, as the left panel of Figure 9.11 shows, the ellipse for [ç] has a near vertical orientation, then points below it will be probabilistically quite close to it. At the same time, there is an intermediate region at around $m_2 = 1,900$ Hz at which the points are nevertheless probabilistically closer to [ʃ], not just because they are nearer to the [ʃ]-centroid, but also because the orientation of the [ʃ] ellipse in the left panel of Figure 9.11 is much closer to horizontal. One of the important conclusions that emerges from Figures 9.10 and 9.11 is that it is not just the distance to the centroids that is important for classification (as it would be in a classification based on whichever Euclidean distance to the centroids was the least), but also the size and orientation of the ellipses, and therefore the probability distributions, that are established in the training stage of Gaussian classification.

As described earlier, a closed test involves training and testing on the same data and for this two-dimensional spectral moment-space, a confusion matrix and "hit-rate" for the male speaker's data are produced as follows:

```
# Train on the first two spectral moments, speaker 67
temp = fr.sp == "67"
x.qda = qda(fr.m[temp,1:2], fr.l[temp])

# Classify on the same data
x.pred = predict(x.qda)

# Equivalent to the above
x.pred = predict(x.qda, fr.m[temp,1:2])

# Confusion matrix
x.mat = table(fr.l[temp], x.pred$class)
x.mat
     C   S   f   s   x
 C  17   3   0   0   0
 S   3  17   0   0   0
 f   1   0  16   1   2
 s   0   0   0  20   0
 x   0   0   1   0  19
```

The confusion matrix could then be sorted on place of articulation as follows:

```
m = match(c("f", "s", "S", "C", "x"), colnames(x.mat))
x.mat[m,m]
x.l    f    s    S    C    x
  f   16    1    0    1    2
  s    0   20    0    0    0
  S    0    0   17    3    0
  C    0    0    3   17    0
  x    1    0    0    0   19
```

The correct classifications are in the diagonals and the misclassifications in the other cells. Thus 16 [f] tokens were correctly classified as /f/, one was misclassified as /s/, and so on. The hit-rate per class is obtained by dividing the scores in the diagonal by the total number of tokens in the same row:

```
diag(x.mat)/apply(x.mat, 1, sum)
   C      S      f      s      x
0.85   0.85   0.80   1.00   0.95
```

The total hit-rate across all categories is the sum of the scores in the diagonal divided by the total scores in the matrix:

```
sum(diag(x.mat))/sum(x.mat)
0.89
```

The above results show, then, that based on a Gaussian classification in the plane of the first two spectral moments at the temporal midpoint of fricatives, there is an 89 percent correct separation of the fricatives for the data shown in the left panel of Figure 9.11 and, compatibly with that same figure, the greatest confusion is between [ç] and [ʃ].

The score of 89 percent is encouragingly high and it is a completely accurate reflection of the way in which the data in the left panel of Figure 9.11 are distinguished after a bivariate normal distribution has been fitted to each class. At the same time, the scores obtained from a closed test of this kind can be, and often are, very misleading because of the risk of **over-fitting** the training model. When over-fitting occurs, which is more likely when training and testing are carried out in increasingly higher dimensional spaces, then the classification scores and separation may well be nearly perfect, but only for the data on which the model was trained. For example, rather than fitting the data with ellipses and bivariate normal distributions, we could imagine an algorithm which might draw wiggly lines around each of the classes in the left panel of Figure 9.11 and thereby achieve a considerably higher separation of perhaps nearer 99 percent. However, this type of classification would in all likelihood be entirely specific to this data, so that, if we tried to separate the fricatives in the right panel of Figure 9.11 using the same wiggly lines established in the training stage, then classification would almost certainly be much less accurate than from the Gaussian model considered so far: that is, over-fitting means that the classification model does not generalize beyond the data that it was trained on.

An open test, in which the training is carried out on the male data and classification on the female data in this example, can be obtained in an analogous way to the closed test considered earlier (the open test could be extended by subsequently training on the female data and testing on the male data and summing the scores across both classifications):

```
# Train on male data, test on female data
y.pred = predict(x.qda, fr.m[!temp,1:2])

# Confusion matrix
y.mat = table(fr.l[!temp], y.pred$class)
y.mat
    C  S  f  s  x
C  15  5  0  0  0
S  12  2  3  3  0
f   4  0 13  0  3
s   0  0  1 19  0
x   0  0  0  0 20

# Hit-rate per classification
diag(y.mat)/apply(y.mat, 1, sum)
   C    S    f    s    x
0.75 0.10 0.65 0.95 1.00

# Total hit-rate
sum(diag(y.mat))/sum(y.mat)
0.69
```

The total correct classification has now fallen by 20 percent compared with the closed test to 69 percent and the above confusion matrix reflects more accurately what we see in Figure 9.11: that the confusion between [ʃ] and [ç] in this two-dimensional spectral moment-space is really quite extensive.

9.7 Classifications in Higher Dimensional Spaces

The same mechanism can be used for carrying out Gaussian training and testing in higher dimensional spaces, even if spaces beyond three dimensions are impossible to visualize. However, as already indicated, there is an increasingly greater danger of over-fitting as the number of dimensions increases; therefore, if the dimensions do not contribute independently useful information to category separation, then the hit-rate in an open test is likely to go down. Consider as an illustration of this point the result of training and testing on all four spectral moments. This is done for the same data as above but, to save repeating the same instructions, the confusion matrix for a closed test is obtained for speaker 67 in one line as follows:

```
temp = fr.sp == "67"
table(fr.l[temp], predict(qda(fr.m[temp,], fr.l[temp]),
fr.m[temp,])$class)
    c  s  f  s  x
c  20  0  0  0  0
s   0 20  0  0  0
f   0  0 19  0  1
s   0  0     0  0
x   0  0  2  0 18
```

Here, then, there is an almost perfect separation between the categories, and the total hit-rate is 97 percent. The corresponding open test on this four-dimensional space in which, as before, training and testing are carried out on the male and female data respectively is given by the following command:

```
table(fr.l[!temp], predict(qda(fr.m[temp,], fr.l[temp]),
fr.m[!temp,])$class)
    c  s  f  s  x
c  17  0  0  3  0
s   7  7  1  1  4
f   3  0 11  0  6
s   0  0  0 20  0
x   0  0  1  0 19
```

Here the hit-rate is 74 percent, a more modest 5 percent increase on the two-dimensional space. It seems then that including m_3 and m_4 does provide only a very small amount of additional information for separating between these fricatives.

An inspection of the correlation coefficients between the four parameters can give some indication of why this is so. Here these are calculated across the male and female data together (see section 9.9. for a reminder of how the object **fr.m** was created):

```
round(cor(fr.m), 3)
        [,1]    [,2]    [,3]    [,4]
[1,]   1.000  -0.053  -0.978   0.416
[2,]  -0.053   1.000  -0.005  -0.717
[3,]  -0.978  -0.005   1.000  -0.429
[4,]   0.416  -0.717  -0.429   1.000
```

The correlation in the diagonals is always one because this is just the result of the parameter being correlated with itself. The off-diagonals show the correlations between different parameters. So the second column of row 1 shows that the correlation between the first and second moments is almost zero at − 0.053 (the result is necessarily duplicated in row 2, column 1, the correlation between the second moment and the first). In general, parameters are much more likely to contribute independently useful information to class separation if they are uncorrelated with each other. This is because correlation means predictability: if two parameters are highly correlated (positively or negatively), then one is more or less predictable from another. But, in this case, the second parameter is not really contributing any new information beyond the first and so will not improve class separation.

For this reason, the correlation matrix above shows that including both the first and third moments in the classification is hardly likely to increase class separation, given that the correlation between these parameters is almost complete (-0.978). This comes about for the reasons discussed in Chapter 8: as the first moment, or spectral center of gravity, shifts up and down the spectrum, then the spectrum becomes left- or right-skewed accordingly and, since m_3 is a measure of skew, m_1 and m_3 are likely to be highly correlated. There may be more value in including m_4, however, given that the correlation between m_1 and m_4 is moderate at 0.416; on the other hand, m_2 and m_4 for this data are quite strongly negatively correlated at -0.717, so perhaps not much more is to be gained as far as class separation is concerned beyond classifications from the first two moments. Nevertheless, it is worth investigating whether classifications from m_1, m_2, and m_4 give a better hit-rate in an open test than from m_1 and m_2 alone:

```
# Train on male data, test on female data in a 3D space formed from m_1, m_2,
and m_4
temp = fr.sp == "67"
res = table(fr.l[!temp], predict(qda(fr.m[temp,-3],
fr.l[temp]), fr.m[!temp,-3])$class)

# Class hit-rate
diag(res)/apply(res, 1, sum)
   C    S    f    s    x
0.95 0.40 0.75 1.00 1.00

# Overall hit-rate
sum(diag(res))/sum(res)
0.82
```

In fact, including m_4 does make a difference: the open-test hit-rate is 82 percent, compared with 69 percent obtained from the open-test classification with m_1 and m_2 alone. But the result is also interesting from the perspective of over-fitting raised earlier: notice that this open-test score from three moments is higher than from all four moments together, which shows not only that there is redundant information as far as class separation is concerned in the four-parameter space, but also that the inclusion of this redundant information leads to an over-fit and therefore a poorer generalization to new data.

The technique of **principal components analysis** (PCA) can sometimes be used to remove the redundancies that arise through parameters being correlated with each other. In PCA, a new set of dimensions is obtained such that they are orthogonal to, or uncorrelated with, each other and also such that the lower dimensions "explain" or account for most of the variance in the data (see Figures 9.9 and 9.10 for a graphical interpretation of "explanation of the variance"). The new rotated dimensions derived from PCA are weighted linear combinations of the old ones and the weights are known as the *eigenvectors*. The relationship between original dimensions, rotated dimensions, and eigenvectors can be demonstrated by applying PCA to the spectral moments data from the male speaker using **prcomp()**. Before applying PCA, the data should be converted to z-scores by subtracting the mean (which is achieved with the default argument **center=T**) and by dividing by the standard deviation[5] (the argument **scale=T** needs to be set). Thus, to apply PCA to the male speaker's spectral-moment data:

```
temp = fr.sp == "67"
p = prcomp(fr.m[temp,], scale=T)
```

The eigenvectors or weights that are used to transform the original data are stored in **p$rotation**, which is a 4×4 matrix (because there were four original dimensions to which PCA was applied). The rotated data points themselves are stored in **p$x** and there is the same number of dimensions (four) as those in the original data to which PCA was applied.

The first new rotated dimension is obtained by multiplying the weights in column 1 of **p$rotation** with the original data and then summing the result (and it is in this sense that the new PCA dimensions are weighted linear combinations of the original ones). In order to demonstrate this, we first have to carry out the same z-score transformation that was applied by PCA to the original data:

```
# Function to carry out z-score normalization
zscore = function(x)(x-mean(x))/sd(x)

# z-score normalized data
xn = apply(fr.m[temp,], 2, zscore)
```

The value on the rotated first dimension for, say, the fifth segment is stored in **p$x[5,1]** and is equivalently given by a weighted sum of the original values, thus:

```
sum(xn[5,] * p$rotation[,1])
```

The multiplications and summations for the entire data are more simply derived with matrix multiplication using the **%*%** operator.[6] Thus the rotated data in **p$x** is equivalently given by:

```
xn %*% p$rotation
```

The fact that the new rotated dimensions are uncorrelated with each other is evident by applying the correlation function, as before:

```
round(cor(p$x), 8)
      PC1 PC2 PC3 PC4
PC1   1   0   0   0
PC2   0   1   0   0
PC3   0   0   1   0
PC4   0   0   0   1
```

The importance of the rotated dimensions as far as explaining the variance is concerned is given by either **plot(p)** or **summary(p)**. The latter returns the following:

```
Importance of components:
                          PC1     PC2     PC3      PC4
Standard deviation       1.455   1.290   0.4582   0.09236
Proportion of variance   0.529   0.416   0.0525   0.00213
Cumulative proportion    0.529   0.945   0.9979   1.00000
```

The second line shows the proportion of the total variance in the data that is explained by each rotated dimension, and the third line adds this up cumulatively from lower to higher rotated dimensions. Thus, 52.9 percent of the variance is explained alone by the first rotated dimension, PC1, and, as the last line shows, just about all the variance (99 percent) is explained by the first three rotated dimensions. This result simply confirms what had been established earlier: that there is redundant information in all four dimensions as far as separating the points in this moment-space are concerned.

Rather than pursue this example further, we will explore a much higher dimensional space that is obtained from summed energy values in Bark bands calculated over the same fricative data. The following commands make use of some of the techniques from Chapter 8 to derive the Bark parameters. Here, a filter-bank approach is used in which energy in the spectrum is summed in widths of 1 Bark with center frequencies extending from 2 to 20 Bark: that is, the first parameter contains summed energy over the frequency range 1.5–2.5 Bark, the next parameter over the frequency range 2.5–3.5 Bark, and so on up to the last parameter that has energy from 19.5–20.5 Bark. As **bark(c(1.5, 20.5), inv=T)** shows, this covers the spectral range from 161 to 7,131 Hz (and reduces it to 19 values). The conversion from Hz to Bark is straightforward:

```
fr.bark5 = bark(fr.dft5)
```

and, for a given integer value of **j**, the following line is at the core of deriving summed energy values in Bark bands:

```
fapply(fr.bark5[,(j-0.5):(j+0.5)], sum, power=T)
```

So when, e.g., **j** is 5, then the above has the effect of summing the energy in the spectrum between 4.5 and 5.5 Bark. This line is put inside a for-loop in order to extract energy values in Bark bands over the spectral range of interest and the results are stored in the matrix **fr.bs5**:

```
fr.bs5 = NULL
for(j in 2:20){
   sumvals = fapply(fr.bark5[,(j-0.5):(j+0.5)], sum,
   power=T)
   fr.bs5 = cbind(fr.bs5, sumvals)
}
colnames(fr.bs5) = paste("Bark", 2:20)
```

fr.bs5 is now a matrix with the same number of rows as in the original spectral matrix **fr.dft** and with 19 columns (so, whereas for the spectral-moment data, each fricative was represented by a point in a four-dimensional space, for these data, each fricative is a point in a 19-dimensional space).

We could now carry out a Gaussian classification over this 19-dimensional space as before although this is hardly advisable, given that this would almost certainly produce extreme over-fitting for the reasons discussed earlier. The alternative solution, then, is to use PCA to compress much of the non-redundant information into a smaller number of dimensions. However, in order to maintain the distinction between training and testing – that is, between the data of the male and female speakers in these examples – PCA really should not be applied across the entire data in one go. This is because a rotation matrix (eigenvectors) would be derived based on the training and testing set *together* and, as a result, the training and testing data are not strictly separated. Thus, in order to maintain the strict separation between training and testing sets, PCA will be applied to the male speaker's data; subsequently, the rotation matrix that is derived from PCA will be used to rotate the data for the female speaker. The latter operation can be accomplished simply with the generic function **predict()**, which will have the effect of applying *z*-score normalization to the data from the female speaker. This operation is accomplished by subtracting the *male* speaker's means and dividing by the male speaker's standard deviations (because this is how the male speaker's data was transformed before PCA was applied):

```
# Separate out the male's and female's Bark data
temp = fr.sp == "67"

# Apply PCA to the male speaker's z-normalized data
xb.pca = prcomp(fr.bs5[temp,], scale=T)

# Rotate the female speaker's data using the eigenvectors and z-score
# Parameters from the male speaker
yb.pca = predict(xb.pca, fr.bs5[!temp,])
```

Before carrying out any classifications, the **summary()** function is used as before to get an overview of the extent to which the variance in the data is explained by the rotated dimensions (the results are shown here for just the first eight dimensions, and the scores are rounded to three decimal places):

```
sum.pca = summary(xb.pca)
round(sum.pca$im[,1:8], 3)
                        PC1   PC2   PC3   PC4   PC5   PC6   PC7   PC8
Standard deviation    3.035 2.110 1.250 1.001 0.799 0.759 0.593 0.560
Proportion of variance 0.485 0.234 0.082 0.053 0.034 0.030 0.019 0.016
Cumulative proportion  0.485 0.719 0.801 0.854 0.887 0.918 0.936 0.953
```

Thus, 48.5 percent of the variance is explained by the first rotated dimension, PC1, alone, and just over 95 percent by the first eight dimensions: this result suggests

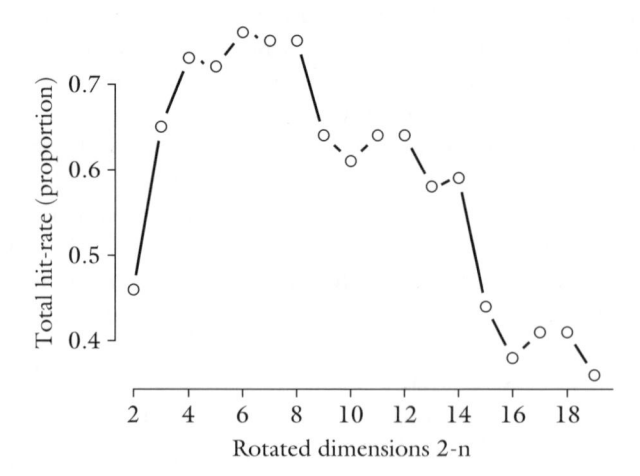

Figure 9.13 Hit-rate in classifying fricative place of articulation using an increasing number of dimensions derived from principal components analysis applied to summed energy values in Bark bands. The scores are based on testing on data from a female speaker after training on corresponding data from a male speaker.

that higher dimensions are going to be of little consequence as far as distinguishing between the fricatives is concerned.

We can test this by carrying out an open-test Gaussian classification on any number of rotated dimensions using the same functions that were applied to spectral moments. For example, the total hit-rate (of 76 percent) from training and testing on the first six dimensions of the rotated space is obtained from:

```
# Train on the male speaker's data
n = 6
xb.qda = qda(xb.pca$x[,1:n], fr.1[temp])

# Test on the female speaker's data
yb.pred = predict(xb.qda, yb.pca[,1:n])
z = table(fr.1[!temp], yb.pred$class)
sum(diag(z))/sum(z)
```

Figure 9.13 shows the total hit-rate when training and testing were carried out successively on the first 2, first 3 . . . all 19 dimensions, and it was produced by putting the above lines inside a for-loop, thus:

```
scores = NULL
for(j in 2:19){
   xb.qda = qda(xb.pca$x[,1:j], fr.1[temp])
   yb.pred = predict(xb.qda, yb.pca[,1:j])
   z = table(fr.1[!temp], yb.pred$class)
   scores = c(scores, sum(diag(z))/sum(z))
}
```

```
plot(2:19, scores, type="b", xlab="Rotated dimensions 2-n",
ylab="Total hit-rate (proportion)")
```

Apart from providing another very clear demonstration of the damaging effects of over-fitting, the total hit-rate, which peaks when training and testing are carried out on the first six rotated dimensions, reflects precisely what was suggested by examining the proportion of variance examined earlier: that there is no more useful information for distinguishing between the data points and therefore fricative categories beyond this number of dimensions.

9.8 Classifications in Time

All of the above classifications so far have been static, because they have been based on information at a single point in time. For fricative noise spectra this may be appropriate under the assumption that the spectral shape of the fricative during the noise does not change appreciably in time between its onset and offset. However, a static classification from a single time slice would obviously not be appropriate for the distinction between monophthongs and diphthongs, nor perhaps for differentiating the place of articulation from the burst of oral stops, given that there may be dynamic information that is important for their distinction (Kewley-Port 1982; Lahiri et al. 1984). An example of how dynamic information can be parameterized and then classified is worked through in the next sections using a corpus of oral stops produced in initial position in German trochaic words.

It will be convenient, by way of an introduction to the next section, to relate the time-based spectral classifications of consonants with vowel formants, discussed briefly in Chapter 6 (e.g., Figure 6.21). Consider a vowel of duration 100 ms with 20 first formant frequency values at intervals of 5 ms between the vowel onset and offset. As described in Chapter 6, the entire F1 time-varying trajectory can be reduced to just three values either by fitting a polynomial or by using the discrete cosine transformation (DCT): in either case, the three resulting values express the mean, the slope, and the curvature of F1 as a function of time. The same can be done to the other two time-varying formants, F2 and F3. Thus, after applying the DCT to each formant number separately, a 100 ms vowel, parameterized in raw form by triplets of F1–F3 every 5 ms (60 values in total) is converted to a single point in a nine-dimensional space.

The corresponding data reduction of spectra is the same, but it needs one additional step that *precedes* this compression in time. Suppose an /s/ is of duration 100 ms and there is a spectral slice every 5 ms (thus 20 spectra between the onset and offset of the /s/). We can use the DCT in the manner discussed in Chapter 8 to compress each spectrum, consisting originally of perhaps 129 dB-values (for a 256-point DFT) to three values. As a result of this operation, each spectrum is represented by three DCT or cepstral (see 8.4) coefficients which can be denoted by k_0, k_1, k_2. It will now be helpful to think of k_0, k_1, k_2 as analogous to F1–F3 in the case of the vowel. Under this interpretation, /s/ is parameterized by a triplet of DCT coefficients every 5 ms in the same way that the vowel in raw form is parameterized by a triplet of formants every 5 ms. Thus there is time-varying k_0, time-varying k_1, and time-varying k_2 between the onset and offset of /s/ in the same way as there is time-varying F1, time-varying F2, and time-varying F3 between the onset and offset of the vowel. The final step involves applying the DCT to compress separately each such time-varying parameter to three values, as summarized in the preceding paragraph: thus, after this second transformation, k_0 as a function of time will be compressed to three values, in the same way that F1 as a function of time is reduced to three values. The same applies to time-varying k_1 and to time-varying k_2, which are also each compressed to three values after the separate application of the DCT. Thus a 100 ms /s/, which is initially parameterized as 129 dB-values per spectrum that occur every 5 ms (i.e., 2,580 values in total since for 100 ms there are 20 spectral slices), is also reduced after these transformations to a single point in a nine-dimensional space. These issues are now further illustrated in the next section using the **stops** data set.

9.8.1 Parameterizing dynamic spectral information

The corpus fragment for the analysis of dynamic spectral information includes a word-initial stop, C = /b, d, g/ followed by a tense vowel or diphthong V = /a:, au, e:, i:, o:, ø:, oɪ, u:/ in meaningful German words such as *baten, Bauten, beten, bieten, boten, böten, Beute, Buden*. The data were recorded as part of a seminar in 2003 at the IPDS, University of Kiel, from three male and four female speakers (one of the female speakers only produced the words once or twice rather than three times, which is why the total number of stops is 470 rather than the expected 504 from 3 stops × 8 vowels × 7 speakers × 3 repetitions). The sampled speech data were digitized at 16 kHz and spectral sections were calculated from a 512-point (32 ms) DFT at intervals of 2 ms. The utterances of the downloadable **stops** database were segmented into a closure, a burst extending from the stop-release to the periodic vowel onset, and the following vowel (between its periodic onset and offset). The objects from this database in the Emu-R library include the stop burst only (which across all speakers has a mean duration of just over 22 ms):

stops	Segment list of the stop burst
stops.l	A vector of stops labels for the above
stopsvow.l	A vector of labels of the following vowel context
stops.sp	A vector of labels for the speaker
stops.dft	Trackdata object of spectral data between the onset and offset of the burst
stops.bark	Trackdata object as **stops.dft** but with the frequency axis converted into Bark
stops.dct	Trackdata object of the lowest three DCT coefficients derived from **stops.bark**

The procedure that will be used here for parameterizing spectral information draws upon the techniques discussed in Chapter 8. There are three main steps, outlined below, which together have the effect of compressing the entire burst spectrum, initially represented by spectral slices at 2 ms intervals, to a single point in a nine-dimensional space, as described above.

1. *Bark-scaled, DFT spectra (**stops.bark**)*. The frequency axis is warped from the physical hertz to the auditory Bark scale in the frequency range 200–7,800 Hz (this range is selected both to discount information below 200 Hz that is unlikely to be useful for the acoustic distinction between stop place of articulation and to remove frequency information near the Nyquist frequency that may be unreliable).
2. *Bark-scaled DCT coefficients (**stops.dct**)*. A DCT transformation is applied to the output of step 1 in order to obtain Bark-scaled DCT (cepstral) coefficients. Only the first three coefficients are calculated, i.e., k_0, k_1, k_2, which, as explained in Chapter 8, are proportional to the spectrum's mean, linear slope, and curvature. These three parameters are obtained for each spectral slice resulting in three trajectories between the burst onset and offset, each supported by data points at 2 ms intervals.
3. *Polynomial fitting*. Following step 2, the equivalent of a second-order polynomial is fitted again using the DCT to each of the three trajectories thereby reducing each trajectory to just three values (the coefficients of the polynomial).

Steps 1–3 are now worked through in some more detail using a single stop-burst token for a /d/ beginning with a perspective plot showing how its spectrum changes in time over the extent of the burst using the **persp()** function. Figure 9.14(a), which shows the raw spectrum in Hz, was created as follows. There are a couple of fiddly issues in this type of plot to do with arranging the display so that the burst onset is at the front and the vowel onset at the back; this requires changing the time axis so that increasing negative values are closer to the vowel onset and reversing the row order of the dB-spectra. The arguments **theta** and **phi** in the **persp()** function define the viewing direction.[7]

```
# Get the spectral data between the burst onset and offset for the second stop
from 200 to 7,800 Hz
d.dft = stops.dft[2,200:7800]

# Rearrange the time axis
times = tracktimes(d.dft) - max(tracktimes(d.dft))

# These are the frequencies of the spectral slices
freqs = trackfreq(d.dft)

# These are the dB-values at those times (rows) and frequencies (columns)
dbvals = frames(d.dft)
par(mfrow=c(2,2)); par(mar=rep(.75, 4))
persp(times, freqs, dbvals[nrow(dbvals):1,], theta = 120,
phi = 25, col="lightblue", expand=.75, ticktype="detailed",
main="(a)",xlab="Time (ms)", ylab="Frequency (Hz)", zlab="dB")
```

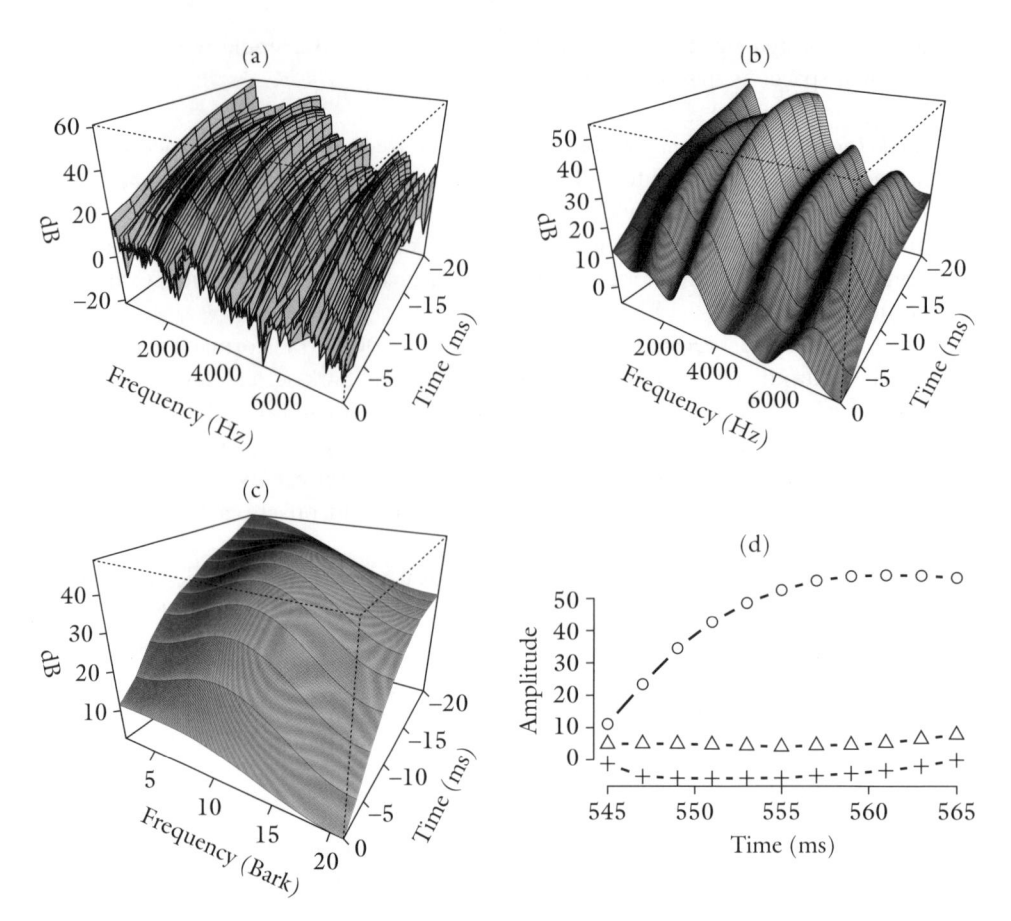

Figure 9.14 (a) spectra at 5 ms intervals of the burst of an initial /d/ between the stop's release ($t = 0$ ms) and the acoustic vowel onset ($t = -20$ ms); (b) the same as (a) but smoothed using 11 DCT coefficients; (c) as (a) but with the frequency axis proportional to the Bark-scale and smoothed using three DCT coefficients; (d) the values of the DCT coefficients from which the spectra in (c) are derived between the burst onset ($t = 545$ ms, corresponding to $t = 0$ ms in the other panels) and acoustic vowel onset ($t = 565$ ms corresponding to t $= -20$ ms in the other panels). k_0, k_1, and k_2 are shown by circles, triangles, and crosses respectively.

Figure 9.14(a) shows that the overall level of the spectrum increases from the burst onset at $t = 0$ ms (the front of the display) towards the vowel onset at $t = -20$ ms (which is to be expected, given that the burst follows the near acoustic silence of the closure) and there are clearly some spectral peaks, although it is not easy to see where these are. However, the delineation of the peaks and troughs can be brought out much more effectively by smoothing the spectra with the discrete cosine transformation in the manner described in Chapter 8 (see Figure 8.22, right panel) to obtain DCT-smoothed Hz-spectra. The corresponding spectral plot is shown in Figure 9.14(b). This was smoothed with the first 11 DCT coefficients, thereby retaining a fair amount of detail in the spectrum:

```
d.sm = fapply(d.dft, dct, 10, T)
persp(times, freqs, frames(d.sm)[nrow(dbvals):1,],
theta = 120, phi = 25, col="lightblue", expand=.75,
ticktype="detailed", main=" (b)",xlab="Time (ms)",
ylab="Frequency (Hz)", zlab="dB")
```

The smoothed display in Figure 9.14(b) shows more clearly that there are approximately four peaks and an especially prominent one at around 2.5 kHz.

Steps 1 and 2, outlined earlier (9.8.1), additionally involve warping the frequency axis to the Bark scale and calculating only the first three DCT coefficients. The commands for this are:

```
d.bark = bark(d.dft)
d.dct = fapply(d.bark, dct, 2)
```

d.dct contains the Bark-scaled DCT coefficients (analogous to MFCC, Mel-frequency cepstral coefficients in the speech technology literature). Also, there are three coefficients per time slice (which is why **frames(d.dct)** is a matrix of 11 rows and 3 columns), which define the shape of the spectrum at that point in time. The corresponding DCT-smoothed spectrum is calculated in the same way, but with the additional argument to the **dct()** function **fit=T**. This becomes one of the arguments appended after **dct**, as described in Chapter 8:

```
# DCT-smoothed spectra (one per time slice)
d.dctf = fapply(d.bark, dct, 2, fit=T)
```

d.dctf is a spectral trackdata object containing spectral slices at intervals of 5 ms. Each spectral slice will, of course, be very smooth indeed (because of the small number of coefficients). In Figure 9.14(c) these spectra, smoothed with just three DCT coefficients, are arranged in the same kind of perspective plot:

```
freqs = trackfreq(d.dctf)
persp(times, freqs, frames(d.dctf)[nrow(dbvals):1,],
theta = 120, phi = 25, col="lightblue", expand=.75,
ticktype="detailed", main=" (c)",xlab="Time (ms)",
ylab="Frequency (Hz)", zlab="dB")
```

The shape of the perspective spectral plot is now more like a billowing sheet and the reader may wonder whether we have not smoothed away all of the salient information in the /d/ spectra! However, the analogous representation of the corresponding Bark-scaled coefficients as a function of time in Figure 9.14(d) shows that even this radically smoothed spectral representation retains a fair amount of dynamic information. (Moreover, the actual values of these trajectories may be enough to separate out the three separate places of articulation). Since **d.dct** (derived from the commands above) is a trackdata object, it can be plotted with the generic **plot()** function. The result of this is shown in Figure 9.14(d) and given by the following command:

```
plot(d.dct, type="b", lty=1:3, col=rep(1, 3), lwd=2, main =
"(d)", ylab="Amplitude", xlab="Time (ms)")
```

It should be noted at this point that, as far as classification is concerned, the bottom two panels of Figure 9.14 contain *equivalent information* – that is, they are just two ways of looking at the same phenomenon. In the time-series plot, the three Bark-scaled DCT coefficients are displayed as a function of time. In the 3D-perspective plot, each of these three numbers is expanded into its own spectrum. It looks as if the spectrum contains more information, but it does not. In the time-series plot, the three numbers at each time point are the amplitudes of cosine waves at frequencies 0, 0.5, and 1 cycles. In the 3D-perspective plot, the three cosine waves at these amplitudes are unwrapped over 256 points and then summed at equal frequencies. Since the shapes of these cosine waves are entirely predictable from the amplitudes (because the frequencies are known and the phase is zero in all cases), there is no more information in the 3D-perspective plot than in plotting the amplitudes of the half-cycle cosine waves (i.e., the DCT coefficients) as a function of time.

We have now arrived at the end of step 2 outlined earlier. Before proceeding to the next step, which is yet another compression and transformation of the data in Figure 9.14(d), here is a brief recap of the information that is contained in the trajectories in Figure 9.14(d).

k_0 (the DCT coefficient at a frequency of $k = 0$ cycles) encodes the average level in the spectrum. Thus, since k_0 (the top track whose points are marked with circles in Figure 9.14(d)) rises as a function of time, then the mean dB-level of the spectrum from one spectral slice to the next must also be rising. This is evident from any of Figures 9.14(a, b, c), which all show that the spectra have progressively increasing values on the dB-axis in progressing in time towards the vowel (compare in particular the last spectrum at time $t = -20$ ms with the first at the burst onset). The correspondence between k_0 and the spectral mean can also be verified numerically:

```
# Calculate the mean dB-value per spectral slice across all frequencies
m = fapply(d.bark, mean)

# This shows a perfect correlation between the mean dB and k₀
cor(frames(m), frames(d.dct[,1]))
1
```

k_1, which is the middle track in Figure 9.14(d), encodes the spectral tilt, i.e., the linear slope calculated with dB on the *y*-axis and Hz (or Bark) on the *x*-axis in the manner of Figure 8.13 of Chapter 8. Figure 9.14(d) suggests that there is not much change in the spectral slope as a function of time and also that the slope is negative (positive values on k_1 denote a falling slope). The fact that the spectrum is tilted downwards with increasing frequency is evident from any of the displays in Figure 9.14(a, b, c). The association between k_1 and the linear slope can be demonstrated in the manner presented in Chapter 8 by showing that they are strongly negatively correlated with each other:

```
# Function to calculate the linear slope of a spectrum
slope <- function(x)
{
   lm(x ~ trackfreq(x))$coeff[2]
}
specslope = fapply(d.bark, slope)
cor(frames(specslope), frames(d.dct[,2]))
-0.991261
```

Finally, k_2, which is the bottom track in Figure 9.14(d), shows the spectral curvature as a function of time. If each spectral slice could be modeled entirely by a straight line, then the values on this parameter would be zero. Evidently they are not and, since these values are negative, then the spectra should be broadly ∩-shaped, and this is most apparent in the heavily smoothed spectrum in Figure 9.14(c). Once again it is possible to show that k_2 is related to curvature by calculating a second-order polynomial regression on each spectral slice, i.e., by fitting a function to each spectral slice of the form:

(4) $\quad \text{dB} = a_0 + a_1 f + a_2 f^2$

The second coefficient of (4), a_2, defines the curvature and, the closer it is to zero, the less curved the trajectory. Fitting a second-order polynomial to each spectral slice can be accomplished in an analogous manner to obtaining the linear slope above. Once again, the correlation between k_2 and curvature is very high:

```
# Function to apply second-order polynomial regression to a spectrum – only
a₂ is stored
regpoly <- function(x)
{
   lm(x ~ trackfreq(x) + I(trackfreq(x)^2))$coeff[3]
}

# Apply this function to all 11 spectral slices
speccurve = fapply(d.bark, regpoly)

# Demonstrate the correlation with k₂
cor(frames(speccurve), frames(d.dct[,3]))
0.9984751
```

So far, then, the spectral slices as a function of time have been reduced to three tracks that encode the spectral mean, linear slope, and curvature also as a function of time. In step 3 outlined earlier, this information is compressed further still by applying the discrete cosine transformation once more to each track in Figure 9.14(d). In the command below, this transformation is applied to k_0:

```
trapply(d.dct[,1], dct, 2, simplify=T)
63.85595  -18.59999  -9.272398
```

So, following the earlier discussion, k_0 as a function of time must have a positive linear slope (because the middle coefficient, −18.6, that defines the linear slope, is negative). It must also be curved (because the last coefficient that defines the curvature is not zero) and it must also be ∩-shaped (because the last coefficient is negative): indeed, this is what we see in looking at the overall shape of k_0 as a function of time in Figure 9.14(d).[8]

The same operation can be applied separately to the other two tracks in Figure 9.14(d), so that we end up with nine values. Thus the time-varying spectral burst of /d/ has now been reduced to a point in a nine-dimensional space (a considerable compression from the original 11 times slices × 257 DFT = 2,827 dB-values). To be sure, the dimensions are now necessarily fairly abstract, but they do still have an interpretation: they are the mean, linear slope, and curvature each calculated on the spectral mean (k_0), spectral tilt (k_1), and spectral curvature (k_2) as a function of time.

This nine-dimensional representation is now derived for all the stops in this mini-database with the commands below and it is stored in a 470 × 9 matrix (470 rows because there are 470 segments). You can leave out the first step (in calculating **stops.dct**) because this object is in the Emu-R library (and can take a few minutes to calculate, depending on the power of your computer):

```
# Calculate k0, k1, k2, the first three Bark-scaled DCT coefficients (this object is
available)
# stops.dct = fapply(stops.bark, dct, 2)

# Reduce k0, k1, and k2, each to three values
dct0coefs = trapply(stops.dct[,1], dct, 2, simplify=T)
dct1coefs = trapply(stops.dct[,2], dct, 2, simplify=T)
dct2coefs = trapply(stops.dct[,3], dct, 2, simplify=T)

# Put them into a data frame after giving the matrix some column names
d = cbind(dct0coefs, dct1coefs, dct2coefs)
n = c("a0", "a1", "a2")
m = c(paste("k0", n, sep="."), paste("k1", n, sep="."),
paste("k2", n, sep="."))
colnames(d) = m

# Add the stop labels as a factor
bdg = data.frame(d, phonetic=factor(stops.l))
```

We are now ready to classify.

9.9 Support Vector Machines

Or are we? One of the real difficulties in classifying velar stops is that they are highly context-dependent, i.e., the place of articulation with which /k, g/ are produced shifts with the frontness of the vowel, often ranging from a palatal, or post-palatal,

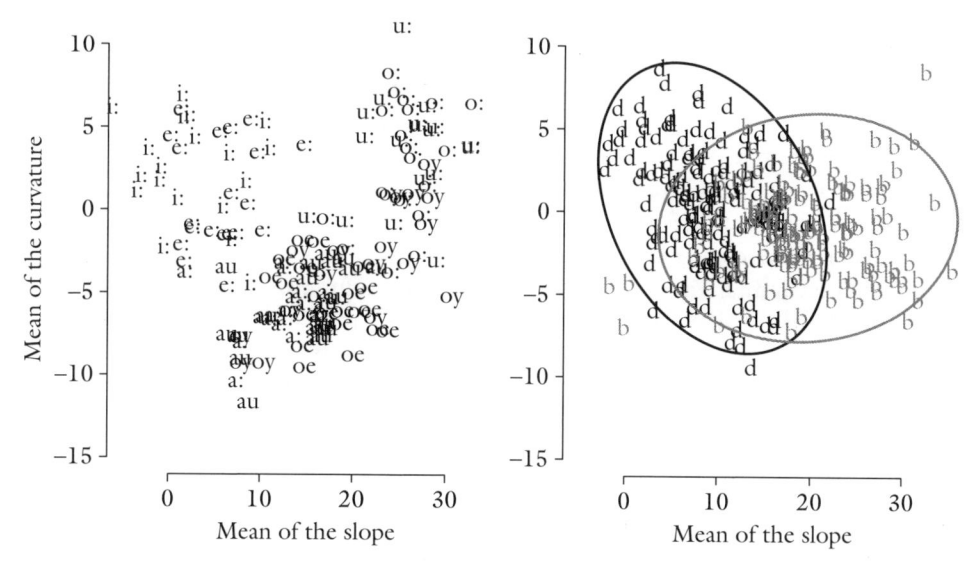

Figure 9.15 Left: distribution of /g/ bursts from seven speakers on two dynamic DCT parameters showing the label of the following vowel. Right: 95% confidence ellipses for /b, d/ on the same parameters.

articulation before front vowels like /i/ to a post-velar production before /u/. Moreover, as theoretical models of articulatory-acoustic relationships show, this shift has a marked effect on the acoustic signal, such that the front and back velar allophones can be acoustically more similar to alveolar and labial stops (e.g., Halle et al. 1957) respectively rather than to each other.

This wide allophonic variation of /g/ becomes evident in inspecting them on two of the previously calculated parameters. In Figure 9.15, the display on the left shows the distribution of /g/ in the plane of parameters 4 and 7 as a function of the following vowel context. On the right are ellipse plots of the other two stops on the same parameters. The plot was created as follows:

```
par(mfrow=c(1,2)); xlim = c(-5, 35); ylim = c(-15, 10)
temp = stops.l=="g"; xlab="Mean of the slope"; ylab="Mean of
the curvature"
plot(d[temp,c(4, 7)], type="n", xlab=xlab, ylab=ylab,
bty="n", xlim=xlim, ylim=ylim)
text(d[temp,4], d[temp,7], stopsvow.l[temp])
eplot(d[!temp,c(4,7)], stops.l[!temp], col=c("black",
"slategray"), dopoints=T, xlab=xlab, ylab="", xlim=xlim,
ylim=ylim)
```

It is evident from the right panel of Figure 9.15 that, although /b, d/ are likely to be quite well separated on these two parameters in a classification model, the distribution for /g/ shown in the left panel of the same figure is more or less determined by the vowel context (and follows the distribution in the familiar F2 × F1 vowel formant plane). Moreover, fitting a Gaussian model to these /g/ data is likely to be inappropriate for at least two reasons. Firstly, they are not normally distributed: they do not cluster around a mean and they are not distributed along a principal component in the way that /b, d/ are. Secondly, the mean of /g/ falls pretty much in the same region as the means of /b, d/ in the right panel of Figure 9.15. Thus the ellipse for /g/ would encompass almost all of /b, d/, perhaps resulting in a large number of misclassifications. Given that a Gaussian distribution may be inappropriate for these data, we will consider another way of classifying the data using a **support vector machine** (SVM) that makes no assumptions about normality.

The development of SVMs can be traced back to the late 1970s, but in recent years they have been used for a variety of classification problems, including the recognition of handwriting, digits, speakers, and faces (Burges 1998) and they have also been used in automatic speech recognition (Ganapathiraju et al. 2004). The following provides a very brief and non-technical overview of SVMs – for more mathematical details, see Duda et al. (2001).

Consider firstly the distribution of two classes, the filled and open circles, in a two-parameter space in Figure 9.16. It is evident that the two classes could be separated by drawing a line between them. In fact, as the left panel shows, there is not just one line but an infinite number of lines that could be used to separate them. But is there any principled way of choosing the line that *optimally* separates these categories? In SVM this optimal line is defined in terms of finding the widest so-called **margin** of parallel lines that can be created before hitting a data point from either class, as shown in the right panel of Figure 9.16. These data points through which the margin passes are called the **support vectors**.

The right panel in Figure 9.16 is a schematic example of a *linear* SVM classifier in which the categories are separated by a straight line. But there will, of course, be many instances in which this type of linear separation cannot be made. For example, it is not possible to separate linearly the two categories displayed in one dimension

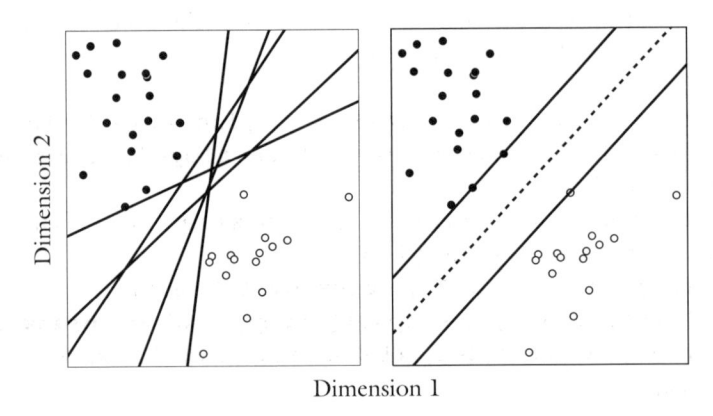

Figure 9.16 Left: two classes on two dimensions and the various straight lines that could be drawn to separate them completely. Right: the same data separated by the widest margin of parallel lines that can be drawn between the classes. The solid lines are the support vectors and pass through extreme data points of the two classes. The dotted line is equidistant between the support vectors and is sometimes called the optimal hyperplane.

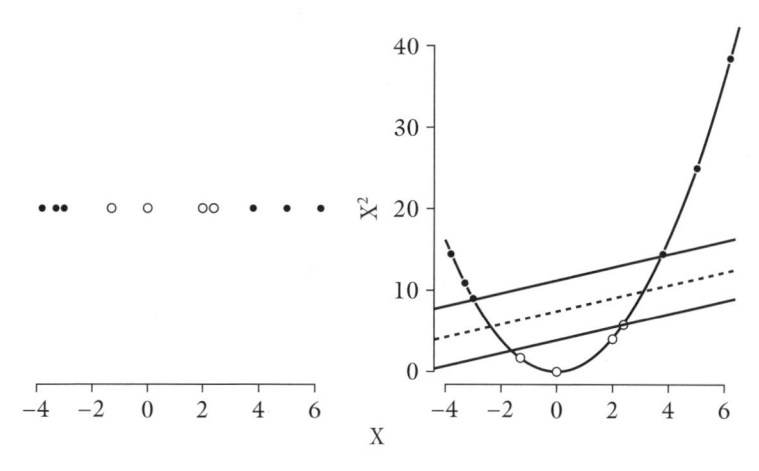

Figure 9.17 Left: the position of values from two classes in one dimension. Right: the same data projected into a two-dimensional space and separated by a margin.

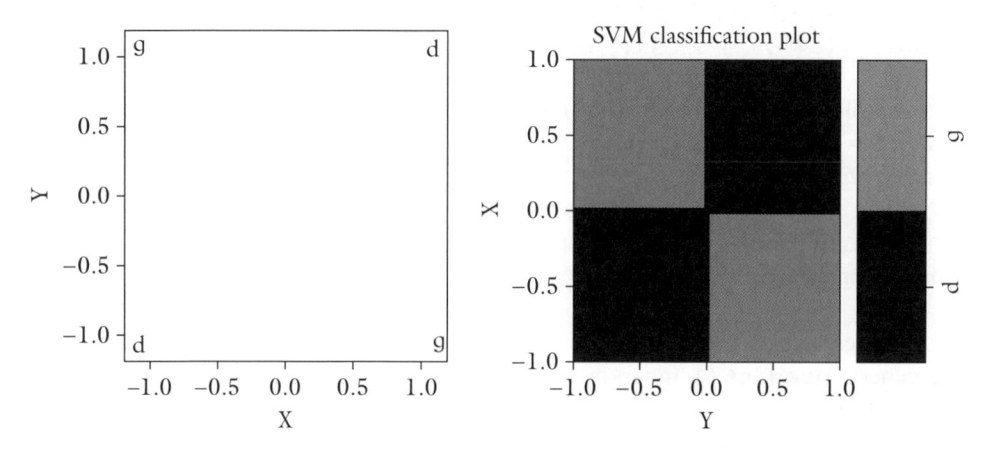

Figure 9.18 Left: A hypothetical exclusive-OR distribution of /b, d/ in which there are two data points per class and at opposite edges of the plane. Right: the resulting classification plot for this space after training these four data points using a support vector machine.

in the left panel of Figure 9.17, nor can any single line be drawn to categorize the exclusive-OR example in the left panel of Figure 9.18 in which the points from the two categories are in opposite corners of the plane. Now it can be shown (see e.g., Duda et al. 2001) that two categories can be separated by applying a *non-linear* transformation that projects the points into a higher dimensional space. The function that does this mapping to the higher dimensional space is called the **kernel**: although there are many different kinds of kernel functions that could be used for this purpose, a few have been found to work especially well as far as category separation is concerned, including the **radial basis function** which is a type of Gaussian transformation (and the default kernel for **svm()** in **library(e1071)** in R). This is also the same as the sigmoid kernel that is used in feedforward neural networks.

A schematic example, taken from Moore (2003), of how projection into a higher dimensional space enables classes to be separated using the same sort of margin as in Figure 9.16 is shown for the data in Figure 9.17. As already stated, it is not possible to separate completely the classes on the left in Figure 9.17 with a straight line. However, when these data are projected into a two-dimensional space by applying a second-order polynomial transformation, $x \rightarrow x^2$, or informally by plotting the squared values as a function of the original values, then the two classes can be separated by the same kind of wide margin as considered earlier.

For the X-OR data in the left panel of Figure 9.18, the separation with a margin can be made by applying a kernel function to transform the data to a six-dimensional space (Duda et al. 2001). It is of course not possible to draw this in the same way as for Figure 9.17, but it is possible to make a classification plot to show how **svm()** classifies the regions in the vicinity of these points. This is shown in the right panel of Figure 9.18. In order to create this plot, the first step is to train the data as follows:[9]

```
# The four points and their hypothetical labels
x = c(-1, -1, 1, 1); y = c(-1, 1, -1, 1)
lab = c("d", "g", "g", "d")

# Bundle all of this into a data frame and attach the data frame
d.df = data.frame(phonetic=factor(lab), X=x, Y=y)
attach(d.df)

# Train the labels on these four points
m = svm(phonetic ~ X+Y)
```

A closed test (i.e., a classification of these four points) can then be carried out using the generic **predict()** function in the same way as was done with the Gaussian classification:

```
predict(m)
1 2 3 4
d g g d
Levels:  d g
```

Thus the four points have been correctly classified on this closed test. A classification plot could be produced with the same function used on the Gaussian data, i.e., **classplot(m, xlim=c(-1, 1), ylim=c(-1, 1))**. Alternatively, there is a simpler (and prettier) way of achieving the same result with the generic **plot()** function which takes the SVM model as the first argument and the data frame as the second:

```
plot(m, d.df)
```

After training on these four data points, the support vector machine has partitioned the space into four quadrants so that all points in the bottom-left and top-right quadrants are classified as /d/ and the other two quadrants as /g/. It would certainly be beyond the capabilities of any Gaussian classifier to achieve this kind of (entirely appropriate) classification and separation over this space from such a small number of data points!

We can now compare the classifications using an SVM and Gaussian classification on the same two-parameter space as in Figure 9.15. A support vector machine is a two-category classificatory system, but it can be extended to the case when there are more than two classes using a so-called "one-against-one" approach by training $k(k-1)/2$ binary SVM classifiers, where k is the number of classes (see Duda et al. 2001 for some further details).

We begin by comparing classification plots to see how the Gaussian and SVM models divide up the two-parameter space:

```
detach(d.df)
attach(bdg)

# Train using SVM on parameters 4 and 7
p47.svm = svm(bdg[,c(4, 7)], phonetic)

# Train using a Gaussian model on the same parameters
p47.qda = qda(bdg[,c(4, 7)], phonetic)

# SVM and Gaussian classification plots over the range of Figure 9.15
xlim = c(-10, 40); ylim = c(-15, 10); col=c("black",
"lightblue", "slategray")
ylab = "Parameter 7"; xlab="Parameter 4"
par(mfrow=c(1,2))
classplot(p47.svm, xlim=xlim, ylim=ylim, col=col,
ylab=ylab, xlab=xlab)
text(c(25, 5, 15, -5), c(0, 0, -10, -8), c("b", "d", "g",
"b"), col=c("white", "black", "black", "white"))
classplot(p47.qda, xlim=xlim, ylim=ylim, col=col,
xlab=xlab, ylab="")
text(c(25, 5, 15), c(0, 0, -10), c("b", "d", "g"),
col=c("white", "black", "black"))
```

There are similarities in the way that the two classification techniques have partitioned the plane: the regions for /b, d, g/ are broadly similar and in particular /g/ engulfs the /b, d/ territories in both cases. But there are also obvious differences. The /b, d/ shapes from the Gaussian classifier are much more ellipsoidal whereas the SVM has carved out boundaries more in line with the way that the tokens are actually distributed in Figure 9.15. For this reason, a separate small region for /b/ is produced with SVM classification, presumably because of the handful of /b/-outliers at coordinates [0, − 5] in the right panel of Figure 9.15.

The reader can manipulate the commands below by selecting columns 4 and 7 to see which approach actually gives the higher classification performance in an open test. In the commands below, training and testing are carried out on all nine dimensions. Moreover, in the training stage, training is done on only six of the seven speakers; then the data values for the speaker who is left out of the training stage are classified. This is done iteratively for all speakers. In this way, a maximum amount of data is submitted to the training algorithm while, at the same time, the training and testing are always done on different speakers. (If not already done, enter `attach(bdg)`.)

```
# A vector in which the classificatory labels will be stored
svm.res = qda.res = rep("", length(phonetic))

# Loop over each speaker separately
for(j in unique(stops.sp)){

# Logical vector to identify the speaker
temp = stops.sp == j

# Train on the other speakers
train.qda = qda(bdg[!temp,1:9], phonetic[!temp])

# Test on this speaker
pred.qda = predict(train.qda, bdg[temp,1:9])

# Store the classificatory label
qda.res[temp] = as.character(pred.qda$class)

# As above but for the SVM
train.svm = svm(bdg[!temp,1:9], phonetic[!temp])
pred.svm = predict(train.svm, bdg[temp,1:9])
svm.res[temp] = as.character(pred.svm)
}

# Confusion matrix from the Gaussian classifier
tab.qda = table(phonetic, qda.res); tab.qda
         qda.res
phonetic   b   d   g
       b 116  16  23
       d   8 133  16
       g  23  22 113

# And from the SVM
tab.svm = table(phonetic, svm.res); tab.svm
         svm.res
phonetic   b   d   g
       b 120  15  20
       d   8 131  18
       g  16  21 121
```

```
# Total hit-rates for the Gaussian and SVM classifiers
n = length(phonetic); sum(diag(tab.qda)/n);
sum(diag(tab.svm)/n)
0.7702128
0.7914894
```

So in fact the scores (77 percent and 79 percent) are quite similar with both techniques and this is an example of just how robust the Gaussian model can be, even though the data for /g/ are so obviously not normally distributed on at least two parameters, as the left panel of Figure 9.15 shows. However, the confusion matrices also show that, while /b, d/ are quite similarly classified in both techniques, the hit-rate for /g/ is slightly higher with the SVM (79.6 percent) than with the Gaussian classifier (71.5 percent).

9.10 Summary

Classification in speech involves assigning a label or category given one or more parameters such as formant frequencies, parameters derived from spectra, or even physiological data. In order for classification to be possible, there must have been a prior training stage (also known as supervised learning) that establishes a relationship between categories and parameters from an annotated database. One of the well-established ways of carrying out training is by using a Gaussian model in which a normal distribution is fitted separately to each category. If there is only one parameter, then the fitting is done using the category's mean and standard deviation; otherwise a multidimensional normal distribution is established using the parameter means, or centroid, and the so-called covariance matrix that incorporates the standard deviation of the parameters and the correlation between them. Once Gaussian models have been fitted in this way, then Bayes' theorem can be used to calculate the probability that any point in a parameter space is a member of that category: specifically, it is the combination of supervised training and Bayes' theorem that allows a question to be answered, such as: given an observed formant pattern, what is the probability that it could be a particular vowel?

The same question can be asked for each category in the training model and the point is then classified, i.e., labeled as one of the categories based on whichever probability is the greatest. This can be done for every point in a chosen parameter space resulting in a "categorical map" marking the borders between categories (e.g., Figure 9.19) from which a confusion matrix quantifying the extent of category overlap can be derived.

An important consideration in multidimensional classification is the extent to which the parameters are correlated with each other: the greater the correlation between them, the less likely they are to make independent contributions to the separation between categories. The technique of principal components analysis can be used to rotate a multi-parameter space and thereby derive new parameters that are uncorrelated with each other. Moreover classification accuracy in a so-called open test, in which training and testing are carried out on separate sets of data, is often improved using a smaller set of PCA-rotated parameters than the original high-dimensional

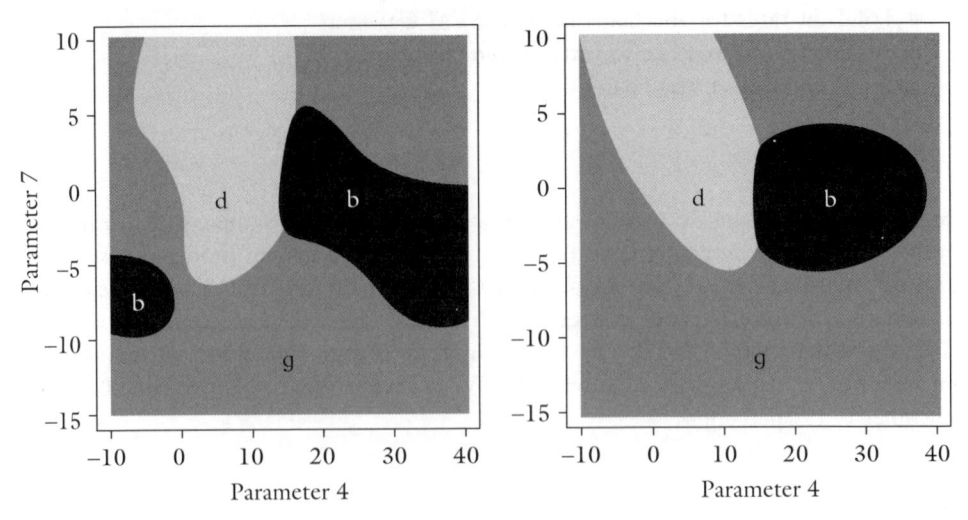

Figure 9.19 Classification plots from a support vector machine (left) and a Gaussian model (right) produced by training on the data in Figure 9.15.

space from which they were derived. Independently of these considerations, an open-test validation of classifications is always important in order to discount the possibility of over-fitting: this comes about when a high-classification accuracy is specific only to the training data so that the probability model established from training does not generalize to other sets of data.

Two further issues were discussed in this chapter. The first is classification based on support vector machines which have not yet been rigorously tested on speech data, but which may enable a greater separation between categories to be made than using Gaussian techniques, especially if the data do not follow a normal distribution. The second is to do with classifications in time: in this chapter, time-based classifications were carried out by fitting the equivalent of a second-order polynomial to successive, auditorily scaled, and data-reduced spectra. Time-based classifications are important in speech research given that speech is an inherently dynamic activity and that the cues for a given speech category are very often distributed in time.

9.11 Questions

A. This exercise makes use of the vowel monophthong and diphthong formants in the dataset **stops** that were described in some detail at the beginning of section 9.8 and also analyzed in this chapter. The vowels/diphthongs occur in the first syllable of German trochaic words with initial C = /b, d, **g**/. There are seven speakers, three male (**gam**, **lbo**, **sbo**) and four female (**agr**, **gbr**, **rlo**, **tjo**). The relevant objects for this exercise are given below – enter **table(stops.l, stopsvow.l, stops.sp)** to see the distribution of stops × vowel/diphthongs × speaker).

stops.l	A vector of stops labels preceding the vowels/diphthongs
stopsvow	Segment list of the vowels/diphthongs following the stop burst
stopsvow.l	A vector of labels of the vowels/diphthongs
stops.sp	A vector of labels for the speaker
stopsvow.fm	Trackdata object, first four formants for the vowels/diphthongs (derived from **emu.track(stopsvow, "fm")**)

The question is concerned with the F1 and F2 change as a function of time in distinguishing between [aː, aʊ, ɔʏ] (MRPA/SAMPA **a: au oy**).

A.1 Sketch possible F1 and F2 trajectories for these three segments. Why might the parameterization of these formants with the third moment (see Chapter 8) be a useful way of distinguishing between these three classes? Why might speaker normalization not be necessary in classifying speech data with this parameter?

A.2 Use **trapply()** on the trackdata object **stopsvow.fm** in order to calculate spectral moments in each segment separately for F1 and F2.

A.3 Produce ellipse plots in the plane of $F1_{m3} \times F2_{m3}$ (the third moment of F1 × the third moment of F2) for the three classes [aː, aʊ, ɔʏ] in the manner shown in the left panel of Figure 9.20.

A.4 Establish a training model using quadratic discriminant analysis in order to produce the classification plot for these three classes shown in the right panel of Figure 9.20.

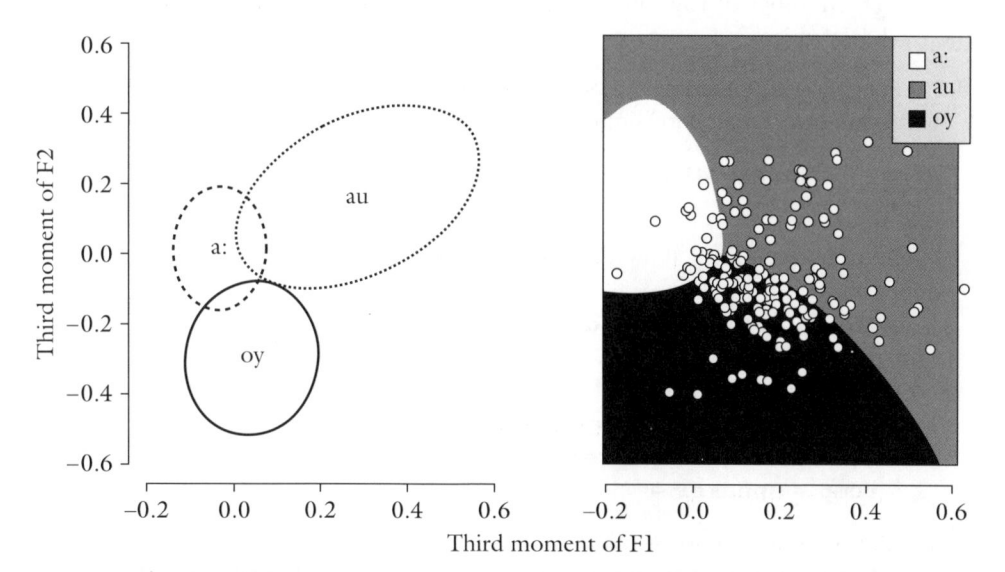

Figure 9.20 Left: 95% confidence ellipses for two diphthongs and a monophthong on the third moment (skew) calculated over F1 and F2 between acoustic vowel onset and offset. The data are from seven German speakers producing isolated words and there are approximately 60 data points per category. Right: a classification plot obtained by training on the same data using quadratic discriminant analysis. The points superimposed on the plot are of [aɪ] diphthongs from read speech produced by a different male and female speaker of standard German.

A.5 Calculate the third moment for the diphthong **aI** (German diphthong [aɪ], one male, one female speaker, read speech) separately for F1 and F2 in the diphthong dataset:

dip.fm   Trackdata object, F1–F4
dip.l   Vector of phonetic labels

A.6 Use **points()** to superimpose on the right panel of Figure 9.20 the $F1_{m3} \times F2_{m3}$ values for these [aɪ] diphthongs.

A.7 As the right panel of Figure 9.20 shows, the values for [aɪ] are around the border between [aʊ] and [ɔʏ] and do not overlap very much with [aː]. How can this result be explained in terms of the relative phonetic similarity between [aɪ] and the three classes on which the model was trained in (d)?

B. The object of this exercise is to test the effectiveness of some of the shape parameters derived from a DCT analysis for vowel classification.

B.1 Calculate the first three DCT coefficients firstly for F1 and then for F2 between the acoustic onset and offset of the vowels/diphthongs in the trackdata object **stopsvow.fm** described in A. above. (You should end up with two three-columned matrices: the first matrix has k_0, k_1, k_2 calculated on F1 in columns 1–3; and the second matrix also contains the first three DCT coefficients, but calculated on F2. The number of rows in each matrix is equal to the number of segments in the trackdata object.)

B.2 The following function can be used to carry out an open-test classification using a "leave-one-out" procedure similar to the one presented at the end of 9.9.

```
cfun <- function(d, labs, speaker)
{
# The next three lines allow the function to be applied when d is one-
dimensional
  if(is.null(dimnames(d)))
  d = as.matrix(d)
  dimnames(d) = NULL
  qda.res = rep("", length(labs))
  for(j in unique(speaker)){
    temp = speaker == j
# Train on all the other speakers
    train.qda = qda(as.matrix(d[!temp,]), labs[!temp])
# Test on this speaker
    pred.qda = predict(train.qda, as.matrix(d[temp,]))
# Store the classificatory label
    qda.res[temp] = pred.qda$class
  }
```

```
    # The confusion matrix
    table(labs, qda.res)
}
```

In this function, training is carried out on $k-1$ speakers and testing on the speaker that was left out of the training. This is done iteratively for all speakers. The results of the classifications from all speakers are summed and presented as a confusion matrix. The arguments to the function are:

d   A matrix or vector of data
labs   A parallel vector of vowel labels
speaker   A parallel vector of speaker labels

Use the function to carry out a classification on a four-parameter model using k_0 and k_2 (i.e., the mean and curvature of each formant) of F1 and of F2 calculated in B.1 above. What is the hit-rate (proportion of correctly classified vowels/diphthongs)?

B.3 To what extent are the confusions that you see in B.2 explicable in terms of the phonetic similarity between the vowel/diphthong classes?

B.4 In what way might including the third moment calculated on F1 reduce the confusions? Test this hypothesis by carrying out the same classification as in B.2 but with a five-parameter model that includes the third moment of F1.

B.5 Some of the remaining confusions may come about because of training and testing on male and female speakers together. Test whether the misclassifications are reduced further by classifying on the same five-parameter model as in B.4, but on the four female speakers (**agr, gbr, rlo, tjo**) only.

9.12 Answers

A.1 The three vowel classes are likely to differ in the time at which their F1 and F2 peaks occur. In particular, F1 for [aʊ] is likely to show an early prominent peak centered on the first phonetically open diphthong component, while [ɔʏ] should result in a relatively late F2 peak due to movement towards the phonetically front [ʏ]. Thus the vowel classes should show some differences on the skew of the formants, which is quantified by the third moment. The reason why speaker normalization may be unnecessary is because skew parameterizes the global shape of the formant trajectory but in particular because skew is dimensionless.

A.2

```
    f1.m3 = trapply(stopsvow.fm[,1], moments, simplify=T)[,3]
    f2.m3 = trapply(stopsvow.fm[,2], moments, simplify=T)[,3]
```

A.3

```
    m3 = cbind(f1.m3, f2.m3)
    temp = stopsvow.l %in% c("a:", "au", "oy")
```

A.4

```
xlim = c(-.2, .6); ylim=c(-.6, .6)
eplot(m3[temp,], stopsvow.l[temp], centroid=T, xlab= "Third
moment (F1)", ylab= "Third moment (F2)", xlim=xlim,
ylim=ylim)
```

A.4

```
m3.qda = qda(m3[temp,], stopsvow.l[temp])
xlim = c(-.2, .6); ylim=c(-.6, .6)
classplot(m3.qda, xlim=xlim, ylim=ylim)
```

A.5

```
m.f1 = trapply(dip.fdat[,1], moments, simplify=T)
m.f2 = trapply(dip.fdat[,2], moments, simplify=T)
```

A.6

```
points(m.f1[,3], m.f2[,3], col="gray100")
```

A.7
[aɪ] shares in common with [aʊ, ɔʏ] that it is a diphthong. For this reason, its formants are likely to be skewed away from the temporal midpoint. Consequently (and in contrast to [aː]), the third moment of the formants will have values that are not centered on [0, 0]. [aɪ] falls roughly on the border between the other two diphthongs because it shares phonetic characteristics with both of them: like [aʊ], the peak in F1 is likely to be early, and like [ɔʏ] the F2 peak is comparatively late.

B.1

```
f1.dct = trapply(stopsvow.fm[,1], dct, 2, simplify=T)
f2.dct = trapply(stopsvow.fm[,2], dct, 2, simplify=T)
```

B.2

```
d = cbind(f1.dct[,c(1, 3)], f2.dct[,c(1, 3)])
result = cfun(d, stopsvow.l, stops.sp)
qda.res
```

labs	1	2	3	4	5	6	7	8
a:	50	8	0	0	0	0	0	0
au	10	47	0	0	1	0	3	0
e:	0	0	48	8	0	3	0	0
i:	0	0	4	54	0	0	0	0
o:	0	1	0	0	48	0	0	10
oe	0	0	2	0	0	52	5	0
oy	0	11	0	0	0	4	42	0
u:	0	1	0	0	6	0	4	48

```
# Hit-rate
sum(diag(result)/sum(result))
0.8276596
```

Classification

B.3 Most of the confusions arise between phonetically similar classes. In particular the following pairs of phonetically similar vowels/diphthongs are misclassified as each other:

- 18 (8 + 10) misclassifications of [aː]/[aʊ]
- 12 (8 + 4) misclassifications of [eː]/[iː]
- 16 (10 + 6) misclassifications of [oː]/[uː]
- 14 (11 + 3) misclassifications of [aʊ]/[ɔY]

B.4 Based on the answers to A. above, including the third moment of F1 might reduce the diphthong misclassifications, in particular [aː]/[aʊ] and [aʊ]/[ɔY].

```
# Third moment of F1
m3.f1 = trapply(stopsvow.fm[,1], moments, simplify=T)[,3]
d = cbind(d, m3.f1)
result = cfun(d, stopsvow.l, stops.sp)
result
qda.res
```

labs	1	2	3	4	5	6	7	8
aː	58	0	0	0	0	0	0	0
au	1	57	0	0	0	0	3	0
eː	0	0	51	7	0	1	0	0
iː	0	0	4	54	0	0	0	0
oː	0	1	0	0	48	0	0	10
oe	0	0	2	1	0	53	3	0
oy	3	1	0	0	0	3	50	0
uː	0	1	0	0	6	0	4	48

```
# Hit-rate
sum(diag(result)/sum(result))
0.8914894
```

Yes, the diphthong misclassifications have been reduced.

B.5

```
temp = stops.sp %in% c("agr", "gbr", "rlo", "tjo")
result = cfun(d[temp,], stopsvow.l[temp], stops.sp[temp])
result
qda.res
```

labs	1	2	3	4	5	6	7	8
aː	31	0	0	0	0	0	0	0
au	0	31	0	0	1	0	1	0
eː	0	0	32	0	0	0	0	0
iː	0	0	1	30	0	0	0	0
oː	0	0	0	0	29	0	0	3
oe	0	0	2	0	0	32	0	0
oy	0	1	0	0	0	1	29	0
uː	0	0	0	0	4	0	0	28

```
sum(diag(result)/sum(result))
0.952756
```

Yes, training and testing on female speakers has reduced misclassifications further: there is now close to 100 percent correct classification on an open test.

Notes

[1] The sample standard deviation, s, of a random variable, x, which provides the best estimate of the population standard deviation, σ, is given by $s = \sqrt{1/(n-1) \sum_{i=1}^{n}(x_i - m)^2}$ where n is the sample size and m is the sample mean, and this is also what is computed in R with the function **sd(x)**.

[2] The square of the number of ellipse standard deviations from the mean is equivalent to the Mahalanobis distance.

[3] In fact, the χ^2 distribution with 1 degree of freedom gives the corresponding values for the single parameter normal curve. For example, the number of standard deviations for a normal curve on either side of the mean corresponding to a cumulative probability of 0.95 is given by either **qnorm(0.975)** or **sqrt(qchisq(0.95, 1))**.

[4] All the above commands including those to **classplot()** can be repeated by substituting **qda()** with **lda()**, the function for *linear* discriminant analysis which is a Gaussian classification technique based on a shared covariance across the classes. The decision boundaries between the classes from LDA are straight lines as the reader can verify with the **classplot()** function.

[5] z-score normalization prior to PCA should be applied because otherwise, as discussed in Harrington and Cassidy (1999), any original dimension with an especially high variance may exert too great an influence on the outcome.

[6] See Harrington and Cassidy (1999), Chapter 9 and the appendix therein for further details of matrix operations.

[7] The reader will almost certainly have to adjust other graphical parameters to reproduce Figure 9.14. Within the **persp()** function, I used **cex.lab=.75** and **cex.axis=.6** to control the font size of the axis label and titles; **lwd=1** for panel (a) and **lwd=.4** for the other panels to control the line width and hence darkness of the plot. I also used **par(mar=rep(3, 4))** to reset the margin size before plotting (d).

[8] The first coefficient 63.85595 is equal to $\sqrt{2}$ multiplied by the mean of k_0 as can be verified from **sqrt(2) * trapply(d.dct[,1], mean, simplify=T)**.

[9] You might need to install the **e1071** package with **install.packages("e1071")**. Then enter **library(e1071)** to access the **svm()** function.

References

Abelson, H., Greenspun, P., and Sandon, L. (2008) Tcl for web nerds. Accessed from http://philip.greenspun.com/tcl/index.adp on September 28, 2009.

Abercrombie, D. (1967) *Elements of General Phonetics*. Edinburgh University Press: Edinburgh.

Adank, P., Smits, R., and van Hout, R. (2004) A comparison of vowel normalization procedures for language variation research. *Journal of the Acoustical Society of America*, 116, pp. 3,099–107.

Ambrazaitis, G., and John, T. (2004) On the allophonic behaviour of German /x/ vs /k/ – an EPG investigation. *Arbeitsberichte des Instituts für Phonetik und digitale Sprachverarbeitung der Universität Kiel*, 34, pp. 1–14.

Anderson, A., Bader, M., Bard, E. et al. (1991) The HCRC Map Task Corpus. *Language & Speech*, 34, pp. 351–66.

Assmann, P., Nearey, T., and Hogan, J. (1982) Vowel identification: orthographic, perceptual and acoustic aspects. *Journal of the Acoustical Society of America*, 71, pp. 975–89.

Baayen, R.H. (2008) *Analyzing Linguistic Data: A Practical Introduction to Statistics Using R*. Cambridge University Press: Cambridge.

Baayen, R.H., Piepenbrock, R., and Gulikers, L. (1995) The CELEX Lexical Database (CD-ROM). Linguistic Data Consortium, University of Pennsylvania: Philadelphia, PA.

Bailey, G., Wikle, T., Tillery, J., and Sand, L. (1991) The apparent time construct. *Language Variation and Change*, 3, pp. 241–64.

Bard, E., Anderson, A., Sotillo, C., Aylett, M., Doherty-Sneddon, G., and Newlands, A. (2000) Controlling the intelligibility of referring expressions in dialogue. *Journal of Memory and Language*, 42, pp. 1–22.

Barras, C., Geoffrois, E., Wu, Z., and Liberman, M. (2001) Transcriber: development and use of a tool for assisting speech corpora production. *Speech Communication*, 33, pp. 5–22.

Barry, W., and Fourcin, A.J. (1992) Levels of labelling. *Computer Speech and Language*, 6, pp. 1–14.

Beck, J. (2005) Perceptual analysis of voice quality: the place of vocal profile analysis. In W.J. Hardcastle and J. Beck (eds.) *A Figure of Speech (Festschrift for John Laver)*. Lawrence Erlbaum: Mahwah, NJ, pp. 285–322.

Beckman, M.E., Edwards, J., and Fletcher, J. (1992) Prosodic structure and tempo in a sonority model of articulatory dynamics. In G.J. Docherty and D.R. Ladd (eds.) *Papers in Laboratory Phonology II: Segment, Gesture, Prosody*. Cambridge University Press: Cambridge, pp. 68–86.

Beckman, M.E., Hirschberg, J., and Shattuck-Hufnagel, S. (2005) The original ToBI system and the evolution of the ToBI framework. In S. Jun (ed.) *Prosodic Typology: The Phonology of Intonation and Phrasing*. Oxford University Press: Oxford, pp. 9–54.

Beckman, M.E., Munson, B., and Edwards, J. (2007) Vocabulary growth and the developmental expansion of types of phonological knowledge. In J. Cole and J.I. Hualde (eds.) *Papers in Laboratory Phonology IX*. Mouton de Gruyter: Berlin, pp. 241–64.

Beckman, M.E., and Pierrehumbert, J. (1986) Intonational structure in Japanese and English. *Phonology Yearbook*, 3, pp. 255–310.

Bell, A., Jurafsky, D., Fosler-Lussier, E., Girand, C., Gregory, M., and Gildea, D. (2003) Effects of disfluencies, predictability, and utterance position on word form variation in English conversation. *Journal of the Acoustical Society of America*, 113, pp. 1,001–24.

Bird, S., and Liberman, M. (2001) A formal framework for linguistic annotation. *Speech Communication*, 33, pp. 23–60.

Bladon, R.A.W., Henton, C.G., and Pickering, J.B. (1984) Towards an auditory theory of speaker normalisation. *Language and Communication*, 4, pp. 59–69.

Blumstein, S., and Stevens, K. (1979) Acoustic invariance in speech production: evidence from measurements of the spectral characteristics of stop consonants. *Journal of the Acoustical Society of America*, 66, pp. 1,001–17.

Blumstein, S., and Stevens, K. (1980) Perceptual invariance and onset spectra for stop consonants in different vowel environments. *Journal of the Acoustical Society of America*, 67, pp. 648–62.

Bod, R., Hay, J., and Jannedy, S. (2003) *Probabilistic Linguistics*. MIT Press: Cambridge, MA.

Boersma, P., and Hamann, S. (2008) The evolution of auditory dispersion in bidirectional constraint grammars. *Phonology*, 25, pp. 217–70.

Boersma, P., and Weenink, D. (2005) Praat: doing phonetics by computer (Version 4.3.14) [Computer program]. Accessed from www.praat.org/ on May 26, 2005.

Bombien, L., Cassidy, S., Harrington, J., John, T., and Palethorpe, S. (2006) Recent developments in the Emu speech database system. *Proceedings of the Australian Speech Science and Technology Conference*, pp. 313–16.

Bombien, L., Mooshammer, C., Hoole, P., Rathcke, T., and Kühnert, B. (2007) Articulatory strengthening in initial German /kl/ clusters under prosodic variation. *Proceedings of the 16th International Congress of Phonetic Sciences*, pp. 457–60.

Brancazio, L., and Fowler, C. (1998) The relevance of locus equations for production and perception of stop consonants. *Perception and Psychophysics*, 60, pp. 24–50.

Broad, D.J., and Fertig, R.H. (1970) Formant-frequency trajectories in selected CVC utterances. *Journal of the Acoustical Society of America*, 47, pp. 1,572–82.

Broad, D.J., and Wakita, H. (1977) Piecewise-planar representation of vowel formant frequencies. *Journal of the Acoustical Society of America*, 62, pp. 1,467–73.

Browman, C.P., and Goldstein, L. (1990a) Gestural specification using dynamically-defined articulatory structures. *Journal of Phonetics*, 18, pp. 299–320.

Browman, C.P., and Goldstein, L. (1990b) Representation and reality: physical systems and phonological structure. *Journal of Phonetics*, 18, pp. 411–24.

Browman, C.P., and Goldstein, L. (1990c) Tiers in articulatory phonology, with some implications for casual speech. In T. Kingston and M.E. Beckman (eds.) *Papers in Laboratory Phonology I: Between the Grammar and Physics of Speech*. Cambridge University Press: Cambridge, pp. 341–76.

Browman, C.P., and Goldstein, L. (1992a) Articulatory phonology: an overview. *Phonetica*, 49, pp. 155–80.

Browman, C.P., and Goldstein, L. (1992b) "Targetless" schwa: an articulatory analysis. In G.J. Docherty and D.R. Ladd (eds.) *Papers in Laboratory Phonology II: Gesture, Segment, Prosody*. Cambridge University Press: Cambridge, pp. 26–56.

Burges, C. (1998) A tutorial on support vector machines for pattern recognition. *Data Mining and Knowledge Discovery*, 2, pp. 121–67.

Butcher, A. (1989) Measuring coarticulation and variability in tongue contact patterns. *Clinical Linguistics and Phonetics*, 3, pp. 39–47.

Bybee, J. (2001) *Phonology and Language Use*. Cambridge University Press: Cambridge.

Byrd, D. (1992) Preliminary results on speaker-dependent variation in the TIMIT database. *Journal of the Acoustical Society of America*, 92, pp. 593–6.

Byrd, D. (1993) 54,000 American stops. *UCLA Working Papers in Phonetics*, 83, pp. 97–116.

Byrd, D. (1994) Relations of sex and dialect to reduction. *Speech Communication*, 15, pp. 39–54.

Byrd, D., Kaun, A., Narayanan, S., and Saltzman, E. (2000) Phrasal signatures in articulation. In M.B. Broe and J. Pierrehumbert (eds.) *Papers in Laboratory Phonology V*. Cambridge University Press: Cambridge, pp. 70–87.

Campbell, N. (2002) Labelling natural conversational speech data. *Proceedings of the Acoustical Society of Japan*, pp. 273–4.

Campbell, N. (2004) Databases of expressive speech. *Journal of Chinese Language and Computing*, 14:4, pp. 295–304.

Carletta, J., Evert, S., Heid, U., and Kilgour, J. (2005) The NITE XML Toolkit: data model and query. *Language Resources and Evaluation Journal*, 39, pp. 313–34.

Carlson, R., and Hawkins, S. (2007) When is fine phonetic detail a detail? *Proceedings of the 16th International Congress of Phonetic Sciences*, pp. 211–14.

Cassidy, S. (1999) Compiling multi-tiered speech databases into the relational model: experiments with the Emu System. *Proceedings of Eurospeech '99*, pp. 2,239–42.

Cassidy, S. (2002) XQuery as an annotation query language: a use case analysis. *Proceedings of the Third International Conference on Language Resources and Evaluation*, pp. 2,055–60.

Cassidy, S. (2004) The Emu speech database system version 1.9, unpublished document. Accessed from emu.sourceforge.net/manual/index.html on September 28, 2009.

Cassidy, S., and Bird, S. (2000) Querying databases of annotated speech. *Proceedings of the Eleventh Australasian Database Conference*, pp. 12–20.

Cassidy, S., and Harrington, J. (1996) EMU: an enhanced hierarchical speech database management system. *Proceedings of the 6th Australian International Conference on Speech Science and Technology*, pp. 361–6.

Cassidy, S., and Harrington, J. (2001) Multi-level annotation in the Emu speech database management system. *Speech Communication*, 33, pp. 61–77.

Cassidy, S., Welby, P., McGory, J., and Beckman, M. (2000) Testing the adequacy of query languages against annotated spoken dialog. *Proceedings of the 8th Australian International Conference on Speech Science and Technology*, pp. 428–33.

Chiba, T., and Kajiyama, M. (1941) *The Vowel: Its Nature and Structure*. Tokyo Publishing Company: Tokyo.

Clark, H. (1973) The language-as-fixed-effect fallacy: a critique of language statistics in psychological research. *Journal of Verbal Learning and Verbal Behavior*, 12, pp. 335–59.

Clark, J., Yallop, C., and Fletcher, J. (2007) *An Introduction to Phonetics and Phonology* (3rd edn.). Blackwell: Oxford.

Clopper, C.G., and Pisoni, D.B. (2006) The Nationwide Speech Project: a new corpus of American English dialects. *Speech Communication*, 48, pp. 633–44.

Cox, F., and Palethorpe, S. (2007) An illustration of the IPA: Australian English. *Journal of the International Phonetic Association*, 37, pp. 341–50.

De Jong, K. (1995) The supraglottal articulation of prominence in English: linguistic stress as localized hyperarticulation. *Journal of the Acoustical Society of America*, 97, pp. 491–504.

Delattre, P.C., Liberman, A.M., and Cooper, F.S. (1955) Acoustic loci and transitional cues for consonants. *Journal of the Acoustical Society of America*, 27, pp. 769–73.

Disner, S. (1980) Evaluation of vowel normalization procedures. *Journal of the Acoustical Society of America*, 67, pp. 253–61.

Docherty, G.J. (2007) Speech in its natural habitat: accounting for social factors in phonetic variability. In J. Cole and J.I. Hualde (eds.) *Papers in Laboratory Phonology IX*. Mouton de Gruyter: Berlin, pp. 1–35.

Docherty, G.J., and Foulkes, P. (2005) Glottal variants of /t/ in the Tyneside variety of English. In W.J. Hardcastle and J. Beck (eds.) *A Figure of Speech (Festschrift for John Laver)*. Lawrence Erlbaum: Mahwah, NJ, pp. 173–99.

Douglas-Cowie, E., Campbell, N., Cowie, R., and Roach, P. (2003) Emotional speech: towards a new generation of databases. *Speech Communication*, 40, pp. 33–60.

Draxler, C. (2008) *Korpusbasierte Sprachverarbeitung – eine Einführung*. Gunter Narr Verlag: Tübingen.

Draxler, C., and K. Jänsch (2004) SpeechRecorder – a universal platform independent multi-channel audio recording software. *Proceedings of the Fourth International Conference on Language Resources and Evaluation*, pp. 559–62.

Draxler, C., and K. Jänsch (2007) Creating large speech databases via the WWW – the system architecture of the German ph@ttSessionz web application. *Proceedings Language Technology Conference*, pp. 69–73.

Duda, R.O., Hart, P., and Stork D. (2001) *Pattern Classification* (2nd edn.). Wiley: New York.

Edwards, J., and Beckman, M.E. (2008) Some cross-linguistic evidence for modulation of implicational universals by language-specific frequency effects in phonological development. *Language, Learning, and Development*, 4, pp. 122–56.

Essner, C. (1947) Recherche sur la structure des voyelles orales. *Archives Néerlandaises de Phonétique Expérimentale*, 20, pp. 40–77.

Fant, G. (1966) A note on vocal tract size factors and non-uniform F-pattern scalings. *Speech Transmission Laboratory, Quarterly Progress Status Reports*, 4, pp. 22–30.

Fant, G. (1968) Analysis and synthesis of speech processes. In B. Malmberg (ed.) *Manual of Phonetics*. North Holland Publishing Company: Amsterdam, pp. 173–276.

Fant, G. (1973) *Speech Sounds and Features*. MIT Press: Cambridge, MA.

Fletcher, J., and McVeigh, A. (1991) Segment and syllable duration in Australian English. *Speech Communication*, 13, pp. 355–65.

Forrest, K., Weismer, G., Milenkovic, P., and Dougall, R.N. (1988) Statistical analysis of word-initial voiceless obstruents: preliminary data. *Journal of the Acoustical Society of America*, 84, pp. 115–24.

Forster, K., and Masson, M. (2008) Introduction: emerging data analysis. *Journal of Memory and Language*, 59, pp. 387–8.

Fowler, C.A., and Housum, J. (1987) Talkers' signaling of "new" and "old" words in speech and listeners' perception and use of the distinction. *Journal of Memory and Language*, 26, pp. 489–504.

Fowler, C.A., and Saltzman, E. (1993) Coordination and coarticulation in speech production. *Language and Speech*, 36, pp. 171–95.

Ganapathiraju, A., Hamaker, J.E., and Picone, J. (2004) Signal processing. *IEEE Transactions on Acoustics, Speech, and Signal Processing*, 52, pp. 2,348–55.

Garofolo, J., Lamel, L., Fisher, W., Fiscus, J., Pallett, D., and Dahlgren, N. (1993) *DARPA TIMIT Acoustic-Phonetic Continuous Speech Corpus CD-ROM*. US Department of Commerce, Technology Administration, National Institute of Standards and Technology, Computer Systems Laboratory, Advanced Systems Division.

Gibbon, D., Moore, R., and Winski, R. (1997) *Handbook of Standards and Resources for Spoken Language Systems*. Mouton de Gruyter: Berlin.

Gibbon, F. (2005) Bibliography of electropalatographic (EPG) studies in English (1957–2005). Accessed from www.qmuc.ac.uk/ssrc/pubs/EPG_biblio_2005_september.PDF on September 15, 2009.

Gibbon, F., and Nicolaidis, K. (1999) Palatography. In W.J. Hardcastle and N. Hewlett (eds.) *Coarticulation in Speech Production: Theory, Data, and Techniques.* Cambridge University Press: Cambridge, pp. 229–45.

Glasberg, B.R., and Moore, B.C.J. (1990) Derivation of auditory filter shapes from notched-noise data. *Hearing Research*, 47, pp. 103–38.

Godfrey, J., Holliman, E., and McDaniel, J. (1992) SWITCHBOARD: telephone speech corpus for research and development. *Proceedings of the IEEE International Conference on Acoustics, Speech, & Signal Processing*, pp. 517–20.

Goldinger, S.D. (1998) Echoes of echoes? An episodic theory of lexical access. *Psychological Review*, 105, pp. 251–79.

Goldinger, S.D. (2000) The role of perceptual episodes in lexical processing. In A. Cutler, J. McQueen, and R. Zondervan (eds.) *Proceedings of Spoken Word Access Processes.* Max Planck Institute for Psycholinguistics: Nijmegen, pp. 155–8.

Grabe, E., and Low, E.L. (2002) Durational variability in speech and the rhythm class hypothesis. In C. Gussenhoven and N. Warner (eds.) *Papers in Laboratory Phonology VII*, Mouton de Gruyter: Berlin, pp. 377–401.

Grice, M., Baumann, S., and Benzmüller, R. (2005) German intonation in autosegmental-metrical phonology. In S. Jun (ed.) *Prosodic Typology: The Phonology of Intonation and Phrasing.* Oxford University Press: Oxford, pp. 55–83.

Grice, M., Ladd, D., and Arvaniti, A. (2000) On the place of phrase accents in intonational phonology. *Phonology*, 17, pp. 143–85.

Gussenhoven, C. (1986) English plosive allophones and ambisyllabicity. *Gramma*, 10, pp. 119–41.

Guzik, K., and Harrington, J. (2007) The quantification of place of articulation assimilation in electropalatographic data using the similarity index (SI). *Advances in Speech–Language Pathology*, 9, pp. 109–19.

Halle, M., Hughes, W., and Radley, J. (1957) Acoustic properties of stop consonants. *Journal of the Acoustical Society of America*, 29, pp. 107–16.

Hamming, R. (1989) *Digital Filters* (3rd edn.). Prentice-Hall: Englewood Cliffs, NJ.

Hardcastle, W.J. (1972) The use of electropalatography in phonetic research. *Phonetica*, 25, pp. 197–215.

Hardcastle, W.J. (1994) Assimilation of alveolar stops and nasals in connected speech. In J. Windsor Lewis (ed.) *Studies in General and English Phonetics in Honour of Professor J.D. O'Connor.* Routledge: London, pp. 49–67.

Hardcastle, W.J., Gibbon, F., and Nicolaidis, K. (1991) EPG data reduction methods and their implications for studies of lingual coarticulation. *Journal of Phonetics*, 19, pp. 251–66.

Hardcastle, W.J., and Hewlett, N. (1999) *Coarticulation in Speech Production: Theory, Data, and Techniques.* Cambridge University Press: Cambridge.

Harrington, J. (1994) The contribution of the murmur and vowel to the place of articulation distinction in nasal consonants. *Journal of the Acoustical Society of America*, 96, pp. 19–32.

Harrington, J. (2006) An acoustic analysis of "happy-tensing" in the Queen's Christmas broadcasts. *Journal of Phonetics*, 34, pp. 439–57.

Harrington, J. (2010) Acoustic phonetics. In W.J. Hardcastle and J. Laver (eds.) *The Handbook of Phonetic Sciences.* Blackwell: Oxford.

Harrington, J., and Cassidy, S. (1999) *Techniques in Speech Acoustics.* Kluwer Academic Publishers: Dordrecht.

Harrington, J., Cassidy, S., Fletcher, J., and McVeigh, A. (1993) The mu+ system for corpus-based speech research. *Computer Speech & Language*, 7, pp. 305–31.

Harrington, J., Cassidy, S., John, T., and Scheffers, M. (2003) Building an interface between EMU and Praat: a modular approach to speech database analysis. *Proceedings of the 15th International Conference of Phonetic Sciences*, pp. 355–8.

Harrington, J., Fletcher, J., and Beckman, M.E. (2000) Manner and place conflicts in the articulation of accent in Australian English. In M. Broe (ed.) *Papers in Laboratory Phonology V*. Cambridge University Press: Cambridge, pp. 40–55.

Harrington, J., Fletcher, J., and Roberts, C. (1995) An analysis of truncation and linear rescaling in the production of accented and unaccented vowels. *Journal of Phonetics*, 23, pp. 305–22.

Harrington, J., Kleber, F., and Reubold, U. (2008) Compensation for coarticulation, /u/-fronting, and sound change in Standard Southern British: an acoustic and perceptual study. *Journal of the Acoustical Society of America*, 123, pp. 2,825–35.

Harrington, J., and Tabain, M. (2004) *Speech Production, Models, Phonetic Processes, and Techniques*. Psychology Press: New York.

Hawkins, S. (1999) Reevaluating assumptions about speech perception: interactive and integrative theories. In J. Pickett (ed.) *Speech Communication*. Allyn & Bacon: Boston, pp. 198–214.

Hawkins, S., and Midgley, J. (2005) Formant frequencies of RP monophthongs in four age groups of speakers. *Journal of the International Phonetic Association*, 35, pp. 183–99.

Hewlett, N., and Shockey, L. (1992) On types of coarticulation. In G.J. Docherty and D.R. Ladd (eds.) *Papers in Laboratory Phonology II*. Cambridge University Press: Cambridge, pp. 128–38.

Hoard, J.E. (1971) Aspiration, tenseness, and syllabification in English. *Language*, 47, pp. 133–40.

Hoole, P., Bombien, L., Kühnert, B., and Mooshammer, C. (in press) Intrinsic and prosodic effects on articulatory coordination in initial consonant clusters. In G. Fant and H. Fujisaki (eds.) *Festschrift for Wu Zongji*. Commercial Press: Beijing.

Hoole, P., Gfroerer, S., and Tillmann, H.G. (1990) Electromagnetic articulography as a tool in the study of lingual coarticulation. *Forschungsberichte des Instituts für Phonetik und Sprachliche Kommunikation der Universität München*, 28, pp. 107–22.

Hoole, P., and Nguyen, N. (1999) Electromagnetic articulography in coarticulation research. In W.J. Hardcastle and N. Hewlett (eds.) *Coarticulation: Theory, Data and Techniques*. Cambridge University Press: Cambridge, pp. 260–9.

Hoole, P., and Zierdt, A. (2006) Five-dimensional articulography. *Stem-, Spraak- en Taalpathologie*, 14, p. 57.

Hoole, P., Zierdt, A., and Geng, C. (2003) Beyond 2D in articulatory data acquisition and analysis. *Proceedings of the 15th International Conference of Phonetic Sciences*, pp. 265–8.

Hunnicutt, S. (1985) Intelligibility vs. redundancy – conditions of dependency. *Language and Speech*, 28, pp. 47–56.

Jacobi, I., Pols, L., and Stroop, J. (2007) Dutch diphthong and long vowel realizations as socio-economic markers. *Proceedings of the International Conference of Phonetic Sciences*, pp. 1,481–4.

Johnson, K. (1997) Speech perception without speaker normalization: an exemplar model. In K. Johnson and J. Mullennix (eds.) *Talker Variability in Speech Processing*. Academic Press: San Diego, pp. 145–65.

Johnson, K. (2004a) *Acoustic and Auditory Phonetics*. Blackwell Publishing: Malden, MA.

Johnson, K. (2004b) Aligning phonetic transcriptions with their citation forms. *Acoustics Research Letters On-line*, 5, pp. 19–24.

Johnson, K. (2005) Speaker normalization in speech perception. In D.B. Pisoni and R. Remez (eds.) *The Handbook of Speech Perception*. Blackwell Publishing: Oxford, pp. 363–89.

Johnson, K. (2008) *Quantitative Methods in Linguistics*. Blackwell Publishing: Malden, MA.

Joos, M. (1948) Acoustic Phonetics. *Language*, 24, pp. 1–136.

Jun, S. (2005) *Prosodic Typology: The Phonology of Intonation and Phrasing*. Oxford University Press: Oxford.

Jun, S., Lee, S., Kim, K., and Lee, Y. (2000) Labeler agreement in transcribing Korean intonation with K-ToBI. *Proceedings of the International Conference on Spoken Language Processing*, pp. 211–14.

Kahn, D. (1980) *Syllable-Based Generalizations in English Phonology*. Garland: New York.

Keating, P., Byrd, D., Flemming, E., and Todaka, Y. (1994) Phonetic analyses of word and segment variation using the TIMIT corpus of American English. *Speech Communication*, 14, pp. 131–42.

Keating, P., Cho, T., Fougeron, C., and Hsu, C. (2003) Domain-initial articulatory strengthening in four languages. In J. Local, R. Ogden, and R. Temple (eds.) *Papers in Laboratory Phonology VI*. Cambridge University Press: Cambridge, pp. 143–61.

Keating, P., MacEachern, M., and Shryock, A. (1994) Segmentation and labeling of single words from spontaneous telephone conversations: manual written for the Linguistic Data Consortium. *UCLA Working Papers in Phonetics*, 88, pp. 91–120.

Kello, C.T., and Plaut, D.C. (2003) The interplay of perception and production in phonological development: beginnings of a connectionist model trained on real speech. *Proceedings of the 15th International Congress of Phonetic Sciences*, pp. 297–300.

Kewley-Port, D. (1982) Measurement of formant transitions in naturally produced stop consonant–vowel syllables. *Journal of the Acoustical Society of America*, 72, pp. 379–89.

Kohler, K. (2001) Articulatory dynamics of vowels and consonants in speech communication. *Journal of the International Phonetic Association*, 31, pp. 1–16.

Krull, D. (1987) Second formant locus patterns as a measure of consonant–vowel coarticulation. *Phonetic Experimental Research at the Institute of Linguistics*, 5, pp. 43–61.

Krull, D. (1989) Second formant locus patterns and consonant vowel coarticulation in spontaneous speech. *Phonetic Experimental Research at the Institute of Linguistics*, 10, pp. 87–108.

Kurowski, K., and Blumstein, S.E. (1984) Perceptual integration of the murmur and formant transitions for place of articulation in nasal consonants. *Journal of the Acoustical Society of America*, 76, pp. 383–90.

Labov, W. (1994) *Principles of Linguistic Change, Vol. 1: Internal Factors*. Blackwell Publishing: Oxford.

Labov, W. (2001) *Principles of Linguistic Change, Vol. 2: Social Factors*. Blackwell Publishing: Oxford.

Labov, W., and Auger, J. (1998) The effects of normal aging on discourse. In H.H. Brownell and J. Yves (eds.) *Narrative Discourse in Neurologically Impaired and Normal Aging Adults*. Singular Publishing Group: San Diego, CA, pp. 115–34.

Ladd, D.R. (1996) *Intonational Phonology*. Cambridge University Press: Cambridge.

Ladefoged, P. (1962) *Elements of Acoustic Phonetics*. University of Chicago Press: London.

Ladefoged, P. (1967) *Three Areas of Experimental Phonetics*. Oxford University Press: Oxford.

Ladefoged, P. (1995) Instrumental techniques for linguistic phonetic fieldwork. In W.J. Hardcastle and J. Laver (eds.) *The Handbook of Phonetic Sciences*. Blackwell: Oxford, pp. 137–66.

Ladefoged, P. (2003) *Phonetic Data Analysis: An Introduction to Fieldwork and Instrumental Techniques*. Blackwell Publishing: Malden, MA.

Ladefoged, P., and Broadbent, D.E. (1957) Information conveyed by vowels. *Journal of the Acoustical Society of America*, 29, pp. 98–104.

Lahiri, A., Gewirth, L., and Blumstein, S. (1984) A reconsideration of acoustic invariance for place of articulation in diffuse stop consonants: evidence from a cross-language study. *Journal of the Acoustical Society of America*, 76, pp. 391–404.

Lamel, L., Kassel, R., and Seneff, S. (1986) Speech database development: design and analysis of the acoustic-phonetic corpus. *Proc. DARPA Speech Recognition Workshop*, pp. 100–9.

Laver, J. (1980) *The Phonetic Description of Voice Quality*. Cambridge University Press: Cambridge.

Laver, J. (1991) *The Gift of Speech*. Edinburgh University Press: Edinburgh.

Laver, J. (1994) *Principles of Phonetics*. Cambridge University Press: Cambridge.

Lehiste, I., and Peterson, G. (1961) Transitions, glides, and diphthongs. *Journal of the Acoustical Society of America*, 33, pp. 268–77.

Liberman, A.M., Delattre, P.C., and Cooper, F.S. (1958) The role of selected stimulus variables in the perception of voiced and voiceless stops in initial position. *Language and Speech*, 1, pp. 153–67.

Liberman, A.M., Delattre, P.C., Cooper, F.S., and Gerstman, L.J. (1954) The role of consonant–vowel transitions in the perception of the stop and nasal consonants. *Psychological Monographs*, 68, pp. 1–13.

Lieberman, P. (1963) Some effects of semantic and grammatical context on the production and perception of speech. *Language and Speech*, 6, pp. 172–87.

Liljencrants, L., and Lindblom, B. (1972) Numerical simulation of vowel quality. *Language*, 48, pp. 839–62.

Lindblom, B. (1963) Spectrographic study of vowel reduction. *Journal of the Acoustical Society of America*, 35, pp. 1,773–81.

Lindblom, B. (1990) Explaining phonetic variation: a sketch of the H&H theory. In W.J. Hardcastle and A. Marchal (eds.) *Speech Production and Speech Modelling*. Kluwer Academic Press: London, pp. 403–39.

Lindblom, B., and Sundberg, J. (1971) Acoustical consequences of lip, tongue, jaw, and larynx movement. *Journal of the Acoustical Society of America*, 50, pp. 1,166–79.

Lobanov, B.M. (1971) Classification of Russian vowels spoken by different speakers. *Journal of the Acoustical Society of America*, 49, pp. 606–8.

Löfqvist, A. (1999) Interarticulator phasing, locus equations, and degree of coarticulation. *Journal of the Acoustical Society of America*, 106, pp. 2,022–30.

Luce, P., and Pisoni, D. (1998) Recognizing spoken words: the neighborhood activation model. *Ear and Hearing*, 19, pp. 1–36.

Maclagan, M., and Hay, J. (2007) Getting *fed* up with our *feet*: contrast maintenance and the New Zealand English "short" front vowel shift. *Language Variation and Change*, 19, pp. 1–25.

Mann, V.A., and Repp, B.H. (1980) Influence of vocalic context on perception of the [ʃ]–[s] distinction. *Perception and Psychophysics*, 28, pp. 213–28.

Manuel, S.Y., Shattuck-Hufnagel, S., Huffman, M., Stevens, K.N., Carlson, R., and Hunnicutt, S. (1992) Studies of vowel and consonant reduction. *Proceedings of the 1992 International Conference on Spoken Language Processing*, pp. 943–6.

Marchal, A., and Hardcastle, W.J. (1993) ACCOR: instrumentation and database for the cross-language study of coarticulation. *Language and Speech*, 36, pp. 137–53.

Marchal, A., Hardcastle, W.J., Hoole, P. et al. (1991) The design of a multichannel database. *Proceedings of the 12th International Congress of Phonetic Sciences*, 5, pp. 422–5.

Markel, J., and Gray, A. (1976) *Linear Prediction of Speech*. Springer Verlag: Berlin.

Max, L., and Onghena, P. (1999) Some issues in the statistical analysis of completely randomized and repeated measures designs for speech language and hearing research. *Journal of Speech Language and Hearing Research*, 42, pp. 261–70.

McVeigh, A., and Harrington, J. (1992) The mu+ system for speech database analysis. *Proceedings of the 4th International Conference on Speech Science and Technology*, pp. 548–53.

Millar, J.B. (1991) Knowledge of speaker characteristics: its benefits and quantitative description. *Proceedings of the 12th International Congress of Phonetic Sciences*, pp. 538–41.

Millar, J.B., Vonwiller, J.P., Harrington, J., and Dermody, P.J. (1994) The Australian National Database of Spoken Language. *Proceedings of ICASSP-94*, 1, pp. 97–100.

Millar, J.B., Dermody, P., Harrington, J., and Vonwiller, J.P. (1997) Spoken language resources for Australian speech technology. *Journal of Electrical and Electronic Engineers Australia*, 1, pp. 13–23.

Miller, J.D. (1989) Auditory-perceptual interpretation of the vowel. *Journal of the Acoustical Society of America*, 85, pp. 2,114–34.

Milner, B., and Shao, X. (2006) Clean speech reconstruction from MFCC vectors and fundamental frequency using an integrated front-end. *Speech Communication*, 48, pp. 697–715.

Moon, S.-J., and Lindblom, B. (1994) Interaction between duration, context, and speaking style in English stressed vowels. *Journal of the Acoustical Society of America*, 96, pp. 40–55.

Moore, A. (2003) Support vector machines. Carnegie-Mellon University. Accessed from www.cs.cmu.edu/~awm/tutorials on September 15, 2009.

Munson, B., Edwards, J., and Beckman, M.E. (2005) Phonological knowledge in typical and atypical speech sound development. *Topics in Language Disorders*, 25, pp. 190–206.

Munson, B., and Solomon, N. (2004) The effect of phonological neighborhood density on vowel articulation. *Journal of Speech, Language, and Hearing Research*, 47, pp. 1,048–58.

Nam, H. (2007) Syllable-level intergestural timing model: split gesture dynamics focusing on positional asymmetry and intergestural structure. In J. Cole and J. Hualde (eds.) *Papers in Laboratory Phonology IX*. Mouton de Gruyter: Berlin, pp. 483–503.

Nearey, T.M. (1989) Static, dynamic, and relational properties in vowel perception. *Journal of the Acoustical Society of America*, 85, pp. 2,088–113.

Nossair, Z.B., and Zahorian, S.A. (1991) Dynamic spectral shape features as acoustic correlates for initial stop consonants. *Journal of the Acoustical Society of America*, 89, pp. 2,978–91.

Ohala, J.J. (1990) The phonetics and phonology of aspects of assimilation. In J. Kingston and M. Beckman (eds.), *Papers in Laboratory Phonology I: Between the Grammar and the Physics of Speech*. Cambridge University Press: Cambridge, pp. 258–75.

Ohala, J.J., and Kawasaki, H. (1984) Prosodic phonology and phonetics. *Phonology Yearbook*, 1, pp. 113–27.

Öhman, S.E.G. (1966) Coarticulation in VCV utterances: spectrographic measurements. *Journal of the Acoustical Society of America*, 39, pp. 151–68.

Oostdijk, N. (2000) The Spoken Dutch Corpus: overview and first evaluation. *Proceedings of the Second International Conference on Language Resources and Evaluation (LREC 2000)*, pp. 887–94.

Oudeyer, P.-I. (2002) Phonemic coding might be a result of sensory-motor coupling dynamics. *Proceedings of the 7th International Conference on the Simulation of Adaptive Behavior*, pp. 406–16.

Oudeyer, P.-I. (2004) The self-organization of speech sounds. *Journal of Theoretical Biology*, 233, pp. 435–49.

Pereira, C. (2000) Dimensions of emotional meaning in speech. *SpeechEmotion-2000*, pp. 25–8 (ISCA Tutorial and Research Workshop on Speech and Emotion, Belfast, September 2000).

Peters, B. (2006) Form und Funktion prosodischer Grenzen im Gespräch. PhD dissertation, Institute of Phonetics and Digital Speech Processing, University of Kiel.

Peterson, G.E. (1961) Parameters of vowel quality. *Journal of Speech and Hearing Research*, 4, pp. 10–29.

Peterson, G.E., and Barney, H.L. (1952) Control methods used in a study of the vowels. *Journal of the Acoustical Society of America*, 24, pp. 175–84.

Pierrehumbert, J. (1987) *The Phonology and Phonetics of English Intonation*. Indiana University Linguistics Club: Bloomington, IN.

Pierrehumbert, J. (2002) Word-specific phonetics. In C. Gussenhoven and N. Warner (eds.) *Papers in Laboratory Phonology VII*, Mouton de Gruyter: Berlin, pp. 101–40.

Pierrehumbert, J. (2003a) Probabilistic phonology: discrimination and robustness. In R. Bod, J. Hay, and S. Jannedy (eds.) *Probabilistic Linguistics*. MIT Press: Cambridge, MA, pp. 177–228.

Pierrehumbert, J. (2003b) Phonetic diversity, statistical learning, and acquisition of phonology. *Language & Speech*, 46, pp. 115–54.

Pierrehumbert, J. (2006) The next toolkit. *Journal of Phonetics*, 34, pp. 516–30.

Pierrehumbert, J., and Talkin, D. (1990) Lenition of /h/ and glottal stop. In G.J. Docherty and D.R. Ladd (eds.) *Papers in Laboratory Phonology II: Gesture, Segment, Prosody*. Cambridge University Press: Cambridge, pp. 90–117.

Pitrelli, J., Beckman, M.E., and Hirschberg, J. (1994) Evaluation of prosodic transcription labeling reliability in the ToBI framework. *Proceedings of the International Conference on Spoken Language Processing*, pp. 123–6.

Pitt, M., Johnson, K., Hume, E., Kiesling, S., and Raymond, W. (2005) The Buckeye Corpus of conversational speech: labeling conventions and a test of transcriber reliability. *Speech Communication*, 45, pp. 89–95.

Pols, L. (2001) The 10-million-words Spoken Dutch Corpus and its possible use in experimental phonetics. *Proceedings of 100 Years of Experimental Phonetics in Russia*, pp. 141–5.

Pols, L., Tromp, H., and Plomp, R. (1973) Frequency analysis of Dutch vowels from 50 male speakers. *Journal of the Acoustical Society of America*, 53, pp. 1,093–101.

Potter, R.K., Kopp, G., and Green, H. (1947) *Visible Speech*. Dover Publications: New York.

Potter, R.K., and Steinberg, J.C. (1950) Toward the specification of speech. *Journal of the Acoustical Society of America*, 22, pp. 807–20.

Quené, H., and van den Bergh, H. (2008) Examples of mixed-effects modeling with crossed random effects and with binomial data. *Journal of Memory and Language*, 59, pp. 413–25.

Rastle, K., Harrington, J., and Coltheart, M. (2002) 358,534 nonwords: the ARC nonword database. *Quarterly Journal of Experimental Psychology*, 55A:4, pp. 1,339–62.

Raymond, W., Dautricourt, R., and Hume, E. (2006) Word-medial /t, d/ deletion in spontaneous speech: modeling the effects of extra-linguistic, lexical, and phonological factors. *Language Variation and Change*, 18, pp. 55–97.

Recasens, D. (2004) The effect of syllable position on consonant reduction: evidence from Catalan consonant clusters. *Journal of Phonetics*, 32, pp. 435–53.

Recasens, D., Farnetani, E., Fontdevila, J., and Pallarès, M.D. (1993) An electropalatographic study of alveolar and palatal consonants in Catalan and Italian. *Language and Speech*, 36, pp. 213–34.

Reed, M., DiPersio, D., and Cieri, C. (2008) The Linguistic Data Consortium member survey: purpose, execution and results. *Proceedings of the 6th International Language Resources and Evaluation*, pp. 2,969–73.

Roach, P., Knowles, G., Varadi, T., and Arnfield, S. (1993) MARSEC: a Machine-Readable Spoken English Corpus. *Journal of the International Phonetic Association*, 23, pp. 47–54.

Robson, C. (1994) *Experiment, Design and Statistics in Psychology*. Penguin: London.

Rose, P. (2002) *Forensic Speaker Identification*. Taylor and Francis: London.

Saltzman, E.L., and Munhall, K.G. (1989) A dynamical approach to gestural patterning in speech production. *Ecological Psychology*, 1, pp. 333–82.

Sankoff, G. (2005) Cross-sectional and longitudinal studies. In U. Ammon, N. Dittmar, K. Mattheier, and P. Trudgill (eds.) *An International Handbook of the Science of Language and Society 2* (2nd edn.). Mouton de Gruyter: Berlin, pp. 1,003–13.

Schafer, A., Speer, S., Warren, P., and White, S. (2000) Intonational disambiguation in sentence production and comprehension. *Journal of Psycholinguistic Research*, 29, pp. 169–82.

Schiel F. (1999) Automatic phonetic transcription of non-prompted speech. *Proceedings of the International Conference of Phonetic Sciences*, pp. 607–10.

Schiel, F. (2004) MAUS goes iterative. *Proceedings of the Fourth International Conference on Language Resources and Evaluation*, pp. 1,015–18.

Schiel, F., and Draxler, C. (2004) *The Production of Speech Corpora*. Bavarian Archive for Speech Signals: Munich. Accessed from www.phonetik.uni-muenchen.de/forschung/Bas/BasLiteratur.html on September 15, 2009.

Schouten, M.E.H., and Pols, L.C.W. (1979) CV- and VC-transitions: a spectral study of coarticulation, part II. *Journal of Phonetics*, 7, pp. 205–24.

Selkirk, E.O. (1982) The syllable. In H. van der Hulst and N. Smith (eds.) *The Structure of Phonological Representations (Part 2)*. Foris: Dordrecht, pp. 337–83.

Shearer, W. (1995) Experimental design and statistics in speech science. In W.J. Hardcastle and J. Laver (eds.) *The Handbook of Phonetic Sciences*. Blackwell: Oxford, pp. 167–87.

Short, T. (2005) R/Rpad reference card. Accessed from http://polisci.msu.edu/jacoby/apsa07/graphics/refers/Tom%20Short%20Rpad-refcard.pdf on September 15, 2009.

Shriberg, L., and Lof, G. (1991) Reliability studies in broad and narrow phonetic transcription. *Clinical Linguistics and Phonetics*, 5, pp. 225–79.

Silverman, K., Beckman, M.E., Pitrelli, J., and Ostendorf, M. (1992) TOBI: a standard for labelling English prosody. *Proceedings of the International Conference on Spoken Language Processing*, pp. 867–70.

Silverman, K., and Pierrehumbert, J. (1990) The timing of prenuclear high accents in English. In T. Kingston and M.E. Beckman (eds.) *Papers in Laboratory Phonology I: Between the Grammar and Physics of Speech*. Cambridge University Press: Cambridge, pp. 72–106.

Simpson, A. (1998) Phonetische Datenbanken des Deutschen in der empirischen Sprachforschung und der phonologischen Theoriebildung. *Arbeitsberichte des Instituts für Phonetik und digitale Sprachverarbeitung der Universität Kiel*, 33.

Simpson, A. (2001) Does articulatory reduction miss more patterns than it accounts for? *Journal of the International Phonetic Association*, 31, pp. 29–39.

Simpson, A. (2002) Gender-specific articulatory-acoustic relations in vowel sequences. *Journal of Phonetics*, 30, pp. 417–35.

Simpson, A., Kohler, K., and Rettstadt, T. (1997) The Kiel Corpus of Read/Spontaneous Speech: acoustic data base, processing tools. *Arbeitsberichte des Instituts für Phonetik und digitale Sprachverarbeitung der Universität Kiel*, 32, pp. 31–115.

Sjölander, K. (2002) Recent developments regarding the WaveSurfer speech tool. *Dept. for Speech, Music and Hearing Quarterly Progress and Status Report*, 44, pp. 53–6.

Srivastava, S., Gupta, M, and Frigyik, B. (2007) Bayesian quadratic discriminant analysis. *Journal of Machine Learning Research*, 8, pp. 1,277–305.

Stephenson, L.S. (2003) An EPG study of repetition and lexical frequency effects in alveolar to velar assimilation. *Proceedings of the 15th International Congress of Phonetic Sciences* (ICPhS-03), pp. 1,891–4.

Stephenson, L.S. (2004) Lexical frequency and neighbourhood density effects on vowel production in words and nonwords. *Proceedings of the 10th Australian International Conference on Speech Science and Technology*, pp. 364–9.

Stephenson, L.S. (2005) An electropalatographic and acoustic analysis of frequency effects in the lexicon. PhD dissertation, Macquarie Centre for Cognitive Science, Macquarie University.

Stephenson, L., and Harrington, J. (2002) Assimilation of place of articulation: evidence from English and Japanese. *Proceedings of the 9th Australian International Conference on Speech Science and Technology*, pp. 592–7.

Stirling, L., Fletcher, J., Mushin, I., and Wales, R. (2001) Representational issues in annotation: using the Australian map task corpus to relate prosody and discourse. *Speech Communication*, 33, pp. 113–34.

Sussman, H.M., Fruchter, D., and Cable, A. (1995) Locus equations derived from compensatory articulation. *Journal of the Acoustical Society of America*, 97, pp. 3,112–24.

Sussman, H.M., McCaffrey, H., and Matthews, S.A. (1991) An investigation of locus equations as a source of relational invariance for stop place categorization. *Journal of the Acoustical Society of America*, 90, pp. 1,309–25.

Syrdal, A.K., and Gopal, H.S. (1986) A perceptual model of vowel recognition based on the auditory representation of American English vowels. *Journal of the Acoustical Society of America*, 79, pp. 1,086–100.

Syrdal, A.K., and McGory, A. (2000) Inter-transcriber reliability of ToBI prosodic labeling. *Proceedings of the International Conference on Spoken Language Processing*, pp. 235–8.

Taylor, P., Black, A., and Caley, R. (2001) Heterogeneous relation graphs as a formalism for representing linguistic information. *Speech Communication*, 33, pp. 153–74.

Traunmüller, H. (1990) Analytical expressions for the tonotopic sensory scale. *Journal of the Acoustical Society of America* 88, pp. 97–100.

Traunmüller, H., and Lacerda, F. (1987) Perceptual relativity in identification of two-formant vowels. *Speech Communication*, 6, pp. 143–57.

Trochim, M. (2007) *Research Methods Knowledge Base*. Thomson: London. Accessed from www.socialresearchmethods.net/kb/index.php on September 15, 2009.

Trudgill, P. (1988) Norwich revisited: recent linguistic changes in an English urban dialect. *English World Wide*, 9, pp. 33–49.

van Bergem, D.R. (1993) Acoustic vowel reduction as a function of sentence accent, word stress, and word class, *Speech Communication*, 12, pp. 1–23.

van Bergem, D.R. (1994) A model of coarticulatory effects on the schwa. *Speech Communication*, 14, pp. 143–62.

Vance, A. (2009) Data analysts captivated by R's power. Article in the Business Computing section of *The New York Times*, January 6, 2009.

van Son, R., and Pols, L. (1990) Formant frequencies of Dutch vowels in a text, read at normal and fast rate. *Journal of the Acoustical Society of America*, 88, pp. 1,683–93.

Verbrugge, R., Strange, W., Shankweiler, D.P., and Edman, T.R. (1976) What information enables a listener to map a talker's vowel space? *Journal of the Acoustical Society of America*, 60, pp. 198–212.

Watson, C. I., and Harrington, J. (1999) Acoustic evidence for dynamic formant trajectories in Australian English vowels. *Journal of the Acoustical Society of America*, 106, pp. 458–68.

Wedel, A. (2006) Exemplar models, evolution and language change. *The Linguistic Review*, 23, pp. 247–74.

Wedel, A. (2007) Feedback and regularity in the lexicon. *Phonology*, 24, pp. 147–85.

Weenink, (2001) Vowel normalization with the TIMIT corpus. *Proceedings of the Institute of Phonetic Sciences, University of Amsterdam*, 24, pp. 117–23.

Wells, J.C. (1997) SAMPA computer readable phonetic alphabet. In D. Gibbon, R. Moore, and R. Winski (eds.) *Handbook of Standards and Resources for Spoken Language Systems, Part IV, section B*. Mouton de Gruyter: Berlin, pp. 684–732.

Wesener, T. (2001) Some non-sequential phenomena in German function words. *Journal of the International Phonetic Association*, 31, pp. 17–27.

Wesenick, M., and Kipp, A. (1996) Estimating the quality of phonetic transcriptions and segmentations of speech signals. *Proceedings of the International Conference on Spoken Language Processing*, pp. 129–32.

Westbury, J.R. (1994) X-ray microbeam speech production database user's handbook, version 1.0. Accessed from www.medsch.wisc.edu/~milenkvc/pdf/ubdbman.pdf on September 15, 2009.

Wiese, R. (1996) *The Phonology of German*. Clarendon Press: Oxford.

Wrench, A., and Hardcastle, W.J. (2000) A multichannel articulatory speech database and its application for automatic speech recognition. *Proc. 5th seminar on speech production: models and data*, pp. 305–8.

Wright, R. (2003) Factors of lexical competition in vowel articulation. In J. Local, R. Ogden, and R. Temple (eds.) *Papers in Laboratory Phonology VI*. Cambridge University Press: Cambridge, pp. 75–87.

Wuensch, K. (2009) Karl Wuensch's statistics lessons. Accessed from http://core.ecu.edu/psyc/wuenschk/StatsLessons.htm on September 15, 2009.

Yoon, T., Chavarria, S., Cole, J., and Hasegawa-Johnson, M. (2004) Intertranscriber reliability of prosodic labeling on telephone conversation using ToBI. *Proceedings of the International Conference on Spoken Language Processing*, pp. 2,729–32.

Zierdt, A. (2007) Die Entwicklung der Messtechnik für ein fünfdimensionales elektromagnetisches Artikulographensystem. PhD dissertation, Institute of Phonetics and Speech Processing, University of Munich.

Zwicker, E. (1961) Subdivisions of the audible frequency range into critical bands. *Journal of the Acoustical Society of America*, 33, p. 248.

Index

& operator, 75, 102
@ see schwa vowels
==, 125–6, 128–9, 133
!= operator, 75, 81–2, 103, 126–8
-> operator, 76, 78, 80–1, 102
| operator, 74
3D palatographic array, 223
[ç], 301
[x], 301

Abercrombian stress-foot, 98–9
absolute difference, 155, 158, 160
accessing databases, 222–3
ACCOR, 5
acoustic data, 1–2
acoustic offset, 21
acoustic onset, 21
acoustic silence, 282
acoustic vowel space, 46–7
acoustic vowel targets, 47
aerodynamic power, 248
AI see anteriority index
air-pressure variations, 272–3
aliasing, 266, 316
aligning trajectories, 151
allophones, 252–3, 301, 367
alveolar release, 2
amplitude, 264, 307, 364
  of half-cycle cosine wave, 307, 364
amplitude spectrum, 270–1
analysis of EPG data, 248–58
  consonant overlap, 248–51
    VC coarticulation in German dorsal fricatives, 251–8

analysis of formants and formant transitions, 171–219
  Euclidean distances, 190–8
  F2 locus of articulation, 206–13
  outliers, 177–9
  questions and answers, 213–19
  vowel ellipses in F2 × F1 plane, 172–7
  vowel normalization, 183–90
  vowel overshoot and formant smoothing, 198–206
  vowel targets, 179–83
analysis mode, 198, 205–6
analysis of movement data, 160–1
analysis of variance, 9–12
analysis of voice-onset time, 125–32
annotation, 15–17, 39, 74–6
  from the same tier, 74–6
  organization of, 39
annotation files, 20–1
annotation structures, 71–114
ANOVA see analysis of variance
anteriority index, 241–2, 244–9, 259
anterior–posterior movement, 132–3
apparent time study, 196
applying a function segmentally, 144–7, 160
applying routines for speech signal processing, 46–71
arguments, 29–32
arithmetic, 128–9, 140–2, 144
Articulate Instruments, 220, 222, 224
articulation, 206–13
articulatory landmarks, 115, 160, 222
articulatory phonology, 115, 140, 153–5

articulatory stiffness, 159–61
aspiration, 131
attenuation, 51
Australian National Database of Spoken Language, 5
automatic speech recognition, 316, 368
autosegmental association, 79–80, 83, 86–7, 90, 98, 101

background noise, 13–14
background to spectral analysis, 264–88
   amplitude spectrum, 270–1
   dB-spectrum, 272–3
   Fourier analysis, 267–70
   Hamming windows, 273–5
   handling spectral data in Emu-R, 284–8
   pre-emphasis, 281–3
   sampling frequency, 271
   sinusoid, 264–7
   time and frequency resolution, 276–81
backness of vowels, 46–7, 315
balanced design, 10
Bark bands, 355, 358
Bark scale, 189–90, 312–13
Bark-scaled DCT coefficients, 312–16, 361, 363–6
base-names, 34–6, 52
Bavarian Archive for Speech Signals, 4
Bayes' theorem, 327–30, 373
BBC, 5
between-speaker factors, 9–10
bilabial closure, 116
bimodal distribution, 257
binomial distribution, 331–6
binomial expansion, 333
bivariate normal distribution, 342–7
Blackman window, 51
boundary times, 92
branching paths, 97–102
break indices, 77, 90
Buckeye Corpus, 5
building annotated speech databases, 20–45
building annotation structures semi-automatically, 91–6
burst spectrum, 360–2

calculating conditional probabilities, 336–8
calculating DCT coefficients in Emu-R, 306–9
calculating formants, 48–53
calculating posterior probabilities, 338–42

Carstens Medizinelektronik, 115, 117
Cartesian space, 116
categorical dependent variables, 9
categorical map, 373
Celex, 7
center of gravity index, 241, 243–8, 254–9
Center for Spoken Language Understanding, 4
centrality index, 241–3, 246–8
centralization, 190
Centre for Speech Technology Research, xvii
centroid, 188, 193–5, 344–5
cepstral analysis, 306, 310–11
cepstral coefficients, 312–16, 363
CGN, 4
character objects, 29
character vectors, 123
χ^2 distribution, 345
Christmas messages, 196
CI *see* centrality index
citation-form speech, 12, 15, 87, 179, 190
class separation, 354
classes, 74, 123
classification, 327–80
   bivariate normal distribution and ellipses, 342–7
   calculating conditional probabilities, 336–8
   calculating posterior probabilities, 338–42
   continuous data, 330–6
   in higher dimensional spaces, 352–9
   probability and Bayes' theorem, 327–30
   questions and answers, 374–80
   summary, 373–4
   support vector machines, 366–73
   in time, 359–66
   in two dimensions, 347–52
closed test, 330, 352, 354, 370
coarticulation, 12, 179, 251–8
coefficient zero, 305
COG *see* center of gravity index
common logarithms, 143
comparison operators, 126, 142–3
composition, 79
compressed matrix, 223
compressed trackdata, 223
concatenate function, 124, 135–6
conditional probabilities, 329, 336–8, 341
   calculation of, 336–8
confidence intervals, 177
confusion matrix, 350–3, 372

consonant overlap, 248–51
consonant-cluster overlap, 221
consonant–vowel transition, 207
constriction level, 46, 155
contact distribution indices, 241–8
contact profiles, 234–41
continuous data, 330–6
  binomial and normal distribution, 331–6
continuous dependent variables, 9
contract lateralization, 242
conventions for naming files, 17–18
conversion of structured annotation to Praat TextGrid, 86–8, 102
coronal plane, 133
corpora and their place in phonetic analysis of speech, 1–4
corpus design, 6–18
correcting formants, 48–53
correlation, 255, 312, 343, 346–8, 353
cosine transformation, 144, 304–16
cosine wave, 205, 266
creak, 328–9
creating new speech database, 20–1, 32–4
critical Nyquist, 267, 271, 277–8
critically damped movement, 152–9
cross-tabulation, 125
CSTR, 282
cumulative probabilities, 335
curvature, 199, 201, 204, 305, 312, 365

data entry in Emu, 102
data mining, 19
Database Tool (Emu), 21–5, 35–9, 48–9, 52
data-reduction parameters, 246
dB spectrum, 272–3
DCT *see* discrete cosine transformation
DCT coefficient calculation in Emu-R, 306–9
DCT coefficients of a spectrum, 309–12
  and trajectory shape, 311–12
DCT-smoothed signal, 308
De Moivre, Abraham, 331
decision points, 341
decomposition, 306
default argument, 355
default settings, 51
dependent variables, 9
derived signal files, 21
describing tiers, 77
descriptive statistics, 125

designing a corpus, 6–18
  annotation, 15–17
  further issues in experimental design, 9–12
  materials, 7–9
  recording setup, 13–15
  some conventions for naming files, 17–18
  speakers, 6–7
  speaking style, 12–13
details of file structure, 38–9
DFT *see* discrete Fourier transform
DI *see* dorsopalatal index
dialect, 196–8
difference, 288–97
difference spectra, 291–3
differencing, 147–52, 282–3
dimension names, 57, 226
dimensionless number, 300
discrete cosine transformation, 205–6, 264, 303–16
  calculating DCT coefficients in Emu-R, 306–9
  DCT coefficients of a spectrum, 309–11
  DCT coefficients and trajectory shape, 311–12
  Mel- and Bark-scaled DCT coefficients, 312–16
discrete Fourier transform, 268–77, 279, 284, 304
discrete jumps, 266
displacement, 160
displaying formants, 48–53
displaying signal processing in Emu, 59
distribution, 47
DOBES, 4
domain, 7–8
dorsal fricatives in German, 251–8
dorsopalatal index, 241, 243–9, 259
downloadable speech databases, xiv–xv
duration, 74, 81, 122, 127–9, 155–6, 160
dynamic spectral information, 360–6

ear-training, xvi
easy words, 191–3
eigenvectors, 354–5, 357
ELAN *see* EUDICO Linguistic Annotator
ELDA *see* Evaluations and Language Resources Distribution Agency
electromagnetic articulometry, 7, 14–17
  see also EMA recordings
electropalatography, 220–63

analysis of EPG data, 248–58
EPG data-reduced objects, 234–48
overview of, 222–33
palatography, 220–2
questions and answers, 263
summary, 258–9
ellipses, 57, 172–7, 342–7
standard deviation from the mean, 344
in vowels, 172–7
EMA cube, 116–17
EMA recordings, 116–20
see also electromagnetic articulometry
ema5 database, 116–20
emotional responses, 12–13
empty palatograms, 226
Emu, 24–6, 31–4, 39, 72–4, 82–9
Emu-Tcl, 91–6
entering structured annotations with, 82–6
from Praat to R, 32–4, 39
graphical user interface to query language, 82–9
interface with Praat, 24–6, 39
Query Tool, 72–4
reading segment lines into R, 31–2
Emu query language, 88–9
Emu-QL see Emu query language
Emu-R, 90–1, 121–5, 222–33, 284–8
handling spectral data in, 284–8
library, 90–1, 115, 122
vectors, 121–5
Emu-Tcl, 91–6
ensemble plots, 136–9
entering structured annotations with Emu, 82–6
entire formant trajectory, 198–9
EPG data-reduced objects, 224–5, 234–48
contact distribution indices, 241–8
contact profiles, 234–41
EPG objects, 223
EPG plots, 223–4
equality, 125
equivalence, 144
equivalent information, 364
E_{RATIO} values, 196–8
estimation, 333
Euclidean distances, 171, 174, 190–8, 350
relative distance between vowel categories, 196–8
vowel-space expansion, 190–6
EUDICO Linguistic Annotator, 18

European Languages Resources Association, 4
Evaluations and Language Resources Distribution Agency, 4–5
event tiers, 23–4, 72–4, 101
evidence and hypothesis, 327–8
existing speech corpora for phonetic analysis, 4–5
existing speech databases, 21–4
expansion of vowel space, 190–6
experimental design of corpus, 9–12
explanation of variance, 354
extending range of queries, 74–6
 & operator, 75
 != operator, 75
 -> operator, 76
 (or) operator and classes, 74
extracting trackdata objects, 132–3, 160

F2 locus, 206–13
F2 × F1 plane, 46–8, 172–7
vowel ellipses in, 172–7
fast Fourier transform, 268, 277, 280
features, 74
FFT see fast Fourier transform
file output, 102
file structure, 38
file-naming conventions, 17–18
final devoicing, 97
first principal component, 345
first-order differencing, 148
flanking consonants, 198, 207
flipping a coin, 331–3
folding frequency, 267
for-loops, 126, 145, 180, 187, 290, 341, 356
forensic phonetics, 329
formant analysis of vowels, 46–8
formant smoothing, 198–206
formants and formant transitions, 48–53, 171–219
calculating, displaying, correcting formants, 48–53
Fourier analysis, 267–70, 305
Fourier synthesis, 267–70
Fourier transformation, 264, 271
frame, 122
frame rates, 134–6
F-ratio, 12
frequency, 264, 286
frequency resolution, 47, 276–81
frequency warping, 363

frication, 120, 131, 176, 222, 231–2, 238, 288, 302–3
from Praat to Emu to R, 32–4
function frames, 159
function of time, 134, 140, 149, 151, 171, 364–6
functionality, 151
functions, 29–32
fundamental frequency, 47, 59

Gauss, Karl Friedrich, 331
Gaussian normal distribution, 300, 327, 331, 351–2, 357–8, 368–74
German dorsal fricatives, 251–8, 288
German Tones and Break Indices system, 77, 80
gesture duration, 155–6
getting started with existing speech databases, 21–4
Google, 19
grandparent–child relationship, 77–9, 85
graphical user interface, 88–9
GToBI *see* German Tones and Break Indices system

H&H theory, 201
half-cycle cosine wave, 307–9, 364
half-cycles, 304
Hamming windows, 51, 273–5, 280–2
handling segment lists, 121–5
handling spectral data in Emu-R, 284–8
Hann windows, 51, 273–5, 280–2
hard words, 191–3
harmonics, 278–9, 310
Haskins Laboratories, 207
HCRC Map Task Corpus, 5
hearing pathologies, 6
height of vowels, 46–7
hierarchical association, 79–80, 83, 86–7, 95, 98, 101
hierarchical label file, 84–5
higher dimensional space classification, 352–9
hit rate, 350–4, 358–9, 373
homophony, 87–8
hyperarticulation, 190, 201
hypoarticulation, 190
hypotheses, 1, 327–8

incremental sound change, 196
independent variables, 9
indexing, 133, 160

individual utterances, 2
inherent variations in speech production, 11
Institut für Deutsche Sprache, 5
Institute of Phonetics and Speech Processing, 15, 49
integer cycles, 304
intensity, 47
interface between Praat and Emu, 24–6, 39
interface to R, 26–32, 59
  preliminary remarks about R, 26–31
  reading Emu segment lines into R, 31–2
interference, 14
intergestural coordination, 115, 132–9
  ensemble plots, 136–9
  extracting trackdata objects, 132–3
  movement plots from single segments, 134–6
intermediate phrases, 77
intermediate-final feet, 101
interpolation, 313
inter-tier links, 77–82, 99
  and queries, 77–82
intonation, 77, 99–100
intonational-final content words, 99–101
intonational-final feet, 99
intragestural analysis, 115, 139–59
  critically damped movement, 152–9
  differencing and velocity, 147–52
  manipulation of trackdata objects, 140–7
introduction to R, 26–31
introduction to speech data analysis in R, 115–70
  analysis of voice-onset time, 125–32
  EMA recordings and ema5 database, 116–20
  handling segment lists, 121–5
  intergestural coordination and ensemble plots, 132–9
  intragestural analysis, 139–59
  questions and answers, 161–70
  summary, 159–61
inverse Fourier transform, 270
IPDS, 251–2, 360
IPS, 115–16
issues in experimental design, 9–12
iteration, 145

/k/ closure, 120, 125, 128–9
/kl/, 115–70
  clusters, 131, 161
  ensemble plots, 136–9

/kn/, 115–70
  clusters, 131, 161
  ensemble plots, 136–9
Kaiser-window design, 118
Kay Elemetrics Corporation, 220
kernel, 369–70
Kiel Corpus of Speech, 4–5, 172, 301–2
kmeans clustering, 171, 174–5
kurtosis, 297–300

L*, 81–4, 92–6
labeling, 15–17, 21–3, 32
ladiodental fricative, 176–7
language-as-fixed effect problem, 12
Laplace, Pierre-Simon, 331
lateral tongue–palate contact, 254
lateralization, 242
lax monophthongs, 183, 194, 214–15, 276–7
leakage, 274–5
likelihood ratio, 329
line of best fit, 210
linear interpolation, 199
linear links, 77–9, 101
Linguistic Data Consortium, 4–5
linkages, 77–82
Lobanov normalization, 187, 189
locus equations, 171, 207
locus frequency, 206–13
logical operations on trackdata objects, 160
logical operator, 125–6
logical vectors, 126–9, 142, 160, 178, 183, 197
LR see likelihood ratio

Machine Readable Corpus of Spoken English, 5
magnitude of gesture, 152–9
major axes, 345
male–female vowel differences, 184
mandatory arguments, 90
manipulation of trackdata objects, 140–7
  applying a function segment by segment, 144–7
  arithmetic, 140–2
  comparison operators, 142–3
  math and summary functions, 143–4
many-to-many associations, 79, 83, 101
map-task corpora, 8
margin of parallel lines, 368, 370
Markov models, 120

MARSEC see Machine Readable Corpus of Spoken English
mass–spring system, 153–7, 160–1
materials for corpus creation, 7–8
math functions, 143–4
mathematical operations on trackdata objects, 160
Matlab, 118
matrices, 122–3, 127, 133, 135, 184, 288
matrix bridge, 297–9
MAUS see Munich automatic segmentation system
Max Planck Institute, 4, 18
mean, 297–9, 305
Mel scale, 312–13
Mel-scaled DCT coefficients, 306, 312–16, 363
Microbeam Speech Production Database, 5
Microsoft, 13
mid rounded vowels, 75
mid vowels, 75
minor axes, 345
misclassification, 351, 368
mixed-effects modeling, 11–12
MOCHA-TIMIT, 5
monophthongs, 23, 54–5, 183, 194, 199, 209, 214–15, 276–7, 323, 359
morphemes, 97–9
movement plots from single segments, 134–6
movement-data analysis, 160–1
MRPA and IPA for German, xii–xiii
MRPA/SAMPA c, xii, 301
multiple paths, 102
multivariate normal distribution, 342–7
Munich automatic segmentation system, 15, 120

naming files, 17–18
National Institute for Standards and Technology, 13
Nationwide Speech Project, 5
Nearey-formalized formants, 189
neighborhood density, 191
New York Times, 19
NIST SPHERE, 13
NITE-XML, 18
noise, 13–14, 282
nominal F1 frequency, 49
nominal factors, 10

non-Gaussian classification, 327
non-linear links, 77–9, 83, 90, 101
non-linear transformation, 369
non-uniform vowel changes, 184
normal distribution, 331–6
    see also Gaussian normal distribution
N-point window, 275–8, 280
null hypothesis, 212
number of factor levels, 10
number of points per repetition, 264
numeric objects, 29
numeric vectors, 123, 125
numerical operations on trackdata objects, 160
Nyquist theorem, 13, 303, 361

object-oriented programming, 133
obligatory arguments, 137
occlusal plane, 116, 132
one-against-one approach, 371
one-to-many associations, 79, 83, 101
onglides, 179
open test, 330, 354, 358
    Gaussian classification, 358
optimal separation of categories, 368
(or) operator, 74
ordinal factors, 10
organization of annotations, 39
orientation, 178
orthographic transcription, 15, 120
oscillation, 153, 310
outliers, 177–9, 371
over-fitting, 351–2, 357

package statement, 93
packages, 31
palatographic margins, 254
palatography, 220–63
parabolic trajectory, 199–205, 312
parallel objects, 123–6
parallelism, 143–4
parameterizing dynamic spectral
    information, 360–6
parameters, 342–7
parametric analysis, 249
parent–child relationship, 77–9, 83–5, 95, 97–9, 101
parsing, 79, 97
PCA see principal components analysis
P-COG see posterior center of gravity
peak velocity, 152–9

perception of speech, 2, 312, 327
periodicity, 129–30, 206, 284–5
pharyngeal cavity lengths, 184
phase, 264, 266
phonemes, 2–3, 7–8, 16–17, 79–80, 97–9
phonemic contrast, 2
phonetics, 312, 329
phonological distribution, 7–8
physiological experiments, 11
pitch-accents, 80, 83, 88, 90–2, 95
place of articulation, 206–13
place of corpora in phonetic analysis of speech, 1–4
plotting speech data from trackdata objects, 160
polynomial fitting, 361
population means, 331–2, 335, 343
posterior center of gravity, 254–5
posterior probabilities, 329, 338–42
    calculation of, 338–42
post-vocalic dorsal fricatives, 251–2
power ratios, 289
Praat, 24–6, 32–4, 39
    interface with Emu, 24–6, 39
    to Emu to R, 32–4
Praat TextGrid, 17–18, 33–9, 72, 86–8, 102
    conversion of structured annotation, 86–8
prediction order, 51, 370
pre-emphasis, 51, 281–3
pre-stored packages, 31
principal components analysis, 354–7
prior probabilities, 329
probability, 327–30
probability density, 334
proportion, 334
prosodic phrases, 3, 7–8, 12–13, 77, 98

quadratic discriminant analysis models, 340
quantification of similarity, 327
quantile–quantile plot, 338
Queen Elizabeth II, 196
Query Tool (Emu), 72–81, 102
querying annotated speech databases, 20–45
querying annotation structures, 71–114
    branching paths, 97–101
    building annotation structures
        semi-automatically, 91–6

conversion of structured annotation to Praat TextGrid, 86–8
Emu Query Tool, 72–4
entering structured annotations with Emu, 82–6
extending range of queries, 74–6
graphical user interface to Emu query language, 88–9
inter-tier links and queries, 77–82
questions, 103–14
re-querying segment lists, 90–1
summary, 101–3
query-range extension, 74–6

radial basis function, 369
ratio, 288–97
ratio of energy levels, 290–1
ratio of powers, 272
reading Emu segment lines into R, 31–2
Reading EPG3, 220
reading formants into R, 53–8
recording setup, 13–15
rectangular windows, 274–5
reference sounds, 272–3
regression line, 210–12
relating evidence to hypothesis, 327–8
relative distance between vowel categories, 196–8
repetition, 10–12, 264
re-querying segment lists, 90–1
restriction by domain, 7–8
rhythm, 16
right context, 199
Rion corporation, 220
rotated dimensions, 355–6, 373
rotation matrix, 357–8
rounded high vowels, 75
rounding errors, 270
routines for speech signal processing, 46–71
  calculating, displaying, correcting formants, 48–53
  introduction, 46–8
  questions and answers, 59–71
  reading formants into R, 53–8
  summary, 58–9
row names, 134

sagittal plane, 116–17
salient acoustic information, 315
same-tier annotation, 74–6

sample mean, 332
sampling frequency, 271, 310
saw-tooth effect, 305
Scheffers, Michel, 49
schwa vowels, 51, 80, 199
second-order polynomial, 365, 370
segment lists, 21, 72, 90–1, 121–5, 159–60
  handling, 121–5
segment tiers, 23–4, 72–4, 101
segmental application of function to trackdata objects, 144–7
segmentation, 15–17
semi-automatic creation of annotation structures, 91–6
semi-automatic derivation, 120
set of coefficients, 198–200
Shapiro test, 337–8
signal files, 20–1
signal processing, 46–71
significance threshold, 338
silence, 282
sine wave, 266
single paths, 102
single segments, 134–6
  movement plots from, 134–6
single-parameter classification, 341
sinusoid, 149, 160, 264–75, 304
size of window, 49, 59
skew, 158, 297–8, 300, 354
  distribution, 158
slope, 288–97, 305
sociolinguistic investigation, 171
sociophonetics, 196
sociophonic variation in diphthongs, 4
software downloading, xix–xx
solving problems in experimental phonetics, 20–1
solving tasks, 7–9
speaker-dependent constants, 188–9
speaker-independent constants, 189
speakers, 12–13
speaking style, 12–13
specifying tier relationships, 101
spectral analysis, 264–326
  background, 264–88
  discrete cosine transformation, 304–16
  questions and answers, 316–26
  spectral average, sum, ratio, difference, slope, 288–97
  spectral moments, 297–304

spectral average, 288–97
spectral leakage, 274–5
spectral moments, 297–304
spectral slope, 293–6, 311–12
spectral standard deviation, 304
spectral trackdata object, 284
spectrograms, 24–5, 49, 52
speech corpora and phonetics research, 1–19
speech data analysis in R, 115–70
speech frames, 49, 55–6, 59, 134–6, 141–7, 150, 159
speech movement data, 147
speech signal processing, 46–71
speech technology, 363
SpeechRecorder, 14
spontaneous speech, 12
standard normal distribution, 335–6, 343
static palatography, 220–2
steady state, 179
stochastic relationships, 2–3
storing information, 30
strategies for vowel normalization, 186
stress, 198
structured annotations and Emu, 82–6
study of an EMA database, 115–70
subtraction, 129, 335
sum, 288–97
summary functions, 143–4
summed energy values, 356
superimposed jaggedness, 305, 310
supervised learning, 330
support vector machines, 366–73
support vectors, 368
supralaryngeal articulators, 5, 149
SVMs *see* support vector machines
Switchboard, 4
symbolic information, 15–17
synchronization, 115, 132, 135, 137–8, 148, 152–3, 180–1, 236, 297
synthesis mode, 198, 205–6

TalkBank, 4
target vowels, 179–83
task, 7–9
task-dynamic modeling, 115
tautomorphemic vowels, 251–2
Tcl/Tk programming language, 91–6
template files, 32, 34–9, 101
  specifying tier relationships, 101
temporal alignment, 137
testing, 330, 340, 352–3, 358–9, 372

text mode, 95
three-point central differencing, 148–50
tier types, 101
tilt, 366
time normalization, 199
time resolution, 276–81
time tiers, 83
timeless tiers, 83, 87, 101
time-slice classification, 359–66
  parameterizing dynamic spectral information, 360–6
timing, 128
TIMIT, 4–5
tkassp routines, 49–51, 58–9, 272–3
ToBI database, 92, 98
tongue–dorsum closure, 115, 132, 138, 155, 234–6
tongue–palate contact, 17, 241
tongue-tip sensor, 116–20
tongue-tip synchronization, 135, 138
tools for annotated speech databases, 20–45
  creating new speech database, 32–4
  first look at template file, 34–8
  getting started with existing speech databases, 21–4
  interface between Praat and Emu, 24–6
  interface to R, 26–32
  overview, 20–1
  questions, 39–45
  summary, 38–9
trackdata objects, 21, 54, 59, 132–3, 140–7, 159–60
  applying a function segmentally to, 144–7, 160
  extraction of, 132–3, 160
  manipulation of, 140–7
  operations on, 160
  plotting speech data from, 160
training, 330, 340, 352–3, 358–9, 370–2
trajectory shape, 311–12
transitions of formants, 171–219
transparency, 144
trend line, 306
trialing, 333
TT sensor *see* tongue-tip sensor
turbulent airstreams, 264
two-dimensional classification, 347–52
two-dimensional distribution, 47

unrounded high vowels, 75
unsupervised learning, 330

using speech corpora in phonetics research, 1–19
  designing your own corpus, 6–18
  existing speech corpora for phonetic analysis, 4–5
  main issues, 18–19
  place of corpora in phonetic analysis of speech, 1–4
utterance identifier, 127, 143
utterances, 20–1, 32, 36–8

variability, 206–13
variance, 297, 300, 303, 345, 354–7
variation in emotions, 12–13
VC coarticulation in German dorsal fricatives, 251–8
vectors in Emu-R, 121–5
velocity, 17, 147–52
  peak velocity, 152–9
vocabulary, 7
vocal fold vibration, 305, 310
voice-onset time analysis, 125–32
voicing by analogy, 97
VOT analysis, 121–2, 125–31, 142
vowel backness, 46–7
vowel ellipses, 172–7
vowel height, 46–7

vowel normalization, 183–90
  strategies for, 186
vowel quadrilaterals, 57–8
vowel targets, 172, 179–83
vowel undershoot, 198–206
vowel-on-consonant coarticulation, 207–9, 234
vowel-quality distinctions, 172
vowel-space expansion, 190–6

warping, 363
WaveSurfer, 18
window function, 51
window shift, 49
within-speaker factors, 10
word-onset clusters, 115

xassp speech signal processing system, xvii

Zentrum für allgemeine Sprachwissenschaft, 252
zero correlation, 347
zero padding, 280–1
zero value, 149
zero-crossing-rate, 47
zooming, 24–5
z-scores, 355